ON WARS

ON WARS

MICHAEL MANN

Yale

UNIVERSITY PRESS

New Haven and London

Yale University Press books may be purchased in quantity for educational, business, or promotional use. For information, please e-mail sales.press@yale.edu (U.S. office) or sales@yaleup.co.uk (U.K. office).

Set in Janson type by IDS Infotech Ltd.
Printed in the United States of America.

Library of Congress Control Number: 2022945852
ISBN 978-0-300-26681-8 (hardcover : alk. paper)

A catalogue record for this book is available from the British Library.

This paper meets the requirements of ANSI/NISO Z39.48–1992 (Permanence of Paper).

10 9 8 7 6 5 4 3 2 1

Contents

Preface

In 2013 I finished the fourth and final volume of *The Sources of Social Power*, as well as two papers that did not fit into that book. While working on these papers, I realized that although I had always emphasized the role that military power plays in the development of human society, I had never really examined in any systematic way its main mechanism, war. And so for the last eight years I have engaged in a wide-ranging exploration of wars through human history—with a bit of prehistory added, too.

My fascination with war owes nothing to any personal experience of it. Family lore tells me I was born in a hospital basement during the last World War II German bombing raid on Manchester. If so, that was my last experience of war. Conscription in Britain was abolished the year before I would have been liable for it, and by the time I became an American citizen I was too old to be drafted. I have never possessed or fired a gun. Some sociologists study themselves—they write, for example, on their own class, ethnic, or sexual identity—but anthropologists and other sociologists, including myself, are fascinated by the task of trying to understand alien ways of life. For me, one such alien way has been war.

I have to thank the Covid-19 pandemic for enabling me to work single-mindedly if remotely during the last two years of this research project, with the help not only of the magnificent UCLA Young Research Library, but also of the internet resources provided by JSTOR for journal articles, Z-Library for online access to most of the many books I sought, and Wikipedia, useful for swift checking of dates and facts. But I must admit at the start that my reading has been restricted to works in English or French.

I would like to thank my literary agent, Elise Capron of the Sandra Dijkstra Agency, for her support and marketing skills. I am intellectually indebted as always to John A. Hall, as well as to Randall Collins and Siniša Malešević for their seminal works on violence, even if I have sometimes disagreed with them. I thank my UCLA colleagues and graduate students of the Sociology 237 seminars. I pay homage to the classical writers on war from Sun Tzu through Polybius and Ibn Khaldun to von Clausewitz, Ardant du Picq, and Raymond Aron. I must thank a horde of archaeologists, anthropologists, and historians for their very many empirical studies, which I have gratefully looted. I thank political scientists for clarifying the theoretical issues at stake. And I thank two anonymous reviewers of my manuscript for pertinent criticisms that I have tried to address.

Nicky Hart has been my constant companion for over forty years. Without her love, support, intellectual stimulation, and reminders of the sunny side of life, I would not have been able to complete this rather dark project. On similar grounds I would like to thank my children, Louise, Gareth, and Laura. May they—and the whole of humanity—be as fortunate as I have been, in never having to fight or to suffer as civilians in wars.

CHAPTER ONE

Military Power and War

WARS REVEAL HUMAN BEINGS behaving at their worst, killing and maiming each other in very large numbers. It is easy to deplore this. Herodotus quoted King Croesus of Lydia as saying in the sixth century BCE, "No one is stupid enough to prefer war to peace; in peace sons bury their fathers and in war fathers bury their sons." In the eighteenth century Benjamin Franklin said, "There never was a good war or a bad peace." Rebecca West in 1941 put it more pungently when describing armed conflicts in Yugoslav history: "It is sometimes very hard to tell the difference between history and the smell of a skunk." But what determines whether war or peace is chosen? Are wars driven by human nature, the nature of human society, or other forces? Are wars rational? Do they do any good at all? My answer in the broadest terms is that there is an element of rationality in wars but that this element gets entangled to varying degrees within the emotions and ideologies of human beings, especially their rulers, and within the social structures and cultures of human societies. The combination often drives rulers in the direction of wars that are rarely rational and that bring benefit to only a small proportion of human beings. If humans and their rulers were predominantly rational beings, there would be far fewer wars, an ideal worth at least aiming for.

I analyze many wars, hence the plural of my title. Most studies of war have been conducted by historians and political scientists who are international relations (IR) specialists. The latter have focused on wars involving the major powers of Europe since 1816, which period provides quantitative data sets of wars. Their preferred method is statistical, but it is also Euro- and modernity-biased. In contrast, historians study wars in many periods and regions. They also remind us that wars do not come as separate, independent cases to be aggregated into statistical models. They come in sequences, in which experience of the past deeply influences the living. Few historians, however, dare to engage in comparative analysis across different regions or periods of history. I dare do this by drawing on their detailed analyses.

As a comparative and historical sociologist, I cover sequences of war and peace over several regions and periods of history, chosen because they offer well-documented cases containing varied war frequencies— namely, Rome, imperial China, the Mongols, Japan, medieval and modern Europe, pre-Columbian and Latin America, the world wars, and recent American and Middle Eastern wars. *Well-documented* means ample written records exist, but many societies have not left such records. I regret that I have neglected historical South and Southeast Asian wars as well as classical Greece for reasons of length, language, and personal exhaustion. I do not claim that mine is a representative sample of wars. That is not possible to provide, since the total number of wars remains unknown and many known ones are only minimally recorded, as in the colonial wars touched on in chapters 8 and 10. I deal with sequences of wars, for wars rarely come singly, and the past constrains the present. This is the tyranny of history. I present simple statistics where they are available. I focus on interstate wars, but since these are often linked to civil wars and extrastate wars (wars involving nonstate contenders), I discuss them, too, where relevant and where records exist. Military power is also used for domestic repression, which has been a precondition for rulers' ability to make any wars at all, but I will not discuss such repression in much detail.

In the course of history, war has obviously changed enormously in weapons, techniques, and organization. The lethality of weapons has grown exponentially over the last few centuries, and the devastation of airpower was added in the twentieth century and cyberwar in the twenty-first. This required major changes in military organization and tactics. The organization of state armies has become much more complex, and the nature of battle has fundamentally changed. Body-on-body "ferocious" killing has partially given way to "callous" killing from a distance. Soldiers no longer stand upright in battle. They would be decimated if they did. Modern soldiers disperse in small units over larger battlefields, seeking cover, living underground—quite successfully, since their casualty rate has not increased, despite far more lethal weapons. Military medicine has produced a major decline in those dying from their wounds, accompanied by greater consciousness of psychiatric ailments. Yet weapons, especially airpower, have increased the civilian casualty rate, and it is now routine to define the total population of a country as the enemy. In the modern period political and religious ideologies justifying war have penetrated more deeply into social structure. Finally, our evidence has greatly increased in a modern surge in literacy, adding ordinary soldiers' writings and social surveys to chroniclers' narratives in earlier periods.

In contrast, the causes of wars and the nature of war-and-peace decisions have changed much less. The biggest variations have been among different types of war. I distinguish wars of aggression, defense, and mutual provocation or escalation. I also distinguish four main types of aggressive war: (1) in-and-out raiding, (2) using military power to change or strengthen regimes abroad to make them compliant, a form of indirect imperialism, (3) conquest and direct rule over slivers of border territory, and (4) conquest and direct rule of territorial empires. Obviously, a war of aggression leads also to defense by those attacked, whereas many wars mix up elements of more than one type. Also important has been the difference between symmetric and asymmetric warfare, that is, whether combatant forces were near equals in power or grossly unequal. Each of these types of war has had certain common features through the ages, so that generalizations are possible. But there is a historical contrast between raiding and imperial conquest, on the one hand, and regime change and slivers of territory, on the other. The former pair have almost disappeared from the earth in recent decades, whereas the latter pair endure.

As a sociologist I hold to two methodological principles: on the one hand, the need for analytical and conceptual rigor, which is necessarily generalizing; on the other, the need to grasp empirical reality, which is inescapably varied. There is always tension, I hope creative tension, between the two. I start with the universal concepts and one near-universal assumption framing my research. I assume that we humans seek to increase our valued resources—material possessions, pleasures, knowledge, social status, and whatever else we might value—or at least that enough of us do this to give human society its dynamism, its history. And in order to maintain or increase our resources, we need to exercise power, defined as the ability to get others to do things that otherwise they would not do.

There are two different faces of power. First, power enables some humans to achieve their goals by dominating others. This is "power over" others, called distributive power or domination, and it generates empires, social stratification, social classes, and gender and racial domination. These are all drivers of war. Second, however, power also enables humans to cooperate with each other to achieve things that they could not achieve separately. This is "power through" others, or collective power. Human development would not be possible without collective power, people cooperating to achieve their goals, while almost all known societies have contained distributive power relations, that is, social stratification. Collective and distributive power are closely entwined, especially in the minds of rulers, who normally claim that their power over others is wielded to the benefit of all, just as imperialists claim that they bring the benefits of civilization to the conquered—as have Chinese, Roman, European, Soviet, and now American rulers.

In the volumes of my *Sources of Social Power*, I distinguished four sources of power: ideological, economic, military, and political. I have also come to make three adjustments to this scheme. First, I distinguish political power exercised within rulers' domestic domains and "diplomatic," peaceful geopolitical power exercised abroad. Second, I pair ideologies with emotions since both surpass empirical knowledge. Ideologies and emotions "fill in the gaps" between pieces of scientifically and empirically ascertainable knowledge. We do not have objective knowledge of the world, and so we act with the help of generalized meaning systems (such as liberalism, conservatism, nationalism, religion, or family values) and emotional commitments. The two are entwined, since powerful ideologies lead to strong emotions. Third, I have seen these four power sources as means to achieve whatever goals people have. I still believe this, but now I explicitly add that power can be seen as an end in itself, which I will explain more in a moment.

Control over these power resources offers the principal ways in which others can be induced to do things that they would not otherwise do. Wielding ideological, economic, military, and political and geopolitical power is the principal means to achieve desired goals. So to explain war, we must understand why humans choose war rather than use economic exchange, shared cooperative ideologies, or peaceful politics or geopolitics to secure valued ends. In fact, more disputes are settled or simmer by these means, without leading to war. Geopolitics contains two distinct elements: the effect of the geographic, ecological environment on human action, as stressed by late nineteenth-century writers; and the international relations between states and communities, as stressed by today's political scientists. Perhaps the *choice* of war is not quite the right word. Rulers may feel constrained by the warrior role they believe is required of them. War is simply what Roman senators or Mongol khans or French kings or American presidents do, habitually, when they feel slighted or sense opportunity. Indeed, they do often feel they have no choice in particular situations but to go to war.

The vast majority of people throughout history seem to have preferred peace to war, so far as we can judge. They have felt that they could achieve their desired goals better through economic exchange, shared ideologies, or diplomacy than through the exercise of military power. So I am seeking to explain the exceptions, to explain war.

The (IR)Rationality of War

Are wars rational? The basic issue is whether wars do achieve desired and desirable goals. If so, we might call a war rational; if not, it might be irrational. But we must distinguish between rationality of means and ends. Rationality of means concerns efficient decision making, which is measured and calculative, balancing goals against means, probably after some debate, according to the best information knowable at the time, and where the means of war seem to be adequate for reaching desired ends. Irrationality of means occurs when the decision for war is made for hasty, uninformed, emotional, or ideological reasons and when the means are predictably inadequate to achieving the ends. Often the ends sought through war are not reached. But this can happen for many reasons, not all of which were predictable at the time of the decision to go to war. War proved a mistake, but this was not evident beforehand—mistaken, but not irrational.

So I add the legal principle of the reasonable person or bystander. Would such a person have judged that war would achieve its ends? Obviously, rulers who commit to wars always think this is rational behavior. Adolf Hitler thought so when invading Russia, declaring war on the United States, and slaughtering Jews. But few others thought so, including many of his generals. The judgment of rationality rests with contemporaries or later scholars, including myself. There is room for disagreement, but a charge of irrationality may be made where these observers conclude from the available evidence that the desired ends could not have been reached, whatever the later contingencies of the war. For example, this was my own view just before the American invasion of Iraq in 2003, as expressed in my book *Incoherent Empire*.[1] Making the generous assumption that the main goal of the Bush administration was the replacement of Saddam Hussein's autocracy with a democratic state, U.S. forces never had significant Iraqi allies who shared this desire, and they had not prepared at all for confronting sectarian divides among Iraqis. As I predicted, the Americans had to strike a deal with some sectarian groups to rule over others, and a disorderly ethnocracy, not an orderly democracy, resulted. This was an irrational war fought for a delusory goal. So, largely, was the Ukrainian invasion launched by President Putin in 2022. But in most wars the folly is not as glaring as this. Whether there is irrationality of means may be arguable.

Judging the rationality of ends is problematic, since ultimately it involves a judgment about whether war produces "benefit," and for whom. Benefit is contestable. Hitler devised an extraordinarily efficient program to kill Jews, six million of them killed in only four years, a rationality of means perhaps unequaled in all of history. Hitler and his acolytes believed that this genocide was also rational as an end, since they feared that the mere existence of Jews threatened civilization itself. But virtually no one else has believed this or would consider the end to be rational in the sense of bringing any general benefit. To us, Hitler seems maniacal in his pursuit of this goal. But this is an extreme case, and whether and to whom a goal brings "benefit" is often arguable.

We are on somewhat safer ground with the narrower materialist view of rationality as identified by Realist and Marxist theorists. They see wars as mainly aimed at economic gain or geopolitical survival (or both), from which the likely profit or secure survival derived from war may or may not exceed its cost. There are four elements involved in this calculation: weighing (a) the cost in money and (b) in lives against (c) the likelihood of victory and (d) the rewards likely to ensue from victory. In my case studies I try to assess the extent to which each of these elements is taken into account. This kind of economic-military trade-off constitutes instrumental rationality, as Max Weber defined it. Where the costs are predictably greater than the profit, war would be materially irrational. Yet even this measurement is difficult since economic profit, casualty rates, and the chances of victory do not share the same metric, and there is no way of calculating how many deaths suffered are worth how much profit made for what chances of victory. If human life is considered sacred, perhaps no death is worth any amount of profit—the pacifist position.

Yet there is an intermediary position, for proportionality might be applied. As we shall see, soldiers in battle often try to apply this: they will accept risking their lives provided they are not being used as cannon fodder and if there is a good chance that victory is achievable. If they perceive this is unlikely, they will try to subvert orders or mutiny or desert. Under proportionality we might decide, for example, that the twenty-one worst wars and atrocities in history in terms of deaths, which I list in table 10.1, each of which resulted in the deaths of over three million people, could not be considered rational, even if they brought profit for the aggressors. But how many deaths would be worth it? There is no satisfactory answer to this. Great conquerors may pay scant attention to the lives of an "enemy" population, or indeed to their own troops' lives. From their point of view, the choice of war is rational, since it benefits them and their circle. But we may feel that the benefit is not widespread enough to be justified. At a minimum, we must carefully assess what benefit accrues to what proportion of the people, and to judge how rational a war is accordingly. Though we shall find that wars have varied considerably in these terms, in general we shall see that most of them are irrational in terms of such means and ends.

Yet wars may be also aimed at desired but nonmaterial goals, such as glory, honor, assuaging anger, exacting revenge, or pursuing an ideology. Power may also be a valued end in itself. Friedrich Nietzsche wrote: "What is good?—Whatever augments the feeling of power, the will to power, power itself, in man. What is evil?—Whatever springs from weakness. What is happiness?—The feeling that power *increases*—that resistance is overcome. Not contentment, but more power; *not* peace at any price, but war."[2]

Those who command may get intrinsic enjoyment from dominating others, regardless of what other benefits they might experience. They enjoy the emotions they elicit from subordinates and conquered peoples, ranging from adoration and admiration, through respect and envy, to hatred, fear, and sheer terror. Chinggis (Genghis) Khan is reputed to have said, "Man's greatest good fortune is to chase and defeat his enemy, seize his total possessions, leave his married women weeping and wailing, ride his gelding, use the bodies of his women as a nightshirt and support, gazing upon and kissing their rosy breasts, sucking their lips which are as sweet as the berries of their breasts."[3]

Political correctness prevents modern leaders from saying such things, yet power remains an intoxication that might need no other justification. As the philosopher and political scientist Raymond Aron said,

"The satisfactions of *amour-propre*, victory or prestige are no less real than the so-called material satisfactions, such as the gain of a province or a population."[4] These satisfactions are somewhat ineffable, not easily quantified. They may also bring not benefit but disaster to the people as a whole. The pursuit of status, prestige, and honor by "statesmen" for themselves and their state is an important source of war, independent of what other rewards they might get from it. Moreover, a sense of excitement and enjoyment in power may even trickle down quite broadly among the people, as it probably did among the Romans and Mongols and does among many Americans today, proud of their country's military power, which seems to boost their own egos.

When domination and glory are desired ends in themselves, this may fit Max Weber's second form of rationality, *value rationality*, which he defined as "belief in the value for its own sake of some ethical, aesthetic, religious, or other form of behavior, independently of its prospects of success. . . . The more the value to which action is oriented is elevated to the status of an absolute value, the more 'irrational' in this [instrumental] sense the corresponding action is. For the more unconditionally the actor devotes himself to this value for its own sake, . . . the less he is influenced by considerations of the consequences of his action."[5]

His term *value rationality* may seem paradoxical, but it certainly fits Hitler's perversion of rationality. Many powerful groups may be driven by values overriding everything else—values for hatreds, glory, honor, or ideological transformation. Rulers pursuing such ends might calculate precisely the means available for achieving them. But are the ends "rational"? The benefits they bring are usually distributed very unequally; small elites benefit most. They may indicate endless ambition, without a resting place—the malady of infinite aspiration, in the sociologist Emile Durkheim's words. The main problem of an infinite aspiration to conquer is the number of lives it destroys. War is a peculiar activity: it is designed to kill a very large number of people, and this surely requires a very high level of justification. Self-defense is generally considered such a justification, but we will see that this is quite an elastic concept.

So I will tread carefully when dealing with the rationality of war, trying to distinguish means from ends, errors from irrationality, costs from benefits, the odds of victory, and social constraints. I try to assess who benefited and who lost from the wars I discuss—for whom exactly was war rational in the sense of beneficial? The answer is often almost no one.

Defining Military Power

Human societies involve conflict and cooperation among persons wielding varying blends of ideological, economic, military, and political or geopolitical power. These provide the key dynamic of human history toward the development of more and more complex and powerful societies. Conflicts may be relatively peaceful—using mixtures of ideological, economic, or political-diplomatic power—or they may be warlike, resorting to military power. Military power may also achieve desired ends when merely threatened, without war following. The Chinese military strategist Sun Tzu wrote in the sixth century BCE, "The supreme art of war is to subdue the enemy without fighting."[6] War is only one way of achieving ends, and we must ask in what circumstances human groups turn to military power to achieve their goals.

So the first of three additional themes in this book concerns the causes of war—when, where, by whom, and why war rather than peace is chosen or stumbled into. If we want to achieve Immanuel Kant's ideal of perpetual peace, we need to know what to avoid that otherwise might lead to war. I devote eight chapters to examining the causes and rationality of wars through human history.

My second additional theme concerns the culmination of war, in battles, and its cost in terms of death or mutilation. I focus on exploring how soldiers—normally men—are induced to accept such a risk. Why do they fight despite the strong possibility that they will end up dead or physically or psychologically mutilated? Few soldiers actually like battle, so how do they cope with their dominant mental states in battle, which are fear and loathing? Many have argued that soldiers have moral qualms that are important in influencing their behavior in battle. I treat the management of fear, loathing, and moral qualms in three more chapters. These focus mainly on wars from the second half of the nineteenth century until today. Alas, this reduction of focus is necessary because these have been the only wars in which most soldiers have been literate and have thus left written records. I must apologize to sailors for excluding their experiences, but this book is long enough without them. Flyers do get some attention, though obviously only in the twentieth and twenty-first centuries.

My third additional theme concerns whether there has been a decline of war, either throughout human history, or only in modern times, or indeed merely since the end of World War II. In chapter 10 I dissect all these claims skeptically. No long-run or short-run trends can be discerned in the frequency of war. But this is not conventional military history. I neglect tactics, weapons, battle formations, and the like, except when they influence the answers to the questions mentioned above.

Military power is the social organization of lethal violence. It coerces people to do things they would not otherwise do by the threat of death or serious injury. The Prussian military theorist Carl von Clausewitz said, "War is thus an act of force to compel our enemy to do our will."[7] Military power is physical, furious, unpredictable. Above all else, despite the positive lures of army recruitment drives and despite armies' role in alleviating natural disasters, the main point of militaries is to kill people. Since a lethal threat is terrifying, military power evokes distinctive psychological emotions and physiological symptoms. The emotional intensity of approaches to war, and of wars themselves, and of actual battle, is much higher than the relatively pragmatic calm of economies and polities, while ideologies come both hot and cold. Clausewitz added a high level of chance: "War is the realm of uncertainty: three quarters of the factors on which action in war is based are wrapped in a fog of greater or lesser uncertainty. . . . War is the realm of chance."[8] He said this was due to the "frictions" of battle, where nothing goes as planned. The Duke of Wellington said war was "guessing what was at the other side of the hill." These generals suggest a random element in war that obviously threatens our chances of reaching an overall theory of war.

These are the distinctive features of military power, separating it from the other three power sources. This is not to deny an often close relationship between political and military power, and I focus mostly on interstate wars. But wars between communities lacking states, civil wars, and nonstate guerilla forces will all play important roles, and so will contradictions between military and political power revealed, for example, in both coups and "coup-proofing" by rulers who deliberately weaken their armed forces to protect themselves from their own generals. We cannot merge these two forms of power.

Routinized coercion dominates within armed forces. Rank is all. Military power provides the most rigid form of class structure found in human societies. Those of higher rank must be obeyed, to a degree that is unknown in ideological, economic, or political organizations. Soldiers have formally signed away their free will. They cannot freely leave if they find war not to their taste. They are under intense military discipline, which is intended to stifle the urge to cower or flee. Their lives are dominated by orders, however unpleasant or foolish officers might seem, however savage the drilling and disciplining involved. If they do not obey, they will be physically harmed, and sometimes even killed.

There are exceptions. Guerillas and other less formal militaries, like tribal and some feudal forces, are freer in the sense that they may challenge orders and even decide to walk away from combat if they are dissatisfied. In modern armies there are also written codes of conduct that in principle limit the power of higher ranks. You need to be very brave, however, to invoke such codes against your officers. There are differences even among modern state armies—for example, between the rigid discipline of eighteenth-century Prussian forces and the more easygoing American armies of today. Nonetheless, armies wield fundamentally coercive power within as well as without, to create a military culture in which for lower ranks choice, rational or otherwise, may be very restricted.

Yet armed forces have a dual organizational form, combining the apparent opposites of hierarchy and comradeship, of intense discipline and strong esprit de corps, especially in elite regiments. These combinations are cultivated by commanders so that soldiers will not rationally respond to fear with flight, as you or I might. The commanders may also provide alcohol or drugs to dampen soldiers' sense of danger. This is again distinctive to organizations deploying lethal force. But military power wielded externally, over enemy soldiers and civilians, is the most punitive, fearsome, and arbitrary power of all.

Militaries depend on the other power sources: economic supplies and the logistics to deploy them; ideological morale based on varying combinations of solidarity, loyalty, patriotism, and belief that the war is just and can be won; and political resources in the form of conscripted manpower and revenue streams. Yet military power once mobilized has an ultimately autonomous existence, for it alone can lay lives and territories to waste. Mostly it plays an intermittent role. In peacetime, which is most of the time, it may be confined to barracks, guard duties, parades, and exercises. It may slumber as a distinct military caste living in its own communities on the fringes of society. In many tribal or feudal societies and among guerillas, "armies" barely existed at all outside wartime. Yet when war threatens, military power comes onto center stage in explosive bursts, terrifying, destructive, and unpredictable.

The four sources of power are ideal types, and most real organizations combine elements of more than one of them. Some economic organizations wield some lethal power, as in systems of slave labor; and in ideological organizations, heresy may be met with death. There are lesser forms of coercion—employees discharged may be blacklisted by other employers, and someone who quits an ideological movement may suffer social ostracism. If you live in a given political community, you are willy-nilly a citizen-subject of that community, subject to its laws and punishments. Many states inflict capital punishment and all forcibly fine or imprison or inflict physical harm on lawbreakers. All forms of power organization wield some coercion, many of them inflict physical punishment, and a few kill. But armies are far more consistently and lethally coercive—within as well as without, since casualties are suffered by all. Ramsay MacDonald, Labour prime minister of Britain in the 1920s, remarked: "We hear war called murder. It is not: it is suicide." It is both.

There are also more benign aspects of military organization, manifested in enthusiastic enlistment, warm comradeship, handsome uniforms, banners, stirring brass bands, belief in a cause worth fighting for, and patriotism. But in war these are secondary to inflicting death. The enthusiasm shown upon enlistment rarely survives long. This book is not about the glories of military history. War is hell, and militaries train soldiers for hell. Soldiers themselves come to know this. Civilians often do not.

One further definition. *Militarism* combines the power predominance of military elites in society, ideological exaltation of military virtues above ideologies of peace, and extensive and aggressive military preparedness. Militarism comes in degrees: some societies are highly militaristic, others much less so—and so less likely to start wars.

Few rules restrain military power. "Rules of war" are difficult to enforce, even in the era of Geneva Conventions and the International Criminal Court. So far war crimes trials have been conducted only against the losers of wars. The major charge brought against Nazi leaders at Nuremburg was launching aggressive war, and this was also prohibited in principle in the United Nations Charter and in later international treaties. But aggressive war has disappeared as a charge from war crimes trials, which have focused on two other offenses, crimes against humanity and genocide. Since U.S. wars today are mainly aggressive, no American politician could accept that this charge be levied. Numerous norms have also spread concerning "just" versus "unjust" practices of warfare, but there have been many infringements, too. Norms have especially concerned the treatment of fellow officers, of prisoners, and of civilians, especially old men, women, and children, yet these are often breached. The relative paucity of rules or norms is unlike economic or ideological power—and especially unlike political power whose core is law. War is the least lawlike, least predictable sphere of human action—which makes both rational decisions and causal analyses more difficult.

Defining War

A war is a lethal conflict between two groups organized by rival states or communities, or by rival communities within countries riven by civil war. Although interstate and civil wars are often kept apart in analyses, in reality about one-third of wars mix them together. But how big does armed conflict have to be to count as war? Not duels, or brawls, or even a mere skirmish between rival patrols. But where do we draw the line? Do we need to? Most political scientists have followed the "Correlates of War" (CoW) research project, which has produced statistics on wars since 1816. It has defined war as an armed dispute that causes one thousand or more battle-related fatalities inflicted within a twelve-month period. I will not stick rigidly to that, and indeed lesser levels of fatalities have been recently added by political scientists. A word of warning here: two different terms, *casualties* and *deaths* (or *fatalities*), are used for losses. Casualties is the broader term, meaning all soldiers removed from battle by death, wounds, capture, or having gone missing. Unfortunately, some sources stating losses do not make clear which is being referred to.

Setting a required minimum number of deaths makes quantitative analysis easier, and one thousand fatalities has the merit of including only significant wars, but any threshold figure should merely be a rough guideline. A conflict resulting in only five hundred battlefield deaths between two small countries is surely as significant for them as are five thousand deaths in combat between two big ones. Furthermore, many uses of military power fall short of war as defined above yet involve the use or threat of lethal force. So political scientists have introduced an intermediary category between war and peace, "Militarized Interstate Disputes" (MIDs), defined as conflicts in which the threat, display, or use of military force short of war by one state is explicitly directed toward the government, official representatives, official forces, property, or territory of another state. These range in intensity from mere threats to combat short of one thousand casualties. Gary Goertz and his colleagues note that the absence of war does not necessarily indicate peace. The Cold War produced no fighting between American and Soviet forces, but one

might not be inclined to call this "peace." So they enumerate five categories of growing conflict short of war.[9] These are relevant to whether recent history has seen a decline of war, for decline might take the form of
a shift across these categories to lesser violence rather than to full peace.

Statistical analysis of war frequency and casualties is possible only in
the modern period—though rough figures are more widely available. But
statistics have limitations. These count all wars as one, no matter how big
(if it is over one thousand casualties), yet the two world wars dwarf the
twentieth century. Explaining them is likely to be a far more significant
exercise than explaining large numbers of lesser conflicts. Separating
them as single cases also ignores the fact that wars come in sequences,
each one influencing the next. Severity can be measured through the
number of deaths or casualties, but the quality of estimates varies greatly.
Civilian casualties are not included in the CoW measure of war, and they
are often impossible to calculate. Quantification also downplays history
and geography. The wars of different epochs and ecologies probably differ. The most obvious difference through time is the exponentially increasing lethality of weapons, which require major adaptations. As Will
Rogers remarked, "You can't say civilization don't advance, however, for
in every war they kill you in a new way." Each place and period has idiosyncrasies, which makes generalization challenging.

Historical records are biased toward narrating war rather than peace.
War is exciting, peace boring. Can you "narrate" peace? It doesn't
change. Great monuments like castles, triumphal stelae and arches, statues of warriors, and paintings of battles survive, often considered great
works of art, whereas peaceful peasants and workers leave few traces.
Since the winners of wars write the records, they suppress the losers' experiences and extol the glory, not the shame, of war. Nowadays, however,
victors' accounts are challenged. Revisionism is now necessary for the
award of a history PhD, and there is much pulling down of statues of
warriors and slavers. Alas, this is belated criticism. There are periods and
regions for which written records, let alone statistics, of war are not
available, as in much of precolonial Africa. Imperial powers kept tallies of
their own dead but didn't count dead natives. Especially difficult are estimates of civilian deaths caused by war but indirectly, through malnutrition and disease. We can estimate, if to varying degrees in different
periods and regions. But I now turn to a widely accepted generalization:
war is universal because it is human nature.

CHAPTER TWO

Is War Universal?

OW WIDESPREAD IS WAR? Are we doomed to repeat, generation after generation, Plato's observation that "only the
dead have seen the end of war"? Perhaps war is hardwired
into either human nature or human society. All complex societies have had specialized groups of armed persons, and almost all have
raised armies. But have they all gone to war? There are two main sets of
findings on this question: whether war existed among very early human
societies, and variations in the incidence of war across space and time.
They both strongly suggest that war is not genetically programmed into
human nature.

The Earliest Human Societies

Much of the argument concerns the very earliest societies, which, since
the time of the philosopher Jean-Jacques Rousseau, many have believed
lacked war. Others have endorsed Ibn Khaldun's fourteenth-century
statement: "Wars and different kinds of fighting have always occurred in
the world since God created it. It is something natural among human beings."[1] The argument continues today.

Archaeologists are our first witnesses. They have found no remains
indicating organized warfare before discovery of a site in the Sudan
along the Nile River, dated to around 10,000 BCE. In that site twenty-
four of fifty-nine well-preserved skeletons were found in close proximity

to what may have been parts of weapons—suggestive of group combat, perhaps, but not conclusive. Clearer was the discovery of twenty-seven skeletons at Nataruk in Kenya, datable to 8000 BCE. Twelve of these were well-preserved, ten of them showing evidence of a death inflicted by a spear, arrow, or club. The bodies had not been given a proper burial, which suggests that this was not a feud within a single community, but a small war between rival bands.[2] Nataruk was then adjacent to Lake Turkana in a resource-rich environment, so it could have been a struggle between groups over rights to irrigated land or fishing. But there is no indication of who the victims were or whether they were settled there.

In Australia there is evidence in cave paintings of duels between individuals dating to 8000 BCE; there are paintings of group confrontations datable to 4000 BCE. In Central Europe disorganized mass burials of persons conjectured to have died from either battle or execution date from the period 5600–4900 BCE.[3] In Spain rock art similarly suggests a growth in organized violence from the sixth to the third millennium BCE, related to the appearance of agriculture, more social complexity, and the emergence of war leaders, identifiable by their burial goods, commanding groups of warriors.[4] Archaeologists of the early Bronze Age, from around 3000 BCE in Europe, have correlated injuries on skeletons with unearthed weapons of the time to conclude that these were deaths in combat. For a little later period in the Balkans, it is estimated that weapons and body armor represented about 5–10 percent of total bronze remains.[5] Yet in Central Asia there is no clear evidence of war until 3000 BCE. In America the first evidence dates to 2200 BCE. In Japan right up to 800 BCE, only about 4 percent of skeletons reveal evidence of a violent death, and there are no known cases of group deaths from violence. As Hisashi Nakao and his colleagues observe, such gross variations across human communities suggest that war is not built into our nature.[6]

We cannot be certain that these were the first cases of warfare, for such an argument would rest on an absence of earlier finds. Perhaps earlier evidence of war may be found in the future. Yet at present it seems likely that minimally organized warfare began sometime after 8000 BCE, much later in some regions of the world, and it probably related to settled farming.[7] As William Eckhardt had earlier concluded in his review of the literature, "War was a function of development rather than instinct."[8]

Anthropologists have long disputed such issues. Lawrence Keeley claimed that early hunter-gatherer societies were extremely warlike.[9] But Brian Ferguson went through Keeley's early cases one by one, arguing that they had been cherry-picked.[10] He concluded that only a few communities regularly practiced warfare. Azar Gat defended Keeley by assembling data on two groups, Australian aborigines and peoples of the Pacific Northwest of Canada and the United States. He says they offer "laboratories" in which primitive peoples observed by Westerners were as yet "uncontaminated" by the violence of Western imperialism.[11] Contamination makes it difficult to generalize from the experience of present-day hunter-gatherers to prehistoric hunter-gatherers. Recently warlike groups, such as today's Yanomami of Brazil, appear to have developed much of their ferocity in response to Western colonialism.[12] But Gat claims that his two uncontaminated groups were violent, probably more so than modern societies in that a higher proportion of men died as a result of violence.

Gat focuses on hunter-gatherers in Australia, using anthropologists' estimates of killing rates in different regions.[13] The numbers killed in war are given over periods varying from ten years to three generations, yet the estimates of total male population are apparently one-point-in-time figures, and they do not take account of additional comings of age of young men each year. Recalculating their figures to do this would give violent death rates among men of 5–10 percent. These figures are still quite high, comparable to rates found in modern wars. Yet in a band of forty people that contained twelve men of fighting age, if archaeologists dug up three whose wounds indicated a violent death, the rate would be 25 percent—higher than in modern armies but perhaps an artifact of small numbers.

Hunter-gatherer war bands normally numbered fewer than thirty men, and war was occasional and brief. It had to be brief since virtually all healthy adult males in the community participated in them, and if they were away on campaign, there would be no meat or fish for their families. So before any attack was launched, the men would go on a hunting expedition to provide enough food for their families during their absence, but this had to be short. Gat says that in a war involving all adult males, if an armed encounter went badly, most of the adult male population might be killed. The highest death rates were almost never found in set-piece battles, which were often terminated at the first casualty. Instead, the most fatalities occurred in surprise ambushes. The element of surprise could lead to a rout and massacre, followed by the incorporation of most of the women and children of the defeated into the victorious group. In terms of the proportion of a population killed, these episodes have been surpassed in modern times only by genocides in which the women and children are massacred, too. They were quite rare events, however, not typical of normal aborigine skirmishing.

Richard G. Kimber concludes that "aborigines appear to have been no different from other peoples on earth in that, despite a generally harmonious situation, conflict did occur."[14] He also emphasizes the far more massacres committed on aborigines by European settlers in Australia. Lloyd Warner suggested that the death of young males allowed polygynous marriages to continue.[15] Peace would have created major conflict between sex-starved young men and the clan leaders, who typically had more than one wife. Polygyny was common among Australian aborigines, but uncommon among most other hunter-gatherers.[16] Carol Ember and Melvin Ember agree with Gat in seeing Australian aborigines as rather warlike, as were the fishing communities of northwest Canada, attributed to fixity of settlement around natural harbors, which generated a healthy surplus.[17] The Calusa of southern Florida were a more extreme example of a warlike fishing community, engaged in large-scale slaving raids, able to support three hundred full-time warriors.[18]

Douglas Fry and Patrik Söderberg provide a broader global survey of twenty-one simple hunter-gatherer societies.[19] In twenty of them, the median level of lethality during a period of one to three years was only three. Of these incidents, 64 percent involved one killer, one victim—a murder or a fight. Only in twelve events among these twenty bands was there a killing of persons from a different band. So war between bands was rare, and homicide was more common. None of these twenty bands was Australian. The twenty-first band was exceptional. It contributed no less than 76 percent (thirty-eight of fifty) of the total number of inter-band disputes, and this included seven strings of related killings, whereas the other twenty bands had only two strings of killings among all of them. The deviant group was the Tiwi of northern Australia. So indigenous Australians were rather aggressive, but elsewhere hunter-gatherers made war rarely or not at all. The reason may be that they were clan societies which generate larger social units sharply distinguished from other clans. Gat has refuted Rousseau's claim that primitive peoples were inherently pacific, but he has not shown that they were very warlike. Warfare was rare.

Some early warfare was rarely deadly, according to anthropologists' accounts of peoples in the interior of New Guinea who had had no contact with white men. The men of two bands would meet in a clearing, sometimes by earlier agreement, and stand in parallel lines facing each other, just inside either archery or spear-throwing range. They would shout and swagger defiance and then throw or shoot. When one or perhaps a few were hit, battle would stop, the men would disperse, and any victim would be carried back to his village. Neither side was capable of the coordination necessary to conquer the other or seize its territory. Slaves were valueless in their economy, and more territory was only of marginal value. These communities had neither the motivation nor the ability to make war. Ritual combats were ways of venting grievances and displaying one's honor and bravery in a relatively safe way.[20] Aggressive behavior might flare up into violence, but this was ritually managed to stop short of anything we might call war.

Such rituals might have been more successful than any achievements made by the diplomats of history or by today's international institutions of conflict mediation sponsored by the United Nations and other agencies. War was avoided over millennia, partly unintentionally, by maintaining a mixed economy of horticulture and hunter-gathering from which war rarely emerged, partly by deliberately avoiding the development of classes and states, developing only what anthropologists call "rank" inequality of status without inherited inequality of material possessions or political power.[21] If we could do without classes and states, there would probably be no more war, an admittedly utopian prospect.

The likeliest conclusion is that pre-state communities contained interpersonal violence but only rarely warfare.[22] Christopher Coker argues the opposite, but only by merging the two.[23] Organized warfare may have emerged first in fixed fishing and agricultural settlements producing substantial surpluses and was enhanced when classes and states appeared. Keith Otterbein says settled agriculture normalized organized warfare, but it was helped by armed bands inherited from previous bands of hunters of large game.[24] War then escalated when peoples were trapped within fertile ecologies like wetlands and river valleys, so they could no longer run away from attackers without major sacrifice. Their lands were worth defending, and outsiders thought they were worth attacking.

Early states were surrounded by mobile "barbarians," hunting and gathering, foraging, practicing slash-and-burn horticulture or pastoralism. James Scott notes that for a very long time most of the world's population lived in such communities, and only a small minority lived under states: the first warring Sumerian states came "only around 3,100 BCE, more than four millennia *after* the first crop domestications and sedentism" because

mixed, decentralized economies predominated.²⁵ To explain the appearance of states and wars, he emphasizes the growth of grain crops, which
ripen all at the same time and are highly visible, impossible to hide. Thus,
they can be taxed, seized, and stored. Armed thugs could do this by force
and become an idle ruling class living off others' surplus, helped by armed
retinues, city walls, administrative records, and wars to acquire slaves—all
serving to cage the people under their rule. So began almost all the world
civilizations. Other anthropologists disagree, seeing granaries as evidence
of collective sharing of resources. David Graeber and David Wengrow
have suggested that in early city-states relatively egalitarian and somewhat
"democratic" political institutions—such as town councils, neighborhood
ward associations, and political assemblies that included many women—
oscillated with institutions embodying more class inequality, aristocracy,
monarchy, and patriarchy.²⁶ We cannot discern which made the more
wars, though threats from outside peoples often forced egalitarian groups
to place themselves under the protection of armed men. If these men
could manage to hold on to power or if outsider "marcher lords," already
featuring kings and aristocracies, triumphed, then history's dynastic empires appeared and the scale of warfare increased.

So more than 95 percent of the 150,000 years of humans living on
earth had passed before the appearance of warring states. This means
that warfare is not genetically programmed into us. Biology is not destiny; we are doomed to warfare not by our genes, but by societies. The
1986 Seville Statement on Violence, signed by distinguished scholars in
biology, psychology, ethology, genetics, and other human sciences, declares that war is not genetically based, that we have not inherited a tendency to make war from our animal ancestors, and that there has been
no natural bias toward aggressive behavior. Nor do some racial groups'
genes dispose them to more or less warlike behavior. Geneticists have
shown that despite superficial differences between human communities
in the shape of the nose, the color of the skin, and so on, human beings
are remarkably similar in their DNA sequences. Currently, about 85 percent of human genetic variability has been found within racially defined
groups, only about 15 percent between them. Malešević provides a detailed critique of essentialist genetic and biological explanations of violence and of explanations in terms of universal, stable, and biologically
uniform human emotions relevant to violence.²⁷

Can we derive answers from our nearest relatives? Gorillas are not aggressive. In a Rwandan forest I sat within a meter of a group of gorillas

without any sense of danger. They ignored my presence although an enormous silverback male brushed against my arm as he came ambling by me. But humans share more genes with bonobos (apes) and chimps. Bonobos are much less aggressive than chimps, but humans are more varied than either. When relations between human groups deteriorate, they can become much more violent and on a much larger scale than relations among chimps. When human relations are good, they are very good, accompanied by much greater payoff from neighborly relations than bonobos manage. Humans do more than just mingle and have sex, like the peaceful bonobos. They trade, share elaborate ceremonies, and generate the forms of cooperation that led to their unique social development. "When it comes to intergroup relations, we beat our close relatives on both the positive and negative ends of the scale."[28] Coker notes that no fewer than seventy species aggress violently against members of their species, but only the human species makes organized warfare.[29] Yet only humans also devise complex, flexible, cooperative divisions of labor. Extreme variability of violence and cooperation seems to be distinctive to our species.

Individuals vary in propensity for violence. We all know people who are aggressive, others who are meek and mild. We will see that a few soldiers like violence, for reasons of either sadism or heroism, but most soldiers do not. In many areas of social behavior, personality differences matter little. The growth of capitalism depends not on a few persons with distinct personalities but on large numbers of entrepreneurs and workers whose personal differences will tend to cancel each other out. But war-and-peace decisions are made by small numbers of persons, sometimes by a single monarch, dictator, prime minister, or president. Because of the powerful social role they occupy, their personalities matter considerably to outcomes of war and peace. Attila the Hun was likely to make war, whereas Edward the Confessor preferred peace, and the history of white America is from one mad king, George III, to another, Donald Trump. Such idiosyncrasies limit general theory.

Yet whatever the human propensity for violence, cooperation has played a larger part in social development. Those who fight die; those who cooperate survive and prosper—a peaceful version of the survival of the fittest. Like most behavioral characteristics, this one involves opposites—we may have a propensity for violence, but we also have one for cooperation (as we do for love and hate, introversion and extroversion, and so on). Gat identifies cooperation, competition, and violent conflict as the three fundamental forms of social interaction and says that

humans choose among them.[30] He offers the paradox that war is both innate and optional, by which he means that it is close to the behavioral
surface, triggered with relative ease. Steven Pinker's bifurcation of human
nature into inner "angels" and "demons" is similar.[31] For war-and-peace
decisions I prefer the metaphor of a balance. Human beings are perched
in the center. If their behavior tilts in one direction, we get war; if it tilts
in the other direction, we get peace. But the question is: What tilts them
one way or the other?

Randall Collins in his brilliant book *Violence* tilts a little toward
peace.[32] Using a host of empirical descriptions of violence drawn mostly
from modern brawls, he suggests that most humans do not like violence
and are not very good at it. Confrontations rarely lead to actual physical
violence. Fights that do break out tend to range bullies against the weak
and are not like those in the movies. They are clumsy, imprecise, and
frenzied, involving more flailing and slapping than solid punching. By-
standers rarely get drawn in, as they often do in the movies. He adds that
in war soldiers are fearful to go "over the top," and they have bowel
problems at the prospect. Violence is "hard," he says, because "humans
are hard-wired for interactional entrainment and solidarity," and this
propensity "is stronger than mobilized aggression."[33] Thus, most people
stick at bluster and bluff. To be violent, Collins says, most people have to
overcome fear and tension, and this happens either in ritualized encounters in which status concerns are primary, as in duels, or in unusual situations when people are "sucked into" what he calls a "tunnel of violence,"
when normal perceptions are distorted, pulse rates accelerate as cortisol
and adrenaline flood the body, and there is forward momentum down
the tunnel produced by a quick-fire sequence of events. One example is
"forward panic," found especially in micro-conflicts in which bullies attack the weak without mercy, but found also in wars, when one army fal-
ters and begins to flee, emboldening the other to rush forward and
engage in a killing frenzy. It is forward panic, he concludes, that leads to
most of the lethality of war.

Yet Collins hedges his bets with a principle of "social evolution"—
the growth of military power organizations. Armies have devised techniques for keeping men fighting, even though they may be afraid—the
entrapping infantry phalanx, perpetual drilling, cultivating esprit de
corps, and an officer hierarchy backed by military police. At first tribal
warfare consisted of short skirmishes and involved much ritual defiance
but considerably less action. Thus, the capacity for violence has increased

with greater, permanent social organization. Violence is not primordial, and civilization does not tame it; the opposite is nearer the truth, Collins says.[34] Civilization makes killing easier, more organized, more legitimate, and more efficient, adds Malešević.[35] Yet armies are highly efficient organizations only before they encounter the enemy. Then all hell breaks loose. Battles are chaotic and terrifying, the soldier sees that the enemy is trying to kill him, there is no escape (as there is in street brawling), and his own survival becomes unpredictable. Fear, anger, uncertainty seize the mind, and reason is subordinated to emotion. As one side flees during an incident of forward panic, the most murderous sentiments among the victors are suddenly induced as fear and uncertainty are released. Anger swells at those responsible for the fear and the deaths of comrades. Their charge forward, accompanied by triumphant cries, reinforces emotional hatred. For Collins serious violence needs both strong social controls and unusual situations.

Variations in the Frequency of War: Gender and Region

Militaries have been overwhelmingly masculine. When we glimpse the mass armies of Rome, China, Japan, pre-Columbian America, Europe, and elsewhere, we must visualize them as dense phalanxes of men, not a female face in sight. Higher officers were older men, while rankers were youngish males. Warrior norms, masculine and machismo, have amplified the gender bias. The sense of honor so important in war has been masculine, "being a man." Irregular guerilla forces throughout history have contained women, but fighting soldiers in regular armed forces have been men. The average male is physically stronger and faster than the average female, so that males on average made better soldiers in the battlefield body slashing, which lasted for most of history. This is presumably why armies were male, and it may be why patriarchy enshrining male dominance became the norm in human societies. Men were armed, women were not. In earlier hunter-gatherer and horticultural societies that lacked war, there was relative equality between the sexes. Maybe Amazon warriors existed, though this has not been proved, but women have mostly predominated among camp followers. In recent times many women have had nonfighting roles, as medics, drivers, clerks, cooks, and computer operators. So is war only part of male genetic makeup?

Women now, however, can equally fire guns and drive tanks, planes, and drones, and more are becoming fighting soldiers. In World War I

many women served as noncombatants in all armies, and some died performing their duties. But in 1917 the Kerensky Provisional Government
in Russia, desperate for soldiers, founded fifteen women's fighting units.
The first Russian Women's Battalion of Death, all volunteers, was sent to
the front and fought with greater enthusiasm than their war-weary male
conscript comrades. Since the men wanted the war ended, they hated
these women, who seemed to want to prolong it. A second Battalion of
Death was disbanded as the Kerensky government changed policy, but
about five hundred of these women went on their own initiative to the
front. A female light cavalry Cossack unit also went, and another unit
was posted to defend the provisional government headquarters in the
Winter Palace. Months later it was overwhelmed by mostly male Bolshevik soldiers. Veterans of such units then fought on both sides in the Russian Civil War, though not in all-female units. Russia led the world in
female death dealing.

In the interwar period women fought in the Finnish, Spanish, and
Irish civil wars, as they probably had in earlier civil wars. In World War
II thousands of women fought in the Red Army and the Serb resistance.
Slav women still led in killing! In the Indian National Army allied with
the Japanese the Rani of Jansi was a regiment of women. Elsewhere, few
fought. British and German authorities in World War II authorized
women to staff antiaircraft batteries but not to pull the trigger, a task reserved for masculinity.[36] In the Vietnam War over one hundred thousand
women fought for the PLF (the Vietcong) and the NVA (the North Vietnamese Army), especially as guerillas and in bringing supplies along the
Ho Chi Minh Trail. They took heavy casualties. From the 1970s about a
dozen regular armies have in principle accepted women into almost all
roles, but in practice women have rarely fought. Since modern killing
rarely requires big muscles (except for infantry carrying loads of up to
forty-five kilos), it is only a matter of time before women will become
equal killers. In the U.S. and British air forces there are already women
drone killers. We are discovering that supposedly masculine and machismo sentiments might not be necessary features of militarism, though
these were ever-present in the armies of the past. Female participation in
war atrocities will come, as it already has in some civil wars. War is not
programmed genetically into human beings or only into men. But culturally and in numbers, it has obviously been male so far.

The human nature of soldiers is largely (though not entirely) irrelevant. What matters is that they obey orders. They are always initially ter-

rified, they would often prefer to flee than fight, but they do usually fight, and only a few desert. They are not genetically programmed to do this; they fight because they are socialized and drilled and disciplined, and because they are trapped in their military formations, especially on the battlefield. Clearly, however, there are personality differences. Some soldiers are braver or more vicious than others.

Exaggerating the frequency and scale of war is widespread. Ibn Khaldun noted that in his time chroniclers grossly exaggerated the size of armies because sensationalism sold.[37] There is a persistent internet myth (whose source is unclear) that of the supposed 3,400 years of recorded human history, only 268 have been entirely peaceful. This is bizarre. Who could possibly know this? Yet even if it were true, it would only mean that somewhere across the world one dispute turned into war every fifteen months. The vast majority of human groups in any given year would be at peace. Scholars have given estimates of wars in Europe over several centuries varying between 1.1 and 1.4 wars per year. Again, that means that somewhere in Europe slightly more than one war was ongoing, so that almost all its very many states were at peace. Ditto with estimates for historical China. Though complex societies containing states and social classes have a propensity to make war, their years of warfare are far outnumbered by their years of peace, and their conflicts are far more likely to have been settled by diplomacy, or they remained as running sores without wars.

For warfare since 1816, we can draw on statistical data that reveal large differences between countries and regions. The CoW criterion of at least one thousand battle deaths in a single year reveals sixty-six interstate wars occurring since 1816. Of these sole or main warring states, 54 percent were European.[38] Yet this is an understatement. If we add the seventy-one CoW colonial wars fought by the Europeans against stateless peoples, their contribution rises to 68 percent. But this still undercounts colonial wars. In the forty-three-year period from 1871 to 1914, the British, French, and Dutch between them probably fought at least a hundred military engagements against native forces—about 2.5 wars per year.[39] Thus, Europeans have probably perpetrated well over 80 percent of all wars since 1816, an astonishing disproportion, considering that Europeans contributed only 15 percent of world population at the beginning and 11 percent at the end of this period.

Europeans were from Mars. Evan Luard pushed back the statistics for war in Europe over another four centuries to the year 1400, and Jack

Levy did it to 1494.[40] They reveal that Europeans' propensity for war remained quite high over half a millennium. In the period 1400 to 1559,
Luard finds an average of 1.4 wars fought per year; from 1559 to 1648,
the average was 1.25 per year; and from 1648 to 1789, he says it was only
0.29—but these were mostly big wars between the great powers that had
a consequent large rise in casualties.[41] Such averages conceal big differences between countries. At the extreme, Sweden and Norway fought no
wars at all after 1816, but in earlier centuries Sweden had fought many
wars, which indicates differences between time periods as well as countries. In the post-1816 data sets, no other continent or region has been
anywhere near as warlike as Europe. Latin America since 1833 has had
only about twelve such interstate wars (see chapter 9).

In the nineteenth century, wars among Africans probably increased—and the scale of warfare certainly increased—as African leaders,
influenced by Western imperialism, conquered empires of their own. We
know that some of this, like that in the Zulu kingdom, was bloody, but
numbers of casualties are unknown. Nonetheless, African interstate wars
have been almost nonexistent since the colonial powers departed (though
civil wars have raged there). Before then, Europe had led in war making,
followed at a distance by Asia, then the Middle East, and Latin America
and Africa lagging behind. The African and Latin American postcolonial
ratios of interstate wars are three to five times less than the global average.[42] My tentative conclusion is that other continents and countries in
modern times came more from Venus than Mars—though not entirely,
for few known societies have been entirely free of war over long periods.

We know of both warlike and relatively peaceful cases in all periods
of history. In ancient Near Eastern history we can perhaps contrast warring Sumerian city-states and then Sumerian dynasties with the more
peaceful Egyptian Old and Middle Kingdoms.[43] There are two likely explanations. First, the economic wealth of Egypt was protected from military predators by deserts, and so states did not have to invest heavily in
fortifications; on the other hand, the wealth of the Sumerian cities was
open to attack from adjacent plains and hills, and so they built up substantial fortifications. But, second, Egypt was mostly a single kingdom,
again encouraged by the ecology of the Nile Valley, whereas Sumer,
though a single culture, was divided into city-states that warred intermittently with each other.

Archaeologists no longer believe in a "Mayan Peace." The Maya of
pre-Columbian Central America appear from their paintings, sculptures,

and texts (now deciphered) to have become highly war-prone.[44] Weapons, a few fortifications, and depictions of violence have been found on Minoan Crete, but they are rare, and violence seems to have been more ritualized than murderous.[45] Graeber and Wengrow connect this to what they see as the political dominance of women in Minoan society.[46]

The Indus Valley civilization may have been the most peaceful of all. A century of excavations has unearthed two major and several minor cities with sophisticated water and sewerage systems, standardized weights and measures, literacy, but no evidence of palaces, temples, armies, wars, armor, weapons (except those designed for hunting animals), or skeletons bearing the marks of violent death. We have depictions of men and gods fighting wild animals, but not fighting other humans or gods. The architecture of the cities suggests a relatively egalitarian and highly cooperative society that was engaged in much trade with Mesopotamia and India, but apparently not in wars. In the decline and collapse of the civilization, there are no ash deposits of burned buildings, nor do citadels reveal the kinds of damage we associate with fighting. Flooding from sea and river seems a likelier cause of collapse. It is possible that future excavations or a successful deciphering of its script will reveal more violence, but at the moment this civilization stands as the longest-lived exception to the ubiquity of war. Part of the explanation might be ecology, for the lands around were relatively barren, supporting few people and no significant rival state, and the few partially fortified settlements found were by the seacoast, where pirates might come from afar. This does not explain why there seem to have been also no civil wars. There were a number of distinct cities, but no evidence of conflict between them.

There have been better-documented but shorter periods of more recent peace. For 250 years, from 1637, Korea was a peaceful "hermit kingdom," avoiding relations with other countries apart from tribute embassies sent to China and opening one port to Japanese merchants. For a further hundred-plus years, Korea initiated no foreign wars, though it was attacked several times. Japan was also self-isolating and peaceful for 250 years from the early 1600s. Switzerland has not declared war since 1531, although it suffered brief civil wars, and some Napoleonic wars were fought by foreigners in Swiss territory. Sweden has not experienced war since 1814. Thus, large differences have existed between regions and periods.

After World War II came an abrupt European reversal. Since then Western Europeans, like Africans and Latin Americans, have fought almost no interstate wars, while the Middle East, Asia, and the United States have taken over martial leadership. In fact, war participation by Western Europeans elsewhere in this period has been almost nonexistent if we exclude Britain and France. The other Europeans were now suddenly from Venus. Before 1945 it might have been thought that war was structurally programmed into European society, but the same generation that had made the most cataclysmic war of all switched to peace—indeed, that is part of the explanation. Thus, "European character" is neither inherently warlike nor inherently peaceful. It has fluctuated according to social and geopolitical context.

We find similar time differences in China. Here we have historical records from the eighth century BCE. Between 710 and 221 BCE (the date of the founding of the unified Qin Empire) there were wars in 75 percent of these 489 years, at an average of about 1.6 wars each year. These figures are comparable to those of martial-era Europe.[47] The Chinese were also from Mars. After 221 BCE, wars involving China decreased, though with big variations between regions. There were also civil wars, where dynastic succession was disputed. But as the Chinese Empire declined, Japan rose, and since Russia also became expansionist in the Far East, warfare revived significantly there. Since 1945 Japan has again been peaceful, while some other East Asian countries have had wars. The United States has also had an uneven record, its military aggression having peaked in the most recent decades. But there has been no war with Canada since 1812.

Conclusion

Given such geographical and historical contrasts, the causes of war do not lie in the evolution of an essential human character, as Coker has claimed.[48] Indirectly, of course, human nature does matter, for that yields hot tempers and aggressive ideological commitments, but these are variably distributed. Instead, the causes of war lie in differing social roles, class and state structures, and institutions and cultures that tilt the war-peace balance and killing ratios one way or the other. I explore this in chapter 4 onward, using historical narratives of six relatively well-documented cases. I have selected one case where wars were always frequent—ancient Rome; two where they began frequent but then became fewer—ancient China and medieval and modern Europe; one that showed great fluctuations—late medieval to modern Japan; one where interstate wars were at first plentiful and then became rare—precolonial and postcolonial Latin America; and one making the most recent and most global wars—the United States. Where possible I discuss their colonial wars too. To these cases I add a brief description of postcolonial Africa in which interstate wars have been rare but civil wars common. I hope that this variety, combined with my global span, protect me from possible charges of modernism, Eurocentrism, or cherry-picking my cases to fit some particular theory. It also allows me to explain why some times and places have been much more warlike than others. But first I explore how others have viewed the causes of war.

CHAPTER THREE

Theories of the Causes of War

THE CAUSES OF WAR are many. They concern the motives and the powers of the rival protagonists—desired ends and available means—the nature of the issues in dispute, escalating interactions, and the broader contexts, ecological, geopolitical, and historical, that might escalate disputes into war. All must figure in an explanation of war.

There have been many motives for making war. Economic motives include seizing wealth, land, and labor, free or unfree, getting tribute, dictating the terms of trade, and the mixed economic-sexual seizing of women. Political motives are aimed at enhancing rulers' domestic political power, rewarding one's clan and clients, and deflecting internal conflicts onto foreign enemies. Geopolitical motives aim to enhance status in the geopolitical system, aid threatened allies, co-ethnics, or coreligionists abroad, preempt perceived threats by others, and avenge earlier insults or defeats. Military motives include enjoying imposing terror, being confident in victory, and self-defense. Ideological motives include aggressive nationalism, forcing religious or political ideologies on others, militarism internalized as a desirable code of conduct, and pursuing redress for a perceived slight, revenge, honor, status, or glory through war. All these motives are goal-oriented and assume some degree of means-ends rationality and calculation.

The number and diversity of motives are striking, and they generally come not singly but in combinations varying through the descent into war. Descent adds interactions between rulers and their armed forces. As Clausewitz observed, war "is not the action of a living force upon a lifeless mass ... but always the collision of two living forces"—and often more than two.[1] Motives alone do not tell us why war happens, since alternative means are available to achieve most desired ends. For example, one can obtain wealth through peaceful cooperation and economic exchange, or by threats or trade embargoes short of war. Why is war sometimes chosen instead? There is not agreement about this among scholars of war.

Political Power: Inside Societies and States

Who exactly makes war-and-peace decisions? We talk of Rome against Carthage or the Chinese against the Mongols or the United States against Iraq. These are unavoidable simplifications, but we should not assign motives to states or nations. The decision makers are always specific human beings, and they are almost always small coteries of rulers and their advisers. Persons have motives and emotions, institutions do not. Elites often contain rival war-and-peace factions—Werner Sombart's *Händler und Helden*, merchants and heroes. They dispute the merits of war versus peace, or war versus trade, or offense versus defense. Their struggles will often decide whether there is war or peace.

In complex societies containing a division of labor, the conduct of war is usually assigned to a professional warrior caste. Warriors have their own motives, which might be more or less warlike (since they are generally aware of the horrors and limitations of war). Some generals might prefer not war but a climate of fear, so that they are given large resources without risking their lives. Political rulers may conversely fear their generals' power to mount coups or rebellions, and so they may deliberately weaken them, reducing the likelihood of making aggressive war; this happened persistently in imperial China (see chapter 6) and was also important in the recent Middle East (see chapter 14).

Historians often emphasize popular pressures on war-and-peace decisions, but I am skeptical. The masses are rarely involved in such decision making since they lack interest—in both senses of the word—in foreign policy. "Popular" pressures can turn out influential pressure groups or mobilize crowds but only rarely the mass of the people. Some pressure might well up from below, but most is organized by pressure groups with special interests at stake, or are stoked by mass media for

whom war fever sells or by students who love to demonstrate. There are
some warrior-dominated societies, like the Mongols and the early Muslim Arabs, and also a few ideological wars in which a mass movement
pressurizes rulers. Yet Hermann Goering, a leader of such a mass movement, dismissed this when arguing with the U.S. jurist Gustave Gilbert
in his Nuremberg prison cell in 1946 before his execution:

> Goering: Why, of course, the *people* don't want war. Why
> would some poor slob on a farm want to risk his life in a war
> when the best that he can get out of it is to come back to his farm
> in one piece? Naturally, the common people don't want war; nei-
> ther in Russia nor in England nor in America, nor for that matter
> in Germany. That is understood. But, after all, it is the *leaders* of
> the country who determine the policy and it is always a simple
> matter to drag the people along, whether it is a democracy or a
> fascist dictatorship, or a parliament, or a communist dictatorship.

> Gilbert: There is one difference. In a democracy the people
> have some say in the matter through their elected representa-
> tives, and in the United States only Congress can declare wars.

> Goering: Oh, that is all well and good, but, voice or no voice,
> the people can always be brought to the bidding of the leaders.
> That is easy. All you have to do is tell them they are being attacked,
> and denounce the pacifists for lack of patriotism and exposing the
> country to danger. It works the same way in any country.[2]

Goering was right, although saying so did not exactly help his
chances of survival! Even in the United States the president and his advisers can manipulate their way into wars. War is the sport of rulers. For
the masses the main curse is war, not who wins it. Yet institutionalized
power relations ensure that the masses follow their rulers into battle,
even sometimes with enthusiasm. They have no alternative sources of
knowledge to what their rulers tell them about the evils of the enemy,
and they are usually ignorant beforehand of how terrible war will prove
to be—for wars are irregular events. In advance, war seems like a masculine adventure story to young men. Reality strikes for soldiers only in
their first battle, while reality dawns on civilian populations, male and female of all ages, only in long, costly wars or when war is fought in their
own fields and cities. Wars may be only superficially popular—but that is

enough to start them, and then they entrap everyone. Soldiers can be trapped by military hierarchy, the battlefield, their own values, or their sense of duty in "getting the job done." Former president Herbert Hoover declared in a 1944 speech: "Older men declare war. But it is youth that must fight and die." War is a conspiracy among old rulers to kill the young. War has also normally been a male activity, although women have generally regarded war as necessary and encouraged their men to fight, shaming them if they don't. Few women have been paci-fists; rather, they were not asked to fight.

The rarity of popular interest in foreign policy has attracted cynical views of war as a political tool wielded by the upper class. Thomas More gave sixteenth-century expression to this in his *Utopia:* "The common folk do not go to war of their own accord, but are driven to it by the madness of kings."[3] Marxists present a modern version: war is a ruling-class strategy to deflect internal class conflicts onto an outside foe. Yet Levy presents evidence suggesting this is rare, and Geoffrey Blainey says a government weakened by domestic strife might want to promote a rally 'round the flag sentiment by conjuring foreign threats but is un-likely to go so far as to declare war.[4] Instead, he finds in the period 1816–1939 that a nation weakened by internal strife is more likely to be attacked by others. It is also dangerous for rulers to arm their subjects. Victory in the 1914–18 war might have boosted Habsburg and Romanov dynasty rule, as was intended by those pressing for war. But defeat brought revolution by workers and peasants bearing guns, as dissenters in both courts had warned. "War fever" does dampen class tensions in the short term, and a quick victory legitimizes rulers, but prolonged war-fare does so only if successful (and even then not always). Today, disputes among nuclear powers cannot rationally be translated into war, but pro-moting fear of the other is useful to preserving one's rule. The current terrorist threat is typically exaggerated, but it places society on a perma-nent threat alert, increasing state power and reducing civil rights while not risking major war.

Marxists are right that the ruling class makes the decisions for war, and other classes die as a result. They are also right to note that in pre-capitalist modes of production with economic surpluses, these were usu-ally extracted from the direct producers by force in the form of unfree labor statuses, such as serfdom, corvée labor, and slavery, all supervised by military power. This was necessary for the rulers to live in luxury or to fight any wars at all. But are wars a rational strategy by dominant classes to deflect class conflict? The rulers would have to be confident that they would win the war quickly—although we will see that overconfidence in victory is normal. It may be more common for rulers to go to war to demonstrate their political strength to rival elites. The deflection of conflict within ruling classes rather than between them might have been more typical.

Political scientists used to argue that democracies do not go to war, but this is not true. Institutionalized democracies do rarely suffer civil wars since they have routinized electoral procedures for regime succession, whereas monarchies and dictatorships are intermittently plagued by succession crises, and democratizing societies in ethnically plural societies are vulnerable to civil war and ethnic cleansing, as I showed in my book *The Dark Side of Democracy*.[5] The "democratic peace" argument has been modified into the claim that democracies do not go to war against other democracies. Levy says, "The absence of war between democracies comes as close as anything we have to an empirical law in international relations."[6] But this comes from focusing on wars between major representative democracies, mostly Western, in the period since 1816. This ignores the earlier war making democracies of history such as some Greek city-states and some early Sumerian city-states—highly imperfect democracies, yes, but so are our own.[7] Modern colonial wars involved many native peoples who had direct democracies in which the whole community or all men decided on war or peace, and anyone had the right not to fight. Such groups often fought against each other. One curious contrary case was the Iroquois Nations' League, which embodied a "Great Law" of peace lasting from 1450 to 1777.[8] During this time the nations kept their own political autonomy and decided their own policies. Yet the individual nations waged war against outsiders, killing, torturing, and even sometimes eating them, but they never warred against each other or collectively, as a league. Finally, whatever constitutions say, in most modern democracies decisions for war are more often made by the executive branch than by parliaments, let alone by the people.

Yet political science has spawned a "triumphalist" democratic school seeing democracies as not only more pacific but more successful in the wars they do fight.[9] Yet Alexander Downes says that Dan Reiter and Allan Stam combine those attacked (called targets) with those joining a war later (joiners), and that they exclude wars in which there is no victor.[10] When targets and joiners are separated, and draws are included (for they indicate lack of success), democratic states, whether initiators, targets, or joiners, are neither more likely to win nor more likely to lose wars. Other political scientists maintain that democracies fight more effectively, having bigger economies, stronger alliances, better decision making, more public support, and better soldier morale. Michael Desch has roundly criticized this, finding no significant relation between war capacity and regime type.[11] He concludes: "The good news is that contrary to some defeatists inside and outside the U.S. government, democracy is not a liability for a state in choosing and effectively waging war. The bad news, however, is that democracy is not as large an asset as triumphalists maintain. In sum, regime type hardly matters."[12] The twentieth-century armies of authoritarian Germany, the Soviet Union, China, and Vietnam enjoyed superior morale to their democratic opponents. When we add Islamist fighters (see chapter 14), ideological morale compensated for the technologically superior armies confronting them.

Economic Goals, Military Means

Seeking material gain is an important cause of war, and military power supplies the means. Calculating the relations between them dominates much theory. Yet why choose war to get richer? War is costlier in money and lives, it is riskier since it may result in defeat or a costly draw, and it makes enemies. On the plus side, victory may yield immediate reward in the form of tribute, but this may last only as long as you can enforce it. Conquest and direct rule may give more secure possession of resources, especially of geographically fixed resources like fertile soils, minerals, or harbors, but their administration is costly. Slaves, normally acquired by war, permit more intensive exploitation than free waged labor. Slavery, however, has costs in its need for coercive supervision and its lack of labor flexibility (you don't lay off slaves when business is bad).

Sexual motives have usually figured in raiding. Raiders typically raped women or carried them off as wives or concubines or slaves. The motives were to satisfy sexual desire, to exercise dominance, or to increase the victors' rate of reproduction, thereby making their group stronger. Rape is also easy for armed men to accomplish. In modern warfare rape remains common; indeed, the highest total of known rapes in a single campaign was perpetrated by Red Army soldiers in 1945, who raped an estimated 2 million German women. Though today rape is still common, carrying women off is much less so, except in nonstate armies. In earlier societies raiding rather than full-scale war was often sufficient to carry off loot, slaves, and women from territories that the raider could not stably control.

For much of history, victors reaped the spoils of war—land, loot, slaves, women. Provided war was not too costly and they survived, rulers and most soldiers could benefit and war might be rational for them in terms of ends. This was Weber's "booty capitalism"—risky but profitable. But the general population back home might not benefit. European expansion into the world was rational in terms of ends for many younger sons and settlers, but not for most of the population. Probably only two European countries, Holland and Britain, made a net long-term profit from their colonies.[13] Perception of profit was what mattered, however, and overoptimism was normal among war makers. The conquistadores, soldiers, merchants, plantation owners, and settlers directly participating in colonial ventures might make a large profit if they survived the battles and diseases. The risks were great, but so were the potential profits, though the financiers staying at home did best. Few Americans have derived material benefit from recent wars. Many, perhaps most, defensive wars are rational in ends if successful, though they rarely bring additional material resources.

Wealth can also be sought by military threats short of war, aimed not at conquest but at tribute or coercing the terms of trade. The different types of empire identified in volumes 3 and 4 of my *Sources of Social Power* involved varying degrees of military coercion. Informal empire, for example, threatens military power but uses it only in short bursts aimed not at territorial conquest but at demanding homage and tribute or dictating the terms of production or trade. "Tributary empires" receive tribute from rulers who otherwise might remain in control of their domains. If they refuse, they may be removed and replaced with more reliable clients. There is also the reverse tributary case, where an empire pays tribute to its neighbors so that they will not attack it. It was cheaper for China to pay off barbarians than pay for military forces to fight them. The United States today can learn from this (see chapter 14). While better-developed societies may make forays against less well-developed ones by virtue of perceived military superiority, they themselves may be tempting targets for less economically developed but militarily skilled raiders, as Rome and China were for barbarian neighbors: they offered a spectacle of such riches that if the barbarians could raid and run away it might be rational to try it. The inhospitable terrain of their homelands and their military mobility gave them motive and opportunity.

Those seeking war for economic gain should be constrained by their material means of making war—the cost in both money and lives of militaries and their effectiveness relative to their rivals. Military power may tempt states into aggression if they perceive easy pickings. Yet many wars are fought between powers or alliances of powers that are evenly matched, and these tend to produce longer, costlier wars. It is less clear why their rulers should rationally choose war rather than other means of increasing rewards. The opposite puzzling case is where lesser powers defy and fight those that are much stronger. Why do they not do the apparently rational thing and give in? On occasion, military tactics may offset inferior numbers. Ever since Sun Tzu's time, military writers have stressed that concentration of forces against the enemy's weakest point in battle matters most, not overall inequality of forces. Yet since both sides are trying to do this, the bigger battalions generally do win, though there are exceptions. Political scientists have also tried to find good reasons for the weak to resist the strong, though only for modern wars.[14]

Most wars are fought between neighbors over disputed border territories, who claim this is rational in both economic and strategic terms. Yet they usually add on moral assertions, bringing emotions into the dispute, especially in "revisionism," whereby one party claims the right to territory it used to own but then lost—as do Russia and China today or the extraordinary pitting of a claim based on one thousand years of Arab land ownership in Palestine against a rival Jewish settler claim dating back to a purported gift by Jehovah himself! Wherever territory is lost, there will be revisionism. Economic interests tend to be quantifiable and capable of compromise, as in splitting the difference in rival territorial claims. But deaths cannot be objectively measured against profit, and if we add righteous emotions, compromise becomes difficult. It is rare to find a war that does not invoke notions of right and justice. Economic power relations do cause disputes, while escalation to war should include calculating costs, benefits, and relative military strengths; yet other motivations, emotions, and situations are necessary to explain why the horrors of war are accepted so often.

Contexts 1: Ecology

I will place war-and-peace decisions amid the contexts of geography and history. Geography was emphasized in late nineteenth- and early twentieth-century geopolitical theory, but recently geography has given way to

politics. Archaeologists suggest that war began when human groups settled fixed natural environments that could support them and which they
called their own—as John Locke had argued. When peoples irrigated
fertile river valleys, they were trapped there by Mother Nature. If they
left, it would be to less fertile land. Their lands were worth defending,
and less economically privileged neighbors with military resources
thought they were worth attacking. The sight of wealthy cities with fertile fields and fat animals lured pastoralists skilled at raiding. So cities
built up their military defenses and perhaps retaliated with punitive raids,
and war intensified. Wars were made likelier by ecological disjunctions
between fertile river valleys, irrigated or not, and savannas, mountains,
and jungles around whose economies generated distinctive military resources. This explanation is not founded only on ecologies, but on how
they generate different economic and military resources for the human
communities located at a specific site.

Moreover, a disjunction between the carrying capacity of the land and
population growth can threaten survival, to which warfare might be a rational response or at least a gamble on one's ability to seize land, or it
would be if starving people were good fighters. Darwinian sociologists emphasize population pressure as a spur to social evolution, but most archaeologists disagree.[15] In ancient Mesopotamia and Mesoamerica, growing
state complexity and more war were correlated with population decline,
not increase.[16] Warlike "Great Migrations" across Eurasia have often been
attributed to population pressure, but recent scholars have argued that
other pull-and-push factors mattered more. The pull was the lure of richer
lands and cities and the push was military pressure from other peoples at
their backs.[17] Climatic changes also mattered. In the thirteenth century the
weather favored Mongol expansion as the normally cold, dry steppes of
Central Asia enjoyed their mildest, wettest period for a thousand years,
which caused an increase in grass, war horses, and Mongols.[18] Mass migration has often led to war, for settlers favor conquest. They want land and its
natural resources at the expense of natives, who might be exploited as laborers or slaves, or expelled and in extremis exterminated. James Fearon
and David Laitin showed the importance for modern civil wars and their
guerillas of ecology.[19] Civil wars have flourished primarily in rugged terrains that allowed the weaker protagonist to hide and survive.

Ecology in interaction with social structures may encourage either
war or peace. Societies in pre-Columbian America lacked both the wheel
and draft animals (llamas were an exception of limited utility), and so

faced more daunting logistics of political and military power. The link between ecology and types of military formations (infantry, cavalry, and the like) and the influence of ecology on campaigns and battles have received much attention from military writers throughout history. Mother Nature does not lead us into war, for war is a human choice, yet choices are affected by ecology's effect on society.

Contexts 2: The Tyranny of History

Karl Marx's *18th Brumaire of Louis Bonaparte* (1852) begins: "Men make their own history, but they do not make it as they please; they do not make it under self-selected circumstances, but under circumstances existing already, given and transmitted from the past. The tradition of all dead generations weighs like a nightmare on the brains of the living."

Marx was applying this striking image to revolutions but it is also apposite to wars. International relations (IR) theories of war tend to lack history. Sequences of wars are neglected in favor of comparison of individual cases taken out of their historical contexts; such theories disregard how the past may influence or constrain present decisions for war or peace. Historians obviously do focus on causal flows through time, although they rarely hazard long-term or comparative generalizations. My cases are not single wars (except for the American Civil War) but sequences of war (and peace) over long periods, the longest being an almost three-thousand-year account of war in China. Past wars weigh on the brains of present decision makers, but not only as nightmares. A major predictor of civil wars is earlier civil wars in a specific locale.[20] The same is true for interstate wars. Sociologists call this "path dependence": the present path depends on, or at least is substantially constrained by, past paths. Though we cannot convert path dependence into a law, it is a tendency in contexts where the past was relatively successful. Past victories lead to increased ambition, overconfidence, and ultimate hubris. Militarism becomes "baked in" to cultures and institutions, so that war becomes seen as normal and even virtuous, making it more likely.

Contexts 3: Geopolitics, Realism

From Thucydides through Machiavelli to contemporary political scientists, geopolitics has been seen as the endless pursuit of power by rival states, inevitably leading to wars between them. "Realism" has been the dominant theory. States are the sole actors in an "anarchic" international space; there is no arbiter above them wielding international law, in contrast to the rule of law that routinely exists within states. Thus, states cannot be certain of other states' intentions, but they reason that the greater their own power, the less likely they are to be attacked. So they all build up their power. This, however, leads to "security dilemmas." To ensure a state's security, its leaders must prepare for possible war, building up military power, perhaps only for defense, but this alarms rivals into escalating their military preparedness, too.[21] Contagious feelings of insecurity make war more likely. It might take only one aggressive community or state, for whatever reason, to begin a process of escalation. Sometimes none of those caught up in escalation might have originally wished for war. Realism can be "offensive" or "defensive." John Mearsheimer, an offense advocate, says states will ceaselessly pursue more and more power, whereas Kenneth Waltz, on defense, says balances of power make states content once they have acquired enough power to survive and feel secure.

Insecurity also means that all protagonists claim to be fighting in self-defense, which is generally considered legitimate. Many rulers whom we might consider to be aggressors paradoxically claim that they are the threatened ones, striking out in fear of other predatory states. German rulers in 1914 declared that Britain was "strangling" them across the world, and that Russian military modernization would soon threaten them on land. Japanese rulers struck out in World War II using the same metaphor, the main strangler being the United States. Such fears were not groundless, although it was the German and Japanese responses that produced war. Since Realists attribute readiness for war as necessary self-defense against the uncertainty of geopolitics, they tend to absolve rulers of blame for provoking acts of aggression. Yet rulers can always try diplomacy instead of war. Humans seek collective as well as distributive power—cooperation, not conflict—to achieve what they desire. And they may pursue their goals using any of the four sources of power, not just military power.

It is true that most geopolitical relations are less rule-governed than relations within states, except for civil wars, palace coups, and repressive rulers who kill large numbers of their own people. But we should treat "anarchy" as a variable, present in varying degrees. Wendt identifies three degrees of anarchy in European history.[22] The most warlike he calls Hobbesian anarchy, where states share almost no norms and perceive other states as enemies. He locates this in pre-1648 Europe. The medium level he calls Lockeian anarchy, where European states perceived others as rivals but accepted norms like the notion of "live and let live," recognizing each other's right to exist. He says this typified the post-1648 Westphalian system of Europe. The lowest level of anarchy he calls Kantian, where states cooperate with each other, influenced by an "other-help" conception based on "collective identity" and shared norms of conduct: war is displaced in favor of cooperation, as in post-1945 Western Europe. I find the first two of his periods problematic (see chapter 8), but real-world geopolitics does contain varying degrees of anarchy. Contrast in this volume the highly anarchic environment of sixteenth-century Japan (chapter 7) with the mild case of postcolonial Latin America (chapter 9).

Realists note an alternative to anarchy. A single hegemonic state can knock heads together to achieve geopolitical order and peace because it has overwhelming military and usually also economic power in its region, as well as leadership regarded as legitimate by other states. It combines what Max Weber called domination and authority. The model cases are Britain in the nineteenth century and the United States since 1945. Yet hegemons are uncommon. If a state seems potentially hegemonic, others may form "balancing" alliances against it. Yet there was no balancing against the hegemony of Britain, the United States, the Roman Republic, or the Chinese Qin dynasty, so there are specific preconditions of balancing alliances. Rulers must be confident that their alliance can defeat the would-be hegemon and that their allies will live up to their commitments, for if some make a deal with the hegemonic power, the others are at greater risk. Anarchy means allies cannot be fully trusted. Indeed, a balancing coalition also requires normative solidarity among the allies, but norms are absent from Realist theory. The allies must also fear the dominant power if they are to combine against it. This has not been so since 1945 in Western Europe, where the United States is seen as protecting those countries from worse predators. The notion of anarchy is useful but variably so.

I am more skeptical about Realists' other core thesis: that states are self-interested, unitary actors rationally pursuing carefully calculated means for pursuing their goals and seeking to maximize their prospects for survival and growth. Thus, we should find that rulers choose war rather than more peaceful forms of power when it can better achieve desired goals. There is, however, implicit tension between Realism's two theses of anarchy and calculation. Anarchy breeds anxiety and fear of others, which rises as the possibility of war looms, but these are emotional states conducive to reckless, angry, or panicking behavior rather than calm calculation. Decisions for war or peace are usually made in highly fraught environments of growing tensions, domestic and foreign. Thus, not all Realists stress calculative efficiency. Waltz argued that states often act in nonstrategic, reckless ways, but he does not abandon rationality altogether; he says that when states act recklessly, the system punishes them, whereas states that act rationally are rewarded by the system. Here rationality of means lies not with the individual state actor but with the hidden hand of the system.[23]

Mearsheimer expresses the commoner Realist view: "Great powers are rational actors. They are aware of their external environment and they think strategically about how to survive in it. In particular, they consider the preferences of other states and how their own behavior is likely to affect the behavior of those other states, and how the behavior of those other states is likely to affect their own strategy for survival. Moreover, states pay attention to the long term as well as the immediate consequences of their actions."[24] States are said to act "with relative efficiency." Bruce Bueno de Mesquita makes this into an "expected utility theory" of war: states go to war when the expected benefits exceed the expected costs.[25] Calculation leads to fairly accurate predictions of when war will bring gain. A few historians concur; Michael Howard says: "Men have fought during the last two hundred years neither because they are aggressive nor because they are acquisitive animals, but because they are reasoning ones. . . . Wars begin by conscious and reasoned decisions based on the calculation, made by *both* parties, that they can achieve more by going to war than by remaining at peace."[26]

Fearon criticizes Realist theorists, saying, "War is costly and risky, so rational states should have incentives to locate negotiated settlements that all would prefer to the gamble of war."[27] I agree. Whatever the anarchical threats, more is needed to push states over the brink into risky, costly war. So he adds three factors that he believes can save the Realist model: states can miscalculate because of imperfect or asymmetric information, whereby one state has private information and incentives to misrepresent it; commitment problems whereby mutually preferable bargains are unattainable because at least one state would have an incentive to renege on a deal; and some issues are indivisible, preventing a compromise.[28] But Fearon's actors remain "genuinely rational, unitary states," and he excludes the role of emotions, ideologies, or power struggles within states, all of which we will see perpetually permeate decision making. Human action is not in fact dominated by instrumental rationality, pragmatic calculation, and understandable mistakes. Margaret Mac-Millan notes that even if a struggle seems material, defenders always try to protect what they hold dear, so that emotions are always involved.[29] Some Realists acknowledge factional power struggles within a state. But they say that these rarely undermine rational strategic thinking and so can be treated as "noise." Mearsheimer says: "Unit-level factors usually do not have much effect on foreign policy-making, and when they do, they do so in ways that are consistent with balance-of-power logic. Domestic political calculations are not likely to undermine sound strategic thinking."[30] This is hard to believe, and we will see that it is not true.

Some political scientists do introduce noninstrumental elements into geopolitics. Richard Ned Lebow, analyzing twenty-six twentieth-century wars, says wars emerge out of periods of dislocating political crises.[31] He identifies three types: crises arising from the ruler's attempt to mobilize domestic and foreign support for war; spinoff crises resulting from unintended secondary confrontations with third parties if accommodation is tried; and brinkmanship crises, the most common type, when a ruler tries to force an adversary to back away from a commitment. Misperception, especially of the resolve of the enemy, is a major cause of war when there is brinkmanship: "As learning and steering capacity diminish, policy comes to resemble a stone rolling downhill; it can neither be rerolled nor can its path be altered."[32] And crises are not conducive to calm rational calculation. If only political leaders did carefully assess the pros and cons of war! Realism, like its competitor, liberalism, is in reality a normative theory that says to rulers, "This is how you should behave if you are rational." But, alas, they often do not.

Most political scientists focus on war between major European powers since 1816, where the statistical data sets can be found. This leads to biases, some of which I have already noted. Here are two more. These great powers had virtually filled up the space of their geographical core, so that this really was a multistate system. Today this has become a world multistate system that offers almost no possibilities for expansion, except extraterrestrially. In these space-filling multistate systems, sometimes states win wars, sometimes they lose, and sometimes they fight inconclusively. But they do not die. It is a board game of diplomacy in which all the players stay on the board. Both Waltz and Wendt say that the death of states is rare.[33] This might be true of major modern states, but it is

false of much of the rest of history. Most wars discussed in this book resulted in an enormous number of states disappearing. Successful states
became bigger through imperial swallowing up of the "vanished kingdoms" of history. The number of disappeared societies greatly exceeds
that of the survivors, on all continents. This presents a conundrum for
defensive Realism: Can states act "with relative efficiency" to ensure
their survival when the vast majority do not survive?

IR theorists say that some geopolitical configurations generate wars
more than others, but they cannot agree on which.[34] Significant correlations (on post-1816 statistical data) between geopolitical configurations
and war are rare. Multistate systems sometimes produce many interstate
wars, as they have historically in Europe, but not in postcolonial Latin
America or Africa. There is no agreement about whether "bipolar" (two
great powers) or "multipolar" (many powers) entities dominate a geopolitical system—or whether an equal or an unequal distribution of power
between states causes more war.[35] Bruce Bueno de Mesquita and David
Lalman examined different distributions of power and the number and internal cohesion of alliances and found no significant correlations with
wars.[36] Nor did decision makers act as if they were constrained by such
variables. Some writers say international trade brings peace, but others
dispute this.[37] A balance of power between many states is sometimes associated with peace, but not among the city-states of classical Greece or the
warring states of ancient China. Balances are fragile. As Kant nicely put it:
"A lasting universal Peace on the basis of the so-called Balance of Power
in Europe is a mere chimera. It is like the house described by Swift, which
was built by an architect so perfectly in accordance with all the laws of
equilibrium, that when a sparrow lighted upon it, it immediately fell."[38]

Power transition theory says that preponderance in power by a single dominant state decreases the likelihood of war, a weak form of hegemony, but if a dissatisfied challenger achieves power parity with the
dominant state, the probability of war increases. Rising powers sometimes do make war, but many don't. Germany spectacularly did so in the
twentieth century, but the simultaneous rise of the United States at the
expense of British power was peaceful. Here the normative solidarity of
Britain and the United States was important, but norms are neglected by
Realism. As for the United States, its rising power had led it into only
minor participation in interstate wars until 1941, when the country had
already risen and was actually attacked. Only after 1945, when the
United States was already hegemonic over most of the world, did Ameri-

can foreign policy embody substantial militarism. We might expect other rational rising powers to wait until they achieved superiority before turning to military aggression, but neither Germany nor Japan did wait. And adding other periods and regions, we see wars occurring in far more varied circumstances than Realism suggests. Something is wrong with the theory if it does not lead to empirically supported conclusions.

Stephen Van Evera analyzes thirty modern wars.[39] He says Realists have mistakenly attributed war to the "gross structures" of geopolitics, like those just mentioned. In his wars, these explain almost nothing. Yet he argues that more "fine-grained structures of power" do help explain war. He identifies four: first-move advantages privileging attack over defense; "windows of opportunity," whereby striking now gives a state a temporary edge; the relative ease of conquest; and cumulative resources whereby aggression yields further resources that enable a state to continue aggressing. Realism should focus on these, he concludes. Yet he actually shows not that these four do lead to war, but that *belief* in them by rulers does. If rulers believe there is a first-move advantage or a window of opportunity or easy conquest or cumulative resources, then war is more likely. This is a useful finding, but such beliefs are false as often as not, agrees Van Evera.

Finally comes entry into battle, an arena of emotions and chaos. Generals strive hard to maintain their rationality here, to implement an initial plan but also to adapt flexibly to changing events. Yet look at two famous generals who doubted their rational ability to accomplish this. Here is William Tecumseh Sherman on causes: "Wars do not usually result from just causes but from pretexts. There probably never was a just cause why men should slaughter each other by wholesale, but there are such things as ambition, selfishness, folly, madness, in communities as in individuals, which become blind and bloodthirsty, not to be appeased save by havoc, and generally by the killing of somebody else than themselves."[40]

And here is Clausewitz on battle: "So-called mathematical factors never find a firm basis in military calculations. From the very start there is an interplay of possibilities, probabilities, good luck and bad that weaves its way throughout the length and breadth of the tapestry. In the whole range of human activities, war most closely resembles a game of cards. . . . War is the realm of uncertainty: three quarters of the factors on which action in war is based are wrapped in a fog of greater or lesser uncertainty."[41]

This had also been expressed by Ibn Khaldun:

Victory and superiority in war come from luck and chance. . . . There are external factors such as the number of soldiers, the perfection and good quality of weapons, the number of brave men, skillful arrangement of the line formation, the proper tactics, and similar things. Then there are the hidden factors. These may be the result of human trickery . . . occupying high points . . . hiding in thickets or depressions [or] rocky terrain and similar things . . . suddenly appearing when the enemy is in a precarious position. . . . These hidden factors may also be celestial matters, which man has no power to produce for himself. They affect people psychologically, and thus generate fear in them. . . . An Arab proverb says: "Many a trick is worth more than a tribe." It is thus clear that superiority in war is, as a rule, the result of hidden causes, not of external ones. The occurrence of opportunities as the result of hidden causes is what is meant by luck.[42]

If they are correct, could humans rationally choose war to achieve their goals? In war as in Clausewitz's gambling metaphor, most players are losers.

Liberalism, Constructivism, Emotions

A rival English or liberal school in IR theory sees geopolitics as dual, involving both anarchical tendencies and benign international institutions and culture. Kant had argued that "perpetual peace" might be attainable under three conditions: representative government, a universal norm of hospitality toward strangers and traders, and an international federation of free states.[43] He took comfort from the fact that in his time representative government, international trade, and international law were spreading, but he accepted that there was a long way to go. Hedley Bull similarly found hope in representative democracy, the economic interdependence of global capitalism, and an international "society of states" centered on the United Nations, all sharing common norms and interests.[44] Comparable institutions restrained anarchy in the past, such as the medieval Church in Europe or Confucian education in China. Liberals say that common norms emerge because states share a fear of unrestricted violence and seek rules on the use of force, the sanctity of agreements, and property rights. Statesmen do pursue their own self-interest, but not at any cost, and the desire for peace is based on its considerable virtues. Liberals stress "international orders," collective agreements between states made to preserve peace, like the Peace of Westphalia in 1648, the Congress of Vienna in 1815, and the United Nations today (see chapters 8 and 15). Some liberals go further today, seeing a "world society" composed of states, nonstate collective actors, and individuals, all recognizing their mutual dependence and shared norms and values—a pacific spin on globalization theory. Yet it is not clear that either global capitalism or representative democracy leads necessarily to peace, or indeed that war is even declining across the world.

A third school of IR theory, constructivism, rejects Realist materialism and stresses social identities, seeing interests not as objectively grounded in material forces but as resulting from ideas and culture constructed in social interaction. Thus, constructivists do not assume rationality. Peter Katzenstein emphasizes "the cultural-institutional context of policy on the one hand and the constructed identity of states, governments, and other political actors on the other."[45] Institutions embody norms, identities, and cultures. Norms give actors their identity. Culture refers to both evaluative and cognitive standards defining how actors operate and how they interrelate. I largely agree, though I call this sociology, while noting that constructivism overplays cultural creation. Social institutions were originally constructed and then adapted by actors over long periods, some becoming deep structures, constraining actors at later points in time—such as the state, the Catholic Church, or capitalism. They are all composed of actors, but actors constrained by institutions that have lasted much longer than themselves. Sociology also contains a "cultural" approach to war, which is closer to constructivism, and it also neglects constraining power institutions, including those relevant to war-and-peace decisions.[46]

Constructivism also allows for emotions, neglected by Realists and some liberals. Lebow in a data set of ninety-four wars between major powers between 1648 and 2008 finds 107 dominant motives among the initiators of wars.[47] A concern for "standing" (status) or honor mostly motivated sixty-two wars, and another eleven were motivated mostly by vengeful territorial revisionism. Insecurity and fear, stressed by Realists, and material greed, stressed by Marxists, Realists, and liberals alike, account for only nineteen and eight cases, respectively. So sentiments of honor, status, and revenge produced over 70 percent of offensive wars and a wish for material gain only 9 percent. His powers are all European except for the United States and Japan since the 1890s and China since 1949. Nor does he discuss the most common warfare over many earlier centuries: the swallowing up of minnows by sharks. Would his findings apply to other contexts?

Overoptimism

War is especially puzzling: when weak fight strong powers rather than negotiate or submit, and when states or alliances of roughly equal powers fight each other, since their war will probably be prolonged and costly. We might expect such rulers to rationally show more caution. At most only one side can win, and often both sides lose more than they win. There would surely have been no World War I if the statesmen had carefully calculated the odds. Van Evera says false optimism by both sides preceded *every* major war since 1740.[48] He and Blainey note that rulers persistently exaggerate their chances of victory, which has led to more wars than Realism would warrant.[49] Of course, all that is needed is for a single ruler to be rash enough to start a war imprudently. This may have been the case with Vladimir Putin in his invasion of Ukraine. Van Evera mainly attributes overconfidence to chauvinist myths embedded in modern nationalism. This emphasizes the nation's virtues and commitments, is ignorant of other nations, and minimizes their strength and virtues. But rulers were overconfident long before nationalism appeared, trapped within the sentiments they have for their own community, contrasted with their negative and inaccurate views of foreigners—this would be the negative aspect of Durkheim's stress on the normative solidarity of societies. Blainey offers a "catch-up" Realist theory: "War can only occur when two nations decide that they can gain more by fighting than by negotiating." But "wars usually begin when fighting nations disagree on their relative strength," and "wars usually end when the fighting nations agree on their relative strengths." Rulers might eventually calculate accurately, but not before they get burned by war and mass deaths. He adds that the initial overoptimism is due to "moods which cannot be grounded in fact . . . by which nations evade reality"—hardly Realism.[50] Quincy Wright wrote: "International conflict is not in reality between states, but between distorted images of states. It is probable that such distortions, stereotypes, and caricatures are major factors in the situations of international conflict. . . . The false images depend not on misinformation about the immediate situation, but on prejudiced conceptions and attitudes rooted in distant history, in the national culture, or in the minds of important persons in the decision-making process."[51]

Obviously human beings are not just calculating machines sometimes prone to errors. We are emotional and ideological creatures, as we know in our personal lives. Sometimes it is not clear that any calculation

of odds is being made in a headlong rush to war down what Collins describes as the "tunnel of violence," in which perceptions narrow as blinkers come down, and a rush of adrenalin overwhelms caution—as also
happens to soldiers in battle.[52]

Ideological Power

It is sometimes argued that human groups distinguish between killing
within their own community and killing outsiders. Aware that the former
raises moral dilemmas, they apply an "internal ethic" to make fine distinctions between murder, manslaughter, self-defense, and legitimate retribution. Such distinctions are not applied to foreign enemies, to whom a
weaker "external" ethical ideology is applied. Yet this argument is undermined by the frequency of civil wars in which worse atrocities occur, and
wars have often ensued in which combatants saw each other as sharing the
same culture. The Sumerian city-states warred with each other yet believed they all belonged to a single ethnic group, the "blackheads." Greek
city-states fought each other and yet shared Hellenistic culture. In Europe
Christians fought Christians and rulers were often kin-related. Human
beings can make war whether or not they consider the enemy as alien.

But some wars seem especially ideological. John Owen identified four
modern waves of ideological warfare: sixteenth- and seventeenth-century
European wars of religion; the wars of revolutionary and Napoleonic
France; twentieth-century wars among fascism, communism, and liberalism; and Islamic wars from 1979 onward.[53] These waves generated intense
ideological polarization diffused through what he calls transnational ideological networks (TINs). I discuss such waves in chapters 8 and 14, accepting the first three, but with skepticism about the fourth. But I add that
empires have legitimated conquest by claiming to be a "superior" civilization, on the basis of ideologies of racism or religion that favor eliminating
or forcibly civilizing supposedly savage or degenerate peoples.

Jeremy Black combines ideologies and emotions into a concept of
"bellicosity"—how favorably rulers view war itself and how entranced
they are by military symbolism. He sees some communities as "warfare-
societies," in which intense militarism ensures "that the relationships between ends and means cannot be comprehensively calculated"—rationality
of means cannot operate.[54] I add that militarists are more risk-accepting of
war. Black says bellicosity is hard to measure and does not explain when
bellicosity intensifies. He says rulers generally have clear ideas of what

they want, but these get inflected by bellicosity and other ideological prejudices, so that the conceptions of alternatives required by rational calculation of means are absent.

I distinguish in my work three types of ideological power: transcendent, immanent, and institutionalized. Some wars—between religious sects, or among socialism, fascism, and liberal capitalism—involve a clash of transcendent ideologies all seeking to remake the world and impose their beliefs on others. Such ideological wars make the enemy seem evil, which increases casualties and atrocities. Second, immanent ideology reinforces the solidarity and morale of a collectivity, including armies. Quite high morale is present in most effective armies, but in chapter 13 I show that some communist forces possessed an excess of both these first two types of militarism, making them more formidable fighters, able to compensate for technological inferiority with a more self-sacrificing morale. But most wars are not so ideological, and transcendent and immanent ideologies do not last long. They settle down into the third type of ideology, institutionalized ideology. In the case of militarism, social actors have internalized the inheritance of past experiences of victory, which bequeaths to further generations baked-in militarist institutions and cultures. Historical practices infuse the minds and institutions of the present. The weight of history is conservative: people keep doing what seemed to work in the past—path dependence. Conversely, if war proves repeatedly unsuccessful, bellicosity should falter. In between the two there is likely to be a cultural lag period when bellicosity endures when it should not, as it did recently in the United States.

All three types of ideology constrain conceptions of self-interest. Commitment to bellicose values such as honor and physical courage may overcome normal human repugnance at killing others and normal fear of being killed oneself. Militarism seduces through rituals, values, and norms—heroic sagas, divine blessing of the banners, colorful parades, brass bands, anthems, medals, and a culture that extols heroism, clothes battles with moral worth, promises glory—even afterlife—to the slain, and confers honor and status on its heroes. Together these stir our hearts, predisposing us to war.

A sense of honor is important. Mark Cooney discusses it among American inner-city gangs. Gang leaders respond violently to any "disrespect."[55] If they do not respond, they lose respect and masculine honor in the eyes of their own gang. Cooney emphasizes that the slightest behavior perceived as disrespectful can be the trigger for violence, even homicide. The responsibility attached to leaders traps them into violence.

They fear status loss within their own gang more than they fear the enemy gang. He says that codes of honor were especially strong among the aristocracy of the past. Their ideology valued the warrior more than the peacemaker, but now honor has slipped down to lower-class gangs.

Yet in all ages his model also fits statesmen, the word revealing a claim by leaders to personify the state. They identify their own career success, personal honor, and status with the state's. They seek, in varying degrees, personal glory and grandeur for their state. Human emotions like ambition, righteous anger, vengeance, humiliation, and desperation are applied to the state. Lebow observes that powerful states are more likely to feel slighted, even humiliated, than weak ones: "Anger is a luxury that can only be felt by those in a position to seek revenge."[56] Weak states are used to being slighted and learn to live with it. Perhaps the main reason the Bush administration launched an invasion of Iraq in 2003 was fury over Saddam Hussein's decadelong defiance and disrespect of the United States. This is felt as both a personal and geopolitical affront. Statesmen or stateswomen believe they lose face personally if they do not respond with toughness to slurs and threats, and they believe that their state will lose face in the system of states. If both rulers in a dispute are imbued with prickly honor, neither will want to be seen backing down, and it is difficult to find compromise solutions to disputes, as we saw in the descent into World War I.

Conclusion

We have seen varied motives, disputes, and contexts as well as different theories of war-and-peace decisions. It is easy to be skeptical about one-size-fits-all theories like Realism. But can we go further in establishing the relative weights of the many components of war-and-peace decisions? At the macro level it is perhaps a struggle of the rather materialist duo of economic and military power versus the potentially less rational duo of ideological-emotional and political power. But this is muddied by wars resulting from interactions between different factions and communities that bounce unevenly, unpredictably toward war or peace. Wars never start accidentally, says Evan Luard, but they often result from the unintended consequences of interactions. Several causal chains may interact contingently, and their conjunction may not have been planned by anyone. All this provoked Raymond Aron into declaring that a general theory of war was impossible. But I will have a shot at one.

CHAPTER FOUR

The Roman Republic

ROME WAS AN EMPIRE long before it was ruled by emperors, and it was almost always at war. Between 415 and 265 BCE, peace seems to have ruled for only thirteen years, and for only fourteen between 327 and 116 BCE.[1] The first emperor, Augustus, claimed in 14 CE that the doors of the temple of Janus, closed during peacetime, had before his reign closed only twice since the founding of Rome. In his forty-five-year reign, he said, it had been closed three times, suggesting that he was a man of peace. Such figures may mislead. Rome became a very large empire, and its regions were not all at war at the same time. In any one region wars were occasional, but there was normally a war going on somewhere. Nonetheless, this is a formidably enduring record of militarism that few states in history could match. Three main explanations have been offered: war was self-defense; it was a consequence of a geopolitical system in which Rome was no more aggressive than others; and Rome was the aggressor because of its militaristic social structure and culture. The third explanation becomes the most appropriate, as militarism became thoroughly baked in to Roman culture and structure, constraining daily actions in ways of which the actors were largely unaware.

Three Explanations of Roman Militarism: (1) Self-Defense

A sense of insecurity certainly looms over later Roman accounts of the city's early years. They imply that Rome had to fight in self-defense or be conquered by other Latin peoples or by tribes descending from the hills and the north. Rome was sacked by Gallic tribes from the Po Valley in 390 BCE, and later authors argued that the ethos remained kill or be killed. This may have been true early on, and then occasionally later as large groups of barbarians came raiding, but Roman authors generalized the argument to cover the centuries. Almost all its wars were deemed defensive and "just." Not everyone agreed. Sallust quotes a letter he says was sent by Mithridates VI, king of Pontus, describing the Romans: "They have possessed nothing since the beginning of their existence except what they have stolen: their home, their wives, their lands, their empire. Once vagabonds without fatherland, without parents, created to be the scourge of the whole world, no laws, human or divine, prevent them from seizing and destroying allies and friends, those near them and those afar off, weak or powerful, and from considering every government which does not serve them."[2]

Tacitus quotes a long speech supposedly uttered by the Caledonian chieftain Calgacus, including this description of Romans: "They have plundered the world, stripping naked the land in their hunger. . . . They are driven by greed, if their enemy be rich; by ambition, if poor. . . . They ravage, they slaughter, they seize by false pretenses, and all of this they hail as the construction of empire. And when in their wake nothing remains but a desert, they call that peace."[3]

Sallust and Tacitus were criticizing Roman militarism but preferred to express it through the mouths of enemies. Cicero was more measured: "Wars were waged with the Celtiberi [Celts or Gauls] for actual existence, not for rule; with the Latins, Sabines, Samnites, Carthaginians, and with Pyrrhus [a Greek king] the struggle was for rule"—that is, wars for rule were wars of choice, not of survival.[4]

War-and-peace proposals were put to a senate composed of rich aristocrats by the two consuls, who had to be in agreement. There was then a thorough debate, provided there was a quorum, at one point fixed at two hundred senators. Total membership was upward of three hundred. New senators were appointed by the consuls, not elected. Debate could last for a whole day. Every senator present had in theory to speak in turn, and because of the time constraint, filibustering was possible. The popular assemblies generally ratified senate decisions, but a proposal could be vetoed by a plebeian tribune. In this respect the republic exemplified Realism's rationality-of-means model, a rule-governed debating system with the merits and demerits of war discussed at length, more than in my other case studies. Debate mostly lacked high emotions because it was focused on the likely gains in wealth and loot from a war, not on violent emotions, unless this was the response to some killings of Romans. They also had enormous confidence in their military means. If the gains were thought great, military means would be provided, while likely Roman losses of life were rarely calculated. Two factors did counsel restraint. First, if the legions were already engaged in war elsewhere, the proposed war would probably be deferred. Second, domestic politics might intervene. Senate rivalry meant that some favored peace out of jealousy of the consul who would be appointed to command the legions and grab the loot. There was careful but limited calculation.

Once the decision was made, specialized priests (*fetiales*) carried the senate's terms to the potential enemy.[5] If their terms were rejected, they would cast a spear into enemy territory, or into a sacred piece of land in Rome symbolizing enemy territory. Both were declarations of war. The ritual invoked the support of the gods and so brought justice to the war. When Latin sources seemed to imply a defensive war, they actually meant a just war. Greek sources, like Polybius, emphasize imperial conquest, not self-defense. Moreover, the terms they offered were nonnegotiable. The enemy must accept them or be at war. So "defense" was actually a provocation to war. The *fetiales* system decayed in the third century, but Roman "diplomacy" continued to be tough. The senate sent ambassadors to offer Roman terms. If those terms were not accepted, a state of war existed—no bargaining.

Attempts at mediation by others were considered insulting. A nonnegotiable stance was less common among the republic's major rivals, Carthage and the Hellenistic states.[6] This was not Roman self-defense; it was more a pretext based on leaders' belief they were divinely privileged.[7] "Defense" included going to the assistance of friendly polities or factions in polities that sought Roman help. The goal was not only to help allies, but also to dominate them afterward. Roman domination was thus extended. Cicero quotes the Roman general Gaius Laelius: "Our people in defending the allies have now gained control of all lands."[8] This "offensive defense" was the dominant Roman policy in campaigns and conquests fought against many peoples: the Marsi, Samnites, Etruscans, Umbrians, Gauls of north Italy, Sabines, Vulsinienses, Lucani, Tarentini, Brutii, Picentes, Sallentines, and the Greeks in Italy. It was highly successful, as the Romans conquered the whole of Italy by 275 BCE. Almost all these peoples eventually disappeared from history through defeat in war. Some wars went through several stages of offense and defense. The wars against the Greek king Pyrrhus of Epirus began when the senate broke a treaty after the Roman fleet menaced the last democratic Greek city-state in Italy, Tarentum. The Tarentine democrats responded fiercely, fearing defeat and oppression, calling on Pyrrhus to help them. He invaded Italy in 280 BCE, recruited Samnite and Lucanian allies, and fought several very costly battles against Rome—hence the expression "Pyrrhic victory." This was a more defensive phase for Rome. But Roman ability to keep on raising legions forced Pyrrhus out of Italy. The Tarentines surrendered in 272 BCE, and Rome completed the conquest of Italy. The way was open to Greece and Sicily.

Most leaders claim their wars are waged in self-defense, usually divinely blessed, and their own people normally believe them. If Romans sincerely believed this, it made a difference in their behavior. But as an explanation for Rome's continuing to go to war, defense was limited mostly to its early years and to lesser phases of its wars of expansion.

Three Explanations of Roman Militarism: (2) The Geopolitical System

The second explanation is Realism's version of self-defense, blaming war on an anarchic multistate system. War is said to have resulted primarily from the insecurities of the geopolitical system, not from the nature of particular states, rulers, or peoples. No central authority existed to which rival states could turn for a diplomatic settlement, and the only way to punish an aggressor was by fighting—a Hobbesian "war of all against all"—the inevitable logic being that the strong defeated the weak. Some ancient authors agreed. Demosthenes said it would be better if all states behaved morally, but they don't: "All men have their rights conceded to them in proportion to the power at their disposal."[9] Thucydides quotes the Athenian response to pleas for mercy from the city-state of Melos: "Right is in question only between equals in power, while the strong do what they can and the weak suffer what they must."[10]

Arthur Eckstein is the main modern exponent of Realism on Rome.[11] He rejects, as most Realists do, "unit-level" analysis, which emphasizes the internal structure and culture of states and communities. The threat from the external geopolitical environment was what mattered, yielding a perpetual Roman sense of insecurity and violent response. After struggles with Latin and Etruscan states, the Gauls of the Po Valley, the

Volsci, and the Samnites, came the Greek city-states in southern Italy, sometimes backed by the Hellenistic monarchies, and then the states of Greater Greece, the Carthaginian Empire, the peoples of the Middle East and North Africa, and the tribes of Europe and the Balkans. Rome was militaristic, he agrees, but this was normal among ancient states and tribes around the Mediterranean, trapped in the same "cruel logic." Rome was merely the most successful.

Nicola Terrenato casts doubt on this.[12] He says that in the sixth to the fourth centuries BCE, Rome, like many Italian communities, consisted of an urban center and an agricultural hinterland dominated by aristocratic clans. The center was gradually becoming statelike, but before the fourth century goals were primarily those of dominant clans, not the city, and Rome's "army" comprised the retinues of aristocrats, fighting for private clan goals, and raids, especially for cattle, were the main type of warfare. Communities lacked clear boundaries and did not occupy the whole space of even that zone of Italy. Yet through exchange with neighbors they came to share some common culture. Most Roman wars with known locations were fought not against other lowland urban centers, but against the tribes of the north and the Apennine Hills, especially the Samnites. Against the Gallic tribes, most war was self-defense in response to raiding, but the Romans repeatedly initiated wars against the Samnites because they blocked Roman ambitions to conquer a realm stretching from coast to coast.

Yet the incorporation of neighboring lowland urban centers into Rome, says Terrenato, was less through warfare than through negotiations, not between states, since this was not yet a multistate system. Neighboring clans, especially those with kin connections in Rome, would negotiate alliances with Rome, often to repress class conflict within their own communities. Rome attracted neighboring aristocracies because it defended their rights against the lower classes and granted them Roman citizenship. This pressure for regime change made it "at worst the lesser evil and at best a golden opportunity" for some elites, who aided Rome's absorption of their own community.[13] This involved faction fighting with clans opposing absorption. He sees "a grand bargain between elites across the peninsula that would be the main catalyst of its political unification."[14] They cared "little for the destiny of any specific state and much about that of their own lineage, they weaved in and out of the various political systems, jumped on passing bandwagons, and jockeyed for position, all the while trying to stay on the winning side."[15]

This is persuasive for the two centuries following the establishment of the republic in 509 BCE. Since many prominent Roman families had non-Roman origins, wars may have been less common than later Romans believed.[16] They were perhaps reading back into earlier history the world of an Italy filled with states they themselves inhabited, and they were neglecting class conflicts within and class solidarities between communities. Terrenato concludes, "The situation in central and southern Italy after the conquest is essentially compatible with a model that regards wide-ranging elite interaction and negotiation as the primary factors that drove the transition."[17] There were wars, but some polities disappeared because their elites sought a change of regime. By 264 BCE, Rome had made more than 150 treaties with polities across Italy, bilateral but asymmetric, embodying a Mafia-type Roman protection racket. After 338 BCE, allied Latin city-states were forbidden to maintain official relations with one another to prevent alliances among them. Rome's tributaries had to contribute military levies and fund their military operations. Roman citizens paid a direct tax earmarked for the military, while allies supported their own levies.[18] The most urbanized rival peoples, Etruscans and Greeks, were divided in fractious city-states.

So in the fifth and fourth centuries BCE Rome expanded across central and southern Italy, a mini-empire becoming more statelike, as were other Mediterranean polities, such as Phoenician colonies (e.g., Carthage), Syracuse, Marseille, and Tarquinia. Terrenato emphasizes "the limited range of options that remained open for those states that were not expanding. For them, small-scale neutrality and independence must have been increasingly unrealistic. . . . It became clear to the elites involved that their only viable choice was to lend their support to whoever offered the better terms. . . . These states began negotiating the terms of their incorporation, especially in central Italy, where they were tightly clustered together."[19]

Terrenato and Scheidel emphasize a shift in early Roman history from diplomacy to Mafioso threats, to regime change, and finally to conquest. It was from then on, with the emergence of real states, that Eckstein's Realism might be applicable, and this was an insecure environment.[20] As William Harris and Mary Beard note, however, almost all Rome's wars were then fought outside its own or its allies' territories, which suggests offensive expansion.[21] One advantage of offensive war is that it lays waste to enemy territory rather than one's own. Harris says that the Romans initiated more offensive wars than the Samnites or the Etruscans once Rome was clearly established.

Eckstein offers some sketchy data on Greek states. He says Athens was at war in two-thirds of the years from 497 to 338 BCE, and other states engaged in war in over 90 percent of years over short periods. At least one of the Hellenistic monarchies was at war for 97 percent of years over a 163-year period. Yet since there were between four and nine monarchies at any one time, the average for any single one of them would be a war in under half the years—still a high rate, however. Three Hellenistic rulers, Attalus I, Philip V, and Antiochus III went to war every year, but over only a twenty-five-year period.[22] Victor Alonso challenges the view that Greek city-states were at war almost all the time.[23] The focus on Athenian-Spartan rivalry obscures the fact that many states stayed out of war for long periods. Argos and Corcyra abstained from war for most of the fifth century, as did Megara, the Achaean Confederacy, and the Common Peace movement in the fourth century. Regions such as Aetolia, Epirus, and Crete adhered to neutrality and non-alignment, as did many of the Greek colonies abroad. Alonso emphasizes the role of diplomacy in mediating Greek conflicts. Though Greeks believed that war was frequently inevitable, they sought to limit its scope and delay its outcome while pursuing diplomacy. Once war had started, they accepted truces, capitulations, and protection of heralds.

Rivals sometimes launched offensives against Rome, but less often, whereas the frequency and duration of Roman wars is unparalleled. Polybius said the Romans were more ferocious than Hellenistic states in dealing with defeated enemies. We shall see that the Carthaginians were not as warlike as the Romans. Eckstein's geopolitical argument has some limited explanatory power, varying and declining through time, but we must add the third theory of Roman wars.

Three Explanations of Roman Militarism: (3) Roman Aggression

This explanation accepts the notion that the geopolitical environment was unstable, but it argues that Rome, propelled by domestic militarism, became the main aggressor. Among classical writers Polybius and Cicero came close to this, and Harris is the main modern scholar.[24] Harris does not see a conscious long-term policy of imperialism, for expansion came piecemeal and opportunistically (which is not unusual in empire building). But success breeds success and there was a consistent thrust of aggression: Rome kept doing it. Dexter Hoyos agrees, as does Erich Gruen, regarding

Roman policy in Italy and the west, but not Rome's relations with the Hellenistic world.[25] Gruen portrays Rome as being long indifferent to the Greeks, unwilling to enter into treaties with them, cautious about entering a region where multiple developed states competed. At this stage there was little thought of annexation in the east. He concludes, "Hellas ultimately fell under Roman authority not because the Romans exported their structures to the East, but because Greeks persistently drew the westerner into their own structure—until it was theirs no longer."[26]

Yet during the second half of the third century BCE Greece was a sideshow. Rome was fully committed in its wars against Carthage. As we will see, this immediately became a major Roman imperial venture into the eastern Mediterranean (followed by a phase of desperate defense in Italy). But in 201 BCE as soon as the Second Punic War ended in decisive Roman victory, the legions began intervening in Greece. Gruen says Rome "blundered" into the Second Macedonian War, 200–196 BCE, yet the senate revealed it was determined to go to war, as it was in the Seleucid War in 192–88 BCE against Antiochus.[27] This major commitment of forces included withdrawing legions from Spain and Gaul, and it produced the first Roman incursion into Asia. The senate was also determined to fight the Third Macedonian War (171–68 BCE) against Perseus. After victory the senate divided Macedonia into four client republics and permanently stationed legions in Greece. In the Fourth Macedonian War, in 150–48 BCE, these legions quickly defeated an attempt to reunite the Macedonian kingdom. Finally, the Achaean League of Greek city-states launched a desperate rebellion against Rome but was quickly defeated in 146 BCE, which culminated in the Roman sacking of Corinth—in the same year the city of Carthage was obliterated. This looks like determined aggression.

Gruen makes some concessions. He says several times that Rome would not tolerate threats to the Adriatic. He agrees that the Punic Wars provoked more Roman imperialism, and he agrees with Harris that when the senate did decide to fight, it fought until victory was fully achieved, whether or not it saw vital interests at stake, and even if the enemy wanted to come to terms, as Perseus did. Gruen concludes that Rome's ultimate "willingness to assume imperial responsibility . . . [was] the effect of numerous individual decisions in ad hoc situations, not a grand design to control the East."[28] Yet I have narrated a cumulative imperialism whose level of aggression steadily increased once imperial control of the Carthaginian territories was completed. Carthage is the missing player in Gruen's account.

There were different stages of Roman aggression. First came the punitive raid, not just to carry off goods and slaves, but also to punish peoples and rulers who would not submit. Roman diplomacy was built on fear, instilled through punitive campaigns. This did not at first involve territorial conquest, only pillaging and destroying to demonstrate that Rome could make uncooperative neighbors suffer. The troops were encouraged to loot but the goal was also to secure cooperative client rulers through regime change or stiffening. Thus, directly ruled Roman territories were ringed by client monarchies, republics, and tribes. But Rome rarely rested satisfied with indirect imperialism. Second, seeking more direct control, Romans invaded to conquer, either installing Roman consuls or stationing advisers and perhaps legions there to supervise the ruler. This brought more systematic plunder and slavery, vital to supply labor for mining and agriculture, the core Roman economic sectors. The third stage was to suppress rebellions, widespread after conquest. The key was swift response to stifle revolt before it spread. Local troops were flung into action. If they failed, a larger army was mustered to crush rebels and install more direct rule. All three types were fought mostly on land. Roman naval power was weak until it took on Carthage. The main function of Roman navies was to patrol coastlines and suppress piracy.

The decision makers for war were in theory drawn from the citizens who served in the legions and paid the taxes, perhaps one-quarter of male inhabitants, and no females. No one else counted. But the decisions occurred within the senate and the popular assemblies. The senate was dominant, and it was dominated in turn by wealthy aristocrats. The popular assemblies also had powers, but they had class-weighted voting systems favoring lesser aristocrats, and the moderately prosperous census classes provided the heavy and medium-heavy infantry. This was a representative system, but weighted by class—and most of the leaders, the consuls in the senate and the tribunes in the assemblies, were aristocrats. The people of Rome could demonstrate, riot, and strike (collectively marching out of Rome), and they always had sympathizers in the popular assemblies, especially on domestic issues like debt and taxes. The assemblies rarely contested senate decisions for war, though they voiced discontent about long-running wars. A few aristocratic senators were disproportionately responsible for Rome's wars.

Evidence of aggression comes from the absence of Roman diplomacy, unlike elsewhere in the ancient Middle East. Amanda Podany details many diplomatic treaties, oaths, and gift exchanges made, and for a time adhered to, between the cities and empires of the Bronze Age in the Middle East region—Ebla, Mari, Mittani, Hittites, Kassites, Egypt, and more.[29] Resolving conflict through mediation and arbitration also featured in Greek and Hellenistic international relations.[30] These procedures seem to have been unknown to the Romans. Romans let Greeks resolve their own differences but themselves rarely participated. Sheila Ager says, "The formal structure of the fetial formula undeniably implies that judgement of some sort has already taken place before Rome even embarks on war. In some sense, Rome has already been to 'arbitration,' for a judgement has been rendered that the enemy is the guilty party. For a mere human to offer his third party diplomatic skills when Rome has already received heaven's judgement on the matter would therefore be at the least superfluous, and . . . might be construed as presumptuous and offensive."[31]

There were a few unjust wars, Romans acknowledged—when Rome was defeated! This proved the gods had not been consulted, for they would have declared defeats to be unjust.

Romans indignantly rejected attempts at mediation. Attempts to negotiate by Greek and Carthaginian ambassadors indicated "the posture of one great power to another, not of a submissive inferior to an acknowledged superior," and were unacceptable.[32] Ager adds that the most a third party could do in a dispute between Rome and a Greek state was to plead mercy for the Greeks. In the later empire, Rome met states of equal powers in the east, the Parthians and Persians, and then had to negotiate treaties. Before then, when dealing with groups who were not enemies, Rome did occasionally conclude nonaggression pacts or recognize each party's distinct spheres of influence, but these were temporary. Hostages were taken but only by the Roman rulers who never offered their own hostages. War sometimes deliberately provoked other states, and Roman dominance expanded through defending and then absorbing allies, but both were claimed as self-defense.[33]

Polybius tells us that those defeated by Rome and who then capitulate: "surrender all territory and the cities in it, together with all men and women in all such territory or cities, likewise rivers, harbours, temples, and tombs, so that the Romans should become actual lords of all these, and those who surrender should remain lords of nothing whatever."[34]

Although the norm was that defeated enemies should be treated mercifully, "the Roman response to the entreaties of the defeated could not be calculated, any more than the responses of soldiers or muggers or rapists to the pleas of their victims. . . . That, for the Romans, demonstrated the fulness of their power."[35] They paid less attention to acquiring direct control of territories than to instilling fear into their inhabitants. All dissent would be countered with "terror and awe that they hoped to produce in the enemy; and the moral and status issues, such as the need to repress *superbia*, avenge *injuriae*, and maintain the honor or *decus* of the empire. It was on these things that, as they believed, their security depended; it was for these that they fought."[36] The Roman treatment of allies was constitutionally the same as of defeated enemies—their land would be formally confiscated by the Roman state. Some was kept to found colonies for Romans, although most was given back to those perceived as reliable allies. Treaties offered degrees of citizenship to the allies, but Rome alone would dictate matters of war and peace. Trusted allies could rule themselves—but they must provide troops to assist Rome.[37] So the rulers of Rome fought mostly aggressive wars.

Economic Motives

Once the republic was securely established by the early third century BCE, two main motives, greed and glory, drove Romans into war. They came bundled together with political ambition.[38] Economic motives meant looting removable wealth, receiving tribute, seizing farmland, and acquiring slaves. By the first century BCE there were over a million war-acquired slaves in Italy, about one-fifth of the population.[39] Territorial control usually came later to ensure security of control. Rome did not develop more sophisticated policies of economic acquisition because it almost never conceived of a realm of economic power relations separate from other power realms. There was no mercantilism, and military defense of trade simply meant combating pirates, not dictating the terms of trade. Conquest and expropriation, or subordination and tribute taking, not trade on unequal conditions, dominated economic acquisition.

War making depended on funding from those paying the property taxes. Yet with expansion, the upper classes, members of which became governors or officials of conquered states and siphoned off most of the spoils, kept the state's treasury adequate for normal expenses, but not for more. The upper classes did not want a successful general or a popular demagogue using public wealth to finance either tyranny or public welfare. This began a three-way struggle between the senatorial elite, the generals, and more popular forces. The Roman people suffered a loss in power when the property tax was abolished in 167 BCE. Since they no longer funded wars, their voice was marginalized.[40] The taxes, indemnities, and loot expected from a war were carefully assessed beforehand, as Realists would expect, but for the elite's private gain. Of course, they often had limited information, and mistakes were made, as in an invasion of the Arabian desert, wrongly assumed to contain fabulous wealth.[41]

By the time the republic was prosperously established, loot was considered too base to figure in dignified senate speeches. Obsession with booty was a persistent criticism levied against rivals, for they all sought it. Claims to act morally were important in Roman upper-class discourse, but acquiring booty was more important in reality.[42] If civilians tried to stop the looting of their homes or the raping of their wives or daughters, they would be shown no mercy, especially if the legionaries had suffered casualties in the campaign. Defeated enemy soldiers and civilians in their many thousands provided most of the slaves of Rome, and they were sometimes the greatest source of profit from war. Generals profited most but donated some captives to their soldiers. Slave traders following the armies then bought them from the soldiers. Rape generally went unpunished, though it was prosecuted in peacetime and bore the risk of execution (though not if the victim was a slave or prostitute). Ransoming wealthy prisoners was common. Ordinary soldiers might calculate on profit coming from victory—provided they lived—and they received a basic level of pay. Accepting the risk of death seemed normal to citizens at the moment of enlistment, whether conscripts or volunteers. Once enlisted, they had lost the ability to control their lives and were at the mercy of decisions made by the senate and the generals. The booty of war was their compensation for their exploitation by the state and the upper class.

The land and part of the booty went to the state, but most booty was claimed by the soldiers in quantities according to rank.[43] In the third and second centuries BCE, the distribution of the spoils became more unequal and in response, the "Social Wars" exploded, a rebellion by Rome's allies, outraged they were not receiving their fair share and impoverished by the neglect of their farms during their long military service. Discontent with Roman rule and the distribution of spoils had precipitated defections of allies to Hannibal in the Second Punic War. Elites acquiring offices in conquered provinces, especially governors, diverted revenues into their own pockets. This was constantly railed against but was normal practice. Once a territory was conquered, the *publicani*, the public contractors, also arrived seeking profits from army and administration.

A second material motive was for land seized from the defeated, leased to the rich or given to Latins or Roman colonists, or granted outside any formal structure. This began soon after the foundation of the republic, although we have details only from much later. Veteran colonies were designed to stiffen the loyalty of newly conquered territories, producing population transfers of many thousands moving from old to new Roman territories, increasing Romanization and war support among veterans and ambitious civilians.[44]

There were some longer-term economic benefits. Booty did inject much capital into the economy, while slavery increased agricultural yields and wine exports, but this was entirely at the expense of those looted and enslaved. Yet Philip Kay detects an "economic revolution" during the mid to late republic.[45] What I termed in volume 1 of *The Sources of Social Power* the "legionary economy" yielded some more general benefits from better communications infrastructures constructed by the legions, the economic demand coming from the army and the state, and the provision of relative order. An unintended consequence of levying taxes on the conquered peoples was that they had to convert their agricultural surpluses into cash, which encouraged commercialization.[46] Living standards and population rose, though not enormously.[47] On the other hand, the many rebellions brought exemplary repression as tribes and cities were annihilated to deter others from rebelling.[48] But if you behaved yourself, life improved a little. For the Romans, militarism was institutionalized into everyday economic life. Their material greed probably provided the most widely shared motive for imperialism among the different social classes and legionary ranks. It was a conscious choice for acquisition through conquest, but increased trade was also a consequence. There is, however, the counterfactual possibility that economic growth might have been alternatively stimulated by peace.

Ideological Motives: Grandeur and Glory

Like all empires, Romans justified conquests ideologically: their version was that their rule brought peace and the rule of law to less civilized peoples, and so was blessed by the gods. Rome was a state of laws, imposing its order on the conquered through war.[49] Peace was valued, but mainly as propaganda. Although atrocities such as Caesar's near-genocide in Gaul were denounced, there was almost no pacifism. Nor was there transcendent religion justifying or denouncing war. Romans were religious in the sense that they regularly performed rituals to deities in whom they believed, but there were multiple gods and you could choose your own. As was common in the ancient world, Roman leaders consulted the auguries (usually the behavior and entrails of birds) before making decisions. A bad omen might delay battle for a day or two but not stop it altogether. After a defeat, however, it was often said that the omens had been bad. Suetonius quotes Caesar as saying, "The omens will be as favorable as I wish them to be."[50] Roman wars were not usually driven forward by transcendent ideologies, religious or secular, or indeed by high emotions, for emotions were cooled down by the rituals involved in debate and quasi diplomacy, except where rebellions had killed many Roman citizens.

War had become the means to achieve all things material and ideal: wealth, fame, and glory for the leaders, grandeur for the state. Status, influence, political power, refusal to show weakness, and domination for its own sake were shared by senators, generals, and to a lesser extent their soldiers.[51] Tacitus remarked, "The lust for power, for dominating others, inflames the heart more than any other passion."[52] Prestige and glory for the rulers, once institutionalized, becomes grandeur for the state, involving more militarism than material goals, which are restrained by calculations of profit and loss. Greedy generals will make war only if they see profit. But fame, prestige, glory, and grandeur in a militarized society are valued for their own sake, almost whatever the profit or loss. Susan Mattern says honor, revenge, and aristocratic competition were the main forces driving foreign policy.[53] Gruen agrees that economic motives were far less important than status in explaining Roman wars in the Hellenistic world.[54] He sees the Third Macedonian War, for example, as caused by senators' fear of losing face, showing "that Rome was not a helpless, pitiful giant," a rather odd way of expressing it![55] Walter Scheidel explains endless war thus: "Unless we believe in decades of inadvertent mission creep, the aristocratic quest for glory coupled with a pragmatic desire to keep Italian mobilization structures fully operational is the most economical explanation for this outcome." He adds that in 157 BCE, after sixty-eight consecutive years of warfare, when Rome had run out of targets, the senate immediately launched a new campaign in the Balkans to ensure that the people would not be softened by a lengthy peace.[56]

Ambition for glory among the elites was hereditary. Roman commanders, said Sallust, "as they called to mind their forefathers' achievements, such a flame was kindled in the breasts of those eminent persons, as could not be extinguished till their own merit had equaled the fame and glory of their ancestors."[57] The ideology was not transcendental. It had no goals higher than bringing order and profit through Roman rule. But it was immanent, strengthening the solidarity of the lineage and the republic.

Militarism was institutionalized into politics and ideology. Serving in the field became the main way to public office. Polybius says young men had to serve with distinction during ten campaigns before they could stand for public office. Distinction meant showing valor and leadership skills in battle, which Sallust adds made the young keen to make their bravery conspicuous. Promotion through the hierarchy of public offices (from which ascending levels of profit flowed) depended on valor and victory, right up to senate level. Ordinary soldiers could also receive honors and promotions. A medal for bravery or promotion to centurion gave prestige, and its receipt was proudly carved onto tombstones. Some in all classes had war-making incentives. This was not the ageism of modern warfare, whereby old civilians send out young soldiers to die. Rome's aging leaders had already experienced battle themselves. Even the self-declared near-pacifist Cicero, who rose as an intellectual, lawyer, and politician, had done military service (and hated it). When he conquered mountain tribes while proconsul in Cilicia, he demanded a Triumph. He did not get it, but he did get the spoils of office. The highest public officials were the two consuls, drawn from senatorial ranks. One would be delegated ever since the founding of the republic in the mid-fifth century BCE to command the legions in the field together with a professional general. Their term of office lasted only a year, so if they wanted glory and wealth, they had to get on with war quickly.

Generals used the riches won from wars to strengthen their political power in Rome.[58] Rome entered wars even when lucrative pickings were unlikely. Caesar's two invasions of Britain were motivated more by his desire to best his rivals and dominate the senate. Cicero observed, "There is not a bit of silver in that island and no hope of booty except from slaves."[59] Later, Claudius, the third emperor, conquered Britain mainly because victory would overcome his political difficulties. The desire to achieve domination, honor, and reputation came to triumph over money, say Gruen and Mattern.[60] Michael Taylor finds that from 200 to 157 BCE, military expenses were about 75 percent of all state expenses, and that few wars were profitable for the state, since the taxes and loot received from them was less than the military expenses.[61] But war was profitable for the generals extracting loot.

Only about one-quarter of consuls did not engage in war.[62] The other three-quarters hoped to get the highest accolade, the Triumph, when a victorious general marched with his soldiers through Rome, displaying the riches he had looted, providing circus spectacles, showering delicacies and trinkets on the people, while enemies were marched in chains before being enslaved or killed. The victor basked in the adulation of the city. The main restraint on the number of Triumphs was other senators' resentment of their rivals' successes. One-quarter of consuls did get a Triumph. Writers of the Late Republican period such as Livy, Sallust, and Tacitus disapproved, seeing Triumphs as a corrupt degeneration of the simpler, austere ceremonies of earlier times. The fame sought by Roman generals grew through time, a sign of the institutionalization of militarism. Architecture increasingly reflected military glory, as can be seen in surviving triumphal arches and columns and in statues erected to the goddess Victory. Monumental public building meant much was spent on displays of power and glory, just as medieval Europe's cathedrals demonstrated the Church's glory. Taylor says such monuments represented another 10 percent of total state expenses. Again there were mixed motives of self-glorification and intimidating the world and the populace with the grandeur of Rome.[63] But all these forms of greed and glory depended on Rome's having the military might to win wars at an acceptable level of cost. Triumphs required victories.

The Roman Art of War

Citizenship and class jointly structured the way Rome fought wars. There were four legal criteria of class identity: ancestry, patrician or plebeian; six census ranks based on wealth and political privilege, in which the senatorial and equestrian ranks were classified above the ordinary citizens; honors granted so that a self-made man's family could become "noble" plebeians; and citizenship rights ranking freeborn Romans above the partial citizenship given the allies. All these statuses came with rights under law. All male citizens had to fight. They had originally provided their own weapons, armor, and horses, according to the resources specified by the six census ranks. Census taking was established in Rome from the fifth century BCE, and we have numerous census totals recorded from 234 BCE onward. Its purpose was to count manpower available for the legions—all free males above the age of seventeen, not women, children, or slaves—and to allocate it by class. There was a parallel in the same years in Warring States China, but these two cases were, I think, unparalleled mobilizations of military power in the ancient world. The censor was always an official of the highest standing, whose decisions could not be overruled. The census became an overall population count only later, during the empire.

Roman citizen-soldiers had democratic rights, including electing some of their officers. But there was a tension between the inclusive nature of citizenship and class inequalities (as in democracies today). The result then was class struggle and army mutinies, recorded from the fifth century BCE onward. When pay was not forthcoming or when soldiers felt deprived of loot, or badly led, or forced into too many battles, they might resist. We don't know how frequent mutinies were, but they were a refusal to accept disliked conditions of service, not a refusal to fight. But their sacrifices had to be proportional to the chances of victory and rewards, and this indicated soldiers' determination to defend legal privileges.

So these rulers and the citizens were devoted to making war, and they were efficient at it. The republic, once institutionalized, could rapidly extract taxes for war and raise and logistically maintain legions in the field. It probably mobilized a larger proportion of the total population than any other state before modern times, and modern states have much larger state and local bureaucracies. Rome had a very small bureaucracy: only about 150 civil servants in Rome, and perhaps 150 senatorial and equestrian administrators, plus small staffs of public slaves in the provinces. Such a tiny bureaucracy could not effectively govern an empire of around 50–70 million people spread over 100,000–200,000 square kilometers deploying legions totaling between 200,000 and 300,000 disciplined, logistically supported soldiers. But this state was really run by its militaristic class structure, defined by nobility, wealth, and military service, whose combination of collective solidarity and hierarchy of rank conferred considerable infrastructural power. The republic centered on the senatorial and equestrian classes, which shared a common culture and were politically organized in the senate and shared the popular assemblies with heavy infantry and medium-heavy infantry middling classes. All participated in a career structure that tied together army command and political office, providing the spoils of war and political office. The military-political class structure provided the core of the state, not the few "bureaucrats," who were often slaves. As Scheidel says, "The Roman state that arose from these arrangements was one narrowly focused on warfare and little else."[64] This war-addicted republic had an economy largely "off the books," making war for greed and glory. So despite what I wrote in my 1984 article on despotic and infrastructural power, the Roman Republic actually had extensive infrastructural power and a despotic power confined to controlling the poor, the conquered, and the enslaved.

The fighting qualities of the Roman soldier are often exaggerated. As happens in all armies, on occasion the soldiers got frightened, ran, or deserted. There were defeats, those against Hannibal and Mithridates, king of Pontus, being the best-known. Jessica Clark counts forty-three defeats in the second century BCE alone, but she adds that the senate did not always count them as such and always saw them as setbacks on the road to eventual victory.[65] In 53 BCE at Carrhae in modern Turkey, defeat came at the hands of a Parthian army dominated by horse archers. The Roman commander Crassus had scorned advice to attack the Parthians through Armenia and instead marched his troops straight across the desert, engaging in battle without resting his men, in open terrain suited to horse archers. Roman weakness in cavalry meant the archers could not be dispersed. Firing from outside the range of Roman spears during a whole day, they caused substantial infantry losses, although the line stood firm. Now Crassus made the error of sending forward part of his force, breaking up the legions' cohesion. The Parthian heavy cavalry charged and the lines began to disintegrate. The legionaries, their officers, and Crassus were slaughtered. After Carrhae, vengeance was required. To accept defeat was unthinkable. Caesar was preparing an expedition to avenge Crassus when he was assassinated. Mark Anthony did launch a Parthian expedition but was defeated in 37 BCE, having ill-prepared his troops for mountain combat. The senate kept on authorizing attacks on Parthia, and some victories were achieved, but the troops were never able to finish the enemy off. Rome had been more intrinsically bellicose than successful, yet declaring that final victory is inevitable means you carry on aggressing. Roman armies kept coming back from defeats. They had been successful while Roman rulers could tolerate only victory. Belatedly, Parthian persistence taught Romans Realism.

There had been two main military virtues of Roman citizenship (Eckstein and Harris agree). First, it was geared to warfare. It generated comradely bonds among citizen-soldiers, while its legally and militarily entrenched class privileges strengthened legitimate hierarchy. Intense comradeship and unquestioning obedience to hierarchy are the main requisites of an effective army. The citizen body became larger than rival states', expanding to include all classes of free men. Taylor says that the Romans could muster a peak deployment of 175,000 soldiers in 190 BCE (other estimates are higher). By comparison, the Seleucid and Ptolemaic kingdoms spent much less of their wealth on the military and so could mobilize only about 80,000, and though the Macedonian kingdom was more militarized, it was also smaller and poorer and mobilized only 45,000. Taylor notes that Carthage could on occasion mobilize more men than Rome, but they were drawn mainly from tributary states, which had weaknesses.[66]

Citizens were lightly taxed, for their main duty was onerous military service, which evolved into a duration of six to fourteen years (according to need) for the *assidui*, citizens with the property qualification. The draft went smoothly and there were no troop shortages, not even when virtually all *assidui* were called up in the Second Punic War. But then came some reluctance, and in 107 BCE Marius abandoned the property qualification, recruiting poor, paid soldiers who would expect a grant of property at the end of their service. A further change was instituted by Emperor Augustus, who established a volunteer, professional, and paid army with a service obligation of sixteen years. These reforms broke the tight links between citizenship and the army that had provided the republic's coup-proofing.

Legionaries expected a share of the loot, and many could expect land when they finished their service. To satisfy them required victories, a self-reinforcing system. Soldiers who survived could achieve more prosperity and respect from family and neighbors. So Roman soldiers and veterans were an important pressure group for war. They fought well both because rewards depended on victory and because of the brutal class-based discipline, intensive drilling, and citizen esprit de corps of the legions. The legion was superior because of the dual nature of Roman citizenship, which yielded class solidarity at the top and hierarchy down below.

The second advantage of Roman citizenship was its flexibility toward allies. Although Romans viewed peace as something imposed by them on a defeated enemy, repression was limited by a desire to enhance their military manpower, and this was achieved, uniquely in the ancient Mediterranean world, by gradual extensions of citizenship.[67] Eckstein saw the crucial Roman advantage as its "divorce of citizen status from ethnicity or geographical location," which allowed the creation of a citizen body dwarfing other ancient states, coming close to being a "unified nation-state."[68] After allies and former enemies had subordinated themselves to

Rome, they were given a degree of citizenship consonant with their past behavior, present attitudes, and strategic location. A few were granted full citizenship, others had citizen status without the right to vote, others had lesser rights. Those who had fought against Rome might be killed or enslaved and have their property expropriated. This has the look of a highly rational war-making strategy.

It is not entirely clear why Rome adopted this uniquely expansive citizen strategy. The foundation myth was that when Romulus defeated the Sabines, he promised citizenship to Sabine war captives held in Rome. We saw that some early non-Roman elites negotiated their way into Roman citizenship. This happened, for example, in Veii, the nearest Etruscan city. In 396 BCE the Romans took the city. Archaeologists have detected continuity of settlement, and Rome apparently allowed it to operate as before, but under its authority. In 390 Veiians were among four new citizen tribes created after the Gauls sacked Rome, expanding the pool of military recruits.[69] Highly attuned to battlefield advantage, Rome viewed winning wars as more important than preserving the exclusivity and purity of citizenship, in contrast to the Greeks. In Greek city-states like Athens, all freeborn males were citizens, but slaves, foreign residents, and allies could not become citizens. Though the Carthaginians were probably not so restrictive, they had a merchant empire lacking extensive landmasses with large populations. Only when defeated in the First Punic War did they acquire tributary states in Iberia and North Africa in order to field more troops. The reason that the Romans were the most successful warriors was that their social structure, their political rights, and their culture were all subordinated to military efficiency—a truly militaristic society.

By the late republic, citizenship was held by Italians, colonies of Romans established elsewhere, Romans or their descendants living elsewhere, some city populations throughout the empire, and client allied rulers. Women were not citizens since they did not provide military service, though they had legal rights. The grant of citizenship if one proved one's loyalty was a major factor keeping allies loyal—the one area of genuine Roman diplomacy. The allies did not pay taxes, nor did the Romans usually take tribute from them. Instead, allies delivered annual military service. Since this symbolized their subordination, it was important to use allied auxiliaries regularly, another incentive to make war often.[70] The advantages for the allies were that they had a right to loot, while Rome brought peace between them.

Each Roman legion was flanked by allied auxiliaries often outnumbering the legionaries. Without them, Rome would have been weak in cavalry and javelins. That they fought together on the battlefield required close coordination of drilling and tactics, which solidified the relations between Rome and its allies. Most ancient empires fell because rivals took advantage of revolts in conquered provinces. Hannibal tried in Italy to draw away Rome's allies, offering them alliance with Carthage. Some wavered, but they knew he could not give them rights equal to those of Roman citizenship, and they knew that Rome would keep on fighting whatever the odds. Being on the winning side was all-important to them as minor powers. Thus, Rome rarely sued for peace or searched for compromise, even when in dire straits. Three Samnite Wars, three Punic Wars, four Macedonian Wars: by digging deep for victory, Rome kept its allies loyal.[71] The allies initially kept their own languages and culture, but from the first century BCE the allies became Romans in culture, language, taxes, censuses, oaths, baths, architecture, and law.[72] Assimilation was not forced on them, for they desired Roman favor and civilization.

The two military virtues—breadth of citizenship and its extension to allies—brought Rome larger manpower reserves than its rivals. Beard and Eckstein agree, but they claim that Rome's opponents were just as militaristic, focusing as they did on ferocity of culture and praise for warriors. More critical for militarism is the need that other institutions be subordinated to military efficiency. In the nineteenth century Prussia became more militaristic than Austria-Hungary, not primarily for reasons of culture but because it had a military machine dominating the state. Rome's power structures were subordinated to military efficiency. Greek states valued a citizenship restricted by class and ethnicity for political reasons. In Carthage militarism was subordinated to trade. That is why Rome was unusually aggressive and fought and won so many wars.

Each refusal to accept defeat, whatever the cost, brought final victory. Roman militarism was not unique, but it was more relentlessly pursued, more enduring, and more institutionally embedded. War was a reasonable bet for achieving booty and glory. The confidence of legionaries in their superiority made the odds seem more favorable. In periods of defeat, the risk was much greater. Then brutal discipline and intense drilling had to kick in to nullify fear and motivate the struggle for ultimate victory. Roman legions suffered defeats, but they won the wars. For an example, I turn to the third-century BCE Punic Wars, fought against Carthage.

The Punic Wars

The surviving sources on the Punic Wars were all written later than the events described and they are pro-Roman—Polybius the least so. We can combine archaeological evidence, synthesized by Nathan Pilkington, with the largely text-based accounts of Richard Miles and Dexter Hoyos.[73] But because the Roman senate ordered the destruction of Carthage's records after final victory, we know little of its version of events.

Eckstein again sees the Punic Wars and concurrent wars against Greek states through the lens of Realism. He says that the eastern Mediterranean world had been formerly "balanced" between three great Hellenistic powers, the Seleucid, Ptolemaic, and Antigonid successor dynasties to the empire of Alexander the Great. But through internal conflict in the Ptolemaic state, from 207 to 188 BCE the eastern Mediterranean suffered a "power-transition crisis," as the balance ended and anarchy increased. Wars to establish hegemony broke out. Rome, says Eckstein, was pulled into this partly by fear of unrest or of a new hegemon, partly by commitments to its allies, and partly by its long-established traditions of imperial expansion. Carthage was similarly pulled in, he says. Rome's triumphs in the Greek and Punic wars signaled the rise of a new hegemon.[74] This makes some sense, but to understand the Punic Wars we must also examine the different sources of social power within Rome and Carthage.

The city-state of Carthage, on the North African coast in what is now Tunisia, was an offshoot of Tyre, a Phoenician city in Lebanon. The Latin word *punicus* meant Phoenician. Carthage became a self-governing city-state penetrating its hinterland, but for centuries it remained a minor colony. It originally had kings, perhaps elected, but then acquired a constitution with an aristocratic senate and a more popular assembly. Around 340 BCE Aristotle said admiringly that it combined monarchical, oligarchic, and democratic elements and deflected internal conflict abroad by sending groups of citizens to found other Carthaginian states. There was a shared ruling-class culture and shared military-service obligations for citizens of Carthage and its African hinterland. The main differences from Rome were that merchant and aristocratic families could act more autonomously, and military offices were rigorously kept apart from civilian and religious offices; in Rome militarism also dominated the state and religion. Two annually elected "suffets," resembling Roman consuls, exercised judicial and executive power but not military power. Generals were appointed separately, often picked by the officers, and were then ratified by the city authorities. Militarism was not as central to the state and society as in Rome.

Carthage was said by Justin to have invaded Sicily in 550 BCE and again around 525. Herodotus adds an invasion in 490 BCE, defeated at the Battle of Himera. Many scholars have followed them in dating Carthaginian imperialism this early. Hoyos gives a detailed account from Greek sources of the campaign leading to Himera, and Terrenato mentions several wars in Sicily between Carthage and Syracuse through the fifth century.[75] Yet the battle at Himera probably involved men from other Phoenician colonies, argues Pilkington, adding that there is no archaeological evidence for any Carthaginian military venture abroad until an opportunistic invasion of Sicily in 409 BCE, when Syracuse had been weakened by its long war with Athens.[76] Carthaginian forces razed several Greek cities on the island and established at least two settlements, while leaving alone indigenous Sicilian towns. Before this, Carthage had established sufficient control over its African hinterland to support the city and armed forces. Carthaginian rule brought more prosperity to fertile Tunisian land that had been previously underexploited. Rule over the indigenous peoples was not very onerous, enabling the fusion of these Africans into a Carthaginian identity. They became the mainstay of its army, alongside other mercenaries, while citizens dominated its navy. But the port of Carthage remained small and lacked dry-dock facilities until the mid-fourth century BCE. There were merchant ships but no fleet capable of carrying a large invasion force. Perhaps the fleet of 490 BCE came from several Phoenician cities.

Unlike Rome, Carthage then became a major trading state, at first through trade with Athens and other Greek city-states, especially by exporting grain from its own hinterland. Small Phoenician colonies in Sardinia and southern Gaul were also subordinated, sometimes forcibly, though they retained their own political institutions, which indicates indirect Carthaginian rule. C. R. Whittaker and Miles emphasize the nonimperial nature of Carthaginian power even in the third century BCE, and it was for long more a federation than an empire.[77] Rome was the only true empire in the western Mediterranean world. Carthage controlled key ports and had widespread political connections but no imperial system of conquests or annexations. After 350 BCE Carthage maintained large fleets in a big new port facility, dominated more North African territory, and founded colonies in Sicily, Sardinia, and Iberia. This involved troops, although not much war was involved. Miles says Carthage's foreign policy "stands in stark contrast to the power politics" of Rome's plunder and subjugation policies. "There is little evidence of territorial conquest, administrative control, collection of taxes, commercial monopolies or the appropriation of foreign policy." Carthage created a "middle ground on which Phoenician, Greek and indigenous populations interacted and cooperated."[78] Perhaps this is a little too glowing, as Harris argues, for Carthage did wage war, had some militarism in its culture and institutions, restricted citizenship tightly, and dealt harshly with discontent.[79] But Hoyos says Carthage waged far fewer wars than Rome and the effect was to produce generals who were "amateurs" in comparison with the Roman generals (Hannibal excluded).[80] Whittaker went through the attributes of empire—territorial conquest, colonial governance, tribute, and unequal trade.[81] In the fifth and fourth centuries BCE he found only reciprocal agreements with other cities and peoples for port of trade rights favoring Carthaginian ships, since their naval power protected shipping. Military power did not dominate Carthaginian economic, political, and ideological institutions. Much expansion was by private merchant houses with their own small fleets. Think of several British East India Companies, not the British Empire.

This was only a coastal empire, focused on port cities, and the hinterlands needed to supply them. After the invasion of Sicily, troops were stationed there, but there is no sign of political institutions. The population subject to Carthaginian rule in Sicily and Sardinia remained small and largely self-governing. Carthage avoided conflict in Greece and with Rome and played no role in the Italian mainland. Polybius says Rome and Carthage concluded three treaties recognizing each other's spheres of influence, and trade between them produced a Carthaginian merchant district in Rome.[82] In the third treaty, signed in 279 BCE, Rome and Carthage pledged to aid each other in case of a threat from the Greek king Pyrrhus. Since Rome still lacked much of a navy, a Carthaginian fleet would, if required, transport Roman troops across the seas. The treaty was not activated, but it implied a loose alliance. Pyrrhus then entered Sicily, forced Syracuse to submit, and attacked the Carthaginians, pushing them to the west of the island. They were saved by his maltreatment of other Greek settlements in Sicily, which joined with Carthaginian forces to drive Pyrrhus off the island in 276, leaving a balance of power between Syracuse and the Carthaginians, and other Greek and indigenous settlements alongside them. Carthage was still not revealing imperial ambitions and Rome lacked equal sea power. War between them was not inevitable.

Then came a window of opportunity. The Mamertines, "Sons of Mars," a band of Italian mercenaries, had seized Messene, the closest port to mainland Italy, and held it for twenty years. They had slaughtered the inhabitants, for which they were universally condemned as war criminals, and had then run the city as a base for piracy on land and sea. Syracuse finally sent a force that defeated them. The remaining Mamertines, retreating into the citadel, appealed in 264 BCE to both Carthage and Rome for help. The Carthaginians had a fleet nearby and sent some troops into the city, but then they moved out. We don't know why. There was some debate among the Roman senators about the morality of aiding the Mamertines, especially when they themselves had just put to death renegade Roman soldiers, allies of the Mamertines, who had similarly murdered the citizens of Rhegium in Italy. The senate—unusually—failed to reach a decision and passed it on to the popular assembly. Polybius gives a detailed account of the decision. He says the Romans feared Carthaginian power:

> Carthaginian aggrandisement was not confined to Libya but had embraced many districts in Iberia as well. . . . Carthage was, besides, mistress of all the islands in the Sardinian and Tyrrhenian seas: they were beginning, therefore, to be exceedingly anxious lest, if the Carthaginians became masters of Sicily also, they should find them very dangerous and formidable neighbours, surrounding them as they would on every side, and occupying a position which commanded all the coasts of Italy. . . . Should they avail themselves of the voluntary offer of Messene and become masters of it, they were certain before long to crush Syracuse also, since they were already lords of nearly the whole of the rest of Sicily. . . . They felt it was absolutely necessary not to . . . allow the Carthaginians to secure what would be like a bridge to enable them to cross into Italy. The people, however, had suffered much from the previous wars, and wanted some means of repairing the losses which they had sustained in every department. Besides these national advantages to be gained by the war, the military commanders suggested that individually they would get manifest and important benefits from it. They accordingly voted in favour of giving the aid.[83]

The appeal to greed undercuts the claim that this was really self-defense, for the "manifest and important benefits" accruing to Roman citizens meant plunder and tribute, "justified" by the threat of future strangulation. In reality Carthage was not a threat. Polybius's sources were written near the end of the Punic Wars by historians reading back their present into the past. Carthaginian ships had long patrolled the straits, protecting trade from pirates without showing signs of territorial ambitions in mainland Italy, and Carthage was in defensive mode in Sicily, deploying few troops there. If Carthage had been seen as the main threat in Sicily, the obvious strategy would have been to ally with Syracuse against Carthage, but this was the opposite of what Roman forces did.

In 264 BCE a Roman invasion force crossed the straits and took Messene, beginning the first Roman war fought outside Italy. Roman and Carthaginian forces initially avoided each other, and the Romans instead went southeast to attack Syracuse, forcing it to submit to Roman rule. Only then did they turn westward toward Carthaginian settlements, having realized the relative weakness of the Carthaginian presence. It was opportunism aimed at direct territorial control. Carthaginian forces followed the cautious strategy they had pursued against Sicilian Greeks. Defending a few fortified towns, their outnumbered troops hoped to sap the Roman will to continue fighting so that a negotiated settlement could be reached. A treaty delineating separate spheres of interest was possible. Rome could have continued as a northern Mediterranean power, Carthage as a southern, and Carthaginian strategy on the island aimed at preserving the status quo. But Roman goals had expanded into conquering the whole island. Carthaginian leaders felt they could not accept this because as a maritime power trading across the Mediterranean, Carthage needed some control of the straits. Since Roman leaders must have realized this, they knew they were starting a major war with a power whose navy dominated the seas. I suspect a war party in the senate had a longer-term ambition. Polybius's ambivalence might indicate a similar suspicion.

War began, its first phase taking place in Sicily. The Carthaginians poured in reinforcements, and bloody, inconclusive warfare ensued, both in Sicily and in North Africa. Carthage was at first dominant at sea. Rome had the advantage of its expanding citizenship and a much larger population from which it could draw troops for land fighting. Pilkington says Carthage could draw on a maximum of about 200,000 men of fighting age from its African territories and colonies elsewhere.[84] Apart from its African hinterland, the Carthaginians had not acquired landmasses with large populations. Thus, it had only about one-half of Rome's potential soldiers. Carthage had to make up numbers with levies from tributaries and mercenaries, perhaps costly and of lesser loyalty. Carthage had to twice divert resources to suppress rebellions among North African troops. The Romans also detached some of Carthage's tributaries in Iberia and Numidia. Rome had the edge on land.

At first Carthage was a naval power and Rome was not. Yet the Romans again demonstrated an ability to subordinate the economy to war and exploit the resources of Greek city-states that it now dominated in the western Mediterranean. Private finance was mobilized to build fleets whose design was based on a recovered Carthaginian vessel, using Greek craftsmen, while adding improvements such as raised, strengthened prows for ramming and boarding (though these proved vulnerable in storms). Battle performance improved, and in 256 BCE a Roman fleet of over three hundred ships defeated the main Carthaginian fleet, also over three hundred vessels, off Cape Ecnomus in the south of Sicily. There was further fighting for a few years, but Carthaginian soldiers in Sicily, their supply lines cut, surrendered. Later that year a Roman army invaded Africa. The ultimate weakness of a commercial empire now revealed itself. Carthage struggled to find more troops; Rome continued to raise them.

Polybius says the First Punic War was "the greatest war in history in its length, intensity, and scale of operations."[85] But the Carthaginians now sued for peace. The senate exacted heavy terms: a war indemnity paid over ten years and the loss of Sicily and other islands. Polybius concludes rather euphemistically: "It was *not* by mere chance or without knowing what they were doing that the Romans struck their bold stroke for universal supremacy and dominion, and justified their boldness by its success. No: it was the natural result of discipline gained in the stern school of difficulty and danger."[86]

Romans then took advantage of Carthaginian preoccupation with a Numidian revolt to seize Sardinia and Corsica, hitherto Carthaginian. The senate then demanded a further indemnity from Carthage. These unprovoked, treaty-breaking acts made further warfare inevitable, as Polybius notes.[87] So far this had been all Roman aggression.

But this had provoked an aggressive Carthaginian response. Its rulers now sought direct control over further African territories, and they looked to Spain to build up resources to counter further Roman aggression and to pay the indemnities. They already had trading depots along the coast, and they now moved inland through campaigns against indigenous peoples, planting a more direct imperial rule over them, aided by marriage alliances with local elites and new settler cities.[88] This was now territorial imperialism, a defensive response to Roman expansion, though offensive against the inhabitants of Africa and Spain.

The Treaty of Ebro in 226 BCE allowed Carthage to expand in Spain south of the Ebro River while Rome took the north. This was breached by Rome when it supported the city-state of Saguntum, south of the river. The Saguntines had attacked a nearby city-state allied to Carthage, believing they had Roman protection. Carthage's commander in Spain, Hannibal, moved quickly to defeat Saguntum in 219 BCE. He would spare the population, provided they were "willing to depart from Saguntum, unarmed, each with two garments." He needed to pay his army and bribe the wavering assemblies in Carthage with the spoils of the city. They were more cost-conscious than Romans, and Hannibal, unlike Roman commanders, had to contend with an assembly peace faction. The citizens of Saguntum declined his offer and tried to destroy the city, so Hannibal ordered a bloodbath. The senate declared that this was a casus belli and that Carthage had breached the Ebro treaty. Roman ambassadors were then sent to demand Hannibal be handed over and taken to Rome as a war criminal—a typically unacceptable Roman demand, made so that Rome could claim that refusal made this a "just" war. Polybius blames both sides, as do most modern historians. Nathan Rosenstein says that neither Carthage nor Rome wanted war, but neither would back down, whereas Harris blames the Roman senate for using the Saguntines to provoke Hannibal into war.[89] The provocation seems to have been mutual, however.

The Second Punic War lasted seventeen years, until 201 BCE. Hannibal, well aware of Rome's greater potential reserves, struck quickly at the Roman heartland.[90] He took his soldiers and his elephants in Spain over the Alps into Italy. He had support from several Celtic tribes and tried to bring Rome's Italian allies over to his side, releasing all their captured prisoners and promising to restore the freedoms of those who allied with him. At the height of his power in Italy, perhaps 40 percent of Italian cities had promised him their allegiance, though most were more cautious in their actions, anxious not to provoke Roman rage. After Hannibal's great victory at Cannae in 216 BCE, in which Livy asserts 50,000 Romans were killed, Livy says Hannibal told his prisoners that "he was not carrying on a war of extermination with the Romans, but was contending for honour and empire. That his ancestors had yielded to the Roman valour; and that he was endeavouring that others might be obliged to yield, in their turn, to his good fortune and valour together. Accordingly, he allowed the captives the liberty of ransoming themselves."[91]

At this moment Hannibal did not march straight on Rome but offered negotiations, a decision sometimes considered his biggest mistake, since Rome never negotiated. Livy quotes one of his generals urging an immediate march on Rome.[92] Hannibal replied, "I commend your zeal, but I need time to weigh the plan which you propose," to which the general responded, "Assuredly, no one man has been blessed with all God's gifts. You, Hannibal, know how to gain a victory; you do not know how to use it." Yet Hannibal had probably calculated that taking Rome would involve a long siege that threatened supply difficulties while his forces remained static, vulnerable to attack. He wanted not the destruction of Rome but recognition of the equal stature and independence of Carthage. Cannae is also well over three hundred kilometers from Rome.

Hannibal's alliance with King Philip V of Macedon in 215 BCE put pressure on Rome, which faced a possible two-front war. Hannibal marched around Italy for fifteen years, ravaging Roman territory. The Romans resorted to stalling "Fabian" tactics, made famous by the general Fabius Maximus. Hannibal was hurt by the defeat of his brother Hasdrubal, who had brought reinforcements into Italy. When Rome sent legions to detach Carthaginian allies in Spain and Numidia, Hannibal was in trouble, unable to get reinforcements or defend his Italian allies. Again, Roman allies and mobilization policies made the crucial difference.[93] Hannibal also faced a faction in Carthage that opposed sending him reinforcements. The commercial instincts of Carthaginian leaders prompted them to send more resources to Iberian campaigns than to Hannibal in Italy. With the economic resources of Spain, members of this faction believed they might reestablish a balance of power with Rome. Hannibal was eventually recalled to Carthage and lost a final battle with the Romans at Zama in Africa in 202 BCE. His government then sued for peace and exiled him. Carthage, unlike Rome, had not subordinated all its sources of power to war making. Commercial and military calculations remained distinct. Faced with Rome, wavering between them would destroy them.

The Roman senate kept raising new legions. There were no rebellions, no peace factions within the senate, just class solidarity and competition between senators for command against Hannibal, and the fame and spoils that would bring. Over 70 percent of Roman citizens aged seventeen to thirty were drafted to fight, which in modern times, Rosenstein notes, has been equaled only by the Confederate states in the American Civil War. The disasters in Italy, says Livy, did not induce the Romans "to breathe a word about peace."[94] The final peace treaty of

202 BCE stripped Carthage of most of its territories, most of its fleet, and the right to make war without Roman permission, as well as the payment of a huge annual indemnity over a fifty-year period. When Carthage offered to pay this off in a single installment, Rome refused—it was a long-term means of demonstrating Carthage's subordination, a status ploy.[95]

During this war the Romans had avoided a two-front war with Philip V, king of Macedon, only by conceding a treaty favorable to Philip. This was remedied in 200 BCE when they invaded his kingdom. The senate responded to a call for help from the Greek states of Pergamum and Rhodes, which were feeling threatened by a projected alliance between the kingdom of Macedon and the Seleucids, another Hellenistic monarchy in southwestern Asia. These smaller powers feared they would be overcome, and the senators seized the opportunity to use their enlarged armies to achieve conquests in Greece also.

The Romans had won the Punic Wars. Carthage had been defeated, but a war party led by Cato declared repeatedly that "Carthage must be destroyed." The city still had rich pickings, and greedy Romans were keen to take them. Hoyos says no Roman could have believed that Carthage was still a threat.[96] Rosenstein laments, "The Republic's declaration of war on Carthage in 149 stands as a permanent stain on its honour."[97] Polybius and Appian say the senate made a secret decision to attack Carthage, while encouraging a Numidian prince to attack it first. When Carthage resisted, the senate claimed this was in breach of the treaty requiring Carthage to first seek its permission for war. Claiming a just war, a Roman army arrived in Africa in 149 BCE and besieged Carthage. The city offered to surrender, but the Roman generals demanded they hand over all weapons, abandon the city, and found a new city at least sixteen kilometers from the sea—an offer they could not accept. After a three-year siege the city was stormed and looted.[98] Perhaps 150,000 Carthaginians were killed and 50,000 survivors, mainly women, were sold into slavery. Archaeological excavations confirm that the whole city was burned and razed to the ground, not a soul remaining—emotional revenge for past humiliations, out of all proportion to them. The loot did pump wealth into the Roman economy, and taking North Africa into public ownership, the state redistributed it to Romans. In the same year Corinth was destroyed by Roman forces, the pretext being that Roman ambassadors, again offering unacceptable peace terms, had been insulted. Some citizens were slaughtered, the rest enslaved, and the city declared extinct. Yet archaeology reveals a lesser scale of destruction than at Carthage.

The Roman senate showed that it would achieve domination free of any rival. The Punic Wars had revealed an imperialism and resistance to negotiations unmatched by the Carthaginians. The end of Carthage was more than just payback for its earlier victories. Along with Corinth's extinction, it was a dire warning to any people who might contemplate resisting Rome. Eckstein helps us identify a dangerous geopolitical environment, but Harris gives us the reason war triumphed over diplomacy in handling it—an opportunistic but cumulative Roman militarism baked in to its social structure. Carthaginian power structures could not match such single-mindedness.

Endgame of the Republic: Civil Wars

Roman militarism reached its apogee in overthrowing the very republic that had institutionalized it. Roman conquests had increased inequality, and peasant soldiers had fought to their own detriment. While away on military service, aristocrats had bought their lands with the spoils of war and cultivated them with slaves the soldiers had conquered. The new slave-based villa agriculture generated higher yields and economic growth—at the expense of soldiers and slaves alike. Rising expectations of war profit heightened corruption by governors and generals, intensifying electoral bribery for high office. The state had acquired extensive public lands, which the wealthy of Rome could lease to create estates worked by slaves. Many peasant farms could not compete, and farmers were forced off their lands into a poverty-stricken existence in Rome, whose population rose greatly. Their rising discontent was paralleled by that of slaves, who across different regions mounted large-scale revolts in 136–30, 105, and 72–70 BCE (the last famously led by Spartacus).

These conflicts led to more violent Roman politics. During 133–21 BCE, the two Gracchi brothers exploited their power as tribunes of the assemblies to seek radical reforms, backed by a large influx of people voting in the assemblies. The twin political institutions of the republic, senate and assemblies, were now at odds. The Gracchi sought to redistribute lands that the rich had acquired to veterans and landless citizens, and to offer more rights to the allies—the social democrats of the ancient world, fiercely opposed by most senators, who represented the rich. The unequal distribution of the spoils of war generated an enduring polarization of Roman politics between reform-minded *populares* and conservative *optimates*. But the Gracchi brothers were assassinated by *optimates* before their reforms bore fruit. These murders may have been the first political bloodshed in the city of Rome for three centuries, and they reduced the political power of the popular classes.

The senate aborted the reforms but unrest remained. Discontent among allies grew: manpower shortages meant their military service obligations were mounting. They were doing most of the fighting. This provoked in 91–87 BCE the Social Wars of the allied Italian peoples, who demanded full citizenship, equal share in pay and spoils, residence and contract rights, and marriage with Romans. Rome was pressured into granting most of their demands. But this did not end unequal imperialism. The upper classes continued to amass large fortunes, while more legionaries were dispossessed or indebted. The elite destroyed the republic. They "lacked willingness to abide by the norms under which they had grown up" (a parallel for today).[99]

The embedding of Roman armies in the senate, the popular assemblies, and the citizen population as a whole had produced an outcome similar to modern civilian control of the military. Coup-proofing strategies had not been required. But now the social bonds had been broken and wars had increased the power and autonomy of generals, which encroached on the power of the senate. During the 80s BCE, two rival generals, Marius and Sulla, managed in turn to restore order by force and intimidate the senate into appointing them as consuls. They had recruited armies more loyal to themselves than to the state by extending military service to the lower classes, offering them bounties and land upon discharge, and granting more citizen rights to allies. The ensuing civil wars of the period involved much plundering in order to pay the troops and ensure their loyalty to their generals.

Marius was an arriviste populist and used his popular backing to break the rules of Roman politics, including standing for reelection to the consulship on multiple occasions—and winning. Sulla, an aristocrat, was backed by *optimate* senators. In 88 BCE their rivalry escalated into civil war when Sulla violated a constitutional taboo by marching his army into Rome and forcing Marius and his followers to flee the city. After the death of Marius in 86 BCE, Sulla seized control, styling himself "Dictator to Restore the Republic," killing and seizing the property of opponents and distributing it to his own supporters. The institutions representing the dominant classes of Rome had lost their power. Now a general spoke for them.

That began the death throes of the republic, but it did not solve factionalism. Disorder followed the death of Sulla. In 59 BCE two generals,

Pompey and Julius Caesar, joined forces with Crassus, a man of enormous wealth acquired through buying up property confiscated by Sulla. They seized power in Rome and established a triumvirate. Caesar styled himself protector of the Marian legacy and courted popular support with reforms opposed by most of the senate. He was granted an extraordinary ten-year command in Gaul to get him away from Rome, but his string of victories there enabled him to build up a formidable army and wealth. The Gauls, he said, were emotional, impulsive, credulous, fickle, quick to anger, politically unpredictable, and constantly intriguing. They were therefore a threat, needing a firm Roman hand. They certainly got it. Plutarch says his campaign killed a million Gauls and enslaved another million.[100] Think of the horrors such numbers must have involved. His goal was political power in Rome. He needed money from slaves and military prestige to ensure this and to outdo Pompey.

Crassus died at Carrhae, leaving Pompey and Caesar as twin dictators. They both had armies, and Pompey also had a senate majority.[101] The inevitable civil war began when Caesar took his army into Italy in 49 BCE, crossing the River Rubicon. Pompey was defeated and murdered, and the senators opposing Caesar were mopped up. But when Caesar adopted the title *Dictator in Perpetuo*, a conspiracy of sixty senators assassinated him. Caesar's followers won the ensuing civil war, and in 43 BCE came the triumvirate of Mark Antony, Lepidus, and Octavian, ruling different regions. This produced more civil wars, ending with the victory of Octavian, Caesar's great nephew, adopted son, and heir, in 31 BCE. At first Octavian preserved the shell of the senate and assemblies. In 27 BCE a tame senate granted him the titles of Augustus and "First Citizen of the State." He ruled as de facto emperor until 14 CE, followed by many emperors. The republic was finished by its own militarism.

Postscript: The Roman Empire

Under Augustus, Rome became formally an empire. The term *Pax Romana* was coined, referring only to the internal peace of the empire, not its foreign relations, which differs from modern usages of similar terms— *Pax Britannica* and *Pax Americana*. Since Augustus was determined to keep military power pointing outward, foreign wars continued. Glory remained the principal motive for war among the emperors.[102] Conquests all around the Mediterranean followed. The emperors said they made war in order to bring peace to the conquered peoples.[103] The emperors in theory controlled the army, but its practical autonomy threatened them. The development of praetorian guards was an attempt at coup-proofing, but then their loyalty might be problematic. Civil wars were rare, but coups common. There were seventy emperors in total, and only twenty seem to have died of natural causes. Between twenty-seven and thirty-five were assassinated or died in prison, nine died in battle, and five committed suicide.

Militarism slackened as a professional army detached war from citizenship, so that culture and institutions became divorced from military power, as resources became stretched over a vast empire, and as frontiers adjoined regions with little wealth or fierce resistance so that war became not worth the cost. In the east against Persia a more defensive strategy brought treaties and hostage exchanges.[104] But the western empire became vulnerable to militarism. Civil wars broke out between rival emperors whose soldiers were loyal to their generals, who became provincial warlords. No one intended to destroy the western empire. Collapse came as an unintended consequence of their struggles. The barbarians mattered as they became a larger proportion of Roman armies.[105] But for almost a millennium, Rome was perhaps the most successful example of militarism the world has ever seen. After its fall, no European state had equivalent military power for over a thousand years. The only equal was the Chinese Empire. Their secret was not a powerful bureaucratic state, but the embedding of dominant classes in political institutions.

Roman Conclusions

Seven reasons explain why the Roman Republic made war so continuously. One more explains why this did not last forever.

1. Early Roman growth was due to mixed defensive war, Mafia-style protection rackets, and negotiated upper-class alliances in an Italy not yet filled by states, which offered opportunities to expand over other peoples. Then going to the defense of an ally and gaining dominance over both enemy and allied regimes was a mixed offensive-defensive strategy that allowed Rome not to fight on its own territory. Insecurity receded as Rome enforced more regime changes and conquered more territories and peoples.

2. Offensive warfare needs success to become repetitive. Rome was militarily effective because militarily defined classes were

entrenched in the senate, the popular assemblies, and the legions. Politically, the senate dominated, debating the likely gains, though not usually the costs, of proposed wars. But calculations—rationality of means—were dominated by optimism about Roman military power. This proved not to be misplaced since Romans dug deeper and sacrificed more for war than did their enemies. Legally guaranteed rights were held by citizens in return for lengthy service in legions that thus possessed cohesion resulting from citizen solidarity. The privileges varying by social class strengthened legitimate army hierarchy and enabled the intensive drilling, discipline, logistics, and flexible maneuvering of large legionary armies by a very small state. Thus, domestic political power relations produced effective legions, helping lead to success in aggressive wars.

3. Romans granted varying degrees of citizens' rights to allies, thereby reinforcing their loyalty and more than doubling the size of Roman armies. Battlefield success was enhanced by prioritizing military power over exclusive citizenship, unlike Rome's Greek and Carthaginian rivals. This involved "society" in its two senses, one modern, meaning a collective body of citizens, the other relating to the original Latin root word *socius*, a confederation of allies.

4. Allies' allegiance required Roman victories. Client peoples fear above all the defeat of their protector. If they sense weakness, they may change sides. But Rome kept on winning. Roman rulers scorned diplomacy, which meant that they could not counter possible grand alliances among their rivals by means of negotiations. They issued demands and refused compromise, while defeats merely made them dig deeper into manpower reserves than their enemies could. That gave allies confidence in Rome's ultimate victory. This wavered only temporarily under Rome's greatest challenge, Hannibal's invasion of Italy.

5. This combination of causes meant that Roman militarism became baked in to its economy, ideology, and politics more than in other states around the Mediterranean. Scheidel agrees: "The four sources of social power—ideological, economic, military, and political—were unusually tightly bundled together: members of the same narrow elite acted as political

leaders, military commanders, and priests, and controlled the largest private fortunes."[106] Roman success was not due simply to a better military, disconnected from society. All sources of power were sacrificed to war making. This eventually brought success even after reverses in battle, which generated territory, wealth, and slaves for Romans; it intensified a bellicose culture transmitted across generations; and it subordinated economic, ideological, and political institutions to military needs. This was no longer war by careful, pragmatic calculation of cost, as in Realist theory. It was war whatever the cost. Repeated wars were due primarily to domestic power structures.

6. Benefit accrued mainly but not only to the upper classes. The dual pursuit of greed and status through glory, the two being closely entwined, also brought political office, becoming the main motives of politician-generals and soldiers alike, justifying the risk of death. Romans saw conquest, not trade (coerced or not), as the major mode of economic acquisition. Carthage mixed the two and was militarily weaker for it.

7. Rulers carry on doing what works, and Roman militarism and imperialism intensified with success. Ambition grew from achieving mere dominance over neighbors to conquest and territorial empire. By the time of the Punic Wars, Rome was the major aggressor around the Mediterranean. Any people that defied Rome would be destroyed—*Carthago delenda est*, and Corinth too. Such ferocious retribution involved an unusual phase of emotional amplification of imperialism. An autonomous ideology, however, was not a characteristic of Roman imperialism. Rather, militarism was built into everyday life experience, especially into the economy and the political career structure, seemingly natural and taken for granted. The proximate cause of wars of aggression was victory in earlier wars. Path dependence helps explain why Romans kept on making war. We will see that this was merely one of the most extreme forms of conquest imperialism, commonly found in historic warfare.

8. But war making eventually weakened the republic, intensifying inequality and discontent, opening fissures between the senate and popular assemblies, overturning the coup-proofing links between citizenship and the army, and allowing generals

to build autonomous power bases. Military power was deployed in Italy and in Rome itself in civil wars whose winners became dictators, destroying the republican polity. Militarism had become suicidal for the republic.

The Roman upper classes were the main beneficiaries of war, followed by legionaries who survived intact, merchants trading with the legions and in conquered provinces, and foreign upper classes who switched allegiance when they perceived Rome would win. The allies took heavy losses but benefited if they got Roman citizenship. Defeated peoples suffered massacres, rapes, pillage, and slavery. The Romans destroyed hundreds of "vanished kingdoms." The region benefited a little from Roman economic growth, but whether more peaceful development might have occurred across the Mediterranean had Rome shared power with Greeks and Carthaginians is unknowable. Less tangible was the Roman contribution to civilization—law, literary works, mosaics, sculptures, aqueducts, baths, straight roads—but achieved with great loss of life. Overall, these wars probably benefited few of the peoples around the Mediterranean. Rationality of ends was mostly confined to Roman elites and their dependents.

CHAPTER FIVE

Ancient China

ETWEEN 710 AND 221 BCE, 866 wars are mentioned in the Chinese annals, but many were probably minor skirmishes (MIDs). Over the period 656–221 BCE, there were 256 wars involving "great powers"—one every 1.7 years. In the last phase of the Warring States period, 356–221 BCE, there was a war every 1.4 years. Most of these encounters probably met the CoW standard of one thousand battle deaths in a year, although exaggerations are common in the records, and we can rarely be sure about army size or casualty rates. The number of polities was reduced from over seventy in 771 BCE to about twenty in the mid-fifth century BCE. The Warring States period then saw this reduced to just one, the empire of Qin.[1]

So there were many "vanished kingdoms," and the likelihood of any single polity being at war grew through time. Dingxin Zhao says that fifteen of the twenty wars whose casualties surpassed 20,000 occurred at the end of the Warring States period.[2] Yet such statistics only indicate that, on average, somewhere in China a war was occurring between at least two states. In any single year until near the endgame, most states were not at war. Nevertheless, *The Art of War*, by Sun Tzu in the sixth century BCE, begins, "Warfare is the greatest affair of state, the basis of life and death, the Way to survival or extinction." The questions for this chapter are: Why so many wars, why so many state extinctions, and were wars rational in terms of either means or ends?

Before 771 BCE the Western Zhou Chinese monarchy had expanded through quasi-colonial conquest of mostly stateless agriculturalists and hunter-gatherers. As in early Roman Italy, there was not yet a multistate system. The Zhou launched wars because they could win them, for they had greater economic and military power than their neighbors. They did not seize great wealth. Slaves and military conscripts were the main prize, and Zhou settlers might develop more intensive agriculture in conquered areas. Many peripheral peoples bowed to reality by submitting to threats without going to war. Their elites' daughters might be married off to Zhou aristocrats as a symbol of their absorption into the Zhou realm. Rule was feudal, though different from European feudalism. As their realms extended, rulers shifted from being mere heads of clans and lineages and stabilized their conquered realms by "enfeoffing" kin and allies in small walled towns and military colonies, in which these became lesser replicas of the king, while their own hereditary "ministers" became lesser replicas of themselves—the typical devolution of power we find where feudal regimes are unable to directly control large territories. The eldest son of the principal wife or concubine inherited lordship, though younger sons received lesser hereditary office at court or served as soldiers and might be enfeoffed in more peripheral towns.[3] Younger sons agitated for more conquest.

Armies were formed of lineage levies whose core was aristocratic charioteers. A clan chief might have a few full-time soldiers, but most were conscripted peasants. As in other feudal regimes, as Marx said, armed force was necessary to extract surplus from the direct producers so that the upper classes could live well and not fight wars at all. Yet exploitation had its limits. The core class problem in near-subsistence agrarian societies was that taking too much of the surplus or too many of the peasants as soldiers or slaves harmed the productivity of farms on which rulers depended to fight their wars. They could not squeeze too hard. Taxes were moderate and armies small and confined to a campaigning season when farm labor was less important. But peasants were also taken as corvée labor, given the great height and depth of city walls found by archaeologists. Warfare remained key for aristocrats, their culture bellicose. Mark Lewis says, "Defense of one's honor was the primary spur to battle," but as Zhao adds, there were also economic, political, and geopolitical motives. Lacking much evidence, we cannot disentangle them.[4] Then the kings' power weakened in a typically feudal way as power shifted downward through this hierarchy of lineages. They lacked the infrastructures to control their vassals or stop their feuding. They began to suffer defeats by incoming peoples.

The Spring and Autumn Period, 771–476 BCE

In 771 BCE came disaster. The Zhou, racked by a disputed succession, saw their capital sacked by men they called uncivilized—barbarians. The survivors fled eastward, where the Zhou lords set up their own polities as "dukes" over which the king retained only a symbolic kingship. Ritual deference was shown to him, and no one else could claim the title of king. The indigenous people of the new domains either were conquered and enserfed or submitted to ducal power to keep their freedom. Since these states were founded by military power and continued to extract the surplus by force, militarism continued. China was divided into many independent lordships—one chronicler says there were 148, but there were at least 70, most of them tiny; a few acted as overlords to their smaller neighbors.

States were at first rudimentary, and ministers and officials were dependent on personal relationships between dukes and their vassals. The duke could assign offices to his vassals but had little power over them once they were installed. An effective vassal enjoying high office might acquire enough retainers to challenge the duke, and so might cliques of discontented vassals excluded from office. Dukes were male, although dowager queen mothers might govern as regents on behalf of a boy successor, a practice surviving right through to Cixi, the final dowager of the Chinese Empire, who died in 1908 just before the fall of the last dynasty.

Civil wars were caused by a duke's failings, especially in war, by the absence of a direct male heir, by the accession of a boy or apparent weakling, or by the rise of a discontented lineage group. Palace coups were more common, when discontented kin killed a duke and seized his throne. Zhao finds that about half the dukes of three major states were assassinated—an extraordinary proportion, which might seem to render irrational the pursuit of political power, except that there was no escape—even kin who sought only a quiet life were killed in coups, as were the kin of those staging unsuccessful coups. The domestic fears of insecure dukes fueled foreign wars, for to secure domination at home required soldiers acquired in war, and victories abroad brought loot for retainers and loyal soldiers, who could then be deployed domestically. Thus, war was the way to acquire resources for extracting the surplus from those who actually produced it. This Marxian circular process reinforced the lure of war.

Geopolitics was fairly anarchic, yet so was domestic politics, which often led to civil war between rival lineages. Chinese thinkers believed war was inevitable because of either human nature or the nature of society. The primary value was political order, as is usual in disorderly societies. War imposing order was therefore righteous but generally brief. These were highly class-divided societies in which the masses shared little of the culture of their rulers. Peasants saw little of the state. Taxes, military service, and corvée labor were extracted by local vassals.

There was a shared culture among elites in the core zones. One enduring diplomatic form was the hegemon—a duke coming to exercise some authority over other rulers through arbitration of disputes and convening of assemblies to issue agreements. An edict of 657 BCE proclaimed, "Let there be no damming of irrigation water, no withholding sales of grain, no changes of heirs apparent, no promoting of concubines to replace wives, and no involvement of women in state affairs." Another declared: "Let not office be hereditary, nor let officers simultaneously hold more than one office, and in the selection of officers let the object be to get the proper men, and let not a ruler take onto himself to put to death a great officer. . . . Make no crooked embankments, and impose no restriction on the sale of grain, and let no boundary markers [be] set without announcement." These were probably good intentions rather than actual practice, although Cho-yun Hsu says this was an "interstate community," adding a liberal tinge to Realist geopolitics.[5] Yet hegemony was not heritable, struggles over the next hegemon were common, and all five of the hegemons were from different ducal houses. These hegemons do not fit political scientists' usage of the term since they had nothing like the powers exercised by the British and American empires—or of later emperors of China. They were uneasily perched as first among equals in an arena that still had "empty" spaces for expansion.

There were short-term peace agreements and even attempts at enduring ones. In 579 BCE the rulers of Qi, Qin, Jin, and Chu convened a conference at which they agreed to pursue peace and limit army size. Alas, this was only rhetoric. In 546 Hsiang Shu, a Sung diplomat, lobbied Chinese courts to negotiate a treaty to end all wars. Wanting to seem to be on the side of virtue, fourteen major rulers drew up an agreement. A dispute then erupted over who should sign first. Some then refused to sign, and the signers ignored it anyway. Hsiang Shu presented a signed copy to his chief minister, who responded that war was an inevitable tool of statecraft. To seek to abandon it was folly. He tore up the treaty in front of him.[6] In 541 BCE a peace conference received the news that Lu forces had just invaded the small state of Ju. There was a proposal that the conference punish the delegate from Lu. But the chief minister of Jin responded: "Territory is defined by battle. It belongs to one state at one time, to another state at another time. Where is the constancy? . . . Supporting large states at the expense of the small ones is the way a leading state has acquired its leading status. What else is useful? Which state has not lost some land? Which presiding power can pass judgement?"[7] It was not far from Hobbesian anarchy. War was normal, baked in to culture and institutions.

Yet one secular tendency appeared amid the confusion: the swallowing up by dominant rulers of lesser ones through war, mafia-like protection rackets, and a few marriage alliances. Eventually there were only twenty, including seven much bigger than the others. The ensuing Warring States period saw space-filling geopolitics in which "great powers" alternately fought and negotiated with each other, rising and declining amid two centuries of balancing alliances and instability. These unstable balances of power defeated all attempts by individual dukes to maintain dominance temporarily achieved.[8] All the while, smaller domains were vanishing.

The aristocrats saw war and militarism as normal. Victory brought both glory and material gains, in the form of more territories and peoples, which could be converted into a bigger military for further wars. But dukes also fought wars if they felt slighted, to defend their honor or right a wrong or recapture territory lost by defeat in a past war, or when they felt threatened at home and sought to demonstrate strength through war. An army raised could be turned to domestic repression. As in Rome, there were many motives for war, but we lack the knowledge to rank them in importance. When war was so baked in to social life, it was not so much "chosen" in preference to the other sources of power; it was the normal way in which conflicts were settled. It is difficult to discern how much careful calculation of means was involved in war decisions, but calculations had to include the likely responses of other states that might be supposed allies or enemies. Diplomatic luck and skills were important.

Warrior motives deriving from religious or secular ideologies were absent, which was not the case in Europe. For repeat victors, conquest was self-sustaining—though there were always more losers than winners, as the declining number of states confirms, which would not seem to indicate much accurate calculation by most of them. Aristocratic culture glorified lineage, patriarchy, blood, war, oaths, and covenants of fealty. Codes of honor in battle were shared, making warfare not too costly for the aristocrats, as was true in medieval Europe. Some rulers fought in person, though it was more common to use kin as generals. Conquest was justified as spreading order and civilization to the uncivilized.

Once horses were domesticated, aristocrats' chariots dominated warfare. Their weapons were of bronze, which only the wealthy could afford. Armies were around 5,000 to 25,000 men in the Spring and Autumn period, campaigns lasted a few weeks, and most battles were decided in a day. Though the bigger states often clashed with each other, until the Late Warring States period the ecology of China enabled states to partially deflect their conflicts onto mutual expansion through conquest of, and rule over, less well-developed peoples on the peripheries. Only the central zone was filled with states. The incentive to make aggressive war increased for Zhou states adjacent to the periphery.[9]

Up to the mid-sixth century, an archipelago of city-states expanded control over stateless and tribal peoples, the "country dwellers," while major states annexed minnows. "Early hegemonic rivals typically attacked the lesser states that were sandwiched between them and largely avoided direct confrontations."[10] Victories dominate surviving annals, for the annals of defeated rulers usually vanish. The conquerors of the country people founded walled towns fed from their hinterland, the "well fields," which were distributed among friendly indigenous people, military veterans, and other settlers. The towns were inhabited by the "people of the state [or city]." Around them the "people of the field" or "country people" might owe labor service or payment in kind to the cities, but not initially military service, in order to keep them disarmed. City fortifications became stronger and included lateral barriers to the free flow of people within the city, which suggests authoritarian control.[11] It was a form of Gumplowicz's "super-stratification," a class structure imposed by the victors of war over the vanquished.[12] The peoples farther away lived in so-called empty spaces outside the control of states, which were inhabited by "those who will not come to court," less "civilized," lacking "duty" or "moral instruction." The notion of a state as a bounded territory arose in the fifth century BCE. Before then, the walled towns formed a network of nodes, each sustained by a rural periphery of uncertain boundaries. The non-Zhou peoples, like the "uncivilized" Rong and Di, were gradually absorbed. They began as farmers, shepherds, and mountaineers, but by 400 BCE they had disappeared as separate peoples from the records. Military service, corvée labor, intermarriage, and cultural assimilation had generated a single people calling themselves the Hua Xie, the Chinese.[13]

Dukes made war to acquire wealth and peoples, to increase their population and specifically their army size, but also to acquire status and glory, just as Roman aristocrats did. Again, these motives were closely interwoven. Polities were identified by the name of the ruling dynasty, a ducal house, not a state. Offensive war was incentivized, for it might bring loot or conscripts, and it spared one's own agricultural base from devastation. Sun Tzu in his *Art of War* advised the Wu king, "When you plunder a countryside, let the spoil be divided amongst your men; when you capture new territory, cut it up into allotments for the benefit of the soldiery."[14] His recommended distribution was very unequal: "If he is a noble he will receive 10,000 mou of land; if he is a farmer, artisan, or merchant he will be permitted to seek service at court; if he is a slave or bound to menial service he will be freed." But most settlers benefited, as did younger sons with meager inheritances. They were risking their lives but were militarily dominant and lived behind defensive walls. The expected utility of war was high—the only avenue of advancement.[15] War was rational in terms of ends achieved by the surviving winners— obviously not for the losers.

Concentration of power in the ruler and his court grew with the extension of state control into the hinterland, as military power translated into political power.[16] Army service was originally owed only by the nobility and the people of the state, but it was then extended to the country dwellers in return for granting them fuller property rights to the land, so that military power became baked in to the economy of China. As the size of states increased, armies grew to up to 50,000 men, mainly peasant infantry armed with newly available iron weapons, cheaper and stronger than bronze weapons. The exploitation of iron brought about what is often described as a military revolution, though its diffusion from Anatolia across Eurasia took seven hundred years. But the aristocratic chariot disappeared. Larger armies required more drilling, and manuals describe complex battle formations. Armies required more logistical support, so states acquired new functions, such as censuses to determine conscription and taxation. Taxes were usually only up to 10 percent of income, but in a subsistence economy that could be severe. County administration replaced lineage patronage, which indicates more political centralization, as do fewer civil wars and palace coups. Leading ministers were less aristocratic than dependents of the monarch. More intense warfare required greater agricultural productivity, assisted by irrigation projects. Trade increased. These were small steps toward resolving the feudal military paradox: costlier warfare might lower the agricultural surpluses needed to finance it. War was initially bad news for the conquered, many of whom were enslaved, but it might eventually bring economic and other civilizational benefits—provided the conquered did not rebel, for then they would be slaughtered.

The Warring States Period, 475–221 BCE

The states now began to form permanent administrations and had frontiers dotted with walls and forts. Wars became costlier in money and lives, for fewer easy preys remained. The space-filling core grew, though expansion brought new peripheries. Army size by the end of the Warring States period ranged up to several hundred thousand men, much bigger than forces in Rome or Europe before Napoleon. Soldiers were drilled to be capable of shifting formation rapidly, as they were in European armies only from the sixteenth century CE.[17] Casualties rose, as little mercy was shown to the defeated. The dead and prisoners alike would be beheaded and the heads presented to the generals, who rewarded soldiers according to the number. There are accounts of "taking sixty thousand heads." After the battle of Changping in 260 BCE, the Qin victors claimed to have inflicted 450,000 casualties on the defeated Zhao. Such figures may be inflated, but drilling and killing had skyrocketed.[18] The risk of death or mutilation for soldiers rose, but most were conscripts who lacked free will. They were fed and minimally paid, and they might as veterans be awarded a small farm on conquered land, the silver lining for the survivors.

Because of the growing lethality of war, sophisticated literature on war strategy and tactics arose, like Sun Tzu's *The Art of War,* advising generals how to win without fighting and how to practice ambushes, feints, and deceptions of one's own strength, to strike where the enemy is weak and never where he is strong—tactics intended to avoid murderous frontal pitched battles. They were widely read among elites. Their stratagems might mean that states weaker in material resources could defeat the bigger battalions. The end product was more losers than winners, which suggests much miscalculation. The distinction is often made between a "Chinese way" of war and a "Western way," expressed in a contrast between Sun Tzu and Clausewitz, particularly the latter's emphasis on annihilating the enemy through frontal assault. The contrast is real enough between them, but today both are required reading at West Point and the Chinese Military Academy.

Nonetheless, periods of negotiated peace lasted much longer than wars, and so there was tension between a preference for institutions guaranteeing peace versus opportunities to intervene in dynastic succession crises and in peripheries. Peace was rendered fragile as rulers used peacetime to introduce military reforms, which led their rivals also to improve their militaries—the Realist security dilemma. By the mid-fourth century BCE, all seven surviving major states had implemented reforms suggested by "legalist" theorists to gear the economy and the state more tightly to war needs. A mass of peasants owing military service replaced lineage-organized militaries.[19] Militarism now affected the people more intensely.

The surviving large states had institutionalized militarism, internalizing "glory" as an end, making them confident of success in the next war. Indeed, they were overconfident, for when they lost—and all but one eventually did—they might disappear as autonomous states. So from 419 BCE, with a bigger jump after 317 BCE, wars resumed, costlier and fiercer, producing greater chances of death for soldiers and greater debts for states. Defeat might destroy quite major states.[20] During the fourth century BCE, rulers began to style themselves as kings, and deference to the Zhou monarch collapsed. By then professional soldiers rather than the dukes went into battle. Dukes could play with the lives of others.

This phase was probably more ruthless than it was in medieval Europe, where Christendom and kinship networks meant that a petty prince conquered by a major kingdom might be treated mildly. He might pay an indemnity and swear loyalty to the new king. Though this also sometimes happened in China, in other cases the defeated aristocracies and soldiers were put to death or enslaved en masse. One cause of the decline of the aristocracy in the late Warring States period was the killing of so many of its families.[21] Multistate alliances grew, seeking peace through deterrence but periodically activated for war.

During the Warring States period peripatetic intellectuals sold expert advice to rulers.[22] The sayings of some survive, philosophers like Confucius and Mencius, legalists like Shang Yang and Han Fei, and military writers such as Sun Tzu and Sun Bin. Despite their many differences, most reacted to the Warring States period by arguing that China was destined to be one realm under a single state: "all under heaven," ruled by the "Son of Heaven." They believed in Realist style that only a hegemonic power could enforce peace over all China.[23] This view drew on the Zhou ideological legacy of universal kingship, now with the cosmic resonance of returning the natural world to its proper course. None of these intellectuals defended the autonomy of individual states. They hoped that one day one ruler would come, and realistically, he could come only through war.[24] This belief encouraged several thrusts by individual states for hegemony across the central China region. Yet all failed, until Qin.

Confucius (born 551 BCE) said little about war, but he taught that creating the moral person and the good society involved five virtues: benevolence, charity, and humanity; honesty, uprightness, and the ability to tell right from wrong; knowledge; faithfulness and integrity; and propriety, ceremony, ritual, and worship. He emphasized filial piety and strict ritual adherence to one's given social role, a conservative program aimed at protecting society from uncertainty and disorder, the greatest threat to good government and social harmony. Action by both the individual and the government should aim at morality, not profit or utility. Yet only an elite of morally and intellectually superior men could refine their innate moral goodness or overcome innate badness and decide policy. Since states could not create such a man, this elite must have some autonomous power from the ruler. This idea later bore fruit in a Confucian bureaucracy.

Confucius said that a ruler is morally obliged to maintain peace, by force if necessary, while for the people war is a justified last resort to remove inhumane kings. But when asked to give a ruler advice about the conduct of war, he refused. When questioned on the purpose of government, he replied, "Give the people enough to eat, and enough soldiers to defend them, and they will have confidence in you." But which of the two should be given up first? Confucius replied, "Give up the soldiers." Yet rulers could ensure victory in war through just and humane policies that would win popular support.

Mencius (active in the fourth century BCE) denounced war: "In wars to win land, the dead fill the fields; in wars to seize cities, the dead fill their streets. This is what we mean by teaching the earth how to eat human flesh." The ruler had been installed by heaven solely for the benefit of his people, and human nature tends toward and desires goodness. The truly good ruler would be looked up to even by the people of neighboring states, who will "turn to him like water flowing downwards with a tremendous force." To wage an expedition for the improvement of people's lives was acceptable, but he added: "In the Spring and Autumn Annals, there are no just wars. They merely show that some wars are not so bad as others." Mo Tzu (ca. 480–ca. 390 BCE) condemned aggressive war on both utilitarian and moral grounds. Aggressive war did not pay, except for a few winners, and their peoples rarely benefited, since war required high taxes. He criticized the moral double standard of violence being illegitimate within a state but legitimate in interstate relations; aggressive war was morally the same as murder. He favored defensive war, however, giving expert advice to rulers on defensive fortifications, and his supporters formed a militia to help small states resist big ones. Alas, they were on the wrong side of history, as armies became bigger and bigger, and sharks swallowed up the minnows.[25]

Few Confucians were pacifists. They gave two legitimate reasons for making war. First, China was the universal state, of greater moral authority than any rival. So if a foreign ruler refused to perform rituals of submission, war against him would be just. Second, wars were just if they helped reunite "all under heaven," restoring the unity of China. Xunzi (born ca. 300 BCE) remarked, "Human nature is evil, and goodness is caused by conscious [or intentional] activity." He saw the military stratagems of Sun Tzu as working only against a state in which ruler-subject relations had broken down. "For a tyrant to try to overthrow a good ruler by force would be like throwing eggs at a rock or stirring boiling water with your finger." Virtuous rulers would win wars over despots since their soldiers and people would be more committed. Virtuous rulers would not fight against other virtuous rulers—an ancient variant of democratic peace theory. Sun Tzu said the moral ruler benefits from a "moral law" that "causes the people to be in complete accord with their ruler, so that they will follow him regardless of their lives, undismayed by any danger." An immoral ruler at odds with his people will fail regardless of his skill in the art of war. Sun Tzu added, "If one is not fully cognizant of the evils of waging war, he cannot be fully cognizant either of how to turn it to best account."[26] There is a parallel here with Waltz's version of Realism in which those states that act wrongly will be punished by the system. If only that were true.

Legalist theorists subordinated morality to politics. The early Zhou period was seen as having been a time of plenty and peace—"the people were few whereas goods were plenty; hence people did not compete," said Han Fei, blaming population growth for ruining that idyll. Scarcity produced greed, conflicting interests, and war. Legalists saw the state as the only source of order and morality, so all should be subordinated to it. Since no one can say who deserves the title of "superior man," the ruler could not rely on a ministerial elite. Ministers were concerned only with their own interests, and a ruler must be absolute and create an order in which only those who benefit society through agriculture and war should be rewarded and promoted. Those who fail should be punished. The meritocratic yoking together of agriculture and war under an authoritarian ruler would yield a successful and orderly state. Reward and punishment should be the twin "handles" of policy, said Han Fei. The ruler must subordinate his ministers to strict bureaucratic controls. Yet the *Han Feizi* text is full of references to weak and incompetent rulers as well as great rulers who annexed many states but whose successors then lost all. "The intrinsic contradiction between an institutionally infallible and humanly erring sovereign is the major source of tension in the *Han Feizi*," says Yuri Pines.[27] Yet Han Fei seems to imply the resolution of the tension: the incompetent ruler will fall, and the most competent one will eventually produce "all under heaven." But even military strategists such as Sun Tzu and Sun Bin claimed to abhor war. The latter's *Art of Warfare* declares: "Abhorrence of war is the highest military principle. A distaste for war is the most basic principle of the True King. Between heaven and earth there is nothing more valuable than man. [Thus,] you must go to war only if there is no alternative."[28]

Chinese theorists often speculated on the causes of war. One example is in Wuzi's *Art of War*, written around the turn of the fourth century BCE.

> There are five matters which give rise to military operations. First, the struggle for fame; second, the struggle for advantage; third, the accumulation of animosity; fourth, internal disorder; and fifth, famine. . . . There are also five categories of war. First, righteous war; second, aggressive war; third, enraged war; fourth, wanton war; and fifth, insurgent war. Wars to suppress violence and quell disorder are righteous. Those which depend on force are aggressive. When troops are raised because rulers are actuated by anger, this is enraged war. Those in which all propriety is discarded because of greed are wanton wars. Those who, when the state is in disorder and the people exhausted, stir up trouble and agitate the multitude, cause insurgent wars."

And he offers solutions: "There is a suitable method for dealing with each: a righteous war must be forestalled by proper government; an aggressive war by humbling one's self; an enraged war by reason; a wanton war by deception and treachery; and an insurgent war by authority."[29]

War was considered righteous when dedicated to order or the restoration of order. But if order already existed, there could be no righteous war.

The major states seem more pragmatic than the intellectuals. They alternated wars and peace conferences, making and switching alliances—all rather Realist. Yet Sun Tzu stated, "Peace proposals unaccompanied by a sworn covenant indicate a plot," which implies that sworn covenants might be relied on.[30] But why did wars continue when casualties increased and their expected utility declined? The risk of death and debt might outweigh possible gains. Part of the answer is that rulers were not at risk themselves since they hired generals who were professional soldiers, mostly younger sons enjoying upward mobility through soldiering. Defeated rulers of states whose soldiers had fought with honor and then surrendered might be enfeoffed by the victor, given title to their lands but in the victor's realm. There was a Realist calculation: attack when the rival seems weak or when a minor or a woman succeeds, or when he or she is already engaged in a war on another front. But there was also overoptimism about the chances of victory, as their final comeuppance revealed.

Rulers also had to face new threats from the periphery. "Uncivilized" nomads and seminomads of the north and west became more formidable enemies once horses and camels were dressed with saddles and stirrups. This development produced horse archers with durable composite bows and iron-tipped arrows. The twin military "revolutions" of iron and cavalry are emphasized in Peter Turchin and his colleagues' analysis of the diffusion of military technology across the globe in early historical times, though the diffusion of iron was slow because of the complex smelting techniques required.[31] It did not reach the Americas or Australasia. It is not known whether tools or weapons, if either, came first. Cavalry's striking range was greater than "barbarian" peoples' capacity to institutionalize political rule, so their initial threat was raiding. Chinese frontier states then realized they must field horse archers, and they built great walls for defense and to fence off newly conquered territory from barbarians seeking their lands back. Chinese pressure also tended to consolidate the barbarians into larger military federations that mimicked the Chinese in seizing grazing lands for cavalry horses and iron deposits for weapons and tools.[32] The Chinese adapted in turn, taming wastelands and thereby enabling new settlements and more soldiers. Thus, frontier states gained a military advantage, as they had bigger populations and armies than the states of the old core.

In the sixth century BCE, China was dominated by four states, Qi, Jin, Qin, and Chu, all located on the peripheries, ruled by "marcher lords" who could combine agricultural infantry and pastoral cavalry. I showed in volume 1 of *The Sources of Social Power* that marcher lords became a major feature of early empires, and Turchin and his colleagues have confirmed this as a general feature of early historical warfare.[33] In China these four peripheral states were joined in the fifth century by two states along the southern periphery with mixed Zhou-barbarian populations or barbarians who had adopted Zhou culture and institutions.[34] The Warring States period saw the sharks protecting, dominating, and then swallowing up minnow states in a kind of "offensive defense"—expansion through defending allies—which we have seen was also the Roman strategy. A Jin minister observed: "If we had not taken over the smaller states, where would be the gain? Ever since the reign of Wu Gong and Xiang Gong, Jin annexed many states. Who bothered to investigate?"[35] Surviving, unmutilated soldiers benefited from victory, while the losers died or suffered. Most peasants probably didn't care who ruled them.

There was also path dependence. War had worked in the past for these states, baking in the institutions and culture of militarism. States carry on down the path that has brought them success. Many states for whom war had not brought success had vanished. For successful states, the pursuit of power and glory became intrinsically desirable, bringing respect, high social status, and profit. Victors left a legacy of literature and monuments glorifying war. Bellicosity dominates the historical record because the winners wrote it. The meek inherit neither the earth nor its history.

Lewis says: "The chief activity of these states was combat. . . . They were states organized for warfare."[36] Militarism had several sources: the need to extract a surplus from the peasants, an ecology enabling outward expansion, the increasing integration and bureaucratization of state, army, and economy, and Legalist ideology urging the moral imperative of commitment, obedience, and sacrifice for one's state.[37] Zhao detects four main regional war zones, each seeing one state located on its periphery dominating the smaller states of the central core. Three of these states were also located in more defensible ecologies, having better borders and fewer neighbors than their rivals. Between 403 and 350 BCE they had also implemented the military and economic state-strengthening reforms urged by legalists.

But why was the final outcome of these wars different from that in Europe? Unlike Europe, all the Chinese states were eventually con-

quered by one of their number. There were far, far more losers than winners. They should have heeded Sun Tzu:

> He who knows the enemy and himself
> Will never in a hundred battles be at risk;
> He who does not know the enemy but knows himself
> Will sometimes win and sometimes lose;
> He who knows neither the enemy nor himself
> Will be at risk in every battle.[38]

Few rulers could meet such a high standard.

European attempts at continental hegemony failed, unlike Chinese
endeavors. This is generally explained by "balancing theory": a state's
aiming at hegemony was countered by a balancing alliance of the other
states. The Habsburgs, Louis XIV, Napoleon, and Hitler were all frustrated. Indeed, this had happened to several would-be hegemons in
China before Qin. Balancing theory sometimes worked. But Hitler was
not in fact thwarted by a balancing alliance within Europe, either in the
1930s, when Britain, France, the Soviet Union, and minor powers failed
to agree to an alliance, or during World War II, when Western Europe
was rescued from afar by the United States and the Soviet Union. During the Cold War the United States again rescued Europe, this time
from the Soviet Union. Europe wasn't very different from China. Victoria Tin-Bor Hui notes the failure of fifteenth-century Italian city-states
to balance against France and the Habsburgs and the failure of the Hellenistic empires to balance against Rome, which picked them off, one by
one, as we saw in the last chapter.[39] The Qin conquest of China was just
another example of such balancing failure. We will see another failure in
Japan. Balancing failure seems more common than success.

Zhao adds two reasons for political-military dominance.[40] First,
China lacked religious institutions capable of restraining the state comparable to those of Christianity in Europe and Islam in Muslim countries. Chinese elites did not believe in transcendental divinity, or in an
afterlife. Ancestral cults legitimized first the Zhou royal line and then the
aristocratic order. Neither the Confucian nor legalist tradition advanced
transcendent ideologies, for both emphasized order and obedience to the
state. Daoism preached quietism. Later, Buddhism was more controlled
by rulers than Christianity was in Europe. None of these theories promoted individual rights. Second, economic actors lacked autonomy.

China had no independent merchant associations, guilds, or autonomous cities, as Europe did. Cities were ruled by state officials. Economic acquisition through conquest rather than trade was prioritized. Rulers knew they should promote economic well-being to get a revenue base to finance large armies. They interfered with existing markets and promoted economic infrastructures, production, and trade. The economy was somewhat statist (insofar as a near-subsistence peasant economy could be) and did not offer a counterweight to the militaristic state. The absence of autonomous economic and ideological power institutions is important in explaining Chinese state militarism.

In the fourth century BCE balancing began to fail. In 221 BCE the state of Qin finally conquered the others and founded the first empire over China. Qin dynasty rule proved short-lived, but the successor Han dynasty lasted four hundred years and institutionalized a single imperial state across the core of China. This expanded through many dynasties into the twentieth century CE. The sequence of feudal expansion, collapse, reconstitution, and then consolidation into fewer states is reminiscent of both Europe and late medieval Japan. In the end China, like Japan but unlike Europe, was unified into a single state.

Why did Qin and not another state achieve hegemony? Ecology mattered: Qin was at the extreme north and west of the Warring States. It may have had the advantage of a marcher lord position at the cusp of the pastoral-agricultural divide, like almost all the later conquerors of China, for the effectiveness of the pastoralist horse archer was now becoming evident. Moreover, it did not face rival states on two of its four sides. On the other two sides a single mountain pass conferred a strong defensive position. To the north and east it could expand against lesser foes, acquiring their populations to increase the size of armies. Qin was outside the main line of fire of most wars.[41] Its rulers waited for most of their rivals to weaken each other before they attacked. Qin's final assault had a good chance of victory, but an even better chance of avoiding defeat, because of its good defensive position.

Qin's geopolitical strategy was also important. Hui emphasizes the "clever," "devious," and "Machiavellian" stratagems of Qin rulers, "dividing and ruling" among opponents, waiting for them to weaken each other in warfare. The chroniclers stress the varying diplomatic talents and personalities of kings and dukes, the varying military talents of their generals, and their advisers' complex scheming. Yet it strains credulity that Qin rulers should have enjoyed a monopoly of intelligent strategy lasting over the 135 years of Qin's ascent, and they did fight more wars than their rivals. Yet since their territorial gains were piecemeal and opportunist, they did not unduly alarm rivals. In this period its fifty-two expansionist wars encountered only eight allied balancing responses. In 266 BCE the appointment of Fan Sui as a senior minister ushered in a policy shift. He urged "irrevocable expansionism," arguing that the way to dominance was to wage war against one's neighbor in alliance with more distant powers that could force the neighbor into a two-front war. This could expand the state, and "each inch or foot gained was the king's foot or inch."[42]

Rulers were well-versed in geopolitical alternatives. Balancing against a would-be hegemon was called vertical strategy, whereas horizontal strategy favored conciliating the leading power and sharing in its rise. Horizontal strategy assumed from past experience that no state could remain ascendant for long, so it was not risky to side with a more powerful ruler. That was soon proved wrong, but Qin had not seemed an existential threat until too late. Qin had led an alliance defeating the last previous attempt at hegemony, by the Qi king who was about to assume the Zhou title of Son of Heaven. So Qin forged an alliance with five others, defeating Qi. Now there was only one other ruler of comparable strength to Qin, the Zhao ruler, as well as five weaker others. Zhao might have organized a balancing coalition, but states not directly threatened by Qin preferred to stay neutral. Zhao was trying to swallow up another state when Qin attacked it, so Zhao had to fight on two fronts, Qin on only one. After fluctuating fortunes lasting three years, Qin triumphed. The last remaining states might have allied with each other. But once Zhao was defeated, they wavered between vertical and horizontal options.[43] For some, coming to terms at that point seemed the better fate. Terms were granted confirming the local powers of rulers if they accepted Qin sovereignty.

Broader domestic reforms also underlay Qin victory. Hui contrasts the "self-strengthening" character of Qin reforms with the "self-weakening" reforms of European states. The Europeans operated in a monetary economy permitting loans, sale of public offices, tax farming, and hiring mercenaries. She sees these as "easy" but "self-weakening" means of waging war, since they weakened the rulers' control over powerful civil society groups. The most successful European states from the seventeenth century onward did not weaken themselves in this way. Holland and Britain developed state-enhancing tax and financial institutions and achieved hegemony through global empires, though not in Europe itself.

The legalist reform movements of the fifth and fourth centuries BCE sought to forge new relations between the warring states and their populations, parallel to Rome and resembling the European states of the nineteenth and twentieth centuries. Yet this was not participatory citizenship. It was a form of authoritarianism sidelining the aristocracy and extracting military service from peasants in return for easing serfdom and granting leasehold tenures and eventually property rights. This might be seen as a lessening of coercive extraction of the surplus, but it was significantly called "lodging the army among the people," which baked the coercion of militarism in to everyday life. Meritocratic military reform also meant soldiers could rise through the ranks. Generals came increasingly from unknown families.

Under Shang Yang, chancellor of Qin, the reforms went deepest and the populace was mobilized for mass sacrifices. He declared, "The means by which a ruler encourages his people are offices and rank; the means by which a state arises are agriculture and war." The goal was to create a single class, "men of service in farming and warfare." If agriculture is the sole source of energy, and warfare its only outlet, the people will risk death to serve the state. The state produces energy and manpower for battle. The effective ruler makes the people "forget their lives for the sake of their superiors" so they "delight in war" and "act like hungry wolves on seeing meat." For Shang the most useful outlet of energy is war. There must "always be another war to fight, another enemy to defeat." Surpluses must be consumed by war, for settling into enjoyment of the surplus would lead to self-interested squabbling and idleness. Lewis observes that this "sucks in more and more resources to be consumed in wars that no longer serve any purpose save to keep the machine running."[44] This is war for its own sake.

The Qin ruler Shi Huang was a megalomaniac who claimed heavenly powers and declared that his dynasty would reach to the end of time and the limits of space. He had nourished this ideal secretly. Now, to transcend his humanity and become immortal, he ascended Mount Tai to communicate with the highest god. He inscribed his triumphs in verse on the peaks of mountains throughout his realm. Six have survived. They declare blessings had been bestowed on all within the four seas, "wherever sun and moon shine," "wherever human tracks reach," even extending to the beasts and the plants. The range of his power and beneficence was universal.[45] The path to that end had been repetitive, baked-in warfare.

Conclusion

Ancient Chinese polities inherited a feudal mode of warfare. Inequalities between polities encouraged the strong to conquer or demand fealty from the weak, and wars of conquest could be fought against weaker peripheral peoples. Sharks swallowed minnows, but they were more cautious about other sharks. Coups, rebellions, and civil wars between lineages threatened rulers, giving them political motives to raise armies, demonstrate strength in foreign wars, and use their armies to crush revolt and extract the surplus from the peasants. Honor, revenge, humiliation, and the like intermittently added more emotional, less material motives, though the annals rarely delve into character except when scandals were involved. Inheritance norms gave incentives for younger sons, as they did in Europe, but here lineage rivalries were also important. War gave ambitious young men opportunities for upward mobility after the age of chariot warfare. Conflict between major polities was often "deflected" onto weaker ones, making it less deadly for major polities.

This resulted in the path-dependent growth of militaristic institutions and cultures baked in to state power, in to warrior ideologies and ambitions for greed and glory across the generations—as in the Roman Republic. Neither religions nor cities and merchants could counterbalance warriors. Although Confucians were generally more pacific than legalists, both advocated that order-enforcing states fight "just" wars. Ideological power did not undercut state power, as the Church in Europe sometimes did. Major states then turned against each other, fighting costlier wars. Victorious states carried on fighting, eventually overconfidently, and all but one plunged to defeat. Rationality of both means and ends weakened. "Mistakes" were not occasional but systemic, because a mishmash of motives and opportunities intervened: greed, demonstrating political power at home, pursuing honor and righteousness, anger, and revenge. The result was either overconfidence in victory or a more resigned view that war was the only way for human beings to settle disputes and for China to become reunited—which Confucian and legalist theorists endorsed. All four power sources are necessary to explain the patterns of war in China.

There came a fourth century BCE "arms race" to integrate economic and military power as legalist reforms brought the masses into war in return for economic concessions. There was a little support for liberal theory in the many treaties and intermittent recognition of a hegemon, but

Qin unified China through conquest. In the Changping campaign Qin's harnessing of economic to military power gave it more staying power than Zhao, but campaign contingencies were decisive in the end. Realism has dominated IR theory of war in the post-1816 context of struggles between fairly equal major powers, all of which survived. Ancient China was a different context, more typical in the history of a world where the strong swallow the weak, and the weak cannot retreat into guerilla warfare. It had finally brought only one winner out of the seventy-plus who had begun in post-Zhou China. The fundamental contradiction in ancient Chinese warfare was that, on the one hand, rulers practiced much military and diplomatic calculation, aided by much military, economic, and political expertise, yet the result was the defeat and disappearance of all but one ruler. Realism sets a much higher standard of calculation of means and ends than was realistically possible here.

Who benefited? The dukes and vassals of victorious states might benefit during their lifetimes, if they were not cut down by coups or wars. Settlers moving into conquered lands might benefit, while rulers and peoples who submitted without fighting did not lose much. Limited economic privileges came in return for more military service, as more lives were risked in ever-larger armies that suffered greater casualties. Chinese cultural civilization was largely for the upper classes. Qin unification was seen as likely to bring order to China, but it is finally impossible to say whether the millions of casualties and the devastation produced by hundreds of wars were justified by the much later creation of a somewhat more peaceful and very long-lasting realm. One can conjecture an alternative path of development, through a more peaceful multistate Chinese civilization, but this seems a long way from the reality of ancient China. But although rulers thought they were pursuing rational purposes through wars, most lost their realms and lives. Peace and diplomacy might have produced better outcomes, but both geopolitics and domestic power relations blocked this path to development.

CHAPTER SIX

Imperial China

For most of its over two-thousand-year history, the Chinese Empire was the leading edge of human civilization. It made war quite frequently. Tonio Andrade says that from 800 to 1450 the rates of war of China and Europe were similar.[1] Then, between 1450 and 1550, warfare decreased somewhat in China while increasing in Europe, but convergence resumed between 1550 and 1700. From the 1750s a "great military divergence" grew, when Chinese warfare was at its lowest level ever. Overall Chinese figures, however, conceal large differences between macroregions. The east and southeast saw relatively few wars, and a distinctive form of tributary diplomacy emerged instead. In the north and west relations between China and its neighbors were far more warlike. Realist theories cannot explain this difference. In fact, as we shall see, it was due primarily to different ecologies generating different internal social structures and external relations. In the north and west an empire populated mainly by agriculturalists and city dwellers abutted savannas and steppes populated by pastoralists. This produced different configurations of power and far more conflict between them. But through time and wars the steppe dwellers and the farmers merged into a single, larger empire. Abstract theories of war cannot deal with such variation in space and time.

The Imperial Chinese State

The first Qin emperor, Shi Huang, crushed resistance and greatly expanded his realm through war, while burning the books of those who had opposed war. He standardized the written language, penal code, calendar, weights and measures, and cart axle rod lengths. He built roads, canals, and monuments with mass corvée labor. Today we marvel at his mausoleum near Xian, built by perhaps 700,000 workers, with 7,600 full-size, lifelike, beautifully sculpted terra-cotta soldiers and their horses (more are apparently not yet unearthed). After failing to reach immortal health through imbibing the potions of magicians and sages, he seems to have believed that this army would protect him in the afterlife. He is the first of the great conquerors of history I shall discuss, driven onward by his sense of destiny, subordinating all to universal domination, including megalomaniacal exploitation of labor. His regime became steadily harsher, more militaristic, and less popular. He buried many Confucians alive. Massive infrastructure projects and further conquests brought benefit to only a few. After his death, his dynasty collapsed amid insurrections; it was replaced by the milder western Han dynasty (206 BCE–8 CE), which rejected severe legalism in favor of the moralistic tones of Confucianism.

The imperial state began to acquire its long-lasting forms. The royal court was divided into an inner and an outer part, separating the personal household of the emperor from the central administration of government. The inner court was confined to members of the imperial family and their concubines, eunuchs, and staffs. Membership in the outer court was at the discretion of the emperor, yet its agencies had some autonomy because they were strongly rooted in the provincial gentry class. The Han and then the Tang increased the central bureaucracy to 153,000 officials, ten times larger than the Roman Empire's bureaucracy that ruled a slightly smaller population.[2] By modern standards this is still tiny. In 2019 in the United Kingdom, which had a similar population, there were 5.4 million public employees. Modern states pursue many functions unknown to early states.

The Han introduced examinations for entry into the bureaucracy. Under the Tang dynasty (618–907 CE) these became systematic, testing candidates' Confucian knowledge and literacy. The northern Song (960–1127) extended the system to almost all officials, and this lasted right up to 1905, though of less importance during the two ex-barbarian dynasties, the Yuan and the Qing. Since almost all literate males came from gentry families or from the children of dependents educated by these families, a national gentry-bureaucrat class with a common Confucian culture emerged, which dominated the outer court while also anchored in local class power. In an attempt to increase bureaucratic powers, officials could not serve in their own region. Yet this was undercut by officials', often powers of patronage, which led to corruption contrary to Confucian norms. Confucians also educated most emperors and their families. This created a rooted and quite cohesive agrarian state, comparable to the Roman senate and assemblies in their representing the dominant classes of Roman society. Republican Rome had a representative system, and China did not, but both had strong connections between provinces and central government, which reinforced cohesion among the upper classes and mobilized large, well-organized armies. Sizable ancient empires needed comparable links between the central state and provincial class power. Otherwise, they would devolve into feudalism—and some did. But not China.

Zhao sees a balance of forces between emperors, Confucian scholars, and bureaucratic officials in a "Confucian-Legalist State."[3] Legalism provided the law and punishment, Confucianism the morality. This "amalgam of political and ideological power" allowed emperors to "strengthen state authority and . . . penetrate the society." Military power, he says, was required less. Political elites curbed the generals' power and kept economic power holders localized.[4] Confucianism permeated higher education and the bureaucracy. Allied to strong gentry identity, its advocacy of low taxes and laissez-faire economics limited the emperor's ability to make war. This dual state tamed all challengers, including bandits, rebels, barbarian conquerors, Buddhism, Daoism, and commercialization. True, heredity or competence might fail and a dynasty collapse amid civil war, but when its victor founded a new dynasty, essentially the same state was reconstituted. The merger of central state and the gentry class was too useful to rulers. Rafe de Crespigny adds that the ideology of a Zhou-Han-Sui-Tang line of descent legitimized a single state, while it also had an economic core.[5] The central plain, crisscrossed by rivers and canals, offered a solid base to rulers, fertile and revenue yielding.

Nonetheless, civil wars and wars between states within China lasted for almost five hundred of a two-thousand-year history. For a quarter of its life, the universal empire was aspirational. When Chinese dynasties were solidly entrenched, they still had to contend with rival rulers around their borders.[6] Sometimes imperial family life became a bloodbath. Despite a norm of inheritance by the eldest son, when emperors had multiple wives and concubines, it was often unclear which son might inherit, and a kinsman or ambitious general might claim the throne. In such civil wars there was only one winner but often several losers. Only half the emperors died in their beds or abdicated by choice; the other half died through assassination, by forced suicide, or in an uprising—and the entire royal family might then be killed off. The second Qin emperor murdered all his siblings as he ascended the throne. Thirty-one Tang dynasty family members had been styled heirs apparent, but only nineteen of them reached the throne, twelve being murdered. Yet, after succession crises, an established emperor might count on fairly stable rule. Ex-barbarian dynasties were more precarious, as their rules of succession were fuzzier and aristocratic rivals all commanded troops.

Chinese ideologies lacked a transcendent divinity. Order was valued above any ultimate notion of truth. The emperor was the Son of Heaven, but if he did not keep order, he was perceived as having lost the mandate of heaven and could be overthrown. Occasionally, rebellions generated mass millenarian religious movements, such as the Huang Lao, the Yellow Turban, the Five Pecks of Grain (which demanded minimal taxes), the Taiping, and the Muslim rebellions. Underlying them was protest against exploitation. This was also occasionally so in medieval and early modern Europe. But only the last two Chinese cases, both in the nineteenth century, had an avowedly religious goal—to establish a Christian or Muslim state. Religious ideology was also unimportant to the nomads and seminomads attacking China, though farther west in central Asia some were fired up by Islam.[7]

War-and-Peace Decisions

Traditionally, Chinese foreign policies were seen as Confucian-dominated, favoring peace.[8] This is now regarded as exaggerated. But there are several competing theories, mostly varieties of Realism. Yuan-Kang Wang offers a structural Realism like that of Eckstein on Rome.[9] Focusing on the Song (960–1279) and Ming (1368–1644) dynasties, he stresses geopolitical anarchy and lack of trust in other states. "Confucian pacifism" had little role, he says, for foreign policy was geared to calculating the material capabilities of China relative to its rivals. Rulers chose offensive war when strong, and defense, compromise, and harmony when weak. What mattered was the relative balance of "troops, horses, grain production, government budget, fiscal balances, and domestic rebellions."[10] Although Song and Ming officials passed through the Confucian exam system, this had little effect on whether they launched wars. Wang does not explain why some dynasties were more warlike than others. He omits the Yuan and Qing dynasties from his Realist analysis on the grounds that, as ex-barbarians, they were not Confucian. But this omits the most aggressive regimes of all.

Zhenping Wang offers a toned-down Realism.[11] In barbarian-Tang relations rulers attempted to calculate balances of power resources; sometimes they tried to understand the social dynamics of rival kingdoms, and sometimes they decided that they must use soft, not hard power. They had to assess allies and enemies, opportunists lying and dissembling. Thus, alternative decisions might be equally plausible and errors likely. Local officials in frontier provinces had different priorities from those of the central authorities, and outcomes were often decided by the balance of power between factions. De Crespigny says modernists favored military expansion and state intervention in the economy to secure more revenue for wars, while reformists favored localism, less government, low taxes, and no costly wars.[12] During the early Han and Tang dynasties, Zhenping Wang distinguishes doves, hawks, and centrists.[13] Factions were often "ins" versus "outs," however, possessing or excluded from the spoils of office. War-and-peace decisions were often the by-product of domestic struggles. The temperaments of rulers also mattered. Strong emotions surged, such as desire for vengeance if feeling deceived. Finally, the fortunes of battle were uncertain. This is a more realistic Realism. Rulers try to be rational, but often they fail.

Alistair Johnston offers an ideological version of Realism. He says legalism, not Confucianism, dominated Ming policy. It had a "parabellum" model: "If you want peace, prepare for war." Security threats must be met by force, the people must obey their rulers, foreigners are rapacious and threatening, and violence must be the response to them. One attacks when strong, but defends or seeks accommodation when weak. The Confucian model was an ideal, but most practice was parabellum—not because of geopolitical anarchy but the martial culture internalized by officials. Yet he exaggerates the role of legalism, less important in officials' education than Confucianism, and he mischaracterizes Confucians as pacifists.[14] As we saw in chapter 5, Confucians offered mixed messages on war and peace.

Peter Lorge doubts whether any moral philosophy was heeded by rulers.[15] The texts offered ideals that Confucian-trained officials endorsed in principle but considered marginal to practical politics. Military power remained the way to hold China together. The military absorbed above 70 percent of state revenue, all dynasties were created in war, all declined through military decay, and all fell to rebellious generals claiming the throne. He concludes: "Chinese empires were not created by the cultivation of virtue, a fundamental cultural orientation to political order, or ideological pleas for ethnic unity; they were created by decades of war and political strife. Organized violence was applied toward political goals intelligently and ruthlessly, with the targets of that violence almost exclusively the power elite, the men and women who held significant political, military, cultural or economic power."[16]

This is effectively a military Realism, but applied to domestic struggles as well as external wars. Lorge believes our sources are biased by literati who downplayed militarism. Jonathan Skaff agrees, for the Tang literati elite (618–907) presented "an incongruent image of a society with a value system seemingly opposed to frontier aggression that nonetheless implements a strategy of military expansion."[17] Beautiful poetry concealed violence. Yet the frontiers required doses of both military action and diplomacy, hard and soft power.

A military and political offshoot of this approach would help explain why the founders of dynasties and their immediate successors generally launched more offensive wars than later successors. They had already demonstrated martial skills when seizing the throne, they had troops needing employment, and their victories gave them the political power to levy taxes and conscription for war. But gradually the Confucian gentry-bureaucrat class pressured successor emperors toward conservative, low-tax, and low-conscription policies, and away from war.

Tributary Diplomacy in East and Southeast Asia

This region saw relatively few wars. China became the dominant partner in a tributary system comprising China, Japan, Korea, and Vietnam; distant polities participated more loosely. David Kang says that between 1368 and 1841 only two major wars occurred between these core states, though two Chinese civil wars also spilled across frontiers.[18] In this period the borders between the four states were relatively uncontested. But we should add a few more wars: a Ming occupation of Vietnam between 1406 and 1427; the Ming defeat of a Japanese invasion of Korea in the 1590s; two Manchu Qing invasions of Korea in the 1630s against a

Korean king who supported the rival Ming dynasty; a brief 1662 Qing invasion of Myanmar to capture a Ming pretender to the Chinese throne; Qing incursions into Myanmar in the 1760s; and a brief Qing incursion into Vietnam in 1788.

There were also naval engagements against pirates, as well as Admiral Zheng He's famed five voyages around South Asia to Africa in the early fifteenth century, which intimidated coastal peoples into paying tribute to the emperor. His fleets were large, carrying about 27,000 persons, half of them soldiers, about the same overall numbers as in the Spanish Armada 150 years later. They were deployed in three brief wars, one against pirates, one to defend a Sumatran tributary ruler against rebels, and one of retaliation against a Sri Lankan kingdom that had opposed his presence during an earlier voyage. But the admiral died in 1433 during his fifth expedition, and the voyages were abruptly ended by the imperial court after a struggle between the eunuchs who had backed him and Confucian officials concerned with the cost. The "Treasure Fleets" had come back with little treasure. The Yongle emperor had spent lavishly, leaving large debts. The voyages had been for glory as much as economic profit. His successor, Xuande, stopped them, more on grounds of economy than of military weakness. He also feared that far-flung trade would give merchants too much power. The reduced Chinese fleet could still achieve victories in naval engagements against pirates, the Portuguese in 1512, and the Dutch in the 1620s.

Thus, China in this region fought only about a dozen land wars, in addition to smaller naval engagements, which lasted in total about forty years over a six-hundred-year period, a very small proportion. Two-thirds of the land wars were undertaken by ex-barbarian dynasties, and two were the spillover of Ming versus Qing civil wars. So this was broadly a defensive, diplomatic imperialism, mostly at peace, especially under Han Chinese dynasties. Kang notes that between 1368 and 1841, under twenty interstate wars were dwarfed by wars elsewhere with northern and western barbarians (252 cases), by defense against pirates (60 cases), and by conflicts among other states and unruly border tribes with occasional Chinese intervention (number unspecified). In this region state and interstate institutions favored diplomacy far more than war.

Was this due to China's weakness, its inability to overcome its rivals, as Realists suggest? Feng Zhang's population and GDP estimates suggest not.[19] China had ten times the resources of any single rival and over twice the resources of all the regional rivals combined. Kang says China had "the military and technological capability to wage war on a massive scale," potentially defeating all rivals.[20] That meant those rivals could not threaten China, which we will see was not the case in the north and west. Moreover, the main foreign actors involved were established states with agrarian economies similar to China's: known, predictable actors. Underlying this was the fact that China did not have expansionist goals in this region and was very rarely provoked into military action by others. Here was a satiated power. Of course, there were lesser economic and political factors involved. Bigger wars required higher taxes, flouting Confucian (and Daoist) laissez-faire economics, and were opposed by much of the gentry-bureaucrat class. The court's fear of its generals also reduced military budgets as a coup-proofing strategy. Overall, however, foreign states in this region were not powerful enough to threaten China, so why bother? I examine first the exceptions, when it did bother.

There were four Sui dynasty attempts between 598 and 614 CE to subjugate the main Korean kingdom. Their failure led to the fall of the dynasty. There were two Tang invasions between 645 and 668 in support of the Korean Silla kingdom, the second one being largely successful, although Silla kept its independence. David Graff says these were the only wars against foreign states during the period 300–900 CE.[21] After another three hundred years came the period of Mongol expansion and establishment of the Yuan dynasty in China itself. Between 1231 and 1257 came eight invasions of Korea, with varying outcomes, and then two failed invasions of Japan in 1274 and 1281 by Kublai Khan. Hurricanes destroyed his fleets as they arrived at Japanese shores. Like many mighty warriors, he found nature mightier still. These invasions were a part of the almost continuous wars of aggression the Mongols waged to extend domination over much of Asia. They were neither Han Chinese nor Confucian.

After three hundred more years came a successful 1592 Han Chinese intervention in Korea by a Ming dynasty army of 50,000, equipped with heavy cannon and flanked by substantial naval forces. This was to aid Korean forces against an invasion by a Japanese 160,000-strong army launched by Hideyoshi, who had just reunified Japan by force and believed his battle-hardened army could beat anyone. He also needed to find employment for it. Chinese intervention was an activation of the tributary system, but it was also self-defense, since Hideyoshi had sworn to move straight through Korea and conquer China, installing himself as regent. After heavy losses in his first campaign, Hideyoshi tried again in 1597 with an army of 150,000. In response the Ming raised their forces to almost 100,000. The China-Korea alliance won again, the Ming cannon destroying the Japanese arquebus-equipped infantry (this was a war of guns), while the Chinese and Korean navies controlled the seas. Total Japanese casualties were reported as 80,000, the Ming as 38,000, the Koreans as 200,000 militia plus several hundred thousand civilians.[22] The war devastated Korea and involved atrocities against civilians and captive soldiers. No one gained except Tokugawa Ieyasu in Japan, and he gained by not fighting. Defeat weakened his Japanese rivals, enabling him to found the Tokugawa dynasty (see chapter 7).

This war revealed the formidable military power of the Ming, but there was no attempt to take over Korea. Ji-Young Lee says the court considered annexation but preferred "coercive diplomacy through tribute practices to extract Korean compliance."[23] Japan itself was protected by its seas and was now isolationist. It did not return to Korea until the 1890s and to China until the 1930s. China never again contemplated an invasion of Japan. The bias of China in this region was toward peaceful tribute, while Japan remained insular.

Chinese dominance over Vietnam had lasted a thousand years. Kang and his colleagues have a data set of wars and lesser disputes from 1365 to 1789.[24] This reveals a broadly tributary system as Vietnamese rulers ritually recognized their lesser status—with one major exception. In 1400 Ho rebels massacred the ruling Tran clan and seized the Vietnamese throne. The Tran heir (or perhaps a pretender) fled to the Chinese court and asked for help. After a long pause, during which the Chinese investigated what had happened, the Ming Emperor Yongle agreed. He was experienced in wars against northern barbarians and was known for aggressive policies. He sent the Tran prince back to Vietnam with armed Chinese guards. Once over the border, the small force was ambushed and all were killed. Yongle saw this as an outrageous violation of tributary relations mandated by heaven. Confucian principles demanded revenge, bolstered by righteous outrage at the killing of the Chinese.

An invasion force of 200,000 entered Vietnam in 1406. The lure of loot was important among the soldiers, but the court's motives were honor and revenge. Yongle ordered that after the war was won and a Tran installed on the throne, the army would leave—just regime change. But though victory came swiftly, the army stayed for twenty years. Heaven's mandate turned into naked imperialism and mass looting.[25] This provoked fierce Vietnamese resistance. It was a question of survival for Vietnamese elites, not so crucial and then not so profitable for the Chinese after most of the loot had been taken. After several rebellions, in 1427 an overextended Chinese army of occupation was defeated. There had been debates at court between factions urging leaving or staying. Now they left. Profit had been submerged by the costs of repeated wars for a not very desirable target. Beijing later recognized the son of the victorious rebel as the legitimate ruler and regular tribute missions resumed, borders were settled, and peace endured. Vietnamese elites had no ambition to attack China, and they could now turn southward to destroy their long-term rival, the Champa kingdom. The Vietnamese accepted a largely notional tributary status and peace endured.

The Pacific island of Taiwan, not hitherto Chinese, was occupied in 1662 by Ming forces seeking a secure base after their defeat in China by the Qing. In 1683 the Qing invaded, defeated the Ming remnants, and annexed the island—a Chinese civil war spilling out abroad. They stayed there to prevent the Portuguese from using it as a naval base. But China never tried to annex the Ryukyu island archipelago kingdom (which was wealthy through trade), the Philippines, Borneo, or other lands occupied by militarily weaker peoples. The Moluccas had supplied spices for centuries and were formally tributary states, but they were left alone. Tributary trade was preferred to conquest as the mode of economic acquisition.

Between 1370 and 1500, 288 tribute missions came from seven lesser Asian states to the Ming court—more than two per year. The system was termed "all under heaven" or "harmonious world." The emperor's duty was to maintain cosmic harmony through the performance of ancient religious rites cultivating popular obedience and moral virtue.[26] He also had to impose rites of homage and tribute on other peoples. Foreign rulers should "observe the subordinate integrity of loyalty, obedience, and trust-worthiness for serving China," while China should show "moral excellence, humaneness, and grace for loving smaller and inferior" peoples.[27] China could legitimately launch punitive expeditions against a state defying the Confucian diplomatic system, and the threat rarely led to war. This was not the Confucian triumph of pacifism described by John Fairbank, nor was it governed by Realist principles, as Yuan-Kang Wang suggests.[28] His model applies better in other regions of the empire, as we will see. The elaborate rituals also served to dampen emotions, though doubtless those performing them might have felt humiliations that they had to try to repress.

But in any case lesser states often benefited from ritual submission. They did not have to worry about war with China and could deploy their forces elsewhere. The legitimacy of foreign rulers was bolstered by an investiture ceremony performed by the emperor. The Chinese court derived domestic prestige and legitimacy from the repeated presence of foreign ambassadors doing homage at the feet of the emperor, strengthening factions favoring diplomacy over those favoring war. Once a state did homage, it could participate more in the world's biggest trading network. Tribute trade was only a small part of all trade, but it played a key role. Typically, ambassadors would do homage at court while merchants did business in ports. If you did not pay tribute, this opportunity was not available.[29]

For the Chinese the main reward was peace, for China usually gave more valuable gifts to foreign states than it received. Exchange of hostages and marriages of Chinese princesses to foreign rulers furthered relations.[30] "Kowtowing" to the emperor, forehead on the ground, was the most expressive ritual. In the mission of British Ambassador Macartney to China in 1792–94, he bowed but refused to kowtow, and his mission was a failure. Emperor Qianlong wrote to King George III: "Our Celestial Empire possesses all things in prolific abundance and lacks no product within its borders. There is therefore no need to import the manufactures of outside barbarians in exchange for our own produce."

The system was a formal hierarchy with China at the top, yet it permitted much informal equality.[31] Subordinate states were free to choose their own domestic policies. In this region after the Yuan dynasty, China sought direct imperial rule abroad only once in Vietnam (described above) and once in Myanmar. The Chinese never sought to export Confucianism, though some neighbors did embrace it.

Tributary diplomacy was built to avoid war. Chinese rulers mediated conflicts between other powers, while never submitting to mediation themselves. They said they were bringing civilization to Asia, and neighbors sometimes appeared to accept this. But despite the submissive rituals, these neighbors rarely viewed the system in Confucian terms, except Korea, a Confucian country. In dual-language agreements, the duties of foreign rulers appear more stringent in the Chinese text than in the other language—mutual complicity to evade clarity for peace and honor. Lee says the contrast between Korean acceptance and Japanese rejection of Chinese hegemony was due not only to the sea, but also to Korea's being Confucian.[32] In contrast, Japanese political legitimacy rested on traditional reverence for the Japanese emperor and for Japan as "the country of the gods," with no reference to China.

IR specialists see hegemony as the principal means of countering geopolitical anarchy. A state possessing it enjoys preponderant military and economic power over all others and leadership that includes some consent and legitimacy—dominance and authority. China had both. Realist hegemonic theory focuses on domination, as does Yuan-Kang Wang, whereas other IR theories emphasize authority. Liberal theory stresses acceptance of some constitutionalism and a rule of law that constrains the hegemon as well as the lesser states. Power is embedded amid a system of rules and institutions that restrains its exercise, and the states bind themselves to consent and agreed-on rules and institutions.[33] For Gramscians hegemony is broader, "based on a coherent conjunction or fit between a configuration of material power, the prevalent collective image of world order (including certain norms) and a set of institutions which administer the order with a certain semblance of universality." Thus, it is seen "as the necessary order of nature," spanning economic production and class exploitation as well.[34] Both Gramscians and constructivists stress the diffusion of legitimacy among the population as a whole.

All these conceptions bear the marks of modernity and do not quite fit imperial China. The model cases are American power over much of the world since 1945 and British nineteenth-century liberal imperialism. In military power the United States has been far more dominant than China was, and Britain ruled the waves. Both spread liberal capitalism globally, and their economic power included possession of the world's reserve currencies. In contrast, China did not try to influence the economies of other states. Nor did hegemony extend downward to the peoples, who were of no concern to the court. Tribute involved relations between rulers, extending downward only as far as aristocracies and major merchants. Chinese hegemony was narrower, more conservative, and less ambitious than modern examples: it was oriented to peace. The relationship with Korea was the most spectacular success. It saw over two hundred years of peace and virtual political independence in exchange for occasional trips to perform rituals of submission at the Chinese court. This was hegemony for peace.

Yet peace also brought stability and economic development. Its diplomatic rituals fit liberal better than Realist theory. The answer here to "who benefited?" was almost everyone. The Chinese Empire was largely satisfied in this region. The potential gains from further expansion seemed minimal and its costs unacceptable, as Kublai Khan's failed Japanese and Vietnamese forays had revealed. All the power sources reinforced the same geopolitical logic, and ideological power relations provided the rituals by which this could be achieved honorably. But this could not be replicated in other regions.

The North: Barbarians and Civilization

In China, empire emanated almost exclusively from the northern frontier. Over the course of 3,600 years, all but one of a dozen unification events originated in the north. Seven of them were rooted in the northwest, especially the Wei River valley: Western Zhou (twelfth century BCE), Qin and Han (third century BCE), Sui (sixth century CE), Tang (seventh century CE), Yuan (thirteenth century CE), and the communist takeover out of Shaanxi (twentieth century CE). The Manchu Qing came from the northeast (seventeenth century CE), and the Shang (sixteenth [?] century BCE), Western Jin (third century CE), and Northern Song (tenth century CE) from the north-central area. Two further unifications merely of northern China—Northern Wei (fourth century CE) and Jin (twelfth century CE)—originated from the northwest and northeast, respectively. The Ming regime (fourteenth century CE), centered on the Yangzi basin, was the sole outlier.[35]

Northern China exemplified the Eurasian economic divide between predominantly nomadic pastoralists to the north and predominantly settled agriculturalists to their south. On the agriculturalists' Middle Eastern southern flank lay pastoral Arabs. Pastoralists had horses or camels, but the agriculturalists had the wealth and then the iron to equip chariots and infantry. Then, with the advent of stirrups and saddles, mounted archers required only horses and the recursive bow with iron-tipped arrows to become highly effective soldiers. Pastoral aristocracies began their expansion. Ibn Khaldun said the military difference was that the pastoralists developed the technique of swift attack and withdrawal, whereas the agriculturalists advanced steadily in closed, massed infantry formations, retreating if necessary inside fortifications organized by bureaucratic states.[36] The Chinese called the pastoralists "uncivilized," normally translated as "barbarian." Larger nomadic and seminomadic confederations often had a political center, yet that center was mobile. The khans moved around their domains, the better to control them.[37]

Note that the horse and iron were unknown in the Americas before the Spanish arrived, and so American wars lacked this contrast and the dynamic that flowed from it.

Marcher lords who learned to combine the two military forms could become conquerors, emerging from the fringes of Chinese civilization in more mixed pastoral-agricultural surrounds, learning the military skills of both sides—early practitioners of "combined arms warfare." Nowhere was this clearer than in north China. That list of conquerors given by Scheidel, quoted above, contained only two barbarian dynasties, the Yuan and the Manchu, but almost all the dynasties were to some degree descended from barbarians who had become ex-barbarians.

War was much more frequent here than in the southeast, and the region absorbed the vast bulk of Chinese military expenditure. The Chinese had to deal with the consequence of their own success. Agrarian productivity and wealthy cities attracted the cupidity of their pastoral neighbors who could trade, raid, or exact tribute payments for not raiding. Most of the time they chose trade, tribute, and diplomacy, but their striking speed and range led to raiding by small war bands owing loyalty to their leader, taking back loot, women, and slaves at low cost but some risk, especially when it brought large-scale Chinese retribution. From childhood, nomadic pastoralists were skilled horsemen, and in hunting they became skilled archers—natural horse archers experienced in skirmishing between clans and tribes. Di Cosmo says the image of the "natural warrior" can be taken too far, and nomads and seminomads were not fighting most of the time, yet the contrast with China is valid.[38] They did not really "choose" war; it was part of their way of life. Chinese armies consisted of massed peasant infantry, many armed with crossbows, as well as mercenary cavalry drawn from barbarian peoples. But agriculture does not teach military skills, and Chinese society was normally more peaceful. The peasant had to be trained to fight, which required permanent conscripted forces and taxes, and states. Criminals were often recruited as soldiers. Though the Chinese population was much greater, the barbarians could raise tribal hosts of up to one-quarter of a total population, and the cost to their khans was minimal.[39] War was costlier for Chinese states, and they usually had low taxes.

Different ecologies made for inequality between the two economies, yet their relatively equal military power enabled acquisition by force. Chinese armies often defeated tribal confederations in fixed battles, but the nomads then might retreat into endless steppes where the Chinese had not the logistical ability to follow because they were dependent on provisioning by supply trains, whereas the nomads could live off pastureland. Since cavalry horses had become the crucial weapon, Chinese armies needed more horses than their own ecology could provide. They traded many products with the barbarians, but the main Chinese demand was for horses (camels were second). They could trade with some barbarians to acquire horses to defeat other barbarians; they could get horses by seizing and ruling pastureland; or they could use barbarian soldiers to attack other barbarians. Chinese forays into the steppes often relied on recruits from the very peoples they were combating. But horse archers might need ten mounts, and their price was high and the quality of those offered for sale was often quite low.[40] Since trade was insufficient for Chinese military needs, it was not clearly preferable to go to war. Such dilemmas maintained the rough equality of military power between the two sides and kept their relations simmering for two millennia.

When China fell into disorder, the pastoralists were less threatened, and tribal confederations might then weaken. Chinese aggression consistently enhanced the power of khans leading tribal federations. Barbarian factionalism was endemic—anarchy within as well as between. It also allowed lesser chieftains to flout treaties negotiated by their leaders. Before the tenth century, cycles of raiding that invited punitive retaliation predominated. Barbarians did not initially seek the conquest of agrarian China, but growing military power enabled some of them to move from the steppes into terrains mixing pastoralism and agriculture—and to capture iron mines and foundries to make weapons, for Chinese states often banned weapons exports. Thus began conquests by multitribal barbarian armies. But victorious khans grew keen to acquire the institutions and culture of "civilization," which the khans blended into their own practices. Many had served as officials or soldiers in China (like the barbarians attacking the Roman Empire). The most successful khans founded permanent administrations, extracted taxes from sedentary populations, acquired literacy, and claimed the title of emperor.[41] They were "ex-barbarians." There seem to be no examples of states emerging spontaneously within pastoral societies. They all came from interaction with sedentary states.

Around imperial borders, raiding and retaliation were frequent, wars and conquest occasional. Scheidel estimates over five hundred nomad incursions over the two thousand years from 220 BCE and almost four hundred in the opposite direction by China.[42] According to an eleventh-century calculation, between 599 and 755 CE, Turks in Mongolia accounted for 55 percent of the 205 recorded attacks on Sui and Tang China, or 0.72 per year. But pastoral nomadism "was characterized by permanent instability. It was based on dynamic balance between three variables: the availability of natural resources, such as vegetation and water; the number of livestock; and the size of the population. All of these were constantly oscillating. . . . The situation was further complicated because these oscillations were not synchronic, as each of the variables was determined by many factors, temporary and permanent, regular and irregular. Thus, even annual productivity of pastures varied significantly because it was connected to microclimatic and ecological conditions."[43]

Chinese warfare was often reactive, sometimes defensive, sometimes punitive expeditions to deter further raids, sometimes conquest and incorporation of enemy territories. Conquest was seen by the Chinese as an exasperated final step to eradicate raids. They sometimes erected defensive walls around recently conquered territories—like the Great Wall. This was a reaction against barbarian pressure, but it was also defense of lands acquired through conquest. But borders were not very stable. Sometimes sections of the Great Wall were inside Chinese territory, sometimes not. But geopolitics was not entirely anarchic, for it had a rough cyclical logic.

Dealing with the seminomadic Xiongnu was unfinished business from Qin unification. The western Han dynasty launched wars against them in the north and in Central Asia, aimed at cutting the links between these regions. The wars eventually succeeded, though the cost in lives and money was tremendous.[44] Incursions deep into Xiongnu territory led their khans into adapting agriculture, permanent states, literacy, even siege engines and navies. Some styled themselves as rival "empires" to China. The Chinese court might trade, appease, or marry Chinese princesses to barbarian princes. It might divide and rule, defend, aggress, found military colonies, or resettle difficult populations. None would work indefinitely, and this meant shifting flexibly between diplomacy and war. Sometimes the Chinese made shrewd choices, sometimes disastrous ones—usually because of overconfidence or emotions overriding pragmatism.

On both sides war-and-peace decisions involved debate. In China the inner court (the emperor, eunuch officials, and dependents) tended to be more warlike than the Confucian gentry-official stratum of the outer court, who sought to keep taxes down, yet under the Tang dynasty eunuch factions warred with each other. Chinese rulers found decisions difficult given nomad volatility. They divided over whether to believe a khan's promises, or whether he could control tribes under his nominal command. Tribal leaders had to engage in diplomatic negotiations or minor wars with tribal rivals, and only the skilled or lucky ones rose to the top. How long they or their successors could stay there remained uncertain.[45] Emotions of anger, hubris, fear, and vengeance inflected rationality, while preserving honor was important for all.

Ethnic stereotypes sometimes intensified hostility. The Chinese told tribal rulers that their "cultural inferiority" meant they should submit. A Song high official called the Khitans "insects, reptiles, snakes, and lizards," adding, "How could we receive them with courtesy and deference?" Ming officials said the Mongols had "the faces of humans but the hearts of wild beasts"; they were "dogs and sheep whose insatiable appetites and wild natures made them unenculturable." Han China was the head of a person, barbarians the feet. When they refused to submit, it was like a person hanging upside down. Racism made calculative decisions more difficult.[46] When the Chinese had to negotiate because of weakness, however, they usually showed pragmatism in hiding their racism.[47] Barbarians regarded the Chinese as herds of sheep to be pushed around at will.[48]

Confucianism was alien to the barbarians, and tribute was simply given to the stronger. When China was strong, it exacted tribute from barbarians; when weak, it paid tribute (in all but name). Tribute encouraged trade, which within limits was mutually useful. But tribute was also sometimes paid by China even when strong, since bribes for peace were much cheaper than war. The Xiongnu and later Turkic groups swore fealty to the emperor in return for cash. Ying-shih Yu calculates that between 50 and 100 CE the value of goods received by barbarians from the Chinese was equal to 7 percent of imperial revenue, or 30 percent of the imperial payroll.[49] Song and Ming paid lesser indemnities.[50] Critics at court insisted that this dishonored China, and the payments consolidated the power of tribal rulers.[51] When the Chinese demanded tributary submission, barbarians and ex-barbarians balanced a loss of honor against the gains it brought. Some pragmatically submitted, others proudly refused.

Testing Realism: The Song and the Barbarians, 960–1279 CE

Song dynasty wars were usually fought against ex-barbarian peoples who had adopted Chinese practices. Can their wars be explained by structural Realist theory, as Yuan-Kang Wang argues?[52] He says the northern Song state was weak, especially compared to the first century of the Ming dynasty (1368–1449). Thus, he says, the Song fought mainly defensive wars or sought accommodation with the barbarians, whereas the stronger Ming fought largely offensive wars.

The Tang dynasty had fought aggressive wars against barbarians up to about 760 CE, but it paid a price for territorial expansion. The gap between the central officials and those in frontier districts grew into political incoherence.[53] Military governors far from the capital acquired autonomy, which resulted in rebellions. The biggest was launched by general An Lushan, who commanded over 100,000 troops along the northern frontier. He rebelled in 763, and it took fourteen years and millions of deaths for Tang forces to finish off his forces (see table 10.1). Meanwhile, the Tang lost most of their western lands as neighbors seized on Chinese disunity to grab territory. A reduced tax base and smaller armies weakened the dynasty. A partial revival occurred in the early ninth century, but then an uprising was suppressed by a general who killed the entire royal family and declared himself Emperor Taizu of the Later Liang dynasty. After his death, his domains disintegrated as warlords founded their own states in the period of the Five Dynasties and Ten Kingdoms.

One warlord took control of the central plain in 960, styling himself the first of the Song dynasty. He remained threatened by the ex-barbarian Khitan Liao, ruling formerly Tang lands on both sides of the Great Wall. The Khitan ruled over a mainly Han Chinese agricultural population and blocked Song access to horses. The Khitan north was ruled according to tribal principles, while its south had a Han Chinese administration.[54] Geopolitics was not entirely anarchic. Most rulers preferred peace to war, and embassies, audiences, and gift exchanges proliferated. When war broke out, "The basic rule," says Edmund Worthy, was "cease aggression before annihilating an actor."[55] Rather, the goal of war was to compel allegiance and homage, expressed in honorific titles conferred on subordinated rulers.[56] These were ways of defusing conflict while mutually preserving honor and status.

Yuan-Kang Wang says that the Song mounted aggressive war when strong, and defended or accommodated to the enemy when weak—and the latter situation predominated.[57] Some Song advisers did urge this.[58] But most Song endorsed the Confucian orthodoxy that a war was just if a foreign ruler refused to pay homage to the Son of Heaven or if the goal of war was to retake formerly Chinese domains. Previously Han lands in the north were ruled by the Khitan Liao, the Tangut Xi Xia, and later the

Jurchen Jin, all ex-barbarian empires. In the south lay ten small Han Chinese states. The Song intended eventually to reunify all China, but they knew this was beyond their powers at the time. They focused on re-claiming the southern states and, in the north, the state of the northern Han and the region known as the Sixteen Prefectures, which was fertile and strategic but had been lost by the Tang dynasty to the Liao. The Song felt entitled to these "lost territories."

Taizu, the first Song emperor, calculated carefully. Seeing that he lacked the power to retake the Prefectures, he attacked the small Chinese states to the south, mopping them up one by one. Lorge says there was no advance plan.[59] The court was divided, and Taizu was tentative. Yet he was a proven general and politician, flexible and opportunistic. He had first focused on stopping northern Han raids, but victory eluded him since the Liao supported the northern Han. When it became clear that the southern Han rulers could not unite against him, he went instead for the weakest of them, and conquest of the others followed. Strengthened by the resources of these regions, he then turned northward, carefully built up his forces, but then unexpectedly died. Taizu fits the Realist model, an unusually talented ruler and general who was in command of his court. Not so his successors. His younger brother, Taizong, succeeded Taizu. He knew that many at court thought Taizu's son should have been made emperor. Taizong was weak, unpopular, and incompetent. He chose to attack the northern Han, says Lorge, mainly because he thought victory would firm up his domestic political position. He would show that he really was the Son of Heaven. Personally leading the Song forces, he destroyed the northern Han state in 979 and achieved a victory over Liao forces in a narrow pass unsuited to Liao cavalry strength.

The court knew, however, that victory had really come from Taizu's careful military buildup, so Taizong felt he had to win his own war. "His clear political motivations for invading overrode his military judgment," observes Lorge.[60] Emboldened by his recent victory, and despite the mis-givings of his generals, Taizong ordered an invasion of the Prefectures. But his troops were tired and unpaid, and supplies were sparse. They were routed in badly chosen flat terrain that benefited the Liao horse ar-chers. Taizong then turned inward to secure his political position by al-ternative means, murdering all royal rivals, removing most generals, and expanding the Confucian bureaucracy. Yet he still craved legitimacy and pressed for a new offensive. In 986 an opportunity seemed to come with the accession to the Liao throne of an eleven-year-old. His mother, the dowager empress, became regent, which Taizong thought signaled weakness. So he ordered an invasion. The swiftness with which his forces advanced threw off the prepared campaign plan and led to confusion among his generals. The Liao launched a crushing counterattack ably led by the dowager empress herself. Taizong had not known she was an experienced general. Lorge says Song and Liao military strengths were fairly equal, and the main reason the Liao generally won was better leadership, more consensus at court, and a more consistent policy of border defense.

Taizong died in 997 and was succeeded by his third son, Emperor Zhenzong. Neither he nor any subsequent Song emperor commanded armies in the field. Yet he had not abandoned recovery of the Prefectures. In the year 1000 Song armies launched an offensive against their other northern neighbor, the Xi Xia, believing that victory there could lead to a Prefecture offensive. Again, they were overconfident. The Xi Xia cavalry repulsed them, and a stalemate resulted. Song policy in the north had been unrealistically aggressive. A series of inconclusive wars followed, and the Song constructed a network of canals, which Lorge calls "The Great Ditch of China," intended to foster economic development but also to strengthen defenses against marauding cavalry.[61] In 1004 came a major Liao attack that captured much Song territory before the Liao's inability to storm Song cities forced a halt. This series of wars gave the Liao gains but was costly in lives and damage to the countryside. Even so, the Liao had succeeded in stabilizing the frontier and retaining the Prefectures.

It seemed like a stalemate, and both sides agreed to end the war in the Chanyuan Covenant of 1005, a treaty ensuring 120 years of peace. It allowed both parties to take back small amounts of territory. The Song made large annual payments of silver and silk to the Liao and removed assertions of civilizational superiority from their public discourse. The Liao did better since the Prefectures remained in their hands. But the payments were not crippling, only 1–2 percent of the cost of the last war. Paying for peace was a sensible way of using the greater resources of China.[62] This reflected less a Chinese weakness than it did a preference for a cheaper policy than war, one that appealed to the tax-averse gentry class. Most at court recognized that bribes and walls were better than wars.

Peace brought mutual benefit. The Liao used the payments to build a new capital and buy needed Song goods. Unequal trade then enabled the Song to recover 60 percent of the value of the payments.[63] Peace also enabled the Song to focus on reforms that touched off a remarkable pe-

riod of technological innovation, population growth, economic development, and cultural flowering. The Song almost achieved a breakthrough
into an industrial revolution—seven centuries before Europe managed it.
The Song capital, Kaifeng, grew to over a million people. Reforms of education and administration enhanced state infrastructural powers and enabled the literate gentry-bureaucrat class to share an imperial identity
that, notes de Weerdt, survived all subsequent dynastic upheavals in
China.[64] Thus, the Song boosted the chances that future upheavals
would end up restoring the Chinese imperial state.

Its domestic achievements eased succession problems, and peace
made possible reforms cementing civilian control of the military,
through the removal of generals from foreign policy decisions.[65] A supreme military council was headed by a chancellor who had no actual
control over the army. The army was divided among three marshals, each
reporting separately to the emperor, so he (and his advisers) provided the
only unity of command. Generals were limited to a single-term posting,
and the emperors protected themselves with large bodyguard armies stationed in and around the capital. All this was coup-proofing, to prevent
generals from accumulating enough power to threaten the emperor. Just
to be on the safe side, the emperor had some generals executed. The
constant change in generals weakened the army, yet the measures
worked in increasing political cohesion. There were eight more emperors during the 167 years of the northern Song and only three brief failed
attempts at usurpation. During the 252 years of the successor southern
Song dynasty, there were only two short-lived periods of rival claimants.
Combined, the two Song dynasties were the longest-lived dynasty of
China. Whatever the Song failures in interstate wars, they had success in
domestic growth, stability, coup-proofing, and avoiding civil war.

A war party emerged, however, urging war against the supposedly
less powerful Xi Xia tribes. Yet in 1040 the Xi Xia inflicted two more
battlefield defeats on the Song. The Liao now debated whether to join in
the war and finally eliminate the Song, who would have to fight on two
fronts. The Liao emperor contented himself with increasing Song tribute payments, preferring subsidized peace and balance to the cost and
risk of war. Wang says balance-of-power logic suggests that Song and Xi
Xia should have allied together against Liao, but Song Confucians saw
the Xi Xia as rebel vassals and refused to recognize their legitimacy. "In
this case," Wang concedes, "cultural variable supplements structural realism by explaining behaviors contrary to structural logic."[66]

But the Prefectures retained their allure. The accession of Emperor Shenzong in 1067 brought another revisionist. He began with a campaign against the Xi Xia, as a prelude to moving into the Prefectures. His 1081 campaign was not decisive, so he ordered an attack again the next year. The Song army was routed. Losses in the two campaigns were reported as 600,000. Shenzong died in 1085. His successor was a boy, and the dowager empress abandoned the offensive and ceded territory to the Xi Xia. When the boy came of age, he ordered war against the Xi Xia. The 1097 offensive was a success, recovering territory until stopped by Liao threats of intervention. Most of the newly captured territory was soon returned to the Xi Xia.

The region was then transformed by the rise of another northern ex-barbarian dynasty, the Jin, originally a Jurchen people. In alliance with the Song, they destroyed the Liao in 1125. Again the Song chose the wrong ally, for they should have formed a balancing alliance with the Liao to contain the more powerful Jin. In the event of their victory, the Jin had promised the Song the Prefectures. Yet while Jin forces had won their battles, Song forces were twice defeated by the Liao—overconfidence again. The Song military weakness revealed, the Jin granted them only six lesser Prefectures in return for large Song subsidies. Two years later, the northern Song were finally finished off by Jin armies.

Since their early offensives against the southern states and the northern Han, the Song had repeatedly gone on the offensive but lost, through desire to show strength subverted by rash overconfidence. They did then move to defense out of weakness, as Realism suggests, but it was largely self-induced, owing to their failed offensives and coup-proofing to weaken their generals. After a last offensive failed, the Song retreated southward to form a southern Song dynasty, still economically strong and technologically creative. In the military sphere they developed the first effective gunpowder weapons and a navy able to suppress coastal piracy.[67]

The Jin rulers to the north embraced Confucian institutions and culture but faced rising Mongol power to their north.[68] The southern Song launched two campaigns northward, in 1206–8 and 1234, in attempts to reconquer the lost provinces. The first one was against the Jin, who the Song believed were in a state of collapse. Not so—the Song armies came fleeing home. But obsessed with finishing off the old Jin enemy, Song rulers failed to see the greater threat of the Mongols. A Jin-Song alliance would have been Realist balancing, but instead the Song launched an invasion of Jin in alliance with Mongol forces. This finished off the Jin. In

1234 the Song launched a campaign to win back Honan, then occupied by Mongols. Officials advised against this war, citing army weakness and logistical difficulties of campaigning in devastated Honan, but an impulsive, revisionist emperor, egged on by hand-picked advisers, overruled them. The army was destroyed. The Song continued to irritate the Mongols with revisionist claims yet held on stubbornly for forty more years. The Mongol forces overthrew them in 1279.[69]

So the Song offer only limited support for Wang's structural Realism. The initial problem comes from seeing the Song as weak. The Song did not believe they were weak; in fact, they were resolved to show strength, and I have chronicled seven offensive wars by them. The founder of the dynasty, Taizu, behaved like a Realist, assessing the odds, carefully preparing his forces, and achieving successes. Yet his successors launched six offensive campaigns, lost four, and achieved only one victory; one was a draw. They were more effective in defense and in peace, which permitted economic and political development—indeed, they almost broke through into industrialism—the "Song Miracle." Technological advancements included improvements in agriculture, creation of movable type, development of various weapons from gunpowder, invention of the mechanical clock, devising of compass navigation, improved shipbuilding and a permanent fleet, issuance of paper money by the government, and porcelain production. All this produced a population explosion and improved living standards. The Song did not dig as deeply into the economy for military resources as some other dynasties, which was probably a mistake, given their environment, their defeat, and the subsequent economic stagnation of China. But it was partly a choice, a coup-proofing strategy to weaken the generals—a contradiction between political and military power. Peace, not war, brought benefit for most Chinese.

The northern and southern Song did strengthen military defenses, deterring enemy attacks and stalling invasions, giving the dynasties long life during a period of increased barbarian pressure. Wang views this as a sign of weakness, but it was a recognition of military realities given ecological conditions. Campaigns typically pitched infantry-dominated Song armies against horse archers. So Song forces were better in terrains that were rough, forested, or crisscrossed by rivers or canals. The ex-barbarians were better on open plains but weak in siegecraft. The Song carried supply trains, the ex-barbarians preferred to live off the land, but different ecologies shifted logistical possibilities. In this zone of varied landscapes, when one ruler aggressed, he or she usually moved out of favorable terrain into terrain favoring the enemy. This slowed down offense or brought defeat. The more the Song advanced northward, the greater the terrain aided cavalry; the more the ex-barbarians advanced southward, the more their cavalry got bogged down by canals and cities. Defensive warfare triumphed on both sides and was responsible for the longevity of Song rule. So reliance on defense was due partially to coup-proofing, which produced military weakness, and partially to different forms of military power aided or hindered by the terrain.

There were also two Song strategic failures. Their Achilles' heel remained a yearning to rebuild the imperial unity of China, specifically to restore the Sixteen Prefectures, reinforced by Confucianism, which was not pacifist on this issue. Ambitious, overconfident emperors and advisers embarked on offensive campaigns against the ex-barbarians, emboldened by the perceived righteousness of their claims. Second, in the decisive campaigns, when the northern Song attacked the Jin and the southern Song allied with the Mongols, they made the strategic mistake of rejecting balancing alliances with the enemy of their most powerful enemy.

Sometimes Realism works, but with the Song it mostly does not. The Chinese and ex-barbarians alike were ruled by despotic monarchs with varying preferences, abilities, and characters. Being despots, they had the power to choose their advisers and execute critics, subordinating careful calculation of foreign realities to a desire to show strength at home. Debates over war and peace, however, were often secondary to domestic issues. "Reform" factions tended toward revisionism, "anti-reform" factions were conservatives who favored the status quo, low taxes, and defense or cash payments to the enemy. If the Song military underperformed, that was due mostly to a combination of overconfidence and coup-proofing. War-and-peace decisions and campaign performance might be the indirect outcome of domestic political struggles.[70] Campaigns were usually carefully planned, but the plans rarely survived contact with the enemy or the terrain. Peace also had its own virtues, for it led to economic development and greater political stability.

Coup-proofing, deliberately weakening their militaries to safeguard their political power, was commonly also practiced in the Han, Sui, Tang, and Ming dynasties.[71] "A proven general by his very nature was a political hazard." China was too big to be stably ruled by a single monarchical state. Succession crises were inevitable, and rival generals could challenge the state. The most a ruler could do was enforce obedience on localities too small to challenge him and to divide the military into units too small to allow generals regional power bases.[72] This might mean a less effective military, but it also lessened the chances of civil wars—much like the coup-proofing by authoritarian rulers in the postwar Middle East and North Africa (see chapter 14).

The First Khan Emperors: The Yuan Dynasty

The Mongols overthrew the Song and seized the imperial throne. For several centuries "barbarians" had been acquiring Chinese characteristics, but now steppe and field came under a single yoke. Through repeated wars Chinggis (Genghis) became the Khan of Khans of the Mongols in 1206. Major khans had long believed that their rule in the steppes was sanctioned by heaven. Then they had extended this blessing to sedentary realms as well. From the tenth century their victories had led them deeper into China. The Khitan Liao and the Jurchen had accepted the Song emperor as an equal. Not so Chinggis, who claimed a heavenly mandate to conquer the whole of China as both Son of Heaven and Khan of Khans. He claimed he was predestined to rule the whole known world, hence his choice of title. "Chinggis Khan" means "Oceanic Khan," implicitly ruler of all lands between the Pacific and the Atlantic. He did not "choose" war; it was his destiny. All must pay homage. "Insults against the Mongol nation and the imperial family were as pitilessly avenged as personal slights. . . . When an Onggirat prince voluntarily submitted to Genghis Khan, the latter decided to reward him with one of his daughters in marriage. The daughter did not appeal to the prince: 'Your daughter looks like a frog and a tortoise. How can I accept her?' commented the Onggirat . . . an impudent answer for which he paid with his life."[73]

Chinggis rose ruthlessly to the top. He himself fought in battle, though not particularly bravely. But his campaigns were carefully prepared with the help of a council of generals, and Chinggis was an effective commander, trusted by his officers, who were therefore loyal to him. Despite his anger, he was rarely rash or impulsive, and his diplomatic skills, especially his ability to exploit differences among his enemies, was exceptional. He lost some battles but, like the Romans, he and his men kept on fighting, to found through conquest the biggest land empire the world has ever seen. During his reign, fewer than one million Mongols with an army of just over 100,000 ruled half of Asia.

How could so few rule so many? Precariously. Like many of the empires of history, but unlike Rome or Han China, this empire was not one of direct rule. Chinggis ruled over barbarians more indirectly, through subordinate khans and other rulers, extracting tribute and troops from them. These could come to resemble regular taxes, however, and Chinggis also used the existing imperial bureaucracy to rule over his Chinese subjects, especially the taxation system. He moved masses of skilled persons, including soldiers, away from their home areas; this was the Mongol policy of ruling through strangers in order to compensate for their small numbers and avoid local resistance.[74] On top of that were various devices designed to increase his powers of surveillance—moving his capital and court around the empire and devising a postal system with staging posts that provided an efficient means of communication between the court and country and enabled troop movement and long-distance trade. These were not paved roads, however, unlike Rome's or the Incas'.

These techniques increased the emperors' control of their territories, yet military power directed from the center was always the principal tool. The core of Chinggis's army was long-service loyalists on whom he could rely, drawn like himself from relatively lowly origins, who had become an aristocracy enriched with the spoils of war. This was a meritocracy, for neither heredity nor ethnicity counted for much. Aristocratic status was achieved through performance in war. Chinggis led a small but quite cohesive state as long as he lived because of his reputation, yet constant offensive warfare was necessary to keep the spoils flowing. Otherwise, Mongols would fragment into their component peoples and clans, squabbling and skirmishing. Chinggis was enabled but also trapped in almost perpetual conquest by the ambition of an aristocratic elite whom he needed to keep on rewarding, and the members of that elite similarly needed to reward their dependents. The same lure of tribute, which trapped rulers into perpetual war to reward their followers, has been noted among the Aztec rulers of Meso-America.[75] There, too, offensive warfare was baked in to the culture and institutions of Aztec society (not so much the tyranny of history, but the tyranny of their own histories!).

The illiterate Chinggis issued written laws, focused heavily on the military. One declares, "Every man, except in rare cases, must join the army." If he could not afford a horse and weapons, "every man who does not go to war must work for the empire without reward for a certain time" as a laborer in military logistics. Every Yuan household with young men had to supply at least one to the army. Their main material reward was loot, including slaves, for another law stated that Mongol households were forbidden to have Mongols as slaves or servants. Looting had rules:

"It is forbidden, under death penalty, to pillage the enemy before the general commanding gives permission, but after that permission is given, the soldier must have the same opportunity as the officer and must be allowed to keep what he has carried off if he has paid his share to the receiver for the emperor." Han Chinese regimes with conscription required that one in seven to fifteen households (according to dynasty and period) provide a soldier. Chinese households could also pay a substitution fee so that a waged soldier could be hired instead. Yuan society was much more mobilized for war than the Han.[76]

At first Mongol military strength rested on horse archers, who combined the mobility of light cavalry with the lethality of the recurved composite bow. Chinggis, however, was quick to adopt the skills of his enemies. He developed a more hierarchical, permanent, and centralized army command structure, and he recruited Chinese infantry, siege engineers, ships, and sailors. Though Mongol conquests involved mass atrocities against those who resisted (detailed in chapter 10), quick submission brought benign consequences, including religious toleration (absent in Europe), multicultural creativity, and increased long-distance trade helped by the postal system stretching across Eurasia. Mongol civilization left many positive legacies for Eurasia even after its empires collapsed. Whether these benefits were worth the death of around 10 million people is another matter.

Much depended on the ruler, and succession was often disputed. Shortly after the death of Chinggis, civil wars split up the empire into four khanates, although the sense that this was a single imperial civilization endured.[77] Chinggis's grandson Kublai Khan inherited the Chinese khanate, and he overthrew the southern Song in 1271, claimed the Chinese throne, and founded the Yuan dynasty. He took the titles of both emperor of China and Khan of Khans, which also trapped him in wars to exact homage to maintain his grandeur, distribute loot to his followers, and exact tribute and taxes for himself and his clan. This entwining of ideological and material incentives resulted in almost continual war, for not all neighboring rulers would yield. Homage was primarily a problem of honor and autonomy, for it did not carry very burdensome obligations. The first sedentary people joining the Mongol camp, the Uyghurs, set the precedent: their khan paid homage to the Mongol khan in person, sent relatives as hostages, paid light taxes, sent military recruits, and participated in the Mongol postal system. This allowed him to carry on ruling his lands, in the khan's name.

Kublai Khan had great early success. The cost almost bankrupted the state, but economic was subordinated to military power. Calculative military-economic trade-offs were rare since he just kept aggressing, fearing the supposed "humiliation" and tribal grumbling if a ruler defied him. Pursuing honor and grandeur, he was pushed on by earlier success and materialistic followers. Sometimes those refusing submission expressed defiant insults, sometimes they murdered his envoys.[78] If so, Yuan wars were brutal: resisting city populations were massacred to persuade others to surrender. But if they swore loyalty, they kept their positions and provided the khan with troops.[79]

Yuan ambition clashed eventually with Mother Earth. In Japan, Java, Annam, and Champa (in Vietnam), the Yuan withdrew after repeated reverses revealed that Mongol troops were unsuited to either jungle or open-sea naval warfare. Tropical diseases devastated these steppe dwellers. This affected Kublai deeply, and he declined to his death. The dynasty fell less than seventy-five years later. Disputed successions were the bane of barbarian states, since there were no clear rules of inheritance, all prominent Mongols commanded troops, and Han Chinese rulers might interfere. Civil wars weakened the dynasty, and it fell to the Ming Chinese dynasty.

The first two Ming emperors destroyed the last Yuan resistance. Their successors had very varying capacities. The third emperor, the bellicose Yongle, expanded the empire back to the old Tang borders through five strenuous campaigns in Mongolia. The Xuande emperor strengthened the empire's administration. But he was followed by the hapless Zhengtong emperor, who in 1449 personally commanded his forces at the Battle of Tumu Fortress. His army of half a million was destroyed by a Mongol force of supposedly only 20,000, and he was imprisoned. Thereafter, administrative power usually lay with the Confucian scholar-bureaucrats, rather than with the emperors.[80]

Wang shows that the Ming in the period 1368–1449 initiated most of the wars with the barbarians.[81] Then war became rarer. In the period 1450–1540 wars were closer to police actions.[82] Ming policies of accommodation revealed a desire for peace based mainly on what Zhang calls "expressive rationality": they wanted peace with honor, as a moral value that elicited deference.[83] The Mongols were more instrumental. When feeling strong, they attacked; when accommodating, they performed deference to benefit materially from tributary payments, but they were not interested in acquiring Ming culture.

Wang says that from 1449 up to its fall in the 1640s, a weak Ming state sought peace. It was certainly corrupt, but if it were weak, it would not have survived so long.[84] Until the 1550s this was peace through strength. Then came a faltering, but a revival arose in the 1590s, when the Wanli emperor won multiple wars. The Ming decline came suddenly, in the 1640s, when its policy was neither defensive nor accommodating. Disastrous offensives posed a bigger problem; these were caused by court factionalism and an irresolute emperor, Chongzhen, seeking to exude strength.[85] Beset by contrary advice, he repeatedly dithered before finally heeding the advice of civilian officials ignorant of warfare; he ignored the views of seasoned generals whose power frightened him, and he had the best of them executed. Coup-proofing continued to weaken military power. In a monarchical system the ruler's capacity, bellicosity, and choice of advisers all matter. The fall of two great Han Chinese dynasties, the Song and the Ming, goes against Realism. They were undone by overconfident aggression aimed at manifesting strength internationally and domestically, rather like the Habsburg and Romanov monarchies in 1914, striking out precipitously.

Han Chinese wars were sometimes defensive, sometimes they launched punitive expeditions to deter further raids, sometimes they sought to conquer and incorporate enemy territories in order to provide extra depth to defense. This third option was obviously imperialistic, but the Han saw it as an exasperated final step in eradicating barbarian raids. Some aggressive wars aimed to reunify Han China through the recovery of lost territories. All were justified by Confucian precepts, on the grounds that they would bring peace. But the barbarians and especially the ex-barbarians really were a threat. This was a clash of "civilizations," as occurred repeatedly across northern Eurasia, intensified by a security dilemma as both Han China and its enemies enhanced their militaries in fear of the other, but where on both sides, especially among barbarian leaders, there was also a security dilemma within. To refrain from war might invite rivals to challenge their rule. Thus, wars were much more frequent in the north than in the south and southeast, where neither a clash of civilizations nor international and domestic security dilemmas ruled.

More Khan Emperors: The Qing Dynasty

Conflict between settled agriculturalists and pastoralists also permeated Inner and Central Asia. The Mongols, Tibetans, and Uyghurs there were physically and culturally non-Han. Han dynasties sometimes attacked them but rarely stayed for long. Ming armies had campaigned there after 1368, gaining nominal overlordship in Yunnan, Mongolia, Tibet, and Xinjiang, but Ming influence then waned. In the northeast the Qing Manchu dynasty (formerly Jurchens) overthrew the Ming and seized the Chinese throne in 1644. They viewed other Mongol-descended tribes not as "aliens," difficult to integrate culturally into the empire, as the Han had, but as ethnic relatives who could be integrated if they swore homage to the Qing ruler as lord of all the Mongols. Under three emperors, Kiangxi, Yongzheng, and Qianlong, the Qing secured control over Tibet, Xinjiang, and Mongolia, taking the Chinese Empire to its largest size since Chinggis.

Kiangxi launched several attacks eastward. He commanded his armies personally and mobilized different supply trains for several armies operating together in wars of encirclement. Peter Perdue emphasizes his ambitious goals, his scorning defense, his overruling the more cautious strategies of his main advisers, whether Han or Manchu, convinced that only personal victory in battle could justify his claim to be the Son of Heaven.[86] The Yongzheng emperor was more cautious and economical with Qing resources, but when provoked into aggression he rashly outran his supply lines and suffered a major defeat.

The greatest Qing conqueror was Qianlong. To achieve and uphold the integrity of the greater empire represented for him the ultimate political goal. It showed that the Manchu claim to power was part of the *zhengtong*, or "true line of rule," and that the Qing "occupied a legitimate place in the historic transmission of Heaven's mandate," says Mark Elliott.[87] They differed from Han Chinese predecessors in that martial achievement dominated their rituals, artworks, and monuments. Yet they were also calculative in their military and political methods. A dual state structure separated the Han bureaucratic administration of China proper from the Qing banner system created for the Manchu homeland and the Inner Asian frontier. Manchu soldiers, called bannermen, dominated the inner court, and eunuchs were replaced by bond servants. Military decisions were made by a secretive Grand Council of Manchu aristocrats, who spoke a language that the Han Chinese could not understand. The armed forces were divided into an elite force of Manchu bannermen and a Green Standard militia composed mainly of Han Chinese. Despite Zhao's notion that the barbarians were incorporated into the Confucian-legalist state, they respected Han ways only when it assisted their rule, just as Buddhism was used in Buddhist areas.[88] Yet although Confucian bureaucracy was subordinated to the Manchu ruling class, it was essential to their stability, for it enabled control of their domains in a way much closer to direct territorial imperialism than their ex-barbarian predecessors had managed.

Qing wars were driven, like the Yuan wars, by the need to compel homage toward a ruler who was both the emperor of China and the Khan of Khans. The Qing normally preferred trade through "tea-horse frontier markets" as opposed to war, provided the steppe peoples formally submitted. Honor was the usual sticking point. While careful to sign treaties with a Russian Empire also expanding into Central Asia, Qianlong launched his armies against "mere barbarian chiefs" who had "humiliated" and "wounded" the vanity of a universal sovereign.[89] Against the Zunghars, the last adversary, in a daunting logistical environment of savannas and mountains, it "was the first time that a logistic system had been created that allowed a Chinese empire to fight a sustained war far into the steppe and bring the enormous material wealth of China to bear in a devastating way."[90] Perdue says it was possible only because of the commercialization of the eighteenth-century Chinese economy.[91] The Qing armies penetrated deep into the Zunghar heartland, where Manchu bannerman cavalry pinned down the enemy and the Han Chinese Green Standard forces' cannon and muskets finished them off. The Qing did not attack only when they were strong. Their militarism could create whatever military strength was needed, whatever the cost—as had Rome's.

In the campaign of 1761, an army of 100,000 killed almost all Zunghar males, and women and children became bonded labor for Chinese families. The number of Zunghar dead or missing totaled half a million. A later Chinese estimate was that a smallpox epidemic contributed 40 percent of these deaths and the genocide of males about 30 percent, whereas about 20 percent escaped abroad. Normally, if a steppe people surrendered, its aristocrats and soldiers were incorporated into the victor's clan, while others became slaves or bondservants. Women, children, and older men were rarely killed. This genocide was exceptional, and due to Qianlong himself. He urged: "Show no mercy at all to these rebels. Only the old and weak should be saved. Our previous military campaigns were too lenient. If we act as before, our troops will withdraw, and further trouble will occur. If a rebel is captured and his followers wish to surrender, he must personally come to the garrison, prostrate himself before the commander, and request surrender. If he only sends someone to request submission, it is undoubtedly a trick. . . . Massacre these crafty Zunghars."[92]

Some historians regard Qianlong's reign as a Chinese Age of Enlightenment because he was a great patron of the arts (and a mediocre poet). There was nothing enlightened about his campaigns, although they did expand Qing territory by over 1.5 million square kilometers.

The Zunghar khanate was renamed Xinjiang province, as it is known today.[93] What today's Chinese rulers are doing there is but a pale shadow of their predecessor's deeds.

This did not end Qianlong's ambition. Wars were also fought against the Jinchuan Tibetans in 1747–49 and 1771–76. These campaigns were unexpectedly difficult, for the Jinchuan had adapted their warfare to mountain terrain. The first war achieved little. The second cost 62 million taels (a weight of silver), compared to 23 million in the Zunghar wars, and 50,000 Manchu died. Eighty percent of expenses went to logistics to supply the armies with food, uniforms, tents, handguns, gunpowder, and, above all, the horses, oxen, and carts to carry them over long distances. The campaign mobilized 200,000 soldiers and 400,000 civilian laborers: "The Qing dynasty was able to effectually mobilize the whole government structure and a large part of the population in order to fulfill its ambitious imperial projects in spite of a narrow financial base and a thin bureaucratic network."[94] This was total war, involving infrastructural power superior to anything Western states had yet mustered.

These wars were motivated more by vengeance, glory, and grandeur than by a cost-benefit calculus of profit. The conquered regions were always a drain on the treasury. For Qianlong conquest of the new territories was a glorious enterprise, worthy of the ages, adding luster to his rule. He boasted of his campaigns in his "Record of the Ten Perfects," stating: "The ten instances of military merit include the two pacifications of the Dzungars [Zunghars], the quelling of the Muslim tribes, the two annihilations of the Jinchuan, the restoring of peace to Taiwan, and the subjugations of Burma and Vietnam; adding the recent twin capitulations of the Gurkhas makes ten in all. Why is there any need to [add] . . . trivial rebellions in the inner provinces?"

Expansion was spurred on by anger at insults, such as a usurper to a local throne failing to seek his blessing. He responded with outrage: "The majestic Great Qing holds unified sway over center and periphery alike, and now this renegade tribal usurper dares to see himself as our equal?!" Qianlong extracted whatever resources were needed. He felt he must keep his Manchu soldiers fighting, for he wanted to be able to continually reward them and did not want them to soften into Chinese ways. Elliott comments, "The second half of Qianlong's reign was a veritable orgy of martial revelry. Some of his dynastic chest-pounding took poetic form. Qianlong composed more than 1,500 pieces on themes of war and battle relating to his ten campaigns." Giant triumphant stelae dotted the landscape.[95]

As usual among the Mongols, subsequent rule was not cruel if a people did not rebel, as the Qing drew together agriculturalists and pastoralists. The conquered peoples' ethnic cultures, descent myths, and lineage histories were all officially recognized.[96] Whereas the Ministry of Rites dealt with tributary foreign states in the east, the Court of Colonial Affairs dealt with the Inner and Central Asian peoples.[97] The Colonial Court made Inner Asian peoples Qing subjects without making them Han Chinese, and local chiefs became officials of the Qing Empire. Tibetans ruled Tibetans, Uyghurs ruled Uyghurs, and Mongols ruled Mongols, each allocated to administrative districts, banners, and "tribes," subject to fixed taxes, conscription, and rituals—somewhere between direct and indirect imperialism.[98]

Along the Burma-Myanmar borderlands in the south, frontiers were unclear, straddled by warlords, some of whom owed fealty to China, some to Burma, others to no one. Conflict and banditry were endemic. The Ming dynasty fought small defensive frontier operations there, while Qing arrival brought border incursions in pursuit of Ming rebels. After a century of relative calm, Qianlong responded with his military forces to requests for help from his vassals in the Shan border states. His economic motives were not as important as the grandeur that he believed arose from defending vassals, teaching upstarts lessons, and securing battle glory. Borderland provinces rarely paid their way, subsidies went from center to periphery, and there was no state mercantilism, which was not the case with Western imperialism. Borderlands were expected to pay for some of their defense, so that taxes on the local economy, such as salt extraction and agriculture, were important but did not dominate policy.[99]

The Manchu knew little of Burma's jungle terrain or of its rulers' resolve. Three wars were fought between 1765 and 1769, each deploying larger forces that contained increasing numbers of elite bannermen. These were defeats due to ignorance of the terrain, tropical diseases, and overextended supply lines cut by guerillas—the same problems suffered here by the Yuan. Manchu casualties in all three totaled 70,000. Eventually a peace treaty was signed that was favorable to Burma. Qianlong perversely boasted he had acquired a new tributary state, adding these campaigns to his list of "Ten Perfects." But in a private letter he confessed bitterly: "Myanmar has awful conditions. Human beings cannot compete with Nature. It is very pitiful to see that our crack soldiers and elite generals died of deadly diseases for nothing. So [I am] determined never to have a war again [there]."[100]

In southwest Yunnan, whose peoples owed the Qing nominal allegiance, the Qing aimed at political centralization, imposing "civilization" on "barbarians," "soothing," "pacifying," and "instructing" "bandits" who threatened China's unity.[101] Qianlong also wisely accommodated local religions, ruling through the Dalai Lama and "Yellow Hat" Buddhists, investing himself with Buddhist titles while delegating powers to Buddhist or Dao institutions.[102] He achieved a small increase in political control.

In Qianlong's old age, the Chinese Empire became a satisfied hegemon. Small Manchu numbers and the power of the Confucian education system ensured that some were sinicized. But long-lasting peace saw armies decay and leaders skimming off taxes. The combination sparked rebellions and fragmented warlord rule. After 1600 European military power had begun growing, as it refined guns originally invented in China. Qing dynasty forces were still able to launch a successful combined land and naval assault in the Sino-Russian Border War of 1652–89, however, driving the Russians out of this disputed northern territory. But an "Age of Parity" after 1700 swung military power from China to Europe. Andrade sees "mild" Chinese military stagnation in 1450–1550 becoming "significant" in 1760–1839, when China had fewer wars than in any prior period.[103] By the nineteenth century the Europeans were far stronger. The Qing had fought less well-developed enemies, expanding techniques for fighting tribes in savannas and mountains—not relevant for fighting Europeans. Then they made barely any wars at all. Like the Japanese, they had become sitting ducks. Unlike the Japanese, they were not spared the time to respond. The virtues of peace came at a cost.

Conclusion

The Chinese Empire was created and expanded through conquest, like the other imperial civilizations of history. But distinctive here was its longevity, its vitality, and its relative stability. Over two millennia this was the most technologically inventive, educated, and culturally creative civilization on earth, one that almost broke through to an industrial society six to seven hundred years before Europe did. The combination of centralized monarchy and an empire-wide gentry-bureaucrat class stabilized state power, providing social order and a dominant class–state alliance that could survive and reemerge after periods of instability caused by external and civil wars. The Confucian dynamic of the empire leaned more toward peace than war, but the empire's size coupled with the normal problems of hereditary monarchy—court intrigues and disputed successions— produced intermittent bloodbaths and civil wars before stability re-emerged. Rulers wanted to show strength, if necessary through war, to bolster their domestic positions and to reveal themselves as the true Sons of Heaven, but most of the early rulers of dynasties were more warlike than their successors. They already had capable armies and needed to find them employment. Yet in the long run the gentry-bureaucrats pressured emperors against raising taxes, and this made wars more difficult. Peace was preferred by most, and peace generated most of the flourishing of this remarkable civilization.

As the state stabilized, however, there emerged large regional differences. In East and Southeast Asia peace resulted largely from Chinese tributary diplomacy. Han Chinese rulers could have chosen further imperialism, but they settled for rituals of homage paid by foreign rulers. This increased trade and was cheaper than war. This was not an anarchic region, for Chinese rulers did not fear their weaker neighbors, and vice versa, for diplomacy lessened Chinese threats to them, increased their domestic legitimacy, and enabled them to focus on problems elsewhere. This was hegemony for peace, minimalist compared to modern hegemonies but effective in preserving relative peace over long periods. There was no parallel region in the Roman domains. Rome kept on fighting offensive wars across all its frontiers—as did the two non-Han Mongol and Manchu dynasties of China.

The frontiers of the north and west differed, seeing at first perpetual conflicts between steppe and field dwellers. Han farmers and urban dwellers waged war against nomadic and seminomadic peoples whose horse archers enabled low-cost raiding. Chinese insecurity led to wars with a larger defensive component than Roman wars, although what was originally self-defense sometimes escalated into imperial conquest and rule—by either side. The diplomacy of the east and southeast did not work here. The barbarians could be bought off, but even trade was permeated by militarism, since the scarcest commodity for China was warhorses and for the barbarians iron weapons, each found in the other's territories. War decisions across this Eurasian fault line balanced economic goals and military means as Realists suggest, but amid an ecology unusually conducive to war.

Most Chinese wars were reactive to barbarian pressure, whereas war, tribute, and trade were all viable means of economic acquisition. Given such dilemmas, the motives and abilities of emperors and khans made a big difference. Confucianism provided mixed messages, a pacific bias undercut by demands for homage and territorial revisionism. Choices were inflected slightly by racism and substantially by emotions like pride, humiliation, hatred, and, above all, honor. Sun Tzu and Sun Bin both regretted that war was so common. Sun Bin said that "a distaste for war is the kingly military instrument," and "you must go to war only when there is no other alternative."[104] The notion of geopolitical "anarchy" made some sense in the north and west, but it was enhanced by the ecological-sociological context, and barbarian society itself contained anarchic tendencies. Moreover, successful rulers waged wars without much calculation, digging deeper into resources to achieve victory at whatever the cost. They made reality more than conformed to it.

Domestic politics greatly influenced war decisions. Strong rulers made wars, but so too did weak ones striving to prove their fitness. Factionalism often pitted a more warlike inner court against the low-tax, Confucian gentry-bureaucratic class of the outer court. Barbarian confederations appeared, conquered, split, and disappeared. The fault line between the two was increasingly muddied by Chinese dividing and ruling, and by barbarians shifting from mere raiding to territorial conquest—and acquiring Chinese civilization. Two ex-barbarian dynasties conquered the entire empire, and the second one, the Manchu Qing, destroyed the remaining barbarians, abolished the agricultural-pastoral gulf, and instituted a single multiethnic China, satisfied, conservative, relatively peaceful, with a gradually decaying military. China was then hegemonic all around its borders for just over a century, before being assaulted by foreign imperialists, though a twentieth-century counteroffensive has come from Chinese nationalists and then more strongly from communists.

Realist explanations of Chinese wars are based on anarchic geopolitics and military-economic calculation. Sometimes this model works—but sometimes not. It downplays important causes of war from ecologies, class and ethnicity, domestic politics, ideologies, emotions, the blessings of peace, and variable human competences and desires. The main ex-barbarian fallibilities were political factionalism and overconfidence in war; the main Han fallibility was a contradiction between wars necessary to strengthen their political power and the need to preserve their political power by coup-proofing, which weakened the military. The main macro-determinant of war was the level of objective threat to China, stronger in the north and west than in the south and southeast. But all four sources of social power, in addition to the ecological environment, help explain imperial China's war-and-peace decisions.

CHAPTER SEVEN

Medieval and Modern Japan

Τ HE FREQUENCY AND INTENSITY of war fluctuated greatly
through Japanese history. The civil wars of the sixteenth century and the interstate wars of the twentieth century are
well-documented and together frame a long period of peace.
In the sixteenth century there were many "vanishing kingdoms"; more
than seventy political lordships, or daimyo, were reduced, mainly
through war, to just one ruling the whole of Japan. In the twentieth century the intensification of Japanese imperialism in Asia culminated in the
Great Pacific War and the downfall of Japan.

Medieval Warfare

As we saw in chapter 2, war arrived late within Japan. The two-hundred-
kilometer sea crossing between Japan and the Asian mainland deterred interstate war until the nineteenth century. Yet civil wars racked Japan, and
in medieval times there were also wars of "deflection," whereby weaker
indigenous peoples were conquered. During the Heian period (794–1192
CE) a war defined by the CoW standard of one thousand battlefield
deaths occurred about once every ten years and rarely lasted longer than a
season. There were more small-scale clashes (MIDs) between clan families, warrior bands, and peripheral peoples. The next centuries saw
power decentralization. The divine emperor and the imperial aristocratic
court represented ideological power, but they yielded military power to a

145

shogun and his allies. The army "moved from a conscripted, publicly trained military force to one composed of privately trained, privately equipped professional mercenaries."[1] These professionals became known as samurai, at first mounted bowmen, then also armed with spears and swords, commanding part-time peasant infantry.

Although the samurai were of lower social status than the imperial aristocracy, they became the main bearers of military power. From the Genpei War (1180–85) onward they dominated the aristocracy. Law and order, day-to-day governance, and tax collection were in practice delegated to local lords, the daimyo. Yet the land formally belonged to the imperial and shogun authorities, which had in theory assigned it to each clan. Once peripheral territories were occupied, the ecology of conflict on these confined islands became unlike that in China. Only rarely could war now be deflected on to less powerful peoples, and so wars between the clan alliances of the major daimyo lords were largely zero-sum wars.

The Kamakura dynasty (1192–1603 CE) saw intense civil wars, but there were also two attempted Yuan Chinese invasions of Japan at the end of the thirteenth century. The invaders were already having difficulty storming entrenched Japanese coastal positions before their fleets were devastated by storms. They retreated, leaving trapped Yuan forces to be massacred. China and Japan then left each other alone until the 1590s. Armed struggle was confined within the archipelago but grew. Armies expanded from a hundred or so to fifty thousand in the 1550s, and prolonged warfare prevented economic growth. The daimyo had not solved the problem of how to feed a growing population while provisioning a military without harming the peasantry. They found it difficult to finance armies and keep peasants productive.[2]

Civil wars mobilized armies composed of the daimyo's kin, vassal samurai, and retainer foot soldiers. The vassals swore fealty to the lord and paid him taxes extorted by credible threat of force from the peasants beneath, recognizably feudal elements. Vassal loyalty was often calculative, and shifts of allegiance resulted from bribes or loss of confidence in a daimyo's military capacities. The famed samurai honor code did not much constrain behavior. Warriors rendered service and expected proper reward. "Fourteenth-century warfare transcended all contemporary boundaries and subverted political, intellectual, and social norms."[3] Karl Friday debunks literary traditions of speeches before battle, agreements to fix time and place of battle, dueling between champions, and respectful treatment of prisoners of war and civilians.[4] Instead, he says, warfare was more ferocious than in medieval Europe because of distinctive features of Japanese feudalism. Land was formally owned by the state, but the possessing clan had the right to control and draw taxes from it. Politically, a clan's influence at the imperial and shogunate centers protected its rights. Yet if it wiped out an enemy clan, it could claim possession of its lands, which the central authorities then ratified. Prisoners were decapitated, their heads displayed in victory parades. Stephen Morillo thinks this explains why ritual suicide was prevalent among losing samurai, while unknown in Europe.[5]

Ideological power could not regulate wars. In contrast to the monolithic dominion of the Church in Europe, religious authority was divided between numerous schools and sects. None was powerful enough to impose ethics on warriors—indeed, armies of Buddhist monks joined in.[6] As imperial and shogun power declined, the state could not restrain war. As in China and Europe, this decline meant autonomy for local lords and ensuing small wars. Lowborn warriors were promised land and loot, lowborn monks were mobilized for revolutionary war, and the samurai dominated the aristocrats. Wars were described as "the lower ranking overthrow the higher ranking." This was material conflict over control of land and its population and taxes, but it also invoked issues of status and honor.[7]

The Warring States Period and the Triumph of the Triumvirs

In the Sengoku (Warring States) period (1467–1590, though exact dates are debated) civil wars intensified, involving perhaps 250 small, independent daimyo domains mobilizing limited forces in countless skirmishes. Before the development of firearms, the leading daimyo were often in the thick of the action. If they were killed, their forces usually submitted. In the sixteenth century more powerful daimyo were able to impose more control over the fighting men and material resources of their domains. They began to swallow up lesser lords. Mary Berry says the main precipitants of war were loose rules of dynastic succession and vassalage in a society where central power was still declining.[8] A strong lord could choose his successor without a contest; otherwise, succession could be disputed between sons or nephews, each supported by vassals. Outside daimyo might also intervene. A century of often savage warfare was triggered by succession crises in four major military households. Unlike those in Europe, some issues in medieval Japanese society, says Berry, "stood outside the universe of statute, precedent, contract, and executive right—outside, that is, the universe of conventional expectation and duress that make the rule of law intelligible. By their very nature, succession decisions resisted the workings of law ... for no review of evidence, no consultation of statutes, no invocation of past practice, no exploration of the natural order could settle them unequivocally."[9]

Only warfare could settle disputes not confined to material issues. It involved

> feelings of pride and anger that spawned mortal grudges in a society preoccupied with honor. ... Jurists sometimes condoned the grudge; chroniclers and diarists made it a narrative frame to interpret conflict; and warlords and soldiers did battle in its service. Sanctioned or not, the grudge satisfactorily organized ideas and actions that required no translation into other terms—of law or religion, of ideology or economics.
>
> Elite families turned recklessly to violence to avenge insult, enhance prestige, secure their stakes in land, and sate the appetites of opportunistic retainers. None intended to remake the world or even to fight very long; all were after marginal gains that would eventually cost most of them everything. ... Violence was a perfectly normal extension of political fights. ... The final years of the Warring States brought an unparalleled escalation in violence, the ravaging of cities and monasteries, and a geometrical increase in casualties as muskets and mass conscription made the gentleman's war obsolete. Hundreds of thousands of troops, representing a majority of able adult males, were brought to arms ... fired by losses, by the seeming need to avenge mounting numbers of dead and legitimate the purposes of their leaders. ... Something that started as an elite contest over prestige ended by obliterating an old world and forging a new one none of the players could have forecast."[10]

This vivid account suggests that calculation of material goals and military means was highly inflected by grudges, vengeance, and savagery, all of which ended in mutual self-destruction, for wars destroyed most of the daimyo. Only for a few winners was there rationality of ends. All rulers attempted rational calculation of means, but most did not succeed. War was not at all rational for civilians, especially peasant farmers, whose homes and crops were looted and burned, inducing famine and disease. William Farris adds laconically, "Violence, pillage, arson, kidnapping, and forced conscription are not conducive to demographic, agricultural, or commercial expansion."[11] Winnowing of states, as in China and Europe, was at the expense of lesser daimyo and major ones made overconfident by past victories.[12] After 1550 wars were fought by daimyo seeking regional, then national, hegemony. Hundreds were eliminated, down to only the triumvirs, and then only one, who ruled all Japan—a process that resembled (though more rapidly) the development of China.

John Bender calculates the numbers of the vanished among seventy-eight daimyo on whom he found data in the period 1467–1600. Of these, 60 percent were eliminated by force.[13] The remaining 40 percent survived by submitting to the winners under threat of war, able to keep some or all of their estates. Survival rates were higher in more isolated and poorer regions. Lack of economic resources prevented the losers from assembling armies and did not arouse cupidity in others. The lowest survival rates were in the richest region around the capital, Kyoto. In this region of small daimyo, all were vulnerable. Bender says that sixteen of the seventeen daimyo around Kyoto were eliminated by war.

Eastern Honshu, quite near Kyoto, was the ideal launching pad for attacks on the capital. The clan of Oda Nobunaga, the first of the triumvirs, came from here. After successful campaigns against rival daimyo in his own region, Nobunaga seized the capital in 1568 with an army of 60,000. He eliminated or accepted homage from the local daimyo and installed an ally as shogun. The shogun and the court were largely symbolic figures, but they brought legitimacy to his rule, and so they had enough power to jockey for advantage with him. Nobunaga then used the wealth of the Kyoto region to finance more wars, bringing thirty of Japan's sixty-six provinces under his sway, and he pressured the shogun into "voluntary" exile, becoming shogun himself.[14]

A successful daimyo needed an economic power base, given mostly by fertile soil and trade. Poor daimyo were unlikely to dominate. But where economic growth occurred without military improvement, this merely aroused the cupidity of neighbors. The competitive pressures of war stimulated some into economic reforms designed to increase military power. Since daimyo needed fortifications, weapons, uniforms, and supplies, some encouraged traders and artisans into their service, and a few even took measures to encourage peasant productivity, sponsoring irrigation and other projects.[15] Berry emphasizes the introduction of

cadastral surveys of the land, which enabled clearer, more equitable conscription and tax obligations that were geared to land productivity.[16]
Defeat loomed for those who did not reform, as was the case in China in
the late Warring States. Cadastral reforms also required political skills in
handling the different interests of the various classes involved.

The elimination of daimyo came mainly from defeat in battle or capitulation to threats. During the sixteenth century, armies got much bigger, their organization more complex, their drilling more intense. Paid
professional soldiers replaced conscripts. Firearms had been imported
from China in the twelfth century but saw little use. But when Portuguese firearms were imported in 1543, they quickly went into mass production. The guns forced the daimyo back, to command from the rear.
Siege warfare involved sophisticated engineering. Most campaigns aimed
at devastating enemy territory, living off the land while destroying the
enemy's subsistence; but killing the enemy clan was more important than
seizing territory. The coup de grâce was the storming of the enemy's fortress. The defeated daimyo would be abandoned by his vassals, which
made retreat into guerilla warfare impossible, except as bandits.

Nobunaga achieved his many victories aided by an elite core of
skilled, upwardly mobile captains, mostly from his own province, who
had flocked to him early because of his military reputation and who were
well rewarded for victory. His armies then increased through victories. If
a daimyo defected to him before battle, he could lead his troops alongside Nobunaga's, and he might receive new estates after victories. If he
capitulated early in a campaign, he and his troops might be absorbed into
Nobunaga's vassal bands, but under the command of the core captains,
and he might lose some estates. A fully defeated daimyo would die, and
his estates were given to Nobunaga's vassals and allies.

Although the resource base and army size mattered, in some battles
smaller forces triumphed. At Okehazama in 1560 an invading Imagawa
force of 25,000 to 40,000 was defeated by Nobunaga's 2,000–3,000 in a
surprise attack on forces sheltering from driving rain, unprepared for
battle. Nobunaga possessed military skills in abundance, while the
Imagawa demonstrated folly, failing to post scouts and pickets in enemy
territory. Their daimyo was killed, and many of his vassals changed sides,
foiling the succession of his heir. After 230 years dominating their region, they vanished. Comparable fates awaited most clans.

Yet most battles were fought by armies of fairly equal strength. Thus,
advance intelligence, tactical skill, fatigue, the terrain, and the weather

could all tilt the balance one way or the other. At Nagashino in 1575, Nobunaga quietly moved his forces into close range of the enemy, into a position flanked by a river on one side and mountains on the other. This meant the enemy could not effectively use his superiority in cavalry on the flanks. If he joined battle (which he should not have done), he had to charge headlong into Nobunaga's firearmed infantry. They did, and they were decimated. Skill triumphed over folly. Nobunaga did suffer reverses, but he had such self-confidence and relentless drive, backed up by the loyalty of his captains, that he triumphed. In war, leadership skills matter.

There was much diplomatic maneuvering around promises and threats. If threatened, a daimyo might be weakened by a factional dispute over the best course of action, and the enemy might bribe or threaten one faction. Military leadership involved knowing when to retreat, compromise, or fight. Fighting on one's own, without allies, was unwise, for it invited enemy alliances smelling victory and spoils. Isolating one's rival was all-important. If one attacked him, one should first secure promises from others of alliance or neutrality. There was much changing of sides by subordinate daimyo, even during battle. Alliances involved treaties, hostage exchanging, and intermarriage, but alliances lasted only as long as they brought gains. Loyalty was not to be relied on. Some daimyo were better than others at such scheming—none better than the triumvirs. Nobunaga and his captains managed to overcome several larger hostile leagues of daimyo and warrior monks. The tactic was to pick on one of them and prevent others from arriving to offer help. This was fertile ground for rational calculation, yet most daimyo ultimately failed.

The sources portray Nobunaga not as an exemplar of calm calculation, but as ruthless, intemperate, impetuous, and unpredictable, preferring terrorizing over negotiations. Emotions often dominated his actions. He reacted to a difficult year in 1571 by killing the entire population of a temple fortress. "Nobunaga dispelled years of accumulated rancour," noted a chronicler. He distributed the temple domains to his soldiers and hoisted enemy heads on pikes, saying, "You cannot imagine my happiness that I have slain them all, for I hated them deeply." The next year he destroyed a confederation of religious sects, slaughtering 40,000 people, making no distinction between enemy soldiers and civilians, men and women. He had declared beforehand, "The confederates make all kinds of entreaties, but as I want to exterminate them root and branch this time, I shall not forgive their crimes." He said he "gave orders to slaughter men and women alike." "This kind of bloodthirsty language occurs frequently in reports from campaigns," observes Jeroen Lamers.[17] All three triumvirs were driven more by skill inflected with strong emotions. Geopolitics was fairly anarchic, perhaps more so than in any other case in this book. Underreported peripheral areas where most daimyo survived probably saw fewer wars, but elsewhere there were few normative constraints. Fear and ambition led to aggression, for it was better to fight on other peoples' lands than on one's own. It was difficult to calculate the odds of victory, since economic, military, political, and geopolitical strategies all figured. But, as is true of most of my cases, fighting was seen less as a choice and more as what a leader did. If aggressing, one chose only when to attack. If defending, honor compelled resistance. More ideological warfare was fought by warrior monks.

Power was pursued through militarism baked in to culture and institutions by the normalcy of war. Path dependence meant that daimyo who gained territories and people sought more victories, which eventually led to their own defeat and the disappearance of their domain. The vanished kingdoms far outnumbered the victors. This was rationality of ends for only a few. Although the primary goal was acquisition of land and people, domination for its own sake was also evident. Violence was the great intoxication of rulers, as Berry has already confirmed. All this resembles war in other cases. Scheming culminated in wars in which recklessness might help, for unpredictability was a useful asset in anarchic geopolitics.

In 1571 Nobunaga, his lieutenant Toyotomi Hideyoshi, and the Tokugawa clan, the triumvirs, began an ambitious joint strategy to dominate Japan. Under Nobunaga terror tactics dominated, but they provoked hostile reactions that might have derailed further ambitions. But contingent events intervened. Nobunaga and his heir died suddenly in 1583 in a surprise coup launched by a dissatisfied general. Hideyoshi avenged his death, becoming head of the Oda clan and shogun. He had begun life as a simple farmer, then become a soldier. He rose rapidly through the ranks, possessing a combination of charm, charisma, and acuity in political and military strategies and tactics that had induced Nobunaga to place great trust in him. "Arrogance, ambition, and daring—not prudence—led Hideyoshi to leadership."[18] His policies were less tyrannical than Nobunaga's, for he sought to conciliate neutrals and those who defected from his enemies, allowing them some autonomy under a "federal" style of rule, confirming their rights over their own vassals, often offering them lands in return for ruling in his name. One letter from him read, "Because of your assistance to me, I bestow upon you all rights to Shisō in the province of Harima. This area shall be your domain in full." He also pursued at least twenty acts of attainder for treason, however, confiscating daimyo estates, and achieving many partial confiscations and transfers of land. Only a daimyo who remained faithful had no need to fear punishment.[19] There was continuity in religious policy, however: the "religious policies of Nobunaga, Hideyoshi, and Ieyasu were all predicated on the primacy of secular authority"; "in early-modern Japan there would be no independent, religious sphere operating outside of state control."[20]

But Hideyoshi self-destructed in the 1590s, dying near the end of his two failed invasions of Korea (see chapter 6). With bad timing, he had recently killed his nephew, the heir-apparent, for his own son was only a child. He was quickly deposed by Tokugawa Ieyasu, who seized the shogunate and showed no mercy to defeated clans. Hideyoshi could be either cruel or conciliatory, according to his perception of the needs of the moment. He himself claimed to value patience: "The strong manly ones in life are those who understand the meaning of the word patience. Patience means restraining one's inclinations. There are seven emotions: joy, anger, anxiety, adoration, grief, fear, and hate, and if a man does not give way to these he can be called patient. I am not as strong as I might be, but I have long known and practiced patience." A model Realist!

Japan was finally unified through violence and two contingent deaths, and the Tokugawa dynasty was declared in Edo (Tokyo) in 1603. The triumvirs unified Japan, where so many warlords had failed, first because of the ruthless aggression of Nobunaga, then because of a timely switch from terror to milder politics under Hideyoshi, and finally because of Ieyasu's patience when he stayed out of the invasion of Korea, which sapped the strength of his main rivals. The sequence seems important—and contingent.

The reforms of Hideyoshi and Ieyasu focused on reducing violence. They did not establish national taxation, regulate banking or commerce, establish a national police force, organize public works or engineering projects, or have education or welfare policies. Revenue came from the shogun's own domains, vast from his having seized defeated lords' lands. Daimyo rights to tax their own domains were confirmed. The unifiers banned Christianity, regulated temples, shrines, and monasteries, and restricted foreign trade—all of which they believed had brought conflicting ideologies into Japan. They repressed pirates, and Dutch traders were confined to a few port enclaves. There was minimal contact with the outside world. Local rule remained with the daimyo, but pacification belonged to the shogun. The daimyo's right to war in pursuit of his interests was abolished. The shogun assumed the right to transfer and redistribute daimyo landholding, removing dissident daimyos to peripheral areas and positioning reliable allies around them. Daimyo castles were destroyed by decree. Samurai were denied tenure rights in land and forced to live by their lords' castles, severed from both villagers and their own subvassals. Commoners were banned from bearing arms, while migration, political mobilization, and unregistered travel were also prohibited. Supreme judicial authority was vested in the shogun's court.[21] The traditional rights and privileges of classes and status groups were confirmed providing they refrained from violence—daimyo, samurai, monks, priests, merchants, artisans, and peasants. Daimyo increased control over their domains, retaining control over local levies and administering local justice, commerce, agrarian affairs, and religion.[22] Samurai and radical clerics were the biggest losers, as the samurai were subordinated to their lords, and the monks were defeated.

These unification policies were popular because there was a reaction against the Sengoku period, whose last battles had seen armies of over 100,000. Ieyasu collected 35,000 enemy heads after the final battle of Sekigahara in 1600. Many battles were decided by daimyo changing sides just before or during the battle, which resulted in the massacre of abandoned daimyo. Use of arms had pervaded villages, cities, and monasteries, aiding sectarian religious warfare, peasant rebellions, banditry, and myriad violent quarrels over property lines, water and forest rights, debts, commercial privileges, inheritances, taxes, runaways, and wives. The unifiers feared violence might engulf them too, so they focused on policies against violence, popular among most classes, who were desperate for peace and aware that Japan had once been united.[23]

The contributors to John Ferejohn and Frances Rosenbluth's volume stress war weariness and yearnings for unification, especially among peasants oppressed by taxes and military service.[24] Farris adds class relations.[25] On the one hand, the daimyo were caught in a race to integrate military and economic power in forms analogous to legalist reforms in China. They encouraged commerce in order to tax it, lessened the tax burden on peasants, and banned armies living off the land, which also safeguarded peasant livelihoods. There was demographic and economic growth after 1550 as improved irrigation, cultivation, and trade raised production above subsistence. They had made steps toward resolving the paradox of efficiently provisioning the military without unduly damaging the economy. Second, peasants for their part pressured their daimyo by using "weapons of the weak"—"striking, absconding, hiding, bribing, negotiating, and in the last resort fighting."[26]

Demilitarizing reforms contributed to success. In the 1587 "Sword Hunt" ordered by Hideyoshi, troops entered villages and temples and confiscated swords, spears, and guns. Peasants, townsmen, and priests were forbidden to bear arms. The Separation Edict of 1591 decreed that armies would consist only of professionals. Conversely, the samurai were denied the right to farm. Farmers and soldiers were now kept apart.[27] The reforms were aimed at curbing lawlessness in the countryside; they enabled peasants, artisans, and merchants to focus on being productive, and under Hideyoshi cadastral surveys were greatly improved.[28] The triumvirs had created a military organization that brought less harm to peasants and townspeople and integrated economic and military power.

Tokugawa Peace, 1603–1868

Unification produced a spectacular reversal of history: almost no wars over 250 years. The only ones occurred at the beginning of that span, when Ieyasu was still fighting to establish his rule. There were three thousand local incidents of violent peasant protest, mainly over taxes, mostly at the beginning and the end of the Tokugawa period, and they were quickly suppressed. Barrington Moore says Japanese peasants in this period played a passive role in historical change, unlike their Chinese or Russian counterparts.[29]

From peace, not war, came growth in commerce and cities and a relatively advanced agrarian society containing protocapitalist tendencies. The military decayed as soldiers were scattered in small units across the country. Non-samurai forces were disbanded, and the samurai wore but rarely unsheathed their swords.[30] There was almost no military training, and soldiers exercised only police functions. Those accorded the highest social rank were samurai wielding swords, then bowmen and pikemen, and the lowest were those bearing guns. Military prestige was thus inversely related to the ability to kill. Toy soldiers ruled. The system preserved "the façade of a military government. But it was not a machine fit to fight a war. . . . The strength of the Edo government lay not in its capacity to fight but in its capacity to prevent a fight from starting."[31] A precondition was the absence of foreign threat. When in the 1850s foreign navies confronted Japan with serious intent, its military could not resist.

Meiji and Taisho Informal Imperialism, 1868–1904

The Tokugawa peace ended in the violence preceding and accompanying the Meiji Restoration of the 1860s. Subsequently interstate wars became more frequent than in any other period of Japanese history, occurring on average once every 2.5 years. This was a second remarkable transformation. Our evidence suddenly improves, and we can see clearly the influence of domestic politics on decisions of war and peace.

After 1854 Japan was forced by American and British naval powers into signing "unequal" trade treaties, opening up trading ports to foreign ships and merchant houses. They were unequal in two senses. First, they gave rights of extraterritoriality to foreigners residing in these entrepôts, who were subject not to Japanese law but to the laws of their home countries. They could not be indicted by Japanese courts even for murder. Second, the treaties specified Japanese tariff levels for imported and exported goods, whereas the colonial powers were free to fix their own tariffs. These inequalities were deeply resented, as they had been in China, but enforcement was by foreign warships, against whom resistance was fruitless.

Some realized that foreign pressure would only mount. Westerners were encroaching on Chinese sovereignty, carving out territorial enclaves outside Chinese jurisdiction. Japan might be the next victim. Hence the reform movement of 1866–68, which deposed the shogun, put down consequent rebellions, and inaugurated the reforms known as the Meiji Restoration, adapting a mixture of Western models of modernization under the rubric "strong military equals strong nation." Militarism was at first self-defense.

Japan benefited from its island ecology, and the Western imperialists were focused on China. For three decades Japanese elites were left alone to reform, an essential breathing space that China and India had lacked. Japan already had a commercial economy, and the reforms accelerated economic growth. Yet the country was hindered by a lack of natural resources and export markets, as well as overpopulation. This pushed toward coveting the resources of Korea, Manchuria, and northeastern China and sending Japanese settlers to all of them. This made Japanese imperialism more likely, although the main motive remained self-defense. Military reforms modeled on French and British examples coupled with the communications revolution enabled the Japanese to join the overseas imperial powers.

Japanese elites expected to expand outward as Western nations had. Up until the 1890s, the dominant Japanese policy was informal imperialism—opening up markets, if necessary with threats, to give Japan the same unequal rights that the Western powers enjoyed. Britain, France, and the Netherlands had substantial Asian colonies. Russia was moving into north China and Korea, building railroads connected to its far eastern provinces. The United States, France, Germany, and Britain were moving beyond Chinese treaty ports into "spheres of influence" in the interior, building railroads, mines, and factories, and leasing lands complete with extraterritorial rights. Many Asians believed this was a step toward partitioning coastal China into colonies. In this world, commented one Japanese statesman, "the strong ate the meat of the weak." This geopolitics was not anarchic, since the imperial predators collaborated with each other—the strong in league against the weak. A resource-poor country like Japan might be later forced into similar submission. Japan wanted to join the imperial age, and China was the obvious target, for as the Japanese resident minister there remarked, "When there is a fire in the jeweller's shop, the neighbours cannot be expected to refrain from helping themselves."[32] China's tributary states could be picked off. Korea was weak; Taiwan was almost stateless.

The first escalation came in 1876 as gunboat diplomacy forced an unequal treaty on Korea, which ended Korea's status as a Chinese tributary, opened three ports to Japanese trade, and granted extraterritorial rights to Japanese in Korea. The second move came in 1894, when the Korean monarchy failed to cope with a rebellion. China sent in an army to restore order, so Japan invaded, too. Japan easily won its short war, for its officers were better trained and acted cohesively, unlike the squabbling Chinese generals—a reflection of broader structural differences between the two sets of elites. The Chinese mobilized 600,000 men, the Japanese 300,000; but about 35,000 Chinese were killed or wounded, and Japan lost only half that. Japan showed restraint elsewhere so as not to alienate Westerners. Britain was willing to use Japan to "balance" against Russia, and it largely repealed its unequal treaties with Japan that same year. Other powers followed by 1899. Japan now had a freer hand in Korea without colonizing it, and Japan received an indemnity from China, joined its unequal treaties, and annexed Taiwan.

These were the fruits of a cheap victory. Japan was moving from fear of other imperialisms to seizing its own. As the world filled up with empires, it was best to take advantage of the window of opportunity before it was too late, and that involved participation in global capitalism. Japan paid for its wars by borrowing on the London market, and its Chinese indemnity was invested there. British financiers were investing in Japanese imperialism.[33] Self-defense had been the original motive, but capitalist greed and national status came to replace that motive in what was becoming a normal imperial state.

But there are different forms of imperialism. In explaining which form triumphed, we must delve into the sources of power within Japan, where Realism cannot take us. Japanese historians distinguish "liberals" from "nationalists" or "militarists" in debates over foreign policy. Almost no one was liberal in the Western sense of favoring only open markets— nor was the West itself. In Japan those favoring informal empire confronted those favoring colonies or protectorates. Should expansion in Korea and Manchuria be achieved by negotiating concessions or by conquest; should Japan pause at the Great Wall or go beyond it? The foreign service favored the first set of options, and the army the second. They battled for influence in the Diet (parliament) until that mattered no more and at the emperor's court. Within the cabinet the posts of war and navy ministers could be held only by a general and an admiral on the active list. They had direct access to the emperor without having to go through the prime minister, while the army or the navy could prevent the formation of any cabinet by refusing to fill these positions.[34] At that point, this power made little difference to Japanese policy, which was still cautious.

The Japanese government first tried indirect rule in Korea, through the Korean monarchy and local elites. Yet they could not find reliable Korean clients, and conflict with Russia was growing. In 1898 Japan had been forced by the other powers to cede to Russia the Kwantung Peninsula in Manchuria, taken from China in 1895. Japan and Russia now had competing railroad-building projects in Manchuria. Britain remained more concerned about Russia, and it signed a naval treaty with Japan in 1902. Since the United States and France took their lead in the region from Britain, Japan would not face interference from them. Japan was now the strongest foreign power in Korea, but its rulers were frustrated at Russian meddling in a country claimed as "the keystone of national defense."[35] Japanese expansionism had obvious economic and strategic motives.

Escalating Imperialism, 1905–1936

The military saw that once Russia finished its projected railroads and ports in its far east, the balance of power would shift toward it. So Japan's second escalation was a preemptive strike in 1905 on Russian forces in Siberia and Manchuria, taking advantage of a window of geopolitical opportunity. This was intended to ease national security fears by replacing Russian with Japanese domination there. No one else intervened.[36] The West did not expect a decisive outcome, but Japan triumphed. The main Russian fleet sailed thousands of kilometers from the Black Sea to the Sea of Japan. At Tsushima it sailed overconfidently too close to Japanese coastal batteries and underestimated Japanese naval skills, suffering "an annihilation with scarcely a parallel in the history of modern sea-warfare."[37] The Russian army did better in Siberia and Manchuria, though Japan gradually prevailed in a war in which machine guns and barbed wire apparently made defense superior to offense; Japanese generals were prepared to take extremely high losses in their assaults on Russian positions. Both powers mobilized over a million men, and they put over half a million men into battle. Japan probably lost about 80,000 dead, Russia about 70,000. About 20,000 civilians also died. This was a terrible war.

Japanese soldiers' diaries and letters reveal conscripts who found battle gut-wrenching and longed for their villages and loved ones. They fought determinedly so that the war would end and they could return home to restore the family farm. Discipline was fierce, and the ideal of "fighting to the last man" was pressed, but Japan had signed the Geneva Conventions, and soldiers obeyed orders to treat prisoners well. Military service made many realize that they were "Japanese," rather than having only a local identity.[38] But this was not ideological war. For the Japanese leaders it was calmly rational, although the experience for the soldiers in battle was not remotely that. But beset by the 1905 revolution, the Russian government wanted the war ended and made concessions that gave Japan unchallenged, indirect rule in Korea and the Kwantung Peninsula. The rest of Chinese Manchuria would be run by deals between the Japanese military and local warlords. It was the first victory inflicted by non-Europeans over a major European power, and many oppressed peoples celebrated. This war had been preemptive, but so had been Prussia's nineteenth-century wars and the U.S. war against Spain of 1898. In Japan it was proof war might work if carefully chosen.

There remained no serious threat to Japanese national security. The powers all had implicitly agreed-on imperial spheres of influence—Russia in Siberia and northern Manchuria, Japan in southern Manchuria, Korea, and Taiwan, the United States in the Philippines, France in Indochina, Britain in the Yangtze Valley, south China, and South Asia, Germany in the Shantung Peninsula and scattered Pacific Islands. They collaborated in China, together fighting off Chinese resistance. Might this be an acceptable balance of power? Could Japan settle for what it had, plus a gradual expansion of informal imperialism and increasing participation in international markets? After 1905 Japan's rulers doubted the wisdom of using force to expand the Japanese sphere of influence. A less risky alternative was to guarantee the neutrality of the region through international agreements giving market access to all foreigners. This would avoid Russia's seeking revenge and lessen military expenditures.

A third escalation came in 1910. Japan increased troop strength in Korea and quietly annexed it. This step was unprovoked but easy, and the main Japanese political parties supported it. Liberals had hoped to achieve regime change through client Korean reformers, but these had failed to overcome local monarchists and nationalists. The Japanese claimed to have been sucked from regime change to direct rule to establish order. The 170,000 Japanese settlers in Korea also demanded protection. For Japan's peasant-farmers, the lure of settler colonies was strong, and so imperialism acquired a social base. The Western powers protested, but Japan ignored them. Annexation was meant to decrease Japanese insecurities, but it alarmed the other powers. In response, the Japanese High Command demanded and got higher military budgets. A security dilemma was ratcheting Japanese militarism upward.[39] So far, a Realist explanation of its modern wars works quite well.

Japan added on a typical imperial mission, however: Koreans were "uncivilized" and "backward," living in "filth, squalor, and indolence," their politics dominated by "passivity, corruption, and toadyism." There was enough shared ethnic heritage and cultural affinity to make their "uplift" possible. Japanese colonialism was not yet as racist as European and American.[40] Japan could transport a large army across the sea to repress resistance, and settlers then followed, given conqueror's privileges, purchasing farms at knockdown prices and dominating profitable sectors. The main colonial actors "were not powerful metropolitan business interests but restless, ambitious, frugal elements from the middle and lower strata of Japanese society." Although trade with Korea was not enormous, the Japanese handling it made big profits.[41] Settlers and some business interests encouraged imperialism.

The Korean economy flourished under the Japanese. Manufacturing rose from 6 percent of GDP in 1911 to an astonishing 28 percent in 1940—far outstripping China or India or anywhere else in Asia apart from Japan itself. Annual GDP growth rate between 1911 and 1939 was around 4 percent, as it was in Taiwan and Japan itself in the same period, double Western rates of growth.[42] Some of this must have filtered down to the local population since average Korean life expectancy is said to have risen from twenty-six to forty-two years over the life of the colony. The Taiwanese became taller, also a sign of improving health. Japanese rulers saw that colonial empire worked. In 1912 the government claimed that "countries . . . turn toward Japan as the sunflower toward the sun."[43] The cultivation of geopolitical status had become an important motive; human societies tend to keep on repeating practices that work—as Japanese colonies clearly did. Resources gained through war had been cumulative.

World War I and the Bolshevik Revolution then dislocated Asian geopolitics. Germany was removed by defeat, Russia was weakened, and France and Britain needed time to recover. The Japanese government had wisely chosen the Allied side in the war and was rewarded with the small German colonies of Shantung, Tsingtao, and the Micronesian islands. Shantung was a possible jumping-off place for expansion in Manchuria or north China. In 1915 the Japanese government made "Twenty-one Demands" on China, which to Chinese nationalists and other powers presaged more Japanese expansion. By the 1920s Japan had a colonial empire in Taiwan and Korea; an informal empire in Manchuria and parts of north China; and substantially free trade with the rest of Asia, the British Empire, and the United States. Its expansion had involved threats and short wars in an unbroken run of success. There was consensus in Japan that it must defend its "line of sovereignty"—Japan plus its colonies—while protecting a broader but unclear "line of interest." Expansion might extend participation in international markets, by expanding its "line of interest" in Manchuria, north China, and Fukien (the Chinese province opposite Taiwan), or by extending the "line of sovereignty"—colonies.

The 1920s favored liberal informal empire. World War I saw the triumph of the liberal powers, followed by the League of Nations, and the Washington Naval Treaties of 1922.[44] The Naval Treaties limited the size of navies, thereby ending British dominance in Asia and allowing Japan to play the United States against Britain. The United States was at this point Japan's largest trading partner and supplier of foreign capital, and most Japanese politicians favored a policy of market expansion in addition to informal empire in China, not more colonies. Shidehara Kijuro, the dominant foreign minister of the 1920s, favored cooperation with other powers. Expansion would be at the expense of China, but he hoped for Chinese consent in an Asian revival led by Japan. Growing Chinese nationalism made this delusory. Japan was expanding too late in world-historical time. This was still the age of empires, but the more advanced colonies were being confronted by nationalism—as the British were finding in India.

The nationalist government in China sought to cancel its unequal treaties. Shidehara, supported by Japanese consular officials and most big businesses, said he would bend to British and American pressure to renegotiate them, provided China pay its debts to Japan. Other Japanese politicians, supported by Japanese business interests in China, resisted renegotiation, while conservatives feared a republican virus spreading from China to Japan.[45] But liberal politicians had popular support to reduce the military budget since this meant lower taxes. And the more Japan industrialized, the more dependent it became on the international market. Economists counseled conformity to its rules, and since Japan depended most on the markets of the British Empire and the United States, it would be unwise to alienate them.

So economic debate shifted toward classical economics, open markets, the gold standard, and deflationary policies. Japan was not on the gold standard in the 1920s, and liberals urged its reinstatement, which was opposed by those favoring a statist path of development. Empire, arms, and authoritarianism were advocated by "German" conservatives, whereas liberal admirers of Anglo-Saxon civilization favored parliamentary politics and informal empire. The "Germans" were drawn more from oligarchs, the army officer corps, and state bureaucrats, the "Anglo-Saxons" were more influential among the political parties and the civilian middle class.

The middling levels of the officer corps were the most extreme, and those in the Kwantung Field Army in Manchuria became imbued with self-confidence and ambition from its military victories. They saw Japan leading pan-Asian resistance to the West, through "total war," advocated by Lieutenant Colonel Kanji Ishiwara, a military theorist who saw history as cycles of short, sharp, decisive battlefield encounters followed by "wars by annihilation or exhaustion" fought by whole peoples to the

death. Japan's previous wars had been short and decisive, requiring attacking élan and high morale. But the modern industrial state was making such war obsolete. A period of wars of annihilation would now
follow, leading to a final encounter between the United States and Japan,
the leader of Asia. Ishiwara's vision of a final war matured through the
late 1920s to the early 1930s. He wrote: "The last war in human history
is approaching. . . . 'Titanic world conflict, unprecedented in human history' . . . the gateway to a golden age of human culture, a synthesis of
East and West, the last and highest stage of human civilization."[46] In
readiness for this final triumph, Japan had to expand in Manchuria and
China to build a self-sufficient industrial base on the Asian mainland,
preferably with Chinese cooperation. Japan could be a great power, "har-
moniously joining Japan's financial power and China's natural resources,
Japan's industrial abilities and China's labor power."[47] Ishiwara proposed
that the Japanese run high-tech Manchurian industry, the Chinese run
small business, and Koreans do the farming![48] Economic policy, he explained, should be aimed at long-term military buildup, not at yielding
profit for bankers or corporations. Acquire resource-rich colonies, build
a "military-industrial complex," and strengthen military influence in
Tokyo, preferably without alienating other powers. War might come,
but, as Tomosaburo Kato, the navy minister, said, "unless we have the
money, we cannot make war."[49]

Those favoring colonies or protectorates argued that Japan could expand into the vacuum left by China's decline. This was their neighborhood, and the other powers were far away, except for Russia, which was
weakened by revolution. Corrupt Chinese warlords should be gobbled
up before Chinese nationalists did so—another supposed window of opportunity. An expanding Japanese sphere of influence in northeast China
would give breathing room and long-term resources. Japan had to grow
in Manchuria, or it would be forced out. Such arguments dominated
army planning circles.[50]

There were domestic pressures, too. Victories had given aggression a
popular base. The ex-servicemen's association had 3 million members,
and "patriotic societies" recruited broadly. Conservative oligarchs and
bureaucrats favored social imperialism as a way of hanging on to power.
The Soviets were consolidating in the north, while leftists were active in
coastal China. Conservatives and the army played up the threat of Bolshevism.[51] Settler and business interests in China promised riches for everyone, and demands to subsidize settlers were fueled by the media.[52]

This coalition proclaimed the "defence of the Asian race" against the West.[53] Media exaggerations of the welcome given to Japanese settlers in Korea and Taiwan contrasted strongly with the U.S. Oriental Exclusion Act of 1924, which banned all Japanese immigration. The Japanese were shocked by the "yellow peril" scare.[54] Japan had failed to get an antiracist clause added to the League of Nations charter, since the other great powers either had racist empires or were internally racist, as was the United States. Western "liberalism" was hypocritical, the Japanese correctly argued.

The choice between these options was decided not by rational calculation of Japan's "national interests," but by the changing balance of political power between left and right within Japan. Leftists and liberals made headway in the 1920s. A cheap food policy depressed prices for peasant farmers, fueling rural riots. Workers agitated for greater rights, forming labor unions boosted by the Bolshevik Revolution and by popular demands to reduce the military budget. Political parties began to dominate the lower house of parliament during the 1920s. Universal male suffrage was introduced in 1925, and civil citizenship rights were increased.[55] Big business mostly supported liberalism until the mid-1930s, since it depended on Anglo-American trade. Most of these developments seemed to favor liberal geopolitics.

Yet there were conservative countertendencies. The franchise overrepresented rural areas whose politics was dominated by landed notables. The Meiji reforms had included little land reform, and tenants were enmeshed in conservative state-run co-ops.[56] Many rural households depended on military wages or were tempted by the lure of settler colonies. The Peace Preservation Law permitted the police to repress socialist and communist parties and unions and to interfere in elections on "public order" grounds. The legal code did not tolerate "outsiders" (i.e., national unions) in trade disputes, and workers had to agitate shop floor by shop floor, which weakened their ability to maintain the membership gains and strike levels of the early 1920s.[57] Japan developed a dual economy with a widening gulf between agricultural and manufacturing wages, making worker-peasant collaboration difficult. Much of the middle class, at that time enfranchised, abandoned its brief alliance with workers, fearful of Bolshevism. Conservative and liberal parties, controlled by the upper class and supported by the middle class, contended for power; leftists, workers, and peasants were largely excluded. All this was set amid the emperor system of the Meiji constitution, which was biased toward ideological harmony, obedience, and patriarchy. The Japanese state became more cohesive and more militarist.

Finally, the extraneous Great Depression tilted Japanese politics rightward. With exquisitely bad timing, the liberal Minseito Party government began deflating the economy to return Japan to the gold standard, just as the Depression hit. This slashed demand and investment, worsened recession, and produced a run on the yen. The 1931 British withdrawal from the gold standard was seen as the fall of the international liberal order. Japanese bankers began selling yen for dollars, confirming nationalist accusations of treason. The government raised interest rates and abandoned reforms, including votes for women and concessions to unions and tenant farmers. Liberalism was halted. The government fell in December, the normal fate of governments of both right and left engulfed by the Depression. Without it, Japan might have avoided aggressive militarism.

Militarism Rampant, 1936–1945

The government shifted to the right, and by 1936, 62 percent of strikes were settled by the "sabre mediation," notes Sheldon Garon. This deterred worker dissent, and, faced with such violence, the unions split and were later absorbed into the "patriotic societies."[58] Liberals shifted rightward. By the late 1930s the economy was dominated by a military-industrial complex that struck corporatist compromises with the government.[59] The subordination of both labor and capital to militarism boded ill for the peace of Asia.

Street demonstrations were in the 1930s dominated by violent ultra-nationalists led by young officers and former colonial settlers who received covert support from inside the High Command. Minseito Prime Minister Osachi Hamaguchi was assassinated in November 1930 and died of his wounds nine months later. The former finance minister Junnosuke Inoue was also killed, and other politicians and zaibatsu (corporation) chiefs followed. Assassins, if brought to trial, were given light sentences because of the "purity" and "sincerity" of their motives. The leftist Social Masses Party garnered 9 percent of the vote in the 1937 elections, but to avoid assassination its leaders embraced "popular imperialism."[60] In public almost everyone favored imperialism.

The economic policies of the new conservative government proved effective. Korekiyo Takahashi, the finance minister, took Japan off gold, lowered interest rates, introduced deficit financing, and boosted counter-cyclical government spending, an "intuitive Keynesianism" (of the right, not the left) that revived industry. Japan exported its way out of depression.[61] This boosted conservatism, and more government spending went to the military. In 1935 Takahashi pushed through a reduced military budget, which earned him an assassin's bullet.[62] Military spending rose under a government dominated by rightist bureaucrats. They introduced more controls on industry, ending market allocation by the price mechanism in iron, steel, and chemicals—state-dominated capitalism for military purposes. These developments produced a quicker economic recovery than liberal capitalist economies managed. As in Nazi Germany, the economic success of an authoritarian regime made a "military Keynesianism" popular.[63] Exclusively "war parties" are rare in modern politics. Parties usually focus more on domestic goals than war posturing, but success or failure in them will lead to questions of war and peace. The economic good fortunes of conservatives, and the bad fortunes of liberals, contingently boosted the lure of war in the 1930s. Such linkages in earlier history must have often tilted the balance between war and peace.

Market-oriented expansion presupposed low-tariff international trade for Japan, which depended on importing equipment from the United States, raw materials from the British Empire, and oil from the United States and the Dutch East Indies. In return, Japan exported textile goods. But the Depression, followed by global protectionism, hit this hard. Japanese fears grew of an "ABCD encirclement" by America, Britain, China, and the Dutch. Exports to Manchuria and north China rose rapidly, boosting arguments for direct imperialism there. The "resource imperialism" of Taiwan and Korea might be extended in Manchuria and north China, which were seen as lifelines for Japan to avoid "strangulation" by the liberal empires. Minerals could be better secured by occupying the territories they lay in than by uncertain markets.[64] So for both domestic and foreign reasons, the shift toward liberalism and informal imperialism in the 1920s was reversed in the 1930s, as the state bureaucracy was militarized.

The Army Ministry and the Foreign Office had been fighting a turf war over Manchuria since 1906. From 1926 Chiang Kai-shek was reviving Kuomintang fortunes in China, egged on by nationalists to restore Chinese authority over former Qing territories in Manchuria and north China. Japanese settlers and businessmen there felt threatened and asked for more protection. The foreign service resisted and was denounced as sympathizing more with the Chinese than with its own citizens. Provocations by Japanese and Chinese nationalists destabilized both governments.[65]

With hindsight, the escalation of Japanese military imperialism through the 1930s might seem inexorable, but it was not. There were long-term factors, but a more contingent role was played by Japanese soldiers taking foreign policy into their own hands, ignoring policies formulated in Tokyo. In 1928 Japanese soldiers killed the Chinese warlord ruling Manchuria. The General Staff refused to condemn this, but in the liberal period this was seen as a mistake and led to the demise of the conservative government that had failed to stop it. More important were the incidents of 1931, 1935, and 1937, constituting a fourth wave of escalation that coincided with rightward shift in Japan. The Kwantung Field Army had attracted ambitious young officers seeking action. In September 1931 they faked a sabotage of the main railroad line and persuaded the army (against the wishes of the government and their own commander) to attack the larger armies of the local Chinese warlords. They won the ensuing battles and overran Manchuria. Ishiwara was the senior staff officer involved, though senior military and court figures were complicit. Ishiwara saw the Manchurian invasion as a short, decisive war building up resources for a later "total war." He judged correctly that other powers would not intervene. The Soviet Union was in the middle of a Five Year Plan, and the West was preoccupied with the Depression.[66]

The Manchurian invasion angered some in Tokyo, including Emperor Hirohito. The liberal Minseito government ministers opposed it, but they had to acquiesce because the action had been successful. A series of failures to stand up to the armed forces followed.[67] The last government staffed by party politicians fell in May 1932. Informal empire in China had involved negotiating deals with local Chinese warlords and capitalists.[68] Some cooperation in Japanese-occupied areas of Manchuria and China occurred, but most Chinese businessmen feared alienating Chinese nationalist sentiment.[69] Lacking reliable allies, the Japanese attempted more direct colonial rule, setting up the puppet state of Manchukuo in a further incident, claiming they had liberated the "Manchus" from China.

Manchukuo alienated the Western imperial powers, the League of Nations, and world opinion. But as Ishiwara predicted, they offered only words. Japan quit the League, and the fuss subsided. But there were unintended consequences. Japan had left the community of states sponsoring the "rules of war," and a backlash came from China. Japanese rhetoric to the contrary, most inhabitants of Manchuria considered themselves

Chinese, and they were considered as such by other Chinese—the legacy of the Qing Empire. Whatever "anti-Manchu" sentiments might have lingered in Chinese republicanism were swamped by anti-Japanese sentiments.[70] Boycotts of Japanese goods by the Chinese finished off Shidehara's moderate diplomacy.

Manchukuo's new government was a partnership of Japanese military officers and capitalists. Borrowing from German World War I and Soviet models, they pioneered a mixed public-private economy with five-year plans. Manufacturing production rose fivefold and GDP rose by 4 percent per year between 1924 and 1941—the normal rate across Japan's early empire.[71] With order restored and the economy vibrant, Japan moved toward less direct rule through Manchurian elites. Manchukuo was described as a "brother country," a "branch house" of the Japanese family. Back in Japan the public read sanitized accounts of colonial progress. One million Japanese settlers entering Manchukuo in the 1930s reinforced imperialism and provided symbols of upward mobility for Japanese peasants. "Manchurian colonization was a social movement before it became a state initiative," says Louise Young.[72] But reality differed from the propaganda. Settlers had to be pressed into part-time soldiering to defend occupied areas from "bandits" (dispossessed peasants). This proved a long way from the "paradise" proclaimed by the Japanese media. Settlers who failed and returned to Japan turned their discontent against those opposed to pouring more resources into the colonies.

After the initial media war frenzy subsided, Manchukuo's contribution to the Japanese economy seemed less than promised. Support for informal empire began to revive in the home ministry and Foreign Office, and army budgets were attacked in the Diet during 1933–35.[73] But when the militarists realized that Manchukuo could not alone provide an autarkic economy, they schemed for north China as well. The solution to the problem of inadequate colonies was seen as more colonies. A purge of "dangerous thought," initially launched against communists, then engulfed socialists, liberals, and internationalists. In 1936 an old rule was reinstated that only serving officers could be military ministers, which gave the High Command a veto within the cabinet and more access to the emperor. The destruction of the Foreign Office was secured. Its diplomats had been walking a tightrope between instructions from Tokyo, the need to work with local Chinese, and conformity to the norms of the treaty ports. As Tokyo shifted rightward, in 1937–38 the diplomatic corps was disbanded, its roles handed to a military-dominated authority.[74]

The military was now in control of a cohesive state seeking further colonies. The navy favored southern advance across the Pacific, recognizing that this carried a risk of war with Britain and the United States. The admirals supported a holding operation in the north to contain the Soviets and Chinese. Most army officers focused on expansion in north China but were divided. "Total war" advocates like Ishiwara sought a "national defense state" to build up Asian resources to challenge the West. This involved dominating China. A second "control" faction sought a deal with the Soviets while strengthening Manchurian defenses. This view was prevalent among General Staff officers who believed Japan could not take on another great power as well as China. A third, "imperial way" policy urged war against the Soviets. It downplayed the contribution of material factors such as production capacity or army size. Such "economistic" calculations were despised. "Decisive battles" would be won by offensive élan. The military knew it would be inferior in numbers and perhaps technology. But Japanese *seishin*, "spiritual mobilization," could triumph over material difficulties. A study group analyzing defeats by Soviet forces in 1939–40 concluded that the Japanese were only about 80 percent as effective in technology and organization as Soviet troops, and "the only method of making up for the missing 20% is to draw upon spiritual strength."[75] This paralleled the Nazi worship of the national spirit. So did the harsh discipline and ferocious fighting spirit that treated enemy soldiers and civilians brutally. But whereas the Wehrmacht cultivated rather egalitarian comradeship between officers and men, Japanese differences of rank were profound. But blitzkrieg, the sudden, overwhelming offensive, would win the day, as it was claimed it had in 1894, 1905, and 1931, and as it had for the Nazis between 1936 and 1940. These debates were not resolved, and policy documents typically combined references to all three strategies while remaining vague about resources needed. But all factions wanted war and territorial expansion in Asia, as well as more military control of the state.[76]

Once again, soldiers on the ground decided the issue. In 1935 Japanese army units, acting without orders from above, created two new puppet regimes in north China and one in Mongolia. This put an end to the negotiations between Japan and the Chinese nationalists. A fifth escalation then began after an incident in 1937 at the Marco Polo Bridge near Beijing. Though fighting between Chinese and Japanese units stationed there may have begun accidentally, the General Staff sent in Japanese army and naval units to escalate it, supported after the fact by Prime Minister Prince Fumimaro Konoe and the emperor.[77]

These military escalations precipitated a full-scale war with China that then evolved into the Pacific War, which lasted until Japan's total defeat in 1945. The war seemed promising in 1937. The Chinese nationalist government lacked the infrastructural power to rule all the country, and it had to retreat. Konoe and army staff officers hoped one swift blow would knock China out of the war. Konoe said he would deal with Chiang Kai-shek only on the battlefield and at the surrender table. He saw Chiang's regime as the obstacle to Chinese acquiescence in a Japanese-led Asian revival, liberating Asia from Anglo-American capitalism and Soviet communism. The Japanese did not yet rate Chinese communists as significant opponents.

Ishiwara and total war advocates opposed this war, recognizing the mobilizing power of Chinese nationalism. Ishiwara warned it would "be what Spain was for Napoleon, an endless bog."[78] He saw China as eating up resources needed for Japan's future, and the war did drain the Japanese economy and manpower. So he was removed from the General Staff. But he did not have a solution either. Like others, he had hoped for Chinese acquiescence in a Japanese leadership of Asia, but he had been misled by Chiang's appearing to seek a deal—but in reality only until he had finished off the communists. Though Chiang and the Japanese both wanted to extirpate communism from Asia, there could be no agreement between them. Most Chinese now saw the main imperial enemy not as the West but as Japan. The United States increased its loans to China.[79]

In Japan the sources of social power had been fused under military dominance. The remaining political choice was between military rule and a quasi-fascist corporatist state, but neither could quite triumph. The Japanese system had relied on the common interests, culture, and modernizing intent of oligarchs, bureaucrats, capitalists, and the educated upper middle class to generate policies of development. But the state had been taken over by a military favoring the anti-parliamentary corporatism sweeping other states of the period, claiming more technocratic expertise and concern for the national interest than disputatious parties had.[80] A few of these were fascists. In other countries fascism was a mass movement mobilizing from below. Japanese fascist groups lacked mass support and did not coalesce into a single movement; Hirohito declared that he would not accept in cabinet or court posts "any person holding fascistic ideas."[81]

After early Japanese victories in China, the army got bogged down. Chinese forces avoided big battles and cut the supply lines of an overextended enemy. The war proved costlier and more difficult than anticipated. Japanese forces were overconfident victims of their own ideology of racial superiority, and this led them into atrocities alienating many Chinese who might otherwise have joined them. Atrocities had been absent in Japan's previous wars, but ideology-infused emotions were beginning to cloud material interest and rational strategy.

In Southeast Asia Japan had pursued a market-oriented strategy in the early and mid-1930s to secure oil from Java and Sumatra, as well as some informal empire in Vietnam. With a neutrality pact signed with the Soviets in 1939, the navy's strategy of expanding southward was embraced. When Hitler overran France and the Netherlands, their colonial possessions in Vietnam and the East Indies seemed to beckon. "Seize this golden opportunity! Don't let anything stand in the way," urged Army Minister Hata Shunroku in June 1940.[82] It seemed another window of opportunity. Since leaders did not expect Britain to last long against Hitler, its Asian colonies might also be acquired. An alliance with Germany and a strike southward was pushed by much of the navy, though not by its head, Admiral Isoroku Yamamoto, who knew Japan could not defeat the United States. But the army was coming around to the notion that defense in the north and offense in the south would be the best strategy.

Japan still depended on foreign imports, especially oil. Though its "resource imperialism" in Manchuria, north China, Korea, and Taiwan provided 20 percent of mainland Japanese GDP, the temptation to strike out for the oil of the Dutch East Indies grew. In 1938 the United States began shipping military supplies and credits to nationalist China, and the British planned a railroad from Burma to ship supplies to the nationalists. This contributed to a stalemate in the China War and increased Japanese hostility to the Anglophone powers.

In August 1940 Japan founded the Greater East Asian Co-Prosperity Sphere for developing Asia peacefully. Yet the next month it joined the Axis alliance and invaded Vietnam—oddly, an attack on the territory of a supposed ally, the French Vichy regime. The main intent was to cut off supplies to the Chinese nationalists. Again, local officers on the ground exceeded their orders and were successful. The sticking point remained China. Since 1932 the Stimson Doctrine had declared American hostility to Japan's invasion of China and Manchukuo. Yet Japan received 80 percent of its oil from the United States. The problem, one U.S. diplomat complained to Roosevelt, was that "we have large emotional interests in China, small economic interests, and no vital interests."[83] Yet the United

States continued to demand that Japan return to the pre-1931 status quo, which almost all Japanese leaders saw as abandoning Manchukuo and 170,000 Japanese settlers. It would be disastrous for Japan's economy and politically for any government that accepted these terms.[84]

The U.S. administration was alarmed by Japanese aggression in China, its alliance with Hitler, its occupation of Vietnam, and the obvious threat to British and Dutch possessions in Southeast Asia. It had prepared possible war plans against Japan ever since 1906, and these were later to provide the blueprint for its Pacific War strategy.[85] But lacking the military power to implement them, it had first fought an indirect proxy war by subsidizing China's resistance to Japan. Now it turned to flexing its economic power resources more directly. Its response to a possible Japanese southward advance was not to come to terms, as the Japanese had hoped. In May 1941 Roosevelt embargoed almost all exports to Japan from the United States or the British Empire. Oil was crucial. Japanese companies had already secured approval for licenses for gasoline from the United States for another nine months and crude oil for thirty-two months, but freezing Japanese assets in the United States would prevent Japan from paying for or getting it. Roosevelt approved this perhaps without realizing the consequences, though Assistant Secretary of State Dean Acheson did. Roosevelt's position remains unclear, though he had appointed the hawkish Acheson to escalate pressure on Japan. The official story is that Roosevelt discovered only in September that Japan had received no oil since July.[86]

The effect of the embargoes was the opposite of that intended. Liberals could not understand militarists for whom the embargoes were "an assault on the nation's very existence."[87] The embargoes precipitated a desperate fling. Japanese planners estimated that the navy could last without oil supplies for between six months and two years. They also saw that the United States was expanding its Pacific fleet. Since Japan could not win a long war, a short but devastating offense against American and British power was needed. When Admiral Yamamoto failed to persuade the emperor to avoid war, in May 1941 he proposed attacking Pearl Harbor as the best strategy. This was tested in war games in September and adopted as policy in mid-October, the fifth and final escalation.

Civilian leaders were not informed by the High Command, and so they did not know of the plan to attack Pearl Harbor. Prime Minister Konoe was authorized to negotiate but not to make concessions. If he could not negotiate a peace, Japan would attack. Both sides toyed with the possibility of compromise in late 1941, but it foundered mainly on China. The issue of Manchukuo might have been detached from the rest of China, allowing Japan to remain there while quitting China. Alternatively, a withdrawal from China might occur in stages over some years. On the Japanese side, however, the army was absolutely opposed to any withdrawal, and its influence on the government and the emperor was increasing.[88] It was curious (from a Realist point of view) that the higher priority than war against each other seemed to be, for Japan, the war against China and, for the United States, the war against Hitler. So why did Japan continue to antagonize the United States by its southward moves? And why did not Roosevelt compromise over China and build up his commitments to the struggle against Hitler? This would also give the United States time to build up its military resources so that it could later deter Japan from aggression.[89] But the confrontation was really between Japanese militarism and rising American consciousness of its own imperial potential. Neither allowed backing off. There were mutual misunderstandings. Japan and the United States embodied different forms of imperialism and different visions of threat: where the United States feared "brutal totalitarianism," the Japanese saw "liberal strangulation" by global economic tentacles. Both were only exaggerating the reality the other posed.

The initial success of Hitler's Operation Barbarossa in Russia pushed Japanese rulers over the edge. Japan had to seize this window of opportunity. But why had Japanese militarism passed beyond the bounds of reason? Only inordinate slices of luck could have brought a good war for Japan, as some Japanese leaders knew. Irrationality is difficult to explain. It is usually the residual in our explanations. But here it brought on war across the Pacific. In October Konoe, having failed to negotiate a compromise, was replaced by General Hideki Tojo, an army hard-liner. On November 25, 1941, White House officials concluded that war was inevitable. Secretary of War Henry Stimson recorded in his diary, "The question was how could we maneuver them into the position of firing the first shot without allowing too much danger to ourselves."[90] Secretary of State Cordell Hull insisted Japanese forces be withdrawn from all of China, including Manchuria, as a precondition for normalizing relations. This was unacceptable. On December 1 the emperor approved the Pearl Harbor attack. On the seventh it began, a surprise attack, simultaneously with attacks on Australian, British, and Dutch forces in Malaya, Sarawak, Guam, Wake Island, Hong Kong, the Philippines, and Thailand. Japan would conquer an empire or go down fighting. Tojo managed both.

Few in the United States had expected such a reaction. This was one example among many of diplomacy where both sides refuse to back down while expecting that their own pressure will force the other to do so. Instead, the opposite happens: each ratcheting up of pressure hardens the response of the other. The U.S. ability to read Japanese diplomatic codes warned them an attack was coming, but no one knew where or when. Some expected landings in the Philippines, not an attack on U.S. territory. Pearl Harbor and its fleet were seen as the springboard toward Japan, not a vulnerable asset. The attack destroyed all the battleships in the harbor. For Roosevelt it was "a day of infamy." American leaders could not believe that Japan, a country with about 5 percent of U.S. heavy industrial capacity, would attack its sovereign territory.[91] Indeed, it is not easy to understand this when Japan was already fighting in China. But American economic warfare and its hard line on China had strengthened Tokyo militarists and brought the navy to agree to secure oil by force.[92] Tojo saw that the embargoes would strangle Japan and the United States would only grow stronger. The chances of success in war were not great, he conceded. But America would reduce Japan to "a third-class nation after two or three years if we just sit tight." Peace under American domination or war against the odds but with honor—that was the choice.[93]

The Japanese could have backed down, and American leaders reasoned that they would. But it would have been rather like Britain backing down in 1940. Japan had a militarist regime with a half-fascist ideology, to which any backing down would have been dishonor, "a colossal loss of prestige," an insult to the memory of all who had died in China, and long-term subordination to the United States, says Ian Kershaw.[94] It had also enjoyed a string of triumphs in war that was being continued in Hitler's sequence of military successes. So it pulverized the American fleet, seized British, Dutch, and American colonial possessions, and established a defensive perimeter across the Pacific to secure the oil of Borneo and Sumatra. Japan could then negotiate to secure access to all these markets from a position of strength, helped by Germany's irresistible force in Europe. Japanese leaders were hopeful of victory in a short offensive war, pessimistic about a longer war. Yet they believed the United States would sue for peace after the first devastating blows, and then they could compromise. Admiral Tomioka Sadatoshi later conceded "such optimistic predictions . . . were not really based on reliable calculations." Overconfidence also resulted from the militarists' despising "soft" liberal democracies. Caged by their own society, they exaggerated Japanese *seishin* and took American mouthing of Wilsonian liberalism at face value. Had they appreciated the reality of American imperialism, they would have realized that the United States had never been averse to using its military in "wars of choice." Yamamoto was right on both counts: the attack on Pearl Harbor was the best strategy, but it still wouldn't work.

A conspiracy school says Roosevelt wanted the Japanese to attack, so that he could get American global domination after the war—a theory that is plausible but lacking evidence, and it would require a visionary strategy of which few politicians are capable. But the destruction of a quarter of the American Pacific fleet in its home port, and the occupation of a dozen countries across an American sphere of interest, caused national outrage. The Senate voted unanimously for war, and the House had one dissenter, the pacifist Jeannette Rankin, who declared to boos and hisses, "As a woman, I can't go to war and I refuse to send anyone else." U.S. officials rejected compromise not only because it would demean its reputation, but also because it had no need to. Japan could not hurt the U.S. mainland—and that made the Pearl Harbor attack stupid. Americans could fight a war with no danger to the homeland. The Japanese could not. So Japanese rulers got a conflagration across the Pacific and their own destruction, while Americans got an economic boom and a global empire. Early Japanese successes contributed to eventual defeat, for by the spring of 1942 its imperial forces were overextended, scattered over thousands of kilometers from Burma to the southwest Pacific. This headlong advance was a strategy infused with *seishin*. Many Japanese officers thought it was folly. The better strategy, they argued (an argument endorsed by some later historians), was to stop short of this and either merely take over the European empires or establish an imperial perimeter that would be defensible for a few years, by which time both sides might want peace.[95] Indeed, they might even be allies against Soviet communism. But these officers were overruled by the leadership.

Appropriately, the last great battle of the war involved the Kwantung Field Army, the cause of so much trouble. The Red Army, joining the war in the east, overpowered it, killing 80,000 Japanese. Pacific War casualties had been appalling. The Chinese suffered most: 3.75 million nationalist and communist troops were killed or went missing, and 15–20 million civilians died, mostly from war-induced famine and disease, though Japanese atrocities accounted for several million. Indian and Burmese civilian losses amounted to several million from famine and disease. Around 800,000 Japanese civilians died, mainly in callous U.S. bombing

raids, about 140,000 died at Hiroshima, and 88,000 perished in the firebombing of Tokyo—a maneuver chosen because Japanese homes were
built of wood. As Major General Curtis LeMay, in charge of the bombing, said, the population was "scorched and boiled and baked to death."[96]
There were far more civilian than military deaths in the Pacific War.

Just over 2 million Japanese troops, about 160,000 Americans, and
120,000 British Commonwealth troops were killed in the Pacific War including 20–30 percent death rates among allied POWs. Japanese atrocities included massacres, surgical dissections of unsedated humans,
reprisals on whole villages and cities, deliberate starvation, and forced
labor unto death. The most notorious examples were the Nanjing massacre of 1937 of perhaps 200,000 Chinese civilians; the "Three Alls Policy"
instructing Japanese forces to "Kill All, Burn All, and Loot All" in China,
approved by Hirohito himself; bacteriological and chemical warfare ex-
periments conducted on Chinese civilians who were invariably killed; the
use of biological and chemical weapons beginning in China in 1939; and
the "comfort stations," where Chinese and Korean women were forced
to serve in brothels as prostitutes for the soldiers.

These atrocities occurred because Japan had withdrawn from the
rules of war, though there were no rules against bombing civilians. In no
previous wars had Japan practiced such atrocities, but in the army a culture of brutality, fanaticism, and racism had built up, including the beliefs
that the Chinese were subhuman and surrender was treason. Assassinations in the 1930s had made the killing of civilians normal. Army logistics became murderous. Living off the land meant extorting subject
peoples' produce, causing starvation, disease, and death. The ideals of the
Greater East Asian Co-Prosperity Sphere were destroyed by wartime occupations. The never-surrender cult spun off into the belief that POWs
did not deserve to live. Japanese army discipline was sadistic and involved
terrible beatings. When trapped on Pacific islands, with no possibility of
retreat, Japanese soldiers chose death. On ten islands the average death
rate was an astonishing 97 percent. In Okinawa it was "only" 92 percent.
These are death rates unparalleled in any other war discussed in this
book. American death rates were under 5 percent but rose to 11 percent
in the battle for Okinawa.[97] In 1945, when the Tokyo leaders knew defeat
was imminent and inevitable, they still refused to surrender until the
United States dropped what the Japanese believed were only the first
two of many atomic bombs on Hiroshima and Nagasaki—in reality the
Americans had only these two.[98]

The mayhem of the Asia-Pacific War was a far cry from the calm calculation of Realism or the beneficence of liberalism. Its combination of
folly and evil is difficult to comprehend. Even if the big battles had gone
better for Japan, it is difficult to see a different outcome. The Battle of
Midway in June 1942 is often seen as decisive, narrowly going against
Japan—ten accurate bombs out of thousands dropped on the Japanese
fleet made the difference. But the Americans had many thousands of
bombs to drop. Even if Japan had won this battle and seized Australia,
the United States would have regrouped, built more carriers and planes,
dropped more bombs, and pushed them back again. Between 1941 and
1945 the Japanese produced 70,000 planes, no mean feat, but at the cost
of civilian suffering. The United States produced 300,000 while its civilians prospered. Ford's Willow Run assembly lines produced a B-24
bomber every sixty-three minutes. And the United States got the atom
bomb. It had acquired the economic and military power and the ideological will to become the world's greatest power. From that point on it
would act accordingly, while still mouthing the ideology of a Wilsonian
charitable association.

Conclusion

We have seen great variations in war in Japan. Its distance from the Asian
mainland made foreign wars difficult for many centuries, but civil wars
increased, resulting in the sixteenth century in over a hundred vanished
kingdoms. Warring rulers thought they were making rational choices,
but they were almost all mistaken. Only the triumvirs and their vassals
survived, and then only one of them. They were the most capable military-political rulers, helped by luck. The drive toward unification proved
popular. It came first from the most ruthless general, then from one who
combined impulsive generalship with astute diplomacy. He and the third
triumvir developed reforms aimed at peace and insulation from the
world. Japan then entered modernity after 240 years of peace in reaction
to foreign imperialism. There was long-term logic in the rise of modern
Japanese militarism. Like the early Roman Republic, the Meiji Restoration began as self-defense, but repeated victories in war combined with
fear of class struggle at home developed a militaristic culture baked in to
political, economic, and ideological institutions. The short-term consequence of the Restoration was remarkable economic development aided
by a militarism that was ultimately to undermine it. Foreign wars came

thick and fast. Abundant documentation enables a nuanced view of war and peace since the Meiji Restoration. Had I equally rich data on earlier societies, I might have found comparable factional struggles, contingencies, and ambiguities of outcome. The annalists had told patterned evolutionary tales. Abundance of data leads to a less coherent narrative.

The Japanese military was suited to direct imperialism in the neighborhood until it began overreaching in China. There was support for "social imperialism," one of the few cases where popular pressures in wars were substantial, though conservative oligarchs manipulated peasant support for imperialism. Peasants provided soldiers and most colonial settlers, boosting popular imperialism. The organized working class weakened under repressive labor laws, and conservatives and bureaucrats intimidated middle-class liberals into accepting authoritarian government. Junior army officers were violent at home and abroad. The Meiji Constitution mattered, as factions struggled over access to the emperor, which was vital for approving policy. Victories abroad increased the prestige of the armed forces in Tokyo and at court.

But the rise of the Japanese empire was not predetermined. There were five Rubicons that might not have been crossed: against China in 1895, in Korea in 1910, in Manchuria in 1931, in China in 1937, and at Pearl Harbor in 1941. The Great Depression that began in 1929 added an external shock, which aided the drift rightward. Earlier aggressions had been cautious; and the 1931 aggression in Manchuria was launched independently by mid-level military officers, which reflected changes in the balance of power within Japan that freed the military from civilian control. The 1930s baked-in militarism led to the next aggression, the full-scale invasion of China, which was again precipitated by soldiers constraining facts on the ground. By this point the Japanese military was more than a rational instrument calibrated to security fears at home and profit abroad. It was the dominant power actor, with its own definition of national interest and honor and with its own savage martial values. The final aggression at Pearl Harbor was suicidal. The deadliest war in human history was governed on the Axis side more by militarist ideology and emotions than by calm economic-military calculation. Belief in the superiority of offense over defense and seizing windows of opportunity became baked in to military strategy and prevented realistic assessment of the odds of victory. Realism was now irrelevant to any explanation of Japanese militarism.

This perverted the Meiji Restoration, a "strong military" dominating a "wealthy country." This had long-term structural causes, but equally important were fluctuating balances of power abroad and at home, the accidents of war, and military provocations. Had power struggles in Tokyo had a different outcome, a different "Greater East Asian Co-Prosperity Sphere" might have appeared, centered on a Japanese indirect and informal empire dominating East and Southeast Asia, but with an increasing role for a reviving China. But within Japan itself had arisen a logic of intensifying militarism, until the moment in 1941 when Japan catastrophically overreached.

After atomic bombs and unconditional surrender came another abrupt shift. Under American direction, Japan abandoned war and embraced democracy, albeit one where elections produced one-party rule for four decades. Japanese ideologies shifted substantially in the absence of militarism and a much-reduced emperor worship, developing a capitalism with only limited state coordination of enterprises. Although some virulent nationalism remains and prevents the apologies and reparations that postwar Germany has offered, most Japanese seem content to be citizens of a peaceful economic giant. Japan has increased its military spending every year for the last nine years while keeping it just below the 1 percent of GDP agreed to in 1945. (In 2023 it is projected to slightly exceed 1 percent for the first time.) But the size of that GDP made this rather pacific power the world's ninth-highest military spender in 2019. More Chinese aggressive moves may determine much more.

The history of Japan reveals the importance of domestic power struggles in decisions of war and peace. It also shows that those who continue to live by the sword will eventually die by it, undone by overconfidence. Conversely, it also shows the pacific effect that devastating victory around 1600 and devastating defeat in 1945 both brought.

CHAPTER EIGHT

A Thousand Years of Europe

EUROPE PROVIDES THE MOST richly documented history of warfare. From the tenth century until 1945, Europe may have had more interstate wars than any other region of the world, although this impression could result from more available data. These seem to raise four questions.

1. Why was war so important in Europe?
2. What was the role of war in the "vanishing kingdoms" of Europe?
3. What were the causes of war in different phases of European history?
4. How rational were decisions to make war rather than peace?

The Importance of Origins

As in China and Rome, origins were crucial. Europe experienced incoming waves of barbarians before and after the fifth-century collapse of the Western Roman Empire. They were not distinct ethnic groups, despite the labels "Visigoths," "Huns," "Saxons," and so on that are always pinned on them, but loose groupings of tribes and warriors collecting thousands of followers as they moved; these polities were "forged on the march."[1] If raiding was successful, it turned into conquest. By war or threat of war, they forced homage on elites and unfree labor on peasants. Desiring "civilization," they Christianized and intermarried with the post-Roman population.

The first successor states in Western Europe were large ex-barbarian kingdoms built on Roman foundations. Under pressure from outside and from their fissiparous succession practices, they fragmented, their taxation powers weakened, and living standards fell.[2] Goths, Franks, Burgundians, and others had come as conquerors but then had to defend against newcomers. War making was bred into post-Roman Europe. The Franks came the closest to reestablishing political unity within Europe, but the division of their realm into three parts undercut this. The ecology of Europe, with its forests, its stone castles and its lack of pastoral plains, protected it (except for Hungary) from barbarian horsemen, but in the seventh century the Muslims invaded and founded enduring states. In Spain they destroyed the Visigoth kingdoms and drove the Christian lords into the north. Later, Muslims conquered the Balkans, from where they kept up the pressure until the seventeenth century. So the defense of Christendom added to continental militarism.

Across Christian Europe fragmentation and defense against raiders led in the tenth and eleventh centuries to the devolution of states to local castles and bands of armored knights, who commanded retinues of peasant infantry and archers, amid a rather Hobbesian anarchy. Brigandage abounded. In reaction, peace movements, known as the Truce or the Peace of God, were led by clerics asking that lords not kill clerics, women, children, the elderly, and sometimes anyone unarmed. Numerous lords did so pledge, and had they acted on their words, this would have been a formidable peace movement. The solution to Hobbesian anarchy eventually came through the creation of larger states operating a Mafia-like feudalism. In the meantime, kingship was subordinate to lordship. "States" had very few functions and lacked taxation powers. To make war, kings with extensive personal estates could finance mercenaries, but most relied, especially for cavalry, on the retinues of their vassals. These men held their estates in return for providing the king with these retinues. Thus, kings had an incentive to make war in order to acquire new lands, which they could distribute as rewards to existing and new vassals, who in return would provide more soldiers. This circular process made war more likely, though it was waged by soldiers owing loyalty more to the lords than to the king. So highly decentralized military power dominated Europe.[3]

Peasants placed themselves under the protection of a lord. If they did not, they would probably suffer the violence of that or another lord.

Some cities survived in leagues of city-states armed with militias and mercenaries. Elsewhere, the castle, the domain, vassalage, the knightly retinue, the servile conditions imposed on the peasants were the institutions of what is generally called feudalism. War and unfree status were the price the people paid for order. Thus, Jeremy Black says, "War appeared natural, necessary and inevitable, part of the divine order, the scourge of divine wrath and the counterpart of violence in the elements, as well as the correct, honourable and right way to adjudicate disputes."[4]

Militarism and the Church jointly infused culture. Transnational chivalric ideals coupled heroic prowess in violence with honor, piety, consciousness of the duties of rank, *courtoisie* toward ladies, and protection of the poor. This was only for those with noble blood, that is, of aristocratic descent and possessing a supposed nobility of spirit.[5] Courtly literature narrated the chivalrous behavior of the knights of King Arthur, the heroes of Valhalla, the paladins of Charlemagne—although recent warriors figured too, such as Otto the Great, Richard the Lionheart, Bertrand du Guesclin, and El Cid. The culture was more religious than that of medieval China or Japan. Chivalric ideology was not transcendent, since all could distinguish between romantic myths and the reality of war, but it played an immanent role, strengthening ruling-class solidarity. War was also infused by aesthetic elements, at least among the upper classes. Knights were beautifully caparisoned, their comportment dignified and gentlemanly. Clerics often criticized the actual behavior of knights, and the literature was normative: knights *should* do these things, but often they did not, a contradiction embodied by Sir Thomas Malory, author of *Le Morte d'Arthur*, who wrote his masterpiece during prison terms for violence, extortion, and rape. Malory depicts Galahad as the only knight who can attain the Holy Grail since he is pure, completely without sin, unlike Gawain, Lancelot, and Perceval, who fail to achieve this unattainable model of perfection, despite conduct that is chivalrous. Pure virtue was not for this world.

There were three supposed sources of order: the Church, princes, and knights. The clergy believed they embodied religion, learning, and peace. The prince claimed a divine duty to establish order and justice, defend the realm, and conquer enemies. But this also required knight enforcers who were "fiercely proud of their independence, exulting in their right to violence and in their skill at exercising it."[6] Such institutionalized ideology gave young men, especially younger sons and bastards, incentive to join in aggressive ventures, driven by greed for land, wealth, and serfs, and by the quest for honor and glory. As in Rome, successful militarism in each generation baked it in for the next one. In any case, rulers lived off surplus extorted by force by their retinues from the peasantry.

Medieval Warfare

By the late eleventh century, the former lands of the Frankish Empire contained polities of varying types, around which lay a periphery of weaker polities, tribes, and self-governing communities. Many were defined as *terra nullius*, nobody's land, ripe for the claiming. Rulers of the core could conquer, enserf, and colonize their peripheries, offering land and booty to accompanying knights, farmers, artisans, and traders, circumstances resembling the early history of China, except that here priests were also winning wealth and souls, providing some normative solidarity through Western Christendom. Younger sons and bastards lacking inheritance were overrepresented. The promise of land with serfs in a newly settled area that lacked rigid status differences was a strong material inducement.

After Rome's collapse, the four sources of social power became uncoupled. Political power lay with princes, but there was not much of it. They lost much military power to their vassals. Ideological power was monopolized by the Church, and economic power was decentralized, shared among feudal lords and townsfolk. By 1000, Western Europe was what I termed in volume 1 of *The Sources of Social Power* "a multiple acephalous federation" composed of these complex interactive networks.

Over the next three and a half centuries, says Robert Bartlett, the core swallowed up the periphery, the sharks swallowed the minnows, feudal states with noncontiguous domains either consolidated them into one territorial domain or were swallowed up, and the victors developed more central administrations.[7] The Norman conquest of England is an obvious example. After victory, Normans were installed in lordships across the country, reinforced by the judicial and military power of the Norman king. Turchin detects several bands of core states stretching across Europe, each swallowing its periphery.[8] Western Europe was not yet composed simply of major states, as it would later be. For the warriors of the core, war was profitable and rational, but it did not usually need much calculation, for the odds were stacked in their favor. Rulers were also glad to get rid of wellborn, armed young men without inheritance prospects causing trouble at home: war abroad to achieve peace at home was a low-risk deflection strategy. Armed men could be dispatched to conquer new lands, just as accompanying traders could acquire new markets and priests new souls, while farmers and artisans sought upward mobility impossible back home. Iberians were an exception since the Muslim enemy was their equal, especially when it was reinforced from North Africa. The Church provided legitimacy that war was moral. There was a risk of death, but the odds were favorable against less well-organized foes, and consolations were offered in the afterlife. Yet the primary motive for expansion was economic but feudal: wellborn men lacking inheritance sought land and its peasants, from whom they could extract rent and labor. Honor derived from achieving this. In this quasi-colonial expansion, some settler groups became autonomous, founding new states on the periphery, as Visigoths and Franks did in Spain, as Normans did in many places, and as knightly orders did on Europe's eastern borders. Crusaders pillaged Constantinople and colonized the Holy Land, but after ruling and squabbling there for almost a hundred years, they foundered against Islamic rulers who enjoyed the logistical advantages of proximity.

The Holy Roman Empire was distinctive, a federation of mainly Germanic but also some Italian rulers who elected their emperor. A Diet of rulers was intermittently called to address crises, and standing tribunals heard legal disputes between members. The empire uniquely saw a persistent three-way power struggle among the emperor, the individual rulers, and the popes, whose powers were threatened by the emperor's Italian domains. This three-way struggle produced much switching of sides and balancing to prevent any one of them from becoming dominant—highly calculative sequences of wars that resulted in a much higher survival rate of small states. Though shaken by religious wars in the sixteenth and early seventeenth centuries, this federation of many states survived until the nineteenth-century absorption by Prussia of Germany, and by Piedmont of Italy. But elsewhere in Europe, state swallowing had been a more cumulative process through the centuries.

Monarchs were anointed by God but benefited from earthly fear of the disorder that followed the perennial weakness of monarchy: disputed successions. Since ruling families intermarried across Europe, claimants might include foreign princes, and civil wars were internationalized. When Henry I of England died without a male heir, several rivals claimed the throne. His nephew Stephen of Blois quickly crossed the Channel and seized the throne, reigning as king 1135–54. But a civil war, "when Christ and all his saints slept," lasted through most of his reign, fought against the Empress Matilda, who as the daughter of Henry I had a more direct claim to the throne but was a woman (in the highly patriarchal society of Europe). The war finally ended in compromise. Stephen recognized Matilda's son as his successor, Henry II, the first Angevin monarch, a strong, even tyrannical ruler. The barons muttered but did not rebel, fearing more civil war. But the third Angevin, John, went too far, importing mercenaries to help him dominate his barons. The barons forced him to sign the Magna Carta in 1215. There were now upperclass constitutional restraints on English monarchs.

Western Europe was a single ideological community—Christendom, whose infrastructures penetrated every town, every village. War was more normatively regulated than in feudal periods of Chinese and Japanese history, and monarchs were normally secure in their beds, there being few palace bloodbaths. The Church legitimized monarchs, discouraging insurrections. Dissidents attacked the monarch's "evil counsellors," not the monarch, while peasant rebels naively believed that the monarch would listen to their grievances. The papacy also legitimized the power of prince-bishoprics and monastic orders. European monarchs were restrained both by the transnational power of the Church and by the contractual element in lord-vassal relations. Royal armies were composed of the largely autonomous retinues of vassals, and princes could not be confident that if they declared war, lords would turn out to fight. Many princes and vassals held noncontiguous lands acquired through marriages and inheritances. Sovereignty was often ambiguous, and in conflicts vassals might choose sides. Some did so for pragmatism— bribery or calculations as to who would win—others for dynastic connections. Before the sixteenth century there were virtually no ideological wars within Christendom, and even in crusades against Muslims, religious zeal was often subordinated to greed. Within Christendom wars were not usually fought to the death of many aristocrats. Defeat led more often to ransoms and homage.

The period 1400 to almost 1600 was dominated by dynastic wars between rival princely families.[9] Every child born to every prince anywhere in Europe might change the balance of power, and every marriage was a diplomatic triumph or disaster, observes Howard.[10] Gains were twofold: acquiring new territory and its resources and taxes, and inducing rulers to do homage. Twice English negotiators in peace talks with the French said they would agree to let the French king control disputed lands if he would do homage for these lands to the English king. Twice the French refused the deal—in this case honor outranked material acquisition. Matters of honor were the most frequently stated casus belli. Disputed succession caused or was the pretext for most wars, as was the case in most monarchical systems of rule (as in China and Japan). If a prince or a baron died without a direct male heir, or if a woman, a boy, or a seeming weakling inherited, this gave opportunity to kin-related lords, often living abroad, to enlarge estates, prestige, and power. Monarchical succession issues led to both civil and interstate wars, a cause of war rare in modern republics and constitutional monarchies. Such wars were risky ventures, but succession crises were opportunities for huge gains of lands and serfs that might not occur again during a lord's lifetime—a true window of opportunity, as Realists say, though the opportunity was high-risk—and lords were trained to accept the risks of war. In any case, claimants might first try litigation and bribery through arbitration by a higher authority, such as the papacy. War was only the continuation of litigation by violent means.

An example of litigation was the success of Philip the Good (not good in the modern sense, since he had at least eighteen mistresses). This Duke of Burgundy paid homage to the French king yet became his near-equal in power through acquisition of territories by wars, purchases, marriage alliances, and victory in a disputed succession in the 1420s against his cousin Jacqueline, Countess of Hainault. Her disadvantage was that as a woman without an heir, she could not herself rule her estates in Flanders, nor could she find a powerful enough man to become her husband and "protector." She had married and then separated from the Duke of Brabant, considered too weak and too close a relative, so this marriage had needed a papal dispensation. This had still not been granted when she married the powerful Duke of Gloucester, brother of Henry V of England. This forced her to change tack and petition the pope to annul her previous marriage. Pressured by Philip and her rivals in Flanders, the pope refused, which annulled her marriage to Gloucester. War was avoided, since without the English she could not muster enough military support. Instead, a peace agreement was imposed, stating that Philip's claim was strong enough to grant him administration of her estates while she lived, and inherit them when she died. Poor Jacqueline, ground down by patriarchal norms of succession.

Through the late Middle Ages the major monarchies of western and northern Europe became more statelike. Then came a "state-swallowing" phase whereby bigger states swallowed up the smaller. Norman Davies has studied thirty vanished kingdoms in Europe.[11] His cases are too diverse and sprawl over many centuries, from Visigoth Toulouse to the Soviet Union, but he distinguishes five ways in which they disappeared: implosion (only the USSR), conquest (ten to twelve of his cases), dynastic merger (three to four cases), liquidation, which is difficult to separate from conquest (three cases), and "infant mortality," a very short-lived state unable to establish roots (one case). Conquest and liquidation dominated. War was the main cause of state mortality.

He identifies no fewer than twelve successive Burgundian realms, vanishing and resurrected with differing territories between 410 and 1477. Burgundies were either destroyed in battle, partitioned by more powerful neighbors, or subordinated to the kingdom of France or the German Empire by marriage alliances or threats of war. There was often a tipping point when vassals would desert the duchy and declare allegiance to someone else. Yet some Burgundian domains continued to exist as part of other realms or as small independent rump states. Resurrection occurred through the temporary weakness of the neighbors or shrewd or fortunate marriages and vassals switching allegiances. The greatest Duke of Burgundy was the last one, Charles *le Téméraire*, usually translated as "the Bold," but "the Reckless" would be the correct translation. He began expansion by using the wealth of his core domains to buy up territories, but then he switched to wars to consolidate his dispersed domains into a single territorial state. But he became reckless, alienating all his neighbors at once. He lost a series of battles against them and was killed in battle in 1477, leaving only his daughter as heir. The king of France and the emperor offered their sons in marriage; the emperor won and swallowed up Burgundy. Burgundy continues to be famous today despite having no administrative status within France because of the swallowing of its fine wines. In earlier centuries, swallowing had usually been more violent.

The United Kingdom has involved a sequence of stages not yet finished. The Normans conquered the Anglo-Saxon kingdoms of England in the eleventh century and then, as Anglo-Norman feudal lords, they conquered much of Wales and Ireland, eliminating some chiefdoms and persuading others that only English rule could guarantee their protection. The English built strong castles to entrench their rule, but it took until the reign of Henry VIII to establish English-language administration and law over Wales. More fractious resistance in Ireland led to civil wars. Then the sixteenth-century schism of Christendom (discussed below) spread to the British Isles. In the 1640s on the Irish battlefields of the Civil War, the Catholics and Royalists were destroyed by Cromwell, which led to a "Protestant Ascendancy" over the largely Catholic Irish in the following century. But since Catholicism was deeply implanted in the Irish population, many Irish lords were offering only token allegiance to the Protestant Ascendancy. The island continued to simmer.

The independent Scottish kingdom, assisted by French and Spanish monarchs, survived repeated wars with England but became divided by its own sixteenth-century religious schism. Yet when Elizabeth I of England died childless, the Scottish Protestant King James VI was her most direct successor. English political leaders had anticipated this, and, fearful of a disputed succession, had already negotiated his succession as James I, the first of the Stuart dynasty. Fighting in Ulster (Northern Ireland) culminated in the "Flight of the (Catholic) Earls" abroad. English domination of Ireland and Scotland strengthened with the crushing of three Catholic Jacobite uprisings, in Ireland in 1689 and in Scotland in 1715 and 1745. The appeal of the Jacobites was limited by their Catholic leanings, while the Scottish clan lords, like feudal lords, could choose their allegiance. Many chose the likely winners, the English, like my mother's clan, the Campbells.

The "Plantation of Ulster" established settlements of English and Scottish Protestants, which forced Catholics off their lands. An Irish uprising with French assistance was crushed in 1798, followed in 1800 by the Acts of Union, which created a single United Kingdom of Great Britain and Ireland. Its empire came to rule a quarter of the world, with considerable input from Scots. The Irish potato famine further lessened the popularity of British rule in Catholic Ireland. After a period of peaceful Anglo-Irish struggle over home rule within the Westminster Parliament, another Irish rising, in 1916, was repressed, but subsequent guerilla warfare forced the British government to grant Irish independence, except for majority Protestant Ulster in the north, which remained in the retitled state, the Kingdom of Great Britain and Northern Ireland. This state remains today, but rival national sentiments, divisions over union with Europe, and the folly of English leaders—all more peaceful causes—have generated a Disunited Kingdom, including the looming possibility of Scottish independence. War, dynastic accidents, and the choices of vassals had predominated earlier, before they were trumped by religious divisions.

In Europe, as elsewhere, the winners of the wars wrote history, whereas the losers were usually absorbed into the winners' culture. Europeans' collective memory of war in history was glorious and profitable, and their institutionalized culture was bellicose, so they kept waging war—selectively recorded path dependence. In the east, the winners were the Romanov, Habsburg, and Ottoman monarchs. In the north, Danish and Swedish expansion brought them successive regional dominance. Peoples were swallowed up by the Spanish, French, and English empires, as Catalans, Provençals, and the Welsh could attest. The swallowers were states, not the earlier bands of lords.

Phase One: The Hundred Years' War

There were three main phases of war in Europe. The first feudal phase is exemplified by the Hundred Years' War, fought between English and French rulers. France was divided into many baronial domains and cities that pledged allegiance to either or both kings, since the English dynasties had originated in France and still had many French domains. During the reign of the incompetent Edward II, England lost most of its possessions in France. His son Edward III determined to strengthen his position at home by fighting successful wars. He first fought a successful war against the Scots. Then when Charles IV of France died in 1328 without a direct male heir, both Edward and Philip, Count of Valois, claimed the throne. Philip had the advantage of being in Paris and had himself crowned king there, as Philip VI. Relations worsened and war was declared in 1337. Edward invaded in 1340, focusing first on securing the loyalty of Low Country lords. Both sides claimed a legal dynastic claim to the Crown and expected that lords in France would help them. The loyalty of their soldiers was dynastic, to their lord or prince, not their country. Much of the population was indifferent about which dynasty ruled them. When the church bells rang for victories, the crowds cheered, but when the taxes to pay for war were raised or when their sons were taken for soldiers, they preferred peace. But the people had negligible power in war-and-peace decisions. Parliaments representing the upper classes had just a little.

Campaigns were intermittent over a century. In the Crécy campaign of 1346 Edward had about 15,000 professional soldiers, the French had a more mixed force of mercenaries and vassals, perhaps 40,000 strong. At Poitiers in 1356 around 6,000 English confronted about 11,000 French.

As a result of these battles, Edward was able to recover the domains in France that his father had lost in return for renouncing his claim to the French Crown. At Agincourt in 1415, 6,000 to 9,000 English under Henry V confronted 12,000 to 30,000 French. All three battles produced asymmetric casualties. The English won all three, thanks partly to their Welsh longbow archers, who could fire more rapidly than French cross-bowmen, but also partly to well-chosen defensive positions. The English suffered fewer than 1,000 killed at Agincourt, and probably only a few hundred at Crécy and Poitiers. The French lost several thousand each time. At Agincourt 1,600 French knights and perhaps 8,000 infantry and archers lost their lives. At the final battle of the war at Castillon in 1453, both armies were under 10,000, and the casualties were again asymmetric, but this time they favored the French, as they had also at the preceding small battles of Orléans, Patay, and Formigny. In all seven battles most casualties came from the killing of troops beginning to flee, in what Randall Collins has called "forward panic."

Yet battles were expensive and monarchs had limited resources. In theory war would bring land and serfs, and so more taxes for the monarch, but that depended on victory. In the meantime, one might borrow from bankers. Debts to them were often defaulted, but this lowered the chance of borrowing again. Vassals might rally around their king's call to arms, but if war dragged on, opposition at court and parliaments appeared, and sometimes popular discontent. Struggles between war and peace factions began, crosscut by struggles between "ins" and "outs" at court. For the English Lords Appellant, exclusion from power was primary, and their favoring war was secondary, in their attack on Richard II's "false counsellors." In contrast, the French Marmouset faction was more focused on the war, consistently advising Charles V to refuse battle and let the English exhaust themselves in marches and skirmishes. The consequence was cyclical warfare. A campaign would be ended by financial stress. A period of peace would ensue, during which resources were built up again. Then might come another campaign.

Most campaigns consisted not of large battles but of sieges, ambushes, and *chevauchées*, mounted raids, by small forces. The largest was the campaign leading up to Crécy, in which the whole English army spread out while marching across the French countryside, stealing whatever they could carry, burning what they could not, raping and killing all who objected, devastating a swathe of territory forty-three kilometers wide over a length of a thousand kilometers. Such atrocities contrasted starkly with chivalric ideals. The English wanted to join battle, the French wanted to avoid it. But the *chevauchée*, which Edward had seen Scots raiders practice in the north of England, was designed to show that the French king could not protect his subjects and so did not deserve to rule. Eventually, this forced him into battle on ground that Edward had chosen. Edward won, as did the defense in almost all the pitched battles of the Hundred Years' War.[12]

Chevauchées were useful when fighting abroad. The French king could with some difficulty finance his army by taxation and through his vassals. The English, like all medieval armies fighting abroad, had to live off the land. As always, those suffering most were local civilians. The infrequency of campaigns also led to bands of discharged mercenaries ravaging areas of France, with names such as Smashing Bars and Arm of Iron, extorting, raping, and murdering. Between 1356 and 1364 over 450 localities were forced to pay ransoms to them. There were two main motives, greed for wealth and sex, and the desire to inflict such terror on the inhabitants that they and their supposed protectors would submit. In this war both the English and French complained about the taxes required, but the French also suffered whole regions of pillage, rape, famine, and consequent disease. Neither people benefited from the war. It was not rational in terms of their ends. Indeed, few benefited other than finally the French king and his clients. Their state got control of the territory we know as France.

Wars were interspersed with treaties, typically stipulating that one side should control a disputed region in exchange for an indemnity paid to the other. States were cash-strapped, barons and cities enjoyed autonomy, and defections occurred as vassals tried to judge which side would win. Succession crises, civil wars, peasant revolts, campaigns against the Scots and Flemish, and the Black Death intermittently disrupted the balance of power. Joan of Arc gave a brief ideological boost to the French armies. The fortunes of war swung around, but the French had the advantage of fighting on home turf while the defection of the Duke of Burgundy from the English cause in 1435 led to the final victories of the French Crown. Six hundred years to the day after the victory at Agincourt, English nationalism was rekindled with exhibitions and commemorative services in churches around the country. No one dared tell them that the French had won the war.

This war lasted so long that it saw two military revolutions. It began as a war of feudal levies led by mounted knights and then shifted toward infantry-archer commoners, in effect professional soldiers, signing on re-peatedly for campaigns. War became deadlier as fewer gentlemanly rules prevailed. Since infantry and archers were cheaper than knights, they could be recruited and expended in larger numbers. The expense of war brought a little more power to the tax-authorizing parliaments and estate assemblies. Finally, the war saw the start of a second revolution, when cannons operated by specialists were introduced, which proved decisive for the first time at Castillon. As cannon gun barrels got longer and pow-der improved, there was more state investment in weaponry and a greater ability to knock down the castles of the barons, and major states became consolidated.[13] The war started with princes fighting in battle. By its end they had retreated to the rear or remained in their courts.

Decisions for war and peace were made by the prince, usually in con-sultation with his principal barons. When taxes had to be raised, assem-blies representing the upper classes might be consulted, though these were often manipulated by bribery and threats. The prestige and political skills of the prince or his principal counselors were important. Howard says European decisions for war reveal "a superabundance of analytical rationality" since humans are "reasoning" creatures.[14] He offers no evi-dence for this claim. Luard lists 229 wars during the period 1400–1559 and says he *never* found any serious attempt to calculate in advance the chances of victory.[15] The combatants had clear goals, but they were care-less about how they achieved them, for to fight was honorable if in a just cause, whatever the outcome. Righteousness outweighed prudence. War was what you declared when your honor had been affronted or when you saw an opportunity to claim long-nurtured rights. Either might bring economic rewards. The prince hoped he could raise the necessary mon-ies and men, and then "in hope and in faith" he sent his forces into battle with however many turned up. Luard probably exaggerated, but the means of war were not often carefully calculated. Overoptimism was widespread, as we shall see in most of my cases.

War was in theory the way to wealth, but at the same time it was a source of honor and glory, requiring courage. As in the case of Rome, it is difficult to separate greed and glory. John Lynn comments that honor pervaded war, interpersonal disputes, and tournaments alike: "Honor is best interpreted as reputation, and for the knight this meant appearing as an example of the warrior virtues. Aristocratic men of medieval and early modern Europe valued their honor so highly that they gambled their lives to maintain it even in what would seem to modern eyes as frivolous matters. Men could fight for no other reason than to avoid any suspicion of cowardice. In fact, a sense of masculine honor led to the common, almost casual nature of violence."[16] So emotions were less idiosyncratic and personal, more the product of monarchical and aristocratic culture.

Calculation was difficult since it was unclear how many men a prince could turn out. If 5,000, he went with them; if 10,000, he could be more ambitious. The cost of mercenaries could be calculated, but hiring them might involve powers of taxation that only some rulers had. Rulers took care to assemble specialists—miners, carpenters, blacksmiths, cooks, and so on. Once total numbers were known, the logistics of assembling and transporting them to the campaigning zone (which for the English involved hiring ships and their crews), supplying them, and provisioning and stabling thousands of horses were all carefully planned. Getting the soldiers into the campaign and toward battle was the zone of calculation, the phase of domination by the quartermasters, as was the case in all the wars I have chronicled.

Once in battle, calculation became difficult again. The absence of much drilling meant that orders were not easily changed and tactics could not be flexible. Outcomes were attributed by chroniclers to commanders' tactical mistakes, ill-disciplined knightly jostling for a chance at glory, or interacting with unexpected battlefield ecology. This was a war of movement in which commanders had difficulty controlling their lieutenants and were often unsure of the enemy's position or the local ecology. Battles turned on failing to spot sharpened stakes concealed in ditches, or cavalry getting bogged down in mud or marsh, or enemy forces hidden by a wood or a hill emerging suddenly to attack flanks or rear. Crécy, Poitiers, Agincourt, Baugé, Patay, and Castillon were all examples of these contingencies. Defense was usually better than attack if undertaken in well-chosen positions. The combination of honor, overconfidence, impetuosity, lack of drilling, difficulties of maneuvering troops in battle, frequent mistakes, variable élan, and unexpected terrains limits rational choice theory's credibility as an explanation of the conduct of medieval war.

Warfare was not all Hobbesian anarchy, however. It was partially regulated through kin networks and shared Christian norms, even if these were not always respected. Anyone could aggress but only if he had legal cause.[17] There were norms of conduct in war. In 1513 the Scottish king James IV gave the English a month's notice of his invasion of northern England, in accordance with his understanding of the rules of war.

We see this as irrational, for it gave the northern English lords time to assemble their forces, at a time when Henry VIII and his army were away fighting in France. Gentlemanly behavior proved James's undoing. At Flodden in Northumberland he was killed and his army routed, supposedly with 10,000 dead.

Norms concerned campaigns, battles, ransoms, prisoners and civilians, truces, and the division of spoils. These all appeared in Henry V's 1415 Agincourt campaign. Henry, like Edward III before him, had decided on war for basically political reasons. His father, Henry IV, had uneasily weathered numerous rebellions, and he determined to secure a reputation for strength with victories abroad. The English landed unopposed in France despite the invasion's being well advertised, for the French king Charles VI could not finance a large force to sit idly by waiting for the English to show themselves somewhere along the coast. The first action was the siege of the port city of Harfleur, necessary for resupplies from England. Eventually the city surrendered and opened its gates to the English, but the terms of surrender included the proviso that if the French army arrived to lift the siege in two weeks, the surrender would be rescinded. Henry agreed—such agreements were common in sieges. The city gates stayed open, and Henry could have marched in. But he waited, honoring the agreement. The French did not come, and so he took the city and then marched north.

In the weeks following, a larger French army shadowed Henry's soldiers as they advanced northeastward, ignoring opportunities to ambush the straggling English columns. The two armies were in implicit agreement to wait until they both showed readiness by drawing up in battle formation, which the English did near Agincourt and the French accepted. The legitimacy of one's cause was demonstrated by proper military comportment—for this was a struggle over who was the rightful king of France, divinely anointed. That involved agreeing implicitly to the rules of war.[18] The English won the battle and captured many prisoners. Before the campaign had begun, English ransom norms had been announced. Henry declared he would take a third of the receipts. Captains were entitled to a share of the ransoms gained by their own troops, and prisoners of high rank would be handed over to the Crown in return for compensation being paid to the captor. Aristocratic honor meant that knights should choose ransoming over killing each other. Nor should they kill prisoners.

Yet at Agincourt, on Henry's direct command, the English massacred their prisoners after the first French attack failed. This was in keeping with his ruthless character (Shakespeare's portrayal of him is Tudor propaganda), but the English claimed this action was the result of their seeing a second attack being prepared. Outnumbered, they did not want to spare soldiers for guard duty, or risk losing control of the prisoners. The French did marshal their troops for a second attack, then hesitated and fled. Contemporary chroniclers seem not to have condemned Henry. There were norms and agreed-on exceptions. Both sides spared for ransom the wellborn and wealthy. At least 320 French were ransomed at Agincourt, with the wealthiest removed to England. When the French king John II was captured at Poitiers, his ransom equaled the English king's taxes for three years. That the French paid it, rather than choose another king (as the Chinese probably would have done), indicated the legitimacy of monarchy. Defeated aristocrats were rarely deprived of their estates except in civil wars. Some did get killed, but not many, so when the major states had swallowed the minnows and turned to fighting each other, it was still not very dangerous for the lords.

It was different for expendable foot soldiers and the poorest knights—or nonnoble women, who were often raped. War for the lower ranks was risky but an acceptable alternative to dire poverty. By the time of Agincourt, the army was waged, although only for the duration of the campaign. Most then reenlisted for the next one. It was a summer job, the campaigning season when armies could live off the countryside. The wage for an archer was sixpence per day, a living wage, even if only half as much as the lowest men-at-arms. Above that, payment varied by aristocratic rank. Loot offered more profit. The Duke of Gloucester opposed a peace treaty with France, declaring "the poor knights, squires and archers of England, who are idle and sustain their estate by war, are inclined to war."[19] Looting was not dishonorable and was a motive for launching wars into others' lands.

European armies were minimally drilled—unlike Chinese armies since about 400 BCE. Crossbows and artillery could not manage repetitive volleys of fire; the first line would fire and retreat to reload behind the second line, who would step forward and fire, and so on. In the seventeenth century most European armies finally did adopt volley fire and were highly drilled. They then overtook the Chinese in cannon technology. Before the seventeenth century, had they ever met, Chinese armies would have destroyed the Europeans, and not only because they had much bigger numbers.[20] European logistical organization was minimal. The soldiers lived off the countryside or from their pay, buying food from merchants who followed the armies. Supplying large armies was difficult.

Civilians were rarely in principle considered the enemy. Peasants were looted and maltreated because that was the lot of peasants, but merchants of countries at war traded with each other, and passports were issued to travel to the enemy's country. Massacres were inflicted on heretics and on stormed resisting towns, as was traditional. Wars were settled by treaties, which were sometimes kept, sometimes not. When the English commander in France, the renowned John Talbot, Earl of Shrewsbury, was captured at Patay, his release required that he never wear armor in battle again. His honor compelled him to comply. At Castillon, then in his sixties, he charged at French cannons. His horse was hit by a cannonball, and he fell to the ground, where he was finished off by a foot soldier with an axe to his bare head.[21] This was a continent of war and gentlemen's agreements.

Phase Two: Religious Warfare

Violence was ratcheted upward in the sixteenth and early seventeenth centuries by two changes, one in ideological power, the other in economic-ecological power. Christendom had been the guarantor of order in Europe, although perennially riven by the contradiction between Christ's message of salvation for all and the worldly power, wealth, and corruption of the Church itself. Heresies had appeared throughout medieval times and been savagely repressed. Now perceptions of Church corruption grew. Luther's nailing of his Ninety-five Theses to the door of Wittenberg Castle Church in 1517 was then the catalyst for schism, since it became linked to broader underlying forces. Simplifying complexity for the sake of brevity, there was an elective affinity, as Max Weber argued, between Protestantism and emerging merchant capitalism, but there was also a geopolitical affinity between Protestantism and the princes of northwestern Europe.[22] These were Protestantism's two main constituencies of support.

For over 150 years after Luther's defiance, Europe saw major conflict between the Catholic Church and Protestant sects, all possessing rival transcendent ideologies claiming divinely inspired truth and seeking to impose it on others. Religious toleration was rare in Europe (unlike the Mongol Empires). Jews survived, but at risk of pogroms. Yet most states came to contain both Protestants and Catholics. In states whose rulers adhered to Catholicism, thousands of Protestant heretics were killed after torture on the rack or public burning at the stake. Burning could produce up to an hour of screaming, depending on the quality of the wood, as the victim died in front of a baying crowd. Protestant rulers also burned Catholics, and both burned single women denounced as witches. ISIS executions today pale by comparison. Decapitation was then the swiftest and kindest form of execution, reserved for aristocrats or those to whom the king granted leniency.

Doctrinal conformity mattered. Whether you lived or died might depend on whether you would affirm that in the Eucharist the body of Christ was actually present or merely symbolized, or whether only the priest or the whole congregation could fully participate in the ceremony, or whether the Eucharist should be celebrated at all. Though the people were largely ignorant of such abstruse doctrines, they might be attached to traditional rituals or a Marian cult or, on the Protestant side, to simplicity of worship or hatred of clerical corruption. A Protestant intelligentsia consisting of what Owen calls a transnational ideological network (TIN) published pamphlets and translated the Bible into national vernaculars that were smuggled abroad.[23] This was a version of the "two-step" theory of communication, passed in this case from the literate to the illiterate. The literate, defined as those who could sign their names in parish registers, were overwhelmingly male. Male literacy rates in England and Germany doubled in the first half of the sixteenth century, to the range of 16–20 percent. By 1650 this had increased to 33 percent, and by 1700 to over 50 percent. That rise was a precondition for the spread of Protestantism across Europe, but the Protestant religion also asserted that the people should be able to read the word of God, the Bible. Most literate men could read short pamphlets of the intelligentsia, and communication to the masses was through sermons delivered in churches, chapels, and public squares to literate and illiterate alike. Though Owen suggests Catholics had their own TIN, their networks were mainly through the Church and the holy orders, and Catholic countries had much lower literacy rates.

Protestantism and Catholicism could mobilize mass movements. War became inevitable when Catholic and Protestant rulers sought to forcibly convert dissidents. This provoked neighbors to intervene to protect their coreligionists, which led to regime-change wars. So began the first of four waves of ideological warfare that Owen identifies over the last five hundred years. He focuses on forcible regime change. In the period 1520 to 1678 he finds seventy-nine states targeted by such interventions, of which thirty-one cases had been preceded by civil war or strife in the target country. Luard lists all eighty-nine wars waged between 1559 and 1648.[24] Half were fought over religion, half were more secular. Luard again finds little calculation beforehand of the odds of victory: "Over-optimism distorted judgements: faith in the national destiny, or in God's benevolence, or in the righteousness of the cause brought persistence in the wars which in the end brought ruin to the country."[25]

Sixteenth-century flare-ups culminated in the Thirty Years' War of 1618 to 1648. Rulers did not take to the field except for King Gustavus Adolphus of Sweden, and the generals remained out of range of the guns. Armies mixed conscripts and mercenaries, typically over 100,000 men, though only up to 30,000 could be mobilized for a single battle. Though the main direct motives were religious hatreds, it was the nature of the war that produced most casualties. Infantry and most cavalry were armed with muskets, backed by artillery batteries. Since soldiers still stood upright in battle, casualties mounted. But civilian casualties were worse. Armies lived off the land, pillaging vast swathes of territory to survive. As the war dragged on and new armies entered, the land could not provision all soldiers and civilians, and so civilians died. Famines and plagues as well as the sacking of villages and cities caused massive civilian deaths. Germany was the main theater of war. Twenty percent of its total population may have died, a figure that reached 60 percent in war zone provinces. Total casualties were around 8 million. Notorious episodes were worsened by religious hatred, such as the massacres committed by a Catholic army at Magdeburg in 1631 and by Cromwell's Protestants at Drogheda in 1649. In earlier periods sporadic outbreaks of heresy had brought occasional horrors, but this period saw persistent savagery, part religious, part survival, part motivated by greed.

The second cause of the war was a geopolitical shift within the continent. Almost all Europe became involved. The war included geopolitical balancing against another perceived attempt at hegemony by the Holy Roman Emperor, whose Habsburg dynasty at that point also ruled Catholic Spain, much of Italy, and the Spanish Netherlands. Scheidel argues that any attempt at hegemony was doomed to fail, but that is not how the other states saw it.[26] The Habsburgs seemed to particularly threaten German princes of the federal empire. Resistance began in Bohemia and then spread to Protestant princes of north and western Germany, who were then aided by the major Protestant states of Holland, Denmark, Sweden, and England. These states had been empowered by two economic-ecological shifts. Agricultural technology could now turn over the heavier, rain-watered soils of the northwest, while open-seas navigation generated trade from the Atlantic and Baltic that rivaled that from the Mediterranean. Protestant rulers and noble clients also profited by the seizure of monastic estates. Geopolitical power was shifting from the Mediterranean to the northwest of Europe for ecological-economic reasons. This proved a lasting European trend.

The beliefs and dynastic problems of rulers also mattered. In England, Henry VIII's marriages and reproductive problems left him unable to produce a male successor. This forced him toward Protestantism, since the pope would not annul his serial marriages. Henry was a wavering Protestant, commanding the burning of fervent Catholics and Protestants alike. The short-lived rule of his one son, the boy Edward VI, briefly burned Catholics. His successor, Mary, burned Protestants, but Elizabeth finished off all but secret Catholics. These were all commitments to a value rationality that today would be considered unreasonable.

Geopolitical balancing crossed religious lines in only two cases. First, Protestant Hungary allied with the Muslim Ottoman Empire to counter Catholic Austrian and Polish attacks. Subsequently, Habsburg armies fought for the Catholic cause, while Swedish, Danish, Dutch, and English forces mixed geopolitical and religious reasons for intervening on the Protestant side. The geopolitical goal of English rulers was to prevent an alliance between the two major Catholic powers, the Habsburg Empire and France. When this policy worked, the English need to join the wars lessened. Since the Habsburg Empire was challenged by its Protestant princes, it built up large armies. And since that menaced French rulers too, the alliance dreaded by Protestants never materialized, and Catholic France prioritized geopolitics over religion, once its internal Huguenot (Protestant) problem was settled by compromise. To counter the power of the emperor, the French king helped finance the Protestant armies, and then in the 1630s French armies fought alongside them. This coalition turned the tide, and Habsburg hegemony was thwarted. French rulers obviously did calculate the odds of alternative options. Other rulers were not without calculation, but they allied with coreligionists.

Thus, the war had several causes: mutually hostile religious ideologies, a shift in economic exploitation of different ecologies, geopolitical shifts, and the domestic politics of rulers. The war was worsened by military and ecological factors, but now Europe remained a multistate system. Rome could not return, says Scheidel.[27]

Three treaties, signed in 1648 by 109 European state delegations, sealed what was essentially a Protestant-French victory. The treaties, known as the Peace of Westphalia, established a precedent for ending wars through a diplomatic congress. In theory there was now peaceful coexistence among sovereign states, backed by a balance of power and a norm against interference in each other's domestic affairs. These principles became the norms of modern international law, although they have often been flouted in practice. The treaties confirmed the Latin tag *Cuius regio, eius religio*, "whose realm, his religion"—each ruler could choose the religion of his (or her) lands, firming up monarchical power and boosting the more statist Lutheran and Anglican versions of Protestantism. Europe remained Christian, but that no longer signified a single faith. Most of the treaties' clauses confirmed the sovereignty of Germany's many tiny states. The settlement caused mass migration of minorities to states controlled by their coreligionists, which increased the homogeneity of states, thereby making it easier to raise proto-national armies and reducing dependence on foreign mercenaries. Many extol the "Westphalian System" as a newborn geopolitical system, but this is exaggerated. Nor was it a shift from a Hobbesian to a Kantian form of anarchy, as Wendt argues.[28] It was a return to limited warfare, if between larger armies. Indeed, the consolidation of states and their finances into war machines continued through the centuries before and after 1648.

Kalevi Holsti and Evan Luard show that between 1648 and 1789, the number of wars declined a little.[29] Most wars were between the major powers, typically lasted several years, and were inconclusive. The main issues were disputed borders, followed by control of maritime trade and strategic naval ports; dynastic issues had fallen to third place. No wars were now fought over religion. Wars became more capital-intensive, so states became more revenue-conscious and centralized. Mercantilism saw the wealth of the world as finite, and more wars were conducted for economic goals. Rulers believed that acquiring more territory would provide more soldiers and taxes, while navigation would secure more wealth through expansion into the world. Sovereigns and their advisers initiated action, the people being irrelevant, except that the more prosperous classes represented in the English Parliament and Dutch merchant elites played an important role, helping establish a "blue-water" naval-centered policy, focusing less on European commitments. This was to favor the island British in their global struggle against France, since France was split into "two Frances," one facing the continent, urging army expansion, the other facing the Atlantic, favoring naval expansion. French rulers never quite managed both at once.

In reaction to the wars of religion, war became more regulated. The effects on civilians lessened. Army size increased as armies developed their own depots and supply chains, no longer living off the land. Aristocratic honor and rules of war restrained savagery. Cities were not sacked, nor their inhabitants slaughtered. There were debates among intellectuals about the causes and conduct of wars and numerous treaties ending wars, and international agreements over ransoming prisoners were applied to common soldiers as well to as aristocrats. Emeric de Vattel, an early theorist of international law, claimed that "the Nations of Europe almost always carry on war with great forbearance and generosity." Eighteenth-century wars were usually fought for clear and limited goals and ended with negotiated treaties. Wars were planned; they rarely occurred as a result of misunderstandings, confusions, or accidents. This period did resemble Realist rational calculation of means. Yet war did not do much good for the people.

Wars were just if committed by a legitimate ruler for a legitimate cause that could not be achieved through institutional legal recourse. Hugo Grotius declared, "Where the power of law ceases, there war begins."[30] Yet war was still considered normal, and rulers' geopolitical ambitions remained: Swedish and French monarchs attempted regional hegemony, and major rulers conspired to partition the minor out of existence. For "Louis XIV and his court war was, in his early years at least, little more than a seasonal variation on hunting," notes Howard.[31] Louis himself said, "I shall not attempt to justify myself. Ambition and glory are always pardonable in a prince."[32] Material considerations were not primary among noble officers. They raised their own regiments, and the expense normally outweighed spoils received. Noblemen and monarchs pursued *la gloire* to demonstrate their honor and status. Montaigne wrote, "The proper, sole, and essential life [for] one of the nobility of France is the life of a soldier." Courage was prized, but it had to be visibly demonstrated, and so the casualty rate among officers was high.[33]

The soldiers were drawn from the lower classes by the pay. Officers considered them men without honor, without aspirations for social status or commitment to the cause, the dregs of society. They had arrived there through conscription or poverty and rarely showed initiative in battle. Only coercion could make them face the enemy. So intensive drilling and harsh discipline ruled European armies in the seventeenth and eighteenth centuries, ending the yelling that had whipped up the spirits of soldiers in earlier battles. Soldiers had to hear officers' orders. Disciplined, repetitive, rhythmic collective movement reinforced regimental cohesion through "muscular bonding," which helped soldiers confront death as a collective physical unit.[34] Many preferred to desert.

Rulers of the major powers tried to calculate the odds of victory but, given the rough equality of power among them, mistakes were normal. Little could be predicted of the behavior of allies, consent to war taxes over long periods, or the commitment of soldiers. Mediation was not used to prevent wars, but if wars dragged on inconclusively, it became a way to end them.[35] This was limited rationality.

Phase Three: The Colonial and Bourgeois Revolutionary Eras

After 1500 came overseas imperialism. Conflicts between the first two imperialists, Spain and Portugal, were settled by papal intervention (see the next chapter). Later, naval wars were fought between Spain, France, Holland, and Britain, partly over trading rights and monopolies, partly over colonies. Though Europe was now full of great powers and their clients, their wars could be deflected onto weaker colonial peoples, reducing their zero-sum nature. Success in war in Europe entwined with naval technology to generate transoceanic empires. The European powers had world-historical good luck since the major Asian empires were stagnating or declining, while those in the Americas and Africa had not yet risen far.

Repeated wars within Europe had nurtured armed forces able to pour intensive firepower on an enemy. Improvements to guns and drills enabled naval batteries to deliver coordinated, continuous fire, while the integration of infantry, cavalry, and artillery became superior to that of non-European forces. New weapons and formations were backed up by reorganized state finances relying more on private capital. Those who lent money to the state could secure low-risk profit. Yet the degree of military superiority varied greatly. It was quickly achieved along coastal Africa and in the Americas (see the next chapter). But superiority came slowly and unevenly in Asia, where the Europeans encountered gunpowder empires and kingdoms mobilizing large, quite well-drilled armies whose rulers were quick to adapt to Western ways of war. European navies, sometimes of states, sometimes of private enterprises, and sometimes privateers—pirates—dominated the seacoasts, pressuring local rulers to become their clients. Some rulers were only too pleased with client status. For example, in India the last century of the Mughal Empire saw much military violence and political chaos, as succession disputes raged and Persian and Maratha warlords and bandits joined in. This chaos made the much stabler political rule and fiscal reliability of the British East India Company seem attractive to many Indians, especially those involved in production and trade. Indeed, says Dalrymple, its ability to get access to unlimited reserves of credit ultimately "enabled the Company to put the largest and best-trained army in the eastern world into the field" and to defeat even relatively well-organized Indian states. European forces provided their military core, but they could not have conquered such large empires without the greater numbers provided by their levies of native soldiers.[36]

Kaveh Yazdani analyzes the fall of the Indian states of Mysore and Gujarat.[37] Mysore's rulers recognized the danger the British posed and embarked on rapid military modernization helped by European mercenary officers and étatist industrialization. Yet they were under continuous British pressure and had too little time. They won the first war against the East India Company and drew the second war, but they were defeated in the third, losing their independence in 1810. The British undermined Mysore industries a decade later. Gujarat was in some ways the opposite case, a strong merchant oligarchy but a weak state, and so it was easier to militarily dominate. The Europeans tended to escalate from regime change to territorial conquest, pressured, they claimed, by unreliable, corrupt local rulers, but fundamentally because they could, except at the far edge of their logistical reach, when confronted by two major, if stagnant, powers—China and Japan.

Did wars inspire economic development in Europe, increasing the rationality of war? We can first consider the development of European science and technology with the aid of Leonid Grinin and Andrey Korotayev's list of inventions.[38] They do not discuss whether innovations coincided with periods of peace or war, but the nature of the innovations can tell us something. From 1100 to 1450 came clocks, spectacles, mechanization of water wheels, and horse-powered drilling machines, while free labor and autonomous capitalism enabled rational profit-seeking first exemplified in Italian luxury manufactures, accountancy methods, and Renaissance artistic and scientific achievements. None was related to or caused by war. From 1450 to 1660 the pace accelerated, through open-sea navigation, artillery improvements, more coordinated armed

forces, windmills, water power, and commercialized agriculture, all resting on a new mechanical view of nature—a mixture of economic and
military drivers. The seventeenth century saw constitutional political regimes, mass literacy, the rationalization of state finances and banks, large
mechanized shipyards, global trading companies, and naval dominance—
responses to pressures from all four sources of power, but including substantial military elements. But from about 1760 the Industrial Revolution
centered on economic developments of machinery, factories, fossil
fuel technology, steam power, chemical processes, and revolutionized
transport—all of mainly economic inspiration. Grinin and Korotayev
and many others stress competition among European states as inspiring
innovation: first Italy, Spain, and Portugal dominated, then Holland and
England, then Britain alone. Yet much of the diffusion of technologies
was peaceful and transnational. Scientific ideas and technological practices spread transnationally across the continent, as did the inventors and
skilled artisans themselves. War had no place in this aspect of the diffusion. Competition among states and capitalists brought much creativity,
but war brought creativity largely to war-related economic sectors.

Were there positive, unintended spin-offs from military development? As Charles Tilly and I have argued, the cost of warfare in taxes
and indebtedness led to political concessions of more representative government, which proved beneficial to the voicing of domestic policy
grievances. That was the first silver lining of the dark clouds of war,
traded off for the second silver lining, reforms to state finances that enabled new relations with finance capitalism using institutionalized debt
to more reliably fund wars (the main breakthroughs were Dutch and
British). There were also lesser economic boosts. Gunnery improvements imparted metallurgical and chemical knowledge useful for other
metal products, military uniforms boosted textiles, and naval developments were simultaneously boosting war and trade. Yet the first stimulus
to the European economic breakthrough—the European Miracle—came
from greater commercialization of agriculture, which was largely unre-
lated to the military or war. This boosted population, workers' wages and
farmers' profits, and consumer demand for metal, textile, and pottery
goods—the three major early industries. Domestic trade based on market principles continued to grow substantially. International trade grew,
organized more on mercantilist principles, which sought to establish monopolies by force. This did bear the imprint of war and produced winners, like British capitalists, and losers, like Indian textile producers.

European global expansion always produced losers as well as winners. Take the plantations and factories of sugar production, models for the factories of the Industrial Revolution—but staffed by slaves. Imperialism itself, although highly profitable for a few, killed, enslaved, and exploited far more. The possibility that major investment in military sectors of the economy "crowded out" private investment in more productive sectors is often suggested but difficult to prove. But it did not add much benefit for the mass of the people of the imperial nations until the end of the nineteenth century. Nor did wars between the major European powers bring benefit for the people. Though there were economic spin-offs from war, they were not the central cause of the economic breakthrough to industrialization. War was rarely rational in terms of ends for most people during this extraordinary period of growth.

Harnessing militarism to science and capitalist finance and industry did deliver clear military superiority from the end of the eighteenth through the nineteenth centuries, producing increasingly one-sided colonial battlefields. Yet stable postconquest rule proved more difficult than in many earlier empires of history. In temperate zones colonial settlers could replace native peoples' rights to land, and in a pre-nationalist era they could persuade some native elites to desert their former ruler and collaborate if they perceived the Europeans would win. Ideology as a driver of war shifted from religion to race. Racist beliefs were not new among imperialists—as we saw in China. But European imperialism involved transoceanic travel and contact with peoples who looked very different from Europeans. The combination of supposedly inferior civilization and different physiognomies evoked the systemic model of racial superiority that still flourishes today. This weakened the empires politically and ideologically, preventing the assimilation of natives that the Roman and Chinese empires had achieved. Racism was the ideological wild card that shortened the life of European empires. There were also many rival European empires, an additional weakness because their existence was conducive to war between them.

Wars between Europeans now included colonial theaters. The Habsburgs and Romanovs struck landward to the east, while Portuguese, Spanish, Dutch, French, and British rulers all went overseas. Prussia deviated, a major power through swallowing neighbors in Europe (plus later some colonies). But there were enough colonies to go round. Even a war's losers might get lesser gains. The colonial deflection of war helped the powers delay the endgame of China and Japan, war to the

death and only one surviving state. Instead, there was balancing, led by
Britain and Russia, against the centrally located states, successively the
Habsburgs, France, and Germany, all seeking continental hegemony.
Balancing was made easier by the geography of the two fringe powers.
Britain with its island protection had developed a formidable navy and
industrial capitalism, while Russia had its enormous landmass, population size, and winter. Neither could be easily invaded, neither rivaled the
other in Europe (though they did in central Asia), and, if allied, they
could deter a central power from fighting a two-front war. Unlike the
last ancient Chinese states, they were not tempted into a deal with the
French. Napoleon could not overcome their alliance, nor did Hitler later
(though he chose to confront the United States as well).

France lost most of its eighteenth-century wars; its debts and weak
taxation destroyed state finances and undid the monarchy. The revolution
added a new wave of ideological wars between absolute monarchy, constitutional monarchy, and republics.[39] Absolute monarchies ruled in Russia,
Austria, and Prussia, constitutional monarchies controlled Great Britain
and Holland, and republics in the Americas had overthrown monarchy
but were controlled by a slave-owning upper class under constitutions
designed to protect them from monarchy or the mob. But in France the
propertied classes lost control, which deepened ideological struggle.

Between 1770 and 1850, Owen identifies sixty-two attempts at regime change in Europe. Twenty-eight were preceded by civil war or
lesser strife in the target country and thirty-six, a majority, were French
interventions. Interventions shot up in the 1790s and remained high in
the 1800s before declining after 1815, although they were briefly
boosted by the 1848 revolutions. Europe was again stunned by ideological warfare. The shock was not confined to the carnage of war, though
this amounted to between 2.5 million and 3.5 million military deaths,
and civilian deaths anywhere between 750,000 and 3 million. There was
also shock at the revolutionary and nationalist ideologies unleashed by
the French armies. The French revolutionaries had developed a republic
of universal suffrage, executed their king and all the aristocrats they
could catch, raised banners of class struggle, and organized a *levée en
masse*, military mobilization arousing citizen nationalism.

Napoleon Bonaparte tamed this revolution, restored slavery to the
colonies, and politically restructured France. His attempted conquest of
Europe continued *realpolitik* struggle between the great powers, but it
was carried to new heights by nationalist ideology. As the manifestation

of one of the great conquerors of history, Napoleon's personality mattered. Harold Parker identified six main motivational elements: his desire to be master of all situations; the noble officer ethic of glory, dazzling fame, and honor; enthusiasm for historical persons personifying masterly qualities; his own brilliant victories and achievements seen as part of this lineage; the opportunity to match past renown in the eyes of his own and future audiences; and a compelling belief in his own destiny. He had declared, "I am of the race that founds empires," and he had encouraged the vision of himself as "the new Charlemagne," flaunting replicas of the sword and crown of Charlemagne, and conquering Germany and Italy as Charlemagne had done.[40] He consecrated his life to glory, to domination in itself. His ends were less instrumental than value-laden. In contrast, in mobilizing means he was highly rational, capable of mastering complex and dynamic political and military situations—though he could not master England, and he invaded Russia against the advice of his counselors. His boundless goals and his extraordinary military record, his Russian folly and Wellington's comment on Waterloo as "the nearest run thing you ever saw in your life," did not mean that the fall of his hegemony was inevitable, but it lasted only about ten years. The multistate system was restored.

The scale of warfare had skyrocketed. In 1812 Napoleon mobilized 600,000 troops for his Russian campaign, and two years later the German states and Russia combined to mobilize a million. Napoleon conquered continental Europe, raising commoners to kings; he was welcomed by liberals abroad until disillusion set in over French domination. The overturning of the Bourbons in Spain had collateral effects in Latin America, where revolutions arose against Spanish rule, as we will see in the next chapter. European crowned heads trembled in fear of the guillotine. Thus, the 1815 Congress of Vienna aimed at repressing radicalism so that monarchy could rest safe. The participants' calculations were weighted by fear more of domestic class struggle than of interstate warfare. Since war might bring revolution, peace was better. France was stripped only of Napoleon's conquests and otherwise restored so as to bolster the power of the restored monarchy. Authoritarian monarchies developed top-down versions of mass mobilization armies. A second fright from the 1848 revolutions led to monarchies introducing limited degrees of representative government under top-down controls. For the second time, transcendent ideologies led by a would-be hegemon had been countered. Europe was experiencing a cyclical sequence of wars.

In the 1780s Germany still contained over three hundred states, their existence largely protected by the Habsburg Holy Roman Empire. But Napoleon crushed the empire and abolished the ecclesiastical and many of the secular states and the imperial free cities. Most were absorbed into a French-dominated confederation, but the Congress of Vienna abolished this and decreed that Germany in 1815 consist only of thirty-eight states and four free cities, in addition to the great powers of Prussia and Austria. Then Prussia's victories over Denmark and Austria in the 1860s enabled it to swallow up dozens more states, more often through military intimidation than actual battle. This culminated in the final act, the defeat of France in 1870, when Bavaria and Württemberg "voluntarily" joined the Prussian federation, having seen what happened to the Hanoverian and Saxon rulers who had resisted. By then most German elites agreed that unification was necessary since small states could no longer protect them. In Germany war had been the main destroyer of the vanished kingdoms. Italy too was unified by the Kingdom of Sardinia-Piedmont and Garibaldi's republican forces through a series of small wars against Austria and the other states, though the final capitulation of the Papal States was through intimidated negotiation. States had continued to vanish violently.

Between 1816 and 1992, Tanisha Fazal finds that 66 of the existing 207 states "died," in the sense of losing control of foreign policy to another ruler. Only 11 died after 1945. Of the dead, 40 percent had been buffer states, and 50 of the 66 deaths (76 percent) occurred through military violence. About half of these were later resurrected, such as the countries conquered by German forces in World War II. But 35 (70 percent) of the permanently disappeared states died violently, predominantly German, Italian, and Indian. She attacks IR models like "balancing" and does not find that rival major powers sought to preserve buffer states between them, since these were the most likely to die. Instead, a major neighboring ruler would preempt another neighbor to acquire a buffer state they both desired, even when this meant the two would become direct neighbors with no buffer between them. Major rulers were just greedy, and war was still the primary cause of vanishing kingdoms.[41]

The number of wars in Europe between 1815 and 1914 declined as a response to the revolutionary period, though only by 13 percent.[42] Wars were also shorter. The Crimean War of 1853–56 was the deadliest because it involved several powers. Several Russian-Ottoman skirmishes occurred, and then Crimea saw intervention by Britain and France for balancing reasons, to prop up the Ottoman Empire and prevent Russian control of the Black Sea. The war produced over 500,000 military deaths, two-thirds of them from disease. Russian and Ottoman civilian deaths are unknown. None of the other five European interstate wars of the century killed many civilians. The Austro-Prussian War lasted only seven weeks but killed over 100,000 soldiers, mostly Austrian; the two Schleswig Wars of 1848–51 and 1864, pitting Prussia against Denmark (and its allies), killed under 3,000 soldiers; the Franco-Prussian War of 1870–71 killed about 180,000 soldiers (three-quarters of them French); the 1878 Austrian seizure of Bosnia-Herzegovina from the Ottomans cost just over 3,000 Austrian soldiers' lives, two-thirds from disease, while Ottoman deaths are unknown; and the Balkan Wars of 1912–13 killed about 140,000. These were quite short wars with decisive victors. Except for the Balkan Wars, they were not very ideological and are largely explicable in Realist terms. Yet during the nineteenth century civil wars grew in the Austro-Hungarian and Ottoman empires and in Spain. Holsti classifies wars by their most dominant issue. He says wars of national liberation against empires were in this era the most frequent, dominant in 37 percent of wars. Territorial issues declined from 25 to 14 percent, while commercial and navigational issues declined from 14 to 4 percent.[43] British-regulated free trade combined with pragmatic use of tariffs by other states had largely replaced protectionist wars.

Further afield, Europeans were perpetually at war, yet rarely against each other. There was a big if uncountable rise in the number of colonial wars fought against the natives of other continents. Owen does not mention that all his three ideological rivals, authoritarian monarchies, constitutional monarchies, and republics, embarked on identical wars of conquest, all installing repressive authoritarian rule over native peoples. He excludes regime changes in the colonies, saying, "I limit targets to sovereign states because such cases are most relevant to IR theory."[44] This is conforming to an academic discipline rather than explaining the nature of war. He also excludes most early interventions by the British in India and the Dutch in Southeast Asia since these were by private companies. At its height in 1803 the British East India Company had an army of 260,000—twice the size of the British army at the time. It fought numerous wars, including big ones against the Gurkhas, Gujarat, and Mysore, imposing regime change on them.[45] Owen does not include regime change imposed by Europeans in the Americas or by Japanese. The excluded cases were ideological wars since the colonial powers claimed they would elevate the savage and decadent races by imposing civilization and the true word of God on them. Thus, Owen misses the longest-lived wave of ideological regime change, colonialism.

There proved to be not much economic profit in most colonies, but the aggressors did not want to be left out of the race—just in case. The struggle was also for imperial status, a "place in the sun." Deflecting war onto the native peoples avoided major conflict with other imperial powers. The "Scramble for Africa" might have threatened this, but in 1885 fourteen powers—eleven European states, and Russia, the Ottomans, and the United States—signed the Treaty of Berlin, which allowed the signatories to claim an African territory if they could effectively patrol its borders. This set off a race by powers focused on their own expansion rather than disputing anyone else's. Despite a few MID incidents, almost all Africa was claimed without inter-imperial wars. At the very end of the nineteenth century, two non-European powers joined in: Japan attacked imperial dependencies of China, and the United States joined the attacks on China and destroyed the remaining Spanish Empire. Imperialism was globally triumphant, at enormous human cost, by 1910. Then it fell apart.

The Two World Wars

This period culminated in the suicide of imperialism in the two deadliest and least rational or profitable wars in history. As Table 10.1 reveals, World War II had the highest absolute fatality rate and the highest annual rate of fatalities, as well as the greatest genocidal component, of any war in history. World War I had the second-highest annual level of fatalities in history. There was little rationality on display in either of them. I discuss soldiers' experience of them in chapter 12, but here I deal briefly with causes.[46]

In the decades before 1914, Europe seems to have had a stable geopolitical order centered on two great power alliances: the central powers, Germany and Austria-Hungary, ranged against the Triple Entente of Britain, France, and Russia. A balance of power between them seemed to have secured peace in Europe. The two Balkan Wars of 1912–13 enlarged Serbian ambition, to the alarm of Austria-Hungary. But the major powers were sharing the spoils of Africa and Asia, the Anglo-German naval race ended in 1912, and mass armies might deter war. But the great powers and their clients were filling the entire space of Europe so that any war between them would be disastrous.

In July 1914 the Austrian Archduke Franz Ferdinand was assassinated in Sarajevo by a cell of Serb nationalists, who bungled the operation but almost by accident managed to kill him. Trouble between Austria-Hungary and Serbia was predictable, likely to lead to a Third Balkan War. But the assassination crisis escalated during the next thirty-seven days to the Great War, which engulfed almost the whole of the continent plus colonies elsewhere. The two alliances held up, but in war not peace, as Russia, France, and then Britain joined the Serb side, and Germany joined with Austria-Hungary. This has been viewed by Realists as a failure of balancing alliances amid power transitions, an inability to cope with the destabilizations posed by Serbia's rise in the Balkans, Russia's rising military power, the decline of the Habsburgs, and the transformation of Prussia into a globally ambitious Germany. German rulers have been usually blamed most for the escalation, especially by encouraging Austria-Hungary to fight. Yet the tyranny of history meant that war remained the default mode of diplomacy for all the powers. If negotiations broke down, war was still normal. The cult of the offensive sweeping high commands brought further danger. Thus, once the crisis in Serbia hit and war loomed, the trigger-happy mobilizations of Russia, Austria, and Germany reinforced one another too quickly for the diplomats to open effective channels of negotiation—and Britain's ultimatum to Germany to deter any invasion of Belgium came too late.

Almost all rulers believed the war would be won quickly by swift offense. None had made plans for the massive industrial and military mobilization that proved necessary. Nor had they made a plan B for a negotiated peace: unconditional surrender or nothing, which yielded decision making to the generals.[47] Of course, the war showed how wrong they were, for in the battles of 1914–18 defense triumphed over attack on the Western Front, producing calamitous casualties, though there was very little movement of fronts (see chapter 12). These might be considered understandable mistakes, except that the example of the carnage of the U.S. Civil War was before them. Those who pressed for war believed with arrogant condescension that this had been due to Americans being amateurs at war (see chapter 11).

In volume 2 of *The Sources of Social Power* I offered a half-serious "cock-up/foul-up" theory of how European states entered this war, emphasizing miscalculations on all sides.[48] This now seems the orthodox view, argued in different ways by Christopher Clark and Thomas Otte.[49] Clark lays much of the blame for the war on the Russian hasty military mobilization. But he emphasizes mainly the microprocesses of diplomacy by all powers. He concludes that the actors were "watchful but unseeing, haunted by dreams, yet blind to the reality of the horror they were about to bring into the world." They were sleepwalkers, fallible, unimaginative, miscalculating and misjudging situations. But additionally these were not unitary states. Decision making in all of them was fragmented among different agencies, ministries, and embassies. The powers of the monarchs were uncertain, their courts were riven by intrigue, deception was common, and leaders gave differing official and unofficial information to the press. All this made assessments of other states' reactions to changing events difficult. Should the Kaiser's statements be regarded as German policy, or those of the chancellor, or those of leading German ambassadors or generals, since they all differed? Some decision makers did warn of the likelihood and dire consequences of war but were outmuscled in the political intrigue.

Otte's blow-by-blow account of the onset of war is similar. He concludes:

> Abstract concepts, such as the "balance of power" or the "alliance system" did not cause Europe's descent into war. Nor did states in the abstract propel the Powers along the path towards war. . . . Individuals acting in response to external and internal stimuli, and to perceived opportunities and threats, were central to the developments in July 1914. Their hawkish or dovish views on the perceived realities of international politics, and how they manoeuvred in the space given to them within the existing political arrangements in their respective countries, hold the key to understanding how and why Europe descended into world war."[50]

His cast list is 160 men (no women) spread across Europe—monarchs, presidents, prime and foreign ministers, diplomats, generals, some of their staffs, as well as one cell of Serbian terrorists. This amounted to quite a lot of people, but drawn from a very narrow social stratum. Otte lays much of the blame on their failings, portraying them as men of limited vision and abilities, inadequate to the task confronting them. Some were ditherers, others reckless. Like Clark, Otte suggests that decision making was haphazard. As we have seen so often in the run-up to wars, whose policy won out month by month in a fast-developing crisis depended more on political power within each capital than on calculative realpolitik. Gross errors proliferated.

Austria-Hungary lacked coherent decision making, and discussion between the two capitals, Vienna and Budapest, was slow. A war party in Vienna triumphed with a *Balkanpolitik* vision focused on punishing Serbia for the assassination and its claim to a Greater Serbia. By war the honor and status of the monarchy could be saved and nationalist insurgents repressed, and little attention was paid to the wider consequences. This was aggravated in Berlin by factional divisions. Prowar generals like Helmuth von Moltke and Erich von Falkenhayn had privileged access to the monarch, hated France, and thought war would stop the rise of both the capitalist class and socialism in Germany. The Kaiser was ruled by a desire to assert German and his own personal honor and prestige. The result was that a few German leaders foolishly gave Austria carte blanche in Serbia, promising German support whatever Austrian actions might be. Yet Austrian aggression against Serbia would probably bring in Russia. But since others in Berlin feared Russia's growing military strength, they reasoned that Russia should be confronted before its current military modernization was complete—a window of opportunity. There were varied German motivations, domestic and foreign. These were also apparent later, during the war, when the proponents of unrestricted submarine warfare won out, thus bringing a reluctant President Woodrow Wilson into the war.

Otte also blames Austria, whose court war party was hell-bent on punishing Serbia, to preserve the prestige, even the survival, of the Habsburg dynasty. The assassination of the archduke was a tragic blow, for he had been a moderate in Vienna, and his death fatally weakened the peace party whose reforms had been lowering the ethnic tensions of the empire. Now hard-liners, especially generals, led the way to war.[51] Otte sees their actions as the first great provocation. In St. Petersburg a more defensive mentality contended with those arguing that aiding the Serbs could maintain the prestige of the Romanovs—and perhaps avoid revolution. Some sought control of the Black Sea and the Bosphorus. There was a disconnect between politicians and generals, and a foolish belief that military mobilization could be kept secret. Otte sees the Russian mobilization as a second provocation. French diplomacy was obsessed with bolstering Russian commitment to the Franco-Russian alliance, which might deter a German attack. In London the pacifist wing of a divided Liberal cabinet threatened resignation if the government uttered military threats. Their resignation would have brought down the Liberals and forced an election that they would probably lose. This domestic political fear prevented Foreign Secretary Edward Grey from issuing deterrent threats to Germany.

Were these all just "mistakes"? Cumulatively, they surely confound Realist theory. The balance of power had seemed rational during peacetime, when it was not needed, but the rapid downward spiral to war was too much for it. A combination of fear and feckless brinkmanship among decision makers in the capitals resembled declining Chinese dynasties launching aggressive war. No statesman would back down, for reasons of great power status and personal honor. This meant less careful calculation of alternative policies or of the odds of victory. All the rulers were caged within their own states and nations, exaggerating national resolve and unity, minimizing the enemy's, particularly one with a different political system. They believed threatening war would deter the enemy from going to war. So they tried brinkmanship to gain leverage. That strategy was irrational because they all followed it and so no one backed down.[52]

The dominant view of the development of war-making capacity through history sees greater and greater complexity, made manageable by bureaucratic state control.[53] True, the armed forces had rigid command structures (blurred a little by rivalry between the services), yet this was not so of rulers' decision making. The states contained numerous institutions. Army High Commands were coherent bureaucratic organizations, but some had autonomy from monarchs and politicians, particularly over mobilization policy. The German chancellor seemed not to know that the High Command's "defensive" mobilization plan involved seizing railheads in Belgium, which would probably force France and Britain to declare war (and it did). Russian rulers were ignorant of their High Command's mobilization plans. Some countries had contending courts and parliaments, courtiers and politicians, while in others parliaments and cabinets contained bickering parties. Foreign services had their own networks. Five great powers and several minor powers with very varied constitutions had little understanding of each other. The 160 persons Otte identified were scattered across institutions, all trying to shape foreign policy—only half the number of Roman senators who made decisions for war, but these had met in a single chamber to collectively and openly debate policy. The Chinese imperial court had two principal loci of decision making, the inner and outer courts, often factionalized, but with decision making far more concentrated than in Europe in 1914. Absolute monarchs, dukes, daimyo, and dictators across

Eurasia had small councils of state, perhaps containing contending views, but able in a single room to argue directly with each other. The First World War resulted from multiple interacting causes, structural, personal, and emotional. It was not accidental, for the escalations were willed or structurally induced, but it was a series of feckless reactions to fear, benefiting no one and destroying all three monarchies that had started it—the triumph of irrationality of ends, perhaps the most extreme of all my cases.

The slide to World War II differed. Decision making was more coherent, for this was naked aggression encountering survival defense. But this was primarily an ideological war. German revisionist demands for the restoration of lost territories were important, a consequence of the first war and a necessary cause of the rise of Nazism. But Hitler and the Nazis added to it a transcendent ideological vision of a Thousand-Year Reich stretching right across Europe, and then the world. The period 1910 to 2003, says Owen, contained the third wave of ideological wars.[54] World War I does not really fit his model since ideologies barely figured, though nationalism was whipped up by the war. But between 1917 and 2003 Owen lists seventy-one cases of wars imposing regime change. The United States fought twenty-five of them, the USSR nineteen, and Germany six. He largely omits Japan, yet Japan forcibly changed regimes in seven countries. From 1918 to after 1945 almost all wars were substantially ideological. From the Allied intervention against the Bolsheviks to the Soviet invasions of Poland and Iran in the 1920s, to the Japanese invasions of China and Manchuria, the Spanish Civil War, and Italian intervention in the Horn of Africa in the 1930s, to World War II, motives for wars were couched within transcendent ideologies. State socialism, fascism, Japanese militarism, and capitalist democracy all led rulers to impose their rival forms of world order. Then the Cold War narrowed down the conflict to state socialism versus capitalist democracy.

In the run-up to World War II, ideological power played an important role in preventing the traditional balancing alliance among Britain, France, and Russia, which might deter Nazi Germany. There were obstacles in Eastern Europe, notably the opposition of Poland to Soviet troops passing through its territory in case of war, and the capitalist powers were not confident of the ability of the Red Army, so soon after its disastrous purges in 1937. Yet for them antisocialism proved a more alluring ideology than antifascism, and this overwhelmed the rational geopolitics of balancing. Britain and France did little to secure Soviet support for a collective deterrence of Hitler, which led Stalin—fearing their lack of determination to fight—into his Non-Aggression Pact with Hitler.[55] But then Stalin obstinately clung to his belief that Hitler would not open a two-front war by invading the Soviet Union, despite the mountain of intelligence reports of a German military buildup on the frontier. For Hitler, the second front made sense now, before the Red Army was restored to its former level of efficiency and before the United States might join the war. But Stalin "remained in complete denial," says Kershaw. Even as the invasion began, he believed that it was launched by German officers without authorization from Hitler. If he spoke to Hitler, all would be sorted out, he said. Kershaw calls this "the most extraordinary miscalculation of all time"—though there is a lot of competition for that honor.[56] Yet Stalin was a murderous dictator, with whom no one dared argue—sensibly so, for he shot eight of his generals after the front collapsed. The balancing coalition did come later, at least between Britain and the Soviets (for France had submitted), helped by the United States. Hitler had finally knocked geopolitical sense into Stalin. In 1943 Stalin tried again to interest Hitler in a joint pact, but Hitler's genocidal plans prevented this.

Hitler's state comprised a vast array of institutions, divided between state bureaucracies, the Nazi Party, and the Nazi paramilitaries, all spawning rival satrapies. Yet Hitler's charismatic dominance and the "leadership principle" meant that in practice they sought to "work toward the Führer," trying to anticipate what he would have wanted them to do, which was always the most "radical" option.[57] This produced a cohesive environment backing up Hitler's prejudices and decisions. Mussolini and Japanese military leaders provided weaker versions of this. The means pursued were irrational, however, dominated by fascist ideology: war was virtuous and its new martial breed of men could overcome the odds. Nazism also came to apply its ruthless militarism to exterminating "lower" races—Jews, Slavs, gypsies, and others. Mussolini went along with this and wanted imperial prestige from colonies in Africa more than any economic benefit they would bring. Japan provided a half-fascist, half-racist version of conquest imperialism. The Axis powers valued martial values more than did the liberals or state socialists, and this led their leaders to underestimate the enemy's bellicosity if attacked. Hitler thought liberal Britain and France would not declare war if he invaded Poland, since they had tolerated his other aggressions. He was right that French forces could be beaten, but that victory was due to the brilliant tactics of his generals. It might have gone otherwise. After the fall of France, he expected Britain to come to terms—indeed, some British revisionist historians have argued that its leaders should have done this in order to preserve the empire. Yet British geopolitical understandings focused on the need to defend imperial honor, and this inevitably took British leaders into the war. In the vital cabinet meeting in 1940, before Churchill had acquired significant authority as prime minister, even appeasers like Lord Halifax came around to the view that they had to fight.[58] Preserving honor was predominant in both the autocracies and the democracies. Of course, as Kershaw notes, this was confrontation between two political extremes, not typical of other modern wars. The four autocracies he discusses conferred far more power on a single leader than did the two democracies, the United Kingdom and the United States. But one should not generalize that autocracies are more likely to go to war than democracies.

Hitler expected the "rotten Bolshevik" regime of Stalin to collapse once he invaded Russia, and then he could finish off Britain. Of course, neither happened. That the obdurate resistance of Soviet and British forces turned into victory required the entry of the United States into the war. Although the Roosevelt administration was already assisting the British before its formal entry into the war, this was on a small scale and was geared to American economic interests in gaining entry to the markets of the British Empire and exhausting British gold reserves. The American declaration of war in Europe came on December 11, 1941, after Hitler's declaration of war on the United States earlier that day and four days after the Japanese attack on U.S. territory at Pearl Harbor on December 7. As we have seen, overoptimistic ideology deluded Japanese decision makers into believing that the United States might have the stomach only for a brief struggle after Pearl Harbor. Here I deal with Hitler's reasoning.

Some historians have seen Hitler's decision to declare war on the United States as utterly irrational. Brendan Simms and Charlie Laderman say it was a calculated gamble.[59] Kershaw offers a more nuanced view. These authors agree that Hitler felt that war with the United States was inevitable at some point in the future and that he thought it was better to start it preemptively, specifically by unleashing all restrictions on U-boat commanders when sighting American ships. (His unleashing order came two days before his declaration of war.) His decision must be seen in the context of his ideology, however. As Kershaw asserts, Hitler

had consistently declared that he sought world conquest. Hitler also believed that Jewish capitalism was his main global enemy, dominating U.S.
governments. So "inevitability" came not from purely geopolitical calculations, but from his ideological commitment to world conquest and the
elimination of a nonexistent Jewish world conspiracy. Nor was victory
over the United States achievable. Hitler could not hurt the continental
United States, apart from his U-boats offshore. But even their threat was
eliminated over the next two years. His declaration of war also only
made it more likely that Roosevelt would fight in Europe as well as
across the Pacific. As tensions had mounted with Japan, Roosevelt was already transferring naval units from the Atlantic to the Pacific, and the
Pearl Harbor attack might have led the United States to neglect Europe,
giving Hitler time to finish off Britain and Russia, and tolerating a minor
level of American aid to them in the meantime. Hitler's declaration also
removed all opposition in Congress, which had up till then resisted
Roosevelt's attempts to join the war in Europe. Kershaw adds that Hitler's temperament and dictatorial status also influenced him. He made
the decision "swiftly, and without consultation"; he was "headstrong,"
"rushing into Japan's arms," "ecstatic about Pearl Harbor." Joachim von
Ribbentrop, echoing Hitler, said, "A great power doesn't let itself have
war declared on it, it declares war itself." Hitler was impressed by Japanese "audacity"; that was his kind of move. His colleagues privately criticized his "dilettantism" and "his limited knowledge of foreign countries."
They said of the declaration, "We couldn't be more surprised," and it was
"politically a mistake." Kershaw concludes that from Hitler's point of
view, his decision was "rational" but not "sensible."[60] But we don't have
to adopt Hitler's definition of rationality. That would also have us describing the Holocaust as rational, from his point of view. His declaration of war had strong ideological, impulsive, irrational, false, and even
suicidal currents. His misperceptions were due to a caging ideology:
trapped within the worldview of his own Reich, he could not have an accurate perception of the outside enemy.

World War II was an ideological war like the wars of religion. The
aggressors were irrational, and there was at first a desperate defensive rationality shown by the Allies, especially by the Soviet people. Those who
were communists or Jews could expect to be murdered after a Nazi victory, while all Slavs could expect to be enslaved. No wonder they fought
like hell. Another ideological struggle between the United States and the
Soviet Union then inherited the earth. This was not anarchic geopolitics,

for only two major powers were clashing through competing ideologies involving conflicting ways of structuring the world.

Finally, we can ask whether these wars produced much benefit. World War I killed about 20 million people and World War II 75 million. World War II did quash fascism, a major benefit. MacMillan also identifies substantial spin-off benefits from these wars, arguing like Arthur Marwick before her that mass-mobilization warfare, demanding mass sacrifices by the citizens, brought rewards to them afterward.[61] But that neglects the great variety of aftermaths, and it misreads the nature of military power. I noted that military power combines strict hierarchy with intense comradeship. These writers focus only on the comradeship. But mass-mobilization warfare brings both hierarchy and comradeship to the mass of the people. Consequences varied according to whether armed forces were victorious or defeated. One army collapsed during the first war, the Russian. What collapsed was hierarchy, the ability of officers to coordinate action or discipline their soldiers. Indeed, many junior officers joined together in comradeship with their soldiers to achieve a socialist revolution—which promised much, always praised comradeship, but delivered more pain than benefit. The other defeated powers saw attempts at revolution, but these failed because military and political hierarchies mostly remained in place. There was a boost to center-left regimes after the war, and they began to deliver reforms but they were overwhelmed by a fascist revival conjoining hierarchy and comradeship. Army veterans were the core of all fascist movements, which also had large paramilitaries.[62] Fascists too brought much more pain than benefit.

Things were better for the victorious countries in the first war. There was less pain and large promises were made, but again the hierarchies remained in place. MacMillan argues that World War I produced a surge in women's suffrage. In the United States, minor participation in the war did contribute a little to the push in a long sequence of victories for women in a growing number of states, as they secured equal rights amendments, though not at the federal level. Yet in Britain suffrage had been promised by the Asquith government before the war and was delayed by the war. Women property owners got the vote in 1920, other women followed in 1929. But Frenchwomen did not get the vote until after World War II, Russian women got a delusory vote, while improvements for women in Germany and Italy were undermined by fascism, a more powerful legacy of the first war. Nor were there many new welfare programs among the combatant countries. The promise of "homes fit for heroes" after the war was kept only for a few. In Britain Labour Party participation in the wartime government did lead to a surge in its vote, which continued through the 1920s. But it achieved little and was badly broken by the Great Depression. It became a major party again in the election of 1935. Everywhere, promises of political rights to colonized peoples made in 1914 were broken. Indeed, the victorious powers got new colonies formerly ruled by the Germans and Ottomans, renamed "Mandated Territories of the League of Nations." To the victors go the spoils.

MacMillan is on firmer ground with World War II, after which some peoples saw full employment, some redistribution of wealth, and some welfare reforms. Yet these gains were less likely in the combatant countries than in the neutral or occupied Scandinavian countries.[63] Of the combatants, Britain benefited because of Labour's shrewd participation in the wartime government. Churchill's Tories ran the war, and Labour managed the home front—and used their ministries to plot reforms after the war. Labour's massive victory in the 1945 election and its subsequent reforms ensured the British welfare state. So this achievement was due to political power relations as well as to the war. Most Americans did benefit economically from the wartime boom, but they gained least in welfare benefits afterward (except for veterans). The Soviet Union never recovered its growth rates of the interwar period. Colonized peoples did gain since they had enjoyed a wartime license to kill white people, and they saw that the whites had been weakened by the war. Successful independence movements, starting with India, grew into an unstoppable global wave.[64] Wars often have unintended silver linings for some, but these rarely figured in the original calculations for war; the Indian nationalists were an exception, for they had joined the British war effort on condition of getting independence afterward.

MacMillan also cites technological innovations, relying on a few stimulated by war, ignoring those that were not, such as vaccines, antibiotics, X-rays, movies, and television. Even some that she does emphasize, such as medical triage, computers, and jet engines, would have probably been developed without the war, if at a slightly slower pace. But who knows what alternative technologies might have flourished in peacetime? And do these rather scattered benefits and inventions justify almost 100 million dead human beings? The benefits of war, even those originally unintended, have been much exaggerated.

Conclusion

1. Europe's early origins paralleled those of Republican Rome and ancient China. In all three cases the need for self-defense in a decidedly anarchic multipolar context produced a militarized ruling class exercising a Mafia-like protection racket that forced the lower classes to provide taxes and soldiers. But states did not fill in the whole space of the region. Endemic small-scale wars of conquest of stateless and tribal peoples by the core states were inevitable.

2. So war was normal, and bellicose ideologies were rooted in the cumulative effects of past historical victories. Continued success by the major states of Europe baked in the institutions and culture of militarism, which, as in Rome and China, added to motives of material gain values such as honor, status, glory, and power in itself. There were major personality differences among rulers—as in the contrast between Edward II and Edward III—but their emotions derived more from the general culture of honor.

3. Christendom provided limited regulation of war in medieval and early modern Europe. Aristocrats shared a transnational culture and were highly intermarried. Church institutions were as powerful as any state until the sixteenth century. For aristocrats and other wellborn men, war was normatively regulated; it yielded a lower chance of death, which in any case would be rewarded in heaven. War seemed rational to them. But it was not for most of the people, especially if war was fought over their land.

4. The core powers expanded through conquest of lesser peoples and states, first on the western European periphery, then across the world and in central Europe. Sharks swallowed minnows, "deflecting" wars between each other from zero-sum to positive-sum for rulers. The dominant classes of major states gained through these phases of colonial expansion. Younger sons and bastards were especially keen on war. Expansion across other continents came with good fortune at the moment when their most powerful states were stagnant or in decline and Europe was filling up with states. Rivalry between the major states fueled revolutions in military organization

and technology, which provided the ability to control sea-coasts and settler colonies and to secure compliant native regimes. This culminated in an alliance between militarized states, technology, and industrial capitalism that from the late eighteenth century was able to conquer most of the world.

5. The breakthrough culminating in the Industrial Revolution—the "European Miracle"—owed little to interstate wars. In any case, neither brought much immediate benefit to the European population as a whole, though it did in the long run—but much less for the conquered colonial peoples.

6. A sense of civilizational entitlement to eliminate, enslave, and exploit colonial peoples was buttressed by a belief that the European population possessed the one true word of God, and by racial theories of superiority based on visible physiognomy. This was the most enduring ideological justification of warfare found among Europeans. But racism weakened empires unwilling to acculturate native peoples, unlike both the Roman and Chinese empires.

7. From the sixteenth century came three waves of transcendent ideological warfare: wars of religion, revolutionary and nationalist wars, and twentieth-century struggles, which originated in Europe but then spread to the world, among fascism, state socialism, and capitalist democracy. The third wave continued after 1945 (see chapters 13 and 14). These wars were particularly vicious, for transcendent ideologies claimed the right to impose certain values on an enemy denounced as evil or savage, though the savagery was mostly the aggressor's own. These produced short-lived reactions in treaties and institutions to restrain wars, which led for a time to cautious interstate wars embodying more pragmatic, delayed-reaction rational Realism—though not in the colonies. Such waves and reactions remind us of how varied are the causes of war, even within a single civilization. But interwave geopolitics was like a game of chess where only the pawns can be taken off the board, white pawns in Europe, black pawns elsewhere.

8. Wars against the pawns were rational in terms of ends for the dominant classes and settlers of the major powers, although in such lopsided wars calculations of means were often unnecessary. Luard concludes his survey of wars through six hundred

years of European history by flatly rejecting rationality of means: "It does not appear that there has been, in most periods, any serious attempt made to balance possible gains against likely costs, or even accurately to assess the likelihood of victory. Governments that resort to war are not usually in a mood for calculations of this kind. They are often filled with passion, indignation, vengefulness or greed; inspired by patriotic estimates of the quality of native fighting men, weapons, and strategies; and so inflated with over-optimistic conceptions of the prospects of success."[65] This would seem to be exaggerated, though truer of western than central Europe, where I noted the calculative nature of the three-way struggles waged over the Holy Roman Empire.

9. As in Republican Rome, ancient China, and medieval Japan, defeat in war multiplied vanished kingdoms, though this was much more belated in central than western Europe. If survival is the basic goal of rulers, as Realists say, almost all failed. Maybe their most important goal was the survival not of their state but of themselves. Yet they could have lived if they had freely paid homage to the strong. Weaker states acted rationally when they submitted to threats from the powerful, or when they voluntarily accepted subordination and absorption, perhaps through marriages. Yet those choosing war overconfidently acted irrationally, and Luard and van Evera say they were in the majority. Delusions also drove states with fairly equal powers to war against each other. In the three ideological waves, European rulers were driven by ideology as well as geopolitical calculation, though between these waves more caution and negotiation occurred. Yet in general militarism was so baked in to culture and institutions that war became what rulers did when they felt insulted, wronged, entitled, or self-righteous in seizing the opportunities provided by succession crises. Most wars were not fought after careful rational calculation of means in relation to ends. Balancing alliances was rarely effective in the long run, as stronger powers repeatedly swallowed weaker ones. Yet some successful balancing occurred between the greatest powers.

In most of Europe before 1945, war was not primarily a rational instrument of policy, except where sharks could easily swallow minnows—which was both morally dubious and not requiring careful calculation of the odds. Overall, the most striking feature of European wars was their varied sequencing through time—from limited but impulsive dynastic wars to wars within more calculative great power systems, to ideological wars, to global colonial wars, to two of the most devastating and least rational wars in human history. Through all these wars, few people benefited.

CHAPTER NINE

Seven Hundred Years of South and Central America

Precolonial Empires: Aztecs

Postcolonial Latin America has had a low rate of interstate wars and good data sources. Yet the period of colonization had been extremely bloody. In the sixteenth century the Portuguese and Spanish sailed to the New World and heard credible stories of cities of fabulous wealth. Spanish conquistadores, driven by greed and relative poverty (being mostly from poor regions of Spain), and militarily confident through the successful Spanish war record in Europe, embarked on conquest—the first major attempt at overseas empire by a European power. The goals were material—gold, silver, and land and labor—though legitimized by Catholic Christianity. There was a risk of death, but the potential gains were great. Priests saving souls, if necessary by forced conversions, came later.

They conquered numerous indigenous communities. I focus on the Aztecs in Mexico and the Inca, whose core lay in Peru. Earlier civilizations had existed in these regions—the Olmec, the classic Maya, Teotihuacan, Toltecs, and Zapotecs in Central America and the Chavín, Moche, Huari, and Tiwanaku in the Andes. These had left impressive monumental buildings, especially temples, and indications of states, dominant classes, occupational specialization, trading and artisanal networks, religions with theatrical public ceremonies, and agriculture yielding surpluses for quite dense populations. But Central America was neither a single core region nor a single dynastic tradition, and states repeatedly rose and fell.

The Aztecs were descendants of the Chichimeca peoples, who entered central Mexico from the north from about 1150 CE, and the Inca inhabited the Cuzco Basin from the eleventh century. From the fourteenth century, our information on both begins to improve, hence the seven hundred years of this chapter title. The Aztec elite were literate, and illustrated books were produced by professional scribes and included maps, histories, censuses, financial accounts, calendars, ritual almanacs, and cosmological descriptions. Almost all were destroyed after the conquest as "books of the Devil" by order of the Catholic Church. Some survived, however, supplemented by codices written soon after the conquest either by native Nahuatl speakers or by Spaniards who had interviewed Aztecs.[1]

Around 1325 the city of Tenochtitlán was founded as the capital of the peoples known as the Nahua or Aztec. They had a long history of serving as mercenaries in other states' wars and were at this time turning their militarism toward their own conquests. A century later, in 1428–30, came the formation of the Aztec Triple Alliance between the city-states of Tenochtitlán, Texcoco, and Tlacopan, neighbors in the Basin of Mexico. The Triple Alliance remained the core of what is generally called the Aztec empire, ruled by nine kings of Tenochtitlán dynasties during the ninety years up to the arrival of the Spanish in 1519. This young empire had emerged in a region of small city-states with a typical radius of about ten kilometers; some were probably republics with representative institutions (perhaps dominated by oligarchies), but most were monarchies, the ruler elected by four leading nobles who chose as kings men who were close kin of the previous ruler, who were proven warriors but not too old for campaigning, and who had daughters who could be married to other rulers to cement alliances. Marriage alliances and tribute were sometimes chosen in preference to war. Few successions seem to have been disputed. In this respect, the political system worked. Nobility was achieved by prowess in war. The cities warred sporadically with their neighbors, sometimes for conquest, but more often to elicit homage from tributary cities—a predominantly indirect form of empire. Alliances between cities to deter more aggressive groups were also common. The Basin of Mexico was unusually fertile, supporting a dense population; its great lakes also permitted quicker communication by water than by land and made possible both a larger heartland of empire and a larger army than the

Triple Alliance's rivals'.[2] Numerical superiority was always their main military weapon.

Led by the Aztecs of Tenochtitlán, the Alliance defeated many city-states, replacing their rulers, raping their women, capturing their men, and distributing estates and their workers to their own nobles and warriors. This achieved their two main aims, to seize lands and labor and to worship the gods by sacrificing captives. But with polities lying farther away, they relied more on exacting tribute and corvée labor from cities that could otherwise rule themselves. The Triple Alliance fielded a formidable army, its core noble units well drilled, and all young men received military training. But there was no standing army, and warriors had to be mobilized for each campaign. All the Aztec kings engaged in aggressive war, and all but two apparently expanded the empire. Ross Hassig states, "Politically peace did not mean amiable coexistence, but subordination. In essence, for the Aztecs, everyone was either a subordinate or a target. Peace was achieved by hierarchy."[3] Though they suffered defeats, on balance the Triple Alliance triumphed through the size of the forces they could field. War was rational for them and highly calculative, but not for the defeated. It was zero-sum. In the province of Morelos, although war and tribute exactions had a positive effect on textile production (of uniforms), and perhaps on agricultural productivity, they lowered general living standards. Inequality widened, given the generosity of tribute given by rulers to their warrior nobles.[4]

According to the norms of the region, rulers needed a casus belli to justify mobilizing their army. They could always find one—maltreatment of their ambassadors or merchants (often used as spies), refusal of an imperial request, balking at paying agreed-on tribute, maltreatment of an Aztec bride—or, indeed, any perceived slight or insult. The Aztec ruler would then mobilize, summon his allies, each of whom would march separately to an agreed-on spot on the enemy's border, and they would join together in battle, each contingent fighting separately under its own lord, all of whom were issuing commands in their own varied languages. The army, though very large, could not have been very well coordinated.

The Aztecs spared those who quickly surrendered, contenting themselves with tribute.[5] They exacted it from over four hundred cities as both regular payments and as extras destined for special needs, such as war or monument building. Some of these cities would in turn exact tribute from other cities. Rulers had to swear allegiance, pay tribute and corvée labor, and provide levies for Aztec wars in their vicinity. The clients could retain their political autonomy if loyal. If not, they would be massacred and replaced by men chosen from among the defeated ruler's kin, who would be married to an Aztec princess to strengthen their loyalty. This economized on military resources, and garrisons were stationed only in insecure areas and at the locals' expense. In a continent lacking the wheel and draft animals, logistical difficulties blocked more direct rule. But the Aztecs were skilled at what they could do.

There was almost no attempt to acculturate subjugated peoples. They did not become "Aztecs" but retained their existing identities, gods, languages, and military levies. Exacting regular tribute and levies reinforced and routinized subordination, encouraging Aztec rulers to keep on going to war. This was of course resented by client rulers. They grumbled and were intermittently rebellious, but usually they complied, as the Aztecs remained strong and won their wars. Rival city-states always existed just outside the borders of empire. To dominate the central valley required making wars elsewhere. They knew they had to extract material rewards for their followers and clients. Polygynous marriages ensured that royal families and their demands got bigger, and the dangers of royal factionalism grew.[6] Only victories would cement the ruler's reputation and his followers' loyalty. Since men would follow a successful leader, conquerors were trapped by their own success, compelled to continue conquests by a mixture of Durkheim's notion of the "malady of infinite aspiration," the need to keep on rewarding followers and kin rivals, and fear that the ambitious militarism they had cultivated might produce threatening kin rivals should their conquests end.

Power was legitimated through intense and aesthetic religious rituals. The core of solidarity in each city was provided by religious ceremonies in which all social classes repeatedly performed rituals. War itself was ritualized. Aztec warriors in battle dressed and were armed according to their noble rank, which was determined by how many prisoners they had taken in previous battles. The Spanish soldiers had never before seen enemies doing ritual dances as they advanced into battle, decked out in bright colors, covered with paint, jewelry, feathers, elaborate headdresses and hair styles, some resembling jaguars, eagles, or other creatures with religious significance. The warriors focused not only on killing enemy soldiers but also on wounding and capturing them, for captives were sacrificed to the gods, which provided spectacular ceremonial and political proof of Aztec dominance and conferred fame and visible symbols of achievement on the captor. In attack the aim was to seize a city's marketplace and destroy and burn its main temple. The defenders lost heart as their god fell to a more powerful deity. The main symbol of conquest was a burning temple—"victory in symbol and defeat in fact."[7]

The Spanish were appalled by the savagery of one Aztec war ritual. Aztecs had inherited from other peoples a belief that the sun god needed to drink human blood to survive. If he died, darkness would envelop the earth and all life would end. The only reliable source of quantities of blood were prisoners of war. So prisoners were delivered to the gods by having their beating hearts ripped out, their blood spilling out over the temple steps in the presence of the people. A new ruler had to deliver larger numbers to show he was approved by the gods. This gruesome militarism was baked in to Aztec culture and institutions. Cases date from at least 1199 until the ceremonies seen by the Spanish in 1519. Camilla Townsend says that Nahuatl memoirs reveal ceremonies conducted in an atmosphere of reverence, not savagery, yet this indicates just how baked in savagery was.[8] Of course, the Spanish were also appalling toward native peoples who resisted them.[9] These were rival ghastly forms of rationality.

The Aztecs also fought a more limited and regulated form of war called "flower war."[10] When conflict occurred with a city-state alliance considered by the Aztecs to be of relatively equal power, like the Tlaxcala, the two sides might agree to send out an equal number of warriors drawn from their elite noble units to an agreed-on battlefield. These warriors would engage in combat but seek to wound and capture an opponent, not to kill him—rather like Roman gladiators, except that some of the captives were later sacrificed to the sun god. It was a way of establishing relative dominance without much actual killing. It was also an opportunity to train men and to deploy one's main force elsewhere, without risking attack from this enemy. One flower war supposedly lasted eight years, but these wars could escalate into an intermediate form of combat that involved commoners who could be captured and sacrificed, as would happen to captives of all ranks in full-scale wars.

In 1519–21 the Aztecs met their match. When confronted by the conquistadores, they proved inferior in tactics and weaponry. Their open infantry formation, permitting each soldier space to fight independently, could be broken up by the close-order Spanish *tercio* formation, which mixed together pikes, swords, crossbows, and muskets, supported by artillery and cavalry. By that time cavalry was a declining force in European warfare, but Spanish horses proved intimidating in open terrain in a continent without horses. Cavalry turned Aztec retreat into carnage. Firearms and crossbows were superior to the arrow and dart projectiles of the Aztecs, and Spanish steel armor and weapons were superior to Aztec thick cloth armor and wooden weapons tipped with obsidian.[11] But this was not enough to secure victory. The Aztecs adapted, focusing on ambushes in rocky or forested terrain unsuitable for horses, developing longer spears, and ducking and weaving when they saw that bullets came in straight lines. The Spanish were but few, massively outnumbered. They could break up enemy attacks and inflict heavy casualties but not press home conquest. They could add greater unity and clarity of purpose. When the Spanish arrived, the indigenous peoples argued about what to make of them, but they thought they were too few to effect conquest. In contrast, the Spanish knew exactly what their purpose was: to seize gold, silver, and land.

Yet the major Aztec weakness was political: lack of control over allies and neutrals.[12] Ironically, Moctezuma was embarking on an attempt to control captured cities through governors and garrisons when the Spanish arrived.[13] The Aztec system worked well as long as the Triple Alliance remained more powerful than any local rival. But once the Spanish revealed military superiorities, discontented clients and rivals saw their opportunity to overthrow their oppressive overlords. This was especially true of the Tlaxcala, long rivals of the Aztecs and still independent but impoverished. Like some other city-states, they had more representative political institutions, and we know that the issue of whether to fight or ally with the Spaniards was hotly debated in them.[14] The clincher was probably when Hernán Cortés promised them an equal share of the booty. Their native allies, including Tlaxcala's army of 20,000, gave the Spanish equal numbers in battle and the means to effect conquest. But the Tlaxcala had made a pact with the devil.

Moctezuma, the Aztec leader, was first puzzled by the Spanish; he then seemed to realize his own political weakness, which might explain his not fighting in 1519. His spies told him that more Spanish ships were arriving at the coast, and it was now clear that his forces would suffer massive casualties even if they managed to achieve victory. He suspected this would destroy his reputation as a war leader, and he and perhaps the empire would be overthrown.[15] Without a show of defiance from their absolute ruler, other Aztecs lacked the legitimacy to command prolonged resistance. Moctezuma was reduced to offering the Spanish massive tribute if they would only leave, underestimating their ambition and avarice. Military superiority and defection of elites from native rulers became repeated features of European conquests. Lacking the bonds of national-ism, local elites would assess the strength of the Europeans compared to their local rulers and side with whoever they thought would win. If some rulers sided with the Europeans, victory would result.

There were also, however, contingencies evident during 1519–21. The Spanish were almost destroyed as they tried to escape from Tenoch-titlán on *La Noche Triste*, June 30, 1520, when Cortés lost over six hundred Spaniards and several thousand of his local allies. Then in September 1520 smallpox struck the indigenous peoples who lacked the immunity possessed by surviving adult Spaniards, which added to the locals' sense of the invincibility of the Spaniards.[16] Epidemics of smallpox, measles, and influenza, in addition to consequent famines, finished off Aztec morale and resistance the next year. Among the victims of smallpox was Moctezu-ma's successor, Cuitláhuac, who had shown some fight. The native popu-lation continued to decline, from perhaps 10 to 15 million in 1519 to just 1 million a century later. So if not Cortés, then another Spaniard, and if not a Spaniard, then an Englishman or a Frenchman. From now on, the Europeans were on a murderous roll.

The Spanish conquest of the Maya was much slower, lasting over two centuries, because of the fragmentation of Mayan polities in this pe-riod and their ability to retreat into terrains to which the Spanish *tercio* and horses were unsuited. Native allies were found, but European dis-eases again proved the most lethal weapon, since the Maya had no im-munity either.

Precolonial Empires: Inca

In South America we know less of the Inca since they had no written lan-guage, but oral traditions, sagas, and early Spanish sources provide much information. My principal sources have been María Rostworowski de Diez Canseco, Terence D'Altroy, Gordon McEwan, and Fernando Cer-vantes.[17] The Inca originated as a tiny kingdom in the twelfth-century Cuzco Basin, defending themselves against the neighboring Chanca, then turning to raiding and finally subordinating them. Then they ex-panded. Each ruler, the Sapa Inca, was expected to expand the empire and demonstrate success in war as evidence of his fitness to rule—a com-mon motivation among monarchs. But a more personal motivation for war resulted from the custom of split inheritance in royal succession. A new Sapa Inca was elected by those with most royal blood on both maternal and paternal lines, but he inherited only the office, titles, and control of the army. His predecessor, although deceased, retained all the wealth acquired during his reign, now controlled and managed by his clan. So the new Sapa Inca was motivated and able to make war.[18]

From about 1438 the Sapa Inca were defeating other peoples in battle, notably the coastal kingdom of Chimor. Like the Aztecs farther north, they were the most warlike people in their vicinity, yet they more often intimidated opponents with a show of force that persuaded them to pay homage without fighting. Inca generals usually gave opponents the choice of homage or death, and sagas describe peoples succumbing without pitched battle. Rostworowski says that in the early stages of expansion, Inca rulers strengthened ties with allies and conquered populations through generous gift giving—luxury and prestige items and women, cemented by generous banquets.[19] Rulers defeated in battle were executed, but their children might be educated in Inca culture and then returned home as client rulers. Rulers who paid homage remained in place. Rebellion was treated severely, sometimes by extermination or deportation and seizure of lands and property, accompanied by much raping. One man later remembered, "When they resisted for a few days, the Incas put all of them, large and small, to the knife, and when this was seen and understood by the rest of the people, they submitted out of fear."[20] Some captives were thrown into dungeons with wild animals, and any survivors were enslaved. At least six Inca rulers conquered new territories, the principal conqueror being Túpac Inca Yupanqui. Opponents generally had smaller armies, were less well-prepared for battle, and were apparently unable to form balancing alliances among themselves—another case of a core mopping up its periphery.

Elaborate religious ceremonies were held before battle. The army was predominantly subject peoples, each serving under its own lord, following orders in its distinct language, although a small elite force, at first of pure-blood Inca, was developed. Armies can have been only loosely organized, and the main tactic seems to have been to overawe the enemy with the sheer size of a force, like the Aztecs. Scholars estimate them at between 35,000 and 140,000, sometimes comprising several armies in the field at once.[21] Most generals were of royal Inca blood, which made rulers wary they might challenge their own power. They did coup-proofing by executing overly successful generals and adding supposedly more loyal ethnic groups to the elite force. Wars of succession involved rival half brothers intermittently claiming the throne.[22]

The Inca had a somewhat indirect empire, yet there was a formal administrative hierarchy, consisting of the Sapa Inca; his council, composed of royal family members and a high priest at the summit; then the governors of the "four quarters" of the empire, each divided into provinces, and then into a decimal structure of local offices. This state could collect taxes, organize corvée labor, and conduct censuses, but it is unclear how uniform it was, since most administration was in the hands of regional and local nobles. But they did have a major communications advantage: a magnificent road system covering the long spine of their empire.[23] They were built by local corvée labor, which alongside military service was the main form of taxation. Two main roads ran north to south along an empire stretching over five current Latin American countries, one down the coast, the other along the Andean highlands. The roads stretched over a total length of about 40,000 kilometers (today's French autoroute system covers only 12,000 kilometers). Roads were from one to four meters wide, often lined with low walls. Some stretches were just tracks, but others were paved, and there were many bridges, causeways, and stepped sections in hilly terrains. In the absence of wheeled vehicles, steps were fine even for load-carrying llamas and alpacas. In the empire's core regions, stone terracing and hydraulic works increased agricultural productivity. The quality of the surviving roads, terraces, and buildings around Cuzco, constructed without cement or iron tools, remains extraordinary even today.

The roads partially compensated for the dispersed political structure, allowing swift movement of tribute payments, troops, and information. A twenty-four-hour system of relay runners, each running 1.4 kilometers, could deliver an oral message or a quipu (colored ropes knotted together in ways that revealed information) at a rate of 240 kilometers a day. There were lodging stations every 30 kilometers, as well as food stores for the troops so that they did not have to live off the land (and so despoil it), and a network of small fortresses. In some regions relatively few Inca-style stone buildings have been found, suggesting an indirect empire there.[24] Yet there was a move toward a little more direct rule as military policy shifted toward pacification, resettling restive peoples, replacing them with compliant peoples, and fortifying frontier hot spots with garrisons.[25] Tamara Bray suggests the Inca used the roads "to subvert pre-existing relations of exchange," an attempt to steer local economies into the imperial model to prevent local alliances among other peoples, while encouraging dependency on the Inca state.[26] The Inca fought fewer wars than the Aztecs, the Mongols, or the Romans once their empire was established. D'Altroy says that in the final decades of the empire, threats came largely from insurrections, not invasions, as is suggested by the commitment of small forces to the perimeter and large ones to internal garrisons and armies of pacification.[27]

The Spanish invaders enjoyed similar superiority in weapons as they had in Mexico, even as their numbers were smaller. They had two great strokes of luck, however. First, Spanish epidemics arrived before the Spanish did (having spread from Mexico and Central America), in 1528 killing off the Inca ruler, his designated heir, and many others. It was not clear which of two sons, the half brothers Atahualpa and Huáscar, should succeed. It was agreed that one would take the north, the other the south. Both then built up regionally based forces, and a civil war broke out, which ended in Atahualpa's victory in 1532, at the very moment when the Spanish under Pizarro arrived—the second stroke of good luck. The two regionally entrenched Inca factions still existed. Again, there was a difference between the Spanish, driven by relentless avarice focused on the seizure of gold, silver, and land, and the divisions and uncertainties of the Inca. Both Inca factions tried to enlist Pizarro's support, but he double-crossed them both. Borrowing from Cortés's tactics, he invited Atahualpa and his elite guard to a feast in the Inca's honor in the main square of Cajamarca. Suddenly, armed Spanish soldiers emerged into the square and massacred the unarmed Inca. Atahualpa was imprisoned and later murdered. Pizarro then kept his successor hostage and killed the remaining leaders of both parties and finally the last Sapa Inca. He had overthrown an Inca Empire with greater administrative resources than the Aztecs without having fought a single serious battle.[28]

Battles did come later, in 1536, when Spanish atrocities against native populations provoked uprisings. But when the last two Sapa Inca were killed, no alternative leader possessed the religiously sanctified prestige to coordinate a major resistance movement. Rostworowski says the generous gift giving of the Inca came back to bite them, for "as the state grew, so did the number of lords who had to be satisfied."[29] New conquests generated revenues but also demands from new clients expecting gifts. So Inca rulers had to increase land and labor taxes. Yet this alienated those who were already allies, and many rebelled, making the disastrous decision to ally with Pizarro. Spanish-borne epidemics then finished off the resistance. Those who fought on retreated to the jungles and mountains, but the end was now inevitable.[30] The Inca were destroyed in intermittent wars over a forty-year period, their empire looted of its gold and silver, which was melted into ingots for the conquistadores and the Holy Roman Emperor.

The Iberian conquest of Central and South American empires was nearly inevitable, given their relative youth and political weakness. Spanish weaponry and solidarity compared to the fissiparous tendencies of Aztec and Inca alliances, the relentless avarice of waves of colonists against the uncertain responses of the locals, and Europe's stealth weapon, the epidemic, added to the power inequality. The extraordinary monumental buildings, mainly religious, of pre-Columbian America tend to disguise their relative political and military weakness.

Few benefited from the conquest. Perhaps half the conquistadores survived and got booty or land, whereas half died or left disappointed. Their leaders became immensely rich, and the king of Spain, entitled to one-fifth of all the spoils, did best of all. Since they created no wealth, destroyed much, and killed hundreds of thousands, their gains were achieved entirely at the expense of the indigenous peoples. Today, the conquistadores might be charged as war criminals by international courts, but the papacy, greedy for souls, thought otherwise. Popes organized treaties between the two Crowns of Spain and Portugal to settle their territorial disputes, giving Brazil to Portugal while Spain received the rest. This spared Latin America the inter-imperial wars that scarred North America and Asia. The two sets of Catholic colonists could exterminate the remaining indigenous peoples in peace, although there was increasing criticism of their brutality within the Church and in Spain that reached even up to the Holy Roman Emperor himself. As elsewhere, moral qualms were felt afterward, too late.

Postcolonialism

"God is in heaven, the king is far away, and I give the orders here," said the colonists. As in North America, they grew discontented with their monarch, encouraged by new liberal republican ideology. The Spanish Empire collapsed when Napoleon invaded Spain and deposed the Bourbon king. In the ensuing power vacuum in the Americas, Creole settlers (those born there) tried to seize the royal administrations from the ruling *peninsulares* (born in Spain), which led to a flurry of civil wars. In 1815 the Bourbons were restored to the Spanish throne and Ferdinand VII declared himself an absolute monarch. This drove most colonists toward demanding independence, although some royalists held out until 1833. Ten Spanish successor states were recognized as sovereign by the Church and by the two relevant great powers, Great Britain and the United States. Two of these states, Gran Colombia and the Central American Federation, soon broke up into several smaller ones. In contrast, Portuguese Brazil stayed whole. The Portuguese king had fled from Napoleon and now ruled in Brazil as emperor. Excluding tiny British, French, and Dutch colonies, there were fifteen sovereign states in Latin America. They are my subject matter.

Explanations of War in Postcolonial Latin America

All these countries except for Costa Rica and Panama possess armies, but their main activity has not been to make interstate war. As Stanislav Andreski noted: "Militarism has become introverted in the Latin American republics: with few opportunities to fight for their countries, soldiers remained preoccupied with internal politics and the search for personal and collective advantage. Instead of inter-state wars there was military violence within states, in domestic politics."[31] He argued that militaries were too large for police functions and too small for interstate wars. Robert Holden says the region contained much violence: "killing, maiming, and other acts of destruction committed by rival *caudillos*, guerilla 'liberators,' death squads, and state agents such as the armed forces and police."[32] Latin Americans are not more pacific humans, but they have rarely launched interstate wars. Correlates of War data since 1830 reveal only a few, mostly in the nineteenth century, though these data exclude most of the wars waged against indigenous peoples.[33] By the mid-1880s the power of the indigenous peoples had been destroyed, although the Caste Wars of Yucatán lingered on into the twentieth century. Subsequent violence has been mostly provided by civil wars between political factions, regions, and classes—and, recently, drug-related gang wars.

Comparing the region with other regions in the world between 1816 and 2007, CoW statistics provided by Douglas Lemke, Charles Gochman and Zeev Maoz, and Tassio Franchi and his colleagues reveal the rate of interstate warfare in Latin America to be three to five times less than in Europe, and rather less than in Asia.[34] David Mares says that after World War II, Latin America was only "in the middle of the pack" for wars, since its three wars put it above Africa's two, Northeast Asia's one, and North America's zero.[35] But it is absurd to say that the United States has had no wars, and Mares also separates Northeast from Southeast

Asia, saying they do not share similar security concerns. Not so. The Korean and Vietnam wars were both confrontations between communist and capitalist authoritarian regimes, both involving the United States, the Soviet Union, China, South Korea, and France. They should be joined into a single regional case. Correcting for these omissions leaves only postcolonial Africa below Latin America in interstate wars—and Africa has had many more civil wars. Most Latin American wars have also been waged by small armies over short periods and at low cost, financed more by debt than by taxes, having less effect on society. World Bank data for 2020 put Latin American defense spending at 1.2% of GDP, half that of the global average of 2.4%. Military spending has been on modernization, not a search for superiority over one's neighbors.[36]

Latin America has barely participated in wars outside the continent. In World War II Brazilian soldiers did fight in Italy, suffering almost one thousand casualties. When German U-boats sank Mexican ships in 1942, President Manuel Ávila Camacho declared war, seeing this as the solution to internal social divisions, but his attempt at conscription was met by social unrest, and Mexico sent no soldiers. In 1944 it sent one air force squadron to the Pacific theater. The pilots were low-cost national heroes, for the United States supplied the planes and only five pilots died in action.[37] Finally, Colombia sent 5,100 soldiers to the Korean War, and 163 died there. For all these reasons Latin American history is often described as a "Long Peace."[38]

Mares prefers to call it a zone of "Violent Peace," observing that a simple dichotomy between war and peace neglects intermediate MIDs ranging from mere bluster to use of force in smaller combats. Using CoW data, Gochman and Maoz suggest that from 1816 to 1976 in the whole of the Americas, including North America, there were 183 MIDs. But this figure was much lower than Europe's total of over 500.[39] In the period 2002–10, only Western Europe had fewer MIDs. Western Europe had zero, Latin America fifteen, Central Europe thirty-five, and the Middle East, South Asia, the Far East, and Africa all had forty or more.[40] There were no Latin American countries among the top-ten initiators of MIDs during the two periods where we have data, 1816–1976 and 1993–2010.[41] So I would not agree with Mares unless he was also including civil and gang wars.

One-third of MIDs in the region have been border disputes and have rarely been settled by one armed encounter.[42] Until the 1980s, all Latin American countries had unresolved minor border disputes, and these sometimes triggered MIDs but rarely war.[43] Most have now been settled. Recent examples are a dispute between Nicaragua and Colombia over two small islands, settled in 2012 by the International Court of Justice; a dispute between Peru and Chile over maritime boundaries, settled by the ICJ in 2014; a dispute between Bolivia and Chile, settled by the ICJ in 2018; and a dispute between Costa Rica and Nicaragua over the Isla Calero region, settled by the ICJ in 2018. There has also been a dispute between Colombia and Venezuela over Colombian guerillas operating from over the Venezuelan border. Only the disagreement between Britain and Argentina over the Falklands (Malvinas) brought war—a small, undeclared one—and has not been settled. Jorge Dominguez and David Mares tersely summarize this: "Territorial, boundary, and other disputes endure. Interstate conflict over boundaries is relatively frequent. Disputes sometimes escalate to military conflict because states recurrently employ low levels of force to shape aspects of bilateral relations. Such escalation rarely reaches full-scale war. Interstate war is infrequent."[44] So there are two main questions: Why were there so few wars in Latin America, and why have there been Militarized Interstate Disputes eventually resolved through diplomacy?

Previous Explanation

The most influential explanation of why there have been relatively few wars is Miguel Centeno's.[45] He emphasizes the weakness of Latin American compared to European states. He departs from the Tilly-Mann theory of the development of the state in Europe. In the famous words of Tilly, "War makes states and states make war."[46] Centeno says this barely happened in Latin America. Since its states fought few wars, they remained too feeble to fight more of them. They found it difficult to increase taxes for war, and they leaked resources through corruption. "Simply put, Latin American states did not have the organizational or ideological capacity to go to war with each other."[47] Moreover, the dominant landowning class favored a weak state unable to interfere with its power and wealth. He acknowledges two exceptions: Chile and Paraguay have possessed coherent states and militaries. So he stresses states' domestic politics, not their geopolitical relations, as IR theorists do.

He also perceives a lack of militarist ideology. After counting street names, statues, memorials, and coinages, he says that, compared to North America or Europe, their iconography "is much more focused on cultural and scientific figures, pays less attention to political symbols, and lacks the mythology of a people at arms uniting through sacrifice."[48] He adds class, ethnic, and religious restraints, too. Racial-ethnic diversity within each country generated a weak national identity that discouraged popular mobilization for war. Between the *peninsulares* and Creoles at the top and later white immigrants, and between those immigrants and ex-slaves, slaves, and indigenous peoples, lay enormous gulfs that involved notions of "civilization" as well as ethnicity and class. The elites had much more in common with each other than they did with their populace. They had Spanish or Portuguese blood, they were Catholic, and residents of all but one state spoke Spanish. Of course, shared Catholicism had not prevented states in medieval Europe from going to war.

His explanation is largely true. But does war require a strong state? One need only consider oneself superior to the rival. Why should a weak state with a ragtag, underequipped, undersupplied, incompetently led army not attack another state it believed to be even feebler? Since most states are overconfident about making war, a sense of relative weakness is rare. A weak fiscal base did hinder lengthy war making. Any state can finance a brief war, but if the tax base cannot be increased, then rulers must borrow to continue a war, and debt can only mount up to when creditors doubt whether they will be repaid. Then the war maker must negotiate. European militarism had the advantage of going through a feudal stage of warfare, which called on vassals who were largely self-financing. Then, when rulers perceived the military superiority of mercenaries over vassals, they developed some state capacity and more productive taxes, and there were plenty of mercenaries for hire. There were neither vassals nor roving mercenaries in America. There could be Latin American wars, but short ones.

Sebastián Mazzuca focuses on state capacity. He says the major states of Europe were "born strong," whereas weakness was a "birth defect" of Latin American states. Yet the last chapter showed that European states had also shared this birth defect, but some became much stronger, owing to a militarism that swallowed up smaller states. In contrast, Latin Americans did not swallow each other up. Mazzuca says that whereas European development was "war-led," Latin American was "trade-led." Although warrior rulers in Europe were able to eliminate peripheral patrimonial power brokers, seen as rivals for the control of land and people, in trade-led Latin America, to battle against peripheral power brokers might bring on civil war, which would torpedo investment, production, and export-led growth. Instead, rulers appeased the peripheries through promises of future shares in economic expansion. There were three kinds of patrimonial factions, he says, port interests, rival parties, and regional caudillos, all favoring fiscally starved, "patronage machine" states, unable to fight wars for long. The weakening of states was reinforced by a period of transnational free trade led by external powers far more powerful than any in Latin America. So for him the low rate of war was due to a distinctive balance of domestic class and regional forces in an era of free trade, an argument made mostly in terms of economic and political power relations.[49]

Geopolitical explanations are added by IR specialists. First, they say interstate wars remained rare because Latin Americans were relatively insulated from the wider international system and did not get embroiled in wars not of their own choosing, unlike states elsewhere. Second, some argue that interstate war became rare thanks to the deliberate creation of balances of power in South America in the late nineteenth century. Robert Burr gives as an example Chile, which, after defeating Peru and Bolivia in the War of Confederation in 1841, sought to maintain a balance of power in its region by an understanding with Argentina while also improving relations with Brazil as insurance against a future conflict with Argentina.[50] Chile also strengthened relations with Ecuador, which was strategically located at the rear of its traditional enemy, Peru. Chile even tried friendship with Colombia. The other states made their own diplomatic moves—all insuring themselves with defensive alliances against the possibility of war against rivals. We will indeed see balancing against rulers seeking regional hegemony. The question remains: Why did these often fail elsewhere and lead to war, especially in Europe, but peace mostly endured in Latin America? Third, IR theorists argue that international regional institutions emerged in the nineteenth century and blossomed in the twentieth, fostering peace and international mediation when wars broke out. Holsti says that during the period 1820–1970, eight South American states used such procedures to settle their disputes no fewer than 151 times.[51] We have glimpsed the importance of the ICJ in settling recent disputes. Europe was also multistate, but its wars rarely ended with mediation or arbitration by outsiders. But *why* did this happen more in Latin America?

Mares offers a modified Realist rational-choice explanation: force is used when its costs are less than or equal to the costs acceptable to the leader's principal constituencies of support.[52] The cost of using force is the sum of the political-military strategy, the strategic balance, and the force employed. The costs that the leader's constituencies will accept are reduced if the leader lacks accountability to them. Politicians consider employing force only to meet the interests of their core constituencies. This stress on domestic politics is uncommon among Realists. He argues that in the twentieth century weaker states tended to precipitate wars and MIDs, usually in response to domestic pressure. Mares also rejects several other IR explanations.[53] Neither power equality nor a preponderance of power reduces the chances for war or serious crises. The balance of military power was not a major factor in Latin America. U.S. hegemony or democracy or authoritarianism cannot explain interstate war or peace here. They have sometimes fueled war, sometimes restrained it, while democracies have sometimes fought each other.[54] Douglas Gibler says democracy is not the underlying cause of peace. Rather, peace results from the stabilization of borders, which also consolidates democracy.[55]

Many of these explanations make sense, but I will insert them into the history and ecology of Latin America. First, the "tyranny of history" here was that these children of two empires had inherited the entire space of the subcontinent. This was already a multistate system. It was not like Europe, where one or several core states could expand outward at the expense of other peoples, in the process strengthening their states and armed forces. In a formal sense the successor states filled up the whole of Latin America. There was no *terra nullius* between them. Expansion here was possible *within* each state's boundaries, however, over jungle or mountainous or desert terrain where the settlers had not penetrated, or over indigenous settled peoples who after the initial conquest phase were displaced by the settlers. Second, these states had mostly inherited the boundaries of either the Portuguese Empire or a former Spanish viceroyalty, or *audiencia* (a law court jurisdiction), or *caja* (a treasury district). Regina Grafe and Maria Irigoin stress the *cajas*, noting, "The break-up of the empire occurred along the lines of territories where the regional treasuries were located."[56] Thus, most of the successor states already had functioning if rudimentary administrative, judicial, or fiscal systems over their territories, though sometimes these had fuzzy borders. Even new republics like Paraguay, Uruguay, and Bolivia, which had not been distinct viceroyalties, had been distinct *cajas* or *audiencias*. Mazucca rejects such continuity by focusing only on the level of the viceroyalties.[57] Only Central America, which fragmented into small republics, had not been a viceroyalty, *caja*, or *audiencia*.[58] The others were literally "successor states" with administrative continuity and legitimacy, while the boundaries between the Brazilian and the Spanish empires had been set by papal mediation centuries earlier.

Thus, states accepted in principle the legal doctrine of *uti possidetis*, Latin for "as you possess"—new states should retain the same borders as preceding ones. All rulers benefited from this, since it confirmed their sovereignty over mountainous, jungle, or savanna areas in which they had no real presence. The political ecology of the region was one of center and periphery *within* each state rather than between them, and so expansion required lesser states, taxes, and armies. David Carter and H. E. Goemans find across the world that borders inherited from previous administrations are less often disputed.[59] From 1955 *uti possidetis* became a globally accepted norm.[60] It could not entirely prevent border disputes here. Though Spanish viceroyalties had been split up during the Wars of Independence, there were occasional attempts to re-create them whole, citing a rival *uti possidetis*, though these were successfully resisted by others. In sparsely settled regions without apparent wealth, like the Amazon basin and the Atacama Desert on the Pacific Coast, precise boundaries had seemed unnecessary before independence, and lines drawn vaguely on a map by the Spanish or Portuguese Crown were easily disputable. Moreover, settlers in border zones tended to arrive from whichever country had the most accessible routes there, so that in some remote areas a claim to settlement might rival the old imperial maps. So there were border disputes.

Many studies show that territorial disputes are more difficult to resolve, more likely to be repeated, and more prone to incur fatalities than other types of issues. Control over territory is the heart of political power, and claims bring an emotional, even sacred, element of sovereignty. In Latin America the sovereignty of each state in its core areas was recognized, and so the elimination of states through wars of conquest *never* happened, nor was it aimed at—which was so different from Europe and China. This was why wars were limited and why even the most decisive war defeat, suffered by Paraguay, did not result in its elimination.

The social ecology of settlement also meant that few population centers lay close to the disputed borders, and so deeply entrenched rival settler communities were rare. Ecology also had military consequences. If a region did become disputed, the rival countries would try to establish a military presence there—a fort or a few huts with barbed wire and a flagpole. Each rival would send out patrols to probe the other's installations. Sometimes these patrols would collide, shooting and perhaps causing a casualty or two. Such an MID incident might be exaggerated back in the capital, perhaps escalating further, occasionally to war. On the other hand, ecology and demography made the military logistics of most cross-border incursions difficult and costly. Early "imperial" projects for a Gran Colombia and for a single Central American Republic were defeated more by obdurate ecology than force of arms. Wars involved small forces operating over large, underpopulated areas—armies were like fleas crawling over elephants, says Robert Scheina.[61] A peace settlement might confer territories on one party, but ruling there was difficult. A peace treaty might be unraveled by new population movements, discoveries of economic resources, or the construction of new frontier posts. This made major wars less likely but disputes involving MIDs more likely. Social ecology is important in explaining the Latin American puzzle.

New settlements by the borders were few because there was ample land for settlers well inside borders. In medieval Europe and early Spring and Autumn China, a small military expedition and war abroad could be immediately followed by "planting" settlers among less well-developed peoples living there. But here settlers could find new estates or trading opportunities within the country, either on virgin or on Indian land. When in the nineteenth century the republics' small forces got modern rifles and the Indians did not, wars of domestic expansion yielded easy pickings for settlers. Interior areas could be pacified without great cost, and states attempting the conquest of indigenous peoples were generally given a free hand by their neighbors. External meddling was rare, and arming Indians was undesirable since it might threaten all whites.[62] It was different for political disputes among whites, which attracted much neighborly interference since this was much cheaper than war. It might lead to MIDs if not war.

Minnow states were not swallowed up. Though Brazil's size dwarfed the former Spanish republics, much of it was thinly populated jungle and mountain. Argentina had a large population and great potential resources, but it was riven by interprovincial conflicts. Chile was more well-developed, although it was initially quite small, and both it and even smaller Paraguay developed the most cohesive states and militaries. Mexico was a giant, but Britain and the United States would not permit it to swallow up the minnow states to its south. For reasons of trade, these two great powers had an interest in maintaining relative peace.

The Cases of War Post-1833

With these general explanations in mind, I turn to the interstate wars fought after 1833. I exclude defensive wars waged against American, Spanish, and French invasions, but I do include the Falklands War. The total number is fifteen, although four do not meet the CoW standard of one thousand battle deaths. For lack of evidence, I do not include wars fought by colonists against indigenous peoples, nor do I include most civil wars, although some affected interstate wars, as we shall see. Interstate wars were all fought between neighbors. I begin with the two main regions that were most strategic or resource-rich. In the Río de la Plata system, large populations lived not far from disputed borderlands, some containing valuable resources or straddling major communications routes. The sparsely settled central Pacific Coast had some strategic importance for international trade and was found in the mid-nineteenth century to contain valuable mineral resources. There seemed to be opportunity for economic profit through conquest of border territory in these two regions, and the biggest wars occurred there.

The Platine War, 1851–1852

This six-month conflict was fought between the Argentine Confederation and Brazil, which was supported by two dissident Argentine provinces. The war had both geopolitical and economic causes. It was part of a long-running struggle between Argentina and Brazil for influence over Uruguay and Paraguay. It was also a struggle for control of the Río de la Plata system, which fed into the Atlantic Ocean, with its valuable trade routes. Brazil had lost some territories in early postcolonial encounters, and revisionism flourished among Brazilian elites. Uruguay had been created by British mediation as a buffer state to help ease their conflicts, but Uruguay had needed a joint Anglo-French naval blockade of Buenos Aires during 1845–50 to protect it from the aggressive Argentine president Juan Manuel de Rosas. This was the only substantial British military intervention in Latin America until 1982. Rosas was backing the Uruguayan Blanco party, while Brazil's Emperor Pedro II backed the rival Colorados—rival attempts at regime change or strengthening. Rosas had strengthened the Argentine Confederation's central state against the peripheries, becoming an authoritarian ruler and building up a cult of personality. It was believed he sought dominance over most of the former Spanish viceroyalty of the Río de la Plata. This might ultimately mean claiming control over Uruguay, Paraguay, and even bits of Bolivia and Brazil. Brazil was provoked by Argentine expansion amid rival interpretations of *uti possidetis*, for borders were not entirely clear here.

After debates in the Brazilian cabinet and parliament, the government decided to send its small professional army, backed by its more powerful navy, into battle. In early 1851 it helped finance two Argentine breakaway provinces and the opposition Colorado Party in Uruguay, and it signed defensive alliances with Paraguay and Bolivia. Provoked, Rosas struck out. Claiming self-defense, he declared war on Brazil. He had actually provoked the formation of the alliance against him. Valuable riverine territory of uncertain ownership fueled conflict, but it was fired up by a high-risk president with ambitious goals.

A Brazilian force invaded Uruguay. After a series of short skirmishes, there was a decisive battle with Argentine forces at Caseros between armies of about 26,000 men on each side. Losses of about 2,000 dead or wounded were afterward declared, two-thirds of them Argentines. Brazil secured victory and marched its army through Buenos Aires in triumph, which humiliation was hardly likely to secure peace in the future. Victory had confirmed the independence of Paraguay and Uruguay, prevented a planned Argentine invasion of Brazil, and weakened the Argentine Confederation. Brazil then enjoyed more internal stability and economic growth. But Uruguay's civil strife continued, inviting foreign interference short of war. Paying small subsidies to a friendly faction there was much cheaper than war. Argentina also became more united in the early 1860s, followed by a consequent growth of revisionism. Paraguay also grew stronger along the river system, sometimes harassing Brazilian shipping. This might not seem a stable balance of power, but peace lasted for twelve years.

War of the Triple Alliance, 1864–1870

This was by far the longest and bloodiest war occurring in Latin America. It pitted an alliance of Argentina, Brazil, and Uruguay against Paraguay. The Río de la Plata system continued to cause armed conflict; it was underpopulated and inadequately mapped but a key strategic and economic resource. Tension rose in the early 1860s, again precipitated by civil strife in Uruguay. In 1863 Argentina aided a small invading army of Uruguayan dissidents trying to install the opposition Colorado Party in power, while Paraguay supported the Blanco Party government—a regime-change skirmish. Paraguay protested the invasion, and Argentina implausibly denied all knowledge. The next year Brazil joined in the invasion, partly to protect Brazilian trade along the rivers. The Blanco regime fell. Paraguay threatened war, but Brazil ignored this. A secret treaty between the allies claimed that "the peace, safety, and well-being of their respective nations is impossible while the present Government of Paraguay exists." News of their deal leaked out, fueling Paraguayan fury.

Thomas Whigham identifies four principal causes of the war. First, disputed thinly populated but strategically important borders had long been causing MIDs. Second, the political ambitions and nationalisms of Bartolomé Mitre of Argentina and Dom Pedro II of Brazil clashed; both claimed territories and sought more central state powers against peripheral political factions demanding regional autonomy. Third, Uruguay's government remained unstable, presenting a security dilemma in which escalation was not in armaments but in foreign meddling. Fourth, like Chris Leuchars and Peter Henderson, Whigham lays most of the blame on Paraguay's president Francisco Solano López.[63]

Paraguay was ethnically quite homogeneous, and its isolationist policies had cultivated a strong sense of nationhood, the main exception to Centeno's argument that ethnic diversity weakened Latin American states and Mazzuca's argument that peripheral factions weakened them. The indigenous population was largely Guarani-speaking, which the regime recognized as a second national language; it also treated the Guarani culture sympathetically. In this sense Paraguay was enlightened. It also had a powerful presidency. President Carlos Antonio López (1841–62) had sponsored statist development centered on protectionism, infrastructure projects, and conscription. He saber-rattled against Argentina and Brazil but avoided war. But in 1862 he transferred the presidency to his more aggressive son, Francisco Solano López.

In December 1864 Solano López declared war and invaded the Mato Grosso region of Brazil. In March 1865, when Argentina refused his request to march through its territory in order to reach Uruguay, he invaded Argentina as well. The first year of the war went well for Paraguay. The armies of Brazil and Argentina were small and poorly organized. Uruguay had no professional army. In contrast, Paraguay was more militarized, employing near-universal conscription. Whigham estimates that Solano López could count on conscript armies totaling one-third of the Paraguayan male population. He was modernizing them with British assistance, and he had built a chain of forts along the river system. Paraguay punched well above its weight in numbers. Yet it decisively lost the war, as was predictable if the war lasted long, given the disparity in resources between the two sides. He thought this was a window of opportunity, but it soon closed. The alliance's population of 11 million dwarfed the 300,000 to 400,000 Paraguayans. Although Solano López could keep on drafting new recruits without recourse to debt, finally conscripting prepubescent boys, this eventually harmed the productivity of the labor force. In a war of attrition Brazil could draft more, at no great loss to the economy. Brazilian casualties as a proportion of national population were not high because of the enormous size of its population. Argentina's were not high because its commitment to the war was low. But estimates of Paraguayan casualties, though much disputed, are somewhere between 15 and 45 percent of its total prewar population. Bear Braumoeller gives a death rate of 70 percent of the adult male population, which is at the high end of the possible. In proportional terms, this would make it the deadliest war in the world in the entire period since 1816, more deadly than either world war.[64]

Fazal sees Paraguay as "a fairly standard instance of a buffer state" having near-death inflicted on it.[65] But Paraguay was no victim buffer state. Its fate was self-inflicted through its ruler's irrational level of aggression. An overconfident president ordered his army and navy, initially superior, to attack *all* the surrounding powers at once. Solano López overestimated Paraguay's military power and underestimated Brazil's, once mobilized. He might have won a short war, but not a long one, although he could keep on fighting because of large-scale conscription. He had reason to fear the Brazilian and Argentinian rulers, but the traditional Paraguayan diplomacy of playing one against the other could have continued. His aggressive impulses got the better of him. He mistakenly thought Argentina would remain neutral in a war between Paraguay and Brazil even if Paraguayan soldiers marched into Argentine territory, which brought unacceptable dishonor to its rulers. He also denied any autonomy to his senior officers in the field and executed many of his own soldiers. He was utterly reckless in fighting to the bitter end rather than shifting to negotiations after repeated defeats made clear the writing on the wall.

Brazil did most of the alliance's fighting. Yet the war was unpopular in Brazil, and its army was composed largely of ex-slaves, some bought by the government from their owners, others promised land after the war. Paraguayan conscripts showed tenacity, but defeat was already certain when Solano López was tracked down and killed.[66] Nationalistic theories claiming the hand of Britain was everywhere have been discredited. The

foreign powers favored peace (for trade) and stood aside, apart from giving loans to whoever seemed likely to repay them.[67] They were not interested in direct intervention, even in mere gunboat diplomacy.

Paraguay's national output was halved, and the country had to cede
one-third of its territory and all its claims in disputed areas. That it was
not wiped off the map was due to the victors not trusting each other—a
very Realist sentiment. This was the closest the continent came to the
elimination of a state, common in European, Chinese, and Japanese history. But Paraguay was reduced to a buffer state, alongside Uruguay.
There was one sweetener. Paraguay was given the desolate Chaco Boreal
region by the arbitrator, U.S. president Rutherford Hayes. Argentina and
Brazil became indebted by the war, but merchants and planters had benefited, as had Buenos Aires centralizers against those favoring provincial
autonomy. In Brazil victory enabled the first stirrings of nationalism to
emerge, and it strengthened the Brazilian military, which prepared the
way for its coup deposing the emperor in 1889, when a republic was established. A war of this magnitude is bound to effect major changes
among the participants. Concludes Leslie Bethell:

> Solano López's reckless actions brought about the very thing
> that most threatened the security, even the existence, of his
> country: a union of his two powerful neighbours. . . . Neither
> Brazil nor Argentina had a quarrel with Paraguay sufficient to
> justify going to war. Neither wished nor planned for war with
> Paraguay. There was no popular demand or support for war; in-
> deed, the war proved to be generally unpopular in both coun-
> tries, especially Argentina. At the same time little effort was
> made to avoid war. The need to defend themselves against Para-
> guayan aggression . . . offered both Brazil and Argentina not only
> an opportunity to settle their differences with Paraguay over ter-
> ritory and river navigation but also to punish and weaken, per-
> haps destroy, a troublesome, emerging (expansionist?) power in
> their region.[68]

Some wars, including this one, involve a human folly that confounds
rationality. Why did Solano López aggress, and why did he continue
fighting long after defeat was inevitable? I note a similarity between
cases where leaders make overaggressive moves and then keep on fighting when defeat seems inevitable, as in Japan and Germany in the 1940s.

Leaders imprisoned themselves inside an ideology and political institutions that induced the belief that their soldiers would be superior in martial spirit to those of the enemy. So the leaders cannot calculate the balance of potential goal achievement versus the economic costs and military fortunes of war. They go recklessly to their doom, as their behavior becomes erratic, psychologically disturbed, and pathologically destructive to self and the dwindling loyalists around them. Solano López's mental descent amid the desperate degeneration of his remaining few troops accompanied by a mob of refugees is vividly and horrifically depicted in Whigham's last chapters.[69] The participants learned a lesson from this terrible war: even the communications system of the Río de la Plata was not worth fighting for again. Tensions were in future followed by rhetoric, and sometimes MIDs, but then defused by negotiations and eventually settlement.

The War of Confederation, 1836–1839

Parts of the central Pacific coast had unclear colonial boundaries. The Spanish Crown had not bothered to clarify administrative boundaries in such barren and sparsely inhabited deserts. But for the successor republics, boundary issues emerged. Separatism in the south of Peru, northern Bolivia, and Chile made neighborly interference for regime change possible. Disputes here were initially about control of coastal maritime trade and the tariffs that this brought. But the so-called tariff wars between Chile and Peru did not flare up into fighting.

The Bolivian regime seized a time of civil war in Peru to intervene and unite the two countries, claiming the legitimacy that they had both been in the same Spanish viceroyalty. This confederation was potentially the most powerful state on the Pacific coast, threatening the interests of Chile and Argentina. Again, a regional hegemony threatened. Diego Portales, the dominant figure in the Chilean government, declared: "The Confederation must disappear forever from the American stage. We must dominate forever in the Pacific."[70] So he threatened military action, and, as intended, this produced negotiations, mediated by Mexico. Agreement on trade and tariffs emerged, but Portales's demand that the confederation be dissolved was unacceptable to Bolivia. Agreement was then thwarted by a military revolt in Chile in which Portales was murdered. Though the rebels were defeated, many believed Peru had financed them. A Chilean war party strengthened. Interstate war in Latin

America again involved attempted regime change in a neighbor's domestic politics. This was the pretext for Chile to declare war.

The Bolivian-Peruvian Confederation had been recognized by Britain, France, and the United States, but they were ignored. Argentina and Ecuador initially remained neutral. But when the confederation interfered in Argentine internal politics, Argentina declared war as well. The confederation defeated the small Argentine army sent against it, but after fluctuating fortunes, Chilean forces were victorious at the Battle of Yungay in 1839, and the confederation was dissolved. There were about 8,000 total casualties in this war; the final decisive battle, between forces each about 6,000 strong, contributed almost 3,000 casualties, mostly Bolivian and Peruvian.

This was not massive warfare, and it did not attract much popular support, although when confederation forces supposedly committed atrocities in Chile, Chileans rallied 'round the flag. But the people were mostly absent from Chilean politics, excluded by an oligarchy that controlled elections.[71] From the 1830s expanding foreign trade was blending Chilean merchants and mine and land owners into a ruling class that agreed on the interests of the country and themselves. Family connections strengthened elite cohesion in a small country, which, given greater resolve and commitment of resources, was an advantage in war. Chile was the second exceptional case noted by Centeno and Mazzuca, where at least at the level of dominant classes there was some sense of "national" homogeneity. This was the only war in Latin America in which a state—a new, fragile confederation—was dismantled by war.

The War of the Pacific, 1879–1883

The second world war was bigger, causing nearly 12,000 military deaths. Geopolitics was here dominated by economic interests.[72] In 1842 valuable deposits of guano fertilizer were found along the border area disputed by Chile, Peru, and Bolivia. MID disputes dragged on for some time without escalating to war, but the rivalry became more intense with the discovery in the early 1860s of nitrate deposits, and then of silver. But in 1864–66 a Spanish fleet bombarded coastal towns in Peru, Chile, and Bolivia. The Spanish fortuitously produced an alliance among the three. In two small naval battles two hundred to four hundred sailors were killed before the Spanish withdrew. Bolivia and Chile signed a treaty in 1866, each renouncing some of its territorial and mining claims. They agreed to split the proceeds from guano deposits and taxes on mineral resources.

Chile developed the more effective government and capitalist economy, centered on a mining-industrial complex. Its revenue enabled development programs and military expenses. In response to mining pressure, the Chilean government sought to reinterpret the treaty to justify territorial expansion. In 1873 Peru and Bolivia formed a countering alliance, but a Chile-Bolivia treaty appeared to settle their differences. MID incidents arose and then dissipated. But in 1878 Bolivian authorities tried to extract more taxes from foreign mining companies, while Peru's impoverished government nationalized Chilean-owned mines. These provocations caused Chilean hawks to demand war to protect mining interests, and mutual miscalculations made war probable. Bolivia's dictator thought Chile was focused on possible Argentine aggression and so would not fight, while Peru's president decided to honor his country's not-so-secret military alliance with Bolivia, blundering into war ill-prepared. Army sizes grew to about 25,000 on each side, but those mobilized into battle were much fewer. They had modern weapons but obsolete tactics of mass infantry assaults, and they lacked logistical support. The Chileans had better-trained officers and NCOs, but their victory resulted mostly from superior civil infrastructures and political instability in Peru and Bolivia.[73]

The peace treaty of 1883 was dictated by Chile, and it allowed Chile to annex one Bolivian and three Peruvian provinces—and their nitrate deposits. Nine of the fourteen articles in the treaty referred to either guano or nitrates. Chile's acquisition of the deposits became the central source of income for the state, strengthening its armed forces and its political oligarchy—just as defeat weakened the Peruvian and Bolivian states. Chile was now the dominant Pacific power. Since the other powers were beset by internal disorder, they mounted no threat, and Chilean leaders relaxed into cultivating its balance-of-power system.[74]

The peace treaty stipulated that Chile organize a plebiscite after ten years in two of the provinces taken. Chile failed to do this, but subsequent MID episodes brought in mediation by the United States in 1929, which awarded one province to Peru, the other to Chile, and fixed all land border disputes. Maritime boundaries were not settled, and there were two further MID incidents followed by negotiations. In the Santiago Declaration of 1952, Chile, Ecuador, and Peru agreed to a maritime boundary limit of 320 kilometers offshore, but only in 2014 did the ICJ finalize a maritime settlement. Another group of Latin Americans learned through experience of unproductive wars that disputes are better settled through negotiation.

Ecuadoran-Colombian War (War of the Cauca), 1863

Both Ecuador and Colombia had been part of the Spanish viceroyalty of New Granada and the early successor Gran Colombia state. Border disputes thrived on vague Spanish maps in sparsely populated areas. In 1861 the conservative Gabriel García Moreno became an activist president of Ecuador, seeking to lessen class, regional, and language disputes by conferring more power on the Catholic Church. This alienated liberals, who saw the Church as an obstacle to liberty and progress. Similar conflicts had riven Colombia, and after a civil war there, the liberal Tomás Cipriano de Mosquera became president and immediately declared he would restore Gran Colombia and annex Venezuela and Ecuador. Venezuela's well-armed president ignored this, but weaker Ecuador was threatened as Mosquera urged Ecuadoran liberals to overthrow García Moreno and join the Gran Colombia project. When nothing happened, Mosquera ordered his army to the frontier. García Moreno responded by ordering his army to invade Colombia. This sequence of provocative actions by two aggressive presidents revealed systematic miscalculation of one another's likely response. The war was swiftly ended at the Battle of Cuaspad when about 4,000 Colombians routed 6,000 Ecuadoran invaders, killing or wounding about 1,500 of them. Colombian losses are unknown.

Colombian forces then invaded Ecuador, but international pressure brought an armistice welcomed by the two tired sides. International negotiations led to an agreement to return to the prewar status quo. Meddling in each other's internal conflicts—regime change—had been the major cause. This was the last war between the countries. Border disputes also involving Peru eventually resulted in a treaty of 1922 that deprived Ecuador of access to the Amazon. Ecuador was a resentful loser but, being weak, could not resist. A historian lamented that Ecuador was like Christ at Calvary, crucified between two thieves.[75] From 1950 Colombia was embroiled in civil wars and had no interest in external conflict.

Central American Wars, 1876, 1885, 1906–1907

These brief, connected episodes were provoked by attempts to reestablish the early Central American Federation, which were countered by balancing alliances among the other states. Once again, factional disputes within a country sparked military action for regime change. In 1876 Guatemala invaded Honduras in support of liberal rebels there, seeking to overthrow a conservative regime. El Salvador joined with the Hondurans to prevent Guatemalan hegemony. The war lasted a month. Guatemala triumphed. A new liberal regime was installed in Honduras, but there was not Guatemalan hegemony. Armies numbered 2,500 or less, while total losses were 4,000 killed or dead from disease. In 1885 Guatemala made another attempt at federation, Honduras acting as an ally. Their forces invaded El Salvador, which was aided by Costa Rica and Nicaragua. After a war of little more than two weeks, the Guatemalans were defeated and Central America remained divided. Army sizes were well under 10,000, and there were about 1,000 casualties, mostly Guatemalan.

A third, two-month war occurred in 1906 between Guatemala and El Salvador, aided by Honduras, each trying to install its clients, liberals or conservatives, in power in the enemy country. The largest army size was 7,000, and there was a total of 1,000 deaths. The war was inconclusive and ended with Mexican and American mediation. The next year war flared again as Nicaraguan forces attacked Honduras and El Salvador in yet another attempt to re-create a federation. Army sizes were about 4,500 and total casualties after two months of inconclusive fighting were about 1,000. A U.S.-sponsored peace conference agreed to submit claims to binding arbitration by a judge from each country, although this proved a failure. None of these short, small wars succeeded in changing the balance of power, but, although dictators kept on meddling in the internal politics of neighbors, they did not again go to war—until the 1969 Soccer War, which had quite different causes. Here rulers learned through failure that war did not pay.

The Chaco War, 1932–1935

This much bigger war was fought between Bolivia and Paraguay over borderlands in the Gran Chaco region, arid and thinly populated, but thought to be potentially oil-rich. Braumoeller says this was the second deadliest war of the modern era in terms of the proportion of national populations killed (higher than either world war).[76] The Paraguay River running through Chaco provided access to the Atlantic Ocean, important to Bolivia, which was landlocked, having lost its Pacific coast to Chile in the War of the Pacific. Since Paraguay had lost half its territory in the War of the Triple Alliance, both were self-righteous revisionist powers disputing access to the Atlantic. Their rulers were under economic pressure from foreign debts and stalled modernization, and under political pressure from nationalist newspapers and student demonstrators. So the war was partly diversionary as presidents sought to shift attention from their domestic failures. Their fears were of rival elites, not of class struggle. Because Bolivian literacy was just over 10 percent, and under 5 percent of its people were enfranchised, politics did not involve the masses. Miners pressed for workers' rights, but they were sectorally confined.[77]

Paraguay claimed its right by virtue of occupying the Chaco since the Spanish left, but this consisted only of a few government outposts dwarfed by large estates that a cash-strapped government had sold to Argentinian, British, and American investors. Its main economic motive was to continue receiving this income. Most of the Guarani people of the region identified with Paraguay. The glorification of Paraguay's mestizo identity, personified in the notion of the patriotic Guarani-speaking peasant soldier, enabled scientists, missionaries, and anthropologists to write about the indigenous populations without racial slurs, a situation unique in Latin America.[78] Bolivia claimed *uti possidetis*, arguing that in Spanish times the Gran Chaco had been part of its *audiencia*. Since Paraguay's defeat in the War of the Triple Alliance, Bolivia had been the more active in the Chaco region, provoking MIDs between them. Foreign powers attempted mediation, but agreements proved contentious back home, and none was implemented. As diplomacy failed, military preparations began.

Both had small military outposts along the frontiers, and 1927 saw a collision between rival patrols. A Paraguayan lieutenant was killed and his men taken prisoner by Bolivian soldiers. Rhetoric escalated in the two capitals, then subsided, as the liberal government in Paraguay resisted pressure for retaliation. A bigger MID clash occurred in 1928, when a Paraguayan battalion seized a Bolivian post. Two successive Bolivian presidents decided that war would divert national attention from internal disputes with a hostile congress, radical students, and a weak economy. Believing that Bolivia's greater resources, larger population, and German-trained army would bring swift victory, Bolivia's President Daniel Salamanca ordered the army to take three more Paraguayan outposts.[79] In 1929 the Pan-American Union brokered a settlement. The two sides signed a peace accord, withdrew their forces, and exchanged prisoners. The border dispute was not settled, but war was avoided, since neither side felt ready to wage it. Instead, they engaged in an arms-importing race.

In 1931 Paraguayan surveyors found a freshwater lake in the parched Chaco region. Irrigation agriculture might be possible. The Paraguayans constructed a fort to consolidate their presence, which the Bolivians seized in June 1932, provoking a counterattack that drove the Bolivians away. There was pressure in Bolivia for retaliation, and a force of 10,000 men seized the biggest town in the Chaco. This produced a Paraguayan army response, and from May 1933 the Bolivians were forced to retreat. This humiliation brought down President Salamanca in a military coup in 1934. By that time, Paraguay's soldiers held far more ground than their country had claimed. Paraguay's soldiers, though outnumbered, again proved more cohesive and better led, possessing the logistical advantage of rivers and rail lines leading into the remote region. It seemed to be winning the war. Yet it had also incurred heavy losses, faced supply difficulties as it advanced, and exhausted its loans from Argentina. Both sides sought peace and agreed to a cease-fire in 1935. The peace settlement of 1938, assisted by Argentina and the United States, awarded Paraguay three-quarters of the Chaco Boreal and left Bolivia with the swampy northwest, not the desired river port. Diplomatic and strategic blunders and political infighting had left Bolivia with far less land than it had had before the war. In mediated settlements victors usually made some gains and negotiators sometimes favored claims based on occupation rather than ancient maps.

Paraguay lost almost 40,000 men and Bolivia almost 60,000, although mostly from disease. Bolivia mobilized about 10 percent of its population during the war, Paraguay about 16 percent. The loss rates, Bolivia 3 percent and Paraguay 4 percent of total population, were slightly higher than European losses in World War I; the recruitment rate was similar to that in the U.S. Civil War (about 10 percent). This had been a devastating war for both countries. Bolivian mobilization was a remarkable if disastrous achievement in a thinly populated country with a supposedly weak state.[80] At first, recruitment had been easy, especially in cities where a rally 'round the flag sentiment briefly raged, but it got more difficult the longer war lasted and the defeats piled up. Conscription required enforcement, desertions grew, and officers had to put rifles in deserters' hands and push them back into the lines, for if they had shot them, their regiments would have been denuded. Eventually, in 2012, commercially viable oil was found in the area awarded to Paraguay, and natural gas was discovered in Bolivia's. It had proved a pointless war. It lived on in Bolivian resentment and occasional MID incidents, but it was not repeated.

The Leticia War, 1932–1933

This eight-month conflict was fought between Colombia and Peru over disputed border territory in the Amazon rainforest. It began with Peruvian occupation of the small river port of Leticia, connected by the Amazon to the Atlantic, 4,000 kilometers away. The attack was by armed Peruvian soldiers and civilians, perhaps without authority from above. A reluctant Colombian government was forced by urban popular pressure to prepare to retake the port. Similarly, the Peruvian government was pressured to defend it. When Colombian forces eventually reached this remote area, 1,100 kilometers from Bogotá, they retook the port. The forces involved were each about 1,000 strong. The number of persons killed is not known, but it is unlikely to have been more than two hundred deaths on each side, partly to jungle diseases, a motive for them to end the war alongside mounting debt. With the assistance of League of Nations mediation, Leticia was restored to Colombia, but the two governments divided the rest of the disputed zone. This conflict had casualties well short of the CoW minimum, and it is not normally included in lists of Latin American wars.

Ecuador-Peru Wars

From the 1830s to the 1990s a large but sparsely populated Amazonian border zone between Ecuador and Peru saw repeated skirmishes.[81] In 1857 Ecuador attempted to repay its debt to Britain by issuing bonds for this disputed territory. Peru objected, and military skirmishes followed, which went in Peru's favor. The Treaty of Mapasingue in 1860 included considerable Ecuadoran concessions. The treaty was ratified by neither government, however, and the next decade saw thirty-four MIDs between them, all short of war. This was the longest-lived territorial sore in the Americas, arising from border ambiguities in forests and mountains. Peru claimed the border was along the ridge of the *Cordillera del Cóndor* mountain range. Ecuador insisted that its territory extended eastward over the top of the sierras to the Cenepa River, which feeds through the Marañón river to the Amazon and thence to the Atlantic, the access to which Ecuador claimed a sovereign right. Thus, this remote region has strategic significance, especially for Ecuador. Three brief conflicts ensued in the twentieth century, interspersing small MIDs or wars with diplomatic wrangling and mediation.[82]

The War of '41, or the Zarumilla War, began when a large Peruvian force invaded Ecuador, seeing a window of opportunity, a political crisis that brought the main Ecuadoran army into the capital. The Peruvians overwhelmed the much smaller Ecuadoran forces opposing them. About five hundred soldiers died, including only one hundred Peruvians. An armistice was soon signed, followed by the Rio Protocol, brokered by the United States, Brazil, Chile, and Argentina. They threatened Ecuador with ending the talks if it did not sign, which would leave Ecuador to face menacing Peruvian forces. Ecuador had to give up two-thirds of the disputed territory, comprising 220,000 square kilometers, thereby losing any outlet to the Amazon River. So Ecuadoran governments became bitterly revisionist. David Mares and David Palmer say that in all the Ecuador-Peru confrontations, politicians on both sides were pushed by "public opinion" into aggressive stances.[83] The urban classes were more ignorant of the horrors of war than were the politicians, and few of them fought in these mostly peasant armies. Only the financial cost of war might harm them, if it lasted long.

Seventy-eight kilometers of the border remained unclear, however. The actual course of the Cenepa River differed from that shown on the maps. Seizing on this, Ecuador rejected the protocol, which brought further diplomatic wrangling. After 1969 relations between them improved. Both joined the Andean Pact, and they signed economic pacts with each other. Peruvian leaders, democratic and authoritarian, hoped this would settle the dispute. But Ecuadoran political movements, seething with injustice, did not let go of the issue, and military outposts were erected in the disputed area in 1977. The Peruvians responded with threats but not much action, and the two sides backed off without war. But Peru's mild reaction emboldened the Ecuadoran government into repeating its infiltration. There were two more flare-ups into violence.

The Paquisha War of 1981 was triggered by Ecuadoran forces establishing three military outposts on the Cenepa River. It lasted only a week, and there were fewer than two hundred deaths. The Peruvians won because of greater military power. Yet in the 1980s Peru experienced economic crisis and near-bankruptcy, political turmoil, a border dispute with Chile in the south, and a civil war against Shining Path guerillas. So Ecuadoran leaders opportunistically upped their territorial claims and prepared for war. This provoked Peruvian forces to strengthen border defenses. Undaunted, in 1995 Ecuadorans constructed stronger forts inside contested territory. Both regimes were egged on by nationalism among the literate classes demanding to preserve or recapture sacred homeland. Ecuadoran governments, whichever political faction was in control, would not let go of the issue because of a sense of injustice. Mares and Palmer observe, "The external threat posed by Peruvian claims to territory in the Amazon . . . [was] the glue that held the nation together."[84] They mean the middle-class nation.

This led to the monthlong Cenepa War, for which 40,000 soldiers were mobilized, of whom 500–1,000 were killed.[85] The Peruvian air force bombed and strafed. Nine of its planes and helicopters were downed. Ecuadoran forces performed better, the fighting was inconclusive, and both governments tired of the financial costs. Revisionism in Ecuador was assuaged by pride in the army's achievements, which gave the government space to negotiate a compromise. International pressures brought back four international mediators who ruled that the border was the line of the *Cordillera*, as Peru claimed. There were sweeteners: Ecuador was guaranteed shipping access to the Amazon and the Atlantic, received $3 billion in development aid from international financial institutions, and was granted perpetual ownership of one square kilometer of land in the disputed territory to build a memorial to its fallen!

This settlement has endured partly because it allowed economic development of both border regions and increased trade between them. The countries finally learned that negotiation is preferable to military aggression. Mares and Palmer say that "we should not believe that Latin America has reached a state in which the use of force as an instrument of statecraft has been rendered illegitimate or null."[86] I am more optimistic, perceiving that each region of Latin America in turn has learned that interstate war does not pay.

The Soccer War, 1969

This war of 1969 was fought between Honduras and El Salvador. The violence began in riots during a football World Cup qualifying match between them, but the roots of conflict lay mainly in mass immigration. Around 300,000 Salvadoran immigrants had streamed into Honduras seeking a better economic life. William Durham and Thomas Anderson show that this resulted from growing inequality of landholding in El Salvador because of the government's encouragement of export-oriented agriculture, which favored larger landowners and squeezed peasants, many of whom were forced by debts off the land.[87] They migrated to

Honduras, believing they could get land there. Some succeeded. But Honduras also had growing inequalities of land that were squeezing out its small farmers. The two pressures of immigration and landlessness, both a consequence of class struggle between capitalist landlords, who controlled the state, and peasant owners and tenants was diverted into struggle between the two national communities. This was one of the few wars analyzable in Marxist terms as the diversion by state elites of class struggle—and the resulting nationalism was popular, mobilizing much of the population.

This war occurred during the Cold War, as fear of communism fanned the flames. Large landowners and American agribusiness pressured the Honduran government into a land reform that expropriated Salvadoran immigrants who owned or tenanted their land, forcing 130,000 out of the country. This infuriated El Salvador's leaders, terrified by returning angry peasants whom they saw as potential communists. The nationalism that flared up was manipulated by Salvadoran leaders and gave popular backing to an invasion of Honduras. The Salvadoran army advanced and quickly neared the Honduran capital. The Organization of American States and the United States then pressured the Salvadorans to halt, as they may have anticipated, and the OAS negotiated a truce. After contentious negotiations, the immigration dispute was settled in 1980. In the four-day air-and-land war El Salvador suffered an estimated 900 dead, mostly civilians, while Honduras is estimated to have lost 250 soldiers and 2,000 civilians—significant numbers in tiny countries. The war strengthened the powers of both countries' militaries and made the border dispute more difficult to solve. Several peace deals later, there has been no further violence.

Falklands (Malvinas) and the Beagle Channel, 1982–1983

The Falklands (Malvinas) War began when Argentine forces invaded these British-owned islands, desolate and of little economic value, long claimed by both sides, long occupied only by British settlers—there were 1,820 settlers and their 400,000 sheep in 1982. War was started to bolster the sagging popularity of the Argentine military regime, while the British response was dictated by a mixture of the sagging popularity of Margaret Thatcher and her strong Churchillian sense of national honor. Losing the war destroyed the Argentine regime; winning bolstered Thatcher. The total casualties (dead plus wounded) of about nine hundred did not meet the CoW project's requirements of one thousand deaths, but it was clearly a war.

Yet it was part of broader conflicts in this desolate region. Border disputes between Chilean and Argentine rulers had mounted in Patagonia in the later nineteenth century as Argentina had expanded southward, conquering indigenous peoples backed by Chile. *Uti possidetis* offered no solution since the Spanish had not settled this far south, but a treaty of 1881 had set the border at the line of the highest mountains dividing the Atlantic and Pacific watersheds. Yet in Patagonia, drainage basins confusingly crossed the Andes. Should the Andean peaks constitute the border, as the Argentines claimed, or should the drainage basins, as the Chileans claimed? There were some naval MIDs, but both feared that any war might be costly. War had been avoided when the parties agreed in 1902 to binding British mediation, which solved the crisis by dividing the lakes along the disputed line into two equal parts, Chilean and Argentine. In celebration the two countries shared the expense of a giant statue of Christ the Redeemer, erected under the shadow of the highest mountain, marking the restoration of friendship.[88]

There was one remaining issue. Chile possessed four small islands at the southern edge of Tierra del Fuego in the Beagle Channel, which connects the Pacific and Atlantic oceans. Possession had implications for navigation through the channel, and steamships had greatly increased traffic. From 1904 Argentine governments had claimed the four islands. The dispute had festered on through MID incidents, attempts at direct negotiations, and supposedly "binding" international tribunals, all of which awarded the islands to Chile. In 1978 a plan by the Argentine military government to invade the islands had been aborted because of divisions within the military. It was perhaps surprising that the generals then made the decision to fight not there against the weaker enemy, but against the British, a major military power traditionally friendly to Argentina. This choice was made because in the intervening four years the military regime had become unpopular and the war was a desperate attempt at survival.[89] Political goals triumphed, backed, as so often, by an overoptimistic military calculation of odds.

The Argentine war plan of 1982 was to invade the disputed Beagle Islands after success in the Falklands. President Leopoldo Galtieri declared that Chileans "have to know ... what we are doing now, because they will be the next in turn." Indeed, he deployed his better troops on the Chilean border, while lesser units had to deal with the highly professional British forces. He made the not unreasonable decision that the 13,000-kilometer distance between Britain and the islands made any retaliation logistically impossible, while the fait accompli of a bloodless invasion of the islands would persuade the British to negotiate. He believed that international public opinion, and the United States, would regard this as a war of resistance against colonialism. Mares regards this as a "rational policy decision" and blames the British and American governments for not taking the Argentines seriously and failing to credibly signal deterrence.[90] The problem in Britain was that war could not be threatened before the invasion, since almost no one in Britain even knew of the existence of the islands or of British sovereignty over them. But once the invasion happened, the government could count on a rally 'round the flag.

Galtieri had misjudged. He had brought forward the date of the invasion because the British government was growing suspicious of the Argentine military buildup, but this gave the British time to retaliate before winter set in. President Reagan had warned Galtieri that Thatcher was determined to fight. She also had political goals, being unpopular at home before the war. Had Galtieri possessed any understanding of the enemy, he would have realized two things about British conservatism. First, it views sovereignty as sacred, not to be renounced in the face of foreign aggression. In 2020 British conservatives supposedly "reclaimed British sovereignty" from the European Union. Second, conservatism was still in the grip of imperial nostalgia. Britannia could still rule the waves—indeed it could against a third-rate military power. Moreover, the weakness of the colonial analogy was that the entire population of the islands declared themselves to be British. International opinion did not turn against Britain, nor did the U.S. government. Being convinced of the justice of the Argentine case and the dominance of anticolonial sentiments around the world, Galtieri had assumed that the Americans would side with him. But once the British fleet reached the South Atlantic (with refueling and communications help from the United States), Argentina's defeat was predictable. Once landed on the Falklands, the British infantry's superiority was marked.

Galtieri's consequent fall resulted in a democratic government anxious to solve the Beagle dispute. It set up a referendum in 1984 in which 82.6 percent of Argentines voted to implement a papal peace proposal. Argentina and Chile signed the agreement, which awarded the islands to Chile but maritime rights to Argentina, the obvious solution. There has been no challenge to this. Indeed, that 82.6 percent shows how far these Latin Americans have moved away from war and even from MIDs. The Falklands are another matter. The rival claims endure there.

Latin American Conclusions

I have analyzed fifteen interstate conflicts since the 1830s, but my total includes four that did not reach the CoW minimum of one thousand deaths. Even including them means there was a war somewhere in Latin America for one in five years—and only a little more frequently, one in four years, in the period 1834 to 1899. This has not been a warlike region of the world, except for its massacres of indigenous peoples. Three countries never went to war with another Latin American state: Venezuela, Mexico, and Panama. After the War of the Triple Alliance, Brazil solved all its border disputes through diplomacy. Among the thirteen countries experiencing war, there were no serial repeaters—unlike Republican Rome, Greek city-states, early Chinese states, Mongol peoples, medieval and modern European states, Japan from the 1890s to 1945, and the United States more recently. Argentina and Peru fought three wars, five countries had two wars, and five only one. No single "front" had more than two wars. The notion that "states made wars and wars made states" involves an iterative sequence: wars must be made repeatedly if war is to be baked in to the culture and institutions of a country. In Latin America wars were few and generally short, for governments lacked an expandable tax base. The two most serious wars were so damaging that they deterred these governments from making war again. Governments dealt with erratic domestic pressures for war or peace; they protested their grievances; they made threats that quite often led to MIDs, but they generally avoided war. Since 1982 there have been no interstate wars, and that last one involved Britain, an outside power.

All the wars were between neighbors, but there was virtually no raiding over borders in the continent. Nor were there successful imperial conquests, though a few attempts at regional hegemony failed. There were three main substantive causes, each present in six cases. First, some wars attempted Realist geopolitical balancing: an alliance of neighbors to counter what they perceived as one state's drive for regional hegemony— as in the Platine War, the War of the Confederation, the War of the Triple Alliance, the Peru-Bolivian War, the Ecuadoran-Colombian War, and the Central American Wars. These aimed at restoring former Spanish viceroyalties. Yet none was successful—balancing worked. No state was swallowed up by the victor in war, as happened in other continents, although some lost territory. Balancing was made easier by the conservatism of *uti possidetis*, by ecological and fiscal limits on would-be hegemons, and by the common culture of rulers. Balancing was largely a rational response, but as a consequence rulers learned to love peace.

Second, six wars involved rival claims to sparsely settled border regions—the Platine War, the War of the Triple Alliance, the War of the Pacific, the Chaco War, the Leticia War, and the Ecuador-Peru Wars—sparked mostly by a disjunction between *uti possidetis* and newer patterns of settlement on the ground, and exacerbated by fuzzy historic maps. Both sides considered their claims to these slivers of territory morally justified, and disputes were exacerbated if major economic or strategic resources lay there. Nitrates and oil were the main economic interests activated in border wars; strategic interests principally meant access to the Río de la Plata and Amazon River systems and to the oceans, which also brought economic opportunities. So economic power interests predominated in this group of wars. But territorial gains were mostly limited. Little was at stake in most border disputes to justify big sacrifices, and conflict was much more limited than in Roman, European, or early Chinese experience, where states were often fighting for their survival. This was an unintended benefit of European imperialism—it roughly stabilized the borders of the successor countries, with the exception of what we might call the "Horn" of Latin America, the former British colonies of Guyana and Belize, whose borders with their neighbors, Venezuela and Guatemala, remain disputed and whose case is currently before the ICJ in 2022. Of course, no benefit had resulted for the indigenous peoples anywhere in Latin America.

Third, six wars were precipitated by interfering in neighbors' internal politics for regime change or regime preservation—the Platine War, the War of the Triple Alliance, the War of Confederation, the Ecuadoran-Colombian War, the Central American Wars, and, in a rather different way, the Soccer War. This involved a distinctive security dilemma. If state B did not interfere in the factional disputes of its neighbor A, then rival state C might do so, increasing its power in the region. So state B sometimes did intervene first, causing state C to do so as well. This was intended as a cheap way of increasing regional influence, although in these cases it escalated into war. This group of wars had a large unintentional component. But security dilemmas involving arms races were rare because states had low tax bases and so were cost-conscious. Interventions were boosted by the ideological similarity of internal disputes across Latin America, between republicans and monarchists, *peninsulares* and Creoles, regional autonomists and central statists, liberals and conservatives, and finally capitalists and socialists. Shared ideologies led to alliance with neighboring like-minded groups, and so domestic political power relations helped drive wars.

The Soccer War was distinctive, the only case in which class struggle was diverted by a government into interstate war, as Marxists suggest. Other forms of conflict diversion were more common, however, and these motivated the Argentine and Thatcher regimes in the Falklands War, two Bolivian presidents during the Chaco War, and the Mexican president in World War II. All sought to gain popularity through a successful war, but it worked only for Thatcher. This was a second way in which domestic political power relations drove wars.

These causes of war overlapped. Some wars can be partially explained by rational choice theory of calculations of the chances of strategic or economic gains balanced against likely military and fiscal costs and the chances of victory. There was calculative brinkmanship, establishing frontier posts, financing foreign factions, taxing foreign businesses, and general saber rattling to bolster a domestic image of strength, but then drawing back by accepting a truce or mediation. Such gambits often did not play out as calculated, however, since the rival's moves were not easy to predict. And as usual in my cases, overconfidence was rife, the product of rulers trapped inside nationally compartmentalized societies, unable to fully comprehend the opponent's motivations, options, and strengths. Six times the initiator of war clearly lost, and only two initiators won. In five cases there was mutual provocations into war, and five wars ended in a costly stalemate, rational for neither side. This is not a rational balance sheet in favor of war.

Rulers mattered. They varied in aggressiveness, and there were four cases in which aggression was rather irrational and military judgment was distorted by reckless ambition, righteousness, and domestic political needs—the cases of Argentine president Rosas in the Platine War, of all three of the principal leaders in the War of the Triple Alliance, but especially Paraguayan president Solano López, in the Ecuadoran-Colombian War by Colombian president Cipriano de Mosquera, and in the Falklands War by Argentine president Galtieri. Moreover, *all* the regimes that initiated war were overthrown either during or immediately after the war.[91] That was a salutary lesson. There was in the long run a learning process: movement from war to MID rituals posturing strength and resolve to satisfy domestic pressures or leadership pride and sense of honor—but also to avoid war, for almost all states had experienced bad wars. Indeed, Latin American history does reassure liberal theory that in the right circumstances human beings can calculate that war is bad and to be avoided—an example of delayed-reaction Realism, the belated realization that war does not pay.

The mass of the population rarely concerned themselves with foreign policy, and nationalism did not penetrate deeply. As Centeno observes, dominant classes in different countries shared more culture with each other than they did with their own popular classes. Two cases deviated somewhat. Paraguay was more homogeneous, even "proto-nationalist," whereas Chile had a more cohesive capitalist ruling class, and so both punched in war above their weight of numbers. Otherwise, nationalism was sometimes mobilized among the urban middle classes, especially students, particularly when an incident like a lethal attack on a border post might be claimed as a national humiliation requiring vengeance. Strong revisionist emotions could push the rulers of countries that had lost a previous war into rash aggression, as they did Paraguayan and Bolivian rulers. They saw themselves as embodying the nation, so that their emotions and ideologies were both personal and national. Galtieri and Thatcher both embodied this during the Falklands War. Sometimes mass media amplified such sentiments. Henderson argues that border disputes strengthened nationalism throughout the world.[92] Not here. Nationalism in Latin America has mostly been of the harmless variety—World Cup not war fever.

I have again emphasized distinctive social and political ecology, but here as causes of the *low* incidence of wars. Expansion by stronger states over weaker neighbors elsewhere in the world brought many wars of deflection, increasing the apparent rationality of war, as we saw in ancient China and medieval Europe. But in Latin America the deflection of war was mostly within states and against indigenous peoples. Most Latin American states were less concerned with expanding borders than with gaining effective control of their own territories. There were sparsely populated regions with little political authority, but unlike early Europe and China, they lay within states wrested from indigenous peoples. A second ecological effect made interstate wars logistically difficult. Wars required mobilizing and deploying forces over long distances in border areas, often in deserts, jungles, or swamps, far from the capital, barely habitable and disease-ridden. The potential gains were rarely worth the cost. MIDs were far cheaper and let off steam, a mixture of rationality and emotionality. Such difficult logistics also meant that regional guerilla insurrections—which I have not discussed—became easier to sustain and more difficult to crush, increasing the number and duration of civil wars in parts of Latin America.

Unlike their counterparts in Europe, the officers and men had had little experience of war and so did not fight very competently—a good thing perhaps. Yet this was not in itself much of a deterrent to war since to win one had to be only a little less incompetent than the enemy. Wars happened when state elites perceived that the enemy state was even weaker than they were, but as in my other case studies, they were often wrong. One difficulty in predicting relative strengths was the combination of very inexperienced soldiers and the foreign British, German, or French officers brought in to advise them. Rulers tended to place unwarranted faith in these men's ability to transform soldiers' behavior, for in battle the soldiers tended to revert to old ways—as we see today in Afghanistan and Iraq in armies trained by Americans.

Another deterrent was the fact that their low tax base was insufficient to finance long wars or big armies. As Mazzuca argues, rulers could rarely overcome the fiscal resistance of peripheral power brokers exploiting an economy of free trade. War involved debt, crippling after a quite short period. As Centeno contends, debt was probably the main state weakness that made for few wars, and it was the main reason that the wars were short, that after a year or two the combatant states were willing to accept mediation, and that there were no repeating war-mongering states. Thus, the institutions and culture of militarism never really got going. Militarism pervaded the officer caste, not the whole society, and conceptions of military honor and virtue were too weak to sustain warfare in the absence of profit. The rank-and-file soldiers fought for pay, and most civilians stood aside. Losing a war was a disaster, but the winners rarely found that wars paid for themselves. Only the War of the Pacific brought immediate profit for Chile, although the Río de la Plata wars brought long-term trading benefits for the victors. Otherwise, victory was a costly investment in limited territorial gains of dubious worth and uncertain future payoff. Defeats resonated more than victories in popular emotions. Pressure from urban classes could push rulers into saber rattling to show their strength, but few wanted a crisis to escalate into war.

There was little armed intervention by external powers—an Anglo-French naval blockade, minor British gunboat diplomacy to protect its colonies Guyana and Belize, a failed Spanish naval attack, a failed French attack on Mexico, a successful British invasion of the Falklands, and more significant Mexican-American wars. With this last exception, more salient for the external powers was the maintenance of free trade, and for this they had much support among Latin American power brokers who wanted to keep central states weak and starved of funds. Thus, free trade was in this case an indirect cause of relative peace.

Most nineteenth-century wars ended by agreement between the belligerents, but all the twentieth-century wars were mediated or arbitrated by other states or outside organizations. This indicates gradual lessening of conflict, which allowed the parties to recognize the liberal virtues of diplomacy. Clear-cut military victories and significant territorial gains became less likely. Some aggression was launched on the assumption that outside negotiators would soon call a halt, and a swift invasion might change facts on the ground to influence the diplomats. Some argue that the global prevalence of mediated and arbitrated ends of wars and MIDs leads to geopolitical instability by preserving weak states and revisionist aggression.[93] This has not been so in Latin America. Interstate wars have yielded to MIDs, which have also become smaller and milder. Mares and Palmer reveal that the years 2005–9 saw ten MIDs in the region, but eight of them involved only threats or shows of force.[94] Two produced shooting and a few deaths, but not war. The usefulness of the category of MID is clear in Latin America.

The Cold War saw a major change in the late 1940s as U.S. administrations went wholesale for regime change or strengthening through violent repressions of leftists. In 1948, at the end of a civil war, the Costa Rican army was abolished. Since then the country has had no military at all, just police forces. Honduran rulers then debated whether to follow this pacific example. Unfortunately, this was bad timing. The United States was entering Latin America more forcefully, offering military training and better weaponry to combat the supposed threat of communism. Though the real communist threat was negligible, the United States sponsored suppressing all other leftists, too, sometimes out of ideological ignorance, sometimes to protect the interests of American business.[95] Latin American militaries loved this, for it gave them better status, training, and weapons. Conservatives also welcomed it for reasons of perceived class interest. In 1947 the United States had given more bite to the Monroe Doctrine with the Rio Treaty. This laid down "hemispheric defense" doctrine over Latin America. The treaty obliged its nations to help against any aggressive actions by one state against another. Yet this was diverted into anticommunism in the U.S. Mutual Security Programs of 1949 and 1951. So Honduras did not follow the example of Costa Rico. Along with most other states, it remilitarized. The threat was civil wars, left against right, not interstate wars.[96] Although Marxian arguments had relatively little explanatory power in interstate wars in Latin America, they are essential in analyzing such civil wars.

In the post–Cold War period, U.S. hegemony is weakening in Latin America. The United States failed to overthrow leftist President Hugo Chávez in Venezuela, and it vacillated when the conservative opposition appealed for help against his leftist successor. Americans' demand for drugs has also undermined Latin American police powers. This happened first in Colombia, where struggles between leftist guerillas and paramilitaries hired by landlords and backed by rightist governments also became drug wars. These spread to other countries, notably Mexico, where over 100,000 people have been killed since 2006, about 70 percent of deaths inflicted by illegally imported U.S. guns. In 2018 the Mexican total of just over 33,000 drug war–related deaths was the second-highest civil war death rate in the world, greater than either Afghanistan or Iraq, exceeded only by Syria. By 2022 there had been a total of 360,000 drug-related killings in Mexico since 2006. The region's cities also have the highest homicide rates in the world. Privatized wars have replaced civil wars as the main form of Latin American violence. Weak government has protected Latin America from interstate wars, but in some contexts it has intensified civil strife.

But this period has also seen a healthier countertrend: two common market pacts, MERCOSUR and the Andean Community, are moves toward greater regional economic integration. In 1998 all the countries (except Venezuela) signed a framework agreement toward integrating the two customs zones in a single South American Free Trade Area, with thirteen member states. This represents a further step away from war as a means of economic acquisition. Yoram Haftel analyzes Regional Integration Arrangements (RIAs) across the world, including MERCOSUR and the Andean Community.[97] He showed that a broad scope of RIA economic activity and regular meetings of high-level officials helped the peaceful resolution of disputes by reducing uncertainty regarding states' interests, motivations, and resolve. They are effective instruments of interstate bargaining in times of conflict, one more factor in explaining why Latin American war is almost obsolete and why even MIDs are much less frequent. I expect such trends to continue—mafias, not massed armies, will predominate in the near future. Latin America represents an example to the rest of the world. Perhaps Kant's perpetual peace is out of reach, but letting off steam with MIDs that lead to diplomacy represents an achievable goal for the world.

An African Addendum

Although wars in postcolonial Africa are not part of my remit, I briefly note similarities between its wars and those of Latin America. For postcolonial Africa we have data for only fifty to seventy years, compared to two hundred years for Latin America. Both experienced anticolonial wars of independence, followed by few interstate wars. Also shared has been the unintended border benefit of posthumous imperialism. The boundaries of the European colonies were accepted by the newly independent states, so there were few border disputes. Ruling regimes had a shared interest in maintaining peaceful borders, while they dealt with the greater problems of imposing rule inside their borders. The colonial powers had generally pacified a zone around a capital, normally a port, and along communications routes to valuable mining and settler zones, but their authority elsewhere was feeble. The postcolonial states inherited this unevenness and have struggled to expand their zones of control. About half of them have seen civil wars, usually between center and peripheries, which is a higher proportion than in any other region of the world. States have prioritized domestic rather than international order. The Organization of African Unity (OAU), established in 1963, pledged to respect state sovereignty and to avoid intervention in each other's internal affairs. Its Cairo Declaration of 1964 accepted the principle of *uti possidetis*, going further than Latin America. As we see in the next chapter, however, the African Union has been recently intervening in wars against non–state actors.

On border issues, the Horn of Africa has been the main exception, again for colonial-era reasons, since territory had been shuffled between the Abyssinian-Ethiopian Empire and the British, French, and Italian empires. Rival borders could be claimed by the Horn's emerging states, Ethiopia, Eritrea, Somaliland, Somalia, and Djibouti, especially where ethnic differed from political borders, as in the Ogaden region of Ethiopia. The Cold War aggravated these conflicts since the United States and the USSR backed different sides, while the growth of nonstate Islamic terrorism has more recently introduced further armed struggles. The total fatalities in the five or six wars of the region have been at least 100,000 so far. They were the only interstate wars in the continent in which disputed borders were the principal casus belli. Unusually for Africa, these states were also repeat war makers, and the disputes are not over, as the war of 2021 that pitted Ethiopia and Eritrea against Tigray revealed. In 2022 a repeat war seems likely.

The Congo War, most severe during 1996 to 2003, but still simmering, has been by far the deadliest in Africa. This was initially a series of civil wars of regional resistance against Congo's central regimes. Yet they have been exacerbated by intervention by neighboring states supporting local clients who would let them share in Congolese mineral wealth—the main violation of the OAU pledge of nonintervention. Conflict between Hutu and Tutsi groups in the country were also exacerbated by armed Hutu militias fleeing from Rwanda after defeat following the genocide there, pursued by vengeful Tutsi government forces. Nine African countries and many more armed groups have contributed to between 2.5 and 5.4 million deaths, mainly through disease and starvation among civilians.

There have been only six to twelve wars in postcolonial Africa, depending on how you count, half in the Horn of Africa, and the worst in the Congo. Over half of these cases also contained substantial civil war elements. Of the fifty-three African countries, at least nineteen have experienced one or more civil wars, often accompanied by quite high civilian casualties, while another eleven have experienced more minor insurgencies. That leaves twenty-three broadly pacific states, though some of these have experienced coups d'état. Like Latin America, Africa has experienced civil wars, but more and deadlier ones. The elimination of states, common in Eurasia, is unknown. If war between states did threaten, the ecology usually made for difficult military logistics. Governments were even weaker in African than Latin American countries, making civil wars likelier. We cannot attribute the low rate of interstate warfare in these two regions to unusually pacific populations. Rather, they specialized in other forms of violence.

CHAPTER TEN

The Decline of War?

Western Views after the Enlightenment

Has there been either a long-term increase or a long-term decrease in wars in history up to today? My answer is broadly neither. Instead, variation has characterized each epoch. Almost every literate source before the late eighteenth century saw war as an inevitable and sometimes desirable feature of the human condition. In contrast, most European writers since the Enlightenment have claimed that war was declining or was about to decline. Kant started this, saying absolute monarchs made war whereas republics and constitutional monarchies might make peace. Provided the latter expanded at the expense of the former, peace might spread. This began a "republican" theory of peace based on the spread of representative government and the rule of law. He added tongue-in-cheek that universal hospitality to foreigners and a federation of free states would also be necessary for peace, and he admitted that occasional wars might be necessary so that the virtues of peace would not be forgotten.[1]

The French Revolutionary and Napoleonic wars interrupted such hopes. Yet nineteenth-century Europe seemed quite peaceful. Europeans fought colonial wars in other continents, but most social theorists ignored these and advanced optimistic dichotomies distinguishing historical from modern societies—throughout history, warfare and militarism had dominated societies; now peace owing to capitalism or industrialism and free trade would rule. War had brought profit in the past, but it was now superseded by the superior profits of trade. Such arguments were made by Montesquieu, Adam Smith, Jeremy Bentham, Auguste Comte, Henri de Saint-Simon, Karl Marx, and Herbert Spencer. Writers like Joseph Schumpeter and Thorstein Veblen, at the turn of the twentieth century, aware of the rise of militarism in Germany and Japan, treated this as the last vestige of feudalism. Four main reasons for optimism were generally advanced: republicanism, free trade, socialism, and industrial society.[2] These arguments are still heard today.

Some British liberals were conscious of their country's colonial wars but embraced "liberal imperialism." Led by John Stuart Mill, who worked for the East India Company for thirty-five years, they defended colonial wars as bringing civilization to the benighted races (including the Irish, said Mill). Like virtually all imperialists, they said war was necessary to bring peace. French writers endorsed an imperial civilizing vision advocating rather more assimilation of native peoples. Late nineteenth-century Americans said it was the duty of the Anglo-Saxon race to bring civilization and peace to other races. The sociologist Lester Ward, borrowing from Spencer, said war had been responsible for human progress.[3] Through violence hominids had gained dominance over animals, and through war technologically advanced races had gained dominance over the less civilized and had a duty to spread civilization among them. Yet he said war would eventually decline as race differences were overcome by assimilation and miscegenation.[4] William Sumner said war came from a "competition for life" between "in-groups" and "out-groups."[5] But he was a pessimist: not only had war always existed, but it always would. "It is evident that men love war," he concluded ruefully during the 1898 U.S. war with Spain, which he stridently opposed.

Much Germanic theory reflected the fact that Germans were winning wars and had not yet achieved empire but wanted one, while Austrians had an empire and were fighting to keep it. For both, war remained necessary, even virtuous. General Helmuth von Moltke the Elder declared, "Everlasting peace is a dream, and not even a pleasant one; and war is a necessary part of God's arrangement of the world." Clausewitz was more measured, writing: "The fact that slaughter is a horrifying spectacle must make us take war more seriously, but not provide an excuse for gradually blunting our swords in the name of humanity. Sooner or later someone will come along with a sharp sword and hack off our arms."[6] That remains the dominant justification for being militarily prepared for war—just in case, as President Putin has recently reminded us.

Ludwig Gumplowicz said modernity would not bring peace since conflicts between dominators and dominated were endemic to human society.[7] Heinrich von Treitschke, Max Weber, Georg Simmel, Werner Sombart, and Max Scheler saw no end of wars. Treitschke approved of warfare; he attacked liberal theories of peace, which he associated with the hypocritical British. The "slaughter" of enemies was part of the "sublimity" of war, he declaimed.[8]

Weber was a liberal imperialist. Although disliking militarism, he saw imperialism and war as necessary to modernity and to German development. As World War I erupted, he embraced it. His support for the war, expressed in August 1914, was ideological. "Responsibility before the bar of history" meant that Germany had to resist a division of the world between "Russian officials" and "the conventions of Anglo-Saxon society," with perhaps a dash of "Latin reason" thrown in. "We have to be a world power, and in order to have a say in the future of the world we had to risk the war."[9] Once Germany achieved its rightful place in the sun, this would bring more civilization to the world and wars would decline—as the British liberal imperialists had argued and as their American counterparts do today. Weber was not alone. Thomas Mann wrote, "Germany is warlike out of morality." German enthusiasm, however, was a temporary rally 'round the flag phenomenon. A year later Weber had shifted to call for a diplomatic end to the war, and by 1922 Mann was defending the Weimar Republic against militarism.

Scheler saw war as inevitable and desirable. The "genius" of war represented the dynamic principle of history, while peace was the static principle. War exposes the banal rationality and materialism of modern culture. It gives people a higher plane of existence, conferring an existential sense of security inside the national community. Like Weber, he saw war as a battle of cultures. Whereas France and especially England embodied pragmatic, empiricist philosophy, Germany embodied the true philosophy of metaphysical idealism. War awakens a nation to the need to preserve its own culture and is justified when its culture is attacked. England was seeking to impose its mercantile, utilitarian philosophy on Europe.[10] Like Weber, however, Scheler shifted as the horrors of this war became revealed. Simmel saw war and peace "so interwoven that in every peaceful situation the conditions for future conflict, and in every struggle the conditions for future peace, are developing. If we follow the stages of social development backward under these categories, we can find no stopping-place." He called for armed struggle against materialistic Anglo-American "Mammonism."[11]

Sombart saw World War I as ranging the German "hero" against the British "merchant." Merchants were morally inferior, greedy for profit, money, and physical comfort. Heroes were superior in historical significance, motivated by ideals of the great deed and of sacrifice for a noble calling. Since Entente rhetoric claimed this was a war of liberty and democracy against authoritarian aggression, the war was seen as a struggle for civilization on both sides.

So most prominent Germanic intellectuals of this period did not believe war was declining, some approved of it, and others were horrified by its excesses. Though many people today would endorse Clausewitz's view that war is sometimes necessary—and military defense is always necessary—almost no one today celebrates war as intrinsically virtuous. That is undoubtedly progress. Marxists have offered a more optimistic theory. Rudolf Hilferding and Vladimir Lenin perceived a close relation among capitalism, imperialism, and war and believed that overthrowing capitalism would bring peace. Most theorists in Britain and France were in between: they deplored war but conceived of their own wars as purely defensive.

World War I made Russians, Americans, British, and French hope this had been the war to end all wars. The Soviets used military metaphors for their domestic policies—shock troops, work brigades, and the like—but after the failed invasion of Poland in 1920, they believed that a socialist society would bring peace. After the war most British and French writers opposed war but preferred to think about other things. Leonard Hobhouse, the first professor of sociology in Britain, had predicted that the future belonged to higher ethical and peaceful standards, and he had been shattered by the Great War. His response was to turn away from sociology to philosophy. Americans experienced revulsion against World War I, which they saw as essentially European. American sociology also preferred to think of activities other than war.

Germany and Italy had experienced unfavorable wars generating conflicting strands of theory. One militarist strand evolved into fascism, which celebrated war, sometimes in mystical terms, always seeing it as crucial to human progress. Socialists in Germany and Italy deplored war and hoped to abolish it, but they nonetheless felt they needed to form defensive paramilitaries. The Italian social scientist Vilfredo Pareto argued that rights would always derive from might, whereas his countryman Gaetano Mosca said that those who held the lance and the musket would always rule over those who handled the spade or the shuttle. In

France, the critic and philosopher Roger Caillois adapted Durkheim's sociology of religion into romantic nationalism whose celebrations had replaced religious festivals in dragging people out of their mundane lives and giving them a sense of the sacred.[12] He saw war as revealing the inadequacies of modernity, expressed in yearnings for national spirituality.

World War II then saw the victory of a Marxian-liberal alliance combining optimism with moral revulsion against war. It was better not to think about war in Britain, America, France, and Germany alike. Functionalism and modernization theory dominated social theory and ignored war. Political scientists, handmaidens to power in Washington, differed. Most supported American liberal imperialism and offered Realist theories of war as a rational instrument of power. Western Marxists emphasized class "struggle," but the metaphor did not mean actual killing. "Third-world" Marxism did turn toward revolutionary violence, exemplified by China's Mao Zedong and the psychiatrist Frantz Fanon. The war had produced the excellent studies of American soldiers to which I refer in chapter 12, but their legacy in America was to reduce the sociology of war to studies of the military profession. With some exceptions—Stanislav Andreski in England, Raymond Aron in France, Hannah Arendt and C. Wright Mills in the United States—the social sciences outside political science neglected war during the Cold War, and this seemed justified by a decline in interstate wars. Today almost no one in the Global North glorifies war. Nor do many believe that human nature or human society inevitably generates war (or peace).

The Return of Liberal Optimism

The twenty-first century has seen a revival of interest in war in the field of sociology.[13] Yet these scholars' suitably nuanced views have been swamped by a revival of liberal optimism expressed by John Mueller, Azar Gat, Steven Pinker, and Joshua Goldstein.[14] Their books have been well received in a Washington satisfied with the notion of a Pax Americana. Goldstein focuses on the post-1945 period. Mueller sees the decline of war as long-term and still continuing. World War II might seem to create a problem for him, but he shrugs this off, saying that one man, Adolf Hitler, was responsible for it. Mueller emphasizes cultural shifts occurring during the twentieth century that made war "rationally unthinkable" as ever more countries were "dropping out" of the war system. He dismisses the rise of Islamic terrorism as criminal activity responded to by "police action," rather than constituting "war."[15] Gat sees war in nineteenth-century utilitarian terms: war is now inferior to trade in securing scarce resources. He also points to attributes of Western society that strengthen the attractions of peace—mature democracy, the growth of metropolitan life, the sexual revolution and feminism, and nuclear deterrence. All differ from nineteenth-century scholars in identifying a long-term decline of war. Dichotomous views of war in history before and after the nineteenth century no longer exist.

Pinker draws on modern studies of human nature, offering a metaphor of "angels" and "demons" struggling within us, capable of steering us either to peace or to war. He also draws on Norbert Elias, who, in *The Process of Civilisation*, argues that a civilizing process involving self-restraint and impulse management had intensified over past centuries in Europe. Europeans had inhibited their impulses, anticipated the consequences of their actions, and empathized more with others. A culture of honor, embodying the ideal of revenge, had given way to a culture of dignity, embodying control of one's emotions. The book was originally published in German in 1939—bad timing! Pinker seems not to know that Elias came to revise his view. As a refugee from Nazi Germany, and then as a wartime British intelligence officer interviewing hard-line Nazis, Elias thought a "decivilizing process" had begun in the twentieth century, when nuclear war was a distinct possibility.[16] He died in 1990, at the end of the Cold War, too soon to regain optimism.

Liberal theories have been heard before. The contribution of recent writers has been to add empirical data. Gat and Pinker give knowledgeable narratives of violence and warfare through the ages. Goldstein offers data on post-1945 trends in wars and civil wars. Pinker presents a six-phase periodization of decline through the ages. Since he presents the fullest historical statistical data on the frequency of wars and the number of casualties they inflict, which are the simplest measures of whether war has declined, I focus on his data.

Pinker on Early History and the Mongols

Pinker begins with prehistoric warfare that I discussed in chapter 2. In it, he says, war deaths averaged 15 percent and amounted to "up to" 60 percent of the total population, whereas in modern nation-states war deaths have been 5 percent or less. His 15 percent average figure is too high. His maximum of 60 percent is much lower than the maximum in modern cases of genocide—

over 95 percent of the natives in North America and Australia, while in the twentieth century the Nazis disposed of about 70 percent of Jews, the Ottoman Turks and Kurds about 70 percent of Armenians, and the Hutus about 60 percent of Tutsis. So war was not more intense in prehistoric times.

Pinker also exaggerates the worst early historical cases. He puts the total death toll of the An Lushan civil war in eighth-century China at 36 million. This is derived from comparing Chinese censuses before and after the war. Sinologists accept that this was a devastating war, but they add that it also devastated the Tang census administration, which led to severe undercounting of the postwar population. They regard 13 million as a more reasonable total for deaths due to the war, which is bad enough.[17] Pinker also accepts as truth the boasts of rulers of ancient empires like the Assyrians that they had wiped out entire populations in their millions. But these were boasts with the strategic purpose of cowing future opposition. Faced with a city refusing to surrender, the Assyrians might massacre the inhabitants after taking the city, but this was to encourage other cities to submit. Given such a terrible demonstration of Assyrian power, they usually did so. The Assyrians wanted to rule over other peoples, not exterminate them.

Gat adds brief data on Greece and Rome. On Greece he focuses on the Peloponnesian War and derives very high totals of Greek war losses from the military historian Victor Hanson, who follows Thucydides.[18] He concludes that a staggering one-third of the whole Athenian population (not just citizens) died in this war. Yet the classicist Stewart Flory shows that all Hanson's estimates are much too high and observes that Greek historians, especially Thucydides, wrote for literary effect, not statistical accuracy.[19] Regarding Rome, Gat focuses on Roman losses in the first three years of the Second Punic War. He follows Peter Brunt's 1971 estimate of Roman legionary losses in those years as 50,000, which he says was 25 percent of the adult male citizenry.[20] Actually, it was the proportion of those citizens called *assidui*, liable for military service. The Roman response was to lower the property requirement for military service, which immediately enabled them to raise more legions. Brunt also inadvertently doubles the likely proportion of Roman citizens slain by assuming that all the soldiers were drawn from its citizen body. Yet the *auxilia*, foreign allies who were not fully Roman citizens, formed at least half of the Roman armies, sometimes more, as I showed in chapter 4. These wars had high death tolls, but probably not higher than the worst wars of most historical periods. What does support Pinker's argument here is the sheer frequency of wars in ancient Rome, also evidenced in chapter 4, although this was not typical of the whole ancient world.

The Mongols are crucial for Pinker. He claims they were far deadlier than any other human group. He estimates that in their conquests they killed 40 million persons in total. Indeed, estimates of between 30 and 60 million dominate web entries on the Mongols, though these give no evidence and are in fact an internet myth. Scholars of the Mongols—Jack Weatherford, David Morgan, and Peter Frankopan—declare such figures to be preposterous.[21] The real total is unknowable, but much lower, they say. Pinker relies heavily on two massacres in the cities of Merv and Baghdad, which fiercely resisted the Mongols but were finally stormed. At Merv he says that the total killed after surrender was 1.3 million, but this is six times more than its probable population at that time. Pinker's estimate of Baghdad's fatalities is 800,000. Again, this is higher than its total population, which was somewhere between 200,000 and 500,000. Even if we conjecture that refugees from the surrounding countryside flooded into the cities, swelling their populations, there would not have been room in the cities for such numbers. The Baghdad caliph's defiance did the inhabitants no good, particularly his reply to Chinggis's order to knock down his walls: "When you remove all your horses' hooves, we shall destroy our fortifications."[22] Michal Biran concludes that though Baghdad did suffer a terrible massacre, the number of deaths was less than previously supposed.[23] Many escaped death by bribes or through negotiations. One scholar comments that 80,000 (removing a zero) is a much likelier estimate of the casualties in Baghdad.[24] True, higher figures for the two cities were given by contemporary sources, but just as these greatly exaggerated the size of Mongol armies, so they exaggerated their slaughter.[25] The Mongols themselves inflated numbers to terrify others into submission. In a letter to Louis XI of France, Khan Hulagu boasted he had killed over 2 million in Baghdad, an utterly incredible figure. The worst massacres occurred where cities that had surrendered then rebelled again, where the khan's envoys or kin had been killed, or in regions of persistent guerilla resistance, which is consistent with the policy of vengeful calculation I described in chapter 6. This was motivated by great anger yet also calculation, for a massacre might persuade the next city or region to surrender.[26] Compare President Harry Truman's dropping of atomic bombs on Hiroshima and Nagasaki to persuade Japan to surrender. Both were justified by the perpetrators as saving further lives among their own troops. We find the Mongols worse because their killing was ferocious body hacking, whereas Truman's was long-distance callous killing, to which we have grown accustomed. Both policies did induce surrender—a ghastly rational calculation.

The Persian chronicler Joveyni described the varied policies used in the conquest of the cities of Bukhara by Chinggis (Genghis) Khan in 1219, which had been provoked by the defiance there of Sultan Muhammad. The sultan's armies were much larger than the Mongols', but fear of his own generals had led him to disperse his armies, a disastrous case of coup-proofing that weakened his war-fighting ability. The cities and their armies were overpowered one by one. Chinggis first reached the city of Zarnuq and sent an emissary to offer the usual alternatives to the city: surrender or death. The citizens of Zarnuq sensibly chose the former and were spared, losing only some sons to Mongol conscription. The next city was Nur. Its gates were shut while divided counsels reigned in the city. The decision was eventually to surrender. Chinggis accepted this but with one condition. All the citizens were led out of the city; none was killed, but the empty city was looted by his soldiers. Then in Bukhara, the defiant sultan sent out an army to resist. It was overwhelmed. The citizens opened the gates, but the sultan's soldiers in the citadel, fearing the worst, continued fighting. They were slaughtered, as were many citizens, in the general mayhem. The rest were driven out into the fields. Chinggis gave a speech to them, declaring: "O people, know that you have committed great sins, and that the great ones among you have committed those sins. If you ask me what proof I have for these words, I say it is because I am the punishment of God." So the city's notables were all killed, while the young men were conscripted into the Mongol army. The rest of the population were spared. Joveyni mentioned twelve cities taken after fighting by Chinggis in 1220–1221. In one city "all were killed," three cities were "destroyed" (casualties not stated), in one the people were driven out and the city looted, and in the other seven there was only limited killing.[27] Ratchnevsky's account uses many sources and differs in details, but not in the overall policy.[28]

Useful anger endured. In 1273 Kublai Khan began his final assault on Song dynasty rule over China by besieging twin cities. Fancheng bravely endured a long siege, which caused massive Mongol casualties, but it was eventually stormed. The population was put to the sword. Ten thousand bodies were supposedly stacked in view of the nearby city of Xiangyang. Its defenders were terror-stricken, and the commander, Lu Wenhuan, promptly surrendered. Not only was the city spared, but Lu and his troops were incorporated into the Mongol army, Lu becoming a prominent

Mongol general. In 1276 the end of the Song dynasty came as its capital, Hangzhou, perhaps the biggest city in the world at that time, capitulated without a siege after negotiations. The city was spared killing or looting.[29]

Mongol practice after resistance was to divide the population. Elites who had resisted were almost always killed, but artisans and merchants were spared, alongside farmers, for the Mongols wanted to rule a rich land, not a depopulated desert. Nor were women and children usually killed—they might be enslaved, while young males were conscripted into their armies. Much of the remaining male urban population might then be killed.[30] Chinggis was reputed to be skilled at winning over allies and was certainly an active diplomat.[31] Empire builders need war and diplomacy. Indeed, the Mongols were not always seen as oppressors, since they offered a higher level of civilization and order to many regions, as well as religious toleration, and they often poured resources into cities after they had occupied them.[32] Some cities and regions were devastated, but most appear not to have suffered at all. Resistance or submission was the key.[33]

Thus, we should reduce the total deaths inflicted by the Mongols by more than half from the internet myth figure. Though most scholars conclude that it is impossible to estimate the total number of the Mongols' victims, one gives a detailed estimate that takes into account known regional variations and yields a probable death total of about 11.5 million, less than one-third of Pinker's 40 million.[34] A figure of 11.5 million is bad enough, of course—worse in total than the atrocities of any other group of that period. I doubt that this was a price worth paying by humanity for the undoubted benefits of Mongol rule. Yet Mongol killings were not out of proportion to other terrible historical cases, including those in the twentieth century.

Pinker's Worst List

Pinker relies most on a list of the twenty-one cases in history with the highest absolute death tolls in war.[35] These death tolls include civilian as well as battle deaths, in addition to state-induced famines. Table 10.1 shows his list, which he arranges in column 1 in order of the absolute number of deaths: World War II had the most, and the French Wars of Religion had the least. All figures in the table are in millions of deaths. A word of caution: modern figures are more likely to be accurate, whereas in ancient sources inflation of deaths is likelier. Lacking alternative sources, however, we have to go with these.

Table 10.1. Pinker Revised: Highest Fatality Cases (my revisions in parentheses)

Cases	Century	Absolute deaths	Relative deaths	Relative rank	Duration in years	Annual deaths	Annual rank
1. WW II	20th	55	55	9	8	6.9	1
2. Mao	20th	40	40	11	15	2.7	5
3. Mongols	13th	40 (11.5)	178 (52)	2 (10)	100	0.4 (0.1)	13 (16)
4. An Lushan	8th	36 (13)	429 (126)	1 (1)	8	4.5 (2.0)	2 (8)
5. Ming Fall	17th	25	112	4	46	2.4	6
6. Taiping Rebellion	19th	20	40	10	14	2.9	3
7. American Indians	15–19th	20	92	7	408	0.2	17=
8. Stalin	20th	20	20	15	15	1.3	9
9. Middle Eastern Slaves	7–19th	19	132	3	1200	0.1	21
10. Atlantic Slaves	15–19th	18	83	8	408	0.2	19
11. Tamerlane	14–15th	17	100	6	37	2.7	4
12. Brit. India Famines	19th	17	35	12	100	0.4	14=
13. WW I	20th	15	15	16	4	3.8	2
14. Russia Civil War	20th	9	9	20	5	1.8	7
15. Fall of Rome	3–5th	8	105	5	200	0.5	12
16. Congo Free State	19–20th	8	12	18	40	0.3	16
17. 30 Years' War	17th	7	32	13	30	1.1	10
18. Russian Troubles	16–17th	5	23	14	100	0.2	17=
19. Napoleonic Wars	19th	4	11	19	23	0.5	11
20. China Civil War	20th	3	3	21	22	0.1	20
21. France Religious Wars	16th	3	14	17	40	0.4	14=

Notes: Absolute death toll = recorded actual number of deaths, in millions.
Relative deaths = absolute deaths, in millions, as proportion of world population at that time, standardized by the 20th-century population total.
Annual deaths = relative deaths, in millions, figure divided by number of years each case lasted.
= Indicates a two-way tie.

His cases are drawn from all ages of human history, though columns 1–3 show that seven of them occurred during the first half of the twentieth century, including the two deadliest of all, World War II and the killings and famine deaths during Mao's Great Leap Forward in China. My amendments of the death toll from An Lushan and the Mongols (discussed above) are given in parentheses in the table. The "Absolute deaths" column reveals no overall decline in fatalities, and Pinker accepts that. But he prefers to use not the absolute but the "relative" death rate—deaths as a proportion of the total world population at the time, standardized by the twentieth-century population total. Thus, the absolute and relative death rates for the twentieth-century cases are identical, while absolute deaths in the earlier cases are all increased by multiplying them by the twentieth-century global population, divided by estimated global population at that time. Columns 4 and 5 present his results.

This changes the picture since most wars with the highest relative death rates were in the distant past, when global population was far lower. With this adjustment, the deadliest wars in Pinker's list are no longer World War II and Maoism but the An Lushan rebellion in eighth-century China and the Mongol conquests in the thirteenth century, although if my downward revision of the Mongol-induced losses is accepted, the Middle Eastern slave trade rises up to the second spot. Indeed, all of the top eight cases are now from earlier centuries, in line with Pinker's theory. This switch from absolute to relative deaths makes sense, yet the decrease in the relative death rates in the twentieth century was due not to growing pacifism but to an explosion in global population and a large increase in workers in war industries who are not counted as combatants. This does suggest not a decline in warfare but a transformation in the nature of war—as I argue later. Braumoeller adds that controlling only for the population of those countries at war would be a better measure of relative rates, though this is not a perfect measure since countries with larger populations tend to have smaller armies relative to population size and so they kill fewer enemies relative to that size.[36]

Should we not also take into account the duration of each case? World War II inflicted fewer deaths as a proportion of the global population at that time than had the Mongol conquests, the Atlantic slave trade, or the annihilation of Native Americans and Australian aborigines. Yet World War II lasted only eight years (including the Japan-China war), whereas the Mongol conquests lasted one hundred years, and the slaughter of the Atlantic slave trade and of the Native Americans took centuries. Pinker says the slave trade lasted twelve centuries in the Middle East and five centuries in the West. The Middle Eastern slave trade lasted so long that in annual terms its death rate plummets to the bottom of the table. True, there is something horrible about an atrocity that endured for centuries versus one that was far briefer but killed more people, but the latter may be a better measure of how much a society is involved in killing. So I have calculated average annual killing rates based on Pinker's relative figures. On this measure World War II goes back up to the top of the list with a much higher annual relative rate of killing than any other case. The runner-up would be An Lushan if we accepted Pinker's inflated estimate of fatalities. If we use the revised figure of 13 million, this drops it back to eighth position. Similarly, the Mongols drop down to sixteenth on my corrected figures. World War I is then the runner-up, after World War II (even though the count does not include the 50+ million Spanish flu casualties diffused to the world by troop movements at the war's end). These revised figures cast doubt on any general decline of war in the period up to 1945. You can take your pick of which measure to prefer, but the combination would suggest no overall decline in casualties induced by war.

Pinker is also inconsistent. While he combines long-lived but sporadic bouts of killings into a single case, like the Mongol conquests or the two slave trades, he separates six cases in the first half of the twentieth century: the two world wars, the Russian and Chinese civil wars, and the Stalinist and Maoist famines. Yet these all occurred within a fifty-year period, they were all connected, and each one led directly or indirectly to the next. These might make them a single case, or rather a single sequence of cases. So the first half of the twentieth century would contain *easily* the bloodiest "event" in human history, in both absolute and relative terms, without even taking annual rates into consideration. These data refute any notion that warfare declined through human history. They might also suggest that none of these mass killing bouts of from 3 to 55 million fatalities could be regarded as rational or justified, whatever the positive contributions made by the perpetrators to their civilizations.

Have Wars Increased?

Do such figures actually support the opposite view, that wars have been rising through the centuries? Eckhardt saw an "increase in war deaths and deaths per war during the last five centuries. Not only has the total violence of war increased over these centuries, but the average war has also increased in violence."[37] Malešević says war deaths have been continually growing over no fewer than one thousand years.[38] He explains this in terms of the growth of the infrastructural power of state bureaucracies, backed up by the resources of modern capitalism and of science. States have become military precision killing machines, he says. Yet we need to remember Pinker's distinction between absolute and relative fatality levels. Overall, armies have been bigger and casualties higher in modern times than earlier in the millennium, as Malešević and Eckhardt say, but primarily because world population has grown so enormously— from perhaps 450 million in 1300 to 1 billion in 1800 to 7.8 billion in 2020. When the death-rate figures are adjusted by Pinker's relative method, the growth in army size and war deaths disappears, except as we saw for the first half of the twentieth century. When subtler measures are introduced, the pattern becomes more complex, as we will see.

Modern and Premodern Wars

Eckhardt and Malešević return us to a dichotomous premodern-modern theory of war, concerning not the frequency of war but the growing organizational efficiency of warfare. They base this on European history during the last five hundred years (for Eckhardt) and one thousand years (for Malešević). One thousand years covers the transition from feudal agrarian to capitalist industrial and postindustrial societies, from small polities with feeble infrastructural powers, mobilizing tiny armies, to the states with the greatest infrastructural powers in history, capable of mobilizing armies of millions. Eckhardt covers the "modernization" period of this millennium. Obviously, their stark contrasts are correct for Europe during these periods. Malešević very briefly discusses two earlier exceptions, Rome and China, with their large, well-drilled armed forces, despite their tiny state bureaucracies. Yet he stresses the "weakness" of China—a bizarre judgment given the Chinese history I chronicled in chapter 6. Even in the nineteenth century, when the lack of naval forces had made China vulnerable to foreign navies, in land warfare against Russia the Qing were still fighting successful campaigns. Malešević says that the Roman exception was due to the unusually well-developed bureaucratic and professional structure of the legions themselves: not the state but the legions had considerable centralized infrastructural power.

Yet infrastructural power does not merely flow from the central state. It is a two-way relationship between the state and civil society. In this book I reveal several types of such relations. In chapter 13 we will see mass mobilizing communist parties that have thoroughly penetrated the armed forces of the Soviet Union, China, and Vietnam, reinforced by communist rituals and ideology. This enabled them to inflict defeat on higher-tech armies. In chapter 4 I showed that Roman citizenship was the main source of infrastructural power, conferring rights on citizen-soldiers, while the hierarchy of citizen census classes translated directly into army ranks. The state and its legions actually *were* the senatorial, equestrian, and heavy and medium infantry census classes. They shared a common ideology, they were politically dominant through the senate and popular assemblies, and they were economically organized by careers that tied together army command and political office. That class structure provided the state's core, not the few "civil servants" (who were often slaves) or the legions themselves. In chapter 6 I found a different form of this two-way relationship in imperial China. Han Chinese armies up to a million strong were the product not of a centralized bureaucracy (again tiny by modern standards), but of a close relationship between a centralized monarchy and a Confucian gentry-bureaucrat class whose powers stretched from the localities into the "outer courtyard" of the palace. Rome and China had polities that structurally "represented" dominant classes, enabling them to levy the taxes and conscription necessary to support large standing armies and to inflict mass slaughter on the enemy—Caesar killing nearly a million Gauls, the Chinese emperor Yongle mobilizing over 200,000 men to destroy several Mongol peoples, the Manchu emperor Qianlong killing several hundred thousand Zunghars and mobilizing 200,000 soldiers in the field, as well as 400,000 logistical support staff (the Chinese armies bearing firearms). These are glaring exceptions to the premodernity-modernity dichotomy of warfare.

I have also noted some intermediate examples of large, drilled, organized, and effective historical armies, as mobilized by the Aztecs, the Inca, the Mongols, and the early Chinese and later Japanese warring states periods. They had quite weak states, but close relations between the ruler and dominant classes, which enabled their forces to begin conquests; and a ruler's feeling forced to continue distributing tribute and spoils to his soldiers also increased the likelihood of further aggression. The Chinese also had a deal with their peasantry, offering economic reforms in return for military service. The Inca developed their extraordinary paved road system, providing more central control as well as trade. The power of that great engine of destruction, the Mongol army, rested on the two-way relationship between the horsemen of its pastoral economy and the tribal political federations—generating forces that were not large but extremely lethal. The Mongols had their weaknesses, especially their small numbers and the factional disputes of tribal leaders, but I noted their techniques for increasing their infrastructural power, like their postal and staging system, their use of Chinese taxes, and an army-centered set of laws. Yet only when they appropriated the entire Chinese administration system, as did the Yuan and Manchu dynasties, were they able to sustain massive armies for long campaigns (Qianlong's being the prime example). Otherwise, wars had to be shorter while disputed successions still brought them down.

Earlier organization of warfare in Europe and Asia thus deviated from the dichotomous model. Two were the equal of the modern West, others were not so well developed but were well beyond the primitive. The West does not provide the only model for an infrastructurally powerful society effective at large-scale, bloody warfare. Of course, many societies in history did have less well-organized armed forces, and these were much smaller. But history is not a divide between modern and premodern states and armies.

Nineteenth-Century Peace? Europe and Its Colonies

Has there been a medium-term trend toward fewer or less intensive wars? Lars-Erik Cederman and his colleagues show that in the years 1770–1810 the French Revolutionary and Napoleonic wars produced a jump in army size and battle fatalities.[39] Reworking Levy's data on wars between 1475 and 1975, they say the emergence of nationalism at the end of the eighteenth century enabled a large increase in states' ability to inculcate loyalty within mass armies, generating deep tensions between the principles of territorial and popular sovereignty that have driven patterns of interstate warfare ever since. They rule out alternative explanations of increasing war intensity, such as increasing population and changes in weapons technology. Thus, they say, we can trace the roots of the twentieth-century world wars back to 1789. They have no actual data on nationalism, however, and the motivation on the French side was revolutionary rather than nationalist, although this did develop into the notion of the nation in arms.

For France's monarchical enemies, the motivation throughout was counterrevolutionary, which involved rejecting the nationalism espoused by those who at first saw the French armies as their liberators. The settlement of 1815 was clearly counterrevolutionary.

Counterrevolutionary fears did then reduce war in Europe. Pinker sees the period 1815–1914 as a "Long Peace." Blainey agrees: "Historians' explanations of peace in modern times are centered on the nineteenth century. Two long periods in that century were remarkably peaceful. One ran from the Battle of Waterloo to the short wars of 1848. . . . The other . . . ran from the end of the Franco-Prussian War in 1871 to . . . 1914."[40] Gat uses CoW data to identify two subperiods of peace, in 1815–54 and 1871–1914.[41] The interim period of 1854–71 was bloody, containing the Crimean War, three Prussian wars with Austria, Denmark, and France, the Indian Mutiny, the American Civil War, the Taiping Rebellion in China, and the disastrous Paraguayan War. But the before-and-after periods are key to Gat's assertion of a long-term decline of war. Braumoeller, using CoW data, notes the hiccup in the middle but concludes that "the trend in the data is very consistent with the mainstream historical record, which portrays the nineteenth century as a remarkably peaceful one."[42]

Yet all these authors are wrong. The nineteenth century did not contain one long or two shorter periods of peace. Gat counted only "wars between the great powers," the major states of Europe, because these were "the most crucial and most destructive inter-state wars." This also limited Levy's data on earlier periods, which showed that the number of large interstate wars had declined steadily in every decade from the sixteenth to the nineteenth century. Their Eurocentrism excludes the most common form of war fought by early modern Europeans—colonial wars fought against natives of other continents. The nineteenth century culminated this process, for the British, French, and Dutch empires now expanded over virtually the whole world, while the American, Belgian, German, and Japanese empires began their relatively brief ascents—all killing very large numbers of indigenous peoples. These studies have two further biases. First, they include only wars in which over one thousand soldiers were killed in battle in a year, and this understates colonial warfare, which usually consists of sequences of much smaller campaigns. Recent CoW data have been extended to cover MIDs as well, but only for conflicts between states, not for "extrastate" conflicts like most colonial struggles. I have every sympathy for the CoW researchers. It is hard enough to get reliable data on soldiers in the battles of major wars. It would be impossible to get comparable statistics on civilian deaths or on smaller colonial wars and skirmishes. Nonetheless, no analysis based on CoW data alone, however statistically sophisticated, can make claims about the totality of war in the nineteenth century.

CoW data on the period 1816–1997 do include some colonial wars. They reveal 79 interstate wars, 214 civil wars, and 108 colonial wars. Of the 53 million combat deaths these produced over the whole period, interstate wars contributed 32 million, thanks mainly to the two world wars. Without them, civil wars produced more deaths, 18 million, mostly in the period after 1945, and colonial wars contributed almost 3 million, mostly in the period 1870–99. The 1890s saw the most wars in one decade until the 1970s outdid them. Controlled for the size of the population, battle deaths had three big peaks, in the 1860s, the 1910s (World War I), and the 1940s (World War II). With these three exceptions, there was a basically flat rate of deaths as a proportion of population, which Meredith Sarkees and her colleagues say suggests "something discouraging about the constancy of warfare in human affairs."[43] They acknowledge that the first quarter century after 1816 was quite peaceful, but there was no further nineteenth-century decline in warfare. They ask rhetorically, "Was this supposedly, civilized, peaceful century just a time when Europeans stopped fighting each other to conquer and slaughter militarily weaker Asians and Africans?" Their answer is yes, and they are right.

The second bias is that CoW figures are of deaths in battle, excluding the many civilian deaths in colonial wars. Many of these wars killed more civilians than soldiers. In Europe the Thirty Years' War (1618–48) had killed about 8 million people, of which battle deaths represented "only" several hundred thousand. Most colonial wars were also lopsided. Yet estimating deaths is difficult since many resulted from starvation and disease resulting from the colonists' mistreatment of natives—troops burning crops and villages and imposing slave labor conditions with brutal punishment and inadequate nutrition. Those were war-generated deaths. But much death also resulted from mere contact with Europeans through diseases to which the natives had no immunity. Such diseases might have spread anyway without war, as a result of peaceful trading or freer labor relations, although the herding of natives together in slave ships, mines, plantations, and armies worsened the spread of diseases. Separating out deaths consequent on war from mere contact deaths cannot be exact. We cannot put precise numbers on fatalities resulting from colonization.

Most colonizing campaigns also consisted of many small encounters, none individually reaching a thousand deaths; native casualties often went uncounted since they were of little interest to the colonial authorities. So I will quickly review the relatively well-evidenced colonial cases. Deaths are usually estimates of whole campaigns involving small encounters rarely recorded individually. I stress that such estimates are less reliable than CoW data and can indicate only rough orders of magnitude.

In the United States the Native American population in 1500 was somewhere between 4 and 9 million. Only about 600,000 were left in 1800, and only 237,000 appeared in the census of 1900, a population loss above 95 percent since 1500 and 60 percent since 1800. In the Indian Wars lasting through the nineteenth century, Native American losses in battle were around 60,000 inflicted by soldiers and settler militias, though in massacres like that at Sand Creek (described in the next chapter), soldiers killed entire populations, not just braves. Many deaths also resulted from the famine and diseases caused by forced deportations onto barren lands. Native North Americans are absent from CoW data. In South America the greatest early casualties had been inflicted by the Spanish and Portuguese, but we lack evidence on numbers. There were massacres through most of the nineteenth century. The last big ones are known. In Cuba's "Great War" of 1868–78, about 240,000 died. CoW counted only 50,000 battle deaths. In Argentina's "Conquest of the Desert" in Patagonia in the 1870s to 1884, over 30,000 died, but this does not appear in CoW data.

In Africa killing rates of indigenous soldiers escalated through the nineteenth century as the Europeans acquired more lethal guns. Since natives learned not to attempt pitched battles, warfare became hit-and-run guerilla campaigns in terrain posing logistical and climatic challenges, and troop ratios to area and population size were low. Intermittent campaigns were more common than pitched battles during the nineteenth and twentieth centuries.[44] Yet in western Kenya alone between 1894 and 1914 the British fought twenty-two battles, one per year.[45] Soldiers and administrators would arrive in the colonies already fearful of supposedly "savage" natives, holding nervous fingers on the trigger. Their fears were exacerbated by unpredictable violence amid hostile environments. To them, this legitimized massacres, punitive campaigns that destroyed villages, and killing of inhabitants who might be sustaining the rebels. There was, says Bouda Etemad, a "conquest-resistance-repression cycle."[46]

The protracted French conquest of Algeria (1829–47) killed between 300,000 and 825,000 Algerians in many small-scale antiguerilla campaigns and punitive attacks on villages. Alexis de Tocqueville, visiting Algeria, said he had a "distressing notion that at this moment we are waging war far more barbarously than the Arabs themselves."[47] French armies did not respect the difference between soldiers and civilians. CoW data include only two campaigns that total 23,000 Algerian deaths. Worse in relative numbers was the German army's genocide of the Herrero and Nama peoples in today's Namibia at the beginning of the twentieth century. The Herrero were reduced from 60,000–80,000 to only 16,000 in eight years (only 2,000 of the survivors being men), and the Nama loss rate was 50 percent of a total population of 20,000.[48] CoW data total only 11,000 battle deaths among the two peoples. In present-day Tanzania in the Maji-Maji War of 1905–7, the official German report presented to the Reichstag stated that 75,000 Africans died. Other estimates double that, others go up to 250,000 to 300,000—a huge number for such a small region. Some tribes lost over 90 percent of their members.[49] CoW native battle deaths there total only 5,400. In the Belgian Congo during 1885–1908, perhaps 10 million died, mainly through diseases brought about by dire forced labor conditions and repression. CoW native battle deaths in the Congo are only 13,000.

Russian colonial expansion into Asia continued through the nineteenth century. Although not as bloody as earlier campaigns in Siberia, expansion into Central Asia produced Turkmen losses of around 20,000 spread over many smaller campaigns. CoW data include three wars against Kokand and Bukhara with total battle deaths of 7,300. The peoples of the Caucasus suffered many more fatalities from the 1860s to century's end. The Russian census of 1897 recorded only 150,000 Circassians left in their homeland, one-tenth of their original number, mainly reduced by deportations ruthlessly enforced by the Russian army. The Russian government acknowledged that the wars and deportations caused 300,000 deaths. Circassian survivors claimed over 3 million.[50] Circassians do not figure in CoW data.

In India between 1850 and 1914, millions were killed in famines caused by coercive colonial policies. This case figures in Pinker's list of the worst death tolls in conflicts in human history. In Java in 1825–30, the Dutch conquest included devastation of the countryside and over 200,000 deaths.[51] CoW data on battle deaths in this case are the same, the only instance of agreement we will find. In the Bali invasion of 1849, about 10,000 died. This does not appear in the CoW list of wars. In Aceh wars between 1873 and 1914, about 100,000 indigenous people died in battle, through disease, and in terrible conditions in labor camps. CoW

data total 22,200 native battle deaths. There were another thirty-one
Dutch smaller military expeditions in this period, says Henk Wesseling.
The Tahitian population collapsed by 90 percent between 1770, when
white men arrived, and the 1840s. This does not appear in CoW data.
The Kanaks of New Caledonia lost 70 percent of their original population of about 70,000, mainly in the nineteenth century, when French settlers seized their land and imposed forced labor on them. A rebellion in
1878 killed 1,000, and many more were deported abroad. They do not
appear in the CoW list. In New Zealand the Maoris were driven from
their lands, exterminated when they resisted, and contracted diseases.
Their numbers fell from 150,000 at the beginning of the nineteenth century to 42,000 in 1896.[52] The Maoris appear only in CoW data for the
war of 1863–66 against the British; 2,000 battle deaths were recorded.

Australian aborigine and Torres Straits peoples do not appear in
CoW data. Yet after the first contact in 1788 there were many small massacres committed by settlers and armed police, often in explicit "hunting
expeditions." The University of Newcastle, New South Wales, is map-
ping all such cases. It defines a massacre as the killing of at least six unde-
fended people, since if the typical indigenous group was about twenty
strong, the loss of six, 30 percent of the population, was likely to threaten
the group's survival. The project has so far uncovered almost five hundred massacres. Most were committed in the second half of the nineteenth century, but they began as the nineteenth century dawned and
continued into the 1930s. Wikipedia's "List of massacres of indigenous
Australians" details over ninety of Newcastle's cases. They involve casualty rates of between six and several hundred. None entails over one
thousand. R. G. Kimber concludes, "The numbers shot were undoubtedly so great as to cause total or near-total local group extinctions . . . so
poorly recorded that accurate pre-contact populations in the region can
never be known."[53] The indigenous population of Tasmania, numbering
20,000, was completely exterminated. Raymond Evans and Robert
Ørsted-Jensen have gone through the records of Queensland. They estimate 65,000 to 67,000 indigenous Queenslanders shot by police and settlers, an overall death rate of 22–26 percent.[54] In 1887 the ethnographer
Edward Curr estimated that "fifteen to twenty-five per cent fall from the
rifle." If the rate in Queensland was typical of other states and territories,
then total killings across Australia must have been about 200,000, about
the same as the battle deaths in the Austro-Prussian and Franco-Prussian
Wars combined.

This is not systematic coverage of colonial wars. Wesseling estimates that the British, French, and Dutch fought about one hundred campaigns against native peoples in the period 1870 to 1914, and I have mentioned only some of these.[55] Paul Bairoch estimates that between 1750 and 1913 the lives of 300,000 European and 100,000 native colonial soldiers were lost in African and Asian territories, mostly due to disease.[56] He says the total native lives lost in battle was somewhere between 800,000 and 1,000,000. He adds, however, that the total deaths resulting from the wars and subsequent forced migrations and famines might have reached 25 million. Etemad estimates civilian losses at 50–60 million, mostly from diseases spread by the destructiveness of war.[57] Because of the mixed causes of death, the total killed directly by wars is unknown, but by any count there were both many more deaths in battle than recorded in CoW data, and a hugely larger number of civilian deaths induced by war.

So we cannot deduce a Long Peace or two Short Peaces in the world in the nineteenth century. Within Europe that may have been so, but it was Europeans who were inflicting almost all the massacres and genocides elsewhere. Combining all the deaths caused by the wars of Europeans might exceed the death toll inflicted by any single civilization in any previous hundred-year period. The rise of Enlightenment civilization in the West did not bring peace. And then came the two world wars. The paradox of the first half of the twentieth century was that it saw both the most devastating wars in human history and the greatest growth in world peace movements—though of course the former dwarfed the latter. But there was no overall decline in warfare through history, or in the nineteenth century, or obviously in the first half of the twentieth century.

Global War Trends since 1945

Most writers have been optimistic about peace in this period, compared especially with the first half of the twentieth century. This comparison is irrefutable. They are encouraged by the postwar settlement, the end of colonialism, the Cold War, and globalization. In 1945 the Axis powers were forced into unconditional surrender and occupied. Top Axis leaders were charged with war crimes and convicted, except for the Japanese emperor, whom U.S. leaders believed would be a symbol of stability for the country. A blind eye was generally turned to lower-level administrators, and to capitalist and political collaborators. Japanese and German mili-

tary spending was at the time kept at very low levels. Parliamentary democracy in West Germany and Japan, and state socialism in Eastern
Europe, were devised as shields against fascist revival. Welfare states
compromised class conflicts. The United States gave substantial economic aid to Japan and Germany and other Europeans. The Japanese
Empire was abolished, and the war had greatly weakened the European
empires. Anticolonial movements finished them off in the 1950s and
1960s. All encouraging news.

The main war threat became hostility between democratic capitalism
and state socialism, and both sides soon were brandishing nuclear weapons. With a few scares along the way, mutual deterrence ruled. Raymond
Aron expressed the Cold War paradox as "peace impossible, war improba-
ble"; although the Soviet Union and the West had incompatible visions of
the world, they were unlikely to risk nuclear war.[58] The Cold War also
added new security arrangements. In the Far East, the American military
presence turned from the pacification of Japan to its protection from state
socialism. NATO also transformed the United States into the protector of
Western Europe against any Soviet offensive. The Warsaw Pact had a
parallel goal in Eastern Europe. Mutual economic cooperation in Europe
strengthened into the Common Market and then the European Union, its
initial purpose to keep Germany in and the Soviet Union out. These institutions did secure stability, peace, and massive economic development
in Europe and (after wars) in East Asia. The continent of Europe, the
most warlike continent for a millennium, was now a zone of peace.

When the Soviet Union collapsed between 1989 and 1991, this owed
less to American military power than to the breadth of it alliances and its
economic and technological superiority. But that was soon forgotten, as
the United States turned more to military interventions to secure its interests abroad. This was to prove much less successful—because war is
rarely a rational instrument of policy.

Liberal optimists note correctly that the period has seen a declining
number of interstate wars. They have suggested that a relative peace, enduring for over seventy years, might be headed at last toward Kant's vision of perpetual peace. Optimism is understandable within recent
Western Europe, from which war was virtually abolished after 1945, but
only by excluding the former Yugoslavia and Ukraine from that zone.
The full-scale Russian invasion of Ukraine in 2022 blasted apart such
European complacency (see chapter 15). It is also odd that the four optimistic liberals are three American citizens (Mueller, Goldstein, and

Pinker), and one Israeli (Gat, an army major), given that their countries are among the few states still waging war. Mueller's optimism concerned forty years after 1945 in the advanced countries, adding that the negative memory of the "two great exceptions," the world wars, acted as a deterrent to further major wars.[59] Gat calls this the Long Peace.[60] He is optimistic about the future but sensibly refrains from predicting perpetual peace by listing some ways that humans might descend again into war. Goldstein says the decline in interstate wars is deep-rooted, derived from eight causes unlikely to be reversed: the end of the Cold War; U.S. dominance; a global economy; the spread of human rights; the spread of democracy; increased participation of women in politics; the proliferation of NGOs; and growing conflict resolution, including UN peacekeeping operations, which he says have made the biggest contribution to the recent decline.[61] Two of these eight, the global economy and democracy, are repeating nineteenth-century theories, but most of the rest are more recent growths in international and transnational institutions. Goldstein believes that international diplomacy spearheaded by the UN and the United States is gradually bringing peace to the world. He sees U.S. forces as being like UN blue helmets (peacekeepers), putting themselves "in harm's way to maintain peace, to establish conditions for political and economic progress, to be diplomats and educators rather than just 'grunts.' "[62] Washington optimists see this as achievable policy, as do soldiers struggling bravely to implement it. While appreciative of their efforts, I am skeptical about their success, and sometimes about the goals of their rulers.

Data on Post-1945 Wars

For this recent period there is no longer a problem of unrecorded small campaigns, although data on civilian deaths remain problematic. The main data sources up to 2015 are usefully summarized on the web by Max Roser.[63] The number of interstate and extrastate (mostly colonial) wars declined greatly. Colonial wars dropped almost to a vanishing point as wars of liberation converted colonies into independent states. We might suppose that this would lead to more interstate wars, since the number of UN member states increased from 51 in 1945 to 193 in 2020, but the reverse has happened—fewer interstate wars, a very positive sign. Indeed, kingdoms did not vanish, and some were resurrected. Thus, Joel Migdal posed the opposite question: "Why Do So Many States Stay In-

tact?" despite their frequent inability to deliver the goods.[64] Fazal identifies just nine vanished kingdoms since 1945, only one resulting from
war.[65] The others were cases like the German Democratic Republic, the
Soviet Union, and Yugoslavia. The exception was Saddam Hussein's invasion of Kuwait and even that proved temporary. Fazal attributes the
end of state mortality to the global strengthening of a norm against conquest, which the exception proved, for Saddam was countered by an invasion under United Nations auspices restoring Kuwait's independence.
The United States has often invaded states, but absorption was never the
aim—regime change or strengthening was the goal. Except for the
United States and Russia, there have been few wars between states with
grossly unequal powers, traditionally the main killers of kingdoms. The
most positive aspect of the post-1945 period was that one of my four
types of war, wars of conquest followed by direct imperial rule, seemed
obsolete—at least until Vladimir Putin aimed at that in his Ukraine invasion of 2022. And this also revealed a weakness of nuclear deterrence,
which is powerless to stop a major conventional war if the aggressor
chooses to threaten the nuclear option.

Nonetheless, there have been a few big wars. The modern war with
the highest death rate of soldiers as a proportion of national population
was Paraguay's 1860s war. Number two, however, was in the 1950s: Paraguay (again) versus Bolivia in the Chaco War (both wars were discussed
in chapter 9). Number three was the Iran-Iraq war of 1980–88, in which
Iran lost about a million casualties, and Iraq up to a half of that, in a war
of trenches and barbed-wire, like World War I. Numbers four and five
were the two world wars, although if we include civilian casualties, the
wars in the Eastern Congo in 1988–2008 would figure. Additionally, the
wars in Korea and Vietnam killed a million or more in battle, and several
million if we include civilians. The ongoing war in Ukraine might join
this group of big wars. There were also many small wars, especially during the Cold War. The overall number of battle deaths, both in absolute
numbers and especially as a proportion of world population, however,
declined between 1945 and 2013 but then began fluctuating quite
sharply. There were in 2020 more wars but fewer casualties than in recent years, but casualties must have risen sharply in 2022 because of the
wars in the Horn of Africa and Ukraine. CoW data on the initiation of
MIDs show that during the Cold War they reached the highest level in
over two centuries, but they then declined with the collapse of the Soviet
Union. This was the only decrease in two centuries of increases in MIDs,

and they rose again in the period 2012–20.[66] Overall, says Braumoeller of CoW data, the post-1945 period has been neither more nor less deadly than the previous 130 years after 1816. But, he warns, "Given how deadly the first half of the 20th century turned out to be, that conclusion is nothing short of horrifying"—referring obliquely to what might happen next. His second overall conclusion is that the two centuries since 1816 have not seen either a consistent rise or decline of war. There have been short-term rises and declines as well as short periods of no variation.[67]

Other studies have lowered the bar for war. Monty Marshall defines war as armed conflict producing five hundred or more deaths, including an annual death rate of at least one hundred.[68] He also measures "war magnitude" on the basis of a combination of casualties, geographical scope, intensity, and displacement of civilians. There were large fluctuations in magnitude without any overall trend between 1946 and 1985. Then came a sharp decline until 1995, when it leveled off before declining again in 2010. The first known year with no interstate wars was 2015. His data end there. They imply not a seventy-year Long Peace but a thirty-five-year Short Peace, since 1985—and more wars have started since 2015. Yet even a seventy-year period of peace would not be unusual in world history, says Aaron Clauset.[69] Focusing on battle deaths from 1823 to 2003, he concludes that both the recent period of relative peace and the half century of great violence that preceded it are not statistically uncommon patterns in time-series data. The postwar pattern of peace would need to endure for over one hundred more years to become a statistically significant trend. Steven Beard controls for the large rise in world population over the period, and this reduces the proportion killed, but again only from the mid-1980s—which is consistent with a Short, not a Long, Peace.[70] It is too soon to conclude that this represents a long-term decline of war, unless one can plausibly project forward decline in the underlying causes of war.

Civil wars show different trends. If we use the CoW cutoff point of one thousand battle deaths, we find that they rose in the 1930s and grew until the 1990s, when they were the large majority of wars. There was then a slight decline from the early 1990s until 2008. Marshall finds that civil wars increased until 1992–93 and then sharply declined, before rising again from about 2009. The last few years have seen a rise in civil wars, from only four in 2012 to twelve in 2016, to ten in 2019—and I count eight in 2020 and twelve also in 2021.[71] Wars involving non–state actors (extrastate wars), such as ISIS, have recently dominated. Paul Hensel gives data for every two-decade period from 1816 to 2000. Excepting the two periods of the world wars, civil wars plus extrastate wars were always more frequent than interstate wars. But wars relocated. In the nineteenth century, most interstate and civil wars were in Europe, and there were far fewer in the Middle East and Asia. Since most independent states in the nineteenth century were in Europe, this is not surprising. But since 1945 the large majority have been in Africa, the Middle East, or Asia. Europe has seen only two interstate wars since 1950.[72] Wars now seem confined to the developing world, though I show later that this partially misleads. The world is now full of states whose spatial configuration is largely guaranteed by international law and institutions. The internal space within more recent and divided or weaker states is now contested.

The Peace Research Institute Oslo (PRIO) and Uppsala Conflict Data Program (UCDP) have data that use only twenty-five battle deaths as defining war. These increased from 1955 to 1994, almost entirely because of civil wars, followed by a decline until 2003, although this level was higher than almost every year from 1950 to 1975. Between 2003 and 2018 trends fluctuated. The total number of fatalities reached its peak of over 100,000 in 2014, and then declined to 53,000 in 2018, but that is still higher than any other year since 1991.[73] Mark Harrison and Nikolaus Wolf go even lower, counting MIDs with fewer than twenty-five deaths, and even counting some amounting to no more than saber rattling.[74] In contrast to actual wars, these have been increasing, and they now far outnumber actual wars. Indeed, saber rattling has increased in recent years among the greatest powers, Russia, China, the United States, and NATO (which I discuss in chapter 15). Goertz and his colleagues suggest that movement toward milder MIDs is the core of increasing peace in the world.[75] Perhaps rulers are warier of war but bluster and bluff more—a modern equivalent of early tribal societies hurling abuse and brandishing spears and bows, but cautious about actually fighting. That would not be quite perpetual peace, but it might be promising. As we saw in chapter 9, this pattern has increasingly characterized Latin America. On the other hand, blustering has also spread to the great powers, capable of the greatest damage to the world.

These figures reveal more fluctuations than long-term trends, with two main exceptions: a trend toward smaller wars and MIDs, which offers support to liberal theorists; and a trend toward more civil wars, which offers no such hope for the Global South. At a global level there has been no overall decline or increase in war since 1945, although there was a decline between about 1985 and 2014, ended by a recent flurry of wars, mostly in Muslim countries (which I analyze in chapter 14).

Braumoeller explains the post-1816 results geopolitically, in terms of "International Orders"—such as the Concert of Europe after the Congress of Vienna, the Bismarckian period in Germany, and the American-dominated world order after the Cold War.[76] These, he says, brought relative peace, whereas contested orders, such as those seen in the Napoleonic period, around the two world wars, and in the Cold War, generated more wars. This geopolitical explanation neglects economic and political power relations and the transnational waves of ideological power I noted in chapter 8. The Napoleonic Wars involved the transnational spread of revolution, which made war deadlier and longer-lasting. The Concert of Europe of 1815 was counterrevolutionary as well as geopolitical. It withstood a smaller revolutionary wave in 1848. It was then shaken in Europe by Italian aspirations for nationhood, and by the rise of Prussia, owing to its militaristic society and state. Bismarck's main later goal was domestic, to use a period of peace in Europe to consolidate the transformation of Prussia into Germany. He hosted the 1884 Berlin Conference on Africa, which did ensure peace between the great powers, but it encouraged them to partition Africa and Asia by force. World War I did break up this order, though this again requires consideration of domestic sources of social power as well as diplomatic factors (as outlined in chapter 8). The war ended with a wave of revolutions, followed by seventy years of bitter struggle among rulers seeking to impose on the world their own transnational ideologies—state socialist, fascist, or capitalist-democratic—as in World War II, Korea, and Vietnam, as well as countless small wars pitting class against class and leftists against rightists. The Iran-Iraq war and the more recent wars in the Middle East have involved both religious ideology and American imperialism (see chapter 14). The main patterns of recent wars have been due to domestic power relations and transnational ideologies as well as to geopolitics.

Civilian versus Military Fatalities

Civilian casualties were high in many historical cases, caused by "exemplary repression" of peoples who resisted as well by armies "living off the land" of their enemies. In chapter 8 I discussed the seventeenth-century Thirty Years' War and its massive civilian casualties. How many Russian civilians died as a result of Napoleon's invasion of 1812 is unknown, but the number must be large. In general, though, civilian casualties increased during the twentieth and early twenty-first centuries, first in interstate wars, then in civil wars. Air forces bomb civilian areas, and most civil wars are "asymmetric," pitting the heavy weapons of state armies and air forces against guerillas wielding light weapons but hiding among the people (sometimes using them as human shields) or fighting in regions with difficult ecologies. Bombing them has increased civilian casualties. Marshall says the proportion of civilian fatalities has steadily increased since 1954, preponderating from about 1990.[77]

Ratios of military to civilian casualties in recent wars have also varied. In the 2003 war in Iraq, official Iraqi estimates put deaths at up to 460,000, whereas unofficial estimates are higher still. Official estimates undercount because of difficulties in conducting surveys in wartime conditions, morgue officials saying they receive more bodies than the authorities record, and Muslim families often burying their dead immediately, without notifying the authorities. The most plausible range of fatalities in Iraq seems 500,000–600,000, civilians contributing 80 percent of them—a ratio of four civilian to one military death. Yet which deaths do we count? Studies finding civilian-military death ratios of less than one or even one to one, as in Bosnia in the 1990s, are of direct combat deaths only.[78] According to the Watson Institute, as of January 2015 about 92,000 people had been killed in the Afghan War, of which only just over 26,000 were civilians. This yields a civilian-to-combatant ratio of only 0.4:1, but this is a count of those killed directly by enemy action. Crawford adds deaths through indirect causes related to the war, such as famine and disease outbreaks.[79] These add another 360,000 Afghans, pushing up the ratio enormously to about 8:1.

African civilian casualties through civil wars have been much worse. Most of these ten civil wars occurred in poor states with few records, so fatality figures cannot be exact. Guesses have to be made of prewar mortality rates and these compared with the postwar rates. In the deadliest case, in the Eastern Congo between 1988 and 2008, two very different estimates have been given by international organizations, one of 5.4 million killed, the other just under half that figure. The higher figure seems biased by an underestimate of prewar mortality rates.[80] So I have preferred 2.5 million, following Bethany Lacina and Nils Gleditsch, who estimate that over 90 percent of them were civilians, as also in the conflicts in Sudan and Ethiopia.[81] Civilian casualties in Mozambique, Somalia, and Ethiopia-Eritrea were probably in excess of 75 percent, a ratio of 3–4:1,

Table 10.2. Estimated Deaths in Major Wars in Africa, 1963–2008

Country	Years	Total War Deaths	Battle Deaths	% of Deaths Occurring in Battle
Sudan/Anya Nya	1963–73	250,000–750,000	20,000	3–8
Nigeria/Biafra	1967–70	500,000–2 million	75,000	4–15
Angola	1975–2002	1.5 million	160,475	11
Ethiopia (excl. Eritrea)	1976–91	1–2 million	16,000	1–2
Mozambique	1976–92	500,000–1 million	145,400	15–29
Somalia	1981–96	250,000–350,000	66,750	19–27
Sudan	1983–2002	2 million	55,500	3
Liberia	1989–96	150,000–200,000	23,500	12–16
Dem. Rep. of Congo	1998–2008	2.5 million	145,000	6
Ethiopia/Eritrea	1998–2000	300,000	43,000	14

Source: Perlo-Freeman et al., 2015.

and this may also be so of the 2021 war in Tigray province of Ethiopia. Being a civilian in a civil war zone is dangerous across large swathes of Africa. A few small wars have more military than civilian casualties—for example, the 1982 Falklands War and Nagorno-Karabagh in 2020—but the reverse is far more common, provided we count civil as well as inter-state wars and include war-induced famines and disease.

Wars also force refugee flight. Statistics have been collected by the United Nations High Commissioner for Refugees (UNHCR) since 1965. The number displaced by persecution or conflict and fleeing abroad reached 19 million in 1989. It then declined to 9 million in 2005, in the period of hope. But then came a decade of increases, culminating in the highest-ever figures, 29.5 million in 2018, 34 million in 2020, and 35 million in 2021. By the end of June 2022, 6.5 million Ukrainians had fled their country in only four months of war. An additional 8 million were internally displaced. Combined, these figures add up to one-third of the Ukrainian population, an incredible proportion. The total number of refugees in the world, if we add those fleeing within their own countries, is much higher. The highest numbers, 82.4 million in 2020 and 94.7 million in 2021, were again the last ones. The biggest numbers were from Syria, Venezuela, Afghanistan, South Sudan, and Myanmar.[82] Of course, instead of remaining in fear of death in a war zone, refugees flee to camps offering basic subsistence, thanks to the UNHCR, other international agencies, and neighboring governments. This offers a little support to Goldstein's optimism regarding international organizations. But when refugees more numerous than the population of the United Kingdom or France are forcibly displaced, this can offer only a tiny smidgen of hope.

Goldstein says UN peacekeeping troops encourage peace. In January 2020 there were 110,000 blue helmets stationed in fourteen countries, the second-largest military intervention force in the world after the United States, which had about 165,000 troops stationed abroad. UN troops are brought in only when both sides to a conflict wish to be separated, so they have no effect on wars until the endgame. Within this limitation, the UN brings some successes, some failures. About half its brokered peace settlements endure longer than twelve years, but half break down sooner. Unfortunately, peace achieved through negotiated settlement does not last as long as peace achieved by the victory of one side.[83] Border disputes settled by the International Court of Justice have been increasing, as we saw in Latin America. A world without border disputes might be halfway to a world without wars. But we are not there yet, for there are well over one hundred current border disputes. Though most are now fairly dormant, some are not. In 2020–22 border disputes continued in Ukraine before exploding into Russian imperial conquest, and they flared up again between China and India, China and other Pacific nations, Armenia and Azerbaijan, Tajikistan and Kyrgyzstan, and Ethiopia, Tigray, and Eritrea. We have seen various indications of a recent uptick in the number and intensity of wars. We must be cautious about projecting this into the future, but the signs are ominous in some places, especially around Russia's borders and in Taiwan.

Pacific Tendencies in Western Societies

Yet internally the West has become fairly pacific, as Pinker, Gat, Mueller, Goldstein, and MacMillan all observe. Take homicide rates. The average in forty local studies in thirteenth- and fourteenth-century England was twenty-four murders per 100,000.[84] Today in England and Wales it is less than one, in the United States it is five, and the global average is just under seven. Yet fifty cities in the world have homicide rates of over thirty per 100,000, higher than in medieval England. Most are in Latin America, three are in South Africa, but four are U.S. cities (led by Detroit and New Orleans). No European city comes anywhere near this level of violence. Pinker says that U.S. violence is a problem only in southern states and among African Americans. Northern white homicide rates are only double those of modern European countries, he says, not ten times as high. Of course, we could reduce the rates of all the world's cities by excluding the groups committing the most homicides.

Police homicides are also relevant. In the United Kingdom between 2010 and 2019, on average 2.4 persons per year were killed by policemen. Few U.K. police carry guns, but in Germany and France most do. In 2018 French police forces killed twenty-six persons and German police forces nine. In most of the French cases, the victims were unarmed, but the police had feared they were terrorists.[85] American official figures of police killings are unreliable, but the *Washington Post* published a survey of all known cases in 2015 that revealed a shocking total of just under 1,000 killings that year.[86] The annual toll was slightly reduced in a 2021 study, which estimated 30,800 deaths from police violence between 1980 and 2018, an average of 820 per annum.[87] These figures are about double officially recorded rates. Around 80 percent of victims are claimed in police reports to have been armed, though we might be skeptical about this claim, and we don't know whether victims were brandishing a gun when shot dead. In any case, shooting a suspect repeatedly in the back when he or she is fleeing because of reasonable fear of the police is an extremely violent act.

The rise of extremist militias in the United States is also worrying, especially their persistent presence on the fringes of the Republican Party and in the Trump movement, seemingly encouraged by the former president. There are also persistent mass school shootings. Despite all this, the prospects of significant gun control are politically very dim. This is exclusively a domestic problem, for gun toters, even those dressed in quasi uniforms, seem uninterested in foreign wars. The potential for civil war is more threatening, should the deterioration of the U.S. political system continue. America North and South does not support liberal theories of a decline in interpersonal violence, but Europe, Japan, some of East Asia, and Australasia do.

Like Helmut Thome, I stress the role of the state in the decline of violence.[88] Infrastructural power is the capacity of states to actually penetrate civil society and logistically implement its decisions through the realm. Most premodern rulers lacked the infrastructural power to institutionalize procedures for maintaining order. Nor could they disarm the population (though we saw that Tokugawa Japan managed it). Rulers relied on repression, including killing. In contrast, modern rulers have infrastructural power whose institutions routinely preserve order without inflicting lethal violence—except in some authoritarian regimes. In most countries the population has been disarmed—the United States is the exception. In the West most people live peaceful lives. The West does have extremely violent video games, and Hollywood movies are obsessed with guns and violence. There is debate about whether this is simply cathartic fantasyland or a direct expression of a repressed desire to kill. But without conscription, real war has been removed from the everyday experience of young men in the most developed parts of the world. To traditional sports like male boxing and wrestling have been added cage fighting and female fighting. Violence in the ring is real enough, though rarely lethal, and the audience merely shouts. Violence in political and racial demonstrations has increased in recent years. Yet overall, there has been a decline in militarism in the principal institutions of society.

Chapter 1 defined militarism as combining the dominance of military elites in society, the ideological exaltation of military virtues above those of peace, and extensive and aggressive military preparedness. In earlier periods I have found cases of militaristic societies in which we can find all three. This is not so in today's liberal democracies. Nonetheless, military spending in both liberal and illiberal countries has been growing, the United States, Europe, India, China, and Russia taking the lead. World military spending grew every year since the year 2000, except for a slight dip between 2010 and 2014. These figures were adjusted to control for inflation. In 2021 it topped $2 trillion for the first time. Doubtless the 2022 figures will be even higher. The United States alone accounts for 38 percent of the world's expenditures. Yet military spending does not dominate the major economies. Their dollar figures never top 4.1 percent of GDP. Only two of the Arab Gulf state figures are higher than this.[89] Military elites do not dominate even American society, and while its gun culture, violent videos and movies, and the elevation of soldiers into "heroes" are expressions of cultural militarism, this is not institutionally dominant. European countries' cultures are more pacific. But the United States possesses the third element of militarism in spades. Never has a single country had such military overpreparedness, its bases spread over the globe, prepared for and launching military interventions across the world. This combination makes for an uneven and narrow form of militarism, a "regime militarism" rather than the societal militarism of Rome and ex-barbarian dynasties of Asia. And it has required new ways of making war.

From Ferocious to Callous Killing

Following Randall Collins, I distinguish "ferocious" from "callous" ways of killing and note a partial shift in the modern period from the former to the latter, from body hacking to killing from a distance.[90] Ferocity is today found mainly in civil wars in poorer countries, from machete hacking in Rwanda to decapitating prisoners in the Middle East, to bayonet stabbing and raping of Rohingya in Myanmar. Civil wars are often called "low intensity," but even paramilitary bands can terrorize large populations, while the states fighting them are often just as ferocious. There is less long-range killing in civil wars and virtually none by insurgent groups lacking airplanes, tanks, and artillery. But all sides commit atrocities.

Wars in the Global South have been called "new wars" involving asymmetry between states and rebels, military privatization, states losing the monopoly of the means of violence, drugs or precious metals sold to finance arms buying, and seizing resources from unarmed aid agencies. All these are said to be reinforced by economic globalization, and all weaken state sovereignty, offering further opportunities for rebels to intensify violence.[91] Of course, some of these were often present in earlier wars, too, while the link of "new wars" to economic globalization is dubious.[92] Yet asymmetry is real: government forces armed with tanks, airplanes, artillery, intensive professional training and discipline battle against insurgents armed with Kalashnikovs, handheld rocket launchers, improvised explosive devices, off-road pickup trucks, suicide belts, guerilla cells, and morale conferred by populist ideologies. Asymmetry had first allowed Westerners to conquer most of the world. But in the post-1945 period, "weapons of the weak" have allowed poorer political movements to fight back and sometimes outlast much more heavily armed and richer opponents. Thus, in a study on conflicts between strong and weak states measured by their material resources, during the nineteenth century the strong ones won over 80 percent of the wars, but after 1945, the weaker actors have won over 51 percent.[93] This came in two waves, first in anti-colonial liberation struggles, second in post-colonial struggles against the Soviet Union and the United States and allies, in which religious ideologies have sometimes loomed large.

Ivan Arreguín-Toft says the colonial powers often tried "barbarism" to repress enemies they considered "less civilized"—for example, massacres and torture by the French in Algeria and by the British in Kenya.[94] Today some Western special forces do fight ferociously, and torture is not unknown, but in general "they" fight ferocious warfare, while "we" do more callous warfare, an aspect of asymmetric warfare. Swords and spears enabled hacking at the body of another. This requires ferocity, which was valued as a social trait. Tournaments, jousting, archery, and quarterstaff combat trained medieval men for physical combat. Calmness and technical ability have supplanted ferocity as the most important military skill. The deadliest weapons are now wielded by people who never see the enemy they kill, which creates indifference to distant death. This especially characterized World War II, in which the firebombing of Dresden and Tokyo, deliberately targeting civilians, was not seen by the Allies as atrocities. We see our enemies' atrocities, not ours. Our attitude was epitomized in 1945 by the mundane words of William Sterling Parsons, the commander of the *Enola Gay* immediately after he had dropped the first atomic bomb on Hiroshima: "Results clear cut successful in all respects. Visible effects greater than any test. Conditions normal in airplane following delivery."[95] There is no emotion expressed in this log entry, only satisfaction with performance. Parsons's navigator, Ted van Kirk, claimed to have "come off the mission, had a bite and a few beers, and hit the sack, and had not lost a night's sleep over the bomb in 40 years."[96] Today's drones even take the travel out of bombing.

As Pinker, Mueller, Goldstein, and Gat observe, Westerners shudder at torture, rape, and hacking of body parts. We shudder at body-on-body ferocity—but not at our own long-range killings. We try not to see them. We prefer not to go into an abattoir and see the mangling of animals. We prefer not to see torture, and we may turn a blind eye if our side does it. We do not have to see any of these sights. But we still eat meat, and we still make war with missiles and drones; America may still covertly torture perceived enemies, and some of its allies certainly do. We are horrified at the decapitation of civilians inflicted by the Islamic State, but not at the callous killing of civilians by our air forces. Among drone "pilots," the enemy is seen only through satellite images on computer screens. Drone personnel follow carefully scripted procedures concerning the adequacy of their information. Only if satisfied with this do they release their drones' weapons. They show no passion, and ideology is not driving their decision other than the belief that those labeled as terrorists can be legitimately killed. ISIS deliberately targets individuals and groups, civilians as well as combatants, and is proud to show videos of prisoners being decapitated. The United States and its allies do not deliberately target civilians, but accurate bombing depends on intelligence gathering on the ground, and its quality varies. Bombing cannot be always aimed at the right target. Rockets and bombs dropped by planes and drones inevitably kill civilians: they are mistaken for terrorists, they are in proximity to terrorists, or they are part of a wedding party or a hospital or a school that intelligence erroneously sees as an assembly of terrorists. The U.S. military admits to killing very few civilians because to admit to more might alienate Americans, a healthy sign of Americans finding the excesses of war unacceptable. But it is no comfort to those civilians caught up in the crosshairs of U.S. or Russian targeting, and it leads to serious undercounting of the civilian victims of recent wars.

Civil Wars Internationalized

So is this now a polarized world, a civilized, pacific North (the United States and Russia serving as partial outliers) and an uncivilized, warlike South? This is deceptive, for two reasons. First, the profit motives of northern arms companies and governments have led to massive arms transfers from the rich countries to the regimes and rebels of poorer countries. Businessmen and "good union jobs" (as U.S. liberals like to say) are causing death in far-off countries. The total dollar value of arms transfers is unknown since much shady arms dealing exists, but SIPRI estimates it as over $40 billion at the height of the Cold War in the early 1980s. Then it fell to just over $30 billion in 2002–6. Then it rose again to about $35 billion in the period 2007–16, before falling to just over $30 billion in 2021. It must have risen again in 2022. But all these figures are very substantial. The biggest exporter in recent years has been the United States, at 35–39 percent of the world's total, followed by the combined European Union countries at 26 percent (France and Germany led the way), and Russia at 21 percent.[97] Numerous additional countries, such as Britain, Italy, Spain, the Czech Republic, and Israel have important arms industries, and manufacturers usually negotiate major arms sales in collaboration with their government. These deals are important to their economies, and so no government wishes to reduce arms sales. Most countries with military expenditure of 5 percent or more of GNP are poor. They are arming against both domestic and foreign enemies, yet they also view a modern military as conferring geopolitical status, just as do the major powers. They all want to flex military muscles in public. Addiction to militarism by southern warlords is fueled by northern arms lords in a symbiotic relationship.

Second, the northern powers do fight, but mostly through proxies. "Civil war" needs qualifying, for most of these wars are also internationalized. The year 2018 saw fourteen conflicts (six wars and eight MIDs) internationalized, where local war was intensified by foreign intervention, especially by the United States. These conflicts provided over half of all battle-related casualties that year. Internationalized conflicts last longer, and political solutions are harder to find. Foreign interventions usually involve regime strengthening, supporting the government side in a conflict, although this was not true of the United States in its wars against Muslim states, and Russia supports regime change separatists in Ukraine.[98] During the Cold War, NATO troops were not sent into war zones. The first intervention came in 1992 in Bosnia. They have since intervened in Kosovo, Serbia, Afghanistan, Libya, and the seas off Somalia and Yemen. After a period in which African countries had a policy of mutual noninterference, the African Union agreed to a multinational intervention force in 2002. Its gestation was lengthy, but from about 2013 it became a reality.

Recent foreign states' interventions were or are in eastern Congo (by nine other African countries), Mali (by France, Chad, and contingents from many African Union countries, with U.S. logistical support), Somalia (by the United States, NATO, and various African Union countries), Colombia (by the United States), Afghanistan and northern Pakistan (by the United States and thirty-eight other NATO and partner countries), Libya (by seventeen NATO members, including the United States, Britain, France, the United Arab Emirates (UAE), Egypt, Saudi Arabia, Russia, and Turkey), Syria (by the United States, much of NATO, Iraq, Jordan, Turkey, Iran, and Hezbollah), Yemen (by the United States, Britain, France, Saudi Arabia, Egypt, several Gulf states, Iran, and Hezbollah), and eastern Ukraine (by Russia, with the United States and NATO providing massive arms supplies to Ukraine). In 2020 Turkey was heavily involved in the fighting in Nagorno-Karabagh, and in 2021 Horn of Africa countries were involved in the struggle between Tigray rebels and the Ethiopian government. UN and NATO forces are active in numerous countries, but few of them are involved in ground fighting, although they do provide logistical and training aid. This is internationalization of local disputes.

Syria has been by far thc deadliest civil war raging over the last few years, and the United States, Russia, and NATO countries have been fighting there, either directly or through proxies, as are Iranian soldiers, Saudi pilots, and Hezbollah militias. Without the foreigners, the death toll and the refugee flow would be much lower. Libya also remains the site of a confused war between numerous militias, all of whom receive foreign assistance. Access to Libya's oil is an important motive for the foreigners. The war then simplified into one main conflict, between a government in Tripoli, backed by the UN, Turkey, Qatar, and Italy, and a rebel general based in Benghazi, backed by Russia, the UAE, Egypt, Jordan, and France. Russia sent unmarked planes and mercenaries working for the Wagner Group, a private Russian organization (with close Kremlin links), and the Turkish government has introduced ground troops, mostly allied Syrian militias, while U.S. planes and drones bomb jihadists wherever they can find them. According to UN officials, Libyan deaths since 2014 in what is called the Second Civil War have risen to 9,000; another 20,000 have been wounded. Turkey assisted the attack in 2020 by Azerbaijan on disputed territory held by Armenia, while Russia supplied Armenia with antidrone defenses that did not work. The death toll here was over 6,000. Across the world, foreign intervention is also common against non–state actors, especially armed religious groups like Al Qaeda, the Islamic State, Boko Haram, al-Shabaab, and the Lord's Resistance Army, and these movements operate across borders.

The U.S. government sends military advisory teams to many countries and bombs a few; NATO assists. Because the action is far away, the North seems pacific. But the United States, followed by France and the United Kingdom, followed by other NATO members, is not pacific. Their foreign entanglements are distant, and their citizens are rarely conscripted and rarely risk death. American leaders have kept the body bags few through risk transfer militarism. Often peoples do not know where their soldiers are engaged. How many Americans knew that U.S. soldiers were in Niger, until suddenly in October 2017, when four of them were found killed? How many French knew of Operation Barkhane, in which 5,600 French troops have been quartered across five West African countries to counter Islamist insurgents across the Sahel region since 2014 (as well as to protect France's uranium mines)? The total number of French killed is so far about fifty; over 600 jihadists have been killed or captured; and the annual cost is one billion euros. In 2021 President Emmanuel Macron announced plans for withdrawing the French troops. Although U.K. military interventions in the Middle East have become controversial, less publicity is given to small African interventions, to U.K. bases in Kenya and Sierra Leone, and to its Indian Ocean island of Diego Garcia, leased to the United States for its Middle Eastern and Afghan bombing ventures. These military adventures are discrete and far away.

Conclusion

I have questioned rival theories of diminishing or increasing wars through history. I found variation across the world and through time.[99] Intergroup conflict was uncommon in early human communities, but it grew as hunter-gatherers settled into fixed communities and grew again as states and empires emerged. Thereafter war remained ubiquitous but erratic. The Roman Republic was continuously at war. In China I found that war varied greatly by region. In Japan it varied greatly through time. Post-Roman Europe was highly war-prone, but at first wars were small-scale and somewhat rule-governed. Smaller kingdoms were swallowed up by major powers with more formidable militaries, which were later diverted into religious and revolutionary wars. These powers conquered much of the world, annihilating or exploiting its peoples. Neither the Enlightenment nor industrial capitalism brought peace to the nineteenth century, as is commonly believed, for Europeans were exporting war to their colonies. Finally, they precipitated world wars that destroyed their own military power. The nineteenth century was not peaceful, nor was the first half of the twentieth century.

Wars changed after 1945. There were fewer big wars but more small ones and MIDs, mostly beginning as civil wars. The total number of wars and their casualties fluctuated, but through all of the twentieth century civilian fatalities grew. At the beginning of the twenty-first century liberal theorists perceived a trend away from war, but this has subsequently wavered. The two main axes of the recent wave of wars in the Muslim world—conservatives-secularists against jihadists and Sunni versus Shi'a—are worsening currently (see chapter 14). In contrast, wars in Western Europe and Latin America have almost disappeared. Warfare is gone from the relations between the rich countries, just as Mueller argues. Whatever the level of economic conflict among the United States,

Japan, and E.U. countries, it is unlikely they would wage war against each other. If the north of the world were hermetically sealed, optimistic liberal theory would have much traction, although the United States lags, with guns galore, a massive state arsenal, and callous militarism. Yet one type of war, territorial conquest imperialism, seems dead.

Many poor countries remain beset by wars, especially civil wars, however, which show little sign of decline. Rich countries still contribute unhelpfully to these with arms sales, proxy wars, and bombing. That these are deployed far away obscures the militarism and seems to give liberal optimism more support than it deserves. Rich countries have exported militarism far from the attention span and the well-being of their citizens. Terrorism in their backyards, partly caused by their own aggression, should have given them pause, but instead it escalated an emotional "war on terror." Irrationality rules. Gat is wrong to assert that in the post-Enlightenment era, "war has become incomprehensible to the point of absurdity."[100] Much of the world knows of its absurdity only too well—and we are partly responsible.

CHAPTER ELEVEN

Fear and Loathing on the Battlefield I

From Ancient Times to the American Civil War

SO FAR I HAVE discussed wars at the level of rulers' decision making, without the presence of ordinary soldiers who had no role in such decisions. We have seen rulers backing farther and farther away from the battlefield as the range of lethal weapons broadened, enabling them to play war games at the expense of other peoples' lives. They no longer see—and so far you the reader have not seen—mutilated corpses, torn flesh, or gushing blood. I must remedy this neglect and focus on those who have been the greatest sufferers from war, the soldiers, both officers and men. But there is one great methodological obstacle. On earlier wars we lack evidence from soldiers themselves, and this changed only with the advent of mass literacy in the nineteenth century. So after a brief introduction, I offer a short section on the limited amount we do know of soldiers in battle before mass literacy, and then I will discuss soldiers' experience of battle during the American Civil War, the first war in which most soldiers were literate and wrote letters, diaries, and memoirs about their experiences. Then, in the next two chapters, I discuss soldiers in battle in more recent wars.

The dominant image of soldiers in modern culture is of courage and triumph, heroes over cowards, good guys over bad guys. In war movies the heroes with whom we identify almost never die. Supporting actors are expendable, but they usually die cleanly, with good grace. These are "good deaths." Today American soldiers are routinely called heroes by politicians, but soldiers themselves are uncomfortable with hero versus coward dichotomy. They often declare that only those who have experienced battle can understand its reality, and they know that their own deeds fall short of heroic. General Sherman spoke for most during the American Civil War: "I am tired and sick of war. Its glory is all moonshine. It is only those who have neither fired a shot nor heard the shrieks and groans of the wounded who cry aloud for blood, for vengeance, for desolation. War is hell."

Of course, soldiers' experiences in battle have varied. A few seem to actually like battle because they are sadists or because they crave danger and are exhilarated by surges of adrenaline coursing through their bodies. They may hate and fear battle, as I think you or I would. They may fight because they are paid to fight and it is their job, because they believe in the cause, because they want the status of a warrior, because they have obedience drilled into them, or out of loyalty to comrades. Soldiers normally embody complex mixtures of such motives and emotions. The battlefield is emotional struggle par excellence. Obviously, the prospect of being killed or maimed is not something that anyone could relish. Fear of this is the dominant emotion on battlefields. Yet fear can be coped with, even utilized to kill others. A loathing for battle may derive from revulsion at the specter of mangled, bloodied bodies, from moral repugnance at killing or maiming others, or from fear of being killed or maimed oneself. Skulking (keeping one's head down and pretending to fight), nonfiring, mutiny, and desertion are all expressions of repugnance. Yet reactions are affected by the perception of risk: What level of risk of death or maiming do soldiers perceive and accept? Is the degree of risk controllable by them? I explore these issues over the next three chapters.

It is unlikely the same answers apply across all forms of arms, all historical periods, all geographical regions, and all phases of campaigns. I will not discuss the very earliest "battles" of prehistoric humans, which (as we saw in chapter 2) are conjectured to have contained more ritual shouting than bodily combat. Later, when warfare became more organized, we can distinguish a very long stretch of time during which infantry and cavalry combat consisted of direct body-on-body slashing and clubbing—what Collins calls ferocious warfare. This was followed by a comparatively short period from the eighteenth century onward in which most killing has been at a distance, often by unseen enemies. This is emotionless, callous warfare, since the killer is not present at the death, and so he can kill dispassionately. In World War II over 95 percent of British military casualties were inflicted from a distance, and 85 percent of fatalities came from aerial bombing, artillery shells, mortars and grenades, antitank shells, and bullets.[1] Of course, archers inflicted bodily damage from a distance throughout history, as did sling and javelin throwers over a few meters away. An interim period lay between the two eras, in which arquebus and musket were fired over short distances against an enemy seen but only rarely confronted bodily. Naval warfare does not fit so neatly into such a periodization, and airplanes did not appear until the twentieth century. Also modern infantries, though firing over distances, do not usually do so coldly. They are themselves simultaneously threatened from a distance. This involves a distinctive terror caused by the seeming randomness of death.

The first phase in a campaign is recruitment. In modern wars we know that the prospect of death seems abstract and distant to new recruits. Recruits think more often of the guaranteed pay, food, and clothing, inducements laced with some degree of pride and status (especially, they think, in the eyes of women) in fighting for one's country, and a desire for adventure influenced by the manly heroism depicted in stories. The notion of adventure includes fighting but not one's own death. None of this prepares them for the terror of battle.

So after recruitment must follow a second phase of drilling and disciplining intended to prepare the soldier to cope with battle by converting him into an automaton, subordinating himself without question to officers' commands, sublimating his sense of self into a collective identity with comrades or a regiment, felt most directly through the "muscular bonding" that I noted in chapter 8 was a consequence of drilling. Subordination and coercion are the heart of military power; the simplest answer to the question "Why do men fight?" is that once recruited, they are coerced to do so, sometimes rather brutally. The Duke of Wellington marveled at the power of drilling in 1813 when describing his own soldiers: "The very scum of the earth. People talk of their enlisting from their fine military feeling—all stuff—no such thing. Some of our men enlist from having got bastard children—some for minor offences—many more for drink; but you can hardly conceive such a set brought together, and it really is wonderful that we should have made them the fine fellows they are."[2]

Finally, the soldier enters into the third phase, battle—skirmishes, ambushes, guerilla attacks, and set-piece battles, all generating different kinds of fear.

The Long History of Ferocious Warfare

From early history until well into the nineteenth century, restricted literacy means our evidence does not come from rank-and-file soldiers. The armies of Greece, Rome, Byzantium, imperial China, Islamic kingdoms, ancient Israel, and the Incan and Aztec empires have left records that suggest that warrior ideals dominated armies, but we lack the view of the soldiers themselves.[3] The Roman Republic is our best-sourced early case. There we rarely read of resistance to the draft. Its legions were usually successful, which helped commitment, as we saw in chapter 4. The Roman military writer Vegetius said, "Few men are born brave, many become so through training and force of discipline," and extensive drilling enabled Roman armies to show battle-winning maneuverability. Repeated success gave them confidence, partly overcoming their fear of death. Their discipline must have also intimidated the enemy. They were not perfectly tuned warriors, however. Sometimes, as in all armies, amid the confusion of battle they would panic and run, while harsh campaign conditions, brutal discipline, and fear led to much desertion.[4] There were many defeats—but usually on the road to ultimate victory. Aislinn Melchior poses the question whether Roman soldiers suffered from something like posttraumatic stress disorder (PTSD). Of course, she lacks the evidence to answer, but she identifies the three main triggers of PTSD today as witnessing horrific events, being in mortal danger, and killing at close quarters. The legionaries routinely experienced all three. Yet Romans were also habituated to the sight of death. Half their children died very young, criminals were executed in public, sometimes torn apart by wild animals in arenas for sport, and disobedient soldiers might be flogged or stoned to death, sometimes by their comrades. Such inurement might make them stoic, less likely to suffer from psychological maladies, Melchior suggests.[5] But no psychological problems would have been recognized by the Roman authorities.

There were material incentives for armies. They were paid. They could ransom rich prisoners, plunder from the dead and wounded, and plunder and rape in cities they had stormed. Soldiers would carry in their pockets whatever coins or jewels they needed to finance themselves during a campaign because this was the least likely place to get robbed. But after death or when wounded, helpless on the ground, they were easy pickings. From Rome to Gettysburg, soldiers stripped the bodies of fallen foes and in Ukraine they still do so. Rome and China expropriated farms from the defeated and gave them to veterans. In Europe when looting and ransoming died out, "prize money," pensions, or public employment could be allocated to veterans. These were common in China, too. Soldiers also fought for social status. Roman soldiers were given *dona*, medals for bravery, prized badges of honor: they are boasted of on tombstones. Roman auxiliaries were granted some of the privileges of citizenship. Upper-class warriors might receive land or offices or better marriage prospects. War was an avenue of upward social mobility for younger sons, and the risk of death came only occasionally. The dominant experience was boredom, since nothing happened most of the time. That is why battles are so suddenly shocking and disorienting.

The culture of most historic societies viewed interpersonal violence as normal. It demonstrated manhood, which men wish to demonstrate, or cowardice, which they wish to avoid. War was the intensification of brawling, as war today is not. Soldiers had disincentives in the form of flogging or execution if they ran away. Yet peasants obeyed their lords in war as in peacetime; their villages had to fulfill quotas of conscripts; and even in modern societies orders are obeyed because the lower classes are used to obeying.

After recruitment, the second phase was drill and discipline—though not, of course, for guerillas whose looser style of warfare has been an intermittent presence through human history. At the other extreme, Roman soldiers underwent intensive drilling in rhythmic movement, always taught to remain tight with the men on either side of them for mutual protection. Theirs was muscular-bonded ferocity. They described the Gauls and the Germans as fighting in a mass, but each man fighting as an individual, with more spontaneous ferocity than Romans. Alcohol and other drugs were handed out in many armies and navies to still fear and instill confidence.

And so they went into battle, usually fought over a small area for not more than a day. Infantry advanced wielding sling, spear, javelin, axe, or sword, cavalry on horseback. Both may have had bad feelings in stomach or bowels, but it was only within range of enemy archers, against whom they were unable yet to defend themselves, did fear of death dominate. Untrained men (and women) would have mostly turned and fled at this point, but in the rhythm of battle, this was when disciplined soldiers quickened their pace, physically trapped within their military formation, shouting, grimly hunching shoulders, advancing under the partial protection of shields. Those advancing were full of hatred and tension, wanting very much to kill the source of their fear.

When soldiers reached the enemy, the motivation of "kill or be killed" took over for those in the opposed front lines. If a soldier hesitated for a moment, the enemy probably would not, and so death or maiming would come. There is no time for complex emotions—just get your blow in first! Thrust into, don't slash across, the Roman drill sergeants urged. Archers fired from a distance, sling and javelin throwers from close by, but all needed protection. Mounted archers were fearsome, for they could wheel out of range after firing. But most infantry were not engaging the enemy at any one point in time. John Keegan imagined the battle of Agincourt in 1415. Most soldiers were lined up in ranks behind the men in the front line. In an advance they would just be pushing those in front forward, in defense they would be stationary, engaging the enemy only if the front rank began to sustain casualties or became exhausted and faltered. Then the next rank had to move forward and strike.[6]

In this type of fighting, dominant through history, battle was an aggregate of individual or small group combats, men welded together by being physically trapped as a mass, not only by the enemy in front, but also by their comrades behind and on each side. They were trapped into fighting by the coercion of army organization and the ecological environment of the battlefield. The trap was tightest in the Greek phalanx, somewhat less so in the Roman legion, and much less so among barbarians and in medieval battles. Cavalrymen were free until they charged. Then they too became trapped by their momentum toward hand-to-hand fighting. If they faced a solid line of enemy, their horses might refuse to charge into it, and cavalrymen often then dismounted to fight like infantrymen. Their advantage in mobility was used mainly to arrive quickly at the chosen point of attack or to assault open or dispersed enemy formations.

Only as victory or defeat seemed to loom did some freedom of movement come to the surviving infantry. If soldiers saw their comrades being felled and felt themselves being pushed back, or especially when they were pushed sideways by an unexpected flanking movement, fear mounted and might overcome training and discipline. Fear paralyzed military action, as many soldiers became incapable of fighting with or shooting at the enemy. Colonel Charles Ardant du Picq in the 1860s recommended how to combat fear: "Man has a horror of death. . . . Discipline is for the purpose of dominating that horror by a still greater horror, that of punishment or disgrace." But he added, "Self-esteem is unquestionably one of the most powerful motives which moves our men. They do not wish to pass for cowards in the eyes of their comrades." He noted that it was paradoxically those in the rear ranks, the least threatened, who panicked first under this pressure simply because they *could* turn and run, whereas the front lines were trapped front and back by the enemy and their comrades.[7] If flight became contagious, the army degenerated from being a coherent body of men to a "crowd," "a human assembly animated," says Keegan, "not by discipline but by mood, by the play of inconstant and potentially infectious emotion, which, if it spreads, is fatal to an army's subordination."[8]

These were the common features of well-organized enemies throughout history. Yet all battles had peculiarities. At Agincourt the English army was mainly archers, protected by concealed sharpened stakes dug into the ground. The French had not reconnoitered these, and the charging French cavalrymen were surprised, their horses terrified, many of them throwing off their riders. The English archers and men-at-arms then rushed forward with knives and axes to capture (for ransom) or kill and strip the wounded or unhorsed knights and men-at-arms pinned down by their armor or horses. French archers and reserve cavalry at Agincourt, witnessing the collapse of this first charge, had a choice. They hesitated and then fled. The English victors surged forward in what Collins calls a "forward panic."[9] The French had lost their order and, engulfed by panic, were easy targets. The pursuing English had neither fear of the enemy nor loathing of battle to hold them back. A rush of adrenaline induced a killing spree as, released from their own fears, they struck or shot arrows at the backs of the fleeing enemy. By far the greatest volume of killing occurred in flight, as we look from Muye, China, in 1046 BCE to Cannae, Italy, in 216 BCE, to Agincourt, France, in 1415 CE.

In battles fear may have been ever-present, but it was managed by the need for violent self-defense and the physical constraint of the battlefield, until the prospect of defeat induced demoralization. Repugnance at killing in battle was unlikely. Slaughter of old men, women, children, and prisoners did evoke disapproval, but it happened. In siege warfare moral qualms were usually suppressed if city leaders had refused an offer to negotiate or surrender. This made the city population vulnerable to massacre after the city was stormed, according to the norms of warfare. The larger the casualties suffered by the besiegers, the angrier and more pitiless they were when they stormed into the city. Their commanders knew that loot and rape were rewards their soldiers expected, and they turned a blind eye to atrocities. The Jewish historian Josephus describes Roman soldiers sacking Jerusalem in 73 CE:

> When they went in numbers into the lanes of the city, with their swords drawn, they slew those whom they overtook, without mercy, and set fire to the houses whither the Jews were fled, and burnt every soul in them, and laid waste a great many of the rest; and when they were come to the houses to plunder them, they found in them entire families of dead men, and the upper rooms full of dead corpses, that is of such as died by the famine; they then stood in a horror at this sight, and went out without touching anything. But although they had this commiseration for such as were destroyed in that manner, yet had they not the same for those that were still alive, but they ran through every one whom they met with, and obstructed the very lanes with their dead bodies, and made the whole city run down with blood, to such a degree indeed that the fire of many of the houses was quenched with these men's blood.[10]

The sacking of cities brought death and horror to civilians as well as soldiers.

Not much more than this can be deduced without testimony from the soldiers. But we can probably assume that moral qualms were rare, while fear was uneven, exploding in routs.

The Early Modern Period in Europe

Clausewitz in *On War* dealt with wars in continental Europe from about 1740 to 1830, focusing on the transition from what he called ancien régime warfare conducted by kings and military aristocracies to the revolutionary warfare introduced by the French and Napoleon. As a long-serving Prussian soldier, from cadet to general, he had personal experience of wars in this period. The transition began with the *levée en masse* of 1792, when the revolutionaries raised a mass volunteer force to defend France against invading aristocratic forces. Their defense succeeded, and it introduced the notion of "the nation in arms," which led to Napoleon's enormous citizen armies, which he deployed in much looser formations, able to act on their own initiative, as ideological fervor supplanted much drilling. This forced other regimes to respond with their own quasi-citizen forces, while Spanish peasants reacted with guerilla nationalism. As Clausewitz noted, the tendency was toward whole nations and entire states mobilizing for war. Patriotic more than aristocratic honor now drove war forward.

Nineteenth-century technological development made weapons much more lethal. Organized combat centered on lines and columns of soldiers, overseen by junior officers leading them onward. Drilling was reinforced by a deployment trapping them on the battlefield. The famous squares deployed by Wellington at Waterloo consisted of a hollow square or rectangle, each side composed of two or more ranks of infantry. The colors and officers were positioned in the center, alongside reserves who could reinforce any weakening side of the square. The wounded could retreat inside the square without disorganizing the ranks. An enemy attack on the square then trapped the soldiers into fighting rather than running away. It was very effective against cavalry and infantry, but its density made it vulnerable to cannon fire.

Rulers no longer fought. The last English and Prussian kings to command on the battlefield did so in the mid-eighteenth century, but they stayed out of range of enemy guns, as did the two Napoleons, the only nineteenth-century heads of state in the field. Modern heads of state have been desk killers, ordering the deaths of far-off soldiers, including their own. Junior officers and NCOs have been in the thick of the action, setting an example. Wavering would be conspicuous and invite demotion and the charge of cowardice. Many have feared that label more than death.

In this period most soldiers were firing muskets. Bayonet charges brought some hand-to-hand fighting, though this inflicted far fewer deaths than guns. The biggest killers were artillery batteries, whose barrages could last for hours. Tolstoy, who had personally experienced battle, gives us a terrifying portrait in *War and Peace* of an artillery barrage at the battle of Borodino suffered by a Russian infantry regiment waiting for orders to move that never come. The soldiers are stationary in a field, under French cannon fire, and death comes from the air, intermittently, randomly, and suddenly. The regiment loses over one-third of its men, killed or wounded, without being able to fire a shot back. Enforced passivity under fire induces not only terror at the randomness of death but also a petrified sense of loss of personal control. The regimental commander, Prince Andrei, with whom we have identified through the novel so far, sets an example by re-maining standing. He sees a shell drop with little noise two paces away. "Lie down!" cries his adjutant, throwing himself flat on the ground. Andrei hesitates. "Can this be death?" he thinks. "I cannot, I do not wish to die. I love life—I love this grass, this earth, this air . . . " His thoughts are inter-rupted by the explosion, a whistle of splinters as from a breaking window frame, and a suffocating smell of powder. It flings him into the air and he lands in a pool of his own blood.[11]

This is fiction of course, although a brilliant, imaginative reconstruc-tion. Andrei's wounds prove fatal, and we lose our hero. But what was he or his men to do? They were too well trained or cowed by coercion to flee, but they were also trapped within the battlefield, unable to fight back. Where could they safely flee? They were in the middle of a very large army. Cossacks patrolled the rear, killing deserters. Bodies contin-ued to fall, fear persisted, but they did not run. They lay silently on the ground, pretending to ignore the carnage around them. What could be more terrifying than this unpredictable threat to life? Desertion usually occurred between battles, when men could slip off or lag behind unno-ticed. Marshal Thomas-Robert Bugeaud suggested that for every French Napoleonic army of 100,000 men, there were 25,000 skulkers trailing in the rear, dropping away.[12] He exaggerated for effect.

The American Civil War

The first war of the industrial age produced more casualties than all America's other wars combined. But 90 percent of Union soldiers and 80 percent of Confederates were literate, and many of them wrote let-ters, diaries, and memoirs. Since there was then no military censorship, we have a mountain of written evidence from the soldiers, mined by Gerald Linderman, Earl Hess, James McPherson, Chandra Manning, Michael Adams, and Jonathan Steplyk.[13] For the first time we get good information on the battle experience of soldiers, and this is why I have included this single war in a book about sequences of wars.

This was a society experiencing immigration and territorial expan-sion amid differences between two regional ways of life. The North and

Midwest hosted industrial capitalism, mining, and commercial farming, all using free wage labor. The South, whose population was also expanding westward, was dominated by agrarian plantations cultivating tobacco, cotton, sugar, indigo, and rice, using mainly slave labor. The cotton gin had made slavery very profitable, and a rich plantation-based slave-owning upper class dominated the South. Even though fewer than one-third of southern white households possessed slaves, almost all whites depended on the slaveholders for wages, produce, and credit. The legitimacy of slavery was barely disputed, which was not so in the North, where slaves were rare.

The two zones had complementary, not rival, economies. Labor was the only economic issue at stake: slavery versus free labor, but as expressed also in terms of ideological and political power. Southerners saw their civilization as different from that of the North, and South and North interpreted in opposed ways their two sacred scripts, the Bible and the Constitution. But war was precipitated by politics in the new western states. The question was not merely whether each would allow slavery. The issue also affected the balance of power in the House and especially in the Senate. If new states embraced free labor, a Senate majority might in the future interfere with, and even abolish, slavery in the South. Since there was more migration westward from the North than from the South, Southerners felt the pressure of growing abolitionism. As a minority in much of the South, many whites feared emancipation might bring race war and their own annihilation.

It was difficult to solve this clash of politicized ideologies. Most Southerners regarded expansion on northern terms as an existential threat; most Northerners would yield nothing in preserving the Union. Attempts at compromise faltered, and the alternative for the South was secession, which was easy enough to declare. In November 1860 the Republican candidate Abraham Lincoln, known to favor abolition, won the presidency without even being on the ballot in ten southern states. This degree of polarization between North and South, the North being politically dominant, seemed ominous for the South, and it was the touchstone for South Carolinian radicals to declare secession the next month. Yet neither Lincoln nor the Republican Party had proposed abolition, half the Republican Party opposed drastic action, and the Democrats, if they could resolve their factional disputes, still had enough power in the Senate to obstruct any such attempt. Nothing much would have happened quickly. Was secession necessary at this point? Was it not better for the South to wait for emancipation proposals to be put on the table so that it could claim to be the victim of northern aggression, instead of being the aggressor?

The United States was only in patches a militaristic society. Westward expansion had required a small army used mercilessly against Native Americans and Mexicans. Its units were stationed in small forts around the country. One was Fort Sumter, commanding Charleston Harbor in South Carolina. It was a tiny Union garrison in secessionist surrounds, and South Carolina's governor demanded its capitulation. Neither side would yield, yet neither wanted to fire the first shot and be blamed for a war that might follow. Eventually the governor gave the order to fire, and an artillery duel ensued. Its supplies running low, the garrison surrendered. The only loss of life had been accidental, but the damage had been done. Six more states seceded. Four others came later. Neither side doubted that war would come or that it would win it. It was expected to be short, especially by Southerners who dominated the army's officer corps and were convinced of their superior martial spirit. Overconfidence ruled. Large volunteer armies were quickly mobilized, composed overwhelmingly of men who had never fought before: lambs to the slaughter.

Why did the soldiers fight? Initially, they were volunteers, and Hess and McPherson, analyzing their letters and memoirs, say that most endorsed the declared casus belli of their side. McPherson finds two main motives for enlistment: a sense of adventure and a patriotic ideology. This included commitment to duty and honor as part of the rite of passage to manhood. He says that duty backed by conscience was more important among the Union troops, whereas honor backed by public reputation dominated among Confederates. Both sides believed they upheld the ideals of the American Revolution. Confederates fought for independence from tyrannical, centralized government; Unionists fought for the liberties of the Constitution. Few Confederates mentioned the defense of slavery (only one-third of Confederate soldiers' families had any slaves), but during the war more Union soldiers came to extend the concept of freedom to the abolition of slavery. This was a war between transcendent ideologies deriving from the key American contradiction, a country of white male democracy and mass slavery.

This contradiction had been visible for decades as each new territory and state was added to the Union. Rarely would soldiers be so well-informed but so ideologically polarized. Linderman, whose sample was mainly officers, observes: "Manliness, godliness, duty, honor, and knightliness constituted in varying degrees the values that Union and Confederate volunteers were determined to express through their actions on the battlefield. But each, as an impulse to war, remained subordinate to courage," which was "heroic action undertaken without fear," virtuous, favored by a just God, so that "the brave would live and the cowardly would die."[14] Religion conferred legitimacy on both sides. Some thought that a "good death" would be rewarded with eternal life. One man wrote that death was just "the destruction of a gross, material body. . . . A soldier's death is not a fate to be avoided, but rather almost to be gloried in." Another saw "something solemn, mysterious, sublime at the thought of entering into eternity."[15] Linderman agrees that deep conviction characterized the volunteers of 1861–62, but then the war brought disillusionment. Courage was then often described as "futile." Manning emphasizes slavery: "The problem, as soldiers on both sides saw it, was that . . . the opposing side threatened self-government. It threatened liberty and equality. It threatened the virtue necessary to sustain a republic. It threatened the proper balance between God, government, society, the family, and the individual. And no matter which side of the divide a Civil War soldier stood on, he knew that the heart of the threat, and the reason that the war came, was the other side's stance on slavery. From first to last, slavery defined the soldiers' war among both Union and Confederate troops." "Shared belief in the dangers of abolition powerfully united Confederate soldiers and motivated them to fight, even when they shared little else."[16]

Economic motives, she says, were subordinated to the need to maintain southern ideologies of race and sex that upheld the privileges of white men and their obligations toward their families. The racially leveling Republicans would destroy slavery, thereby threatening their families' safety. Even as their discontents with the Confederate government mounted and defeat loomed, they fought on, believing defeat might lead to a race war. Manning says Union soldiers championed the end of slavery a year ahead of the Emancipation Proclamation of January 1863, before most civilians or politicians. They had been stirred by welcoming slaves in Confederate areas and by black comrades fighting bravely. Almost 80 percent of them voted for Lincoln in the 1864 election. Being antislavery did not mean that white Union soldiers favored racial equality. But common soldiers believed in the casus belli proclaimed by their rulers. Thus, the soldiers, though inexperienced and poorly trained, had high morale and fought determinedly.

Yet two influential soldier-scholars have claimed that many or even most American soldiers have not been able to fire their weapons because of moral qualms. I discuss U.S. Brigadier General S. L. A. Marshall's widely cited study of American World War II infantry soldiers in the next chapter.[17] But U.S. Lieutenant Colonel Dave Grossman, much influenced by Marshall, focuses on this war.[18] He says most Civil War soldiers could not bring themselves to fire at the enemy out of moral qualms over killing. This is surprising given the ideological fervor we have just glimpsed. The first proof he offers is that war casualties were relatively few despite infantry firing at quite short range at each other. But this had been normal in musket battles for two centuries. Muskets were not very accurate, and few of these soldiers had been properly trained in firing them, and that typically resulted in firing too high. Grossman suggests this was because of repugnance at killing, but he produces no direct evidence of this. Instead, he relies on a curious piece of indirect evidence: a brief description of abandoned muskets found on the field of Gettysburg after the battle of July 1863, as described by a Major Laidley of the Union Ordnance Department. I quote Major Laidley in full:

> The examination of the muskets, picked up on the battlefield of Gettysburg, reveals a fact that few would be prepared to admit, and speaks in terms which should not pass unheeded, as to the inherent defects of the muzzle-loading system. Of the twenty-seven thousand five hundred and seventy-four muskets collected after the battle, it was found that twenty-four thousand were loaded: twelve thousand contained each two loads, and six thousand (over twenty per cent) were charged with from *three* to *ten loads* each. One musket had in it *twenty-three loads*, each charge being put down in regular order. Oftentimes the cartridge was loaded without being first broken, and in many instances it was inserted, the ball down first. What an exhibit of useless guns does this present!—useless for that day's work, and from causes peculiar to the system of loading.[19]

Grossman says the soldiers' overloaded muskets reveal nonfiring because they found killing repugnant: man is not a natural killer, he says. Malešević agrees: "Killing is, in fact, terribly difficult, messy, guilt-ridden, and for most people, an abhorrent activity," although he hedges his bets, observing that some soldiers become "paralyzed by fear" alongside a "conscious inability to kill other human beings."[20] But Laidley does not mention repugnance or moral qualms. He says nonfiring demonstrates the failings of muzzle-loading muskets compounded by drilling deficiencies of soldiers—"causes peculiar to the system of loading," says Laidley. The main cause of nonfiring was soldiers' failure to properly load the trio of powder, bullet, and wadding. Gordon Rottman adds percussion cap problems.[21] The drill manual for the smoothbore musket listed seventeen distinct physical movements for each round fired, quite complicated for nonprofessional soldiers. Given the noise, the dense smoke coming from the black powder used, and the chaos of the battle, as well as soldiers' tension and fear, these men might have omitted any step. The fear and tension of battle bring rushes of adrenaline and cortisol, the stress hormone. The heart rate accelerates. All this brings distortion of vision and shaking of the hands. Soldiers fire wildly and find it difficult to reload. Emotions have physiological consequences. If a soldier botched his first or second shot, he might discard the weapon and pick up another from a fallen comrade. If he did not notice, he might load a third. If and when he did notice, he might still be deterred from cleaning the charges out of the barrel, for this procedure required a corkscrew-shaped bullet extractor attached to his ramrod. This operation was time-consuming, and the soldier in battle felt disarmed and helpless while thus engaged. Adams says that "at least 18,000 men, in a highly distracted mental state, loaded and over-loaded their weapons, oblivious of never having fired them."[22] Probably some were pretending to fire, as Grossman suggests, but there is no evidence the cause was moral qualms. Anyway, why would they not fire deliberately high rather than not fire at all, which would catch the attention of their comrades?

Paddy Griffith thinks the muskets had been discarded as faulty, often because of bad handling.[23] They amounted to 9 percent of all muskets used at Gettysburg, normal for misfiring muskets in Civil War battles. The soldiers had never been trained in live firing, to economize on ammunition and to avoid alarming nearby regiments by creating the apparent sounds of battle. When battle started, smoke enveloped the men, who could not clearly see the enemy.[24] Soldiers recounted in letters and diaries shooting blindly in the general direction of the enemy, hence the low casualty rate and the high ratio of shots fired to casualties. Since they could not see if their shots hit anyone, they could not correct their aim. High ratios of shots to casualties had also characterized the Napoleonic Wars.[25] Later, deadlier weapons paradoxically increased the ratio of shots to kills.

The soldiers were told to fire only when well under a hundred meters from the enemy. Some officers preferred thirty meters. On average soldiers began firing at 116 meters, as they came under artillery fire.[26] If they obeyed orders, many would die without having fired. It is intolerable to soldiers to be inactive when under fire. They fire in order to relieve this and so the enemy does, too. Griffith says that as firing drills broke down, lines became ragged, and soldiers were out of control, blazing away into the fog, usually too high, until their ammunition was exhausted.[27] Experienced forces, like Wellington's British squares at Waterloo, might wait for the order to fire, but some rawer Belgian and German regiments had not, nor did most Civil War soldiers. The commanders had never marshaled large armies and so did it badly. They ignored the "mixed order" possibilities of column and line attack of the Napoleonic Wars in favor of simpler long lines. This made shock action impossible and lateral coordination difficult, as officers struggled to keep their sprawling battle lines from disintegrating if they attempted maneuvers. They believed attack was superior to defense, but the reverse proved true. These two errors brought carnage.[28] Neither side was well-drilled or well-coordinated, but Union forces were twice as numerous and better supplied—so they won.

In 1868 Colonel Ardant du Picq distributed a questionnaire to French officers, asking about the conduct of their soldiers in recent battles. He was killed in the Franco-Prussian War, before he could write a report of his survey. A book collecting his manuscripts was published posthumously in 1880 and is now a classic of military theory. The appendix presenting his questionnaire survey is widely cited by scholars but contains only seven cases. Presumably other responses have been lost. Two officers complained of wild overfiring in the air, and two complained of skulkers in the rear, but none complained of nonfiring.[29] All soldiers experienced fear, said Ardant du Picq. The army that mastered it longer would win, while the one for whom normal fear turned into terror would lose. As a regiment advanced and came under fire, the choices, he said, were not dictated by instrumental reason. Instead, there were two highly adrenalized reactions, "charge" or "flee." One of the seven officers who responded to his survey describes a single *chasseur* rescuing his regiment by shouting, "Charge," and rushing madly forward. His charge was contagious to his comrades. He also comments: "Modern weapons have a terrible effect and are almost unbearable by the nervous system. Who can say that he has not been frightened in battle? Discipline in battle becomes the more necessary as the ranks become more open, and the material cohesion of the ranks not giving confidence, it must spring from a knowledge of comrades, and a trust in officers, who must always be present and seen. What man to-day advances with the confidence that rigid discipline and pride in himself gave the Roman soldier?"[30] He says overfiring had occurred ever since muskets and rifles had first appeared; it was produced by the soldier's anxiety to relieve his fear by firing when under artillery fire or before the enemy infantry fired at him. He cites Cromwell's famous order—"Put your trust in God and aim at their shoe laces!"—to avoid firing too high.[31]

So at Gettysburg incompetence and fear were more important in producing mischarged muskets than moral qualms. Almost all soldiers fought roughly as they were ordered to. The fighting was often severe, there were no mass flights or desertions during the battle, and the final retreat of the Confederate Army was orderly. Even when final Confederate defeat loomed in the war, there was little surrendering until Lee signed the articles of surrender.

The Union and Confederate armies recruited 3 million soldiers, as well as many black slave laborers for Confederate forces. Between 620,000 and 750,000 died, more Southerners than Northerners. In the three days at Gettysburg, Robert E. Lee lost 28,000 men, 40 percent of his force, whereas Union forces lost 23,000, or 25 percent. The disproportion was the result of Confederates' attacking entrenched Union positions on the crest of low hills. Casualties were as high among the upper ranks, closely accompanying their troops. Lee lost one-third of his generals in the battle. The ratio of shots fired to casualties was about 180:1 in the Union Army. Confederate figures were probably just as high. Attrition rates in battle as well as desertions in camp and on the march forced the addition of raw, untrained troops, and in early 1863 the militaries introduced conscripts and "bounty jumpers" (paid substitutes for conscripted men), who were less ideologically committed. The soldiers were recruited by the individual states. The monuments encircling the battlefield of Gettysburg all commemorate the exploits of state regiments, Union or Confederate, and generals had to tolerate autonomous action from them. Ardant du Picq commented patronizingly on these amateurs: "The Americans have shown us what happens in modern battle to large armies without cohesion. With them the lack of discipline and organization has had the inevitable result. Battle has been between hidden skirmishers, at long distance, and has lasted for days, until some faulty movement, perhaps a moral exhaustion, has caused one or the other of the opposing forces to give way."[32]

Griffith shares his low view.[33] Hastily recruited volunteers and conscripts lacked military experience. The stereotype was that Confederate recruits were farm boys and Union recruits bank clerks. Only a few from the western frontier were likely to have fired a gun. The recruits were drilled for a month and then thrown into battle.

How did they respond? McPherson discusses Marshall and moral qualms.[34] The Sixth Commandment, handed down by God to Moses, bothered many, he says. Hess concurs and says soldiers tried to avoid hand-to-hand encounters and aimed fire at groups, not individuals.[35] Neither suggests that this translated into nonfiring, which was not mentioned in any letters or diaries. McPherson says overfiring was a much bigger problem. It was common for soldiers to say they found killing obnoxious the first time. They might hesitate a moment, but then they shot. There was less of a problem the second time, and none the third time. In face-to-face encounters there might be a momentary pause, but then they fired. At very close quarters they stabbed fast with their bayonets, since to pause might be fatal. Soldiers fired because they found reasons to ignore the commandment, most commonly self-defense. This drove out feelings of immorality. One Confederate said that when he saw the pale face of the Union soldier he had just killed, "I felt strange but cannot say that I am sorry any. When I know he would have killed me if he could." Another commented that despite the scriptures, "My nerve seemed to be as steady as if I was shooting at a beast."

A few confessed enjoying it: "I never thought I would like to shoot at a man," wrote one Union soldier, "but I do like to shoot a secesh" (secessionist). A Confederate artilleryman wrote, "I feel a perfect delight when I see my shell crash among them." A new recruit wrote, "I am heart & soul in the war & its success," and so would be "duty bound" to kill if "such a Cup is however presented to me." McPherson says both sides believed God wanted them to kill a godless enemy. A Union soldier wrote that in one battle he must have fired two hundred rounds: "I was up and firing almost incessantly until the enemy was repulsed. . . . Thank God, that in his strength we drove back the enemy. . . . To God our blessed Father in Heaven be all the glory." Sharpshooters who aimed at inactive soldiers, however, were disliked in both armies.[36]

Naturally, men writing diaries and memoirs rarely admit to skulking. One man admitted to having lain low in a wood through a battle, while a few refused promotion into more dangerous posts. Far more complained of other cowards. One man wrote that on battle day "the usual number of cowards got sick and asked to be excused." Another names nine cowards in his regiment. A Union private watched his colonel rubbing gunpowder on his face to appear combat blackened: "Instantly he was transformed from a trembling coward who lurked behind a tree into an exhausted brave taking a well-earned repose." No one suggested that skulkers might have moral objections to the war—they acted from fear.[37] But the term *skulking* was used broadly. Some described rear soldiers thus, partly from envy, as have frontline soldiers in most wars. This would not be fair to the staff of quartermasters, hospitals, prisons, recruitment offices, or those supporting the General Staff and all the other necessary functions in the rear. These men may have breathed a sigh of relief when allocated to the rear, but their courage or cowardice was not tested. Volunteers also despised conscripts, especially bounty jumpers, and probably exaggerated their cowardice. Skulkers disappeared just before battle, lagged behind, lay low, persistently helped fallen comrades on the ground, faked sickness, and so on. They may have totaled 10 percent of the army, but that is just a guess.

The sense of adventure, a major reason for enlisting, rarely survived the first shock of battle, which was more frightening than they had imagined. Hess gives vivid soldier accounts of random death; bodies torn apart by shells; blood, brains, and other body parts spattered over them; streams and pools of blood; the horrors of the hospital; the burying of mutilated bodies; the Minié ball's grating sound when it hit bone, and the heavy thud when it hit flesh. How did they manage to keep on fighting? Hess stresses that a large majority of Union soldiers were working-class men (poor farmers, laborers, and skilled workers) who came to view war as just another job to be done. Often during battle, a soldier became so involved with the tools and tasks of his trade—loading a musket, carrying out maneuvers—that he had no time to think about the horrors. Moreover, after surviving his first battle, the soldier believed that his chances of survival were good. And "it was a source of wonderment to many men that so much lead could be expended to kill so comparatively few soldiers."[38]

McPherson adds more elevated reasons. Their sense of the cause, honor, and duty endured, he says, enabling killing with little sense of immorality, and motivated half of them to reenlist once their three-year term was up. Linderman is more skeptical about reenlistment, seeing the offer of thirty days' leave back home during the campaigning season as an important sweetener—thirty days of heaven before three years of hell.[39] Yet soldiers' ideological commitment waned, becoming weary cynicism and disillusion. Many felt they had been duped. Hess divides fifty-eight Union soldiers' postwar memoirs into four fairly equal groups. The first stressed ideology and remained committed to preserving the Union. The second he calls "lost soldiers," who "could find no self-assurances of any kind about the war," disillusioned and embittered. The third group consisted of "pragmatists," who rejected the cause but viewed the war as a personal process of self-discovery, and the fourth group were "silent witnesses," who "recalled comradeship, camp life, and other common experiences, but repressed memories of battle."[40] This is a very mixed picture.

New recruits were enthusiastic but low in skills. The survivors improved to peak efficiency in their third or fourth battle. Then enthusiasm and energy began to fade. Such cycles were typical in modern wars. A woman watching new Union recruits marching to war said they displayed "boyish enthusiasm," in contrast to the more experienced, who marched "in a grim silence that was most oppressive."[41] Experienced soldiers knew the dangers, kept their heads down, and did the minimum.[42] Hess says that the relentless pressure of war ensured that almost all would occasionally shirk combat duties without being labeled a coward.[43] Everyone needed a rest. One man said 10 percent of Union soldiers were always brave, matched by 10 percent "arrant cowards," while 80 percent lay between, functioning "within the safe margins of acceptability." Since morale was similar on both sides, it did not much affect the outcome of the war. But the constant jumping from calm to chaos brought rapid mood changes. Hess notes that many soldiers distinguished between moral courage, the conscious desire to do one's duty and preserve one's honor despite the dangers, and physical courage, usually the product of adrenaline and the emotional and physiological stimulation of combat.[44] Battle remained gut-wrenching and gut-spilling. Adams presents a horrific litany of actual deaths:

> Corporal James Quick stumble[s] back as a bullet enters behind his left jaw and exits through the nose. He is just twenty-two. Next to him, Lieutenant William Taylor has been hit in the neck by a bullet that missed the arteries but severed his windpipe. He clasps his hands to his neck, trying to stanch the flow of blood and air hissing through the wound. Private Keils runs past, "breathing at his throat and the blood spattering" from a neck

wound. . . . We avoid Private George Walker because his right arm is off, severing the artery, and blood "on certain movements of the arm, gushed out higher than his head." Blood spurts, too, from a Federal officer shot behind the bridge of the nose; he wanders about, continuing to blink even though both eyes are gone, "opening and closing the sightless sockets, the blood leaping out in spouts.[45]

These were not what defenders of wars call "good deaths," but they were probably typical of battles through the ages. McPherson quotes a Virginia private: "I have seen enough of the glory of war. . . . I am sick of seeing dead men and men's limbs torn from their bodies." A sergeant from Minnesota wrote: "I don't know any individual soldier who is at all anxious to be led, or driven, for that matter to another battle." They were volunteers, but their actions were no longer voluntary.

McPherson says that in the heat and fear of battle, many soldiers' bodies pumped out a "super-adrenalized fury" that provided a "combat narcosis" that "acts almost like a hallucinogenic drug," generating an excitement so strong that it overwhelmed thought of morality, fear, or cowardice. We know now that a rush from the adrenal glands generates sudden energy and strength, a racing pulse or pounding heart, and increased respiration. This may induce soldiers to flight, which in the entrapment of battle was difficult, or to fury, which led men to charge forward yelling. The diarists say this meant "behaving like wild men." "Our men became insane, howled and rushed forward." An Indiana sergeant wrote to his fiancée, "A man can & will become so infuriated by the din & dangers of a bloody fight, that if he ever did have a tender heart, it will [be] turned to stone & his evry desire [be] for blood." The "rebel yell" became feared by Union soldiers. Adrenaline came only in short bursts. But for technical jobs such as artillery teams, the mind was occupied with the sequence of loading, firing, repositioning, reloading, and refiring, a process that relegated fear to the back burners. "My mind was wholly absorbed," one wrote.[46]

Fury was fueled by the desire to avenge the deaths of comrades, and so atrocities resulted. A Union soldier wrote: "We captured about a hundred prisoners and killed about thirty of them. It was fun for us to see them Skip out." Confederates shot black Union soldiers they captured, in addition to their white officers. Rapes were common. Union generals advancing in Confederate territory pursued scorched-earth tactics. Sherman declared: "To secure the safety of the navigation of the Mississippi I would slay millions. On that point I am not only insane, but mad."[47] War is "the most dangerous of all excitements" said Lee, and he remarked, "It is well that war is so terrible—otherwise we would grow too fond of it." But once combat or charging forward ended, the men collapsed in exhaustion, and fear returned.

An incident during the Civil War, though not a part of it, however, puts Civil War atrocities in perspective. On November 29, 1864, hundreds of Arapaho and Cheyenne Native Americans were massacred at Sand Creek, Colorado, by Union cavalry led by a Colonel John Chivington, who declared: "Damn any man who sympathizes with Indians! . . . I have come to kill Indians, and believe it is right and honorable to use any means under God's heaven to kill Indians. . . . Kill and scalp all, big and little; nits make lice." The soldiers' attack degenerated into frenzy. They took scalps and other grisly trophies from the dead bodies, adorning themselves with scalps, human fetuses, and male and female genitalia. Two-thirds of the dead were women and children. Civil War battles never sank so low. Yet two cavalry officers at Sand Creek were horrified. Captain Silas Soule wrote to his mother: "I was present at a Massacre of three hundred Indians mostly women and children. . . . It was a horrable scene and I would not let my Company fire." Lieutenant Joseph Cramer also ordered his men not to shoot. In the Civil War soldiers could not treat white men this cruelly.[48]

After Gettysburg more permanent combat exhaustion set in. Soldiers were weakened, says McPherson, from "the marching, loss of sleep, poor food or no food, bad water, lack of shelter, and exposure to extremes of heat, and cold, dust and mud, and the torments of insects." Contaminated water presented them with the dilemma of choosing death through thirst or disease. "Malnutrition and diarrhea gravely impaired the efficiency of armies, causing depression, lethargy, night blindness, muscular debility, neuralgia, and susceptibility to major diseases. Finally, emaciated men could not march or fight and died."[49] A Virginia captain confessed to his wife: "This has broken me down completely. . . . [I am] in a state of exhaustion. . . . I never saw the Brigade so completely broken down and unfitted for service." Occasionally a unit would not fight. A Massachusetts captain reported, "We, our brigade, have made fourteen charges upon our enemy's breastworks, although at last no amount of urging, no heroic examples, no threats, or anything else, could get the line to *stir one peg*."[50] This was neither reluctance to kill nor cowardice, since the soldiers knew that further charges would be pointless, and they were exhausted. Ideology was now irrelevant—they would have gladly gone home. Freer peoples, like Native Americans, would have gone home if their battles were only half as threatening as this.

Some soldiers also had political discontents. They objected to conscription, seeing this as a "rich man's war and poor man's fight," and Confederates took a dim view of Lee's decision to take the war north into Union territory. Most Confederate soldiers thought they had signed up to defend their own state. Mark Weitz says soldiers on both sides saw enlistment as contractual.[51] If they perceived the government as not living up to its side of the contract, they deemed their departure justified. Unswerving ideological commitment was over. The Gettysburg defeat brought a crisis for the Confederacy, which had to grant amnesty to deserters to replenish the army's depleted ranks. Short-term leaves were also authorized by regimental officers if they deemed it necessary to prevent longer-term departure.

McPherson rejects the argument that nineteenth-century Americans were more violent or accepted death more easily than Americans today. He also downplays training, discipline, and leadership in motivating soldiers to fight, declaring, "Civil War volunteer regiments were notoriously deficient in the first, weak in the second, and initially shaky in the third." "American white males were the most individualistic, democratic people on the face of the earth in 1861. They did not take kindly to authority, discipline, obedience."[52] I view such American cultural tropes skeptically, and the army responded by intensifying coercion. Cowards were occasionally shot, but more often they were court-martialed and shamed. A Union private wrote, "There are few cowards here and those that are, are drummed Before the Regt on dress Parade." A Confederate general threatened "to blow the brains out of the first man who left ranks." A Confederate private wrote that his brigade had to watch a captured deserter, "a wretched creature," getting thirty-nine lashes on his bare back, a punishment that they knew was normally reserved for slaves.[53]

Yet the most common coercion came from comrades. As the first battle approached, so did fear, but it included fear of failing to be worthy of manhood, a coward in full view of one's comrades. It was followed by a sense of relief and even joy when a soldier felt he had surmounted his fears and shot boldly at the enemy. Fear of battle was undercut by fear of being labeled a coward by one's comrades and officers. Hess says Union soldiers thought of the "line ... all in touch, elbow to elbow." "Men fight in masses," a Union officer explained. "To be brave they must be inspired by the feeling of fellowship. Shoulder must touch shoulder." Hess concludes, "If it were possible to pinpoint one factor as most important in enabling the soldier to endure battle, it would be the security of comradeship."[54] McPherson quotes a Union colonel writing of Shiloh: "Those who had stood shoulder to shoulder during the two terrible days of that bloody battle were hooped with steel, with bands stronger than steel."[55] Bonded by shared danger, they were "a band of brothers" whose mutual dependence enabled them to maintain self-respect and function as a fighting unit. If one man became petrified with fear, he endangered the survival of all and drew contempt and ostracism, and he lost self-respect as a man.

Peer-group coercion was more effective than coercion by officers, though soldiers stressed that officers who led from the front challenged their men forward. But the reputation of a coward would follow the soldier and his family even in peacetime, given the recruitment of units from single localities. "Death before dishonor" was a constant refrain in letters. An Ohio soldier wrote that he shook like a leaf before his first engagement, but he resolved to "stand up to my duties like a man, let the consequences be as they might. I had rather die like a brave man, than have a coward's ignominy cling around my name." A New York veteran of two years' fighting responded to his sister: "You ask me if the thought of death does not alarm me. I will say I do not wish to die ... but have too much honor to hold back while others are going forward. I myself am as big a coward as any could be, but give me the ball [bullet] before the coward when all my friends and companions are going forward." These were not the forces of intimate primary groups of the dispersed battlefields of the twentieth century but pressures from larger groups in one of the last wars to be fought in long, dense lines.[56]

Gettysburg was a large battlefield of over 11,000 acres. The Confederate lines of attack stretched eight kilometers in a great arc over fields, woods, low hills, and bluffs. A regiment fought in two or three lines, behind which were reserves. Flight from battle was risky, since military police in the rear shot deserters, while reserve units stiffening a disintegrating line gathered up stragglers and stemmed routs. But in camp and on the march, surveillance was difficult and home not far away. By late January 1863 there had been 185,000 desertions from the Union army— who had not so much run as drifted away.[57] There was "straggling" on the march, "French leave" (returning home without permission for a few days), and long-term desertion. Many Confederate soldiers lacked adequate shoes, clothing, and food and could not keep up with the punishing schedule of marching that Lee's strategy demanded. Others responded to heartrending appeals from their families to return home. Lee estimated that one-third of his force was absent at the Battle of Antietam. Official estimates of desertion were 10 to 15 percent among the Confederates and 9 to 12 percent among Union soldiers, but these figures are considered too low. Very few deserters had moral qualms, far more were driven by fear and discontent with the rigors of army life. Given opportunity, many deserted. Given more opportunity, many more would have.

Conclusion

Chaos and fear, not heroism or moral qualms, pervaded Civil War armies. Ideologically, the Sixth Commandment was nullified by the belief that this was a just, even a divinely sanctioned war. Ideological commitment to a transcendent cause had been the most important reason for volunteering, and it endured as a motive, though it weakened into a sense of duty focused on dogged determination to get the job done. Conscripts were less strongly committed. Almost all were disillusioned as the war dragged on. That they fought on was due to coercion: army discipline and punishment, moral coercion by one's close comrades, and the physical entrapment of the battlefield. A predilection for violence encouraged a few, but more were boosted by rushes of anger-fueled adrenaline. The combination produced much bravery, pushing fear to the back burners. Soldiers could kill relatively easily when being fired at, when ordered to do so by routinized, coercive authority, when under moral pressure from comrades, or when committed to the cause. Their willingness to kill, at considerable risk, was produced not by human nature but by social pressures, social authority, and social and political ideologies. Emotional exhaustion was the universal aftereffect among survivors. Yet most soldiers on both sides were courageous in their grim determination to keep on fighting and get the job done.

Was the war worth almost three-quarters of a million dead, more wounded, and 3 million surviving soldiers experiencing intermittent terror—without including abused civilians or the veterans who later suffered breakdowns? The war formally abolished slavery, and the consequent Thirteenth to Fifteenth Constitutional Amendments made clearer the meaning of freedom, citizenship, and equality. But a better solution would have been two

American countries. Secession would have spared almost a million lives, it would have led to mass flight northward by slaves, and it would have spared Washington from the enduring racist input of southern politicians. Even better would have been decades-long political struggle in the House and Senate over cumulative emancipation proposals. Not even a step on the road to the liberty of African Americans was worth such a price in death, given the southern reaction that was soon to undermine emancipation. Slavery would have collapsed anyway near the end of the century, as soil erosion and boll-weevil infestation destroyed the cotton industry and the profitability of slavery. We have the advantage of hindsight, of course, but that enables us to say that this was a tragedy, unhappily hard to avoid but made inevitable by the overconfidence in war among rulers that we repeatedly find in the history of war.

CHAPTER TWELVE

Fear and Loathing on the Battlefield II
The World Wars

World War I

Infantry soldiers on the Western Front were almost all literate, and many wrote diaries, letters, autobiographies, and novels. Unfortunately, their letters were censored by army authorities, although we can add psychologists' reports on morale. In 1914 professional armies were enlarged by reservists and lightly trained volunteers, a product of initial enthusiasm for the war. But from 1915 or 1916, ever-larger numbers were supplied by conscription. An astonishing 90 percent of young French men and 53 percent of young British men were conscripted.[1] Why did the volunteers sign up? Why did the conscripts not resist? There were four main reasons.

1. Young men had imbibed a culture depicting war as an honorable and heroic duty of masculinity.[2] In the books and comics read by schoolboys, the heroes in combat with whom they identified always survived, to be garlanded with glory. Beautiful women swooned over them. There was a desire for adventure and escape from the drudgery of mundane life. War was not envisaged as bringing death. It did not do so to the heroes in the adventure stories.

2. This was portrayed as a legitimate war of self-defense by the warring governments, local notables, and mass media, and few soldiers had alternative sources of information. The intensification of national "cages" that I charted in volume 2 of *The Sources of Social Power* meant that soldiers, whatever their regional identities, had a "banal" sense of identity as British, German, or French, believing that they shared distinct national ways of life. The authorities had to convert this into a patriotism prepared to defend what they defined as the interests of the nation. This then escalated to the defense of civilization against barbarism, helped by exaggerated stories of enemy atrocities and later by the desire to avenge slaughtered comrades. Such escalation was generally achieved despite the reality that British people had little objective interest in defending the global British Empire, while Germans had little objective interest in Germany's "place in the sun." Still less did British or French colonial troops have an objective interest in fighting for their imperial masters (save for the pay). It was different for Russians and French and others whose homelands were invaded.

3. Volunteers signed on in local units, and their commitment was to people they knew and to local notables to whom they deferred. They were honored and sometimes financed by their local community, while its women pressured them to "Be a Man" and sign up. It was very easy to do and it brought praise—it satisfied desire for the social and sexual status of a warrior. Indeed, many women in Britain collaborated in this by handing out white feathers, a symbol of cowardice, to men who had not signed up.

4. Steady, guaranteed pay was a desired factor at first, because of high unemployment, and it continued to be among the poor.

Hew Strachan suggests four ways in which soldiers were made to continue fighting: through pressure from soldiers' primary groups, from ideological commitment and duty to a cause, from drilling and training, and from punishment for those who deviated.[3] I add three more mundane factors: the battlefield as a trap, task absorption, and a claim of self-defense. All seven had influence, applying to different extents in different contexts.

The soldiers were not initially afraid, for they expected to win quickly, bolstered by their belief in the justice of the cause. Since they were right, they "should" win, in the normal double sense of both moral right and probability. But they had not been prepared for battle, which was not remotely an adventure story. Death came raining down, but not after heroic combat. Seventy percent of deaths came from artillery fired from a distance, killing randomly, not aimed at anyone in particular. It was almost insupportable to cower, unable to influence whether one lived or died. A Bavarian lieutenant described battle as a witches' Sabbath, blown by "a hurricane of fire," "like a crushing machine, mechanical, without feelings, snuffing out the last resistance, with a thousand hammers. It is totally inappropriate to play such a game with fellow men. We are all human beings made in the image of the Lord God. But what account does the Devil take of mankind, or God, when he feels himself to be Lord of the Elements; when chaos celebrates his omnipotence."[4] This soldier shared a sense of common humanity with the enemy, but cosmic forces beyond his power or understanding, conveyed here through Christian metaphors, obliterated this.

Most rulers believed the war would be short, the nineteenth-century norm in Europe. The U.S. Civil War had been long and devastating, but they put that down to the incompetence of the Americans. Field Marshal Helmuth von Moltke the Elder had engineered the Prussian victory over France in 1870. He spat out contemptuously and foolishly of the U.S. Civil War that it was "armed mobs chasing each other round the country, from which nothing can be learned."[5] In the recent Russo-Japanese War, the combination of barbed wire and machine guns had produced high casualties, but Japanese mass offensives had proved successful. European General Staffs drew the lesson that offense would triumph over defense. Yet marked technological improvement in weaponry during the Second Industrial Revolution meant artillery batteries had become massive, rifles were more lethal, and the machine gun could spray death around the battle front. All could be mass-produced in existing factories.

When the war began, soldiers no longer stood up to fight. They dug trenches protected by barbed wire to slow down attackers. Peering up over the edge, they fired from a leaning, mostly concealed position. In this war blazing away in the general direction of the enemy was done from holes in the ground. Offense came with the order "Charge!" The infantry ran bent over or crawled across no-man's-land, exposing themselves to fire, especially from machine guns. They were aided by surging adrenaline, whipped up by collective yelling, alcohol, the example of junior officers, and a sergeant at the rear posted to shoot laggards. It was suicidal. The accounts of British and German soldiers during the battle of the Somme convey a sense of hell on earth as the bodies of friend and foe were torn apart around them. Soldiers said that when they charged, they were "out of their minds," reverting to the "primitive man lurking inside all of us."[6] Benjamin Ziemann says their violence was "overstepping boundaries, a process in which protagonists can lose control of themselves, leaving rational consideration behind. . . . Soldiers in combat can become enraged, act out their anger and enter into a state of frenzy."[7] The killing of prisoners was normal.

As defense proved superior on a static Western Front, the capture of a single field cost many lives. Eastern Fronts differed, since the Russians overmatched the Austrians and the Germans overmatched the Russians. Here routs caused "forward panics" involving mass slaughter or surrender. But both fronts produced awful casualties. A French soldier wrote to his parents: "It is shameful, awful; it's impossible to convey the image of such a carnage. We will never be able to escape from such a hell. The dead cover the ground. Boches and French are piled on top of each other, in the mud. . . . We attacked twice, gained a little ground—which was completely soaked with blood. . . . But one must not despair, one can be wounded. As for death, if it comes, it will be a deliverance."[8] Note the preferred ending, to be wounded or even killed and so removed from the battlefield.

Mass slaughter consists of many single deaths. Here is a man dying from a gas attack, depicted by the British war poet Wilfred Owen:

> If in some smothering dreams you too could pace
> Behind the wagon that we flung him in,
> And watch the white eyes writhing in his face,
> His hanging face, like a devil's sick of sin;
> If you could hear, at every jolt, the blood
> Come gargling from the froth-corrupted lungs,
> Obscene as cancer, bitter as the cud
> Of vile, incurable sores on innocent tongues,—
> My friend, you would not tell with such high zest
> To children ardent for some desperate glory,
> The old Lie: *Dulce et decorum est*
> *Pro patria mori*. [It is sweet and fitting to die for one's country]

This poem was published posthumously. Lieutenant Owen was killed just after being awarded the Military Cross for bravery, one week before the Armistice, at the age of twenty-five.

The chances of being killed were about one in five for French soldiers, one in seven for the British. The chances of being killed, wounded, missing, or made POWs were much higher: 76 percent of men mobilized in Russia, 73 percent for France, 65 percent for Germany, 36 percent for Britain and its empire, only 8 percent for the United States (in its seventeen months of fighting). Why did the soldiers accept such odds? As we saw in the last chapter, morale does not turn on whether soldiers experience fear. They all do. Fear, says Holmes, "is the common bond between fighting men. The overwhelming majority of soldiers' experience fear during or before battle."[9] Especially feared were wounds to the abdomen, eyes, brain, and genitals, which soldiers believed made them unfit for life. Fear has physiological consequences, adrenaline and cortisol rushes, accelerating heartbeat, and even involuntary pissing or shitting in one's pants, common just before battle. Soldiers were caught short, ashamed of shitting in the trench in front of their comrades, climbing out, lowering their pants, and having their heads blown off.[10]

In battle itself, continuous mind-filling action tended to banish fear to the back burners but afterwards was replaced by loathing for the horrors of mutilated, decomposing, stinking corpses, body parts hanging from bushes, and dying cries for "Mum, Mum," "*Maman, Maman*" or "*Mutter, Mutter.*" Such repeated sights, smells, and sounds deadened sensibilities. As a French corporal put it, "Our repugnance became dulled, forced to live in the filth, we became worse than the beasts."[11] Most were emotionally damaged. As Malešević says:

> Although wars are often conceptualised in instrumentalist and rationalist terms, the actual lived experience of the combat zone is principally defined by variety of emotional reactions. All soldiers experience intense emotional reactions in the combat zone. Although fear is by far the most common emotion, the combatants tend to display a wide range of complex and changing emotional responses including both negative emotions such as anxiety, anger, rage, panic, horror, shame, guilt, and sadness as well as some positive emotions including happiness, joy, pride, elation, and exhilaration. Living in an exceptional situation of life and death, the individual actions and responses of soldiers are profoundly shaped by emotions.[12]

Alcohol and tobacco helped deaden the sensibilities, but psychiatric medicine and diagnosis were rudimentary. The British recognized "shell-shock," the French *commotion* (concussion) or *obusite* ("shellitis"), but most higher officers assumed these were covers for shirking. There were ways of not coping—self-wounding to get a discharge or claiming trench foot, which restricted mobility. Soldiers felt envious of those whose minor wounds sent them home. Psychiatric hospital admissions grew as physical casualties increased.[13] After prolonged exposure to battle, the major goal was survival: focusing on self-protection and fighting while trying not to expose oneself to unnecessary danger.

Debate about why they kept on fighting has been liveliest in France. Stéphane Audoin-Rouzeau and Annette Becker stress soldiers' consent—early ideological enthusiasm for war and the complicity of religion in war fever, boosted by soldiers' increasing religiosity in the face of death. In France the war was a "crusade" maintained by a "culture of war" that involved "the expectation of a rapid victory," "the heroism of the soldiers," and the "demonized perception of atrocities committed by the enemy."[14] Letters home, they say, show that most French soldiers believed they fought in a just, patriotic cause, that they were sacrificing in defense of the homeland against a foreign invader.[15] Their findings imply a nationalist religiosity, not religion in itself. After all, half the Germans trying to kill them were also Catholics. But their conclusion is that soldiers freely gave consent to the war, for self-defense is the strongest justification, intensified into a defense of civilization against barbarism. This claim was ideologically reciprocated by Germans, who alleged atrocities by "savage" African and Asian troops deployed by the French and British.

Yet other historians doubt that such transcendent ideology figured in most ordinary soldiers' experiences once they were locked in the trenches. Leonard Smith and his colleagues emphasize a less ideological, more grounded sense of patriotism among French infantrymen who felt they had to expel the Boches (Germans) from France.[16] Being mostly peasants (as all armies except the British were), they knew this required digging trenches every meter of the way. For them defense of the soil of France was not an abstract concept. This view also emphasizes consent, but ideology had become institutionalized in everyday activities.

Frédéric Rousseau has a different view, based on letters, memoirs, and fictional works written by more than sixty soldiers.[17] He accepts that the initial rally 'round the flag response brought enthusiastic enlistment amid patriotic rhetoric. But once soldiers experienced the gruesome realities of trench warfare, patriotism vanished: "The so-called *consent* of the soldiers was expressed within a space of extreme dependence, constant surveillance, and heightened coercion." Several of his soldiers flatly said, "There is no patriotism in the trenches," and Rousseau asks rhetorically, "What is a soldier if not a man oppressed, bullied, dehumanized, terrorized and threatened with death by his own army[?]"[18] He says combatants obeyed more from constraint than consent. As I have emphasized, that is the general nature of military power. Jules Maurin also downplays consent, since by 1916, he says, the infantry, the *poilus* (literally, "hairy ones"), had forgotten why they were fighting. They fought because they were told to by the disciplining hierarchies to which they had been accustomed in their communities. The key was unanimity among the three main authority figures in French villages, priest, mayor, and schoolteacher, from political right to left.[19] François Cochet and André Loez bridge consent and constraint.[20] Coercion did not dominate the *poilus*'s everyday experience, they say. Rather, the military set boundaries, and the culture and patriotism of the soldier became irrelevant under the perpetual pressures of the war.[21] Action outside of obedience was risky. Soldiers could only hang on, grimly fighting with an immanent ideology emphasizing comrades, families, homeland, and their own sense of honor—perhaps in that order.

For British troops defense was not so direct, for they were fighting abroad. Their sense of being British extended to a degree of imperial identity, but more important was that they were used to obeying their social superiors—as Maurin argued for the French. They believed what their rulers said about the necessity of the war since their own knowledge of foreign affairs was almost zero. In the war they maintained deference to officers, provided the officers treated their own authority as normal and did not condescend to them.[22]

The rural Bavarians studied by Ziemann and the Saxons described by Tony Ashworth's British soldiers seem more reluctant warriors who found their Prussian officers abusive and arrogant.[23] They were indifferent to German war aims but were held in place by a commitment to finish a job that had been started, by religious commitment to fight a righteous war, by commitment to their comrades, alive and dead, and by harsh discipline, made bearable by generous leave arrangements attuned to an army of peasants trying to keep their small plots of land viable. It is generally assumed that the German fighting soldier was more effective than those of the Entente, though they collapsed at the very end.

Social pressures enabled armies to hang on once patriotic sentiments had subsided. The fear of letting down one's comrades, *copains*, pals, *Kameraden*, was almost universal, buttressed by the need to assert masculinity.[24] Fear was acceptable, everybody in all armies experienced it, says Rousseau. But cowardice was effeminate, unacceptable to a real man. These were still patriarchal and hierarchical societies. Austro-Hungarians drawn from minority nations had probably the least commitment to their regime. By 1917 many believed they would be better off in defeat, through which they could get their own state. Yet most fought on almost to the end. It was difficult to do otherwise. All the hierarchies were in place, and people did what they were told in a spirit of pragmatic acceptance, because that was how the world worked.

Yet the soldiers were not passive recipients of orders. Ashworth found in British soldiers' letters and memoirs independence of action partially undermining higher authorities' commands.[25] He identified a "live-and-let-live" system involving tacit truces between German and British non-elite infantry along quieter front sectors. Elite units identified with their regiment, honored its traditions, and wanted action, but others preferred a quieter life. The system was helped by the ecology of trench warfare. The distance between enemy front lines was from one to three hundred meters. Sentry and listening posts were closer. The lines stretched over many kilometers. The battlefield of the Somme was ten times the length of Waterloo or Gettysburg, where soldiers had been close to the enemy only when under fire. This had prevented communication between armies. Now armies were encamped close to one another, and at quiet times they could communicate. Each trench heard noises associated with everyday living. "Tommy" and "Jerry" (or "Fritz") could hear each other at breakfast, laughing, singing. In quieter sectors the opposed units remained the same over time, so soldiers could shout each other's names. The men were spread out in fives along the front line, away from close surveillance by officers, each of whom was responsible for soldiers over several hundred meters. Battlefield ecology did not merely entrap, it brought a little autonomy.

Live-and-let-live was a mutual strategy to subvert orders and to avoid getting killed, more a utilitarian exchange than the result of moral qualms at killing—though the famous 1914 Christmas Day truce and football game between German and British troops was inflected with Christian notions of fellowship. Ashworth says the system embodied the sociological "norm of reciprocity"—"do unto me as I do unto you." This required trust that the enemy would honor the implied pact; it involved empathy and "a consciousness of kind." After all, they shared the same trench experience, the same will to live, and the same conflicts with a hierarchy that wanted them to kill and be killed. They also shared a hatred of artillery, for if our artillery launches a massive cannonade, theirs will respond in kind—and get us killed. It would be preferable if neither fired. Both infantries hated "fire-eaters," "heroes" whose aggression would bring fire back onto them. Ashworth describes verbal contracts, mutual inertia, and rituals such as not shelling when food was being consumed, deliberately shelling into no-man's-land, or helping the enemy to predict when the next bombardment would come. Patrols might quietly pass each other in the night and soldiers might shoot to miss. On the basis of the letters and diaries of a few regiments, and allowing for the proportion of quiet fronts and non-elite regiments, Ashworth gives a minimum of 13 percent and a maximum of 33 percent of soldiers involved at least once in the system.[26]

The live-and-let-live approach also occurred on other fronts. Ziemann's study of Bavarians fighting on a quiet front in the Vosges reveals similar practices between German and French troops.[27] Rousseau quotes several French soldiers detailing friendly contacts with the enemy when front conditions permitted.[28] Sheldon tells of a German lance corporal captured in no-man's-land by an Australian patrol. The Australians gave him cigarettes and offered not to take him prisoner if he would return and give them a German steel helmet. He agreed and kept his word, returning with a helmet. They shook hands and returned to their lines.[29] This was the life most soldiers would have wanted.

But on unquiet sectors there was carnage. At Verdun it lasted ten months, consuming 550,000 French lives and 430,000 German lives. The Somme offensive lasted five months. On its first day, 60,000 British soldiers were casualties, 20,000 of them killed. The carnage at Verdun was due to Falkenhayn drawing as many French soldiers within range of his artillery as he could. The French generals supplied the corpses, but the troops did not waver. Over the whole war, on average, 900 Frenchmen, 1,300 Germans, and over 1,450 Russians died *every day*. The British lost "only" 457 men per day. About 40 percent of all soldiers in the war were wounded at least once. Medical improvements since the Napoleonic Wars were canceled out by the graver wounds inflicted by new weapons, so more soldiers died of their wounds than in Napoleon's time.[30] But 30 percent of soldiers operated in the less dangerous rear, which means that overall casualty rates underestimate those of front soldiers.

•Nonetheless, both the live-and-let-live tactic and mass slaughter alarmed commanders into changes. From 1916 the German army developed a more fluid strategy of "defense in depth," and they and the Austrians developed "storm troopers," small commando attack forces.[31] The British also turned toward using more snipers, trench mortars, machine guns, and mines, as well as launching more commando raids. These raids were generally ineffective, but they undermined the live-and-let-live approach, since they could not be ritualized or predicted. Army tactics had countered soldiers' agency. But from 1918 such changes were integrated into a more general use of cover and concealment, freedom of subunits to maneuver, and combined-arms integration, all deployed more flexibly to break the stalemate.

Ashworth comments on Marshall's theory of nonfiring by World War II soldiers because of moral qualms, which I discuss later. He notes that live-and-let-live fits Marshall's claim that soldiers failed to fire their guns, but this was not due to moral qualms. He finds no evidence that "the tension between humane impulses and orders to kill caused paralysis."[32] He quotes several soldiers describing killing in matter-of-fact terms. Audoin-Rouzeau and Becker give examples of soldiers reporting enjoying killing in hand-to-hand combat.[33] But noting that many veterans had become pacifists by the 1930s, they suggest moral qualms plagued many after the war, as I noted regarding the aftermath of the American Civil War. Ashworth says that only a "small proportion of soldiers hospitalised with battle fatigue had a fear of killing."[34] This last point is confirmed by Alexander Watson's study of psychologists' reports. Fear for oneself was much more important than moral qualms.[35]

Smith complains that, since Clausewitz, armies have been seen as overcentralized, and soldiers' responses as mere "friction" in the system.[36] Clausewitz did not see that his "apolitical" army was different from citizen soldiers questioning and negotiating authority. Soldiers were not passive victims, brutalized and slaughtered by the modern war machine. In his study of the 5th French Infantry Division, Smith says soldiers were committed to the war effort. They wanted France to win and were willing to fight to achieve this. But they also believed in the "proportionality" of commands. The risks asked of them had to be proportional to their chances of achieving success. When commands are seen as disproportional, soldiers resist with lassitude, reluctance to follow orders of attack, and grousing. There is a degree of rational calculation in this. The troops decided what was possible on their battlefield, and sometimes they imposed their own solutions of retreat, tacit refusal to advance, or even surrender. Their immediate officers might sympathize and lessen their demands, conveying grousing up the hierarchy and suggesting tactical changes. Tacit negotiations between ranks concerned acceptable responses to combat environments.

Emmanuel Saint-Fuscien shows that a sense of proportionality grew in the French military justice system.[37] This began as repressive but then eased, as executions for cowardice or desertion became rarer (with the exception noted below), and fewer sentences were carried out. At the front, the exigencies of battle weakened hierarchy. Junior officers, NCOs, and men faced the same challenges, and examples of initiative and courage by any of them could inspire the others. Authority became more responsive, more flexible. Military justice moved away from an aloof and authoritarian system to a more interpersonal system suited to the needs of a skilled, democratic army. What a tragedy that this occurred only amid mass slaughter!

And as the war ground on, discontent grew. By 1917 this was fueled in France by hopes of peace induced by the Russian Revolution, the entry of U.S. forces, German retreat behind the Hindenburg Line, political struggle in Paris, and the disaster of Robert Nivelle's *Chemin des Dames* offensive. This produced a psychological threshold above which soldiers would not engage in offensives, which exploded in the French mutinies of April–May 1917. About 45,000 soldiers refused to obey the order to advance in a rippling motion across a broad front. They were prepared to defend their positions but rejected Nivelle's policy of incessant attacks: he had breached their implicit contract to defend France without being cannon fodder. The soldiers' demands ranged from better food and more leave to immediate peace. In sending their demands to their deputies in Paris, soldiers were recognizing the legitimacy of the republic and their own power as citizens. They were also trying to protect themselves from execution. Smith weakens his argument by contrasting French "citizen soldiers" with stereotypes of the supposed "subject soldiers" of Britain (like France, a male democracy), and Germany, half-democratic, many of whose soldiers had become socialists toward war's end. More to the point is that British and German soldiers were serving abroad, trapped within their military deployments, while the mutinous French troops were at home, under one hundred kilometers from Paris. Many had spent their leaves in Paris witnessing strikes and demonstrations.

The crisis was solved by Philippe Pétain's carrot-and-stick strategy: on the one hand, the inevitable execution of "ringleaders," and on the other, the promise of "tanks and the Americans," improvements in living conditions and fewer mass attacks.[38] But all the armies had reached the end of their tethers by mid-1918, except for the recently arrived Americans.[39] Those in the front line, with direct experience of battle, were more likely to suffer psychological trauma.[40] This is also what analyses of PTSD in recent wars reveal (see the next chapter).

Surrendering was risky. Many were killed by captors consumed with rage at the deaths of their comrades, or fearful that visibly escorting prisoners back was too dangerous.[41] Desertion was risky. One had to make one's way through numerous lines and, if one was caught, punishment included possible execution. The rate of British, French, and German desertions was only 1 percent, though higher among ethnic minorities.[42] Because of lesser national solidarity, desertion was greater in Austrian, Italian, Russian, and Ottoman forces.[43] Yet survival chances were perversely seen as better if one stayed, for the army command supplied food, alcohol, tobacco, and better medical help than civilians got. The military unit remained a protective environment, enveloping the soldier.[44]

Watson analyzes British and German soldiers' censored letters home and diaries, in addition to psychologists' and army reports. He says most soldiers coped quite well with appalling front conditions. Endurance was the norm—most men adapted to the war. Resilience, not mental collapse, was commoner, because of a combination of fear of the enemy, military obedience, camaraderie, overoptimism concerning the likelihood of death or injury, religious faith, patriotism, rotation systems enabling rest, and adequate food and munitions. Religion, superstitions, talismans, and incessant black humor gave men the illusion of control of their destinies. As long as men believed in survival and final victory, fear was manageable. This required faith in officers, unit loyalty, and junior officers leading from the front (they had the highest casualty rates). Letters from loved ones added moral and emotional support and reminded the soldiers that they were fighting for hearth and homeland.[45]

The front experience did not intensify moral qualms at killing. We can find in soldiers' accounts occasional respect for enemy soldiers, and appreciation when they withheld fire while medics were picking up the wounded or the dead. There was German gratitude to a British prisoner who, after a sudden change of fortune at the front, found himself protecting his German captors from the wrath of his comrades. But in

Rousseau's and Sheldon's lengthy quotations from French and German soldiers, no one expressed moral qualms about killing. On the contrary, battle intensified aggression. One British lieutenant said of his soldiers, "You only have an impartial interest in strangers even though they are Englishmen, . . . [but] your own men downed, sets you cursing and throbbing with rage and hate." Comments Watson, "Casualties, far from sapping combat motivation, actually strengthened survivors' obligation to keep fighting."[46] Nationalist hatreds declined, replaced by primitive hatred. Adrenaline rushes could convert fear into fury. In their letters, when soldiers describe killing an enemy, he is depersonalized, never described as a human being.[47]

This now seems a pointless war, fought neither for genuine national interests nor for high ideals, but for "reasons of state" mediated by the survival interests of dynastic monarchies and the diplomatic incompetence and cult of "honor" (not backing down) of upper-class leaders who did not themselves fight. This suggests that soldiers' sacrifices were senseless, and that is why we should rage at the rulers, politicians, courtiers, journalists, and generals who urged them on. Never were peoples so betrayed as in World War I, but Europe remained a class-bound continent. Soldiers obeyed their upper-class masters, just as they had done in peacetime. Heavy-industry workers and miners were the most likely to rebel, but most were in reserved occupations. Obedience plus national identity were translated by constant drilling and the enemy's murderous attacks into a belief that national interests were at stake. After all, "they" *were* trying to kill "us." If they had doubts as cynics or class warriors, they were still trapped within the coercive space that is an army in a battlefield.

Obedience required the belief that the war was winnable, and this collapsed near the war's end, temporarily for the French in their great mutiny and for Italians at their great defeat at Caporetto, permanently for Russian soldiers in the east and then German troops in the west, as they lost the sense of their own empowerment, their trust in the competence of their officers, and their confidence in victory.[48] Joshua Sanborn challenges the old assumption that coercion was the only reason Russian peasant-soldiers fought, arguing that they possessed a motivating sense of patriotism.[49] Yet the loss of any realistic hope of victory against the superior German army and the increasing sense of being used as cannon fodder turned at the beginning of 1917 into class rage and revolution.[50] This was the only revolution that occurred during the war.

But by September 1918 German soldiers were exhausted. The failure of their last offensive had shown them how outmatched they were in material resources. Ironically, this was so during their last advances, for they captured such plentiful Entente supplies of food, wine, and ammunition as to cause despair at their own resources. Now the soldiers complained of "Prussian" officers and denounced war profiteers back home.[51] They had become republicans, often socialists. As the Americans piled into the front, they no longer believed they could win, while the British and French and the fresh Americans knew they would win. The German army did not disintegrate as the Russian army had, and some units carried on fighting even in defeat, but many whole units of soldiers and officers came forward in surrender. Watson argues that the soldiers remained in the line until there was an "ordered surrender" from above. Ziemann's view seems better evidenced, that soldiers led the surrenders while many others simply went home.[52] Fear had been contained for four long years, but as the Germans neared defeat, containment collapsed, while for their enemies, nearing victory seemed to make sense of the war again. There was no clear relationship between morale and regime type, contrary to the democratic "triumphalism" to which I referred in chapter 3. Until the end, the Wehrmacht soldier fighting for a semi-authoritarian regime was probably superior to the soldier of the Entente male democracies, but the Austrians commanded by a semi-authoritarian regime and Russians fighting for a fully authoritarian regime performed worse. The losing rulers got what they deserved for starting the war, while the winners botched the peace and made promises about a better society that they did not keep.

The war brought on another bout of slaughter, the Spanish flu pandemic, which lasted three years from January 1918. Its origins are unknown but were not in Spain. Spain had been neutral in the war and lacked wartime censorship, so this was the first country where the flu was freely reported—the grave illness of the king making world headlines. This pandemic infected perhaps 500 million people, a quarter of the world's population, and killed between 20 and 50 million. The pandemic had two mostly military causes. First, military encampments contained soldiers living intimately together in very unhygienic conditions and under severe stress—perfect germ pools carrying off innumerable soldiers before spreading to civilians through global movement of troops home as the war ended. We might call this the "Kansas flu," for it was probably in a military camp there that the flu started. The second cause was military censorship, which successfully concealed the scale of the problem until it was too late to take effective preventive action. Nature was striking back, but the ferocity of the blow was social, the idiocy of war and specifically of military authority.

World War II: Ideological Warfare

World War II was very different, as we saw in chapter 8. It was not a war caused by confusion and miscalculation, like the first war, but by ideology. It was a war of aggression created by the militaristic ideologies of Nazi Germany, imperial Japan, and fascist Italy. The French, British, Russians, and Chinese fought largely in self-defense, whereas Americans had more mixed motives. Allied soldiers were not cannon fodder in the power ploys of rulers, although there were imperial goals sought by British, American, and Soviet elites that were of little interest to the masses. And this time, British colonial soldiers, especially those of the Indian Army, were fighting for their probable national independence after the war.

We should also blame the leaders of Britain and France for their ideological anti-Bolshevism, however, which prevented them from allying with the Soviets to deter Hitler in 1938 and 1939—ideology triumphing over Realist balancing. Although this would have left Hitler in place, it might have avoided a world war and the Holocaust. We can also blame the Roosevelt administration for its provocative sanctions against Japan. Yet these are mere peccadillos compared to the atrocities of the Axis powers from the Nanjing Massacre to the Holocaust. Allied soldiers viewed this as a legitimate war, and it was.

For the first time we have interview surveys of soldiers, mainly American, but Russian too. The first survey concerned the Spanish Civil War of 1936 to 1939. The pioneering sociologist John Dollard distributed a forty-four-page questionnaire to three hundred American volunteers who had fought in the Abraham Lincoln Brigade on the Republican side. Of the respondents, 74 percent said they had felt fearful when first going into action. Fear was greatest just before battle started. Fear of being thought a coward by comrades and officers was dominant at this stage, but when soldiers realized fear was shared by all their comrades, this offered comfort. Ninety-one percent of them said they either always or sometimes felt afraid going into actions. Fear generated strong physiological symptoms. A pounding heart or rapid pulse was felt by 69 percent, extreme muscular tension or a sinking feeling in the stomach by

45 percent, and severe trembling by 25 percent. Involuntary urination or defecation was experienced by 11 percent.[53] I noted this happening in World War I, though I lacked figures there. Probably it had happened in earlier wars. Surveys of American soldiers in World War II produced similar numbers, as we shall see. In battle some soldiers lose control over their urinary or bowel function because the sphincter relaxes as fear takes over the brain, causing a loss in the brain's regulatory function. It happens automatically, without one's knowledge, an example of the fight-or-flight response to a stimulus. Here flight prevailed. The opposite response is the increase in adrenaline that enables fight.

Inactivity fueled fear. The vast majority, 84 percent, said that active task concentration during battle filled the mind and dispelled fear. The second-most cited factor in overcoming fear, at 77 percent, was belief in the war aims. Forty-nine percent stressed good leadership, 45 percent military training, and 42 percent good materiel. These last three responses reveal the importance of feeling oneself a member of a well-organized army with a good chance of winning. Hatred of the enemy was admitted by only 21 percent. Discussion of war aims helped 93 percent, whereas 91 percent said being given knowledge of the whole front made them fight better, even if the news was fairly bad. Dollard did not ask them about moral qualms, and they did not volunteer them. This was a volunteer brigade composed of leftists who had crossed the Atlantic to fight in a distant country for an antifascist cause they believed in—which led to high immanent morale. But Dollard adds: "The soldier in battle is not forever whispering "My cause, my cause. He is too busy for that. Ideology functions *before* battle, to get the man in; and *after* battle, by blocking thoughts of escape. Identification with cause is like a joker in a pack of cards. It can substitute for any other card. The man who has it can better bear inferior materiel, temporary defeat, weariness or fear."

The Lincoln Brigade fought hard, yet in a losing cause, as retreat and defeat increasingly dominated its experience. Of the 3,015 Americans in the brigade, about one-quarter died, but ideological commitment and tight comradeship enabled the survivors to take heavy losses and continue fighting. Immanent ideological power, strengthening solidarity, helped master fear.

World War II was highly ideological. The vast majority of leaders believed their cause was just, whether that meant securing national or racial rights and power in the world (Germany, Italy, and Japan) or defeating fascism (China, Soviet Union, France, Britain, United States). Such beliefs played a significant role in soldiers' conduct, increasing their commitment. There were, however, two different types of ideology in the war. Among the Western Allies we see a fairly "latent" form of "immanent ideology," the belief by the troops that they were fighting a just war in defense of their way of life, but these beliefs were implicit rather than explicit, there being little propagandizing by military authorities. In contrast, the German army, especially on the Eastern Front, the Japanese, and above all the Red Army had explicit "transcendent ideologies" that leaders sought to implant in their soldiers to produce higher, even self-sacrificing morale as they scorned the risk of death. In the subsequent development of the twentieth century, ideologies became "weapons of the weak," which allowed technologically inferior armies to level the battlefield by virtue of superior morale. We will see a direct communist chain of descent in the methods used and results produced from the Soviet Red Army to the Chinese People's Liberation Army (PLA), to the North Korean People's Army (NKPA), to the Vietnamese People's Liberation Front (PLF). I will contrast their way of fighting to that of their enemies in the next chapter. In this chapter I deal with the Wehrmacht and the Red Army, and then turn to the Western Allies.

Wehrmacht Soldiers on the Eastern Front

The Wehrmacht's will to fight right up to the gates of Berlin and the death of Hitler gives the impression of a highly ideological army. But Kershaw insists we see this within the context of German society, for civilian will did not waver. He emphasizes that fighting "down to almost total devastation and complete enemy occupation" is very rare in war. In the last ten months of this war, July 1944 to May 1945, far more German civilians died than in the previous five years; half the military deaths occurred in the same period—2.6 million out of 5.3 million. Even as the Reich was collapsing, the Nazi leadership also intensified the murder of millions of Jews and other *Untermenschen*. Kershaw stresses four reasons for fighting to the death. Above all, "the structures and mentalities of Hitler's charismatic rule" combined the charismatic hold Hitler had over Germans with his personal preference to die rather than surrender. Second, the generals found it impossible to suggest negotiations or surrender after the failure of the Stauffenberg plot. Third, repressive control over German society was delegated to Himmler, Goebbels, Bormann, and Speer, and carried to the local level by the long-term Nazi regional gauleiters. Fourth was the fear of Soviet vengeance for German atrocities against Soviet citizens. Goebbels was already broadcasting that vengeance was happening in East Prussia as the Red Army advanced.[54]

The sociologists Edward Shils and Morris Janowitz offer a different explanation of Wehrmacht dedication: the primary group of close comrades was the main force driving the soldiers to continue fighting even when defeat seemed inevitable.[55] Attachments to anything broader are not nearly as salient to them, nor is general ideology. They present rather thin data to support this application of "buddy theory," and most scholars emphasize the ideological commitment of German soldiers, especially on the Eastern Front.[56] Of Wehrmacht frontline officers, 30 percent were members of the Nazi Party, more than twice as many as among all Germans, while the soldiers' diaries reveal deep racism and a personal commitment to the Führer, as Kershaw suggests. The Wehrmacht, like the Red Army, had political "commissars" repetitively instructing soldiers in Nazi theory in weekly political sessions at company level.[57] This helped soldiers fight to the bitter end and to commit terrible crimes, motivated by demonization of Jews and Slavs and the Führer cult. Robert Cintino stresses Führer worship and the vision of the Eastern Front as a struggle to stem a Jewish-Bolshevik-Asiatic flood menacing Western civilization.[58] Soldiers participated willingly in genocide to help this. Harsh discipline was coupled with licensed brutality toward the enemy. An NCO described Russians as "no longer human beings, but wild hordes and beasts, who have been bred by Bolshevism during the last 20 years." Another wrote, "The great task given us in the struggle against Bolshevism lies in the destruction of eternal Jewry."[59] All this came back to haunt the Wehrmacht in Soviet vengeance.

The conditions of battle on the Eastern Front became awful. The Germans were badly clothed, ill-fed, disease-prone, fighting in mud and snow that made high-tech weapons like tanks repeatedly break down. This produced what Omer Bartov calls a radical "demodernization," which forced the Wehrmacht to compensate for numerical and sometimes technological inferiority with a more brutal fighting spirit. The traumas they experienced led to the belief that "not only was war hell, one also had to be a beast if one wished to survive it." The soldiers acquired a "new concept of heroism, a new self-perception of the combat soldier. . . . There was an anarchic element in this celebration of death and return to savagery among the frontline troops."[60]

Stephen Fritz agrees: the extraordinary staying power of the infan-tryman, the *Landser*, was essentially ideological.[61] The National Socialist state had "redeemed the failures of World War I and had restored, both individually and collectively, a uniquely German sense of identity."[62] Nazi ideas resonated: "Many *Landsers*, previously skeptical of Nazi pro-paganda, confronted what they accepted as the reality of the Jewish-Bolshevik destruction of a whole nation." They had invaded Russia in 1941 with forebodings but overcame them with values centered on de-fending the Fatherland against an international Jewish-Bolshevik con-spiracy. They believed their Aryan racial superiority over Jews and Slavs justified murder. No qualms there. Fritz says they also internalized a distinctive Wehrmacht ideology of pride in an elite German institution that instilled discipline and solidarity. The combination of Nazi and Wehrmacht ideals led them to believe they could transform Germany into a more classless society, already prefigured in an army in which all ranks shared equally in rigorous training, harsh discipline, and the bur-dens of the Eastern Front, and where officers and NCOs led from the front.[63]

Bartov says discipline became "perverted," so that atrocities against civilians and enemy soldiers went unpunished, whereas slight infractions against military regulations might bring execution. At least 15,000 Ger-man soldiers were executed, and more were shot on the spot for deser-tion or skulking—much higher numbers than in most armies of the time. Fritz says the common *Landser*, unable to mitigate his suffering in any other way, lashed out in anger and frustration against the only targets within range, enemy soldiers and civilians, transforming the war on the Eastern Front into a horrific bloodbath. One recalls his "almost drunken exhilaration" in battle. Their letters and diaries express thrill in killing and a sense of freedom from restraint.[64] Battle intoxication was much rarer among Allied troops.

German soldiers in the east also feared for their lives if they surren-dered, given their own massacres of Soviet civilians and POWs. The final days saw units flee into the arms of the Americans, who they correctly believed would treat them better.[65] The Wehrmacht fought a much more savage war in the east than on other fronts, always excepting the uniform massacres of Jews. Some German soldiers and airmen could not understand why the Western Allies were not fighting with them, against communism. But in the east they had helped create an even more ideo-logically determined opponent.

The Red Army at Stalingrad

I will not dwell on the hastily created Red Army during the Russian Civil War. Its aspirations were revolutionary, but its performance was only marginally less chaotic than that of the White foe. In the end it won the war because peasants hated the Reds less than they did the Whites. Nor will I deal with the professionalization of the Red Army during the interwar period, then disrupted by Stalin's purges. But this had not made the Red Army into a particularly cohesive force. Stalin worsened its predicament by trusting Hitler's word and so was completely surprised by Hitler's invasion in June 1941. Initially, the Red Army was routed. Stalin's forced industrialization, however, created a large modern force capable of slowing the advance into Russia of the Wehrmacht. I focus on the moment when it stopped that advance, at Stalingrad in 1942–43.

Our best evidence comes from interviews conducted in January and February 1943 by historians working for the Soviet Commission on the History of the Great Patriotic War. They interviewed soldiers, political officials, and civilians involved in the recent battle of Stalingrad. Obviously, no one in Stalinist times felt able to criticize Stalin or the overall Soviet conduct of battle, but otherwise the transcripts of these interviews seem honest reports of personal experience, not propaganda. Indeed, the absence of references to "the heroic leadership of Stalin," the dominant trope in official Soviet accounts, was probably the reason the transcripts languished forgotten in dusty archives until after the collapse of the Soviet Union. Then they were unearthed by Russian historians. They allowed access to the German historian Jochen Hellbeck.[66]

The transcripts are stunning in their depiction of the horrors of the five-month battle raging from August 1942 to February 1943 and of the sufferings unto starvation of soldiers and civilians. At first the Wehrmacht pressed forward in massive attacks and took almost all the city after savage fighting for every street, open space, factory, apartment, cellar, and staircase. Virtually all the city's buildings were destroyed either by bombing or by street fighting. All seemed lost as casualties mounted in a Red Army trapped between the Germans and the Volga River. Soldiers talked of death or wounding likely to come within ten days of their joining the fight. But fierce resistance slowed the German advance, which allowed Soviet reinforcements to arrive across the river. Tied down in street fighting, the Wehrmacht lost its superiority in mobility, maneuver, and precise artillery barrage. Then fierce Soviet counterattacks in the city and to both the north and the south of the city drove the

Germans back and finally encircled them. Hitler refused his generals' pleas to attempt a breakout and ordered them to fight to the last man. They did fight to the point where they were starving and lacked the fuel necessary to effect any breakout at all. Germany's General Friedrich Paulus then surrendered his 220,000 remaining men. The Wehrmacht and its Axis allies suffered 647,300 casualties in the city—killed, wounded, or captured. It was the most decisive battle of the war, the turning point after which the Red Army, and also the British and American armies, could advance rather than retreat. But at a terrible cost: the Red Army, according to official figures, suffered 1,129,619 total casualties in the Stalingrad battles, of which 478,741 were killed or missing, and 650,878 wounded or sick, a casualty rate of over half the total force. It was worse among tank crews trapped inside their burning infernos. Through the whole war, three-quarters of the 403,272 Soviet tank soldiers were killed. Why did the soldiers nonetheless continue fighting through a period when all hope seemed gone?

The combination of harsh discipline and the penal culture of the army was one reason, traditionally emphasized in the West (and in Germany at the time). Anthony Beevor supports this argument, but most of his sources were German and deeply anticommunist.[67] Catherine Merridale, who interviewed two hundred Red Army veterans, also emphasizes the fear of punishment pervading the army, outmatched only by its hatred of the Germans, whose atrocities were widely publicized.[68] Yet Hellbeck shows this is much exaggerated.[69] Beevor's frequently quoted figure of 13,500 soldiers executed during the battle is wildly inflated. Hellbeck calculates that from August 1, 1942, to January 31, 1943, 447 Soviet soldiers were executed on the Stalingrad Front, which would be no higher than the Italian rate of executions in this war. Roger Reese uses oral histories, memoirs, diaries, and letters, as well as archival military and political reports, to undermine the myth of the "blocking detachments," supposedly executing stragglers in the rear.[70] These detachments did not fire machine guns at retreating soldiers. Armed only with rifles, they rounded up stragglers and fleers and returned them to the front, as occurred in most armies. They arrested a mere 3.7 percent of the soldiers they detained, and 1.5 percent received death sentences.

The High Command and Stalin knew that coercion might be counterproductive, producing disaffection and weakening morale. Because the Red Army was so large, the absolute number of executions was greater than in the other armies. But as a proportion of the army, it was only a little more than the rate in the Wehrmacht. More were punished by service in the "penal battalions" at the front, which often took heavy casualties. But sometimes their penal service lasted only several days before the survivors were returned to their original units and ranks. Many fighting in the penal battalions saw them as no more dangerous than the rest of the front. Even a few months fighting there was better than years in the gulag.

Reese stresses the importance of leadership for morale. He says that before Stalingrad the High Command's failure to adapt to the German blitzkrieg strategy had led to disorganization, forcing Red Army units to choose resistance, surrender, or flight. Soviet soldiers were captured when leadership disintegrated, or were killed when small, cohesive units fought to the end. Soviet soldiers were willing to fight, but like all soldiers, they had to be well led. At Stalingrad there was more effective leadership, and the soldiers responded with intense commitment. The High Command cultivated its own version of the buddy system from late 1942 onward, ensuring that units needing new blood because of high casualties were withdrawn from the line and trained together with the new replacements for some weeks before going back into battle. Merridale says that the U.S. Army did not introduce such practices until after 1945.[71]

Reese says most soldiers believed they were fighting for the nation, socialism, and Stalin, who was usually described reverentially. Even those who had suffered prewar repression did not perceive "evil intent on the part of Stalin or see [repression] as inherent to the economic and social systems."[72] Injustices were blamed on Stalin's underlings (as happened in medieval monarchies). They fought mainly in defense of Mother Russia against truly barbarous invaders. It seemed an obviously just war. Intense hatred was directed against the Nazis, whose atrocities were confirmed by the letters soldiers received from home and later by the devastation wreaked by the retreating Germans. Finally, self-interest often kicked in: they fought to improve their career chances. All this enabled a righteous fury to be directed against Germans. Influenced by communism, the soldiers' nationalism became populist and class-conscious. Socialist ideology came from above and from the commissars accompanying every military unit, but this was met from below by proletarian nationalism. So the army was prepared to fight to the death. This sentiment was matched by some SS battalions, but not by the Wehrmacht as a whole. SS General Max Simon said, "The Russian worker usually is a convinced communist, who ... will fight fanatically as a class-conscious proletarian. Just as the Red infantryman is ready to die in his foxhole, the Soviet tank soldier will die in his tank, firing at the enemy to the last, even if he is alone in or behind enemy lines."[73] Bolshevik gender equality as well as the need to mobilize everyone produced 800,000 women in uniform. A few thousand became frontline troops, unlike women in other armies.

Hellbeck claims that discipline was not just coercion. Its aim was also "to teach self-control" and "transform [the soldier] into a self-sacrificing warrior."[74] It had a "didactic element."[75] He adds, "The interviews also reveal an element at odds with most western depictions: the Communist party's enormous effort to condition the troops. The party was an ever-present institutional force in the form of political officers and ideological messages. . . . Together with the secret police, the party placed the army in an iron yoke. But even when party officials doled out punishment, the intentions were corrective, seeking to instruct, motivate, and remake the troops. . . . The pervasiveness and effectiveness of political involvement in military units set the Red Army apart from other modern armies."[76]

Merridale sees the political commissars as mainly instilling discipline.[77] Hellbeck sees them as instructing and motivating through incessant discussions, lectures, reports, in addition to history lessons on Stalin's supposedly brilliant defense of Tsaritsyn (the former name of Stalingrad) in the civil war.[78] A commissar recalled: "What we did was talk to the men in person and then lead by example, showing them how to fight. And in absolutely every battle the party members were the first ones to throw themselves into the fight."[79] A party bureau secretary in a rifle regiment noted: "We introduced a new idea: every soldier had to start a personal account of how many Germans he'd killed. This was essentially a stimulus for socialist competition: to see who could kill the most Germans. We would check these accounts, and if a comrade didn't have any dead Fritzes, we'd have a talk with him, make him feel the shame."[80] Peacetime shock-work tallies were replaced by lists of enemy soldiers killed and medals earned: "The party changed its criteria for admission. Earlier the litmus test had been knowledge of Marxist theory and a working-class background, but now it was military achievement. The party opened its doors to anyone who could demonstrate having killed Germans in battle. . . . The party assumed more of a military quality and became closer to the people."[81]

The more enemy one killed, the better one's chances of obtaining party membership, together with the privileges this conferred on oneself and one's family. Party membership in the army grew during the war from 650,000 to almost 3 million, and most of the newcomers were inducted on the battlefield after demonstrating killing prowess. One man declared that over three days in October, "I killed 25 Fritzes myself. I was given the Order of the Red Banner. . . . After the battle on October 29, I submitted my application to the party and now I'm a member." Hellbeck (unlike Reese) says that attachment to the primary group of close comrades was relatively low in the Red Army, partly because of the tremendous losses occurring every day at Stalingrad, but partly because the authorities discouraged it as divisive. "The cement that the Red Army command used to bind together diverse soldiers and motivate them to fight was ideology. Preached incessantly and targeting every recruit, it was made up of accessible concepts with an enormous emotional charge: love for the homeland and hatred of the enemy."[82]

Although this came framed in simple Marxism, nationalist vengeance was its core and its strength. Propaganda also came with much information about the progress of the war, especially in the form of newspapers handed out to soldiers, but also trench tours by commissars. The soldiers were told why they were fighting until minutes before battle, and the flow of information resumed when it ended.[83] In the Spanish Civil War soldiers had said how important information was to morale, but most armies do not provide it. But months-long battles made regular lectures and assemblies difficult. Instead came propaganda through example. A commissar says that when a special assault group was formed, two or three party members were assigned to it to provide leadership.

Morale was high. The People's Commissariat for Internal Affairs (NKVD) read millions of soldiers' letters. They found some voiced complaints about exhaustion and the hardship of military service. Some letters reflected defeatist sentiments. During the period from June to August 1942, of 30,237,000 letters examined, 15,469 contained defeatist statements. Soldiers knew their letters were being censored, but defeatism evident in 0.05 percent of cases still seems very low.[84] In fact, the extraordinary dedication of both the Wehrmacht and the Red Army makes a mockery of the democratic "triumphalism" in battle to which I referred in chapter 3.

Many soldiers admitted to intense fear in battle, at first of relentless German attacks, their seemingly countless tanks and planes, and continuous artillery barrages. But they explained how they mastered fear. Hellbeck reports an infantryman in his first battle experiencing "the paralyzing fear he felt when German fire forced him to the ground. But he also noted that the fear evaporated the moment he realized that he had to stand up if he wanted to avoid a senseless death: 'I realized that we might die for nothing. It wasn't bravery or courage (which I had none of). I simply realized that I was going to die unless I did something. And the only chance I had to save myself and others was to advance.' " He "picked himself off the ground and was surprised by the galvanizing effect of the battle cry that reflexively crossed his lips: 'I couldn't say anything other than what anyone would have said in my place. "For the motherland! For Stalin!" ' "[85]

The intense ideological power of populist Marxism made this a distinctive army, most resembling the Wehrmacht in its permeation by ideology, yet surpassing it in the extent of political education, of party membership determined by killing rates, boosted by defense of the homeland (which the Wehrmacht lacked). The Red Army was a terrible war machine, but this was self-defense against a foe who its members knew had massacred millions and who would enslave the survivors if it triumphed. The army's transcendent ideology enabled it to withstand enormous losses and keep on fighting with an intensity surpassing other armies'. Its technology was not much inferior to the Wehrmacht's, and its numbers were greater, but its edge was given by its superior morale. The Germans believed this came from mindless Asiatic racial obedience. Yet obedience was mindful, full of ideas.

The Western Allies: The Lonely Battlefield and Nonfiring

This war involved more widely dispersed battlefields. Its air forces brought aerial firepower, forcing ground forces to scatter, enabling strikes against far-off targets, and substantially increasing civilian casualties. Despite the initial success of tank blitzkriegs, tanks proved rather vulnerable, and artillery batteries and infantry slogging remained the heart of ground warfare. Infantry units often enjoyed autonomy from their officers, and soldiers talked of an "empty" battlefield, where the enemy was rarely glimpsed. General Sir William Slim, who led the Burma campaign, declared, "In the end every important battle develops to a point where there is no real control by senior commanders. . . . The dominant feel of the battlefield is loneliness."[86]

In such fighting soldiers could decide their level of commitment. They might choose not to fire their guns. Nonfiring has figured importantly in discussions of soldiers' motivations because of U.S. Brigadier General

S. L. A. Marshall's wartime reports on the rate of fire of American infantry in the Pacific and European theaters. Though doubts have been raised about his methods, most scholars repeat his conclusions as facts.[87] Marshall's research was based on collective discussions with assemblies of infantry battalions, not interviews with individuals. The virtue of this method was his ability to construct a blow-by-blow account of particular engagements, piecing together each man's experience into a vivid overall narrative of battle seen from the ground up. Marshall published over a dozen narratives of individual encounters stretching from World War II to Korea to Vietnam.[88] They are vivid accounts of engagements that rarely went as planned, giving a graphic sense of battle. They are almost unknown today. Curiously, they do not mention nonfiring, except when units were pinned down by enemy fire.

Yet Marshall also wrote broader reports that give statistics on the rate of firing or nonfiring, which are still quoted. Marshall posed open-ended questions to each battalion and listened to their freewheeling responses. He concluded from this that the percentage of men firing at the enemy "did not rise above 20–25%"—a stunningly low figure. We should increase it a little since he says only about 80 percent of the soldiers had the opportunity to fire. Among these, 25–30 percent would fire, still a very low proportion. He said qualms over killing others prevented firing: "The average and healthy individual . . . has such an inner and usually unrealized resistance to killing a fellow man that he will not of his own volition take life if it is possible for him to turn away from that possibility. . . . At the vital point he becomes a conscientious objector, unknowing."[89]

Marshall gave no evidence for this conclusion but added that weapons serviced by crews—artillery, machine guns, weapons fired from helicopters—were almost always fired because the individual was closely watched by comrades. This particular finding has been repeatedly confirmed by later research. But in the late 1940s and 1950s, Marshall's conclusions made a sensation among military authorities who had worried since the First World War about what they called "passive combat personnel." They didn't want a repeat of the live-and-let-live system. The authorities accepted the veracity of his findings, and they introduced new and rather sensible training methods simulating actual battle conditions, as he had recommended.

Yet Marshall's statistics cannot be accepted. He appears to have plucked them out of thin air. His reports give no details of how he arrived at his statistics. His field notes proved sparse and gave no hint of any quantitative calculations at all. His assistant, Captain John Westover, quotes Marshall as saying statistics were only "an adornment of belief." He adds that Marshall had taken only occasional notes, and, most damagingly, that he never actually asked soldiers about firing! Marshall's own statements about the number of his interviews were also varied and exaggerated.[90] Perhaps soldiers might have given him the general impression of nonfiring, but even this is not remembered by his assistant. Marshall's "statistics" were pure invention.

Yet Malešević repeats Marshall's conclusions as facts and cites six authors who he says confirm Marshall.[91] In fact, three simply repeat Marshall's conclusions. Three, Randall Collins, Dave Grossman, and Joanna Bourke, do produce new information, but this fails to convince. I criticized Grossman already when discussing the American Civil War, and I deal with Bourke's equivocal support later. Collins refers mainly to the pioneering sociological research of Stouffer and his colleagues using large-scale interview surveys of American World War II soldiers and aircrews. Yet they offered almost no findings on nonfiring.

Instead, Stouffer and his colleagues emphasized fear. In one U.S. infantry regiment whose soldiers were individually interviewed in France in 1944, 65 percent admitted that they had failed to do their job properly on at least one occasion because of extreme fear. Stouffer's large surveys of four infantry divisions in the Pacific theater revealed physiological responses of fear very similar to those Dollard observed in Spain. They found 76 percent of soldiers saying they had often or sometimes felt a violent pounding of the heart; 52 percent said they had experienced uncontrollable trembling; about 50 percent admitted to feeling faint, breaking out in a cold sweat, and feeling sick to their stomach; 19 percent said they had vomited; and 12 percent said they had lost control of their bowels.[92] The military psychologist Ralph Kaufman also reported a high incidence of such ailments among Pacific infantry.[93] He saw their fears as a rational response to threat; physiological consequences included damage to the cardiovascular, gastrointestinal, and respiratory systems. Bourke agrees and attacks what she sees as the overly rationalistic theories of social scientists that ignore emotions, somatic surges, fury, petrification, and other destructive emotional responses in battle.[94] As a social scientist, I agree.

Stouffer and his colleagues asked another large sample of soldiers what were the most common errors committed by new replacements and more seasoned soldiers. Blazing away, shooting too much—not too little—before they were able to see the target, was the third-most common error

for both groups, after the sins of bunching up when on patrol and making
too much noise at night. These are all sins of hyperactivity. "Freezing," an
indicator of nonfiring (for whatever reason), came only ninth.[95] Captured
Japanese soldiers' diaries tried to make sense of what they perceived as
American overfiring by saying the Americans were paid according to the
number of times they fired![96] In modern warfare, blazing away is like nonfiring in the sense that both are fear-induced risk avoidance, the point
being not to reveal the location of one's body to the enemy. And who can
blame a soldier for either tactic, given the range and lethality of modern
weapons? This was reasonably fearful behavior, not the result of moral
qualms.

Joseph Blake adds the autobiographies of thirty-three ground
troops.[97] The first horror they usually experienced was the sight of a mutilated corpse, friend or foe. This came before their own first action, and
the sight was often a deliberate softening-up strategy used by officers. As
a consequence, "most men, after exposure to violence, are able to commit
violence with no after-shock. Men report their first kill (after exposure)
casually, as part of an ongoing action, or if they say anything about it,
talk in terms of killing as a 'natural function,' 'instinctive' etc." Blake
quotes the initial ambivalence of the American war hero Audie Murphy:
"It is not easy to shed the idea that human life is sacred. . . . If there was
any doubt in my mind, it began to vanish in the shell explosion that
killed Griffin, and it disappeared altogether when I saw the two men
crumple by the railroad track. Now I have shed my first blood, I feel no
qualms; no pride; no remorse. There is only a weary indifference."[98]

Bourke draws on psychiatric reports and the diaries and letters of
twenty-eight British, American, and Australian soldiers in the two world
wars and Vietnam.[99] This is a small and rather varied sample, and she
does not quantify, but her discussion is acute. In her first pages, she says
that war gave some the sense of awesome power, the "initiation into the
power of life and death." One U.S. veteran says killing was thrilling, calling the bazooka and machine gun a "magic sword" or a "grunt's Excali-
bur" because "all you do is move that finger so imperceptibly, just a wish
flashing across your mind like a shadow, not even a full brain synapse,
and poof! in a blast of sound and energy and light a truck or a house or
even people disappear, everything flying and settling back into dust."[100]

Bourke adds: "This book contains innumerable examples of men like
the shy and sensitive First World War soldier who recounted that the
first time he stuck a German with his bayonet was 'gorgeously satisfying

... exultant satisfaction.' " A lieutenant found that bayoneting Prussians was "beautiful work." "Sickening yet exhilarating butchery" was reported to be "joy unspeakable" by a New Zealand sapper.[101] Ferguson agreed, asserting (though without presenting any evidence) that combat was often seen as exciting, adventurous, even fun, because of the danger: "Many men simply took pleasure in killing"; "Men kept fighting because they wanted to."[102]

Bourke then approvingly presents Marshall's work on nonfiring, although it emphasizes the exact opposite sentiments to those she has just detailed. She recounts just two instances of "passive combat personnel." One was World War I soldiers practicing live-and-let-live. We have seen that this was a rational response to fear, not an expression of moral qualms. Her second case is of World War II American paratroopers caught in a defile by a causeway in Normandy in June 1944. Anthony King gives us more details. This battalion had repeatedly distinguished itself in action. Yet although now receiving incoming fire inflicting casualties, the paratroopers did not return fire, despite urging by their commander, Lieutenant Colonel Robert Cole. The official report said they were pinned down, but Cole was more critical. He said they would fire only if he or another officer was standing right behind them, yelling. "*Not one man in twenty-five* voluntarily used his weapon," he emphasized. But Cole saved the situation by brandishing his bayonet and shouting "Charge!" As he charged forward, a quarter of the battalion immediately followed him, and more joined in as the charge gathered momentum. The German positions were taken, though with heavy American casualties.[103] Cole won the Medal of Honor for that charge, and in the end his men were not as passive as he suggested. Sadly, Cole was killed before he could receive the medal. He did not suggest that moral qualms caused his soldiers to fail to fire.

In the third and most penetrating section of Bourke's book, she never again mentions Marshall or passivity or nonfiring. Nor are there the promised "innumerable examples" of men enjoying killing. Soldiers had more complex feelings about the enemy. Said one: "Face to face with them you couldn't feel a personal hatred, they were like ourselves, manipulated by statesmen and generals and war-mongers. We were—they were—cannon fodder."[104] But this did not stop them from killing. During Allied bombardments they could feel pity for enemy soldiers, while also declaring that they would kill as many of them as they could. Bourke adds: "With occasional exceptions most servicemen killed the enemy with a sense that they were performing a slightly distasteful but necessary job."[105] She says war allows men to commit legitimate killing that in peacetime they would view with horror. They often felt they should feel guilty for killing, but this feeling made them feel their humanity was restored, and this helped them return to civilian life. "Men who did not feel guilt were somehow less than human, or were insane: guiltless killers were immoral."[106]

Thus, moral qualms among Allied soldiers were felt but were massaged into willingness to kill, although rarely with enthusiasm. Reports of German or Japanese atrocities also helped reduce remorse, as did racism among the soldiers in Asian but not European theaters. But Bourke also emphasizes Allied atrocities against prisoners and civilians in all three wars. Most soldiers disapproved of them in principle, for military norms had created a clear distinction between legitimate and illegitimate killing. This "maintained men's sanity throughout the war and helped insulate them against agonizing guilt and numbing brutality."[107] But practices differed. Among Blake's cases, half mention between them twenty-five cases of killing prisoners, and five more speak of it as a general practice. Even when such killing was stopped by an officer, no action was taken against the perpetrators.[108] The issue presented genuine dilemmas for soldiers. Should prisoners be killed if guarding them would remove soldiers from battle, or if they might escape and rejoin their army? Yes, of course, said most—as they had at Agincourt in 1415. They could sympathize with the killers, aware that if ordered to commit atrocities themselves, they might have also complied.

Yet sadism was rare and few frontline soldiers were motivated by deep hatred for the enemy. Bourke sees more hatred in the rear. Women were no less aggressive than men, she says, in a blow to feminist essentialism. A large body of research shows that those firing from a distance had more hateful views of the enemy than those firing at short range; that rear troops expressed greater hatred of the enemy; that frontline troops treated prisoners better than did rear troops; that U.S. civilians hated the enemy more than did U.S. troops; that troops still in the United States hated the enemy more than those in war theaters; and that hatred for the Japanese was stronger among Americans fighting in Europe than among those fighting in the Pacific theater.[109] "Anger comes out," says Collins, "where there is little or no confrontational fear."[110]

Finally, contradicting her earlier remarks, Bourke says extreme aggression was rare. Soldiers described this as men losing self-control: "He lost his head completely," "His blood was up," he was acting out of his real character, they said—just as American Civil War soldiers had said. That murderous aggression was an aberration comforted them. But "survivor's guilt," remorse for having lived while one's comrades died, far outweighed "killer's guilt."[111]

King suggests that Marshall's conclusions had come from his interview with Lieutenant Colonel Cole and a collective discussion with an infantry battalion that had withstood a Japanese assault on the tiny Makin Islands of the Pacific.[112] Marshall reported that only the thirty-six machine gunners of a battalion of over two hundred men fired at the enemy, and dead Japanese were found only in front of these machine gun positions.[113] The battalion had mistakenly thought that the Japanese had already been defeated and had prepared only weak defensive positions on landing on the island. When the Japanese unexpectedly attacked, there was panic and most of them went to ground. The official history offers an excuse for their passivity in terms of the layout of the battlefield, but King doubts this, for the battalion's performance had been inadequate on the previous day when panic had generated massive overfiring. He adds that a subsequent assault on Kwajalein Island saw minimal firing from another battalion in which machine gunners and one active sergeant saved the day. Obviously, there were fallible battalions in the American army. But in Marshall's own account there is no hint of moral qualms, and in his other portrayals of engagements, American soldiers performed quite well—with no cases of moral qualms.

King emphasizes passivity among American troops in Europe.[114] Officers complained of units pinned down by fire, unwilling to reveal their positions by firing back, overreliant on artillery, conceding field fire superiority to the Germans. King lambastes British, Canadian, and American troops in Normandy, blaming poor officer quality and inadequate infantry training. He, Francis Steckel, and Martin van Creveld say that Allied soldiers were inferior to the German enemy, being overly dependent on air and artillery superiority.[115] This was probably true for most of the war, contrary to the democratic triumphalism of Reiter and Stam.[116] Of course, by then the Germans were scraping the bottom of the manpower barrel and facing defeat. But none of these authors makes any reference to moral qualms.

Robert Engen details a survey of Canadian officers in Normandy immediately after a battle. The officers complained about many things, but not nonfiring. Two-thirds thought the rate of fire was adequate, one-third complained of far too much firing. Most officers envied their German counterparts' ability to achieve a limited, controlled, and accurate rate of fire.[117] Craig Cameron's study of U.S. Marines in the Pacific theater finds no evidence of nonfiring or passivity. On the contrary, the Guadalcanal campaign was full of wounded or sick men who should have been hospitalized. A marine would not "crap out" if that would put a heavier burden on his buddies. Marines were an elite force, of course. He says that on Okinawa, a terrible encounter forced more men to leave the lines for the hospital, but without any suggestion of skulking. Cameron concludes that Marshall's "is a specious argument to assuage moral sensibilities among civilians." In reality, he says, "the killer exists in men all along and has simply to be brought out and encouraged. Americans proved as adept and ruthless in the exercise of violence as their totalitarian enemies."[118] Performance and firing rates obviously varied between military units, although moral qualms seem to have been absent.

Ben Shalit, a military psychologist, thought he might corroborate Marshall's nonfiring with Israeli soldiers in Middle Eastern wars. But he failed. Nearly 100 percent of ordinary infantry and elite commandos fired when ordered or when circumstances demanded. He also finds overfiring, which is effective in relieving fear, since the drumming and thudding of the weapon covers up the throbbing of fear within the soldier. Shalit describes the commander of an Israeli commando raid counting the bullet holes in enemy bodies and reprimanding his soldiers: "Is it necessary to drill a man with 25 bullets when 2 would do?"[119]

Finally comes an oft-cited study by the British Defense Operational Analysis Establishment's field studies division, which in 1986 is said to have examined the killing effectiveness of military units in over one hundred nineteenth- and twentieth-century battles. The research compared real data from these battles with hit rates by test subjects in simulated battles using pulsed laser weapons that could neither inflict nor receive harm from a virtual "enemy." The test subjects killed far more of the simulated enemy than the number reflected in the real historical casualty rates. Yet the subjects could experience neither fear nor loathing in this experimental setting, nor the noise, blindness, chaos, and ducking and weaving of actual battle. It was a tension-free game of skill, a demonstration of the superiority of rationality in contexts far removed from reality. Moreover, I have failed to find the original report of this experiment and note that all who have cited it use virtually identical words. It may not exist except as an internet myth, but if it does, we should probably ignore it.

None of these studies mentions moral qualms as a reason for passivity under fire, except for Bourke's account of how qualms are overcome. Fear was the problem, though soldiers could manage it. The generals recognized this was the most they could expect. U.S. General George Patton reputedly said, "Courage is fear holding on a minute longer," and U.S. General Omar Bradley allegedly said, "Bravery is the capacity to perform properly even when scared half to death."

Surveys of American Soldiers: Buddies, Latent Ideology, and Task Completion

The surveys by Stouffer and his colleagues found that American soldiers' primary sense of solidarity and loyalty was not to country, army, or regiment, but to the small group of comrades with whom they shared their life in and out of battle. They fought not to let their buddies down, thus enforcing group norms and supporting the individual under battle stress.[120] "Buddy theory" has been repeatedly endorsed; many soldiers have said how much of their lives they shared with comrades, and how intimate were their relations. Sebastian Junger has vividly expressed this among U.S. soldiers in Afghanistan: "The Army might screw you and your girlfriend might dump you and the enemy might kill you, but the shared commitment to safeguard one another's lives is unnegotiable and only deepens with time. The willingness to die for another person is a form of love that even religions fail to inspire, and the experience of it changes a person profoundly."[121] Of course, Islamist terrorists also experience this.

Soldiers sometimes feared being called a coward by their buddies more than they feared death. Social fear mitigated existential fear, as we saw in the U.S. Civil War. Doubts have arisen in high-casualty warfare, in which primary groups are broken up with the arrival of unknown recruits, as in the Civil War and among U.S. Marines in Okinawa. It was especially so in the German army on the Eastern Front in World War II. Yet these Germans carried on fighting and dying right to the end, driven back even to the gates of Berlin. Bartov thinks this runs contrary to buddy theory, doubly so because the Wehrmacht had been originally recruited on a local basis, which at first intensified buddy relations.[122] Yet for Stouffer and his colleagues, long-term friendships did not much matter. It was their mutual interdependence in battle that generated intimacy. Charles Moskos observes: "The intensity of primary-group ties so often reported in combat units are best viewed as mandatory necessities arising from immediate life-and-death exigencies."[123] The guy next to you covered your back, eased tensions with black humor, cursed entertainingly, lied for you if you disobeyed an order or killed a civilian, cared for you if you were wounded, and if you died he would send your personal possessions to your family. Mutuality in life and death generated intense intimacy, which some described as love. New recruits quickly became buddies. They had to, or they died. The soldier, whatever his commitment to the cause or his obedience to orders, had as his primary goal staying alive. This could not be done without his primary group.

Stouffer and his colleagues also tried to establish how important buddies were. In 1944 they asked combat infantry in Europe what kept them going. The most common response was a drive to end the task or to get the war done (44 percent). Not letting your buddies down came a distant second (14 percent), followed by thoughts of home and loved ones (10 percent), and a sense of duty and self-respect (9 percent). Ideological reasons like overt patriotism totaled only 5 percent. Task completion, duty, and self-respect could be combined into an implicitly patriotic sense of institutionalized moral obligation, a latent ideology among two-thirds of the soldiers. Edward Shils said morale in small groups presupposed "a set of generalized moral predispositions or sense of obligation . . . some measure of identification with the collectivity and some sense of generalized obligation and readiness to acknowledge the legitimacy of its demands in numerous particular situations. . . . The soldiers who thought first of getting the job done must, in some way, have accepted the legitimacy of the 'job' and felt some sense of obligation to carry it out."[124]

This sense of getting the job done enabled focus on each task confronting the soldier, each piece of ground to cover, each set of movements, each sequence of firing, each minutia of ritual. Together they could partially blot out the chaos and terror all around. For the majority of the war, most German soldiers probably performed better than most American soldiers, but this was to change. Peter Mansoor and Robert Rush studied high-casualty U.S. infantry battles in Belgium in November 1944.[125] The casualties in Rush's regiment amounted to 87 percent of its original strength. Both agree with Bartov that such casualties produced the collapse of the buddy system, but they say that nevertheless the GIs grimly held on, focused on task completion each hour of each day, helped by the knowledge that they were advancing into Germany and would win the war soon and go home. The Germans, used to offensive successes, lacked comparable confidence in retreating defense, and ultimately they, not the Americans, collapsed. Battle context matters.

American soldiers shared a taboo against flag-waving patriotism. They declared that such "bullshit" was what civilians spouted, ignorant of the realities of war.[126] They were uncomfortable with civilian notions of "heroism," knowing their own imperfect behavior. They disliked having "heroes" as comrades, since their conspicuous bravery drew enemy fire like a magnet to the whole group. Most American soldiers had a "tacit and a fairly deep conviction that we were on the right side, and that the war, once we were in it, was necessary." This institutionalized ideology was important to Allied troops, as it was early in the Vietnam War.[127] Soldiers were not so committed if they thought the war was either unjust or unwinnable, as was common in the later phases of the Vietnam War.

Morale could not be maintained forever. There was a learning curve. Many novices found it difficult at first to kill a clearly visible enemy, but they almost always did fire, and then they got used to it. They became "battle-wise," effective task-completing soldiers doing their duty, after about ten days of battle, at peak efficiency after around twenty-five days. But combat went on and on. Though historical battles had often brought as many casualties as modern ones, they occurred over much less time—hours or a day or two at most. There was then a long period until the next battle. Soldiers had to gear themselves up for one single traumatic event at a time. In contrast, modern battles have ground on and the outcome remained inconclusive. Beset by constant stress, soldiers declined in fighting spirit. After about forty days of battle, they were emotionally shattered, kept their heads down, and did the minimum. Patrols lay down somewhere safe, imaginary ambushes were claimed, sickness and self-wounding rates increased. Campaign cycle effectiveness was maintained for up to 140 or 180 or 200 days, say different authorities, but then the soldier felt acute incapacitating neurosis, becoming so hypersensitive to shell fire, overtly cautious, and jittery that he was ineffective.

Of British World War II casualties, 10–20 percent were said by the authorities to be psychiatric. Many soldiers exposed to continuous combat virtually broke down.[128] U.S. military psychiatrists said of the soldier: "Mental defects became so extreme that he could not be counted on to relay a verbal order. He remained in or near his slit trench, and during acute actions took little or no part, trembling constantly."[129] Yet most soldiers reduced their commitment, took fewer risks, and suffered. A more extreme indicator of unwillingness to fight is desertion, though it is greatly affected by whether the soldier is near or far from home. Desertion rates in World War II were mostly around 5–6 percent, at the low end for most wars—and lower than in peacetime because soldiers were abroad. German army desertions rapidly increased through 1944 to 21 percent—end-of-war demoralization in addition to soldiers on leave simply failing to return.

The lethality of weapons meant soldiers were no longer standing in massed columns and lines. They would be instantly massacred if they did. They were dispersed in cover over the battlefield. "Where the effective soldier on the linear battlefield had to be an automaton, the effective soldier on the dispersed battlefield had to be autonomous."[130] Military training involved less drilling and more emphasis on task completion, as both Marshall and Stouffer had recommended. Each unit is set a task, each soldier is trained to accomplish a subtask within that. He is taught that to survive, the men of a unit need each other to perform their tasks, which officially encouraged the buddy system. It is hammered into soldiers that if they stay focused on task achievement, they are most likely to survive. Soldiers are comforted if they feel they can control their survival. After long exposure to combat, however, the soldier may perceive that he cannot. Then he loses focus on task accomplishment and his morale sinks.

Fighter Pilots: World War II and Korea

More evidence comes from fighter pilots in World War II. I add pilots in Korea because their experience was similar, and many had also flown in World War II. Fighter pilots are interesting because, unlike the infantry, they are autonomous, up alone in the sky. Even in their standard four-plane formations, the four pilots had to make their own split-second decisions in dogfights.[131] In the Korean War dogfights were even faster, for this was the first war involving jet planes, American F-86 Sabres against MiG-15s.

There was great inequality in killing. Only a few pilots shot down most of the enemy. Aces, those who shot down five or more enemy planes, formed only 5 percent of all U.S. fighter pilots, yet they downed 37–68 percent of enemy planes, a number that varied according to theater. Seventy-five percent of pilots had no kills at all.[132] The British figures for the Battle of Britain are not quite so skewed: 39 percent of pilots shot down at least one enemy plane, 15 percent more than one, and

8 percent qualified as aces, having shot down five or more. Collins suggests this supports Marshall's arguments about nonfiring and perhaps moral qualms.[133]

I disagree. There were four reasons for the uneven distribution of kills.

1. Flying was an extraordinarily taxing job. High accident rates not due to combat killed 6,000 RAF personnel in World War II (including bomber crews).[134] Combat was much more difficult. Making split-second decisions at high speed in a juddering plane was needed to outmaneuver an enemy pilot and to get inside the potential kill zone in his rear, when both planes were traveling at 560 kilometers per hour, and over 725 in Korea. The skill and strength to fire steadily while maneuvering were required to counter the enemy's evasive response and to avoid threats from other enemy planes. The crucial decision-making periods lasted two seconds. "Situational awareness" and the ability to perceive and analyze rapidly moving objects in a three-dimensional environment were rare skills.[135] Pilots rapidly trained and thrust into battle failed to shoot down enemy planes because this skill level was beyond them. One American flyer in Europe estimated that "there were probably 20 per cent or so of our Group pilots on a mission who would aggressively seek combat. Another large block—60 per cent—would, when conditions were right, prove to be moderately effective. Then there were those that were of little use in air-to-air combat no matter what the conditions of encounter happened to be."[136] Similar figures were given for Korea.[137] So skill levels helped produce different firing and killing rates.

2. This produced a statistical artifact. Many novices, especially if low-skilled, were quickly casualties, and so they never fired before they died or were transferred out for poor performance. A continuous flow of short-termers increased the total number of pilots but barely increased the number of kills. A few barely competent pilots did survive long-term, capable of keeping in formation and little else, protected by luck and by comrades.

3. Most World War II missions, especially American ones, were flown in the last two years of the war, when the Luftwaffe and

the Japanese Air Force were largely destroyed. There were now more Allied fighters, which increased the number of pilots who never made kills. Most of their later missions were to escort the bombers over Germany and Japan, to deter the enemy from sending up their last fighters to attack the bombers. Ground flak fire also concentrated on bombers, not fighters. Most fighter missions never encountered an enemy fighter. In their four-year war even the American aces fired in only about one third of missions.[138] In the last two years of the war, the average American fighter pilot could expect to meet a German fighter once in twenty-five missions. This also increased the number of nonfirers and nonkillers.

4. There were selection biases. The best planes were assigned to the best pilots, and the best of the best were given the leader role. The standard American flight pattern (RAF patterns differed slightly) consisted of four planes, a first "element" of the leader and his wingman, plus the leader of a second element and his wingman. The first leader's role was to shoot down enemy planes, and his wingman's role was to protect his back. The second element leader might join in if the opportunity arose, but both wingmen were explicitly forbidden to fire unless an emergency arose. Thus, the best pilots were entrusted with the leader positions, and in Korea the leaders got 82 percent of the claimed kills. On rare occasions wingmen got kills too, but over half the pilots on missions almost never got a chance of downing the enemy.[139] So it was fully intended that only a few pilots would get a disproportionate number of the kills.

A further study is often quoted claiming that half the F-86 pilots never fired their guns, and of those who had fired, only 10 percent had ever hit anything—astonishing figures. This claim was made in an article by two military psychologists, Blair Sparks and Oliver Neiss.[140] But they give no evidence for the assertion, instead proceeding to the policy proposals that dominate their article—more understanding of pilots' psychology (and more employment for psychologists!). It clearly serves the authors' purpose if they can claim such failure. Such a finding would surely be widely discussed, but I found no such evidence or discussion. Until a real study is found, I am skeptical.

A further possible indicator of pilot frailty is the aborted sortie, a pilot turning back from the mission before combat. In World War II the U.S. Eighth Air Force calculated this for bombers. In January 1944, 70 percent of the 6,770 bombers completed their operational missions. Of the 30 that did not, 61 percent turned back for weather-related problems, and 29 percent for mechanical reasons. That means 3 percent of the total number of pilots might have been faking it. The RAF total rate of abortions among fighters was about 10 percent.[141] On landing, the aborting RAF plane was examined and the pilot had to defend himself before a panel of officers. If pilots repeated abortions, alarm bells went off about possible "Low Moral Fibre" and the pilot might be transferred. The social pressures on pilots to perform their duty was intense in segregated airbase communities. This forced some who should have turned back because of plane problems to continue with the mission, and with defective speed or maneuverability they might be shot down.

No study suggests that failure to shoot came from moral qualms. Pilots respected enemy pilots, but during fast maneuvering they rarely saw them clearly. Werrell gives us Korean combat stories for over thirty pilots. Only one says he felt bad after shooting up a MiG. He saw the pilot was in agony, trapped in a burning cockpit. His response was to put him out of his agony by killing him. Yet one norm was shared by both sides: once a pilot ejected, he would not be shot at. Kills meant planes, not pilots. Blake says U.S. World War II pilots describe the plane, not the pilot, as the enemy and even refer to it as "he" and "him."[142]

So it was mainly technical, selection, and mission reasons that made kills so imbalanced, although perhaps around 10 percent of pilots were prevented from engaging in effective combat by fear and tension. They had every reason to be fearful, given the death rate. But once in a dogfight, pilots had no time for fear. Total task absorption brought exhilaration and thrust fear onto the back burners. It was not so for the more passive bomber crews who feared death more, although they were only half as likely to be killed. Mark Wells says that British bomber crews had "occasional reservations" about the civilian casualties they were inflicting, but he does not mention anyone failing to bomb.[143]

A Korean War ace said after his first kills: "I was so excited that the thought of having killed two human beings didn't enter my mind. In the first place, I had been spurred to action out of anger; in the second place, the planes I had just shot down were objects, not people." Sherwood says pilots in Korea enjoyed pleasure and pride in their kills.[144] That all countries' aces were feted as national heroes gave them an incentive to kill. "It's love of the sport rather than sense of duty that makes you go on without minding how much you are shot up," said one.[145] In Korea pilots volunteered to extend their tours and fly on holidays. Casualties in Korea were low, for this was a short war fought with more pilots, many with World War II experience. Deaths were about 10 percent, though a little higher among pilots with kills, and higher still among aces.[146] The pilots in slower fighter-bombers faced ground fire. Sherwood notes that 147 fighters were lost in air combat, but 816 planes of all types were shot down by ground fire.[147]

In World War II, pilot casualties were enormous. RAF Bomber Command (which included fighters) calculated that 51 percent of all aircrew were killed or missing as a result of combat operations, 12 percent were killed in accidents, and 12 percent were shot down and became prisoners of war. Only 24 percent came away unscathed, a very low figure. Casualties in the U.S. Eighth Air Force in Europe were similar: 57 percent killed or missing, 17 percent lost through wounds or accidents, only 25 percent unscathed.[148] German and Japanese pilot casualties were even higher once they began losing the air war. Their courage in carrying on was suicidal.

Despite the greater probability of death, the morale of American air crews was higher than it was among infantry, and fighter pilots' morale was higher than other air crews'.[149] This was due to pride in their skill; the autonomy and freedom they enjoyed in the sky; the ability to fight back against all attacks; their high status as "heroes" during the war; and the segregated, comradely, and controlling community in which they lived. In the caste system of air forces, the aces enjoyed the highest status and had every incentive to keep on claiming more kills.[150] Ideology didn't come into it. In Korea, pilots developed what Sherwood calls "flight suit attitude": "a sense of self-confidence and pride that verged on arrogance. . . . The aircraft of preference was the high-performance, single-seat fighter. . . . This culture placed a premium on cockiness and informality. A fighter pilot spent more time in a flight suit than in a uniform. In his world, status was based upon flying ability, not degrees, rank, or 'officer' skills. . . . Military ancestry and institutional traditions were irrelevant to him; instead, elitism in the Air Force was defined by skill, courage, and plane type."[151]

Drilling and discipline were largely replaced by a teacher-pupil relationship during training. Higher officers then ordered their subordinates to perform the missions, but in the sky they were autonomous. Their high morale gave them that extraordinary courage which has impressed all commentators. They went into battle facing a high risk of death, under great emotional stress, but without flinching. This was the peak of courage, not the sudden adrenaline-charged act of the infantry hero, but a two- to three-hour feat of endurance, repeated many times, without the descending rhythm of commitment of long-serving infantrymen.

Conclusion

This half century contained the two deadliest wars in history, fought by millions of soldiers. There were a few "heroes," adrenaline-fueled soldiers rushing headlong at the enemy, while the other extreme of moral qualms at killing was also rare. Alas, qualms usually came after the war, too late to save lives but disturbing the mental balance of veterans. Soldiers usually believed that this was a just war. In the second war "transcendent ideology" was important in the Wehrmacht and in imperial Japanese forces (as we saw in chapter 7), and was absolutely crucial in the Red Army. Among the Western Allies such overt ideology was rare in either war. Dominant instead was a combination of immanent and institutionalized ideology providing latent patriotic morale, which was linked to a sense of duty in completing a necessary task. Then add buddy pressures and a sense that eventual victory was coming. They were enough to keep fear manageable and restrict shirking to keeping one's head down. In long campaigns the pressure ground the soldier down, often ending in psychological degradation. Since the enemy was experiencing the same decline, the war effort was not threatened. Fighter pilots differed, since for them task completion was enjoyable and kills brought them high status as warriors. These rewards made them genuinely courageous, willing to accept the higher level of risk their role entailed.

This tells us little about human nature, except how malleable it is. But it does tell us how mighty social power relations are, capable of disciplining men into behavior that would be unthinkable to them in peacetime: repeatedly trying to kill others while exposing themselves to risk of death or mutilation. Women had a different war experience. Those in the forces were sometimes exposed to danger, though not in the front lines, except in the Red Army, but most women were required only to offer support to their men and to move into their jobs. But for most men who fought, experiencing war from the ground up was a socially induced hell. The second world war was a rare just war, rational for the defenders and reinforced by a just peace settlement and a balance of power that ensured fewer interstate wars thereafter.

CHAPTER THIRTEEN

Fear and Loathing on the
Battlefield III

Communist Wars

T HE MAIN POSTWAR STRUGGLE was between the United States
and the Soviet Union, which had taken over from fascism as
a rival for world domination. Despite a scare or two, the
Cold War saw mutually pragmatic behavior, scaling down the
threat of nuclear war, agreeing, often implicitly, to understandings that
deflected conflict to confrontation between proxies within each superpower's zone of interest. Overall, American and Soviet foreign policy was
bad news for many individual countries of the south, but it was good
news in diminishing the chances of nuclear war. Fear of another major
war was the main deterrent. Yet there were many smaller, often covert
armed interventions by both sides. Barry Blechman and Stephen Kaplan
found 215 cases between 1946 and 1975 when U.S. administrations used
armed force short of actual war—that is, MIDs—to achieve their political objectives around the world. They were successful at attaining their
objectives in 73 percent of cases after six months, though the success rate
declined to 44 percent after three years, a rather mixed record.[1] Kaplan
found 190 Soviet interventions between 1944 and 1979.[2] Only in Eastern
Europe and Afghanistan were these major interventions; otherwise the
Soviets were rather cautious. Again there were rather mixed outcomes.
But attaining American or Soviet objectives did not necessarily benefit
the peoples at the receiving end.

Chapter 5 of volume 4 of *The Sources of Social Power* analyzed American foreign policy during the Cold War, concluding that in some regions it was irrational, blinded by an anticommunist ideology that saw foreign left-of-center movements as demons or dupes, their activities encouraging communism or anarchy. U.S. administration policy was to undermine them, covertly or openly, by financing, arming, and supplying logistical aid to rightist states and armed groups. Occasionally U.S. forces intervened directly. Such policies perversely pushed liberals and social democrats in these countries further to the left, occasionally into the embrace of the Soviet Union, weakening the chances of implementing much-needed reforms that would have brought the United States more allies and a better business environment for American firms.

There were two major hot wars in the Cold War period, in Korea and Vietnam. Although they embodied a traditional geopolitical struggle between great powers, they were also struggles between rival transcendent ideologies, one seeking an eventually communist world, the other a world of capitalist democracy—although in reality the Soviets did not resemble socialist ideals, nor did their allies, while the United States was not cultivating regimes resembling democracy. The United States was fully engaged in these two wars, as was China in one of them. Soviet participation was less direct, primarily through proxies, covert actions, and sending supplies. The United States treated its enemies in both wars as proxies for a Soviet-led world order. The ideologies were transmitted to their armed forces but to greatly differing degrees, as we will now see.

The Korean War

The Chinese People's Liberation Army (PLA) was highly experienced, first from its long war against the Japanese and then in the Chinese Civil War, ended in 1949. Many soldiers in the final Manchurian campaign of these wars had been Koreans fighting against Japanese subjugation of their homeland. After World War II, the Korean peninsula was divided at the thirty-eighth parallel in a truce between North and South Korean dictatorships, communist and capitalist. Americans advising the South missed an opportunity to pressure for land reform, which would have eroded communist support in the South, perhaps deterring the North's invasion. The United States remedied this error after the Korean War. But two Koreas could have continued to exist without war.

From 1946 to 1950 insurrections swept the South, causing perhaps 100,000 casualties, mainly through massive government repression. So in June 1950 North Korean forces invaded the South to assist the rebels and create a single communist state over the whole peninsula. The North's ruler, Kim Il Sung, perceived that the southern government, led by Syngman Rhee, was weakened by faction fighting and had a corrupt and mutinous army. He was also encouraged by the fact that U.S. Secretary of State Dean Acheson had not included Korea in what was called the U.S defense perimeter. Maybe the United States would stay out of Korea. Kim Il Sung had actually waited too long (for the insurrection was almost over) for the go-ahead from an initially hesitant Stalin, but Kim confidently told him that he could ignite an "internal explosion" in the South. Mao was not involved. Kim's preparations were secretive, thus giving the United States no chance to warn that it might retaliate. Kim assumed a lightning strike would force the Americans, who had a small force in the South, into a conciliatory response. If it did not, he believed Stalin would help him fight. Yet Stalin had no intention of committing himself to war. His idea was to fight through his North Korean proxy. He saw gain in either inflicting a humiliating withdrawal on the United States or in embroiling that nation in a costly war. The latter was the outcome.

The core of North Korea's army, the NKPA, had fought against the Japanese in China and Manchuria. On June 25, 1950, 75,000 NKPA troops swept down the peninsula and captured Seoul after three days. U.S. troops supported the South Koreans from July, but the North Koreans drove U.S. and South Korean forces southward. U.S. forces found themselves embroiled in a civil war far from home under the aegis of the United Nations. When the Soviets, who had earlier walked out of the UN, reappeared and vetoed the war in the Security Council, the United States took the decision to the UN General Assembly, then dominated by U.S. allies. The United States acted in support of an ally, as it would repeatedly do over the next decades, in the hope of stopping the spread of communism and maintaining U.S. power across the world. Vital national interests were not at stake. Anticommunists led by Senator Joseph McCarthy had denounced President Truman as soft on communism, so Truman had to show his toughness for reasons of domestic policy. The Korean invasion came just after a successful Soviet atomic bomb test, the communist victory in the Chinese Civil War, and the Sino-Soviet mutual defense pact. The "who lost China" recriminations roiling Washington could not be allowed to transition into "who lost Korea," although many in Washington knew Syngman Rhee was no democrat. American leaders would not describe their country as "imperial," but they were seeking global domination and like leaders of all empires could not stomach the "humiliation" inflicted by communists on retreating U.S. forces. The global stature of the United States was threatened. So factors both political and reputational, both personal and national, made American intervention inevitable. Kim was on his own.

The NKPA was initially superior. Its core was experienced in mountain warfare, ideologically committed, and faced by a poorly organized South Korean army (ROK) that featured a corrupt officer class and low morale. The NKPA adapted the political practices of the Chinese PLA, which I will detail later—cell organization, collective political meetings, and much ideological instruction, although this was somewhat undercut by its harsh discipline and inequalities of rank. General Douglas MacArthur, commanding U.S. troops in Korea, underestimated it, boasting, "I can handle it with one arm tied behind my back."[3] Yet, keeping to the hills, the NKPA infiltrated between enemy forces, bypassing the roads dominated by American communications and control systems, and forced a series of retreats. Only around the Pusan enclave in the far south were the Americans and the ROK finally able to form a defensive line. The United States was now pouring in forces, followed by other UN contingents, and the NKPA had to frontally attack them. Its losses of men and materiel mounted, but its attacks kept coming, reflecting soldiers capable of great sacrifice. By this time the Americans had shifted their initial disdain for the NKPA and rated them highly as opponents. Defeat for America was unthinkable—but possible.

But in September 1950 General MacArthur launched an amphibious landing farther north behind enemy lines, at Inchon, forcing the NKPA into a two-front war for which it was ill-equipped. Outnumbered as well as outgunned, exposed to massive American bombing, it retreated. The National Security Council recommended that American forces stop at the thirty-eighth parallel, which would be mission accomplished. But Truman listened to the bellicose MacArthur, and the U.S. and UN forces pressed on northward. The North Korean retreat became a rout. Kim told Chinese General Peng Dehuai that his army was collapsing and that he could communicate with fewer than 50,000 of his troops.[4] Advance parties of Americans reached the Yalu River on the Chinese border. MacArthur had favored hot pursuit to prevent the NKPA from having time to regroup. But this also meant that the goal had shifted from re-storing the prewar status quo to "liberating" North Korea from commu-nism. A compliant United Nations passed the necessary supporting resolution. It was folly.

MacArthur was on China's doorstep, menacing Manchuria, which contained much of China's heavy industry. Mao was faced with U.S. domination right up to his border. Chinese pride was infuriated that U.S. soldiers were openly urinating into the Yalu River on the border. Few in Washington believed the Chinese would fight, a belief that was the prod-uct of American contempt for an underdeveloped country with a suppos-edly third-rate army that was allegedly controlled by the Soviets—and Stalin clearly did not want to fight. Some Americans who knew China and Mao cautioned against aggression, but they were purged in the "who lost China?" power struggle. Domestic political factionalism obstructed rational thinking.

Mao was steeped in the "parabellum" tradition of Chinese strategic thought discussed in chapter 6, but with the Marxist twist that armed struggle would solve both class and international contradictions.[5] His foreign policy had been to restore Taiwan by force, but the U.S. fleet had moved to protect it and China lacked an effective navy. Mao had to back down and was transferring troops from south to north before the Korean War loomed. Thus, he had the troops available locally to aid Kim. He thought this was the moment to show Chinese power to the world, sur-prising Stalin and stunning Truman and MacArthur. His covert prepara-tions began just in case force was needed. A Chinese People's Volunteer Force had been formed, supposedly an autonomous army of volunteers, a pure fiction enabling China to avoid declaring war on the United States. The initial plan was to invade and stop near the thirty-eighth parallel. But MacArthur's push northward had been too rapid for this. In accor-dance with parabellum doctrines of flexibility and deception, Mao shifted to an invasion while concealing force size in order to lure U.S. troops into action against what they would believe was only a small Chinese force. Then the Americans would be enveloped and hurled back south-ward, perhaps out of Korea altogether.

In late September and early October 1950, Mao made only vague threats to the United States, and after October 13 he fell silent, feigning weakness. This had the desired effect of luring MacArthur even more rap-idly northward, leaving big gaps between his forward units and his commu-nications and supply center. American forces were now stretched out over large areas along both coasts. In late October, Mao ordered large PLA forces quietly across the border. They moved secretively down the mountain chain, their orders to continue disguising the army's true size. A small Chinese force engaged the Americans and then retreated, giving the impression of weakness. Some Chinese soldiers were sent out to be captured and give false information to the enemy. The idea was to bypass MacArthur's advance units and envelop his force from the flanks and the rear.

The surprise mass attack of November 26 proved highly successful, disorienting the Americans. It led to a defeat at the Chosin Reservoir (Lake Changjin to the Chinese), unprecedented in the history of American forces—the consequence of American overconfidence. There was a hasty U.S.-UN retreat southward, and the Chinese briefly took Seoul, the South's capital. But a counterattack brought the front lines back to around the thirty-eighth and thirty-seventh parallels. The United States by this point had abandoned hopes of seizing the whole of the peninsula and shifted back to the original goal of restoring the antebellum status quo. This was now also the PLA's goal, aware that it did not have the firepower to take more territory. Both limited their aspirations and signaled willingness to negotiate. It took another two years of stalemated fighting to secure a truce.

UN Forces

The contrast between the UN and Chinese armies was marked. The South Korean ROK was the largest component of the allied forces. Its troops began the war in poor shape, their morale low. They gradually improved to the point where they could sometimes handle North Korean forces, though they remained inferior to Chinese forces. Of the foreign UN forces, over 80 percent were American, mostly draftees. Most did not know why they were fighting, nor were they told why.[6] The others were drawn from forty-one countries, mixing professional and conscripted troops. Nearly 60,000 British soldiers constituted the second-largest foreign force. Almost no one in the UN force believed deeply in their cause in the way that soldiers in the American Civil War and World War II had. Indeed, they reacted without much thought of ideology in terms of survival on the battlefield. As one American recalled:

> I didn't feel I was defending the port of Pusan, or the rights of the South Koreans, or the interests of the United States. I was

simply trying to stay alive. To survive from one moment to the next, to survive the day, to survive the next day. Some people are exhilarated by combat. They love it. They seem to thrive on it. I knew people like that. Most people though, ninety-nine percent of them, are scared to death. Including myself. It's only after it's all over that the grand design falls into place, and you begin to see what you had a hand in doing.

The war hero Lewis Millett was among the 1 percent. He described a bayonet charge in terms we have already encountered, overwhelmed by emotions and adrenaline, completely without ideology:

> I know I went berserk. When you hit someone in the throat with a bayonet, another one in the head, you got blood spraying up all over you, nobody's going to stay rational. In a bayonet charge, you're not rational in the first place. . . . You can do things that would normally be impossible. The adrenaline gets in there, and you do things that are just physically not possible. During that attack I stuck a Chinaman and threw him out of the foxhole on my bayonet and stuck him again on the way down. Well, you can't do that normally. Then afterward I was so weak. You could have touched me with your finger and I'd have fallen down. After it was all over I sat down and couldn't get up. I'd used up all this tremendous energy doing all these things, and I was completely drained.[7]

King is scathing about the battle performance of this army, inadequately trained and unmotivated.[8] Once the Chinese arrived on the battlefield, UN soldiers had a tendency to "bug out." They ran away when under attack, and they often went to ground in attack rather than press on to Chinese positions, which would have provided them more cover. Rudy Tomedi confirms this from interviews with U.S. veterans, and so does Brent Watson for Canadian troops.[9] None attributes poor performance to moral qualms, though Watson mentions one Canadian who became distressed after the war: "I knew I killed people, and sometimes I have trouble about that. That's the hard part about remembering. . . . Knowing that I did that and my country didn't really give a shit."[10] Fear made these soldiers passive. The Chinese were scathing about the American infantry. But U.S. forces did not need high morale. They had enormous technological superiority, and the generals used it ruthlessly in the daytime. At night, when the planes, artillery, and tanks were blind, the Chinese were in control and the Americans hunkered down.

S. L. A. Marshall wrote a report on American infantry morale in this war. His methods seem to have been the same as before. He concluded that the rate of fire by American troops in the Korean War was much higher than in World War II, "well in excess of 50 percent of troops actually committed to ground where fire may be exchanged directly with the enemy will make use of one weapon or another in the course of an engagement." He elaborated: "In the average infantry company in Korea, between 12 and 20 percent of the men not only participate actively in the firing, but exercise varying degrees of initiative in on-the-spot leading and taking personal action of a type that betters the unit position and induces cohesion. In addition to this control force, there are between 25 and 35 percent of the men who take some part in the fire action, with varying degrees of consistency, but without otherwise giving marked impulse to the course of events. . . . This showing is a substantial improvement over the participation averages among World War II troops." He added that most of the reasons for not firing were acceptable:

> The infantry soldier, so commonly met with in World War II, who made the stock answer: "I saw the enemy; I didn't fire; I don't know why," is strangely missing from the Korean scene. In fact, this reply was not returned by a single man among the non-firers. Among the reasons given by the non-firers were: "I didn't see an enemy target at any time and I thought it best to hold fire until I did." "Grenades were coming in at such a rate I couldn't get my head up." "There was a rise of earth in front of me which hid their people to view." "I was captured from behind before I saw anyone come against me." "I was helping the sergeant get the machine gun back into operation." "There were so many of them that I held fire, thinking they might pass us by." "My gun was frozen and I couldn't find another." And so on. All of these explanations made sense in the situation.[11]

These are some of the legitimate reasons to not fire in modern wars. Russell Glenn gives an overlapping list of reasons given by soldiers in the Vietnam War.[12] Such lists reduce substantially the residual number of nonfirers driven by either fear or conscience. Marshall pronounced himself satisfied with the U.S. rate of infantry fire in Korea, which is ironic given their poor overall performance, much worse than in World War II.

The buddy system was again much in evidence, especially in defense, but also in exerting some moral pressure against shirking. In one small study, two-thirds of a sample of thirty American soldiers had paired with a close buddy.[13] Most had formed a friendship before electing to fight regularly alongside each other. Raw replacements were usually taken care of by an experienced veteran. A few disliked soldiers were excluded from the buddy system, either because they were "duds," shirkers who could not be relied on for cover, or "heroes," exposing soldiers around themselves to more risk. Both were regarded as selfish and dangerous—as in earlier wars. The Western troops in Korea performed not with great distinction but with adequacy conferred by superiority in weaponry. Ironically, the Turkish contingent in the UN force, which lacked this superiority, was said to have fought the hardest.

The Chinese PLA

The Chinese "volunteers" were overwhelmingly illiterate peasants. Even most officers could not read or write. Their tactics and battle order are well described by Xiaobing Li.[14] We also have evidence from U.S. and UN sources, from Kevin Mahoney, from the recollections of Chinese generals, and from Alexander George's interviews in 1951 with three hundred Chinese POWs, of whom eighty-four were interviewed at length.[15] These sources reveal that the PLA had high morale when it entered Korea. It had won China's Civil War only two years before, having defeated Japanese and nationalist armies wielding superior weapons. The soldiers had received extensive political training telling them that this would be a just war fought with their Korean brothers against American aggression. If they did not fight, the Americans would turn on China next—a plausible communist domino theory. The soldiers thought they were fighting in defense of their homeland. The director of the political department said that after the training, 50 percent of the soldiers were ready "with a positive attitude" toward fighting in the war, 30 percent were "intermediate elements who would fight as ordered, but did not care if there was a war or not," and 20 percent were "in an unsettled state of mind," afraid of fighting the Americans and calling the Yalu River bridge the "gate of hell."[16] As was true in the Soviet Red Army, party members formed much of the first group, and they would play an important role in leading and disciplining the others.

The UN soldiers had been sent to Korea without a clear mission, which produced inferior morale, said General Du Ping, the head of the political department of the invasion. Chinese soldiers were also more experienced in the mountain warfare likely to be necessary in Korea. They believed they would prevail if they could pour superior numbers into any single point of attack.[17] There were many women in both communist armies, but not in combat roles.

The PLA had a cohesion based on relative equality between the ranks, and all its members wore the same uniforms. The PLA had an ideological variant of the buddy system. Soldiers were assigned to a cell of three or four men led by one experienced, politically reliable soldier, usually a party member. The cell held a daily mutual criticism session discussing their experience that day. Three threes (or fours) plus a political officer constituted a squad, which held self-criticism sessions once a week, lasting at least one hour. Companies held such sessions less frequently. In actual battle conditions, meetings were less frequent. Explicit ideology and moral pressure exerted through everyday political rituals are not the norm in modern armies, but they help still fear. The Chinese model "was imbued with an ethical and missionary flavor" different from those of Western armies that had no political or ideological training. They relied on latent patriotism and tried to nurture good professional soldiers, whereas the PLA wanted good communist soldiers.[18] Chinese soldiers found these meetings stressful. Being criticized for military or political failures and having to expose one's vulnerabilities, some said, felt worse than physical punishment. There was moral pressure to be an "ideal communist." George adds that many learned how to cover up and conform rather than truly eradicate "evil thoughts."[19] But this mattered less than that their actions be those of a good communist soldier.

Western media were full of stories that North Korean or Chinese soldiers showing reluctance to attack would be immediately shot, but this was not true. Mao declared that his army "must have discipline that is established on a limited democratic basis. . . . With guerillas, a discipline of compulsion is ineffective. . . . [It] must be self-imposed, because only when it is, is the soldier able to understand completely why he fights and how he must obey. This type of discipline becomes a tower of strength within the army, and it is the only type that can truly harmonize the relationship that exists between officers and men."[20]

Mahoney shows that neither communist army in Korea had violent discipline.[21] Beatings and abuses were strictly forbidden. Although executions were laid down for the worst offenses, they were rarely carried out (as was the norm in most armies by now, and as had long been traditional in China). Public shaming, as described above, and political indoctrination camps were preferred methods of dealing with deserters. Afterward the offender would be returned to frontline duty with the same unit. Party members expected to be punished more severely than non-party soldiers for the same offense. Political officers were in charge of the morale of the troops; they had welfare tasks to perform, and they were expected to be role models in combat.

This military wielded an immanent ideological power unknown to the U.S. and UN armies; it combined extensive teaching of Marxism, patriotic self-defense, and moral pressure, all reinforced by everyday collective rituals and party leadership in battle. Its members believed they were tougher than the cosseted Americans. They were told they would have a quick and easy victory, and they enjoyed surging down the peninsula, scornful of American difficulties with the terrain, darkness, and weather. Chinese infantrymen had the psychological edge, and their more confident self-reliance enabled them to fight on against increasingly unfavorable odds and lengthening supply chains. They relied on weapons of the weak.

The relative size of the armies is disputed. To many Western observers it seemed that sheer weight of numbers was the main factor in Chinese success. Yet Paul Edwards and T. R. Fehrenbach say that after the first few months, the UN and South Korean forces outnumbered the enemy, sometimes by two to one.[22] This superiority was reduced in practice by a lower proportion of fighting troops in U.S. forces. But better discipline gave the Chinese an advantage. Fehrenbach and Watson agree that they were superior in combat in the hills, especially at night. The United States controlled the roads in the daytime, especially through its air force. But in the hills of this mountainous country, and at night, when pilots could not see, the PLA was in control. The U.S. Eighth Army rated the Chinese battle efficiency as good to excellent, but the NKPA only as poor to good—but there was much variation in performance within all armies.[23]

UN and U.S. soldiers repeatedly described Chinese attacks as "human waves," mass frontal attacks by unsupported infantry aiming to overwhelm technologically superior defenders by sheer weight of numbers. A collection of Korean War memoirs by U.S. veterans contains several sensational accounts of what they perceived to be a human wave attack. Here are two of them:

> They kept coming in waves, and I kept firing. I fired my machine gun all night long. Everybody else was firing. And the artillery was dropping all around us. The artillery did a good job keeping them off us. And all night long I'm thinking. These people are crazy. They're dying in droves, and they just keep coming on.
>
> It was a typical Chinese infantry attack. No covering fire. No effort to use the terrain. Just a headlong charge by an enormous mass of men. There must have been five or six hundred of them, screaming and yelling and blowing bugles. But they didn't seem to have enough weapons. Maybe the first row would have had weapons, and the next two or three wouldn't. The second row would grab the weapons from the dead as they came on. . . . I think the only thing that saved us was the artillery we called in. . . . Another thing that stopped them was their own dead. We killed so many that they had to climb over stacks of bodies, and it definitely slowed the attack.[24]

Yet none of the soldiers quoted by Mahoney depicts bodies piled on top of each other.[25] The Chinese "did not throw away their lives in unplanned, chaotic banzai charges, as the Japanese did during World War II, but rather gave up their lives in attempting to stop, and destroy, the advancing enemy."[26] If five hundred or more Chinese attacked them, these UN and U.S. soldiers must have been caught in the eye of the storm, in the narrow sector of the front line chosen for the attack, which was the normal Chinese tactic.[27] Most UN and U.S. soldiers would have experienced such an attack only rarely.

The Chinese never referred to waves. The aim was not to strike headlong at entire enemy lines. Each Chinese regiment had a specialist reconnaissance platoon sent forward to penetrate enemy lines. It would deliberately draw fire to reveal UN positions, especially the weak-point boundaries between different U.S. and UN units. Then light forces would use stealth to get close and suddenly attack at these boundary sectors. The tactic was always to outnumber the enemy at a narrow point of attack, as in classical Chinese military theory. Chinese generals were conscious of their inferiority in weaponry and accepted that they would incur heavy casualties.[28] A Chinese battle manual suggested a superiority of between three and five attackers to each American defender, and a lesser superiority if attacking the less well-equipped ROK.[29] Such attacks created the impression of "waves" of larger numbers than they actually had.

The PLA mounted their infantry assaults at night. Relatively small PLA units would break through, flow around high ground positions held by the Americans, go behind them, and interdict their supply roads. Lack of radio communication created problems, but the PLA forces coped as best they could with a medley of bugle, whistle, and animal noise codes. They also gave detailed information down to the lowest ranks before a battle, and low-level officers could react flexibly to battle conditions. Lower ranks shared more in decision making than they did in the more hierarchical U.S. and UN forces. The memoirs of Chinese generals give insight into campaign strategy.[30] Marshal Peng Dehuai, the head of the PLA invasion force, was mindful of what his soldiers could and could not do. He saw that American command of the seas made Inchon-style landings behind his lines possible. Thus, he had to station troops down both coasts as well as on the front. Peng understood the limits imposed by inferior equipment and by logistical difficulties that mounted as they advanced farther away from their supply bases in China. Eventually trucks had to travel four hundred kilometers to the front. General Hong Xuezhi, responsible for logistics, remembers U.S. airpower as the decisive force slowing down supplies and sometimes stopping the Chinese advance.

Chinese soldiers gradually realized the full extent of their military disadvantages. Their morale declined somewhat, but they remained an obstinate foe prepared to take heavy casualties. Mao and his generals now questioned whether their tactic of "man overcoming weapons" could overcome such gross inequality of firepower. In February 1951 Mao lowered the ultimate goal from throwing U.S. and UN forces out of the peninsula to destroying as many enemy units as possible.[31] When General Matthew Ridgway took over after MacArthur's sacking in April 1951, American forces likewise shifted to "Operation Killer," inflicting maximum casualties rather than holding or taking territory. Ridgway believed he might retake the whole peninsula, but only with casualties unacceptable to the American people—and this has remained an American weakness, a healthy sign of declining militarism in American society, as emphasized by liberal theorists.

After April 1951 some POW interviewees said Chinese soldiers knew they could not win. But the army did not break, which is remarkable given that only one to two years before, the communist PLA had incorporated defeated Chinese nationalist soldiers into its ranks. Of George's seventy POWs who were junior officers or NCOs, two-thirds were former nationalist soldiers. Their commitment might have been doubted, and maybe this was why they had been taken prisoner, but there were few desertions. Yet under growing strain, combat cadres and party members had to take a more active role at the front, taking heavier losses.[32] Squad and company meetings remained active. These sent many complaints up the hierarchy, for better rifles and for air and artillery support. They did get better Soviet rifles, but only promises of airplanes and artillery. Soviet MiG fighter jets did arrive, with the pretense that the pilots were Koreans, but they were fully engaged in combat in "MiG Alley" farther north and could offer the infantry little support.

As battle lines were consolidated, PLA units lacking a modern command and control system could not exploit breakthroughs. U.S. and UN forces learned to retreat after breakthroughs, so that the Chinese intent to cut off whole divisions and destroy them could not be achieved. In a single night only small units could be surrounded in this way. Then in the daytime U.S. and UN forces would counterattack with massive firepower, recapture the land abandoned during the night, and cause large numbers of Chinese casualties. The South Koreans called it "the sea of men" confronting "the sea of fire." The Chinese spring offensive of 1951 stalled amid massive casualties, and in July Mao opened peace negotiations.[33]

They dragged on for two years. Meanwhile, combat continued, but both sides' morale dipped. Generals Peng and Yang Dezhi, in charge of combat operations, mixed attack with a defense more geared to protect the lives of their troops. Defense rested in deep trenches and tunnels protecting soldiers from bombers and artillery. Yang says the trenches stretched 6,240 kilometers, roughly the length of the Great Wall of China, while the tunnels covered about 1,250 kilometers. Li gives slightly smaller numbers.[34] Peng believed trenches and especially tunnels were key in reducing the casualty rate to acceptable levels. Attack remained the same: massed, narrow assaults at night on weak points, with breakthroughs focused on killing enemy soldiers, and then retreating back to safety.[35] Stalemate dominated the final two years, bad for the morale of both sides.[36] Given its technological superiority in conventional weaponry, the United States did not need to deploy nuclear weapons.

Truman had considered it, and Eisenhower rejected a request for them by his generals. There was a stalemate between American weaponry and Chinese morale, and the war ended with a cease-fire in July 1953, with the de facto border between the two Koreas exactly as before the war, at the thirty-eighth parallel. There was no peace treaty and there still is not.

Total casualties were enormous, and the proportion of civilian casualties was higher than in World War II. Total Korean casualties reached 3 million of a total peninsular population of 30 million. Most of the dead were North Koreans—somewhere around 215,000 soldiers and 2 million civilians, the latter due mostly to horrendous U.S. bombing that destroyed all their cities. There were no moral qualms among America's leaders when it came to killing communists. Almost a million South Korean civilians died. U.S. estimates put PLA losses at 600,000 killed or missing and 750,000 wounded, out of a total army size of 3 million, an extraordinary rate of casualties. This is also a high proportion of killed to wounded, reflecting the effect of deadlier weapons and poorer medical facilities. Yet these figures were probably exaggerated. Armies know their own casualties more accurately than the enemy's, and propaganda may get in the way. The Chinese estimated their own total casualties at 1 million, but including only 183,000 killed in action, too low a figure.[37] On the U.S. and UN side, military deaths included almost 46,000 South Koreans, 37,000 Americans, and 7,000 of other UN nations. The Chinese estimate of U.S. and UN total casualties was 390,000, too high a figure.[38] The war ended in a draw, but death had come lopsidedly, claiming far more of those fighting for communism.

The last phase of the truce negotiations involved the repatriation of POWs. It was agreed that they could be repatriated to the country of their choice. This revealed a large imbalance. Among U.S. and UN POWs, 347 chose to be repatriated to China or North Korea. In contrast, almost 22,000 of the North Korean and Chinese POWs chose not to be repatriated to their home countries. Instead, they chose to live in South Korea or Taiwan (ruled by nationalist Chinese). Additionally, almost 25,000 North Korean POWs had been earlier freed to live in the South.[39] All together, 46,000 soldiers in communist armies had in effect "deserted." Of course, they did have the option of living among their own ethnic or racial group, which the American "deserters" did not. But the remarkable morale of the communist troops had required everyday rituals and discipline. Once soldiers were languishing in a POW camp as a prisoner, that cultivation of commitment was much weaker.

So this was an ideological war in two senses: it originated in an ideological civil war within Korea, and it was aggravated by an ideological great power confrontation. On the communist but not the capitalist side the soldiers were led to perceive the war as an ideological struggle through repetitive education and everyday rituals. The combination brought together a rather general Marxian-nationalist ideology, but it was grounded in unit solidarity. This brought high morale. The war came as the North Koreans, then the Americans, and finally the Chinese each seized what it thought in Realist terms was a window of opportunity to launch a surprise attack, without sufficient thought about what response it might provoke from the enemy. Each first strike was successful in the short term, but each brought a response. This was a war of mutual overconfidence, misperceptions, and miscalculations, in which the major decisions seemed to the actors to come from rational assessment of costs and benefits of alternatives, but which proved so inaccurate that they generated a devastating war that served no rational purpose and produced neither result nor peace settlement.

The Vietnam War: American Forces

For U.S. forces the Vietnam War was again intervention in a civil war in a far-off land, a "war of choice" involving no self-defense and no authorization by the United Nations. There was no growing groundswell of domestic support, but after the Johnson administration invented North Vietnamese aggressive actions in the Gulf of Tonkin, the Tonkin War Resolution passed in the House of Representatives by 416 votes to zero, and in the Senate by 88 votes to 2. The goal was to preserve American imperial interests in Asia, more specifically to curb communism and supposedly to bring democracy to Vietnam, although the government of South Vietnam was far from democratic. But despite the anticommunism still roiling the United States, the depth of ideological commitment to the war among U.S. civilians or troops was shallow.

Between 1965 and 1973, 2.6 million U.S. military personnel served within the borders of South Vietnam. Of those, 40–60 percent either fought in combat, provided close support, or were fairly regularly exposed to enemy attack. About 7,500 of them were women, mostly nurses. Peak strength in Vietnam of 543,000 was reached in April 1968. Additionally, about 500,000 sailors and airmen in total were based offshore or in Thailand. It was a young force: the average age of enlisted men was twenty-two, of officers twenty-eight. Approximately 58,000 were killed and 304,000 were wounded, about half of them needing hospitalization. This was a major commitment of American resources.

The battlefield environment differed from that in Korea. American forces had even greater control of the skies, but jungle terrain made enemy units difficult to spot, and in open agricultural regions the enemy hid as guerillas among the people, without uniforms, difficult to identify. There were many small engagements, but only occasionally did the enemy People's Liberation Front (PLF) launch massed attacks. These were rarely successful, although the failure of their Tet Offensive proved a Pyrrhic victory for the Americans. The PLF fought mostly small guerilla engagements. Initially, the Americans were all-volunteer professionals, committed to their tasks, if not in any ideological cause, but believing that a soldier must carry out his mission. This belief was also the best predictor of volunteering for foreign service missions among a 1976 sample of U.S. professional paratroopers.[40]

For the infantrymen in Vietnam, combat was mostly defense against sudden attacks on their bases in addition to patrols and offensive attempts to flush out guerillas into combat. Search-and-destroy missions predominated: "The infantry finds the enemy, the air and artillery destroys them," said one general. This was meant to reduce U.S. casualty rates, but for the infantry it was quite passive combat, and firefights were generally initiated by the enemy. The buddy system was essential for such small unit combat, though officers and men complained that the rotation of individuals rather than whole units (the traditional policy) after a twelve-month service weakened it by continually bringing replacements into the unit. Danger was not continuous. Most patrols never encountered the enemy, although land mines and booby traps were a perennial hazard. When the enemy was encountered, often in ambushes, short chaotic battles ensued and casualties could be high. By 1967, 65 percent of U.S. casualties had come during patrols.[41] The unpredictability of each day proved hard to take.

Moskos interviewed thirty-four U.S. soldiers and talked to many more in field trips during 1965 and 1967, before disillusion set in. He found a rhythm to the level of commitment. As in other wars, the first engagement shattered the soldier's enthusiasm and spirit of adventure. It brought respect for the enemy but in this case enduring contempt for the South Vietnamese ally. U.S. soldiers served in Vietnam for one year. From the third to the eighth month of service, the soldier occupied a plateau of moderate commitment to the combat role. In the ninth and tenth months he was most combat-effective. Then he became reluctant to engage in offensive operations, keeping his head down, sometimes "freezing," while officers with similar tours of duty turned a blind eye. At this point personal safety overrode commitment to buddies. Moskos emphasized that buddies were seen instrumentally, entailing less friendship in the affective sense than mutual self-interest to remain alive. Soldiers eschewed patriotic rhetoric. Nineteen of the thirty-four men said they were fighting to stop communism, but they were hazy about what that was. Moskos says they had a "latent" ideology, seeing the United States as simply the best country in the world, worth fighting for, but when compared to the commitment of the enemy, that was not much of an ideology.[42]

Marshall, with the assistance of Lieutenant Colonel David Hackworth, wrote a brief report on an American infantry division in Vietnam during six months of heavy fighting in 1967 before demoralization began.[43] Using the same methods as before, he came to the opposite conclusion of his World War II report. He says the division needs "no stimulation whatever to its employment of … weapons when engaged." During prolonged engagements, he notes, 80–100 percent of soldiers typically fired their weapons, and most of the nonfirers were in noncombat roles. It wasn't unusual, he says, for one man to use three or more weapons if the fight lasted two hours. The main problem was too much firing. He considers self-control quite good but accepts the inevitability of firing too high, mostly missing. He says, "An outright kill is most unusual." That had not changed for over a hundred years, except that late twentieth-century soldiers were blazing away from cover.

Glenn interviewed infantry veterans, most of whom had been conscripted.[44] In other wars fear had been worse when soldiers were inactive while receiving fire. They relieved fear by firing, even if wildly, thus becoming active. Glenn finds this too. He quotes one soldier: "Courage cannot be separated from the fear that has aroused it. It is, in fact, a powerful urge not to be afraid anymore, to rid himself of fear by eliminating the source of it. And the only way of eliminating it is through the use of fire-power."[45]

Many soldiers reported that once in action, the mind was wholly absorbed. Fear disappeared because one did not have time for it. Of Glenn's 258 veterans, 97 percent said they had fired when required. Since a man might not admit his own shortcomings, Glenn asked them to estimate the proportion of comrades who fired during engagements. The average answer fell to 83 percent. Eighty percent gave fear as the main reason, 15 percent mentioned soldiers' moral qualms. One-third of these were conscientious objectors given tasks not requiring firearms. Most soldiers had occasionally not fired when they might have done, though this was a judgment call—for example, does one fire, revealing one's position, if one glimpses a larger enemy force close by? Not firing was found mostly among raw recruits. More shooters were found, as Marshall had suggested, in small teams firing weapons together, like machine gunners and helicopter crews. Teamwork generated more mutual control.[46]

An additional moral dilemma was prominent in Vietnam. Soldiers again made the distinction between legitimately killing enemy soldiers and killing civilians or prisoners, which was almost universally condemned. But in guerilla warfare, when the enemy does not wear uniform and when women and children sometimes hurl grenades, it was difficult to put that distinction into practice. But it sometimes led to atrocities by rampaging adrenalized soldiers, as in the My Lai massacre in March 1968.

Lieutenant William Calley, the commander of Charley Company, had been told that the village was home to a VC battalion, but he already had a reputation as a vicious killer. American morale was already plunging. This unit was inexperienced in combat, but three weeks earlier had been trapped in a minefield, with two deaths and thirteen wounded, and only two days earlier, a booby trap had killed a sergeant and wounded three others. They had not even seen the enemy. Thus, they saw this operation as revenge but were apprehensive and fearful. Calley and Charley Company rampaged through the village. About half the company apparently perpetrated the atrocities, the other half stood aside watching. Almost the whole village was killed, about five hundred people—the elderly, women, children, and babies. No adult males were found there, or any weapons. Women were gang-raped and their bodies mutilated afterward. Some killing began immediately, but it then mounted as rising aggressive confidence, absolute domination of the scene, and racism combined in the massacres of several crowds of villagers herded together by the soldiers. These horrors were revealed only because they were witnessed from above by a helicopter pilot with a conscience who landed between the soldiers and retreating villagers and threatened to shoot the soldiers unless they stopped. The army at first attempted a cover-up, but major publicity launched first by one determined private soldier forced courts-martial. Yet, outrageously, Calley was the only perpetrator to be

found guilty, of personally killing twenty-two villagers. He initially received a life sentence, but served only three and a half years house arrest
before being pardoned.

A similar massacre of ninety, at the nearby village of My Khe 4, on
the same day is shrouded in mystery, since the soldiers refused to testify.
No one involved was ever charged. Operation Speedy Express killed
thousands of Vietnamese civilians in the Mekong Delta, earning its commander the title "the Butcher of the Delta." There were presumably
other massacres, though probably not on the scale of My Lai. Nothing
has changed since Cicero observed, "Law is silent in times of war." The
nature of the war—stressed soldiers of falling morale, fighting a largely
unseen enemy hiding among the people, taking casualties but often unable to take normal military revenge in open firefight—was likely to have
caused atrocities.

The savagery of this war brought incapacitating anxieties later. The
U.S. Civil War had brought on the maladies described as "nostalgia" and
"melancholia." World War I armies were stalked by "shell shock," World
War II by "battle fatigue," and from 1980 onward the diagnosis was
"posttraumatic stress disorder," or PTSD, in which the soldier has terrible flashbacks, upsetting memories, and incapacitating anxiety caused by
the trauma of battle. Estimates based on diagnoses and interview surveys
of veterans have been available since Vietnam. Of its veterans, 31 percent
are estimated to have suffered from PTSD, and this has often proven
long-lasting. "Roughly 11 percent of Vietnam veterans, over a 40-year
period, continue to suffer from clinically important PTSD symptoms,
either having the full diagnosis or very strong features of the diagnosis
that interfere with function." Twice as many had been recently getting
worse rather than better.[47]

Fear figured in PTSD, but Vietnam veterans' feelings of guilt for
their own actions or inaction worsened their condition. Said a helicopter
machine gunner: "Sometimes I think that now I'm being paid back for all
the men I killed and I killed a lot of them. If there is a judge, I figure I'm
going to hell in a hand-basket." One doctor treating veterans said some
refused to take medication because they felt they deserved to suffer pain.
"We see a lot of feelings of guilt over what they've seen and done during
their experience in Vietnam," he says, "and they don't want to blunt
that."[48] One study of one hundred veterans found nineteen had attempted
suicide, and fifteen more had often considered it. Significantly related
to their suicide attempts were guilt about combat actions, survivor guilt,

depression, anxiety, and severe fear-based PTSD. Logistic regression analysis showed that combat guilt was the most significant predictor of preoccupation with suicide and actual suicide attempts. Many veterans reported that disturbing combat behavior like the killing of women, children, and prisoners occurred while they were emotionally out of control because of fear or rage.[49]

In another study of 603 male combat veterans seeking help at a veterans' PTSD clinic, an astonishing 91 percent reported witnessing wartime atrocities, 76 percent said they had themselves participated directly in killing, and 31 percent said they had participated in the mutilation of bodies. These figures cannot be taken as representative of all Vietnam veterans, only of those seeking help from the PTSD clinic. Behavior they defined as immoral was coming back to haunt them. The researchers found that involvement in wartime atrocities, as perpetrator or merely as witness, caused PTSD and severe depression symptoms independent of degree of exposure to combat. A sense of guilt was also associated with suicidal thoughts and with greater postwar hostility and aggression, even after controlling for PTSD severity. This would suggest that there is something about participating in or witnessing wartime atrocities that is not captured by the fear-dominated definition of PTSD.[50] The 30 percent of veterans who did suffer from PTSD included many experiencing extreme guilt. "Moral injury" rather than "guilt" has become the preferred label among researchers for the enduring psychological, biological, spiritual, behavioral, and social effects of perpetrating, failing to prevent, or bearing witness to acts that transgress deeply held moral beliefs and expectations. A further study of 1,106 Vietnam veterans found 35 percent who reported killing one or more enemy soldiers, 7 percent reported killing civilians, and 5 percent reported killing prisoners of war. After the war all three groups had higher symptoms on most mental health and functional impairment measures—PTSD symptoms, peritraumatic dissociation, functional impairment, and violent behavior.[51] Killing anyone brought on a sense of moral injury later.

So in Vietnam moral qualms did figure in soldiers' response to killing and participation in atrocities, but, tragically, well after these had occurred, usually after the war was over. Moral qualms did not prevent or mitigate the killing or atrocities. They offered no relief to the dead and mutilated Vietnamese, and they brought postwar suffering to many American perpetrators. Such psychological responses had probably emerged after previous wars—but they were rarely admitted by either the authorities or the soldiers themselves, and they were never medically diagnosed. Veterans had suffered in silence. But war is hell, and then you go to hell, said these veterans.

In December 1969, as the war ground on, the United States needed reinforcements, conscription was escalated by the introduction of the draft lottery, and morale fell. It did not help that U.S. troops were finding American arms on the PLF dead. They believed South Korean soldiers were selling them to the PLF. Since many educated whites evaded the draft (like Presidents Clinton and Trump) or managed to wangle safe stateside posts (like President Bush the Younger), new recruits were predominantly working-class men, and African Americans were overrepresented. Their class and racial resentments were enhanced by Nixon's attempts from 1969 to negotiate peace. Why continue risking your life if the war was about to end? Opinion back home also turned against the war. Desertion rates rose, reaching just over 7 percent by 1971, but backed by another 18 percent defined as AWOL, absent without leave. In contrast, in the twenty-first century the U.S. desertion rate has not yet risen above 5 percent. The main motives for deserting were not fear and loathing for battle but the attractions of home and the inability to fit into army life, especially its discipline, which weighed heavily on conscripted soldiers.[52] But desertion inside Vietnam was rare. Where would you desert to? Most demoralized soldiers stayed in the danger zone but took fewer risks. When this was by mutual consent among comrades, it was a passive form of buddy resistance.

The most spectacular consequence of American demoralization was "fragging," soldiers attempting to kill a superior officer, usually with a fragmentation grenade, hence the term fragging. After the Tet Offensive and as Nixon was seeking to make peace, between 1968 and 1972, almost one thousand incidents in Vietnam involved the army or marines; hundreds of officers and NCOs were injured, and at least fifty-seven killed. George Lepre analyzed seventy-one cases in which a soldier was convicted, and he found most were younger than average, many came from "broken homes," and two-thirds of them had not completed high school.[53] Their psychiatric reports said the offenders lacked maturity, had low self-esteem, and were rated as poor soldiers. Drugs were often the cause. Either the soldier was under the influence when he committed the offense or he had been disciplined by the officer for taking drugs. Also the growth in the civil rights movement in the late 1960s and the assassination of Martin Luther King in 1968 exacerbated racial tensions, which resulted in more racially motivated fragging incidents. They more often occurred in the rear than at the front line, where the buddy system often worked across racial lines.[54] Demoralization was setting in as no progress was being made. But peace was made before the army might collapse. Once the Americans left, the PLF bided its time and then quickly rolled over the South Vietnamese army to victory. For America the war had been a disaster. If America had been true to the anti-imperialist values it proclaimed, then it would have supported Ho Chi Minh and his movement in the 1950s when it had been an anticolonial nationalist movement fighting against French imperialism.

The Vietnam War: The Communist PLF

Communist warfare was brought to its most effective level in Vietnam. Long-lasting morale was demonstrated by the PLF, taking up Chinese PLA practices, but also enjoying, like the Red Army, the advantages of fighting in its homeland amid a broadly sympathetic local population. "Vietcong," the commonly used term in the West, was a propaganda term used by the South Vietnamese government to suggest that the movement was really communist Chinese. We have considerable evidence on the PLF. The Rand Corporation was commissioned to do hundreds of interviews of PLF POWs and defectors between 1964 and 1971, and a handful more up until 1974. These were not scientific samples, for the South Vietnamese government (the GVN) decided who would be interviewed. Some probably told the Vietnamese interviewers what they thought they wanted to hear.[55] They are a rich data source, however.

The first official Rand report, by John Donnell and his colleagues, was based on 145 interviews in 1964.[56] The interviewees said that almost all the PLF believed strongly in the justice of their cause. The movement had already defeated the French Empire and Vietnamese feudal landlords. It blended nationalist and socialist goals, the two most popular mid-twentieth-century global ideologies. When American forces arrived in 1965, the PLF saw them as yet more foreign imperialists propping up the corrupt and reactionary GVN. The justice of the PLF cause seemed self-evident. Their land redistribution policies were popular, especially among poor peasants. At this stage communist forces were mainly southerners, although receiving help from the North Vietnamese military.

The interviewees revealed the "three-three" system borrowed from the Chinese PLA. Rank-and-file soldiers were grouped into threes, going

everywhere together, covering each other, sharing the hardships of guerilla warfare. They held *kiem-thao* self-criticism sessions almost daily.
Three threes plus an officer formed a squad of ten who also held *kiem-
thao* sessions two or more times a month. A whole company might have a
session about once a month. All sessions aired recent experiences, what
had worked, what had not worked, and everyone was urged to contribute
to the discussion. As in the PLA, rank differences were slight. These rituals amplified the egalitarianism of guerilla forces, but they also caged soldiers, relying less on the coerced discipline of most armies than on an
ideology combining values and norms, institutionalized as rituals performed by individual units and led into battle by party members. The
value of struggle toward a just communist society, the norm of commitment to the movement and one's comrades, and the rituals of three
threes and *kiem-thao* put considerable moral pressure on the soldiers.

The PLF was supported by much of the rural and small-town population. Violence against civilians was rare, except for captured GVN officials, in contrast to the harsh practices of the GVN and its army, the
Army of the Republic of Viet Nam (ARVN). Desertions were mostly not
for political disaffection but for personal reasons—the desire to return
home and end the physical hardship of war. These interviews revealed
high morale, belief in the cause, and confidence in victory. When John T.
McNaughton, assistant to Defense Secretary Robert McNamara, was
briefed on the report, he had already developed a healthy respect for the
PLF and not for the GVN. He declared: "If what you say in that briefing
is true, we're fighting on the wrong side."[57] He was right. Before American troops entered in 1965, the PLF had been nearing victory, as Mc-
Naughton knew.[58]

Two books discuss the Mekong Delta province of My Tho on the
basis of the Rand interviews. David Hunt analyzed 285 interviews undertaken during 1965–68.[59] He confirms that PLF morale was high in the
"golden years" of the early 1960s, when the PLF organized village meetings with an educational mission, lively discussion, and festive spirit,
which villagers enjoyed. David Elliott, using 400 Rand interviews, confirms this picture of PLF-organized village enthusiasm in the early
1960s, noting the party's reach downward through village farmers', wom-
en's, and youths' associations whose leaders were given extensive political
training.[60] Most armies avoid political education and explicit ideology,
preferring to rely on the soldiers' latent ideologies of national identity,
supplemented by extensive drilling, whose goal is to convert them into

automatons. In the PLF, political education, reinforced by the political officers, substituted ideology and educational rituals for extensive drilling.

The party was selective in admitting members, but it then gave them political training, stressing that they were members of an elite with superior objective knowledge of the interests of workers and peasants, whom they must both serve and lead. In this period their policies received much support. One unsympathetic defector observed: "The people thought they were then enjoying 'real democracy' because the cadres behaved nicely toward them. Before, the villagers bent their heads and were scared when they met GVN officials." Elliott reveals the importance of PLF land reform in bringing peasant support.[61] Military recruits were all volunteers. The policy of "upgrading troops" from village guerillas to district troops to main force regulars was also an effective form of military training through experience.[62]

William Henderson, a former U.S. officer in Vietnam, focuses on fifty-three men interviewed between 1965 and 1968. He emphasizes their resilience in absorbing American firepower in the air and on the ground. He also stresses the three-three buddy system, the *kiem-thao* sessions, and the fusion of political and military structures. Each threesome was supervised by a political cadre, a hardened party militant who reported every three days on the men's conformity with party goals.[63] Said Ho Chi Minh: "With good cadres, everything can be done." Henderson notes, "The soldier was never permitted to be an individual; rather, he was constantly reminded of his duties to his two comrades in the three-man cell, to the squad and platoon, to the people, and to the party."[64] This was a daily dose of moral obligation, although allied to some direct democracy. PLF soldiers had the right to discuss and criticize battle plans.

After the entry of the United States, the PLF had to adapt to its superior firepower. It introduced conscription, but from the militias. After brief military and political training, they were assigned to three-man units alongside two experienced soldiers, one of whom was usually a party member. Mostly young, the newcomers were also inducted into the Party Youth Group, a further instrument of solidarity and control. Any soldier identified as lazy or lacking commitment or who harbored "rightist thoughts" was subject to self-criticism sessions, techniques "designed to bring anxiety to the PLF soldier, who was culturally dependent for security upon his relationship with a group."[65] Such moral pressure entwined military and political ideology and organization. This was "the most sophisticated leadership techniques in use by any army in the world today," says Henderson.[66] It prevented "disintegration, collapse or significant loss of military effectiveness" despite American firepower.[67] This was a version of the "man over weapons" strategy of the Chinese PLA in Korea. Increasing casualties and campaign hardship produced more individual but not collective desertions.

Another official Rand report, by Leon Gouré and his colleagues, differed from this consensus. It was based on 450 interviews conducted in 1965. It is dismissive of the PLF. Interviewees said that intensified U.S. air and artillery power was demoralizing it. B-52 bombs penetrated the shallow bunkers and tunnels of PLF camps, and guerilla ability to hide among the people was reduced as villagers fled from the bombing. The introduction by the PLF of taxation and the draft forced less ideologically committed men into the military, and this also reduced popular support.[68] These arguments were partially confirmed by Elliott, but Gouré uniquely added that PLF cadres were now pessimistic about their chances of winning.[69] Their power within the movement was now based on coercion, not persuasion, he claimed. His report makes no reference to the three threes or the *kiem-thao* sessions. It recommends intensifying American bombing. No qualms about civilians here.

Rand colleagues charged that Gouré was biased. His appointment as head of the project had followed a shift inside the corporation to hardline Cold War policies.[70] He had advocated airpower as a weapon of counterinsurgency long before his assignment to Vietnam, and upon arrival he immediately penned a report favoring more bombing. The air force, delighted, ensured he got command of the next Rand survey. Gouré released interim results after each batch of interviews, and his briefings all had the same message: bombing was sapping the will of the enemy, so bomb more. The air force loved it, though reporters were skeptical, doubting especially his view that villagers whose homes were bombed would blame the PLF rather than the Americans. Another Rand analysis of seven hundred interviews concluded that bombed villagers blamed the GVN.[71] But the blame game was actually complicated. Hunt's interviewees said that at first villagers blamed the PLF for bringing retaliation bombing, defoliation, plowing up of crops, forced relocation of villagers, and the shooting down of anyone running.[72] But they soon switched to blaming the actual perpetrators, the GVN, the ARVN, and the Americans. Many added that the government did not have the support of the people, whereas the PLF did.

The fullest analysis of My Tho province is David Elliott's.[73] This was a heartland of the revolution. But its relatively flat and open ecology made it vulnerable to bombing. Elliott says that to understand the development of the PLF, we must grasp the interaction between the two sides' strategies. Class alliances shifted during the struggle. The PLF land program finished off the landlord class, and their lands were redistributed mainly to poor peasants. This upgraded many of them into the middle peasant stratum. The core of the PLF now became the remaining poor peasants while the support of many middle peasants waned, especially when agricultural taxes were imposed by the PLF. Some went over to the GVN. But the PLF was initially more cohesive, more politically moral, and more popular than the GVN, for the reasons given by Donnell and his colleagues and Henderson above. In early 1965, despite the aid given by the United States to the GVN, the PLF seemed on its way to victory.

So the U.S. military intervened directly, in the belief that another country must not be lost to communism. Ground troops arrived, supported by intensifying bombing of the South and then the North, too. American bombing and defoliation from the air and from artillery on the ground devastated PLF core regions. There were supposedly restrictions placed on bombing civilian areas, but the rules were confused, changeable, disputed, and often ignored. The United States sent in 550,000 ground forces and dropped 7.7 million tons of explosives, dwarfing the 2.2 million tons dropped during the entire World War II (and the 635,000 dropped in Korea). Mao's famous dictum that guerillas swam among the people as fish swam in the sea was countered by General William Westmoreland: "It is necessary to eliminate the 'fish' from the 'water,' or to dry up the 'water' so that the 'fish' cannot survive."[74]

Draining the water had two main thrusts: destroy the economy of any pro-PLF locality, and physically remove the population to "strategic hamlets" in areas controlled by Americans and the GVN. This inflicted appalling suffering on the rural population. It could not "win hearts and minds" (proclaimed as the U.S. strategy), but it worked in the sense that the PLF was deprived of its "water," especially in open agrarian areas like the Mekong Delta. Peasants who were not forcibly relocated fled from the devastation. If they stayed, they were defined by the United States as Viet Cong, to be killed, including women and children. Women, the "long-haired warriors," made a significant contribution to the PLF as soldiers, spies, tunnel builders, and porters.[75] American bombing left the

PLF with fewer fighters, fewer recruits, fewer resources for provisioning them, and fewer social and educational programs. In My Tho the PLF was reduced to a hard core of predominantly poor peasants and their families, living in fear while slowly losing ground, moving and hiding, with little time for assemblies or festive occasions. Most interviews reveal fear, especially of the random death inflicted by unseen B-52s and long-range ground artillery. Casualties mounted. It should have been the end of them.

Three things saved them. One was the support of reinforcements of professionally trained soldiers and munitions from North Vietnam. As the war continued, the northern presence in the PLF grew. The failure of the Tet Offensive had devastated PLF forces, and they required an infusion of Northerners. Exact figures are disputed, but it is likely that toward the end Northerners represented almost half the main force numbers, not including local or guerilla forces. There was also help from the Soviets and China. The Chinese PLA rotated 320,000 troops through North Vietnam to man air defenses against American planes, and PLA and Soviet military advisers raced each other to get to crashed American aircraft to steal their advanced avionics. One Chinese veteran noted that in Vietnam there were two enemies, "the American imperialists in the sky, and the Soviet revisionists on the ground."[76]

Second, the PLF party cadres did not waver. Their casualty rate is unknown. The minimum estimate is 444,000, the maximum over a million. The higher figures may also include civilian victims, although the militia system blurred the distinction. The PLA casualty rate was certainly much higher than those of most armies at war, and given rudimentary medical services, far more of the wounded died than in the U.S. Army. The death rate among cadres was higher still. Given the odds against them, the PLA cadres were foolhardily brave, trapped by commitment to an ideology reinforced by everyday ritual wielding considerable moral pressure. There were always replacements, and the movement just kept going. Given taxation, conscription, and tightening military-political discipline, the PLF was using more coercion, yet Elliott notes that POWs and defectors openly expressed disagreements with cadres' directives, without suffering reprisals.[77]

Third, they retained the sympathy of poorer peasants and others who preferred the revolution to a GVN regime that they still viewed as corrupt and benefiting the rich. They preferred socialist ideology even if their understanding of it was rudimentary. Virtually all viewed Vietnam as a single country, whereas the GVN wanted its division to continue and fought as a stooge of foreign imperialism. It is rare among the Rand interviews to find positive views of the government or its army, in contrast to their nuanced views of the PLF. When PLF armed forces weakened, it was rational for peasants to flee to safer areas or to withdraw into everyday life. This happened in late 1968 after the Tet Offensive, when even the PLF's official history admits "rightist thoughts, pessimism, and hesitancy" appeared. It happened again in 1970–71 when U.S. troops invaded Cambodia and destroyed PLF camps there. In these periods supply lines were badly hit and the soldiers became half-starved.

But at the slightest signs of hope, new PLF recruits appeared, men and women alike, often unexpectedly, willing to fight or provide civilian support. This happened in 1963, in 1967–68 in preparation for the Tet Offensive, and in the 1972 Easter Offensive. Back in the United States, the war required an unpopular draft. Its cost had already aborted President Johnson's Great Society reforms, and it was now weakening the dollar. There was a major antiwar movement led by young men anxious to avoid the draft. Morale was sagging among the troops, many had lost faith in the cause, were contemptuous of the South Vietnamese allies, and no longer thought the war winnable. The Sino-Soviet split had revealed to some in Washington that communism was no longer as cohesive as had been believed. Why bother fighting such a costly war for the corrupt government of a nonstrategic poor country? Although the PLF's Tet Offensive failed, its shock convinced American leaders that the war was unwinnable. The ideological commitment and staying power of the PLF were greater than those of the United States and the GVN. This was indeed a triumph of men and women over weapons. Their weapons of the weak had triumphed.

U.S. Ambassador Maxwell Taylor had in late 1964 expressed puzzlement at PLA persistence: "We still find no plausible explanation of the continued strength of the Viet-Cong if our data on Viet-Cong losses are even approximately correct. Not only do the Viet-Cong units have the recuperative powers of the phoenix, but they have an amazing ability to maintain morale. Only in rare cases have we found evidences of bad morale among Viet-Cong prisoners or recorded in captured Viet-Cong documents."[78]

But the explanation was simple: the United States was underestimating PLF numbers and support. Its estimates of total PLF strength at this time were around 285,000. Their monthly estimates of PLF casualties indicated that this total number could not possibly be maintained. Yet others realized that these estimates were only of PLF main and local regular forces and did not include guerilla militias organized by villages and hamlets. Village militias had rifles and hand grenades. The grenades inflicted 20 percent of all American casualties. Total PLF armed strength was over 600,000, and the entire PLF infrastructure of helpers, including youth auxiliaries and civilian laborers and porters, often women, numbered well over a million. When the Nixon administration finally realized this, optimism collapsed: the PLF could replace their casualties from village militias and northern regiments and fight on indefinitely. The United States could not.[79] As Henry Kissinger remarked in 1968, "The guerilla wins if he does not lose." Yes, but provided he and she believe in the cause.

We don't know exactly how many people were killed in the Vietnam War. The Americans suffered about 58,000 deaths; their allies, the South Vietnamese Army, lost about 250,000. Estimates of PLF casualties vary considerably, but in 2012 the united Vietnamese government said there were about 850,000 PLF combat or noncombat deaths. Even if that figure was exaggerated, the disproportion is evident. The sufferings of the PLF and sympathizers, technologically overmatched, were extraordinary. Yet they kept on fighting, because of high morale and the support of the rural population, whose sympathy was buttressed by organizations that blurred the boundaries between the political and the military, and civilian and the military—a communist version of the French revolutionary nation in arms. It represented the terrible human costs of a thoroughly militarized society.

A postscript: the Chinese PLA invaded Vietnam in 1979, in response to Vietnam's invasion of Cambodia to overthrow the genocidal Pol Pot regime. Two communist armies were now at each other's throats. The PLA had been disrupted by the Cultural Revolution and struggled against the battle-hardened North Vietnamese Army (NVA), which relied mostly on its border regional and militia forces. The Chinese had expected an easy victory, but, confronted by large Vietnamese forces blocking the way to Hanoi, they soon retreated. Though both sides claimed victory, the NVA had the better of it, and they stayed in Cambodia.[80] After revolutionary forces achieve their revolution, they settle down into being more conventional armies, with a decline in their ideological fervor and structural rigor. This had happened to the Chinese PLA, and now it was beginning to happen in Vietnam, too—as it happened also in the postwar Soviet Red Army. The ideological army cannot endure long-term in peacetime.

The Wehrmacht, the Red Army at Stalingrad, the PLA, and the PLF are all cases of a one-party state or movement wielding a transcendent ideology grounded in practice at the unit level, generating morale and leadership that can compensate, up to a point, for technological or numerical inferiority. These are the bravest soldiers, the ones who look death in the face and fight on, whether one approves of their ideology. From their own perspectives they are heroes. They refute democratic triumphalist theorists of soldier morale introduced in chapter 3. The soldiers of the democracies performed worse, not better. When they triumphed, this was due to advanced technology and firepower available to wealthy countries. But this simple contrast between democratic and authoritarian regimes is misplaced. Except for the Wehrmacht, authoritarian armies actually were more complex, since at the level of soldier they had more participatory rituals than did the armies of the democracies, and this led to their higher morale.

Such practices are rare, however. There are many one-party states in the world, but almost none wants to change the world. They merely desire to stay in power, distributing benefits to their supporters, repressing opposition. They use their armed forces more for domestic repression than for war. Since they also live in fear of army coups, they promote officers for perceived loyalty, not military competence. They bribe them, too, for officers can participate in state corruption. To be on the safe side, these regimes add their own supposedly loyal praetorian guards, security police, and militias to counterbalance the army. None of these practices is likely to create military efficiency or high morale. A one-party state without a transcendent ideology may be coup-proof, but it is unlikely to win wars.

American military involvement in Vietnam was a defeat. It might be callously said in its favor that the United States had so devastated Vietnam that it would deter movements in other countries from embracing communism, a very nasty form of deterrence. The Vietnam veteran Tim O'Brien gives an even harsher American epitaph on the war: "A true war story is never moral. . . . If at the end of a war story you feel uplifted, or if you feel that some small bit of rectitude has been salvaged from the larger waste, then you have been made the victim of a very old and terrible lie. There is no rectitude whatsoever. There is no virtue. As a first rule of thumb, therefore, you can tell a true war story by its absolute and uncompromising allegiance to obscenity and evil."[81]

Long-Term Trends in Battle Experience

Over the last three chapters we have seen one universal feature of wars. They inflict a massive number of deaths and mutilations. There have been few "good deaths," heroic, clean, and purposeful. In modern wars death has mainly come suddenly, unexpectedly, as randomly inflicted explosions coming from the skies, bursting apart the human body, blood and gore gushing and body parts flying everywhere. The sounds of battle are men screaming and howling in their death throes or at the horror of lying helplessly on the ground, confronting their own ghastly disfigurements, while the survivors around them are shocked to the core, and potentially suffering the long-term effects of what we call posttraumatic stress disorder. To the soldiers this cannot have seemed like the rational fulfillment of useful goals. Nor was it, as I will make perfectly clear in my last chapter. Of the wars discussed in these three chapters, only World War II had to be fought, and only by one side. We have no reason to believe that earlier wars were any more heroic or cleaner or more necessary. Death had come less often from the skies and only from nearby, but it compensated with more battering and slashing of the body, with the same ghastly results. How different from the environment of the decision makers and the weapons manufacturers pursuing normal, peaceful political and economic life. They are full of hope, achieving their goals, and that is all that matters. It is the soldiers, not the working class, who, aside from their own atrocities, are the most truly exploited persons on the planet.

We have, however, also seen four secular trends through the soldiers' experience of modern battles. First, the ratio of casualties inflicted to rounds fired reveals declining efficiency, despite the weapons' becoming much more lethal. In the musket era contemporary estimates of the ratio of shots fired to casualties varied from one hit per 500 rounds to one hit per 2,000–3,000 rounds fired.[82] I earlier quoted the somewhat lower ratios suggested for the U.S. Civil War. These numbers indicate low ability to inflict casualties, probably due to the inaccuracy of the weapons and the difficulties of firing them. Yet the coming of breech-loading rifles in the late nineteenth century increased the frequency of shots fired, but not the casualty rate, and this trend continued throughout the revolution in firepower that characterized the twentieth century. More and more shots were needed on average to inflict one casualty—10,000 in World War I, 20,000 in World War II, and 50,000 in the Vietnam War. But in early twenty-first-century wars in Iraq and Afghanistan, U.S. forces fired an astonishing 250,000 shots for every enemy killed![83] Equipped with automatic weapons, armies have not become more efficient killing machines—quite the reverse. Overfiring enables soldiers to relieve their fear by activity, spraying bullets in all directions, while prudently retaining concealed positions—as the enemy does, too—not because they are cowards, but because they are reasonably fearful of these lethal weapons. Even the simple Kalashnikov wielded by guerillas and terrorists is a far deadlier weapon than the musket. Expose yourself to enemy fire and you die, unlike most U.S. Civil War soldiers.

Second, Ardant du Picq had observed in the 1860s the increasing dispersion of the battlefield. This continued right into the twenty-first century, reducing officers' direct control over their soldiers. Drilling and discipline no longer have the same influence as in the past, and milder forms of skulking, such as keeping one's head down and doing the minimum, may have increased. Strengthening the buddy system has been one response. Another has been an emphasis on task completion to increase the pride in skills and the sense of duty of soldiers—most notable in the case of pilots.

Third was a very large increase in recorded psychological wounds, probably created by more diagnosis in modern societies. But I have not found evidence that moral qualms have prevented soldiers or airmen from shooting at or killing the enemy. Doubtless civilians like you or me might experience some difficulty unless we were cast into the "kill or be killed" hand-to-hand warfare of earlier times. But trained soldiers rarely do more than hesitate momentarily before killing. Unfortunately, human beings are not inherently pacific, not even in today's relatively pacific civilian societies. Men and probably women too can kill easily if ordered to by institutionalized, legitimate political and military authorities. The norm that civilians should not be killed is acknowledged by most soldiers. If they nonetheless kill civilians deliberately or by accident, they may feel a little remorse for their actions, but rarely enough to deter them from doing it again. They rationalize killings in terms of military necessity and explain the worst atrocities in terms of men "losing self-control" in fearful contexts. Moral qualms tragically come after the war, morally destabilizing former killers.

Fourth was the killing of more civilians. There have been no significant attempts to curb this by introducing tighter rules of war. The euphemistic term "collateral damage" is a callous attempt to sanitize and normalize the killing of innocents (alongside the bizarre expression "friendly fire"). Underlying this is a separation between wartime and peacetime norms. The morality of the latter does not apply to the former.

But if pacifist-leaning soldiers are rare, so are sadists or heroes. I have found two contributions made by human nature in battle. First, the rush of energy coming from the adrenal glands produced by extreme fear or anxiety in battle commonly generates suddenly greater strength, a racing pulse and pounding heart, increased respiration, bodily trembling, and distorted vision. This may induce soldiers to a fighting fury, charging forward, yelling and slaughtering anyone in the way. Alternatively, extreme fear may induce loss of control of bodily functions or terrified flight. Human physiology, like human psychology, is ambivalent about killing—fight or flight.

One human emotion dominates the battlefield—fear. The prospect of death or mutilation terrifies virtually all soldiers. What Durkheim called "altruistic suicide," deliberately sacrificing one's life for others or for a cause, is rare. Islamist terrorists are often exceptions because of their commitment to a transcendent ideology, absent from today's professional armies. But fear of death or mutilation is prevalent in almost all wars. The generals know this yet believe fear can be managed. Although fear can incapacitate the soldier mentally or physiologically, or compel him to flee, most soldiers do stay and fight, at first with rising, then diminishing vigor, keeping heads down and blazing away from cover. Since the enemy is likewise fearful and cautious, battle remains inefficiently balanced.

In modern times numerous factors may overwhelm qualms and manage fear: desire for adventure inflected by patriotism and manly honor, drills and discipline, professional commitment to and absorption in military tasks, confidence in army organization and ultimate victory, commitment to one's buddies, commitment to an ideology, and the perceived virtue of self-defense. Their precise mixture varies among circumstances. Modern Western armies have not been very ideological, although they are permeated by a latent sense of national identity and patriotism. Transcendent ideology has figured more in communist forces, as we have just seen, and among religious forces, as we see in the next chapter. Malešević says of small military and paramilitary forces that soldiers were receptive to ideologies "only when they were successfully couched in the language of comradeship, kinship, neighbourhood, and friendship."[84] Ideologies need more concrete grounding if they are to move soldiers to a high level of commitment. But dealing with large armies fighting over broad fronts, concrete is also provided by patriotic identity, hatred, and repetitive collective and educational rituals. We pin derogatory labels on such fighters, such as "fanatics," "zealots," or "pathological." We do not care to admit that they believe more strongly in their cause and are braver than our own soldiers. Thus, they have greater staying power, withstanding enormous technological inferiority. Among the combatants I have discussed, they are matched in banishment of fear and acceptance of high risk of death only by fighter pilots, who are totally absorbed in a difficult, dangerous, and highly skilled task that yields very high social status. But confidence in the army's ability to achieve ultimate victory is more widely important. If confidence in victory crumbles, so does the army.

Monarchs, dictators, presidents, and parliamentary leaders initiate war, but they do not experience battle. They are callous desk killers, inflicting fear, death, and mutilation from afar on those they define as the enemy, on their own soldiers, and on nearby civilians. This is perhaps the greatest inequality in life chances in the world today. Killing in battle occurs when rulers proclaim it as legitimate, and where their militaries create institutions and culture that enable this to be accomplished in an orderly way so that victory seems possible. Intense military power relations, the combination of disciplined obedience to hierarchy and close comradeship, can overcome human repugnance to killing and the fear of being killed. Military power triumphant can do this; military power enfeebled cannot. I prefer the latter.

CHAPTER FOURTEEN

Recent Wars in Muslim Countries

M OST RECENT WARS HAVE been fought in the Greater Middle East. To explain them, we must understand the relations between two main sets of actors: on the one hand, the Muslim peoples and states of the region, and on the other, the interventions of empires from outside the region. Up to World War II these empires had been mostly British, French, and Russian, and they had destroyed the last indigenous empires of the region, the Persian and Ottoman empires. Then the Europeans were displaced by the United States and the Soviet Union. Their interventions during the Cold War had nothing to do with religion. Instead, the misfortunes of the region were the possession of oil fields and a strategic position between capitalist and communist areas. After the Soviet collapse, the United States was left as the major imperial intervener. From the eighteenth to the early twentieth century, direct or indirect colonial rule in the region by the British and French empires had inspired much resistance. When the imperial torch passed to the Soviets and the United States, they sought only informal empire, not territorial control, using military interventions to strengthen or replace local regimes. They sought global grandeur and oil, though they both claimed their missions were defensive, countering the aggression of the other.

The Soviets tended to help self-described leftist states, whereas the United States helped conservatives and monarchists. Both formally denounced imperialism while pursuing it. Yet even before the collapse of the Soviet Union, the region's leftist regimes, Nasserite or Ba'athist, were degenerating into corrupt authoritarianism, failing to sustain the economic development they had promised. That was also true of other regimes in the region, however, unless they had an abundance of oil, in which case they had development for the powerful, and some crumbs for the masses. The United States, the Soviets, and their clients had failed to bring democratic capitalism or socialism to the region. Increasingly, local opposition movements attacked their rulers as stooges of the imperialists promoting decadent Western secular culture. This led opposition movements to draw on the power resource that they alone possessed—Islam. "Islam is the solution" became the dominant slogan of "Islamism." The West calls this "fundamentalism," a return to the supposedly divinely revealed truths of the seventh century. This increasingly became the main opposition force to unpopular secular regimes.[1]

Islamism is popularly rooted in the everyday practices of the people. It is helped by Islam's independence from the state and lack of an institutionalized church hierarchy, though this is truer of Sunni than of Shi'a sects. Although the imams generally oppose Islamism, they lack much influence.[2] There have been important Islamist intellectuals, and simplified versions of their teachings have resonated widely. Although violent jihadists constitute only a tiny minority of all Islamists, they can elicit enough sympathy among the masses to provide persistent recruitment of young men and women as shock troops.

The Islamist offensive was dual, Shi'a and Sunni. In 1979 the Shi'a Islamic Revolution in Iran overthrew the shah, widely seen in the country as a corrupt and repressive puppet of the United States. A brief struggle for power ensued between a more secular coalition and Islamists, who managed to mobilize the mosques and bazaars to seize power. Their leader, the Ayatollah Khomeini, proclaimed an expansive goal: "We export our revolution to the four corners of the world because our revolution is Islamic; and the struggle will continue until the cry of 'There is no god but Allah, and Muhammad is the messenger of Allah' prevails throughout the world."

Such rhetoric is far removed from reality. Shi'a Islam is dominant in Iran, but Shi'a constitute only about 15 percent of Muslims in the world. Shi'a rule could not possibly extend to "the four corners of the world," and the main focus was national. Khomeini's regime imposed a repressive theocracy on the country, though with democratic trimmings such as elections. Islamist rule at home and some export in the region were spearheaded by the development of the 200,000-strong Islamic Revolutionary Guard Corps, independent of the armed forces, commanding its own separate air force and navy, and in command of Iranian missile development—the biggest "praetorian guard" in history, established by an autocratic regime distrustful of the regular armed forces, in this case considered insufficiently ideological.

Among Sunnis, the Saudi monarchy had embraced Wahhābī doctrine, the most traditional reversion to seventh-century ideals. The Saudi regime used its oil wealth to finance Wahhābī networks of schools, universities, and communications media across the Middle East. From these and other transnational networks emerged small Sunni movements espousing jihad, or holy war, to spread the faith transnationally to Sunni Muslims almost everywhere. The most important movement initially was the World Islamic Front, dominated by Saudis and led by Osama bin Laden, who declaimed in 1998, "Praise be to Allah, who revealed the Book, controls the clouds, defeats factionalism, and says in His Book: 'But when the forbidden months are past, then fight and slay the pagans wherever ye find them, seize them, beleaguer them, and lie in wait for them in every stratagem (of war)'; and peace be upon our Prophet, Muhammad Bin-'Abdallah, who said: I have been sent with the sword between my hands to ensure that no one but Allah is worshipped."[3]

Thus jihadists, holy warriors, had penetrated both of Islam's main sects. The beliefs they sought to impose were sharia law and the hadith, the divine revelations of the Prophet Muhammad, in the Shi'a case buttressed by the authority of the ayatollahs. Jihadists advocated spreading truth through holy war. The declared enemies of jihadi movements like Al Qaeda, the Taliban, and Daesh (or ISIS) are not only secular Muslim regimes but also Western regimes, especially the United States and Great Britain, who were persistently intervening in Muslim countries, and whose supposedly degenerate secular culture was said to corrupt Muslim society. It is common in Western societies, and especially in the United States, to blame Middle Eastern wars on these jihadists, and some Westerners go further and identify Islam itself as a violent religion.

Two political scientists have offered Islam-centered theories of recent wars. The first, Samuel Huntington, announced the coming of a global "clash of civilizations," some defined by their religion, others by culture and language. He analyzed nine such civilizations but gave primacy to what he saw as an unusually aggressive Islam embarking on clashes with neighboring religions, principally Christianity and Hinduism. He was right to emphasize a tense "fault line" between these religions stretching across North Africa, the Middle East, and South Asia.[4] Yet this fault line has produced more communal rioting and MIDs than full-fledged wars. In fact, more armed conflict has occurred within Islam than between it and outsiders, while most wars with outsiders resulted from or were aggravated by Western military aggression, which Huntington ignores.

The second, John Owen, suggests recent wars have formed a single wave of ideological warfare sweeping across the greater Middle East, analogous to the three previous waves of ideological wars in Europe discussed in chapter 8. He counts nine cases between 1958 and 2009, although he included only regime-change interstate wars.[5] This excludes nonstate jihadists like Al Qaeda, and ISIS had barely surfaced at the time he wrote.

In reality, most of Owen's nine wars did not significantly involve religion. Three were initiated by American interventions against relatively secular regimes of the region. The targets were Muslim countries, but religious motives were not evident. Owen erroneously labels two more cases as Islamist: the foreign invasions of Jordan in 1958 and of north Yemen in 1962. Here the intervening states were offering help in civil wars between monarchists and leftist republicans, neither of these being Islamist and each supported by other Muslim states. Britain aided the monarchists, the Soviets the republicans. They also occurred too early to be influenced by the rise of jihadism. In two further cases of civil war in Afghanistan, one side was Islamist, but the other was more secular and was aided by the Soviets in 1979 and the United States in 2001. Islam was important here, but only on one side. The 1980 war between Sunni Iraq and Shi'a Iran did have religious coloration on both sides. An Israeli incursion into Lebanon in 1982 obviously had Jewish versus Muslim aspects—as did several Israeli-Arab wars not seeking regime change— though these primarily involved a material struggle over land. So only three of nine cases had a substantial religious input; four involved U.S. troops, and one involved Soviet troops. They are too disparate to be considered a single wave, and foreign, especially American, imperialism was important. Perhaps Owen was perspicacious, for greater religious input became evident after he wrote—but alongside the return of imperialism.

Consider this list of American military interventions, large and small, in Muslim countries since 1986, excluding operations designed only to secure the evacuation or rescue of Americans from war zones: the 1986 bombing of Libya, 1987–88 attacks on various Iranian targets, 1991 Operation Desert Storm invasion of Iraq, 1992–2003 no-fly zones and bombings of Iraq, 1993 Somali fiasco, 1998 cruise missile attacks on Afghanistan and Sudan, 2001 onward invasion and occupation of Afghanistan, 2003 onward invasion and occupation of Iraq, 2004 onward drone strikes on at least six Muslim countries, 2011 bombing of Libya, 2014 onward military intervention on the ground and air in Syria. These actions were not unprovoked, and I am not here concerned with how legitimate they were. But they reveal that the major player in "Muslim wars" has been the United States.

Robert Pape analyzes suicide bombings and finds they are more likely when people feel their homeland is occupied (especially when the occupier is of a different religion), and when the occupier has far superior military power yet is seen as lacking stomach for the fight, as they suppose democracies to be. He concludes that suicide terrorism is a strategic weapon of the weak, wielded by young men and women seeing themselves as altruists for their group. During the period he studied, suicide bombings were committed by a variety of religious and nationalist groups.[6] Since then, almost all bombers have been Muslims, and their targets have often been nondemocratic regimes, such as Saudi Arabia. But his model does seem particularly appropriate for struggles between Muslim jihadists and the United States.

So there were four types of war fought in the region: Muslim states fighting non-Muslim but nonimperial states; Islamic sects fighting against each other; jihadists fighting against more secular Muslims; and foreign imperialists initiating wars against both Islamic jihadists and unfriendly states. I start with Muslim/non-Muslim wars between neighbors not involving Western imperial intervention.

Muslim against Non-Muslim Neighbors: (1) Arab-Israeli Wars

This was a unique series of wars, the only ones fought between Jews and Muslims and the only ones involving a people fleeing pogroms—indeed, a Holocaust—and founding a new state whose rule involved settler colonialism imposed on an indigenous people.

The state of Israel was founded in May 1948. Up to 2014 there were twelve conflicts between it and surrounding Arab states and movements, each one of which met the CoW standard for a war of over one thousand battlefield deaths. There were also several lesser MIDs in that period. War occurred in about half the years, a very high proportion. Almost all ended in Israeli victories. Because of their defeats, the Arab states were forced into lopsided peace deals with Israel at the expense of the Palestinians. The periods of peace have enabled Israelis to establish more and more settlements over land and houses formerly owned by Palestinians, many of whom were forced into refugee camps. Since 1967, every Israeli government has expanded Jewish settlements in the Occupied Territories. Over 400,000 Jewish citizens now live in the West Bank settlements, including urban East Jerusalem, where Arab residents cannot get building permits to confirm their residence there. In consequence, they are forcibly evicted. There are also lesser Jewish settlements in the Gaza Strip.

In 2022 landgrabbing still continued. A protest over the eviction of Arab property owners from East Jerusalem grew into a riot, and then into armed conflict as the Palestinian Hamas militia lobbed rockets into Israel, and the Israeli military responded with air and artillery strikes on the Gaza Strip. As usual, the casualty ratio was lopsided. Above 230 Palestinians were killed, including 60 children, a sign that most casualties were probably civilians. The Israelis lost twelve dead, including one child. Twenty Palestinians were killed for every Israeli victim. The United States was at first supportive of Israel's "right to defend itself," repeatedly vetoing a UN resolution calling for an immediate cease-fire. President Joe Biden had several private conversations with Prime Minister Benjamin Netanyahu, but he would not speak to Hamas leaders, whom the U.S. government defines as terrorists. But in the Middle East, state terrorism is far more deadly than paramilitary terrorism. Biden may have privately put some pressure on Netanyahu since he faced dissent inside the Democratic Party, but Egyptian leaders appear to have been the negotiators of the eventual cease-fire.

Religious differences are central drivers of these conflicts. The combatants do not try to impose their religion on each other, but both believe they have a divine right to the same land. The Hebrew Bible claims that God promised the land of Israel to the children of Israel, and this is now inscribed in the platforms of several Jewish political parties. To the contrary, say Arabs, the Land of Canaan was promised to Ishmael, the elder son of Abraham, from whom they claim descent. Muslims and Jews also revere holy sites in the same places, such as the Cave of the Patriarchs and the Temple Mount. Since Muslims controlled these sites for 1,400 years, they constructed holy buildings such as the Dome of the Rock and the Al-Aqsa Mosque. Jerusalem is thus the epicenter of conflict. Neither the initial political elite of Israel nor the Palestinian people were renowned for their religiosity, but in an age of nationalism, their ethnic identity as Jews and Arabs has greatly reinforced the struggle.

On the Jewish side, extremism has been boosted by relatively poor immigrant Jews coming from Arab countries, Eastern Europe, and Russia. They seek land and housing and are prepared to seize them from the Arab occupants. Their increasing numbers have improved the electoral fortunes of Israeli conservative and religious parties pressuring for more landgrabs. Many Israeli Jews have also learned a lesson from the Holocaust that differs from the lesson liberals had expected, that this appalling experience would make them more tolerant of minorities. To the contrary, most Jewish Israelis seem to believe that to survive as a people, they must use to the full whatever coercive powers they have—and of course the rhetoric of some Palestinians is to "throw them into the sea." Since Israeli Jews have the military and political power to seize Arab lands, most of them believe they have the right to do so, in the name of ethnic survival. Their ambition is boosted by access to international capital, which has enabled them to build a modern state, a modern military, and modern capitalism—to make the desert bloom. Do we not deserve it? they ask rhetorically.

Palestinians are predominantly poor, desperately dependent in their two enclaves on the Israelis for essential services, abandoned by foreign powers, subjected to continuing ethnic cleansing. Their politicians are deeply divided and have achieved little for them. Many young men and women look in desperation for protection from terrorist militias. When they throw rocks at Israeli police and soldiers, the Israeli response is state terrorism, bringing in return more militia attacks. The resulting twenty-fold disparity in fatalities alienates Palestinians further from Israel and seems to some to confirm the Hamas claim that only armed struggle can bring satisfaction, if not actual gains. So despite the two communities' fierce hatred of each other, Israeli politicians such as former Prime Minister Netanyahu and the Hamas paramilitaries are in effect conspiring together, living off each other's aggression, one to win elections, the other to find new militia recruits, each maintaining power among their own people by prolonging the struggle.

Of course, they have not been the only players. Yet the Arab states found that involvement burned them, while British and French power declined and the Soviet Union collapsed. During the 1950s and early 1960s, France was the main collaborator in the Israeli nuclear program, while the United States tried to restrain that program. But then pro-Israeli American Jews' ability to organize the electoral defeat of U.S. politicians critical of

Israel, the decline of American anti-Semitism, and the growing pro-Israeli sentiments among Evangelicals made Israel the most favored U.S. ally, rewarded with massive economic and military patronage. Until the Afghan and Iraq wars brought temporary U.S. aid there, Israel was for three decades the leading recipient of its aid, amounting to between $3 and $4 billion per year, while aid to the Palestinian authority was only between $130 million and $1 billion. Initially, aid to Israel included much economic assistance, but almost all aid is now military. In 2019 the United States gave $3.8 billion in military aid to Israel, in addition to $8 billion in loan guarantees. But these figures exclude Department of Defense "missile defense" aid, which added another 40 percent to this total.[7] The explicit promise is to give Israel a "qualitative military edge" over all its neighbors. And just as war with the Palestinians broke out again in 2021 came a further $735 million in high-tech weaponry offered by the United States to Israel.

This is unique among U.S. policy failures in the Middle East, the one case where the United States potentially had the power to put pressure on both sides by threatening to withdraw assistance to them both unless they came to the negotiating table. But American presidents have shown less and less inclination to attempt this. In 1981 U.S. aid amounted to nearly 10 percent of the Israeli economy. But the decline in economic aid means that total current economic aid is only about 1.5 percent of all aid. As for Israelis, most leaders have lost interest in any peace process; instead, they have done pragmatic economic deals with some Arab states, and they seem willing to take a few intermittent casualties in Palestine for increases in territory. Peace and genuine settlement of the dispute is now a glimmer on the far horizon. Both sides and the United States could in collaboration bring it closer.

Muslim against Non-Muslim Neighbors: (2) Nagorno-Karabagh

These wars ranged a Muslim against a neighboring Christian country, with no significant imperial intervention. The somewhat secularized Shi'a Muslim regime of Azerbaijan and an Armenia adhering to the Christian Apostolic Church dispute the territories between them known as Nagorno-Karabagh. These territories have been recognized internationally since Soviet times as part of Azerbaijan, although about 75 percent of the population was then Armenian Christian. The Soviets had

damped down disputes between the communities, but in 1988, just before the Soviet collapse, and provoked by a pogrom of Armenians in the
city of Sumgait, a large Armenian movement in the region declared independence from Azerbaijan, aided by the rulers of Armenia, which, although formally a secular state, has a 90 percent Christian population.
The ensuing war lasted until 1994, killing perhaps 30,000 people; around
a million refugees fled from the fighting. Religious artifacts and buildings were targeted and destroyed in that war, but religion was less important than ethnicity in the war. Armenian forces won and gained control
over all of Nagorno-Karabagh as well as some connecting Azeri territories depopulated through ethnic cleansing of Azeris. Christians were now
the vast majority of the people remaining in Nagorno-Karabagh, and
two successive referenda there produced more than 90 percent of votes
(on high turnouts) endorsing separation from Azerbaijan and union with
Armenia. A Russian-brokered cease-fire uneasily held for twenty-two
years from 1994 as Russia, the United States, and France chaired fruitless
mediation efforts. A brief MID flare-up in 2016 claimed one hundred
lives, but no territorial changes resulted.

The Azerbaijan regime remained revisionist, however, and modern-
ized its armed forces. Azeri forces probed briefly in 2016, but in October
2020 they invaded Nagorno-Karabagh en masse. Superior military technology overcame fierce Armenian resistance, especially through drones
supplied by Israeli-Turkish collaboration. Military operations were probably directed by Turkish officers.[8] President Recep Erdogan was aiding a
fellow Turkic people while advancing his own regional power. Armenian
forces had neither drones nor the weapons to shoot them down. Syrian
mercenaries were also recruited by Turkey, some experienced fighters,
some raw recruits. They were cannon fodder for Azeri forces on the
bloody southern front to reduce Azeri casualties—"risk transfer militarism." After forty-four days Russia threatened intervention, and so Azeri
forces stopped. Negotiations chaired by Russia resulted in the cession of
territory, mostly outside Nagorno-Karabagh, which Armenia had held.
This makes communication between Armenia and Nagorno-Karabagh
problematic, since the connecting roads now pass through Azeri-held
territory. Two thousand Russian peacekeepers were deployed for five
years to keep them open. This was a clear-cut Azeri victory costing at
least four thousand Armenian and nearly three thousand Azeri casualties.
A few hundred civilians were also killed. Another bout of ethnic cleansing and destruction of religious monuments saw Armenians fleeing from

the ceded territories, often burning down their houses as they left. Azeris came in to replace them, some reclaiming property their families had once owned. Further MIDs in which a few troops were killed occurred in May and November 2021, Azeris seemingly the aggressors, as they were again in 2022 when about 300 troops, mostly Armenian, were killed. By then the Russian presence was weakening because of the war in Ukraine. What will happen when the Russian troops leave?

The conflict had not primarily concerned religion in the sense of doctrinal or ritual disputes, nor did either state seek to impose its religion on the other community. These were primarily ethnic conflicts, Azeris against Armenians, both now governed by radical nationalist intelligentsia, to decide who would dominate these territories.[9] Nonetheless, since religion is the core of their ethnicity, some religious hatreds were stirred up, as revealed in the destruction of churches and mosques. Azeris were also bolstered ideologically by the righteousness normally possessed by revisionists: this region had belonged to us and was taken from us illegitimately by force. Armenians were bolstered by democratic righteousness, the right of a population to choose its government, as revealed in the referenda. Some also feared a second genocide. Memories of the genocide at the hands of the Turks in 1915 is an important part of Armenian identity and had been stirred up by the Sumgait pogrom perpetrated by Azeris, whom most Armenians call "Turks." The United States was not involved in this war, and though Russia had provided arms to both combatants, it was directly involved only in settling the war. Turkey was heavily implicated, and for very mixed motives. This revisionist struggle may not be over.

Islamic Sectarian Wars

For over a millennium Islam has contained rival Sunni and Shi'a sects, ultimately deriving from a seventh-century succession dispute over who should succeed Muhammad. For most of this long stretch of history, Sunni and Shi'a uneasily coexisted, arguing about historical legitimacy and religious ritual, occasionally fighting each other. The Shi'a, being minorities almost everywhere except in Persia (now Iran), tended of necessity to adopt quietist doctrines, while in Persia Shi'a clergy were usually subordinated to a secular state. Wars broke out when sectarian conflict legitimated geopolitical struggle, as in the many wars during 1559 to 1648 between the Sunni Ottoman Empire and the Shi'a Persian Empire. These wars intermittently continued until 1823. Yet these wars had reflected geopolitical more than religious motives.

Shi'a and Sunni tend to dominate different states. Shi'a predominate in Iran, Azerbaijan, and less substantially in Iraq and Bahrain. The rest of the Muslim world is majority Sunni, who amount to over 80 percent of all Muslims. Thus, in most countries significant internal conflict will pit Sunnis against Sunnis, for the simple reason that there aren't enough Shi'a to form a major movement.[10] The converse is true in Iran (90 percent Shi'a) and Azerbaijan (85 percent Shi'a). There have been two major cases, however, in which a geopolitical struggle between states was amplified by a sectarian divide between them, the Iran-Iraq War of the 1980s, and the simmering Iran–Saudi Arabian confrontation enduring today.

In 1980 Iraqi forces launched an invasion of Iran. For the Iranian regime, this was a war of self-defense, defending especially its recent Islamist revolution. The Islamic Republican Guard provided its vanguard force, advancing in human waves, suffering heavy losses, who were glorified as martyrs. Iran's only ally was the Alawite Shi'a ruling (but minority) community of Syria. On the Iraqi side, help came from many Sunni states and from the United States. Though the government of Saddam Hussein was predominantly Sunni, it was also rather secular. Saddam had launched his surprise attack on Iran believing that this was a window of opportunity, that recent revolutionary chaos had weakened the Iranian military. But there was also a sectarian motive, for he feared the Shi'a revolution in Iran might spark off a revolt in Iraq by the majority Shi'a population whom he kept in a subordinate role. He also hoped to annex an oil-rich province. So the war was both a geopolitical and an ideological sectarian struggle with material goals added. After eight years of slaughter, the war ended in stalemate back at the preexisting boundaries. Superior Iraqi weapons had been countered by superior Iranian morale; a million Iranians and half a million Iraqis were dead—the third deadliest war in modern times in terms of deaths as a proportion of combatant country populations. Iran was then put on the defensive by American hostility but semicovertly aided Shi'a movements elsewhere.

The second major sectarian confrontation came after the 2003 defeat of Saddam and the collapse of Iraq. Shi'a Iran and Sunni Saudi Arabia were left as the dominant regional powers, both major oil powers. Their struggle had intensified as Islamist hard-liners took over in both countries, the ayatollahs in Iran, and Wahhābīs in Saudi Arabia. Both had propaganda and educational networks aimed at coreligionists abroad. They are now the core adversaries in a geopolitical-ideological struggle increasingly involving the United States and three other countries, Bahrain, Syria, and Yemen. The main motive of the two powers has been geopolitical grandeur in the region. Sectarianism, however, clearly dominated their choice of allies and clients. No alliance among any of these states crossed sectarian lines.

The Arab Spring protests in March 2011 had direct sectarian repercussions in Bahrain, where a popular protest movement based mainly in the oppressed 60 percent Shi'a population was crushed by Bahrain's minority Sunni government's armed forces, which included many foreign mercenaries, supplemented by one thousand Saudi and five hundred UAE soldiers. All these forces were Sunni. The regime then destroyed about forty Shi'a mosques, a clear gesture of sectarian repression. This had been a brief civil war between rival Islamic religious communities in which the Sunni government triumphed over a popular insurrection that was largely though not entirely Shi'a.

There were bigger repercussions in Syria, where Arab Spring peaceful protests were met by repression by President Bashar al-Assad. This turned protest into armed rebellion aimed at removing him. The core of his regime was the Alawite Shi'a sect. The resistance was an amalgam of largely Sunni groups, some quite secular, such as the Free Syrian Army and the Kurdish-Arab Syrian Democratic Forces (SDF), and some jihadists, like the al-Nusra Front and ISIS. This war saw the largest recruitment of jihadists, and they increasingly dominated the rebel forces. Samar Yazbek quotes anti-Assad militia leaders she interviewed who voiced murderous sentiments toward Alawites, whom they called "apostates."[11] She managed with some difficulty to conceal the fact that she was an Alawite. Although there was an underlying conflict between most Alawites and many Sunnis, the civil war itself amplified murderous hatreds, exacerbated also by an influx of over ten thousand foreign Sunnis to fight the apostate Alawite regime.

Their factional animosities greatly weakened the rebels, as did their inferior weaponry. Lacking antiaircraft guns, they were helpless against bombing from planes and from helicopters dropping barrels loaded with explosives. The Saudis and Qatar supplied them with simple arms up to 2017. Shi'a Iran and Hezbollah have supported Assad, whose air force was aided by Russian planes from 2015 onward. The secular rebels were helped by an international coalition led by the United States from 2014, but the coalition provided much less aid than Russia did to Assad. The Americans also focused on attacking ISIS, not Assad. Turkish ground forces attacked both Assad and ISIS forces, but they focused most on the Kurdish SDF militia since President Erdogan feared Kurdish resistance movements inside Turkey. Israeli governments have also attacked Iranian and Hezbollah forces. Amid such confusion, the Shi'a-Sunni axis has been only one strand of the conflict. Exploiting the chaos, the Assad regime has been able with Russian help and American distraction to survive, the ostensible winner of a destroyed country. The United States and Saudi Arabia were on the losing side, but the real losers were half a million Syrian dead, as well as the shattered survivors of areas devastated by bombing targeted deliberately at civilians, and at least 7 million fleeing as refugees abroad. The most perverse legacy of this internationalized civil war was the creation of Syrian mercenary forces, young men with or without military experience but with no job prospects in Syria, organized by the Turkish military to fight for pay in Libya and Nagorno-Karabagh, a strategy of "risk-transfer militarism" to protect Libyan and Azeri forces.

The third case of sectarian civil war is Yemen. The Sunni former government of the country controls much of the predominantly Sunni south, although Al Qaeda and ISIS affiliates and regional separatists are also active there. In the north the Houthis, a Shi'a Zaydi sect, from 2004 fought repeated wars against the Sunni government with support from a Shi'a population feeling exploited by the central government. A string of victories culminated in their seizing the capital, Sanaa, in 2014. Because the Houthis had overthrown a supposedly legitimate government, the UN authorized sanctions against them, but not military operations. But war escalated in 2016 when Saudi Arabia and other Sunni Gulf sheikdoms began bombing and blockading the Houthis, who receive help only from Shi'a Iran. The Saudis are backed up by Egypt, Jordan, Sudan, Bahrain, and the United Arab Emirates, all Sunni states, in addition to the United States and Britain, who until 2021 defined the Houthis as a terrorist organization. ISIS also attacks the Houthis as apostates, just as ISIS in Afghanistan now bombs Shi'a mosques. By the end of 2021 the UN estimated that the war had killed 370,000, mostly civilians. Oxfam and the UN estimated that 15 or 20 million Yemenis would not have enough food by the end of 2021. Deaths are resulting from lack of food, inadequate health services, and infrastructure destroyed by Saudi-led aerial bombing and blockades and Houthi artillery shelling. The UNHCR also noted that during 2015–20 over 4 million Yemenis had become refugees. The Four Horsemen of the Apocalypse—Pestilence, War, Famine, and Death—gallop together across Syria and Yemen.

Two more countries saw sectarian violence between Shi'a and Sunnis. In Iraq before 2003, Saddam's regime rested mainly on Sunnis, 35 percent of the population, repressing the 65 percent Shi'a (these figures include Kurds of both sects). Control was reversed after the U.S. invasion, but this sparked a civil war that still simmers. In Lebanon Shi'a represent 60 percent of Muslims, Sunnis 35 percent, but each sect dominates its own regions, and Lebanese Christians outnumber each of the Muslim sects. After a period of broadly successful power sharing, Lebanon descended into chaos, but Muslim sectarianism was not a major cause. Hezbollah is a large Shi'a paramilitary force in Lebanon, pursuing violence there and against Israel. It is not fundamentally sectarian, however, for it cooperates with the Palestinian Hamas paramilitary, which is Sunni. The war in Lebanon is only marginally sectarian. Additionally, atrocities have intermittently occurred against Shi'a minorities in Afghanistan, Egypt, India, Indonesia, Malaysia, Nigeria, Pakistan, and Saudi Arabia.

All these cases reveal that sectarian Islamic aspects of civil and interstate wars have been growing. Iran-Saudi confrontations might be considered a more geopolitical than sectarian ideological struggle. Yet since each side allies only with cosectarians, this suggests more religious input, not so much doctrinal as a question of which community will dominate. This has increasingly involved the United States on the Sunni side, as I discuss later.

Transnational Jihadi Wars: Islamic State

Jihadi wars have received considerable attention because the jihadists have attacked Western as well as Muslim countries. Hezbollah, Al Qaeda and its affiliates, and Islamic State movements variously called Daesh, ISIL, and ISIS (the collective term I will use) have spawned affiliates across most of the Muslim world—in the Middle East, North Africa, and Central and South Asia. Hezbollah is the only Shi'a organization, and it has a legitimate political presence in Lebanon. It is much less radical, its goals limited to Lebanon and Israel. In Syria it is halfway to being a regular army with Iranian state support. The main movements are Sunni, like Al Qaeda, ISIS, and their affiliates. They are nonstate and much more radical. Al Qaeda arose among various jihadi groups who in the 1990s had been repressed by regimes in the region. Al Qaeda then focused on small-scale attacks on the "far enemy," the United States, while seeking to rally local Muslim populations in pursuit of its jihadi goals.

But after 9/11, the initial defeat of the Taliban in Afghanistan, the death of bin Laden, and major counterterrorist security measures, Al Qaeda lost much of its capacity to strike at the far enemy and focused on local struggles. The revival of the Taliban, however, may increase its activism. Here I focus on the Islamic State, which has a broader striking range and is better-documented.

ISIS militants are ideological warriors driven by an aggressive reading of the Quran, calling for a jihad, holy war, against the unbelievers. The Quran says that it is for Christians to choose conversion to Islam, payment of an extra poll tax, or death; Ibn Khaldun repeated this in 1377, and it has again risen to prominence.[12] But this holy war is shorn of the two qualifications expressed in the Quran, that jihad might refer only to wars of defense against unbelievers, and the "escape clauses" whereby those ignorant of the true faith might be given time to repent.[13] ISIS militants seek to force conversions of Christians and Jews and to kill those who refuse or who are "apostates," like Shi'a, Alawites, Yazidi and Druze monotheists, and Kurds, a mostly Sunni ethnic group who are more mystical and tolerant. They also attack Sunni Muslims who have flirted with Western influences. ISIS sees apostates everywhere—selling or consuming cigarettes, alcohol, or drugs, with Western clothes, clean-shaven men, uncovered women, "abnormal" sexual behavior, and voting in an election.

At its peak in 2014, ISIS had taken over about 40 percent of Iraq and 60 percent of Syria, founding a short-lived ISIS caliphate. In it, if Muslims outwardly conformed, they were not in peril. In the capital, Raqqa, "Samer" wrote a diary of daily life. He says public attendance at executions was compulsory. Spectators had to mask their thoughts. "It's very dangerous to let your true feelings show because Daesh is eyeing the crowd; we are utterly in their grip." There were daily floggings. Teenage girls were forcibly married to fighters, and women were harassed by the "modesty police." Arbitrary taxes were levied on shopkeepers.[14] A mixture of coercion, indoctrination, and effective governance meant that locals did not resist a regime that was simultaneously a "mafia adept at exploiting decades-old transnational gray markets for oil and arms trafficking . . . a conventional military . . . a sophisticated intelligence-gathering apparatus . . . a slick propaganda machine."[15]

ISIS denounces Shi'a ritual innovations, such as worship at the graves of imams and processional self-flagellation, which it says have no basis in the Quran or the sayings of the Prophet. Two hundred million

Shi'a are in principle condemned to death or forced conversion, though there are too many of them for this to be practical. Muslim heads of state are targets, for they have elevated man-made law above the sharia law of God. ISIS even persuaded many that the final war between Muslims and infidels had started, in which Muslims would eventually triumph, and the end of days would come.[16] This is a transcendent ideology glorifying atrocious religious war.

ISIS kills men, women, and children and tortures and kills prisoners. Killing allegedly adulterous women and homosexual men, and entire organized sex slave markets, are legitimized by its readings of Quranic texts. Like some customs relating to the Judeo-Christian Old Testament, these reflected practices of ancient societies that are considered horrific today. Its deeds put ISIS in the same atrocity league as the Nazis, while adding the religious incentive that atrocities will be rewarded in heaven. The militants do not feel moral qualms but proudly proclaim their brutality in horrific videos. Their text, *The Management of Savagery*, declares that "the most abominable of the levels of savagery" are better than "stability under the order of unbelief." Their atrocities have a dual rationality, however. They are aimed at intimidating the enemy and at showing those who join the movement they must go to any lengths to achieve the Islamic paradise. There is no turning back.

ISIS appeals especially to Sunnis living under Shi'a rule in Iraq and Syria.[17] It first expanded in Iraq after the American defeat of Saddam Hussein in 2003 handed over a previously Sunni government to Shi'a leaders. Sunni tribal paramilitaries, the Sons of Iraq, were also sidelined by the new government. Some top ISIS leaders had previously served in Saddam's military or security services, and so Ba'athism had returned as jihadism. The ISIS appeal to Syrian Sunnis grew as Assad intensified repression and as the fractious Syrian rebel groups produced chaos. These crises, as well as the collapse of the Arab Spring revolts, made some Muslims speculate on the apocalyptic possibility that the great military leader, the Mahdi, might soon come to bring about the end of days.[18] Ibn Khaldun had poured ridicule on those who in the fourteenth century believed this to be imminent.[19] Some delusions never die.

In Syria the United States gave limited help to the anti-Assad rebels while Assad used his airpower, later reinforced by Russia's, to pour indiscriminate devastation on rebel-held regions.[20] Between them, they unintentionally gave ISIS space to expand in a power vacuum across Syrian-Iraqi borderlands. Their fanaticism yielded superior morale, which enabled them to rout much larger Iraqi government forces. It seems appropriate to describe this with the Arabic term *asabiyya*, greater normative solidarity. But the subventions provided by wealthy Sunnis abroad also enabled them to dominate the poorly equipped secular Syrian rebels. In the ISIS caliphate foreign donations were supplemented by bank theft; selling oil, wheat, water, and antiquities; human trafficking; extracting ransoms for kidnapped foreigners; and imposing taxes on local economic activity.[21] Rukmini Callimachi says that ISIS files in Mosul reveal that "the tax revenue the Islamic State earned far outstripped income from oil sales. It was daily commerce and agriculture—not petroleum— that powered the economy of the caliphate." ISIS at one point had a daily income of U.S. $3 million and an annual revenue of $2.9 billion.[22] In some areas ISIS provided effective police, courts, and city services. It mediated tribal disputes, and its justice was swift. Kidnapping, robberies, and extortion declined, and municipal workers were forced back to work. Some had formerly received their salaries while doing nothing. It also imposed price controls on commodities such as oil byproducts.[23]

Though hated by virtually all Muslim regimes, the jihadists have enough popular support to survive state persecution. Several studies reveal the background of ISIS militants. These are based on three sources: government estimates, captured ISIS records, and in-depth interviews with detained, defecting, or captured militants.[24] Obviously, these are not random samples of ISIS fighters, and the various samples may be presumed to have biases, but they are the best we have.

They were virtually all Sunni Muslims; there were just a handful of Shi'a and Christian converts. About half came from Syria or Iraq and half were from foreign countries—perhaps forty thousand of them, all told. Most foreigners were from Arab countries, but at the peak the largest group came from Russia and the former Soviet Central Asian republics, then from Arab countries, then from Europe, with a sprinkling from much farther afield. Tunisia contributed the largest number of Arabs, and France contributed the largest number of Europeans. So they were a veritable international brigade.

The studies find that they were mainly middle-class and quite well-educated, except for the group who had been detained before they could reach Syria or Iraq, who were mainly working-class and poorly educated. But data obtained from ISIS records indicate that this was truer of the foreigners than of the locals. Yet majorities in all groups had experienced unemployment (most believed this was through discrimination). About one-quarter had a petty criminal past or had spent time in prison—rarely for terrorist offenses, mostly for drug offenses. These, together with other "vulnerabilities" like unemployment, poverty, and family troubles (especially evident among women), made them susceptible to making a major change in their life, and friends and the internet were the main persuaders into leaving. Their internet propaganda depends on video games (the popular war game "Call of Duty" was transformed into "Call of Jihad"), Twitter, and Facebook, as well as short films showing idealized life in the caliphate.

They were overwhelmingly young, in their twenties, and around 80 percent were male. Most had been single when they joined the struggle, but half the men were married by the time they were captured, having been found wives by ISIS. Three-quarters of the women were foreigners and were middle-class. Most of the women became brides thanks to ISIS, and their role was the traditional one of bearing and rearing children and caring for their menfolk. Only a few women fought, while at least two-thirds of the men were fighters.

Scott Atran and his colleagues interviewed seventy young men in Iraqi refugee camps.[25] Most reported that they and most Sunnis had welcomed ISIS as leading a "glorious revolution," implementing divine rule through sharia law. Ninety-three percent commended the Islamic State's provision of effective defense, commitment to religion, and implementation of sharia, which resulted in security, stability, and everyday travel freedom because they abolished checkpoints. ISIS brutality and corruption had then undermined this support. Disillusionment was common in all the interview surveys. Yet most still favored sharia law and opposed democracy, which they said brought only conflict—as it had in Iraq. A desire for public order overpowered desire for liberty and democracy. Ninety-four percent believed that Iran and America conspired to "eliminate our [Sunni] religion." They would support another jihadi regime, should one arise. In Dagestan young people were recruited by an online campaign focused on Muslim humiliation and victimhood, an idealized Islamist life, and the duty of jihad.[26] Farhad Khosrokhavar sees young Muslims radicalizing from a sense of personal humiliation and victimization in line with an Ummah community similarly suffering. Speckhard and Ellenberg report that their interviewees privileged their Islamic identity. Their ideological attachments were not so much religious as political—jihadist, caliphate, anti-Western sentiments, and Sunni rights. But unemployment, poverty, and just "helping" also figured.[27] ISIS recruits had heard of the

military failure of Arab nationalism from the Six-Day War of 1967 onward, and the unraveling of incipient welfare states by neoliberal Arab regimes. Lydia Wilson agrees that the ideological core was not Islamic
doctrine but "a visceral feeling of oneness with the group."[28] Life in the
caliphate was depicted as idealized camaraderie between fighters and civilians, bonded by the fight for true Islam and the threat of death. She interviewed Iraqi ISIS fighters in a Kirkuk jail. They were poor, illiterate, often
unemployed, and from big families. She added:

> They are children of the occupation, many with missing fathers
> at crucial periods (through jail, death from execution, or fighting
> in the insurgency), filled with rage against America and their
> own [Shi'a] government. They are not fueled by the idea of an
> Islamic caliphate without borders; rather, ISIS is the first group
> since the crushed Al Qaeda to offer these humiliated and en-
> raged young men a way to defend their dignity, family, and tribe.
> This is not radicalization to the ISIS way of life, but the promise
> of a way out of their insecure and undignified lives; the promise
> of living in pride as Iraqi Sunni Arabs, which is not just a reli-
> gious identity but cultural, tribal, and land-based, too.[29]

All these studies downplay doctrinal motivations. The main attraction
was the defense of an idealized Islamic community.

Brian Dodwell and his colleagues analyzed over 4,600 Islamic State
personnel records for foreign fighters in 2013 and 2014.[30] Of these, 10
percent had experience in jihadi movements. Four hundred were under
eighteen, considered well-suited to suicide bombing. As in the other
studies, few claimed much knowledge of the Quran. Notes made on their
files by ISIS officials indicated searches for specialized professional skills.
This was in many ways a normal business organization. When asked
whether they wanted a fighting or a suicide role in ISIS, 12 percent
chose suicide, and those were mostly from the Middle East and North
Africa. This contrasted with the 56 percent of recruits who had preferred
suicide, as recorded for six hundred Al Qaeda foreign fighters in Iraq in
2007. These were all from Arab countries, mainly Saudi Arabia, Libya
coming in second.[31] But these are both astonishing totals, proof of
extreme commitment.

ISIS fighters numbered between 30,000 and 80,000 during 2014–16.
Between 2015 and 2017 jihadists operating in Europe killed nearly 350

people.[32] Using big data on the online behavior of thousands of ISIS sympathizers in France, the United Kingdom, Germany, and Belgium, Tamar Mitts found that pro-ISIS tweets were significantly correlated with local anti-Muslim hostility, as were descriptions of an idealized life in ISIS territories and favorable views of foreign fighters. Muslim and anti-Muslim extremists are locked together in an escalating spiral of hatred.[33]

In general, recruits could choose to fight as an individual nonmember, usually for tribal allies, or pledge total allegiance to the group, which brought more pay and status but was a commitment for life. Anyone pledging allegiance and then seeking to leave was denounced as an apostate and killed. All fighters had a two- to three-month course on the Quran on top of their military training and then were sent in roughly equal numbers either to the front or to border patrols.

Outside the short-lived caliphate, jihadi guerillas have shifted the battlefield from jungles and mountains to cities, hiding among civilian populations whom regimes and Americans would prefer not to target, since that might alienate the local population. They use the weapons of the weak, such as Kalashnikovs, machine guns, IEDs, the suicide belt, grenades for street fighting, shoulder-held rocket grenades, and pickup trucks. They are beginning to use drones. The IED involves a spotter looking for oncoming vehicles, and a second person who remotely operates the bomb's trigger. But both are directly communicating through cellphones with a controller far away, perhaps in an internet café.. They were outnumbered and technologically overmatched, especially vulnerable to airpower. Yet high commitment and morale enabled a stream of victories over regular and conscript Syrian and Iraqi forces from 2014 to 2016. ISIS militants provided at least seventy-two suicide bombers between January 2013 and March 2018, and well over one hundred who knew they were likely to die in their attacks. These assassins were venerated as martyrs. High morale was evident in the siege of Mosul, where few ISIS soldiers surrendered. One reason, says Khosrokhavar, is that radicalized Islamists believe that if they engage in jihadist action, God will intervene to establish a universal theocracy.[34] Democratic triumphalist theory is rebuffed. ISIS, an authoritarian movement, generates higher morale.

But American airpower ground them down. Mosul was devastated by bombing and fell in July 2017. More surrenders came in early October 2017, five hundred after eleven days of fighting at Tal Afar, and over one thousand after three days at Hawija. Finally, Raqqa, the ISIS capital, fell on October 21. Foreign recruitment had slowed as the defeats came. Some foreign fighters now vanished in a "meltaway" strategy, others languished in detention centers, often refused reentry to their home country. Michael Knights and Alex Almeida report that in January 2020, 14,000 to 18,000 ISIS fighters and helpers remained in Iraq and Syria.[35] ISIS attacks fell sharply but rebounded in 2019 and 2020, scattered mostly across rural areas, relying on small-scale IED and nighttime attacks on villages and police stations. As the United States and its allies pulled out troops, Iraqi forces proved less effective at coping with them. ISIS is hurt but not finished. Its attempt at a territorial caliphate failed because it played into American strength at fixed-position warfare. Its role in Western countries has declined as state intelligence agencies have intensified their surveillance, and almost all attacks are committed by loners armed only with knives, guns, and vehicles.[36] But the digital caliphate remains vigorous, and the U.S. military in 2020 counted 600 ISIS attacks in Syria and 1,400 in Iraq. Its staying power is greater than that of the United States, although U.S. policy has shifted toward drone warfare, which is less costly and provokes less opposition at home. Khosrokhavar says the "salient trait of jihadism is its flexibility and its capacity to adapt to extreme situations through reorganization. Al-Qaeda and the jihadist movements are the first truly global and transnational type of terrorism to perpetuate itself over time, transform itself in the face of international and national repression . . . and continue its struggle in multiple forms, varying them as circumstances change and constantly constructing new ones."[37]

There are other Islamist militias. ISIS-K is the long-surviving Afghan offshoot, with whom the Taliban government has to deal. But jihadism has grown across the north of Africa. Al-Shabaab operates in and around Somalia, stretching as far as northern Mozambique—though here it seems like a local movement protesting government mistreatment of the region and lacking much Islamist coloration. Originally formed as the armed branch of an opposition movement in Somalia, al-Shabaab declared allegiance to Al Qaeda in 2004. It had success during 2005–12, minimally administering much of Somalia. Its defeat of Ethiopian forces that had invaded to assist government forces brought it nationalist credentials. It expanded activities with atrocities committed in neighboring countries, whose retaliatory crackdowns on their Muslim populations increased the flow of young recruits. Al-Shabaab has been fractious and suffered defections to ISIS, but it still has militants and commits bombings and assaults. It remains stronger in rural areas, where it levies taxes and administers justice.[38] African jihadi networks are also intermingling with other guerilla groups in the eastern Democratic Republic of Congo, whose government has invited in the Ugandan army to help combat them. U.S. advisers have been active in combat against militant groups, as have French forces in Francophone Africa, although President Macron announced in mid-2021 that the French troops would soon be removed. But the Taliban victory in Afghanistan is likely to encourage jihadi activity in many places.

American Interventions

One cannot discuss jihadi wars without mentioning the United States. After 1945 the Middle East saw American-Soviet rivalry, fighting indirectly through proxies, with competing ideologies of global domination. The Soviet collapse in 1991 encouraged the United States into new offensives, fighting "wars of choice" when the nation was not itself threatened. Thus, it became the most aggressive military power in the world. The financial cost is no problem for the United States. As the holder of the world's reserve currency, it can just print more money and take on debt to finance war. The cost of war in lives, however, proved more problematic.

Most recent enemies identified by the United States have been Muslim dictators, Saddam Hussein, Muammar Gaddafi, and Bashar al-Assad, and the jihadi movements Al Qaeda, the Taliban, and ISIS. Unlike the Soviet Union, these are hardly contenders for world domination. The "Axis of Evil"—Iran, Iraq, North Korea—denounced by Bush the Younger involved three lesser states, termed "terrorist" to amplify their threat. The "greatness" of America as the arbiter of world conflict, "the leader of the free world," remains the core secular ideology justifying interventions. American power will bring free market (that is, neoliberal) capitalism, higher living standards, and democracy to benighted peoples. Women's equality has been recently added to the mission statement. The ideology is sincerely believed by American administrations of both parties, the one remaining bipartisan policy in a factionalized polity.

The results of American interventions, usually for regime change, have been poor. Since 1945 U.S. goals have rarely been achieved through war. Korea was a stalemate, leaving the peninsula exactly where it was before the war, and adding great loss of life. Vietnam was a defeat. Most of the East Asian region was won for capitalism not by war but by generous trade agreements: economic power proved superior to military power. Defeat in Vietnam then taught Americans caution for a decade, until they credited Reagan with winning the Cold War, which restored American confidence. Invasions of Panama and Grenada were easy victories over minnows, while Serbia was a victory for NATO bombing allied to Croat and Bosnian forces on the ground, bringing Serbia to the negotiating table. None of these wars was authorized by the United Nations, and as wars of aggression they could be considered war crimes, though there is no authority that could impose a criminal trial on the United States.

The First Gulf War of 1990–91 was a full-scale invasion of Iraq in response to the invasion by Saddam Hussein's forces of Kuwait. So the American-led response had the UN seal of approval, which by 1990 (unlike 1950 in Korea) brought genuine global legitimacy. And it was not anti-Islamic since Kuwait and other U.S. allies were Muslim states. President Bush the Elder brought the war to a halt when he had regained Kuwait and taught Saddam a lesson, for he knew he lacked the political power to form a stable alternative government in Iraq. He had hoped Saddam's defeat would lead to indirect regime change, through an army coup, but none came. There were insurrections against Saddam in the Shi'a south and the Kurdish north, but nothing stirred in Baghdad or the heartland, and Saddam savagely crushed the risings. Over a further decade intermittent bombing by American and British planes failed to stop Saddam from breathing defiance. The hoped-for military coup never materialized.

In 1998 Congress and the Clinton administration increased the pressure by almost unanimously passing the Iraq Liberation Act, committing the United States to work for regime change in Iraq, though the means were not clarified. Seventy-two military coups in Arab states had been attempted between 1950 and 2009, and half had succeeded. This spurred authoritarian rulers to curtail the autonomy of the armed forces—just as Chinese emperors had. Rulers appointed generals on the basis of kinship, ethnicity, and sect; built up alternative armed forces or security police to monitor the military; split up tribes and clans in different regiments; rewarded loyalty through grants from oil revenues or import licenses or milking nationalized companies—all to cultivate the notion that "whatever they have is a gift from the regime." There were also purges. Coup-proofing has generally worked, but at the cost—as in imperial China—of making the army ineffective in battle, a cost that authoritarian rulers in Iraq, Saudi Arabia, Iran, Syria, and Egypt were willing to pay.[39] Saddam could not be overthrown from within, but his armed forces were enfeebled. They and the ruling Ba'ath Party were plagued with corruption, the narrowing of the social base of support, and hostilities between the various forces created by Saddam as counterweights to the army. There was corruption, evasion of conscription, desertion, low morale, and poor performance. It was all effective at keeping Saddam in power, but the record of his armed forces was poor.[40]

The 2000 election victory of Bush the Younger inaugurated a president who lacked foreign policy experience and relied on Vice President Cheney, a hawk who appointed neoconservatives recruited from right-wing think tanks to most of the top foreign and defense posts. The atrocity of 9/11 then further empowered them. That the Taliban government in Afghanistan was sheltering Osama bin Laden, the Al Qaeda mastermind, gave a quasi-legitimate motive of self-defense for intervention shared by both major political parties. Only one representative and not one senator voted against the invasion. In theory, international law would have required the United States first to try negotiations with the Taliban and Pakistan to bring bin Laden to an international court of justice. The Bush administration gave the Taliban government only two weeks to hand over bin Laden, an absurdly short period for realistic negotiations to take place. Yet since the United States does not accept international judiciaries, this is pie in the sky. The Taliban were also provincials, unaware of neocon determination to destroy those who defied the United States. American and British forces invaded Afghanistan at the end of 2001, and then it became the common enterprise of NATO, although Afghanistan was 11,000 kilometers from the North Atlantic.

The hawks then also used 9/11 to claim that Saddam Hussein, the Iraqi leader, supported Al Qaeda and possessed chemical weapons, claims that most experts knew were false. Saddam actually hated Al Qaeda, which had denounced him as an apostate, and he was a fairly secular ruler. But he was foolish, believing that the United States would not invade, not appreciating the effect of his own defiance on the new administration.

It is not clear whether a Democratic administration would have invaded Iraq in 2003. The Democrats in both House and Senate were split. Yet the hawks believed strongly in the mission of American military interventions, and the flawed intelligence they presented on Saddam's alleged weapons persuaded almost all Republicans and some Democrats to support the war. Some hawks (like Cheney) seemed to be pursuing American oil and economic interests, though it was difficult to see what these might be. Unlike the 1990–91 invasion, this one was not about oil. Others put U.S. grandeur first. Yet they all shared the belief that they could bring human rights, free markets, and democracy to the world, no longer deterred by Soviet retaliation. They tried to calculate the war's costs and benefits but they grossly overestimated U.S. power—not military power, which they saw would be overwhelming, but the political and ideological power to establish stable rule after victory. They thought it would be a swift in-and-out operation, never imagining having an army of occupation there for years. Some claimed intervention would pay for itself through oil and other trade deals. But they were ideologically blinded by the perceived virtue of their cause, assuming that the allure of their version of freedom and democracy was so strong that Afghans and Iraqis would welcome U.S. forces as liberators. Cheney declared just before the invasion: "I really do believe that we will be greeted as liberators. I've talked with a lot of Iraqis in the last several months myself, had them to the White House. . . . The read we get on the people of Iraq is there is no question but what they want is to get rid of Saddam Hussein and they will welcome as liberators the United States when we come to do that."[41]

This was mind-boggling given that for ten years the United States had been imposing economic sanctions on Iraq that were backed by bombing, which caused civilian suffering and children's deaths, much publicized by Saddam. How could that have led to massive Iraqi support? But calculations were unnecessary: the flow of history toward democracy would bring swift victory. They were wrong, for public order is a precondition for democracy, as Francis Fukuyama argued.[42] Those young Arab refugees whom I quoted earlier valued public order over democracy. Yet the United States produced disorder.

Robert Draper, working from interviews with administration insiders and newly released documents, emphasizes Bush's own role in the rush to war in Iraq. He says Bush experienced a conversion in 2002, conjoining ideology and emotion to evoke a "piercing clarity of purpose" and an "unchecked self-confidence" "to liberate a tormented people," and "to end a tyrant's regime." Meeting with the reluctant Jordanian king, he snapped: "Saddam is a bad guy. . . . My opinion of him hasn't changed. We need to take him down." Bush's voice rose as he declaimed: "History has called us." Bush kept repeating that Saddam hated America because he hated freedom, and freedom was the sacred heart of America. Draper opines, "His increasingly bellicose rhetoric reflected a wartime president who was no longer tethered to anything other than his own convictions." While speaking to Asian journalists in the Oval Office, Bush pointed to portraits of Churchill, Lincoln, and Washington and said that he was, like them, "a leader who knew who he was and who knew what was right." He was "a good versus evil guy," the one "decider," and he used the power of the presidency to sideline contrary opinions within the administration. Of course, most officials around him were hawks who agreed with him. Bush's rigid naïveté and lack of interest in the costs and consequences of war appalled a few staffers, but they dared not object for fear of losing influence or jobs. George Tenet believed his CIA's role was to serve his "First Customer," the president, so dissenters within the agency were not allowed to express criticism—or concluded it was wiser not to. Secretary of State Colin Powell, the likeliest dissenter, caved in with a speech at the UN declaring that Iraqi trucks using balloons for weather forecasting were in fact mobile chemical weapons labs.[43] UN delegates laughed at him. In retirement, he alone has been contrite. But the ability of an ideological-emotional ruler armed with presidential powers, surrounded by a clique of like-minded advisers, to take the country to war reinforces my belief that democracy is irrelevant to war-and-peace decisions.

The United States invaded Iraq in early 2003. It had failed to get Security Council approval, so this invasion was in principle a war crime. Both invasions of Afghanistan and Iraq brought swift battlefield victories and the fall of the Kabul and Baghdad regimes. But neither brought the desired results, as critics, including myself, had predicted.[44] The wars had little popular resonance in the United States, although most Americans initially believed what their leaders said about the connections between bin Laden and Saddam Hussein and chemical weapons. The British less so. But popular interest was skin-deep and faded in the messy aftermaths. By 2011 most Americans saw the Afghan and Iraq wars as having not been worth fighting, and they repeated this sentiment in 2016.[45] They were right, though this is very hard to say to the Americans and allies who fought there.

American and Allied Troops

Over 2.5 million U.S. troops have done tours of duty in the ironically named operations Enduring Freedom and Iraqi Freedom. The United States and its allies—Britain, Australia, France, and most NATO nations— now field professional armed forces. Their training and commitment have provided greater battle endurance than the American conscript army had showed in Vietnam. Yet allied troops have failed to overcome guerillas wielding weapons of the weak (including cyberweapons). They became an occupation force besieged by guerilla warfare for which they were ill-suited. Apart from the doomed attempt at a territorial state by ISIS, which was playing into the skills of the U.S. military, there was no front and no rear in these wars, little sight of an enemy, and less opportunity to get emotional relief by firing back. Defusing bombs was more time-consuming than engaging the enemy. For the U.S. infantry this is not cal-lous warfare, as it is for its air force and drone operators, and they are liable to fire wildly when danger erupts unpredictably, when explosions come from anywhere and fear-reducing retaliation is rarely possible. Local populations have offered little cooperation out of a mixture of hostility and fear, which adds further stress to the troops.

Junger vividly depicts the extreme. He lived with a platoon of U.S. in-fantry in one of the most isolated and dangerous valleys in Afghanistan, which was reachable only by helicopter. In this Taliban-controlled area, they suffered firefights almost every day, and suffered four dozen deaths. But these were men who had volunteered for the assignment, who thrived on the excitement of battle, and who felt fear only between battles. The men lusted to kill, some claiming they lived for the firefights, which they found "insanely exciting." Some took pride in the word "infidel" tattooed on their chests. They cheered when a scout described a wounded insur-gent crawling along a mountain path toward his own blown-off leg. They admit they are terrible garrison soldiers: ill-disciplined, violent, contemp-tuous of noncombatants. Fueled by testosterone and adrenaline, disturbed by sexual deprivation, they joke about killing and raping (even their own mothers and sisters). Their good qualities are killing efficiency, courage amounting to heroism, and bonding amounting to love. They will sacri-fice their lives for each other. Back home after the war, however, they ex-perience difficulty in readjusting to normal life. Reveling in killing has degraded their psyches, from sadist heroes to victims.[46]

In these wars deaths of allied troops have been few but unpredict-able. Unexpected explosives inflicted over three-fourths of the injuries to U.S. and British troops in Iraq and Afghanistan. Explosions cause atmo-spheric overpressure followed by a vacuum that can penetrate solid ob-jects, so that soldiers may avoid blunt-force trauma but receive an invisible brain injury. Over half the three thousand American soldiers wounded in Afghanistan and Iraq have suffered brain damage of varying degrees. Since their average age at the time was only twenty-three, the trauma will affect their memory, mood, and ability to think for as many as sixty years, perhaps more. Many who might have died of such wounds in earlier wars are now treated but left with enduring physical, psycho-logical, and cognitive injuries. While the Vietnam War had a 2.6:1 wounded-to-killed ratio, the Afghan and Iraqi wars had ratios of about 15:1 because of improved medical treatment. Amid the exhaustion of longer deployments in the war zone, random exposure to harm worsens the fear factor. This is the suffering we impose on our troops.

Modern weapons force soldiers to keep their heads down and fire fairly blindly, forcing the enemy to keep his head down and also fire wildly. In recent wars the vast majority of enemy deaths have been in-flicted by pilots from above and by rockets and drones fired from afar. Since the United States dominates the skies, Americans need not fear death from above, unlike the enemy or adjacent civilians.

In Iraq and Afghanistan, guerilla tactics and an enemy lurking among civilians create morally ambiguous situations, as they had in Vietnam. In the First Gulf War, Charles Sheehan-Miles remembers engaging two Iraqi trucks that caught fire. As one of the occupants ran ablaze from the truck, Miles fired his machine gun and instantly killed him. His immedi-ate response was "a sense of exhilaration, of joy," but a split second later he felt "a tremendous feeling of guilt and remorse." The image of the man on fire, running and dying, stayed with him "for years and years and years." His unit returned home, and he was awarded a medal, yet he felt "probably the worst person alive." He told the chaplain that he wouldn't be able to kill again. "It's not that I couldn't, it's that I knew I could. Be-cause it was . . . it was so easy to pull the trigger and kill people. Yes, I was afraid of what would happen. I was afraid of what it would do to me. What kind of person I would become." He later added:

> In my life, I've only seriously considered suicide once. That was just a few nights after the first time I killed someone. . . . But I didn't return home to the United States in one piece either. I was obsessed with guilt. I dreamed about the night when the trucks blew through our position and we killed everyone in them. I closed my eyes and I could see it, the 24th Infantry Divi-sion in Iraq, the biggest mechanized firing squad in history. I was . . . angry with myself, for that moment of unbridled bloodlust when I killed for the first time.[47]

Timothy Kudo, a Marine captain in Iraq and Afghanistan, wrote: "War makes us killers. We must confront this horror directly if we're honest about the true costs of war. . . . I'm no longer the 'good' person I once thought I was. There's nothing that can change that; it's impossible to forget what happened, and the only people who can forgive me are dead."[48]

The worst known case of allied atrocities in Afghanistan involved Australian troops. To its credit, the Australian military exposed it. Its Brereton Report found "credible information to substantiate 23 incidents of alleged unlawful killing of 39 people by 25 Australian special forces personnel." The victims were civilians and prisoners, and the killings occurred amid a "warrior culture" where "blood lust" and "competition killings" were the norm. Junior soldiers were often required by their superiors to murder prisoners to get their first kill, a practice known as "blooding." They would then plant weapons on the dead to "prove" they had been combatants.[49] But in 2022 similar practices perpetrated in Afghanistan by British special forces, the SAS, were exposed. Killing prisoners was widespread, the frequency alarming some higher officers. Weapons were planted on victims who had been unarmed, and squads competed with each other for the most kills.[50] Special forces induce special techniques.

Serial atrocities like this were otherwise rare, but single incidents were common. All the parties in Afghanistan—the Afghan government, the United States and allied forces, the Taliban and ISIS-K (an affiliate of ISIS)—committed atrocities. Probably U.S. and NATO forces killed fewer civilians than the two Afghan sides—if we exclude bombings. In Iraq, the worst known allied atrocity was the massacre of twenty-four civilians—men, women, the elderly, and children—by U.S. Marines at Haditha. The deaths were first claimed by the military to be inflicted by a terrorist roadside bomb that also killed a marine. But evidence showed that the civilians were innocent victims of indiscriminate fire from marines out of control, believing they were avenging the death of a comrade. They were highly stressed, on their third deployment to Iraq in two and a half years. During their previous deployment, they had fought in the Battle of Fallujah, in which thirty members of their battalion had been killed. Stress and revenge made their evildoing in Haditha more explicable but not excusable.

In 2003 over 60 percent of a large sample of soldiers and marines who had fought in Afghanistan or Iraq said they had killed an enemy combatant, and 20 percent said they had killed a noncombatant, the marines being twice as likely to report this. Most civilians were probably killed not by deliberate targeting, however, but by the practice of spraying around fire in the general direction of where the enemy was supposed to be. Battle experience in the two theaters differed. Only 31 percent of soldiers deployed to Afghanistan reported having engaged in a firefight, compared with 71–86 percent of soldiers and marines who had been deployed to Iraq. Consequently, those who had served in Iraq were significantly more likely to experience PTSD. In both theaters PTSD was positively correlated with the number of firefights a soldier had been in.[51]

Brett Litz and his colleagues have added to PTSD the concept of "moral injury," defined as "the lasting psychological, biological, spiritual, behavioral, and social impact of perpetrating, failing to prevent, or bearing witness to acts that transgress deeply held moral beliefs and expectations."[52] They say that moral injury and PTSD are based on different emotions. The main emotion in PTSD is fear, and in moral injury it is shame and guilt; they cause different chemical reactions in the brain.[53] Moral injury is much more likely to lead to suicide than is PTSD because it is self-hate: "I don't deserve to live." Studies listed by Litz and his colleagues show that PTSD and moral injury often overlap, however. David Finkel estimates PTSD sufferers as 20–30 percent of soldiers in Iraq. The sources of their stress, manifested in erratic, often violent behavior and terrible nightmares, usually involved multiple memories of death or mutilation of comrades and of Afghans or Iraqis, especially women and children. A significant thread permeating veterans' group-therapy sessions was postwar remorse at their own behavior. They recounted throwing women across rooms and kicking elderly men downstairs during house-to-house fighting in which the enemy might be lurking around the next corner, which inspired tension, fear, and sudden violence. There was a common practice of posing for photos with mutilated corpses or skulls. "We never had any remorse for anybody we saw dead. Because fuck it," one said. "I guess I'm trying to learn compassion all over again," replied another. A third recounted how the Iraqi police would bring dead bodies into their post: "They'd throw 'em in the back of a truck . . . we'd all run down there and go take pictures. You know? And one guy—his head was chopped off, his body was all bloated and shit, because it had been sitting in raw sewage, you know? And now I can't get those images out of my mind. At the time, though, it was 'Yeah, this is so cool. This is so cool.' I mean, what were we thinking? Why did we even want to go look at that shit?"[54]

Another soldier picked up a piece of bone from a body. "The femur, or something like that. I got pictures of me looking like I'm taking a bite out of it," he says. "What the fuck was I thinking?" "Exactly," said another. "I had a hard drive that I destroyed. Pictures and stuff like that, next to dead bodies, shit like that. Horrible, horrible stuff. Horrible stuff. Us hanging out with dead bodies. At the time, I mean we were rockin' and rollin', we were mean, mean killing machines. Now I look back and I'm, like, God, what were we doing? What were we thinking?"[55] These are heartrending memories. Yet for others remorse can be bypassed by "psychosocial maneuvers" involving mechanisms of moral disengagement, moral justification, such as "they were terrorists," or "we were preserving world peace," or "the enemy is doing worse": euphemistic labeling, minimizing negative consequences, dehumanizing the victim, and displacing or diffusing responsibility.[56]

A few atrocities led to courts-martial. Where men were found guilty, this was usually because comrades came forward to testify against their comrade, which revealed that many soldiers have a sense of moral limits. Yet President Trump in November 2019 pardoned two officers found guilty of war crimes by military courts, and then invited them onstage as heroes at his fund-raising events. One was awaiting trial, the other had been found guilty and sentenced to nineteen years' imprisonment for directing his soldiers to shoot unarmed villagers, killing two of them. Said Trump, "We train our boys to be killing machines, then prosecute them when they kill!" Only a subsequent storm of protest prevented him from pardoning more perpetrators. A navy petty officer was convicted of sharing a photograph of himself and a corpse with the message: "I have got a cool story for you when I get back. I have got my knife skills on." This was in breach of the navy code of conduct, and he was demoted and stripped of his navy SEAL pin, but Trump reinstated him. The petty officer said he regretted nothing and clearly enjoyed being one of Trump's "heroes," trotted out at his campaign rallies.[57] And yet this president wanted to pull all U.S. forces out of both countries.

Few who committed atrocities had felt moral qualms at the time. But in peacetime the memories of their behavior sometimes tore at their psyches through a remorse that destroyed their mental well-being. The tragedy of moral qualms is that they come too late to reduce the carnage inflicted on the local peoples, civilian as well as military. But afterward American perpetrators suffer as well. PTSD occurs in other armies, too. Simon Hattenstone and Eric Allison interviewed eight British Iraq veterans suffering from severe PTSD that led to violent and irrational behavior after they left the army. They talk with horror of the things they had seen in Iraq, of their own near-deaths, of the gruesome deaths of their comrades or of Iraqis. Only one says he suffers moral qualms over his own actions. He says he no longer acts like a rational man. He frequently gets into fights. "I don't like no one. I don't even like myself. I'm disgusted with some of the things I've done. You take someone's life away, no matter if he's going to kill you, and you don't ever get over it." He talks about his nightmares: the screaming, the shaking, the sweating.[58]

There are no stories of U.S. soldiers failing to fire in Afghanistan or Iraq, nor was there much shirking—only isolated rumors of soldiers parking their Humvees safely for the day while radioing in details of a fictitious patrol, and a few soldiers deserting their posts in combat zones. But desertions have been below 5 percent per annum, overwhelmingly when on leave back in the United States. Surveys of U.S. soldiers have shown morale fluctuating according to their current perception of the success or failure of the mission. The British Armed Forces Continuous Attitudes Survey, conducted annually, reveals declining morale in recent years, but British morale is not helped by widespread public disapproval of its wars. In the United States, opposition to wars seems based less on growing pacific sentiments than on perception of mission failure.

American authorities respond to the dangers confronting their soldiers by three forms of what Martin Shaw called "risk-transfer militarism," transferring elsewhere the risk to its own forces.[59] First it focused on bombing, leaving ground fighting to local forces given U.S. equipment and training. From 2014 to 2019, 39,000 airstrikes were made by U.S.-led coalition forces (including French and British airstrikes). The coalition claimed in its anti-ISIS operations in Iraq that only one civilian had been killed in every 157 airstrikes, a very rare event. But after intensive research across northern Iraq, *New York Times* reporters estimated that the real rate was one civilian death for every five airstrikes, thirty-one times higher than the United States admits.[60] In April 2019 Airwars and Amnesty International estimated that the final assaults on the ISIS capital of Raqqa in mid-2017 killed over 1,600 civilians by bombing and artillery fire. The United States admitted to 180 civilian fatalities. Estimates of ISIS militant fatalities are in the range 1,200 to 1,400, fewer than the number of civilians killed. During their three-year reign in Raqqa, ISIS murdered at least 4,000 civilians in cold blood. They were worse in ferocious killing, but the United States topped them in callous killing. ISIS deliberately kills civilians, and the Taliban kills civilians it suspects have any connections with the enemy. In contrast, the United States does try to avoid hitting civilians, and since the 1990s lawyers specializing in international law have been part of the bombing teams. Yet, predictably, this often fails to prevent civilian deaths.

Second, U.S. administrations outsourced military tasks to private contractors. Blackwater is one of several corporations providing mercenary soldiers for guard units. Four of its men, former U.S. Army soldiers, achieved notoriety in 2007 when they suddenly opened fire and killed fourteen to eighteen Iraqi civilians, including women and children; the men were apparently panicked by a car that would not stop. They received prison sentences for murder or manslaughter, but President Trump pardoned them. These corporations hire labor mainly from poor countries, and these recruits are paid far less than American soldiers or laborers and work for much longer periods. In 2008 U.S. Central Command (CENTCOM) counted over 266,000 foreign workers supporting military operations in the Middle East and Afghanistan—about the same as the number of U.S. troops deployed there. In World War II, 14 percent of all personnel working for the U.S. military had been civilians; now they were half, almost all foreigners. The total stayed above 200,000 until late 2012 and then declined as the United States withdrew most of its troops in the region. In 2008 only 15 percent were U.S. citizens, 47 percent were host nation nationals, and the remaining 38 percent were third-country nationals, especially Indians and Filipinos. Eight percent were armed guards, and the rest were unarmed and in logistics, but still at risk. Over 3,300 contractors in Iraq and Afghanistan died between September 2001 and August 2017, compared with about 6,900 U.S. military casualties.[61] This is another product of risk transfer militarism—let private contractors and foreigners take more of the risk.

The third way to reduce U.S. casualties is through the terrestrial robots and aerial drones of the early twenty-first century. Robots are sent to war zones just as fast as the U.S. military can get its hands on them. By 2010 there were more than two thousand deployed in Afghanistan. Two-thirds of them were used for investigating and detonating IEDs, for which the infantrymen who had previously done this manually are profoundly grateful. The remaining one-third were used for reconnaissance and surveillance, such as handheld robots that enable soldiers to see around corners, again considerably reducing the danger for them. It is often predicted that the battlefield of the future might be dominated by robots, though others believe that cyberwars disabling enemy computer systems will take over from actual fighting.

Aerial drones are far cheaper than piloted planes, and their operators are never killed. More than forty countries as well as several guerilla movements (including Hamas and the Houthis) now use armed drones, supplied mostly by the United States, China, Israel, and Iran. Though these are new weapons, their technology is relatively simple. So far high-tech defense against them, such as Israel's "Iron Dome" system, has been effective at intercepting them, perpetuating the advantage to the more advanced states, but this advantage might not last for new generations of drones. They are another potential weapon of the weak. At present the United States has by far the biggest drone force. It was greatly expanded under Barack Obama, and then expanded again under Trump. Its "pilots" are about 10 percent of all U.S. pilots. American and British operators guide the drones over the Middle East from Kansas, Nevada, Virginia, and Lincolnshire. This is the aerial warfare of the future, an extreme form of risk transfer militarism. We can no longer accuse political and military leaders of sacrificing many American lives; 69 percent of Americans approve of the use of drones, only 19 percent disapprove, and 86 percent of veterans approve.[62] Drone operators are unique warriors, in no danger at all. True, they can fall off their chairs in excitement or get carpal tunnel syndrome from endlessly tapping the keys. Robot weapons might presage an age where few soldiers are at risk on the battlefield, though their operating bases would remain targets. But if only one side can afford them, carnage ensues, as happened among the targets of American wrath and among Armenians in 2020.

The pilots glimpse through satellite video the everyday lives of victims, and they often study them for some time before the decision is made to launch. They see the terrible effects of their own missiles. Psychological studies revealed that in 2010, 11 percent of U.S. drone pilots reported high levels of stress, and 5 percent suffered from PTSD—far less than returning infantrymen from Iraq and Afghanistan. A repeat survey in 2014 also found 11 percent of the pilots reporting high levels of distress, but this time only 1.6 percent had PTSD. The biggest stressors were not related to combat or moral qualms, however, but were "operational," resulting from understaffing, rotating shift work, extra administrative tasks, long hours, and career blockage—stressful perhaps, like many other work-related hardships, but not raising moral difficulties.[63]

Yet their quit rate was three times that of other pilots. There is a shortage of trained drone operators, despite the fact that the task has been opened to women, and the shortage puts more pressure on the operators. They have to work "incessantly," says an RAF drone operator. For fighter pilots, the pressure had been intense but sporadic, whereas drone operating involves tiring concentration for most of an eight-hour shift. Chris Cole says many colleagues could not handle the disconnect between the drone shift and family life at home.[64] U.S. defense secretary Chuck Hagel had proposed a special medal for the best drone operators, but a storm of criticism from the military forced him to withdraw it: those who do not face danger should not get medals. The RAF began to award medals to drone operators in 2019, though without the clasp that certifies danger experienced.

Corey Mead watched U.S. drone pilots train and was impressed by their skills in identifying legitimate targets, deciding when to attack, and precision targeting. He did detect "tension between what members of the military feel is right and what their work requires. I observed this in the discord between trainers' rhetoric about how much they disliked killing people—they repeated this to me frequently—and their unabashed excitement, also expressed frequently, about the times they were able to launch strikes and kill 'bad guys.' Hating killing, but enjoying the chance to kill. The competing impulses may have seemed irreconcilable, but they were everywhere." Mead also notes the contrast between the boredom of 97 percent of the work—long hours of intelligence, surveillance, and reconnaissance—and the remaining 3 percent, which the instructor called the "cool" or "exciting" part, dropping bombs and firing missiles. "This is the job that drone operators wait for, and that wakes them up no matter how sleepy or dulled they are from the surveillance work on their shift."[65] When the crunch came, like "real" pilots before them, it absorbed their minds. Killing was not quite callous indifference, but they had help from desensitizing mechanisms like the expression always used for the victims, "bad guys," and the resemblance of their work to video gaming, a harmless but addictive activity. They knew that sometimes they might hit not just the "bad guys" but also their wives, children, or neighboring civilians. Yet the U.S. Air Force and the RAF have reassured them and the general public by issuing civilian casualty rates that are absurdly low, helping assuage qualms. Yet an internal U.S. military report concluded that civilian casualties in Afghanistan inflicted by drones were higher than those inflicted by manned aircraft.[66]

The Consequences of Interventions

By June 2020 total U.S. fatalities were 52,000, 60 percent of them in the Iraq theater. U.S. wars in Afghanistan, Iraq, Syria, and Pakistan have cost American taxpayers well over $3 trillion since 2001. But this is an underestimate. The U.S. war in Korea had been financed largely by raising taxes on the rich. This was also the case with the war in Vietnam. But America's Islamic wars were not financed this way. Indeed, under Bush the Younger and Trump, taxes on the rich were reduced. Instead, these wars were financed by debt, and by the time the debts are paid off in 2050, the cost of the two wars will have been $6.5 trillion, plus $2 trillion more for all the veteran fighters' health care, disability, and burial benefits. But that is only money, not lives.

Afghanistan provided local allies on the ground for the initial invasion, and the government managed, with NATO help, to hold on to Kabul and half the country for twenty years, although the Taliban revived to control the other half. The United States joined a fifty-year-old civil war and over the next twenty years exacerbated it. In 2020 U.S. forces estimated that the Taliban still had in excess of 50,000 fighters, in addition to several thousand part-timers. The Afghans claimed to kill one thousand Taliban every month, mostly through U.S. bombing. Just as they had in Vietnam, American leaders calculated that such a loss rate would finish off the enemy. They probably exaggerated the kill rate, but, as it had in Vietnam, the enemy kept on replenishing its forces. If an eldest son died, the next one would step in. And the enemy received help from neighbors. The Pakistani intelligence agency provided safe havens for Taliban leaders in Pakistan, and the movement recruited frontline fighters from among the 2 million Afghan refugees and seminary students in Pakistan.[67]

On May 2, 2011, bin Laden was killed by American special forces, perhaps aided by Pakistani officials. The Taliban have shown some hostility to ISIS, and Al Qaeda now has a marginal presence in the country, so the original goal of the invasion was largely achieved. Yet fighting dragged on under Obama because the Afghan government was not strong enough to stand on its own. President Trump's policies zigzagged, but in 2020 negotiations began. Trump said U.S. forces would be withdrawn by May 1, 2021, if the Taliban consented to a peace deal. The Afghan government was excluded from the negotiations and ignored, while it was unlikely that the Taliban would keep their word. But Trump wanted out and he upended the negotiations by withdrawing troops any-way, removing his major bargaining chip. The Biden administration in-herited this no-win situation and swiftly withdrew in July and August 2021. The Taliban now triumphed with a speed that surprised almost ev-eryone. But Afghan forces always depended on U.S. airpower and special forces, calling in U.S. airpower when in difficulties. Now they suddenly could not. Rural areas had been the main battlegrounds of the war, and most villagers there had experienced terrible U.S. bombing and drone strikes as well as brutal counterterrorism operations in which the Ameri-cans turned a blind eye to (and sometimes joined in) the many atrocities committed by Afghan special forces. Much of the countryside welcomed the Taliban victory.[68] Taliban morale and belief in their cause far ex-ceeded those of the government soldiers, who were also aware of the massive corruption in their officer corps. These were the major factors in the ten-day collapse. Though the pictures of Afghans clinging to the U.S. planes leaving Kabul airport eerily resembled the photos of Vietnamese clinging to U.S. helicopters as they left the U.S. Embassy in Saigon in 1975, the Taliban, unlike the NVA/PLF, did not even wait for the last American soldier to leave before they seized Kabul. Both these victors were successful ideological armies.

Withdrawal from Afghanistan was a betrayal that led to the murder of many Afghans who had collaborated with the NATO coalition or the Afghan government. It might also be a terrible step backward for Afghan women and Afghan education in the cities, though in this respect the Taliban are reflecting the traditional values and practices of the country-side. If the Taliban can maintain order and peace, that would probably be preferable for most Afghans to a continuation of a bloody war with many civilian casualties. Peace is better than war. But the Taliban seem unable to repress ISIS-affiliated terrorists, and the economic outlook for the country is dire. The Taliban do not inspire confidence in their ability to manage the economy. Yet U.S. troops were achieving neither victory nor a negotiated deal, and they were unlikely to even if their numbers had been doubled. There was no rational alternative, no point in dragging failure on longer.

I had predicted that outcomes would be worse for these countries than their sufferings under their earlier dictators and that interventions would fuel more terrorism.[69] I predicted that in Iraq the United States would have to rule through the Shi'a and the Kurds, who could win elec-tions because they form a majority of the population—an ethnocracy rather than a democracy. This would fuel sectarian war among Shi'a, Sunni, and Kurds. In Iraq the United States initially had no local allies, for it had relied on a small group of Iraqi Shi'a exiles, among whom Ahmed Chalabi was the most prominent. They had not been in Iraq for thirty years or more and so were quite unknown there. They could not form an effective government, as the U.S. military swiftly realized. But they had just enough influence in Washington to persuade the head of the Coalition Provisional Authority, Jerry Bremer, to dissolve the twin pillars of Iraqi government, the Ba'ath Party and the army, both of which the exiles hate.[70] That had the effect of dissolving all government. As a committed neoliberal, like most of the Bush administration, he also grandly declared that Iraqi industry would be privatized. Regime change would be both political and economic. Eric Herring and Glen Rangwala list a catalogue of American errors: privileging exiles over domestic elites; de-Ba'athification; indiscriminate use of force; little interaction between Iraqi and U.S. officials; inability to provide water, electricity, and employment; privileging American corporations; high turnover of Coalition Provisional Authority staff; torture; and promoting divisions between local and national actors to prevent them from challenging the occupation.[71] Sectarian identities intensified after the occupation began.

But the error from which all these flowed lay deeper: to invade Iraq at all, since substantial local allies on the ground were not available. This meets the standard of irrationality I laid down in chapter 1: the objective observer would judge that the goal of the war could not be met whatever the circumstance. U.S. forces had to fall back on the Shi'a parties, supported by their militias and ironically by Shi'a Iran, which led to ethnocracy, not democracy, and to civil war, Shi'a against Sunni, while Kurds were able to establish their own autonomous administrations in the districts they controlled. Nor could much industry be privatized, for there was enough opposition to this to produce economic disorder. Disorder encouraged jihadists, which culminated in ISIS—an irrational policy from beginning to end. ISIS was crushed, for the moment, however, and the ethnic-religious tensions are currently simmering rather than exploding. Iraq was only a mild disaster. Its governments tottered but survived. ISIS and Shi'a militias are still biting, but these are mostly gnat bites.

In March 2011 came a military intervention for regime change in Libya against Gaddafi's idiosyncratic dictatorship. A rebellion had begun in the east, and Gaddafi's forces were getting the better of the fighting.

He was a repressive dictator, but he had oil and he was neither of the right nor the left, but persisted in defiance of the United States. A UN resolution was passed authorizing member states to enforce a no-fly zone and use "all necessary measures" to prevent attacks on civilians. In practice this became a NATO bombing campaign of government infrastructures, perhaps killing around a thousand civilians—although casualty estimates vary wildly. The Gaddafi government then announced a cease-fire, rejected by the rebels. This was a regional, not a sectarian war. They were all Sunni.

Burned by Afghanistan and Iraq, the Obama administration "led from behind," contributing not ground forces but naval bombardment of coastal cities, aerial bombarding of a hundred targets, and a drone strike destroying Gaddafi's personal convoy moments before his death. Bombing was aided by the French, British, and Canadian air forces. Gaddafi was killed in October, and NATO forces then withdrew. The predictable consequence of this short war was the disintegration of the Libyan state and civil wars between several militias, still ongoing, backed by numerous foreign powers. Without the repressive hand of Gaddafi, the country descended into disorder, civil strife, terrorism, and even slave markets. Thousands of jihadists poured into the country. These outcomes were due mainly to the locals themselves, yet the destruction inflicted by the Western powers made things much worse. In Afghanistan, Syria, Libya, and Yemen, foreign interventions have exacerbated existing civil wars; in Iraq the intervention created civil war. These ventures did not benefit these countries or democracy. They were irrational.

American commitment to rebuild them after the war has been minimal. Between 2001 and 2019 the United States spent $1.5 trillion dollars in Afghanistan. Of this, less than 9 percent went to "reconstruction" programs, and even much of this went to training the Afghan army and police forces. Only 4 percent of the total budget went to civilian projects. "If you look at the overall amount of money spent in Afghanistan, you see a tiny percentage of it went to help the people of the country," Robert Finn, former ambassador to Afghanistan, told U.S. government investigators. "It almost all went to the military and even most of that money went for local militia and police training." The Watson Institute's "Cost of War" concurred: "The majority of U.S. international assistance spending related to Afghanistan, Iraq, and Pakistan is for military or security purposes rather than economic and social development." The institute estimates that between 2001 and 2022, U.S. military and security spending

due to such wars was $8 trillion. Development program funds there to-
taled $189 billion.[72] The institute also estimates that these wars have
killed over 900,000 people.

Of course, in two of these countries U.S. invasions had destroyed
local military and police capabilities. European Union countries spent
mostly on humanitarian and infrastructural projects. Since Afghans knew
the United States would sooner or later go home, corrupt elites felt they
should distribute benefits to their patronage networks while they could.
Especially profitable was inventing "ghost soldiers," men for whom pay
and supplies arrived but who did not actually exist. A senior State Department adviser reported to the investigators: "Afghans knew we were
there temporarily, and that affected what we could do. . . . An elder in
Helmand [said], 'Your Marines live in tents. That's how I know you won't
be here long.' "[73] The Taliban adage was "You have the watches. We have
the time." And so it proved.

Somalia is a miniature Afghanistan. The United States remains involved against al-Shabaab, with only about one hundred troops left there
after Trump withdrew another five hundred, but with CIA operatives as
well, paying mercenaries, drone bombing (sometimes hitting civilians),
and subsidizing a deeply corrupt, unpopular government. This is doing
no good. It is supposedly preventing an al-Shabaab attack on the United
States, for which al-Shabaab has no capability.

U.S. forces were more than twice as powerful as those of any other
state in the world but they had two enduring domestic weaknesses. First,
Americans are squeamish about the cost—not apparently in money but
in the number of U.S. casualties. In the Iraq War of 2003 only 4,000
Americans were killed—compared to 500,000–600,000 Iraqis. In previous wars Koreans, Vietnamese, and Afghans had taken much heavier
losses than U.S. troops. I noted the rise of risk-transfer militarism earlier.
American leaders have managed to keep a low military profile by keeping
the body bags few and unpublicized. Yet this has a military downside.
Enemies believe they can outlast U.S. forces since Americans cannot endure casualties. From Korea and Vietnam to Afghanistan, Iraq, and Syria,
they have been proved right.

The second weakness is fragile popular support for wars. When
Americans learn of interventions involving ground troops, they get excited on the sidelines. They cheer on their team playing away from
home, but they make no sacrifices themselves. I called this in Britain during the Falklands War "spectator sport militarism."[74] They wait with

bated breath in the early stages, cheering on their side in a rally 'round the flag. But this is only skin-deep. Political rhetoric treats U.S. soldiers as sacred, lauds them as "heroes" uniquely "serving their country." Politicians who avoided active military service themselves, like Bush the Younger and Trump, like to bathe in the reflected glory of photo ops surrounded by soldiers displaying medals. But, except in cases that can be plausibly claimed by rulers to threaten national survival, as for Americans after Pearl Harbor and during the period from 9/11 to initial victory in Afghanistan, the troops cannot rely on adoration for long. If things did not go well, we turned our backs. Who wants to support a losing team? The public lost interest and returning soldiers were not greeted as heroes, which they might have been had these ventures been short or successful. Our recent wars have not been driven by deep emotions, insecurities, and ideologies, unlike those of the jihadists. Ours are the ideologies not of the masses but of the elites who decide foreign policy.

The Obama administration revealed lessening resolve, though without major policy changes. Trump, despite his blustering style, and apart from Iran, retreated a little, though impulsively. In 2019 he twice ordered all American troops out of Syria—only to reverse himself after aides implored him to reconsider. He then did suddenly withdraw U.S. troops from the Syrian-Turkish border, abandoning his Kurdish SDF allies to Turkish attacks, forcing them into Russian and Syrian arms, weakening their ability to guard thousands of captured ISIS soldiers and their families. His abrupt and unilateral force reductions in Afghanistan were ill-timed, given his ongoing negotiations with the Taliban. And while he cut back troops in Afghanistan and Iraq to 2,500 each and reduced U.S. forces in Europe by one-third, he steadily increased the military budget: from $767 billion under Obama to $818 billion in 2017 and $935 billion in 2020. This included a 50 percent increase in spending on nuclear warheads. The combination of withdrawal and more military spending makes sense only for domestic politics—drum-beating rhetoric without risk to American lives. It also drains U.S. budgets of an ability to deal with the severe equity problems besetting American society and of flourishing U.S. economic power abroad. The total U.S. development aid budget for 2020 was $19 billion, only 2 percent of the military budget. Under Biden military spending remained flat, and though he removed U.S. forces from Afghanistan, over 40,000 American troops were still stationed around the Middle East in late 2021, including 2,500 active in Iraq and 900 in Syria. Drone operations continued, mainly aimed at Islamist groups.

Three American Blind Spots

American geopolitical choices might appear calculative and instrumentally rational. They are proclaimed as such, since Realist theory's hometown is Washington, D.C. Careful calculation of the resources and likely decisions of allies and enemies, and frequent use of war-gaming and diplomatic-gaming scenarios makes it all seem rational. Yet for seventy years, American policy has had three blind spots stymieing its foreign interventions, refuting any notion that this is rational policy in terms of either means or ends.

First, most American politicians, Republicans and Democrats alike, still believe in an imperial civilizing mission, a responsibility and capacity to bring order, democracy, free enterprise, and general beneficence to the world. Most sincerely believe this, yet it is unachievable and it naturally gets a little corrupted by American interests along the way. Since U.S. allies outside Europe and East Asia are more authoritarian than democratic, U.S. policy is in practice more committed to the capitalist than the democratic mission, and it often uses force rather than inducements. The problem is that in an age of rising nationalist and religious resistance, imperial goals, however beneficently expressed, cannot be attained. The United States can no longer install indigenous client regimes, let alone democracies, that can keep order as effectively as most of the overthrown dictators—or as effectively as other empires in previous centuries. Nor can Americans, amid ensuing disorder, mobilize their economic power to bring the promised vibrant economy. The combination of military violence, political disorder, and economic stagnation undermines American ideological power, exposing it as hypocrisy. Interventionism exaggerates America's powers, and actual military intervention weakens them. Its persistence despite repeated failures can be understood only in terms of the lack of any real military rival. No one *can* withstand U.S. forces in fixed battle. It is otherwise in the case of low-intensity warfare and the political aftermath.

The second blind spot is failure to understand the laws of cause and effect, not just in the Middle East. U.S. governments have identified North Korea as an enemy since the late 1940s. U.S. forces killed 2 million North Koreans—20 percent of the total population—in three years of carpet bombing during the Korean War (as we saw in chapter 13). Whatever their hatred of their own regime, North Koreans hate America with good reason. In the seventy years since the beginning of the Korean

War, the United States has never made a sustained effort to negotiate a permanent peace treaty, hoping that the communist North Korean regime would simply collapse. Is it any surprise that in response North Korean regimes have made a sustained drive to acquire nuclear weapons? They are seen as necessary self-defense—though this is delusional. A U.S. offer of friendship and economic assistance would do better for both sides, as it would have at almost any point during the previous half century.

Similarly, jihadi and other threats have been exacerbated by American actions. Iranian meddling in Lebanon resulted from the failed Israeli-U.S. war against Syria in the early 1980s. In Iraq Iranian meddling followed the U.S. wars against Saddam. In Yemen Iranian meddling resulted from Saudi and UAE attacks on the Houthis, backed by the United States. The main causes of the new jihadi movements obviously lie within Muslim countries. But the main reason terrorists attack Americans and the British is their military interventions (the second reason is perceived discrimination against Muslims in the West, more important in Europe than in the United States). Bin Laden himself gave three reasons for attacking the United States: the presence of its forces in Saudi Arabia, its support for expansionist Israel, and its 1991 invasion of Iraq and the subsequent bombing and starving of children there. He later added the invasions of Afghanistan and (again) Iraq—as, of course, did ISIS.

The effects of bombing and drones are almost invisible to Americans but devastating for the locals. Basra, Raqqa, and other cities are liberated from ISIS but destroyed, having suffered many civilian deaths and lost even more who fled as refugees. The young men from Mosul I quoted earlier hate America for what they say it has done to their country. Millions of Muslims who suffer from these policies will not view the United States as liberators, although many realize that ISIS is worse. Among those millions are thousands who will fight, and hundreds who will accept suicide missions. They lack the resources to conquer or hold a state, but they use the weapons of the weak to sustain long-term asymmetric warfare. If they suffer reverses at home, they encourage Muslims in the West to take up terrorism, which a few are willing to do. The 2019 defeat of the ISIS caliphate reduced the number of new recruits—but not the number of sympathizers, from whom new militants emerge. American drones kill ISIS and Al Qaeda leaders, but new leaders arise. Extreme Islamism is a hydra, the mythological nine-headed water snake. We cut off its most visible head, but other heads rise to menace us. In the Greek myth one is immortal. The solution is not war. It is to moderate U.S. policies in the region.

The third blind spot, especially visible in the Middle East, is conservatism—not conservative in the party political sense, since Democrats support it as well, but in its attachment to tradition, which I have found so important in war making across the centuries. Conservatism represents past, not present, visions of American power. U.S. policy makers act as if this were 1942, when the United States charged in with military power to rescue the world from evil. Subsequent rebuffs in Korea and Vietnam should have cast some doubt on such confidence, but it was boosted again by the fall of the Soviet Union. Yet throughout, definitions of friend and foe inherited from the past are unchanged, even though reality has changed.

In the Middle East, Saudi Arabia and Israel are still seen as the most dependable allies despite alternative ways of getting oil and other energy sources, and when Israel is now the dominant and the only nuclear military power in its neighborhood. Unswerving support for Israel is counterproductive to peace, alienating Arabs across the region, perpetually creating a few Islamic terrorists. Domestic politics helps determine this foreign policy, as we have seen in most other wars. In this case, both U.S. parties fear the electoral consequences of antagonizing pro-Israeli lobbies, and across the Bible Belt there are fervent Evangelical Christians who believe that the Jews must be in possession of the Temple Mount before the "Rapture," the Second Coming of Christ. Shades of the return of the Mahdi! Trump's secretary of state Mike Pompeo hinted that he shares this ridiculous view. There is on the Palestinian side no comparable political lobby.

Of course, the United States must guarantee Israel's right to exist. But behind much Arab hatred lies American support for Israel's continuing aggression, its seizure of lands that have been Arab for a millennium. In the past, a slap on Israel's wrist was delivered for such incursions. President Trump instead endorsed Israeli landgrabs in his so-called Peace Plan of January 2020. Indeed, in order to get Arab states to sign accords with Israel, he gave concessions to them all—high-tech military planes to the UAE, switching to support Morocco's claims to the western Sahara, dropping Sudan from the State Department's list of terrorist states. But approving Israeli expansions makes unviable the Palestinian state to which American foreign policy is theoretically committed. President Biden might return to the slap-on-the-wrist days, but not to genuine peace brokering. There is some shift among younger Americans toward more sympathy for the Palestinians, yet Israelis offer steadily increasing support to settlements in Palestinian lands for which the grinding down of Palestinian society is a precondition. It is difficult to see the end of this ghastly cycle: Israeli expansionism blessed by the United States creates more terrorism, which leads to more repressive Israeli policy, which creates more terrorism, and so on and so on.

Conservatism also ensured that the United States has joined in the sectarian war, on the Sunni side, with the exception of its war with ISIS and its presently faltering alliance with the majority Shi'a Iraqi government. Administrations and Congress would vehemently deny this bias. But consider the evidence. In Iraq it had offered no help to the Shi'a community in the 1990s, though this had presented the most credible opposition to Saddam Hussein. U.S. administrations further support the Saudis and the Gulf sheikdoms—which are Sunni—and oppose Iran and Hezbollah—which are Shi'a—in their struggle for regional dominance. The United States supplies 85 percent of Bahrain's military equipment and from 2002 declared Bahrain to be a "major non-NATO ally." In the 2011 uprising the Americans' "major concern is that a fall of the Al Khalifa regime and ascension of a Shiite-led government could increase Iran's influence and lead to a loss of the use of Bahrain's military facilities." Bahrain is the base of the U.S. Fifth Fleet, whose main purpose, says the Department of Defense, is to counter Iranian military power in the Gulf. The British were also major military suppliers, and in 2012 they supplied to the Bahrain regime a large consignment of weapons suitable for police and paramilitary repression. The Obama administration tried to talk the king into more conciliatory policies, but it did nothing, not prepared to risk the anti-Iran alliance for the sake of human rights. Then the Trump administration removed all human rights issues from its support for Bahrain.

Sunni Saudi Arabia has been an ally since 1945, receiving massive military aid. Since then, it has changed from a weak tribal confederation sitting on massive oil reserves, anticommunist, and needing protection, to a modern repressive state and aggressive military power. Communism is gone and Saudi oil reserves are of less importance for the United States. Iran has been defined as an enemy since 1979, although Iranians take the hostility back to the 1953 CIA- and British-backed coup that overthrew an elected government and installed the shah. In 1980, after the fall of the shah, when Saddam attacked Iran, the United States provided him with billions of dollars in credits to buy arms, coordinated his arms buying in the West, and provided intelligence support. Britain, France, the Soviet Union, and other Sunni states assisted Iraq. Iran was alone, without allies.

In 2015 President Obama supported the Saudi-led offensive against the Shi'a Houthis in Yemen, a much lesser American contribution than in Afghanistan, Iraq, and even Libya and Syria, for it merely involved co-ordinated U.S. military and intelligence support from CENTCOM and U.S. midair refueling of coalition aircraft. The refueling ended amid congressional alarm at civilian casualties in 2018, but U.S. naval ships still aid the Saudi blockade. Britain and France also help the Saudis. The Trump administration's "maximum pressure campaign" against Iran in-cluded U.S. naval forces intercepting vessels carrying arms to the Houthis. In 2019 Trump also handed the Saudis a Patriot air defense battery, and the State Department declared: "We stand firmly with our Saudi partners in defending their borders against these continued threats by the Houthis, who rely on Iranian-made weapons and technology to carry out such attacks." The Houthis say that they are merely defending themselves, though they have begun to extend self-defense into lobbing missiles into Saudi Arabia and the UAE. They usually deny that they are receiving weapons from Iran, but they have occasionally said that only Iran will supply them with weapons. True, since 2015 American adminis-trations have provided over $2.4 billion in emergency humanitarian aid for Yemen, mostly to repair the damage done by allied bombing and blockading.

U.S. policy makers have repeatedly argued that the Houthis are only a pawn in the regional power game of Iran.[75] But the Saudis are playing the same game, and U.S. administrations help them. Growing humani-tarian outrage produced an easing of support under Obama and Trump. The Biden administration then announced three further significant steps, declaring in February 2021 that U.S. offensive operations in Yemen would cease, as would export of precision-guided munitions to the Saudis or the UAE (but other arms sales would continue), and a State Department negotiator would go to Yemen to attempt to bring the war-ring sides together—a welcome breach of the State Department's formal ban on negotiating with "terrorists." But the State Department asserts that its shift has been purely on humanitarian grounds and still regards the Houthis as terrorists. They are defined as terrorists because they are the enemies of our Saudi allies, not because their behavior is any worse than theirs. We should have neither enemies nor allies in this civil war.

We should merely offer humanitarian aid and help for the Yemenis to resolve their differences.

President Trump had intensified hostility toward Iran in 2019 by arbitrarily withdrawing from the 2015 nuclear deal framework agreement among Iran, the UN Security Council, and the European Union. All other signatories declared that UN weapons inspectors' reports showed the agreement was working. But Trump instead intensified U.S. sanctions on Iran and authorized a missile strike on the Baghdad airport that killed General Qassim Suleimani, commander of the elite Iranian Quds Force, a branch of the Revolutionary Guards. This enraged the Iraqi government, which was revealed not to be sovereign in its own land. This series of responses had a negative effect, isolating Iranian reformists and increasing the power of hard-liners, especially those committed to developing nuclear weapons. After all, Israel, its main enemy, already has nuclear weapons. The Biden administration hopes to return to the nuclear agreement, though at the moment both sides insist that the other move first. To move first would be regarded as "backing down," a sign of cowardice! That is how World War I started. Agreement to move simultaneously is the way to solve this and avert possible war.

The United States does not need to choose sides between Sunni and Shi'a. Americans are equally indifferent to Sunni and Shi'a dogma, and Saudi Arabia is even less democratic than Iran. It is an absolute monarchy with no freedom of assembly or speech. Iran has elections to a parliament, though the candidates are vetted for their loyalty to the regime. Yet public demonstrations are frequent in Iran but not in Saudi Arabia. During 2020–21 there were repeated mass demonstrations in the streets of Iran on economic issues, especially by retirees, workers, and farmers. The security forces often responded harshly, but the demonstrations kept on coming. Saudi citizens, still less the foreign workers often held in slavelike conditions, rarely dare to do so. Nor does Iran carve up its dissidents into little pieces. Neither of these regimes could be termed benevolent, but the Saudis are worse.

Externally there are differences, too. U.S. administrations constantly denounce Iranian "terrorism" abroad. The hand of Iran can be detected in two types of intervention. One is helping Shi'a communities—in Syria, Yemen, and Lebanon. Iran is helping coreligionists, just as the Saudis are. The second type of intervention is against the United States and its proxies, in the Persian Gulf and in Afghanistan (if the rumors of Iran paying the Taliban for killing American soldiers are true). But they are, after all, attacking Iranian interests. The United States and China are inevitably rivals, but there is no necessary reason for the United States and Iran to be rivals. And in one respect, Iranian interests are the same as America's. This Shi'a regime is deeply opposed to Sunni jihadists. Its Quds Force has helped combat Al Qaeda and ISIS in Afghanistan and the Middle East. In contrast, the Saudis supply more jihadists than any other country, often recruited through the Wahhābī schools they finance abroad. The economic issues involved are declining in importance. The Saudis have 25 percent more oil reserves than Iran, but these are 30 percent less than U.S. reserves, following shale oil and gas finds. In any case, market exchange is cheaper than war in securing oil, as the Japanese, Chinese, and Europeans know. The Saudis are economic allies, providing profits for Western arms producers and investing their oil profits in the West. There is now a very large joint Saudi and American business lobby in Washington. But the Saudis will continue to invest their oil profits in Western economies. An alternative American policy of mediating between Iran and Saudi Arabia would pay a large peace dividend in the Middle East. The main stumbling blocks to a new policy on the Iranian side are its calls to destroy Israel and its sponsoring of Hezbollah. But if the incentive was there to change tack on Israel, Iran might take it—as Egypt and Jordan had earlier done. There is no good reason against trying it, only the blinkers of tradition and the short-term horizons of powerful interest groups.

The nuclear programs of Iran and North Korea are worrying but have been mainly caused by U.S. policy identifying them as state terrorists. They think the Gaddafi example shows what happens to an enemy of the United States who gives up nuclear weapons. Trump's withdrawal from the nuclear deal and crippling sanctions brought poverty for many Iranians. These measures were supposed to bring Iran to the conference table to accept more stringent American demands. Predictably, the reverse happened, as in most conflicts we have seen. Iranian leaders, their personal, religious, and national honor at stake, refused to "back down." Quite the reverse: they launched attacks on oil tankers docked off the Emirati coast, and more tentatively on a U.S. base in Iraq. In September 2019 the Iranian Air Force launched twenty drones and precision-guided cruise missiles on Abqaiq, an important Saudi oil field and processing center, causing serious damage. Mutual provocation is under way. Iran has recommended work on its nuclear program, and it says it will renounce the nuclear deal. Trump's main motive for the anti-Iran policy was probably domestic: talking tough was popular among his base—domestic politics interfering with rational geopolitical calculation.

For these three reasons, American foreign policy in the region is not rational. We have seen that this is not unique to the United States. I have shown that many rulers' grasps of reality have been feeble. But American militarism is unreal, bad for Americans, worse for the Middle East, the triumph of bipartisan conservatism that is wedded to the past, not present realities or needs. Asked to do the impossible by politicians, U.S. forces coped as best they could, but they could not win. Ultimate failure forced major withdrawal from both Iraq and Afghanistan, and minor withdrawals from Libya, Syria, and Yemen. As I grow older, my behavior comes to resemble American imperialism. I march into a room and then forget why I am there.

Yet U.S. leaders could learn from past failure. They have begun to sidestep their formal ban on negotiating with "terrorist" states and movements, engaging in secretive back-channel communication with the enemy. They could learn lessons from imperial China: paying tribute to barbarians not to attack them was far cheaper than fighting wars against them. American wealth can afford it. Tribute was a Chinese development program for barbarians. The United States should use the economic powers it has, not the military-political powers it lacks. Remember that impoverished Iran cannot offer much economic aid to its allies abroad, and the United States can easily outspend Iran. I am advocating not isolationism but peaceful interventionism.

American leadership can achieve more through "soft power" than war, as Joseph Nye has long argued.[76] U.S. power has often been hegemonic, seen as legitimate by other countries. U.S. diplomats and politicians have repeatedly acted as conflict mediators—as in the Camp David and Dayton accords. U.S. development programs give grants and loans to poorer countries, although it helps to be an ally like Israel, the biggest recipient. In a country as rich as the United States, cash can usually buy off the chances of war. After all, the United States bought the Louisiana territory from France and Alaska from Russia. Development programs offered to North Korea and Iran with strings attached could stop their nuclear programs and make them friendlier. The precedent is that between 1980 and 2018 the United States provided Egypt with over $40 billion in military aid and $30 billion in economic aid so that Egypt would make peace with Israel. The wars in Afghanistan and Iraq have so far cost $3.5 trillion. I am not suggesting ending development programs for friendly countries. That would be only rewarding villainy!

It is a major obstacle to peace that U.S. citizens have suffered so little from recent wars. Wars are far away, casualties have been low in a professional army in which subcontractors and foreign workers also take losses, and drones are the key attack force. This reduces publicity back home, except when jihadists attack on American soil, but this is much rarer than in a Europe that contains discontented Muslim communities, and much rarer than homegrown American militia bombings and school shootings. So counterproductive conservatism endures in Middle Eastern policy, provoking little public interest. This gives free rein to Wall Street and business lobbies involved in Saudi Arabia and to pro-Israeli lobbies. Policy stuck in the past does not work. It is grounded not in Realism but in irrationality. This is not an anti-American rant. It is normal in wars, most of which are irrational.

Conclusion

In its history, Islam has been neither more nor less war-prone than other faiths. The Quran contains brutal passages, just as does the Old Testament. The early Islamic waves of conquest were in contrast to the pacific tendencies of early Christianity.[77] Thereafter Islam may have fought almost as many wars as did Christendom, but it was more tolerant of other religions at home. Most recent wars have been in the Muslim Middle East, although the region has been also beset by Western (secular) imperialism. Religion mattered, for it was a primary marker of community identity, yet these were not religious wars like the Crusades or the Thirty Years' War, in which both antagonists were defined by their religion. Just one side, the jihadists, declared itself favored by divine power and cherry-picked the most brutal passages in the Quran to justify its atrocities. Underlying these wars were three causes:

1. the failure of Muslim rulers, influenced by Western developmental ideologies, to tackle the poverty and corruption of the region, which led neither to liberal democracy nor to socialism but to corrupt authoritarian regimes provoking popular resistance and repression;
2. the rise of distinctively Islamic solutions offered for those problems, generating at the extreme small, murderous jihadi movements brandishing texts from the Quran;
3. imperial interventions, in the Cold War by the United States and the Soviets, then by the United States and Russia, assuming that military intervention could overthrow unfriendly

regimes and bring capitalist democracy (capitalist autocracy in Russia) to Muslims. Instead, it increased disorder, which increased the influence of jihadists as perverted forms of anti-imperialism.

U.S. attempts at regime-change wars since 1990 mostly achieved battlefield victory but failed to establish order, let alone democracy, thus intensifying jihadism. Iraq had few jihadists before U.S. intervention because most Sunnis were satisfied with Saddam's rule and most Shi'a were cowed. In Afghanistan the Taliban had seized power with U.S. help since their more secular enemy had been backed by the Soviets. Before the U.S. invasion, Taliban killings of civilians had been relatively few, but afterward civilian casualties inflicted by all sides rose. Other wars occurred without U.S. ground troops, but only in the two small wars in Nagorno-Karabagh was there no U.S. participation. In other cases, the United States, with British and sometimes NATO support, offered military help to one side in a war. This might have been decisive in the Israeli-Arab wars, but probably not elsewhere—in the Iran-Iraq War and civil wars in Iraq, Libya, Yemen, and Bahrain. U.S. military aid helped destabilize the region, making jihadism more attractive to a small minority of Muslims. Better the United States had acted as a neutral referee, helping settle these disputes through conciliation laced with incentives.

American policy in the region had three blind spots: exaggerating the powers of the U.S. military, failing to distinguish cause and effect in enemy hostility, and inability to adjust policy to cope with regional changes. The United States has sleepwalked its way into aggravating conflicts between Sunni and Shi'a Muslims, and between Muslims and Jews, revealing the irrationality of American policy. Failure is not unique to America, for I have stressed the role of irrational policy making through history. But remedy is at hand: rely more on American economic and diplomatic power, less on military power. That would yield more order and less war in the Middle East, enhance U.S. influence in the region, and lessen jihadi attacks on the West. This would not solve the problems confronting Muslim societies, but it would help.

CHAPTER FIFTEEN

Possible Futures

N O ONE CAN PREDICT the future accurately, yet bleak prospects for war are often suggested: war between the United States and China, nuclear war leading to a "nuclear winter" that will destroy human civilization, the unleashing of biological or chemical weapons, climate change wars, or induced disease pandemics. Since all these dire scenarios might bring utter disaster for humankind, a large degree of Realist rationality is obviously needed in the future.

Danger intensifies with proliferating weapons of mass destruction. Several minor powers might be on the way to acquiring nuclear weapons. Iranians currently see their nuclear program as a potent symbol of their country's status and a necessary form of self-defense against Israel, Saudi Arabia, and the United States. This is already drawing Israeli cyber and bomb attacks on Iranian nuclear facilities (with the complicity of U.S. intelligence agencies). If these drive Iranian nuclear facilities farther underground, Israelis might be tempted into a preemptive nuclear strike. The Turkish president has announced that he is contemplating acquiring nuclear weapons, and Saudi rulers are also rumored to be considering it. Recent Chinese assertiveness may be perceived as a potential nuclear threat in East Asia, which might induce Japan and South Korea to acquire nuclear weapons.

The danger of a conflagration worsens with more nuclear states. The nuclear age has so far contained two main pairs of face-to-face rivals—the United States and the USSR or Russia (for British and French weapons would not be launched independently of the United States), and India and Pakistan. They have stared each other in the face, saber rattling, but deterred by the horrendous specter of nuclear war. Yet with many nuclear powers the balance becomes more fragile, since states—especially those of different types—cannot easily predict the actions of all the others. That is how World War I started. International terrorists present a further threat if they can capture a weapon of mass destruction—more probably biological or chemical than nuclear—which is especially worrying if militants believe that heaven awaits those who kill heretics. It seems scientifically possible for a pandemic to be introduced into an enemy country, though keeping control of its spread might be difficult, even impossible. On a more cheerful note, cyberwars might disarm the enemy without casualties. Nuclear, chemical, and biological deterrence might work, in which case peace will predominate globally; or they will not work, in which case human civilization might end. But given the persistent irrationality of humans starting wars, one cannot be too hopeful.

What if Russia or China and the United States backed by NATO square off against each other? They would all claim legitimacy for their actions. Established powers claim the legitimacy of a defensive posture while revisionists claim they are righting a past wrong. Revisionism of borders is currently the major threat to world peace as self-righteousness envelops the world's three greatest military powers, one hitherto dominant, the other two rising and revisionist.

Putin's Revisionist War in Ukraine

The war of 2022 in Ukraine may have shocked many, but it was fairly predictable and it revealed many traditional features of warfare—mainly the negative ones. Russian revisionism—the demand for "lost territories"— had intensified in recent years, revealed in successive military interventions in Chechnya, Georgia, Crimea, and Ukraine, all formerly tsarist Russian and Soviet territories. Success in earlier ventures under Putin's leadership had led to increasing confidence in the Kremlin that desired ends could be attained by military means. As I have emphasized, the best predictor of new aggression is success in previous aggressions. Hitler had launched an escalating series of aggressions: the Rhineland, Sudetenland, the rest of Czechoslovakia, Poland, France, Britain, the Soviet Union, and the United States, though the combination of the last three proved his undoing. Will Putin's endgame be similar?

Armed conflict in Ukraine erupted in 2014 when the elected president, who had become unpopular when he bowed to Russian pressure and abandoned talks to enter the European Union, was overthrown by massive pro-Western street demonstrations. In response, Russian soldiers in disguise, the "little green men," met with scant resistance as they swiftly occupied largely Russian-speaking Crimea. The West denounced this but did little, apart from limited economic sanctions. It was difficult to see what more they could do, short of full-scale war. In eastern Ukraine armed separatists in Donetsk and Luhansk, the two mainly Russian-speaking provinces of the Donbas region, declared independence. Their militias were aided by more little green men from Russia. Yet they faced determined resistance, and this soon forced Putin into sending in regular Russian forces. Even so, they could not prevail and stalemate resulted. By 2021, 14,000 people had already been killed in a mixture of regular and irregular warfare.

Yet Putin's rhetoric was already going much further. He proclaimed that an independent Ukraine should not exist at all. It is part of Russia, he claimed—as indeed it had been for most of its history before 1991. Many Russians agreed with him. In the buildup to his full-scale invasion of 2022, the normal blend of fear and overconfidence fueled Putin's actions. The understandable part of Russian fears derived from the eastward expansion of NATO, begun in 1999 as Poland, Hungary, and the Czech Republic joined it. Further expansion came as seven more countries joined in the early 2000s: Bulgaria, Estonia, Latvia, Lithuania, Romania, Slovakia, and Slovenia. All these countries wanted to join NATO because they feared Russia, and, except for Slovenia, they had been part of the tsarist empire or the Soviet Union. During this period NATO and the United States took full advantage of Russian inability to mount more than verbal protests. The Kremlin noted that NATO expansion was contrary to American assurances given by Secretary of State James Baker to Gorbachev that NATO would not expand eastward (in return for Russia's accepting the unification of Germany). By late 2021 there were NATO missile sites in Romania and Poland, NATO exercises in the Baltic states, and American military aid to former Soviet states in Central Asia. Russian leaders felt encircled. Alongside the economic policy disasters inflicted on Russia by Western neoliberals, this had weakened the influence of both the West and Russian liberals and it enhanced the popularity of Russian and Slavic nationalists. The NATO expansion was peaceful, since it was at the invitation of Russia's neighbors. But also provocative in Russian eyes was the November 2021 signing of a "charter on strategic partnership" between Ukraine and the United States that called for Ukraine to join NATO; the United States also promised "unwavering commitment" to the reintegration of Crimea into Ukraine. NATO's expansion produced much self-satisfaction in Washington and Brussels: they were cutting Russia down to size.

Some warned that such provocations would be counterproductive once Russian power revived. Backed by nationalist and Slavophile factions, Putin used his popularity as the man who had brought social order to Russia, and he used his authoritarian powers to repress dissent and increase military spending at the expense of living standards. The grim irony of this NATO expansion is that its forces have remained irrelevant to the war in Ukraine, insufficient to deter Putin. In fact, they enraged him. Most Americans had also had enough of war after recent military disasters, and the Western Europeans had even less appetite for war. So U.S. and NATO encirclement could not actually restrain Russia. But this also meant that Russian fears were exaggerated.

In February 2022 blowback came when Russian troops massed along Ukrainian borders and invaded Ukraine across three fronts. This was far more than border revisionism. It was attempted imperial reconquest. Putin's initial plan seems to have been to subjugate the whole of Ukraine. He thought that Kyiv, the capital, would swiftly fall, that he could take over the whole of the Donbas, create a land bridge through southern Ukrainian territory between the Crimea and Russia, and seize the whole of the south of Ukraine, making the country landlocked. Politically, this might result in either incorporating Ukraine into Russia or leaving a puppet Ukrainian state in Kyiv and the west of the country.

Military weakness on the ground in Europe meant that NATO could not send forces into Ukraine. Nor did NATO members wish to use air power to establish a no-fly zone (as they had done in Iraq), since they feared escalation, and Putin hinted that this might force him to turn to the nuclear option. Instead, NATO relied on the economic power of its members and their willingness to supply arms to the Ukrainians. Initially, Putin was not much discomforted by this. His conception of Russian "greatness" was grounded more on military than on economic power, and he believed anyway that he could compensate economically through greater cooperation with China and India. Chinese leaders are conscious of the similarities of Russian claims in Ukraine to their own revisionist claims to Taiwan. They are now also willing to push the envelope against the United States, and so, like Indian rulers, they willingly buy Russian oil at discounted prices.

Russian fears of NATO partly explain Putin's warmongering. Four more factors played important roles. The first was ideological. This was not a war driven strongly by economic motives, though Putin obviously hoped victory would bring economic benefit. His starting point was the ideological identification of himself with the Russian state and people—a common delusion among rulers. Here it came with a primarily military sense of "grandeur" and "honor," emotionally supercharged by shame and humiliation over the decline of Russian power after the Soviet collapse, which he described as "the greatest geopolitical catastrophe" of the twentieth century, a "genuine tragedy" for the Russian people. Russia must erase that tragedy, ruthlessly, brutally. He added that the ongoing collapse of Western hegemony is irreversible: things will never be the same. The battlefield to which destiny and history have called us is a battlefield for our people. Putin believed he could do it and become Russia's new historic savior, honored forever. During the invasion he compared himself to Peter the Great and his western wars—which had lasted twenty-one years! Comparable delusions have been common among dictators insulated from reality by like-minded or yes- men around them. Putin was a throwback to the time of would-be great conquerors of earlier chapters.

Second, in terms of military power, Russian forces and Putin himself had become overconfident because of earlier successes, though these had all been against rather puny powers with no significant airforces. Ukraine had a significant airforce and indeed Russia has never been able to dominate the Ukrainian skies. Russians had become inured to killing civilians as well as soldiers through campaigns in Chechnya, Georgia, and Syria. But the Ukrainians constituted a much more significant military power that had been receiving American arms and training over several years. The flattening of the cities of Grozny and Aleppo were Putin-ordered atrocities reminiscent of earlier conquerors' destruction, as well as of all sides in World War II. Putin and his generals had already shown that in war they did not count the cost in lives.

Third came Putin's personal political motive, his belief—correct if he could achieve victory—that war could bolster his popularity at home, which was just beginning to falter. Playing the nationalism card and demonstrating strength was popular, helped by control of the Russian media. Combined, they generated a strong rally 'round the flag response.

As we have seen, perceived political advantage has been a common cause of war, though it can rebound on the ruler if the war is not a success.

Fourth came generalized political contempt for Ukrainians. Putin was shrewd and instrumentally rational in calculating some of the relative costs and benefits of war. Yet his hatred of and contempt for Ukrainians had been intensified by growing differences between the two political regimes. Since 2004 Ukraine had been moving closer to Western democracy, whereas Putin had intensified autocracy. He also manipulated Russian historical memories of the "Great Patriotic War," calling the Ukrainian government fascist and genocidal, drawing on the fact that some Ukrainian nationalists had thrown in their lot with the Nazis in order to be free of the Soviets. Yet over a million Ukrainians had died fighting in the Red Army, and President Volodymyr Zelensky is Jewish, making him an unlikely candidate for fascism. There are some neo-Nazis among Ukrainian paramilitaries, as in the Azov Battalion. Yet the Ukrainian government had been trying to squeeze them out, while there are also fascists in the separatist militias. There is no evidence whatsoever of genocide by Ukrainians, and the Ukrainian regime is less corrupt and more democratic than Putin's.

Putin, like many aggressors before him, despised his enemies and disparaged their powers. Russian military superiority seemed assured: a shark swallowing a minnow. Had Kyiv fallen within three days, as some Washington military pundits predicted, or within six days, as the Russian generals apparently expected, Putin might have got away with his invasion. The West would have huffed and puffed but done little. But Ukrainians, with modern weapons, fired up by nationalism, fueled by the emotional power derived from defending their homeland, fought tenaciously, with bravery, skill, and solidarity and displayed more tactical agility in the field by granting local commanders autonomy. The hierarchy-bound, arrogant Russians thought the invasion would be easy and so could not adapt to local battlefield conditions. Their folly was clear when they attacked with tanks without infantry support. Initial Russian defeats lasted long enough for anger abroad to grow against Russia, sparking an economic and weapons-supplying counterattack. Putin had unintentionally strengthened the solidarity of his foes. He had expected that declining American will power, revealed during the period of Trump's fawning, divisions among the Europeans, and an inexperienced German chancellor would produce divided responses.

Yet the West's response, led by the United States, was stronger and more united than he had expected. This should not have surprised him after the Ukrainians showed initial resistance, for the Americans and

NATO could now seize the opportunity of cutting Russia down to size without committing any troops of their own. They were able to fight a proxy war, he was not. Western sanctions greatly harmed the Russian economy, even though Western leaders knew sanctions would also hurt their own economies. Supplies of weapons to the Ukrainians also escalated. For the first time since World War II, the German government, dominated by socialists and greens, sent arms abroad and announced an increase of 100 billion euros in German military spending. The whole of Europe joined in the sanctions. Sweden, Finland, and Ukraine announced they would apply to join NATO, while Ukraine, Moldova, and Georgia applied to join the EU. Even those rulers whom Putin had considered his friends, like Viktor Orbán in Hungary and Recep Erdogan in Turkey, were equivocal. Only China and India offered him a measure of economic support.

All this was of his own making. It had not helped Putin that he and his diplomats had spent weeks lying that Russia would not invade. Diplomats are used to being economical with the truth, but they hate being taken for complete fools. Their anger intensified ideological commitment to the principle of self-determination, to which Ukrainians were believed to have a sacred right. Both NATO and Putin had unwittingly strengthened the very threats they had feared. Caught in the middle of their irrational struggle were mangled Ukrainian bodies, devastated cities, and tattered refugee columns—the normal horrors of wars, especially horrifying Westerners as the wartime sufferings of nonwhite peoples in Africa, Asia, and the Middle East had not.

There had been ways to avoid this war, although they were now unacceptable to the parties. It had been reasonable for Russia to desire greater security. Ukraine might have taken the Finnish or Austrian post–World War II routes and been accorded neutrality between NATO and Russia. Since NATO had not originally wanted Ukraine as a member, agreed neutrality might have been part of a good solution. Now, of course, no security guarantees made by Putin are believable. Declaring Ukrainian neutrality would simply be an invitation for a later Russian attack.

Principles, not pragmatism, ruled. Putin's vision of grandeur and NATO's principle of sovereignty: the Ukrainian government must have the absolute right to regain sovereignty over its former territories. Strong principles often lead to war, but they can be compromised by geopolitical pragmatism, motivated by the need to avoid war. There must be negotiations at some point. The only alternative would be a clear-cut victory. Putin was still confident of eventual victory, and he still did hold enough Ukrainian territory to be able to claim a lesser victory, and so was uninterested in negotiations. Paradoxically, the only viable path toward negotiations for the West was to up the weapon supplies to produce either stalemate or recapture of territory by Ukrainian forces, either of which might bring Putin to the negotiating table. In the meantime, mutual mass slaughter ruled.

In the Donbas, with its majority of Russian speakers, the Minsk Accords of 2014, never implemented, could have given it significant autonomy within Ukraine. Events had also gone too far for this solution. Alternatively, plebiscites might have been held whereby regional populations decide for themselves which state they wish to live in, as happened in Europe in the interwar period. Putin opposed these alternatives because he believed he could conquer the Donbas (and indeed the whole country) by force, and then administer his own phony plebiscites. Many locals would probably have voted for union with Russia, but Putin's brutal invasion has probably reduced their number below majority level. Ideally, the main principle involved should have been neither commitment to national honor and grandeur (Russia) nor inviolable sovereignty (the United States and its allies), but the right of peoples to self-determination. But Putin was not interested in that. It may be necessary for Ukraine to give up Crimea and the territories of the former separatist "republics" in order to gain back remaining Russian-occupied areas. Russia would have to agree to Ukraine's joining NATO, for that would be Ukraine's only protection against a further Russian invasion. Yet it is hard to imagine Putin agreeing to that, either. But how much is given up by each side will depend on the fortunes of war.

War is the worst option not only because it is an efficient killing machine, but also because its outcome is unpredictable. Starting a war is extremely risky. Realist theory assumes that rulers' decisions usually have a rational basis. True, Putin carefully planned his course of action over several years. He cautiously assembled his forces for Ukraine over at least several months. He chose what he thought was the right moment to strike, given recent Belarusian dependence on him, European disunity, a new, inexperienced German government, and a soft-spoken U.S. president. Perhaps he waited until after the end of the winter Olympics to avoid discomforting China. These were all indications of instrumental rationality. Yet though Putin is undoubtedly a clever and calculating man, his reasoning had become subverted by emotions, by ideology, by his need for personal political survival, by his need to please nationalist and

Slavophile factions, and by his blinkered contempt for those he defined as his enemies—like many other aggressors of history.

The risk soon became glaring, as Ukrainian forces held on, repelling Russian attacks on Kyiv and Kharkiv, forcing Russian retreat with heavy losses. When this first wave failed, attack was redoubled in the Donbas, reserve forces were moved in, and tactics honed in Chechnya and Syria were resumed. Eastern and southern cities were devastated, not by tanks, but by long-range artillery, missiles, carpet bombing, and cluster munitions. These were overwhelmingly unguided because Russian stocks of precision weapons were diminishing, and so soldiers and civilians were being killed fairly indiscriminately. Cities were razed before Russian forces advanced on the ground—a strategy not likely to win hearts and minds, but effective in death-dealing: a ghastly form of rationality. The performance of the Russian armed forces has been quite dismal, and so far Putin's escalations—a partial mobilization and the lobbing of rockets and drones against Ukrainian cities and civilians—seem signs of weakness rather than strength. Much of this falls within the category of a war crime, although such brutal tactics—including *deliberate* targeting of civilians—had also been the traditional warfare of industrial societies and was used by all sides in World War II. Yet the Russian advance was very slow, and then it stopped. It is unclear how long either of them can continue. It is impossible to give even approximate casualty figures, but fatalities so far have probably exceeded 50,000.

I have stressed the unpredictability of battle, and I cannot predict the outcome of this one (I write in late 2022). The war will probably drag on a while yet, since neither side looks as though it will achieve a rapid victory (provided the West does not falter in its weapons supplies and sanctions), and neither side is interested in negotiating. Perhaps Russian numerical superiority and the indifference of Russian leaders to their large casualty rate will eventually succeed in devastating and conquering the whole of the Donbas. Perhaps Putin might declare victory at this point—or he might not stop. Even if Russian forces were to secure battlefield victory in the east, guerilla resistance and political turbulence would probably ensue there. Of course, most locals may care more about the war ending than who wins it. Kremlin leaders might face years of quagmire in Ukraine, inducing gradual economic and military decay: a Pyrrhic victory. This might eventually affect Putin's ability to continue ruling. A coup against him remains the hope of many for a negotiated solution, though his authoritarian rule seems very solidly rooted. On the other hand, the recent initiative has lain with the Ukrainians, who have made considerable gains in the east and south. But if their momentum continues, this increases the chances that Putin might escalate to a nuclear response, perhaps at first only of battlefield nuclear weapons but still devastating not just for soldiers but also for the surrounding civilian population. The American response to this is unclear. Threats of retaliation have been made, but they have remained vague. But Putin's absence of rationality so far does not inspire confidence in the rationality of his future actions. Yet further Russian expansion is unlikely given the blowback among neighbors seeking NATO and EU membership. They reason correctly that otherwise a Russian victory would lead to more invasions. Rarely does anyone gain from a major war—except the armaments industries. That this has been so irrational a war should not induce surprise. That is a quality shared by most wars. We should not portray Putin as a madman, for his folly is not uncommon among rulers.

Chinese Revisionism

Chinese revisionism has more fronts but as yet has not involved as much militarism. It might, however, be aggravated by the Russian example or if the United States refuses to accept its rise. The current U.S. defense strategy is to be the "preeminent military power in the world," accompanied by "favorable regional balances of power in the Indo-Pacific, Europe, the Middle East, and the Western Hemisphere." Though widely accepted in the past, this now seems provocative to a far more powerful China, especially when intensified by Obama's "pivot to Asia," aimed at China, and Trump's grotesque insults. China's defense strategy proclaims, "China will never follow the beaten track of big powers in seeking hegemony," and "As economic globalization, the information society, and cultural diversification develop in an increasingly multi-polar world, peace, development, and win-win cooperation remain the irreversible trends of the times." While we should doubt such modesty, China is potentially dominant in its region, though not the world, as the United States has been.

There are still great military disparities between these two powers. Current U.S. military spending is probably more than twice that of China (although Chinese statistics are rather opaque). The United States has around six hundred overseas military bases, while China will shortly have three to five. The United States has several military bases close to China, but China has none near the United States (the same disparity exists with Russia). In 2021 China had about three hundred nuclear warheads, and the United States had four thousand. The Chinese aim to reach one thousand by 2030, and they already have the "nuclear triad," the ability to launch missiles from air, land, and sea. The United States had twelve aircraft carriers and two under construction, whereas China had three. The United States has launched many overseas wars in the last sixty years; China has engaged only in border skirmishes—which leads some observers to cast doubt on Chinese fighting ability. But a new arms race is potentially looming over hypersonic weapons, space arms, and cyber-weapons, in which China is no laggard. The fear is that an attack that disabled space satellites or command-and-control systems could escalate in unpredictable ways. At present there are no channels of communication between the United States and China over such weapons as there was over nuclear weapons between the United States and the Soviet Union. Nor is economic power so skewed. In 2019 China's nominal GDP remained only just behind the United States', and it is ahead if measured in gross Purchasing Power Parity; but China has a far bigger population, so its GDP per capita was only one-fifth of the American. Yet its economy will continue to grow.

China currently plans expansion to restore the full extent of former Chinese empires. This revisionism means securing full control of Hong Kong, Xinjiang, and Tibet, plus slivers of territory along the border with India (which the regime dubiously claims is in accordance with the 1890 Anglo-Qing Treaty), the return of Taiwan, and predominance in the South China Sea. These targets lay within the Ming or Qing empires, and past imperial glory is important in modern Chinese nationalism.[1] Regime legitimacy rests not only in economic prosperity and longevity but also in bringing unity and order to Chinese lands. Official Chinese ideology states that one hundred years of submission to foreign powers ended in 1949. Thereafter, Mao made China free, Deng made China wealthy, and Xi is giving China global strength. This national revitalization rests on popular revisionism, though it is boosted by regime manipulation. There is a widespread sense that all these domains are rightly Chinese, bringing a nationalist righteous tone to aggression that is not easy to turn aside. At the same time, as is normal in border disputes, rivals in contested zones feel as strongly in the justice of their case, and India, Japan, and Vietnam are quite substantial powers. Further MIDs are likely on the China-India borders for strategic and status interests.

In Hong Kong Chinese repression has ruthlessly mounted into a tragedy for a population used to far more civil freedoms than mainland

Chinese enjoy. The West has been helpless to intervene, except with rhetoric and economic sanctions that harden Chinese repression. China seems prepared if necessary to run down this great financial and trading entrepôt, currently a valuable economic asset, rather than yield an iota of control. For the Xi regime, domination is a value rationality to which even economic prosperity is subordinated.

The Chinese offensive in Xinjiang is claimed to be aimed at jihadists. The years 2013 and 2014 saw two terrorist attacks by Uyghurs. In response, Xi promulgated a "comprehensive security framework," calling for vigilance toward a jihadi "virus" against which Chinese Muslims must be "inoculated." He urged local Chinese officials to "use the organs of dictatorship" with "absolutely no mercy."[2] The policy seemed vindicated to Chinese Communist Party (CCP) leaders when a few contacts between Uyghurs and Islamist organizations abroad were unearthed, as well as the presence of Uyghur fighters among Middle Eastern and Afghan jihadists. These fighters may have not yet taken jihadism back into Xinjiang, although affiliates of al Qaeda and ISIS have declared a desire to do so. Hence, the forcible "reeducation" of up to a million Uyghurs and Kazakhs is claimed as "counterterrorist preventive repression." It includes deporting thousands of Uyghur young women to factories in distant provinces of China. Such measures may be counterproductive, amplifying what is at present a minimal terrorist threat, an example of confusion of cause and effect.

Most mainland Chinese regard Taiwan as part of their country, stolen away by Japan in 1895, and China prevented in 1950 from taking it back again by the U.S. Seventh Fleet. Chinese rulers might be encouraged into adventurism by the recent imperialism of their Russian ally. The American military commitment to Taiwan has been vague, and the United States does not recognize Taiwan as a separate state to avoid provoking China. Yet in May 2022 President Biden seemingly abandoned this "strategic ambiguity" by promising to defend Taiwan should China attack it. Was he simply going off script, which is a personality trait of this president? The pro-China element in Taiwan is weakened by the Hong Kong repression, and a deal between the two Chinas seems unlikely. The most likely war scenario might be a Chinese regime in domestic trouble turning to diversionary war fever over Taiwan. If this led to an invasion attempt, Chinese forces might accomplish this quickly unless the United States intervened. The U.S. response might depend on its own domestic considerations. It is conceivable but unlikely that a full-fledged war between China and the United States might be the outcome, but unintended escalation into war has happened too frequently in human history to rule this out. Here the UN is of no help to Taiwan, since it recognizes China but not Taiwan, and China is a permanent member of the Security Council.

The Chinese claim to control the South China Sea, which is called its "historical waters." This is a challenge to several Asian countries and to the American fleet stationed there. The claim centers on the islands of Senkaku, possessed by Japan, and two isolated archipelagoes, the Spratly Isles (formerly uninhabited) and the Paracel Isles, each containing tiny islets, rocks, cays, and reefs. Taiwan, Vietnam, the Philippines, and Malaysia all claim some of the Spratlys and have established small bases and airports there. China claims all the Spratlys and is establishing much bigger bases there, which caused the Philippines to go to a UN arbitration tribunal in 2016. The ruling was that no single country had exclusive rights to the isles, but China refused to accept this and has continued to construct artificial islands for military purposes. The Paracels do have a permanent population of about a thousand fishermen on an island controlled by China. But Vietnam also claims the Paracels, and both have produced historical records indicating nominal control there in different historical periods. These islands are important as fishing grounds and have potential undersea oil and gas fields, but their strategic significance is greater, for they lie astride the shipping lanes through which a third of the world's maritime trade passes. The other states contesting the isles cannot credibly challenge Chinese military power, nor do they want to alienate China, so they are reluctant to object to Chinese encroachments. Japan, however, has installed missile batteries on the island of Ishigaki, only three hundred kilometers from Taiwan, part of a package of military upgrades in its small Pacific islands. But in the North Pacific, China is beginning to challenge American military dominance. Material interests are secondary. The main problems are rival claims to geopolitical status and domination.

So Chinese rulers are assertive on all four power sources. Their nationalist ideology defines domestic opponents as traitors and terrorists undermining national unity; they seek Asian and even global economic power serving strategic as well as profit motives; they are embarked on more high-tech weaponry as well as expansion in the South China Sea; and they have a stable authoritarian political order attractive to many other would-be authoritarians, a factor in the faltering of democracy around the world. None of this is deterred by American rhetoric, which is easily parried. To accusations of Chinese repression, they cite American drones killing civilians; to American capitalism, they counterpose the Great Capitalist Recession of 2008 and their own faster recent growth; to the virtues of American democracy, they posit bought American elections, racism, and fighting in the streets. These are not foolish accusations, although the failings of American democracy pale beside the repression exercised by the CCP.

Chinese rulers seem not to want to expand territorial control beyond former imperial boundaries. To the west, they do not want to govern more Muslims. To the north, Russia is a formidable opponent; to the south, so is India; and to the east, so is Japan (if backed by the United States). To the southeast, less powerful regional states would prefer accommodation with China. Its "Belt and Road Action Plan," announced in 2015, will encompass northerly land routes (the "Belt") and southern maritime routes (the "Road") to encourage trade relations with Asia, the Middle East, and Europe, primarily through infrastructure investments and economic aid—economic, not military, power—though China has threatened trade embargoes and sanctions, which are also American tactics, of course. But Chinese rulers lack interest in the form of foreign regimes, unlike their American counterparts. The Taiwanese issue apart, other powers need not fear war with China unless they provoke it. It is difficult for U.S. leaders to accept this expansion of Chinese power, but the peace of the world depends on it. The obvious failure of recent American military aggression has, we can hope, drummed greater Realism into its leaders. Realistically, there is little the United States can do to stem Chinese repression at home or the growth of Chinese power in its own region. Yet it should hold the existing level of defense over Taiwan and counter the Belt and Road program with its own aid and development program. Trump took a giant step backward from this when he took the United States out of the Trans-Pacific Partnership. That decision should be reversed and the partnership deepened. The United States should continue to stand for the virtues of democracy and human rights, though that stance is being undercut by the very visible decay of democracy in America itself.

Material interests should offer restraint, but mutual desire for status and honor by rulers might suggest otherwise. The level of economic interdependence between Western Europe and Russia is quite high, centered on Russia's energy industry, and that between the United States and China is now very high: the United States had over half a trillion dollars of trade with China in 2020, reinforced by a wealth of educational and scientific exchanges and mutual interests over pandemics and climate change. Growing trade between Britain and Germany before 1914 did not stop their warring with each other, but today's interdependence is orders of magnitude greater. As recently as the Cold War period, the Soviet Union was largely autarkic. Autarky no longer exists for any country. I have often doubted rulers' commitment to material interests while making war-and-peace decisions. But for Chinese or American rulers to ignore such an unprecedented level of mutual material interests would be stupidity of the highest order. That might induce a certain degree of hope, except that children's games over who is to dominate the playground, irrelevant to the concerns of their peoples, are baked in to the institutions and culture of geopolitics. Recent rising tensions between the great powers lend some support to pessimistic Realism, which sees wars as ensuing from the inherent anarchy and insecurity of geopolitical space. In the end, however, wars are rarely possible to predict.

Existential Threats

Unfortunately, a far more serious crisis is now in sight, and solving it requires much closer collaboration between all the powers. If no action is forthcoming on the conflicts just mentioned, nothing disastrous would happen. Inactive peace would be good news. But climate change differs. If nothing is done and major mitigation policies are not implemented, it is *certain* natural and human disaster on a global scale will ensue. No problem with predicting here. Doing nothing is not a rational option, 95 percent of climatologists say. According to the estimate of the Intergovernmental Panel on Climate Change (IPCC), if we continue "business as usual," relying on fossil fuels, the earth's average temperature will rise by 2.6°C to 4.8°C above preindustrial levels by 2100. Implementing the 2015 Paris Agreement's "unconditional Nationally Determined Contributions" (NDCs) would still lead to a global temperature rise of 2.9°C to 3.4°C by 2100, which would continue to rise thereafter. Current NDC target levels need to be tripled if emission reductions are to meet the Paris goal of 2°C warming, and increased fivefold for the 1.5°C goal, the real solution. The UN says these gaps can still be bridged, but each year we get further away from a solution except in rhetoric. Yet even the rhetoric is contested, especially by the U.S. Supreme Court, which has proudly privileged "originalist" rhetoric in banning the federal government from issuing climate regulations, relying on eighteenth-century notions of justice—when *no one* could have envisaged the climate crisis we now face.

Accelerating rates of carbon emissions, ice cap melt, seawater and sea acidity rises, heat waves, forest fires, floods, cyclones, and species extinctions beyond previous experience have characterized the last two decades. Emissions for 2020 were the highest recorded, and average temperatures rose by 2°C rather than the 1°C annual rise of the previous decade. The climate becomes more sensitive to greenhouse gases as it warms, so that emission and temperature rises might be exponential. The 2021 report of the UN IPCC confirmed this and found that we are already locked into harmful changes in the ocean, ice sheets, and global sea levels, which will continue for centuries to come, whatever our policies. Using a 784,000-year-long reconstruction of sea-surface temperatures and a paleoclimate simulation that includes atmosphere, ocean, sea ice, and vegetation factors, researchers calculated a range of warming of between 4.78°C and 7.36°C by 2100.[3] Anything over 4°C would be catastrophic, but even the range of 2–4°C would bring widespread disaster. High-emissions regimes like the United States, Brazil, and Australia were recently removing laws designed to reduce emissions. That is suicidal. Reason does not rule in climate change. Short-term sectoral profit backed by ruinous consumerism does, and they will ruin the earth if unchecked. The positive side is that people in rich and poor countries alike are now directly experiencing these disasters, so that politicians are beginning to enact emission-lowering policies. That is already happening in the United States under the Biden administration, China under Xi, and across Europe. But will their measures go far enough, will they even be revoked, and can they lower the rising emissions of poorer countries as they develop?

Climate change has not yet directly produced wars, although sustained local drought preceded both the Sudanese and Syrian civil wars. But if leaders do not negotiate a lowering of greenhouse gases, violent conflict for declining resources will rise. Poor states are unable to take or enforce expensive measures, and they lack the military power to challenge more privileged states, so the specter might not be interstate wars, but massive refugee flows beating up helplessly against the defensive walls of wealthy, privileged countries. One can conceive of mass extinctions of humans more easily than wars. One postapocalyptic scenario would be a halving of the global population through genocides, pandemics, or famines that could produce an era of emissions reductions for the survivors. Yet there is also a potentially brighter scenario. Any successful global response to climate change would have to be achieved by major international cooperation. A byproduct of this would make countries less likely to war against each other. Perhaps the path toward Kant's perpetual peace might be through combating climate change.

Raymond Aron saw only two ways to world peace: a universal state or the international rule of law.[4] Resurgent nationalism is currently moving us away from both. Optimistic liberals see a global civilizing process. They might concede that it is slower and more uneven than initially suggested, but they see present exceptions as blips in the long run. But my history of war suggests that periods of war alternate with periods of peace. This will probably continue for a good while yet. Recent Russian imperialism shocked the world into realizing that even in Europe war is not dead. We cannot explain war or peace by relying on universals like human nature or the essential nature of societies, as historical pessimists did. Nor can we support evolutionary theories of the rise of peace, or Realist theories that assume that rational calculation of odds determines war-and-peace decisions. This is an admittedly uncertain ending, but wars have always been the product of unpredictable human decisions that might have gone differently, and which might do so in the future. I wish I could share the optimism of the liberal tradition. Goldstein concludes: "Today, bit by bit, we are dragging our muddy, banged-up world out of the ditch of war. We have avoided nuclear wars, left behind world war, nearly extinguished interstate war, and reduced civil wars to fewer countries with fewer casualties. We are almost there."[5]

Regretfully, this mixes reality with hope. In the words of an American soldier-president: "Every gun that is made, every warship launched, every rocket fired signifies in the final sense, a theft from those who hunger and are not fed, those who are cold and are not clothed. This world in arms is not spending money alone. It is spending the sweat of its laborers, the genius of its scientists, the hopes of its children. This is not a way of life at all in any true sense. Under the clouds of war, it is humanity hanging on a cross of iron."[6]

Rulers should fully commit to international institutions to combat war and climate change, consider undertaking wars only in self-defense, calculate carefully what is self-defense, calm the emotions and the temper, never demonize potential enemies, consult advisers of varying views, and use soft power unless attacked. If both parties to disputes think only of self-defense, there will be no more wars.

Conclusion
Patterns of War

OST INTERSTATE wars have been irrational in terms of either means or ends, and often of both. Here I summarize the evidence and explain why irrationality has dominated. Most interstate wars that have been rational in terms of ends would be actually termed wars of aggression as defined by the Nuremberg Tribunal and then by the Rome Statute which set up the International Criminal Court. Yet international courts have brought no prosecutions for wars of aggression since Nuremberg. It would bring more peace if they did, for then military interventions might be only those authorized by the UN. This is utopian, of course, since 42 countries have not signed up to the ICC or the Rome Statute (123 countries have), and the nonsigners include the United States, Russia, and China. It would also help if arms sales abroad, other than for policing, were banned, but this is also utopian. I have little faith in the present capabilities of the UN, and major military interventions would still have to be led by U.S. forces, but the outcome of multilateral measures would be better than recent unilateral interventions by the United States and its allies.

War is not universal, but it is ubiquitous, occurring in all regions and periods, if varying in frequency and intensity. Yet years of peace have far outnumbered those of war, and the large majority of interstate conflicts have been settled by conciliation or continue to fester amid grumbling. But boring peace has been considered less noteworthy than exciting wars, from early inscriptions, chronicles, and sagas to today's mass media. Wars sell better than peace. So war is neither genetically hardwired into humans, nor quite as important as it is often represented. Nor is it hardwired only into men. Men have caused and fought virtually all wars, but this is due to their culture and institutions, not their genes, whereas guerilla forces and recent armies have included many women. For over 90 percent of their time on earth, humans fought very few wars, but when fixed agrarian settlements generated states and social classes, organized war became ubiquitous. Societies, not universal human nature, cause wars.

Marxists explain the origin of war as a product of class exploitation. In precapitalist modes of production, they say, peasants were in physical possession of the land, and lords had to extort the surplus from them through force. The reverse Mafia-like sequence was also common, whereby peasants put themselves under the protection of local armed men when threatened by armed men from elsewhere. The result was the same: peasants were forced to yield up surplus to lords, whose privileged lifestyles, castles, fineries, and weapons depended on it. This, I think, is a valid theory pertaining to the origins of war.

Yet military power is only one of the four main ways for humans to acquire whatever material or ideal resources they may desire. I have asked why rulers use military power rather than rely on cooperative ideology, economic exchange, or political diplomacy to attain foreign policy goals. I focused mainly on interstate wars, though including civil and extrastate wars when these intruded. In chapter 10 I found no long-term or short-term trend toward either more or less war, provided we add interstate, civil, and extrastate wars together and note increasing civilian casualties, arms sales, and internationalization of recent civil wars. Overall, war is neither more nor less meaningful today than in the past.

Anarchy and Hegemony

The dominant theory of interstate war has been Realism, which deploys three major concepts: anarchy, hegemony, and rationality. Anarchy contrasts the rule of law within states with its absence in international space. Thus, rulers' anxieties about other rulers' intentions, as well as fears for their own survival amid anarchy, inevitably entail "security dilemmas," by which two or more powers periodically escalate into war. This is often true, especially in wars of mutual escalation. Yet Realists minimize domestic causes of war. Eckstein, for example, sought to explain the Roman Republic's wars almost entirely in terms of geopolitical anarchy.[1]

In chapter 4 I showed this made some sense in the very early wars of the republic, but domestic power relations were much more important causes later on. Most of its wars were wars of aggression, which led first to regime change abroad and then to imperial conquest of peoples who did not threaten Roman survival. Instead, the economic, ideological, and political institutions and culture of Rome had been subordinated to militarism.

Realism minimizes the importance of norms. Almost all wars before the modern period were between neighbors, but so was most foreign trade and ideological diffusion of shared norms, religions, and in the case of trade, agreed-on regulatory procedures. Liberal theorists emphasize pacific norms, like Confucianism, religious injunctions, or United Nations resolutions, which have aimed at limiting or regulating war. Some shared norms do restrain warriors, as in siege warfare or the treatment of prisoners or civilians. These norms often fray, but those who surrender hope the norm will be respected. Shared norms may alternatively embody warrior virtues that favor war, however, as in the feudalisms of China, Japan, and Europe or in modern fascism. Norms may restrain or amplify hostilities.

The opposite of anarchy in Realism is hegemony: peace will follow if a single state has military power coupled with the legitimate authority to set the norms of geopolitics. In many regions one great imperial state emerged out of a plethora of contending small states. Yet to achieve imperial peace, countless lives had been sacrificed in war, and most imperial states continued to make war against newly perceived enemies until their decline and fall. A rare exception was Tokugawa rule in Japan, where peace predominated for 250 years after the dynasty had achieved hegemony, although this was helped by its island ecology, which made wars against foreigners difficult. Hegemony has also been region-specific, as in imperial China's relatively peaceful tributary diplomacy with states in its east and southeast but more warlike relations in other regions. The American informal empire since 1945 was hegemonic over Western Europe, moved toward hegemony after three decades of wars in East Asia, yet was not achieved in the Middle East or Latin America.

So hegemony may sometimes reduce war but is too rare to be the main cause of peace. There are other causes of peace. War is costly, especially one likely to last long. Sometimes balances of power among several states encourage peace. Some rulers have clearly preferred peace, such as the Confucian gentry-bureaucrat class of China, some ancient Greek city-states, eleventh-century Song China, the Iroquois Confederacy, postcolonial Latin

America, recent centuries in Scandinavia, and recent decades in Western Europe. In the Cold War, the United States and the Soviets respected arms treaties and nonintervention in each other's sphere of influence. In all these cases, peace had its own virtues. It permitted extraordinary economic development in Song China and in the postwar world, where it also avoided nuclear war. Though anarchy and hegemony are useful aids in explaining war and peace, the push of anarchy is no stronger than the pull of peace. We have seen perennial tugs-of-war between them.

Rationality

Realists say war-and-peace decisions hinge on rational choice of means and ends. Defensive Realists say that states value above all the goal of survival and so calculate rationally the means of ensuring this. Aggressive Realists say that states calculate the ends of economic or strategic profit from war set against its cost in treasure and lives and the likelihood of military victory. If the odds seem favorable, states will go to war. States will initiate war when militarily strong and choose defense or diplomacy when weak. These hypotheses are plausible, and we have seen some confirming examples of them.

Yet I have preferred to write not of states but of rulers, whether individuals or smallish groups. We have seen that these have made the decisions, and they possess cognition, emotions, and values, which states lack. States, however, are important as political institutions and networks within which rulers operate. These stretch outward into civil society, carrying orders, constraints, and resources two ways between the center and the periphery. So for rational foreign policy there must be both rational decision makers and some overall coherence to the rules and practices of these institutions. The extent of state coherence has varied, and there has not been a consistent historical trend toward either more or less coherence. The Roman Republic had considerable coherence in decisions for war. Senate and popular assembly rules were clear, as they were in some ancient Greek city-states. The Chinese imperial state was fairly coherent with its two courts, one dominated by the emperor and his kin, the other by the gentry-bureaucrat class. The main problems confronting coherence were the relations between them, as well as the sheer size and the succession crises of the empire. In feudal monarchies, coherence depended on relations between the prince and his leading vassals, who enjoyed much autonomy. Their relations might be harmonious or fractious and were intermittently bedeviled by succession crises. In theory, today's representative democracies have clear rules for war-and-peace decisions, but the size and complexity of modern states can subvert this—as in the chaotic multi-institution decision making that caused World War I or the "shadow" neoconservative networks confusing the chain of command in the Bush the Younger administration, both of which reduced the rationality of decision making. A high level of institutional coherence has been quite rare.

Rulers always think their decisions for war are rational in terms of both means and ends, and they will surely try to avoid a war they believe they are likely to lose. It is difficult to probe their motives, which have obviously been varied. Yet we can pose a simple question: Do those who initiate wars win them? Obviously some do not, but that may only indicate understandable mistakes. It might reach the level of irrationality of means if initiators systematically either lost them or fought very costly wars with no victor. Quantitative data are available for wars since 1816, and I can add my own historical cases.

Melvin Small and David Singer concluded that between 1816 and 1965 initiators were victorious in thirty-four of forty-nine wars, which apparently indicates relatively rational decision making. Yet in over half these cases, the initiator was a major power attacking a minor power. Of these nineteen confrontations, the major power initiated hostilities on eighteen occasions and won seventeen. This is hardly surprising, since a war between a shark and a minnow is not much of a risk for the shark. When minnows fought minnows, the initiator won fourteen and lost seven, but when sharks fought sharks, the initiators won three and lost five. So initiating hostilities was less likely to bring victory when the combatants were great power near equals. The authors add that there was only one stalemate war among their cases (which I find hard to believe).[2]

Reiter and Stam found fifty-six of initiators in the period 1816–1988 were winners, and only thirty were losers. The authors had discarded all wars ending in a draw from their analysis, however. Draws are really a loss for both sides, costly in lives and money, which renders the war pointless, even in some cases of self-defense. If we add to the losers the seventeen initiators who fought costly draws, we get forty-seven losers to set against the fifty-six winners—only slight odds in favor of risking war.[3] Lebow in his sample found that initiators won forty-six, lost forty-five, and drew six—poor odds. And the states initiating the nine biggest wars all lost them! In his sample the odds got worse: since 1945 only 26 percent of initiators achieved their goals, rising to 32 percent if success means merely defeating the enemy's forces in the field (as in Iraq in 2003).[4] So when Ralph White studied only twentieth-century wars (after the age of imperialism), he found that aggressors lost twenty and won only five, with five draws—very bad odds. I analyzed in chapter 9 postcolonial wars in Latin America. Initiators lost six wars and won only two.[5] There were also five mutual provocations and five costly stalemates. All eight of the rulers who initiated wars, whatever the outcome, were thrown out of office because of the wars. This sorry record did bring a "delayed reaction Realism"—a belated desire to process conflict not through war but mere MIDs and mediation.

So aggressive war was risky: there was usually only around a 50 percent chance of success. Would you initiate a war with such odds? But millions of people today take on projects with scant chance of success— like opening start-up companies. In the United States they have only a 60 percent chance of survival after three years, 50 percent after five, and only 30 percent after ten. The U.K. figures are 40 percent, 36 percent, and 33 percent. Given the lure of wealth and autonomy, hope springs eternal, as it does in war. Consider also a massive global industry whose customers are mainly losers. Yet the gambling industry is booming. Its gross gaming revenue (GGR), the difference between revenues and payouts, is rising, and GGRs are projected to reach $565 billion in 2022. The industry exists only if there are more losers than winners. Gamblers are risk-accepting; they get excited by the act of gambling, and they are hopeful. So are rulers, especially since in war they are usually gambling with other people's lives. Most war-and-peace decisions are made in a context of risk-induced anxiety, hope, and unexpected interactions that are hardly conducive to reason.

But given the order to prepare for war, generals calculate campaign plans and mobilize resources. Quartermasters' logistics dominate this phase, and it is highly calculative. Then comes contact with the enemy, and all hell breaks loose. As we saw, battle is felt by the soldiers as fearful chaos, from the ferocious body-on-body slashing of earlier history to modern callous warfare in which soldiers blaze away at a distance, keeping heads down, but vulnerable to random death inflicted from the skies. Carefully laid plans can rarely be implemented because of the enemy's unexpected behavior or the unanticipated battlefield terrain—Clausewitz's "friction" of battle and Ibn Khaldun's "hidden causes" of outcomes. Various commanders, including Helmuth von Moltke the Elder and Napoleon, have been credited with the adage "No plan of operations extends with any certainty beyond the first contact with the main hostile force." The outcome of six of the seven biggest battles of the Hundred Years' War was the result of unexpected terrain or enemy action. Most of the battle victories of the U.S. Civil War did not result from initial strategies. The small-scale engagements by U.S. World War II units vividly described by S. L. A. Marshall were decided by unexpected terrain or enemy dispositions, mistakes, acute or fortunate decisions, and bravery by small groups. The decision for war submits rulers, generals, and soldiers to the fickle fortunes of battle. Today the lack of predictability is obvious in Ethiopia, Yemen, and Ukraine.

I recap the extent of calculation of means in my main historical cases. The Roman senate debated war-and-peace decisions at length; it focused on the economic profit war might bring, not on the cost in lives. There were deviant cases, such as Caesar's wars in Gaul and Britain, which were not expected to be profitable. Here the main motives were domestic politics: most senators wanted Caesar far away, where he could not foment trouble in Rome, while Caesar's faction wanted him to command legions abroad and then bring them back to foment trouble in Rome (which he duly did). The senators rarely doubted military victory, so discussion of military odds was confined to how many legions should be mobilized. War was usually endorsed unless jealousies stopped a rival senator from getting the chance to command the armies or unless other wars were ongoing and therefore stretching resources. Senators were sometimes overconfident, and defeat resulted. But their response was to dig deeper into manpower resources and emerge with eventual victory, as in the Punic Wars. The eventual success rate of Roman-initiated wars was high. War for the Romans, however, was not really a "choice"—it was what Romans did, by virtue of their militaristic institutions and culture. In contrast, the goal of economic profit was more important for the Carthaginians, and they did not sacrifice as much for military purposes. So they lost the Punic Wars and were destroyed.

The rulers of the two ex-barbarian dynasties of China, the Yuan and the Qing, behaved like Romans. They also could dig deeper into resources than their enemies because militarism was baked in to their institutions and cultures. Military power restructured the other three sources of power. As in Rome, war was considered the surest way to wealth, political power, and status, honor, and glory alike. War was what Mongols and Manchus, Aztecs (Incas less so), and Arab conquest dynasties did whenever opportunity or insult seemed to arise. They continued aggressing until they reached hubris, sometimes induced by Nature's deserts, jungles, or oceans. This finally constrained them into preferring diplomacy and peace—a delayed-reaction Realism. Until then, rulers were constrained more by institutionalized militarism than by calculation. But perhaps my rather aggressive cases—the Roman Republic and the Mongol, Manchu, Aztec, and Arab dynasties—were atypical.

So I examined the milder two Song dynasties of China. The first Song emperor, Taizu, was a model Realist, fighting and winning offensive wars after cautious initial probes to test whether victory was likely, and carefully building up adequate forces. Yet his successors initiated six offensive wars resulting in only one success, one costly draw, and four defeats. Muddying rational calculation were righteous revisionism demanding the return of "lost territories," attempts to divert domestic political power struggles, an emperor's overweening ambition, or choosing the wrong allies, as in the crucial final wars of the two dynasties (the only major geopolitical cause). Other Song rulers preferred peace or defense over aggression, less because of weakness than because they pursued economic and social development, following liberal, not Realist, precepts, and preferring diplomacy, cultural cooperation, and production and trade. In contrast, the last Song emperors (and the last Ming emperors, too) were relatively weak but hastened collapse by striking out impulsively, in denial of weakness, rather than settling for accommodation. The Song present a mixed bag.

Luard said that most European rulers between 1400 and 1940 who started wars lost them.[6] He surely exaggerated in perceiving *no* careful calculation of means among rulers, but war was mainly what a medieval ruler did when feeling slighted or ambitious or when diverting the turbulence of younger sons or bolstering his or her own domestic power. These motivations and the lure of status, honor, and glory then dictated calling out the barons, levying taxes or borrowing, and setting off for battle with whatever levies showed up, which the ruler could not predict. Again, war was less a choice than what a ruler felt constrained to do in particular contexts. Later European rulers fielded professional armies and navies, but they still mostly warred when feeling slighted or ambitious. It was not always a question of "choice" because conflict stances might escalate into an unintended war. From the sixteenth century came a wave of neomercantilist naval wars with material goals and the belief that the international economy was zero-sum—for one country to gain, another must lose. This was more calculative, although there were also ideological wars in this period, at first religious, then revolutionary-nationalist. Finally, global imperial conquest was launched by Europeans in which the lure of profit fused with righteous ideologies of civilizational and racial superiority.

In World War I no aggressor initially invoked economic goals. Instead, they demanded status in the geopolitical system and the honor of defending allied client states to ensure the survival of their dynasties (though German rulers did hope for more profitable colonies). Many calculations were made by many actors, but war resulted from cascading diplomatic mistakes and incoherent policy formation. A plethora of political institutions produced unpredictability and brinkmanship that perversely meant that no one would back down. Most rulers were confident of victory, but they had a backup belief that this would be a short war, since economies could not support it for long. How wrong they were! So the rulers of Germany, Austria-Hungary, Russia, and the Ottoman Empire, the leading initiators, secured not only their own defeat but also the fall of monarchy itself. Some at the time warned that this might happen, but they lost the domestic power struggle. Yet all the rulers lost heavily in this dreadful war, except for the two outsiders who picked up the pieces, Americans and Bolsheviks. This war was irrational for everyone else.

In World War II rationality was disrupted more by ideology. This obstructed Allied defense strategy in the late 1930s. War might have been prevented or delayed if France and Britain had allied with the Soviets to deter Hitler, as many suggested at the time. There were geographical and political obstacles to this in Eastern Europe, but ideology was the main problem, since most French and British rulers feared communism more than they did fascism. So Stalin, isolated, made his 1939 Non-Aggression Pact with Hitler, and there was no balancing alliance. In the Far East, Japanese rulers despised the Chinese, underestimating their nationalist resolve; and Japanese and American rulers miscalculated each other's reactions and got into an unanticipated total war. War was initiated by German and Italian fascists and Japanese semi-fascists. Their economic motives were subordinated to a vision of imperial conquest achieved by martial ideologies despising the "decadence" of the liberal powers and China, and the "barbarism" of communism. Early successes prevented rational long-term calculation of military and economic odds. The Axis rulers believed their martial spirit would overcome daunting odds of numbers and technology. For them this war embodied Weber's "value rationality," commitment to ultimate values overriding instrumental rationality. Their initiation of war was suicidal.

In the Korean War, North Korean, American, and Chinese rulers all in turn aggressed, underestimating their enemies, blinkered by ideology. They could reach only a bloody stalemate, which achieved none of their objectives and led to a bitterness across Korea that still poisons East Asia. After Korea, U.S. presidents were better at propping up client regimes than at changing them, but in Vietnam they failed to achieve either and suffered defeat through underestimating the ideological commitment and normative solidarity of their opponent. Reagan's pressure on the Soviet Union did help bring about Soviet collapse, but the main causes of that collapse lay within the Soviet Communist Party. The recent spate of wars in Muslim countries has seen some initial battlefield victories for the United States and its allies, yet neglect of political power predictably thwarted goal achievement. U.S. interventions greatly damaged Afghanistan and Iraq and contributed together with other actors to the chaos rending Libya, Syria, and Yemen. The United States has not achieved its goals in any significant war since 1945, apart from the Cold War, a remarkable series of failures by the world's superpower. At the moment Putin seems far from attaining his goals. So from early history to the present day, initiating major war probably resulted more often in failure than success, while there was substantial irrationality of means.

Of course, some wars are rational in terms of ends, initiated for potential or actual profit that was achieved, mostly in raids and in imperial-conquest wars between highly unequal adversaries, while other wars are rational because fought in self-defense with a good chance of success. But benefit in these cases was almost entirely zero-sum: for some to gain, others must lose. In Central and South America, pre-Columbian empires and Spanish and Portuguese empires alike fought wars devastating indigenous peoples, which embodied a ghastly racial form of rationality, bringing benefits to a few conquerors but massacres of the defeated. Spanish and Portuguese imperialisms, like other subsequent European imperialisms, would today be classified as war crimes, and often as genocides. In contrast, subsequent Latin American decisions were increasingly rational because rulers learned from "bad wars" not to make more. There were no serial aggressors here. Instead, rulers learned to move toward lesser MID conflicts and diplomatic mediation.

Some wars might be considered rational in hindsight, having sparked unintended benefits such as economic development, while conquest may bring creativity by blending hitherto distinct social practices. It may also provide more social order. Roman rulers always claimed this, as indeed did most imperialists. Recent scholars have emphasized the creativity generated by the blending of diverse cultures within the Mongol Empire. Yet peace also brings order and creativity. Ibn Khaldun assessed the economic consequences of early Arab wars. The conquerors seized great wealth for themselves and their followers, for "booty was lawful property," but always at the expense of the conquered. Orderly imperial rule, however, did generally boost economic growth and tax returns for the first two generations of a dynasty, but then came decline in both, leading eventually to the collapse of the dynasty in wars: a rather mixed bag.[7] When dealing with early modern European warfare, the Industrial Revolution, and the two world wars, I found that even the unintended benefits of war, though real enough, have been exaggerated and pale beside war's devastation. The counterfactual of whether civilization could have been furthered better through peace may be unknowable. But there is a major countercase. In Song China peace favored major technological innovation and economic development—and it was defeat in war which ensured the end of the extraordinary development under the southern Song.

The post-1945 period has seen extraordinary technological and economic progress in the Northern Hemisphere, but was this due to American hegemony or to the mere fact of peace there—a peace in reaction to the most devastating war in human history. Statistical data drawn from national income accounts are available on the economic impact of wars since 1945. They show that war reduces GDP per capita, even though the main losses, of life and the destruction of physical and human capital, do not figure in these income accounts.[8] We cannot calculate such detail in earlier wars, but chroniclers imply that interstate wars were zero-sum—for some to gain, others must lose—and they stress the devastation of regions in which campaigns occurred. Admittedly, this is far from perfect evidence, and the economic effects of war need much further research. I tried to end my cases with a rough guess at who benefited and who lost. Generally, more lost than won. Given the certainty that war kills millions, my conclusion is that most wars are pointless and irrational in terms of both means and ends. Why are there nonetheless so many of them?

Political Power: Whose Decision?

Most decisions for war, whether made by a representative democracy, an oligarchy, a monarchy, or a dictatorship, were made by a small coterie of rulers, advisers, and other powerful persons—and sometimes by a single

monarch, dictator, prime minister, or president. There is very little democracy in foreign policy. The extreme potential case, thankfully not yet
realized, is the sole authority of the American president to release nuclear missiles that could destroy the world. That might also be said of
both Putin and Xi. A recent example of a consequential single ruler of
the United States was George Bush the Younger. His personal drive to
war in Iraq was discussed in chapter 14. Decisions have been made by
rulers and their close associates, not nations or the capitalist class, with
influential colonial bankers and merchants, arms industries, and media
barons as exceptions. Most capitalists prefer to do business amid peace,
but they adapt quickly to ways of making profit from war. As I showed in
chapter 10, contrary to the views of most political scientists, modern representative democracies have been no less likely to make war, whether or
not this was war against other democracies, provided we include all their
small colonial wars and the direct democracy found among many indigenous peoples. Ideally, democracy should make a difference, but in practice foreign policy decision making is not very democratic.

The people are rarely responsible for wars, not because they are virtuous but because they are barely interested in either sense of that word.
They do not see their personal interests at stake, and they lack interest in
foreign affairs. Representative democracy includes hundreds of elected
persons sitting in parliaments passing laws. Yet they depend for reelection on their constituents, and so they mirror their lack of interest in foreign policy. In the U.S. Congress, for example, few representatives or
senators show much interest in foreign policy. They leave it to the foreign affairs committees. If their chairs and highly respected committee
members agree with the administration, foreign policy is rubber-
stamped, unless powerful interest groups intervene (or a gross violation
of human rights provokes them into moralizing rhetoric). This is why
congressional votes for war in the United States have been so lopsided.
In this country a plethora of think tanks add advice, yet congressional
votes suggest that dissonant advice is ignored.

Of course, public opinion does play a role in most modern societies
(rarely in large historical societies), but it is usually somewhat manipulated by political leaders, entrenched vested interest groups, and media
barons. Where geopolitical relations become fraught, conflict becomes
normalized and foreign threats become "nationalized," in the sense that
the public, lacking much knowledge of foreign affairs, can be fairly easily
persuaded that national interests are at stake, as their leaders claim. As

war looms and as it starts, a rally 'round the flag mentality usually occurs, lasting long enough to persuade leaders that the public actually wants war. Sometimes the result may be complex interactions among leaders, vested interests, mass media, and mass publics, but the initiative in decision making almost invariably lies with the leaders.

Democracy is a desirable system for deciding domestic issues in which the people show interest. But democracy has not proved its worth in war-and-peace decisions. The people have known little about the "enemy" beyond what rulers tell them. In the past people saw war as defense of their lord or monarch. Obedience was their duty, reinforced by institutionalized rituals and by coercion. Today the people often do identify with the nation and its rulers and so can be persuaded that even an aggressive war is self-defense or that the enemy is evil. Americans, for a time, and Russians, under severe censorship, will support a war claimed to be waged in self-defense or good against evil—and leaders invariably assert both.

In some societies men have been addicted to war (and women accepted addiction as normal), as did some pastoralists in northern Eurasia and the Middle East. Decisions for war were made by the khan or emir and his intimates, but there was popular enthusiasm for war. More widespread in human history, however, has been the ethos of masculinity and manliness pervasive in patriarchal societies, including our own, which for most men smothers any pacific tendencies with the smear of cowardice. This has been especially powerful while mobilizing soldiers once war has been decided on. At this stage, women are often complicit in the ethos of manliness—or at least men think they are and so feel they must prove their manliness to them. Fear of demonstrating cowardice in the eyes of comrades and women is then important in keeping men enduring the horrors of battle, as we repeatedly saw in chapters 11–13. This may have been the most popular prop of militarism.

In a few societies, quasi-representative decisions for war have involved many more people. In some Greek city-states, decisions were made by the citizen body as a whole—20–40 percent of adult males. Many were probably involved in some early Sumerian city-states. They were in the state of Tlaxcala, Mexico, in 1519, and among many native American peoples. There was more limited citizen participation in the popular assemblies of the Roman Republic and in twentieth-century liberal democracies. Modern public opinion surveys may give the impression that most people have serious views on matters of war and peace, while politicians "acting tough" may win popular support before the reality of war sinks in. Yet these are generally paper-thin sentiments easily shredded by war itself. Some sectional interests do favor war or peace, and some constituencies willingly supply soldiers because alternative channels of advancement are absent—like the overrepresentation of southern white officers and African American men in U.S. forces, or the role of Gurkhas in British armies.

Yet even in representative governments, decisions for war have been steered by manipulative rulers abetted by special interest groups and compliant mass media (where these exist). In the Roman Republic senatorial elites manipulated the popular assemblies into war. Parliaments in England generally left matters of war and peace to monarchs and their ministers, except during the mercantilist eighteenth century, when merchants and bankers joined in. Nineteenth-century British colonial policy debates reliably emptied the House of Commons, and the people showed little interest in empire except when native atrocities committed against British people were publicized. Hitler's lies about murders of Germans in Danzig in 1939, Roosevelt's distortion of the USS *Greer*'s 1941 brush with a German submarine, and Johnson's lies about the Gulf of Tonkin in Vietnam in 1964 were pretexts for war believed by most citizens. The administration of Bush the Younger, helped in Britain by Tony Blair, fed false information to gullible publics in 2002–3 about Saddam Hussein's supposed links with terrorists and weapons of mass destruction. The Putin government denied in 2014 that the masked men who seized Crimea were regular Russian troops, and in 2020 Putin claimed that Russian mercenaries and Russian planes in Libya were not Kremlin approved, although their weaponry could only have come from Russian army supplies. Putin's lies about his war in Ukraine were many. The U.S. Congress is constitutionally empowered to declare war, but in the twentieth and twenty-first centuries it has usually ratified decisions already made by presidents. Launching World War II was a partial exception, since until the attack on Pearl Harbor Congress had blocked Roosevelt's attempts to join the war. So Roosevelt retaliated with covert means and trickery to supply Britain with aid. In 2001, during the panic induced by the 9/11 terrorist attack, Congress passed—with only one dissenting vote—the Authorization to Use Military Force Act, allowing the president to use force abroad without congressional approval if such conduct was in pursuit of terrorists or those who harbor them. The president decides who is a terrorist. The act is still in force. By 2018 it had been used forty-one times to attack nineteen countries.

Once war is declared, popular support grows in the first months, for "they" really are trying to kill "us." Volunteers sign up in numbers, but rallies 'round the flag, helped by propaganda of the enemy's atrocities, are temporary. Conscription becomes necessary. Soldiers continue to obey the order to fight since they are under discipline and believe that this is the way the world works. Varying degrees of value commitment among soldiers—high in religious and communist armies, and among the conquistadores, quite high in Roman Republican armies and in World War II, lower in most wars with professional or conscripted soldiers—is reinforced by repetitive drilling, harsh discipline, and entrapping battlefields. Yet a secret ballot held the day before battle would probably produce a majority of soldiers voting against battle, except perhaps in elite regiments. Alternatively, the rulers who chose war could do the actual fighting—alas, these are utopian solutions.

People believe their rulers' narratives since they lack alternative knowledge. Popular street demonstrations in favor of war (or peace) do occur, but the demonstrators are small proportions of the population. If war proves unpopular, this is because it is not going well, or because of opposition to domestic consequences, such as conscription and extra taxes or debts. Anticipation of this, especially taxes, is one of the main deterrents to rulers considering war. War-and-peace factions within ruling groups do exist; there is also lobbying by special interest groups, and students and intellectuals mobilize for causes. That is as popular as war-and-peace decisions generally get. So the problem shifts away from why human beings make wars to why rulers do. One inference is clear: the best antidote to war would be direct participation by citizens in popular assemblies to decide war or peace. Alas, this is also utopian.

Political Power: The Nature of Rulers

Since rulers make wars, their preferences and personalities matter. Some rulers focus on stability, the economy, social welfare, or justice and oppose the conscription and higher taxes war requires. Others favor war as profitable or heroic, necessary for grandeur and glory, and willingly raise taxes and initiate conscription. Some strike warrior poses. Rulers' sagacity and war record matter. Sequential victories enhance prestige and vassal loyalty and make future wars more likely. Rulers are capable or incompetent, calm or impulsive, brave or timorous, suspicious or trusting. Contrast three successive Ming emperors—Yongle, the successful warrior; Xuande, the administrative innovator; and Zhengtong, the incompetent. Contrast the cruel warrior Henry V with the mentally challenged Henry VI, or the peace-loving Chamberlain with the bellicose Churchill, or the cautious, conscientious Obama with the erratic, ignorant Trump. Of course, to describe rulers or their policies in terms of just one or two character traits is grossly oversimplified. Stalin was paranoid about domestic opposition but naively trusting of Hitler. Trump was chronically distrustful of others and regarded business and political relations as battle zones, but he was not a militarist abroad. Yet in Latin America I attributed four of fifteen wars to reckless presidents initiating or provoking wars they would probably lose. The chroniclers told "great men" narratives, exaggerated but containing some truth. Since personality differences are contingent, Realists dismiss them as "noise" in their models, but we must not confuse models with explanation.

Monarchs, dictators, and presidents rarely make policy on their own. Most decisions come after rulers listen to opinions at court or in councils or assemblies. Yet outcomes depend as much on the ruler's ability to control the information flow, generally by appointing like-minded advisers, or on the balance of domestic political power, as on accurate perception of external realities. For example, debates over Japanese imperialism in the early twentieth century were settled by political power in Tokyo shifting rightward through domestic crises caused by the Great Depression, repression of the working class, collapse of political parties, and assassinations of prominent opponents. Rulers' preferences shifted from international market nudging to informal empire to territorial imperialism. Since domestic issues dominate political debate most of the time, war-and-peace decisions depend on which faction—conservative or reformist, right or left, centralizers or decentralizers, frontiersmen or men of the core—has acquired influence on domestic issues. Of course, they were almost all from the dominant class and ethnic groups, and they were almost all men. For most politicians, foreign policy is peripheral vision. Bush the Younger came to power primarily on domestic issues, ignorant of the outside world. He let Vice President Cheney make most appointments to foreign and defense posts, and Cheney chose hawks. They and a converted Bush manipulated Congress into wars.

Rulers have launched many wars to shore up their domestic political power. Others find it impossible to back away from a war going badly, which would seem to signal weakness. Marxists stress the diversion of class conflict, but this has been uncommon since war is prone to increase rather than reduce class conflict, especially in defeat. It did figure in the reasoning of monarchs on the brink of World War I, but revolution was the actual consequence, as skeptics at court had warned beforehand. Repression of the working class, *"solving"* class conflict, fueled interwar militarism in Germany and Japan. Diverting intra-elite conflict has been much more common, launched by rulers beset by rivals or seeking to counter an impression of weakness—like Taizong or Edward III and Henry V of England. Such rulers try to factor into their decision making whether this will work, but it depends principally on whether the war is successful. But weak as well as strong rulers launch wars.

Fearon suggests one way conflict escalates. A standard tactic is for one side to strengthen its bargaining power by issuing threats.[9] To carry credibility, these need to involve significant costs and be made publicly, perhaps by withdrawing diplomats, seeking the support of allies, or moving troops. This may provoke the rival to reciprocate. The protagonists now find themselves in a downward spiral toward a war they had not initially intended. They might prefer to back down, but this brings what Fearon calls "audience costs." To back down signals weakness and dishonor in the eyes of the domestic audience. These costs worsen as the crisis escalates, making it harder to avoid war. Fearon suggests honor results from modern nationalism. Yet he is too modest. We saw "audience costs" in all periods, among ancient Chinese dukes, the emperors Taizong and Chongzhen, the emperor Claudius, medieval monarchs, leaders plunging into World War I, General Galtieri, and Saddam Hussein, among others. Rulers face domestic threats from opposition parties, factions at court or in a single party, military coups, or rival pretenders to the throne. So they try to convey strength and honor by not backing down. Monarchs may also wish to prove that they really are the Son of Heaven or anointed by God, as we saw in China and pre-Columbian America. Putin wants to prove he really is a new Peter the Great.

Rulers may also fear their generals and deliberately weaken the armed forces to lower the threat of military coups. So they are less likely to initiate wars, but it may encourage others to attack them. Shah Muhammad II of the Khwarazmian (Persian) Empire separated his massive army into smaller detachments stationed in different cities, in fear of his generals. So Chinggis Khan picked them off one by one and destroyed his empire. The Roman Republic's unending wars conversely enhanced the generals' power, and they eventually overthrew the republic. Subsequent Roman emperors used praetorian guards for protection from the army, with mixed results. The Inca and Middle Eastern regimes sought coup-proofing by reducing the army's autonomous power. Saddam Hussein self-destructed this way. Stalin almost self-destructed, purging his senior officer corps in the late 1930s, thus hamstringing the Red Army. In contrast, few African rulers have devised effective coup-proofing. Between 2000 and 2020 seventeen successful military coups occurred in a continent where militaries are deployed more for domestic than for international purposes. In such cases we see a contradiction between military and political power—each undermining the other. Yet in contrast, stable democratic and communist regimes have both retained civilian control of the military.

Dynastic monarchy has been the most common regime type, with its own rhythms of war. Unclear rules of succession and polygynous marriages all made wars of succession more likely, as was true among the Mongols, Chinese, and Inca. The absence of a competent male heir often led to civil war between claimants, which invited interventions by foreign rulers. Dynasties rarely lasted more than a hundred years, as Ibn Khaldun also noted of Arab kingdoms.[10] In succession crises only one claimant could win, and the others usually lost their lives, but hopeful ambition had bent their perception of the odds. Civil wars lasted for a quarter of China's two-thousand-year imperial history. Such wars rarely occurred in city-state republics like Venice and some elected monarchies, such as the Aztec, where ruling oligarchies had devised agreed-on procedures to choose the next ruler. Modern republics, constitutional monarchies, and one-party states have their own agreed-on rules of succession. Nonetheless, rulers' personalities, preferences, reproductive abilities, and ambition all influence war-and-peace decisions.

The Three Main Motives for War

Three motives for war stand out above the others. Historians often emphasize two, "greed and glory," and political scientists have explained civil wars in terms of "greed and grievance." Those launching aggressive war usually visualize economic benefits and promise them to their soldiers and subjects, but acquiring more territories or tribute and subjects or submissive clients also brings rulers the gratification of greater status and honor in the geopolitical system, both for themselves and for their states, the two being seen by them as identical. Glory is the highest level of status and honor, for it has the advantage, rulers believe, of being eternal, whereas profit is only for now. So status, honor, and glory combine in an ideological-emotional package of motives. In a few societies the populace may share to a limited extent in this—for example, many Roman citizens, many modern Germans and Japanese during their periods of military success, and Americans more recently, though now this package is mixed with nostalgia for a past, more glorious period. But a third main motive is the intrinsic enjoyment of domination over others, found especially in conquest and raiding, and particularly among the great conquerors of history, but often shared by their soldiers, who abused, looted, and raped enemy populations. We have seen these three motives—greed, status-honor-glory, and domination—repeatedly entwining in my case studies in ways not easy to disentangle.

Economic motives (greed) have obviously been important. Balancing economic costs and benefits against casualties and the likelihood of victory is the core of Realism, and rulers—and adventurist bands like the conquistadores—did try to assess these odds. Yet this involves four separate metrics, and there is no way to set lives, the chances of victory, economic profit or loss, and longer-term strategic advantages against each other in any systematic way. They had to make rough assessments.

The cost in lives may have been less of a deterrent to war, as most rulers did not risk their own lives. In history they began in the center of battle formations, well-protected but still at some personal risk, as Crassus, Harold Godwinson, and Richard III all discovered. More accurate archery forced rulers and generals back to command from a vantage point in the rear, and then firearms forced them even farther back. By the twentieth century they had become desk killers, sending out younger men to distant deaths. Few campaigns in any era have been called off because rulers feared heavy losses. Quite the reverse: they were more likely to intensify calls for "sacrifice," which they were not making themselves. Three recent U.S. presidents ordering wars had been effectively draft dodgers—Clinton, Bush the Younger, and Trump. In the past many rulers saw their soldiers as "scum," drawn from the uncivilized lower classes. Their lives could be casually spent. Modern soldiers have also expressed fear of being used as cannon fodder. We saw French troops in World War I demanding their sacrifice be "proportional" to the chances of success, whereas in 2021 Afghan troops fled when their sense of proportionality was shattered by sudden American withdrawal. So the risk of death, the main cost of war, is usually minimized by rulers, making war more rational to them than to soldiers or civilians.

Yet the financial costs of war often did deter rulers. War requires increased taxes or debts, as well as conscription, which are unpopular and take resources from the economy. Many rulers were reluctant to squeeze peasants hard for fear of rebellion or damage to the economy, which would then reduce the taxes and men available for future war. Easy targets and short wars were not ruinous, nor were rule-governed wars with few casualties, but losing or lengthy wars might threaten rulers' downfall. The decision was often for peace. A few astute militaristic rulers, however, devised reforms harnessing military and economic relations together to yield economic growth that could fuel war—like the legalist reforms of the Chinese Warring States, sixteenth-century cadastral reforms in Japan, seventeenth-century fiscal reforms of England and Holland, and twentieth-century military Keynesianism. These were strategies making war more economically attractive to rulers with vision and the political skills to implement reform. Nonetheless, if economic profit was the sole motive of rulers, there would have been far fewer wars.

The Four Types of Offensive War

Offensive wars must be distinguished from defensive wars and from the middling category of mutual provocation and escalation. I divided offensive wars into in-and-out raiding; intervention to change or prop up a regime abroad (informal imperialism); war to seize slivers of border territory; and territorial conquest followed by direct imperial rule.

In raiding, goals appear as mainly material—looting movable wealth, animals, slaves, and women. Successful raiders, however, also enjoy status among their followers, and they enjoy domination in itself, exulting in the fear in their victims' eyes, especially evident in rape. Raiding was normal among "barbarian" peoples possessing military resources. In Asia and Africa their raids continued until the eighteenth century but have now died out except in failed or very poor states. Looting has been perpetrated by modern troops, however, notably by Nazi, Japanese, and Red Army troops in World War II, by Chinese nationalist forces in Vietnam at the end of that war, and by Iraqi soldiers in 1991 and 2003.

Military intervention aimed at foreign regime support or change was frequent in the early phases of Roman and European "informal empires" and in pre-Columbian Latin America. Rule was through local clients. Yet it has persisted through the twentieth and early twenty-first centuries in American military interventions. The goal may be geopolitical, to protect an ally, or economic, for tribute, better access to raw materials or terms of trade, or simply to enjoy wielding dominance over others.

Wars over slivers of border territories have become the most common wars. Aggression here is not always regarded by international law as a criminal act because the contending parties often have a case. Since the collapse of direct empires was followed by the creation of many new or restored states, border disputes and revisionism have grown. They involve mainly economic and strategic goals. Yet "revisionism," a claim to recover "lost" or "stolen" territories, has added righteousness to them. This subverted the pacific Confucian bias in imperial China, and it was prominent in the Hundred Years' War and some Latin American cases. Timur the Great claimed to be only recovering Chinggis Khan's realm. German revisionism led to World War II, to regain territories lost in the first war. Russian revisionism today seeks to recover some of the territories lost in the collapse of the Soviet Union, though this was probably intended as the conquest of whole countries, territorial empire being the final goal. Chinese revisionism today seeks full control of Taiwan, Hong Kong, Tibet, and Xinjiang, and offshore naval expansion—all to restore control over lands and seas formerly dominated by Chinese imperial dynasties. Restoring lost territory was deemed a righteous war by Azeris in 2020, but Armenians maintain a rival revisionism. Israelis and Palestinians find it impossible to negotiate a sharing of their promised but lost lands. Wherever there are lost territories, revisionism stirs, blending motives of moral right and economic and strategic interest. This is the dominant danger of warfare today.

But it is not everywhere. Postcolonial Latin America has seen relatively few border wars, and relatively few interstate wars at all, for three main reasons. First, states had limited fiscal resources, enough to finance a brief war, but raising new taxes was difficult and soon debts and political discontent would mount. Part of the risk of war is that rulers cannot predict how long a war will last. Second, settlement was easier in the ecological heartland of the new states (once indigenous peoples were removed) rather than near borders, which tended to be in mountainous, jungle, or desert regions where the old Spanish maps were often unclear. Since settler expansion was rarely around borders, wars there were less likely. Third, where a newly independent state occupied the same area as a former Spanish provincial, treasury, or judicial district, this strengthened the legal principle of *uti possidetis*—new states should retain the old borders. This assisted mediation of border disputes by outsiders.

African countries also inherited colonial borders, which discouraged border wars except in the Horn of Africa, where the British, French, Italian, and Ethiopian empires had left their own border conflicts to plague their successors. In Southeast Asia, most colonies inherited the territories of former kingdoms, which made postcolonial restoration of sovereignty easier. The successor states of the Habsburg Empire also inherited its provincial boundaries and so rarely fought against each other. Nor did many post-Soviet successor states. The Tajik-Kyrgyz skirmish in April 2021 was an exception, but most post-Soviet wars have been between a revisionist Russia and other peoples, as in the Caucasus and Ukraine.

Wars of imperial conquest add seizure of territory and direct rule over peoples. They have almost died out today, the Russian invasion of Ukraine being the main recent exception. The great conquerors I examined—Qin Shi Huang, Chinggis Khan, Qianlong, the Japanese triumvirs, and Napoleon—all took care in preparing their wars, signs of instrumental rationality. But their goal became conquest and domination for the status, honor, glory, world transformation, and even immortality they believed this would bring—value more than instrumental rationality, using Weber's term.

The conquerors sacrificed countless lives to this vision. They saw their military conquests less as choice than as an obligation to follow their destiny or the will of the gods, as probably did other great conquerors like Sargon of Akkad, Thutmose III of Egypt, Tiglath-pileser III, Cyrus II of Persia, Alexander, Attila, Timur, Asoka, Pachacuti Inca Yupanqui, Aztec kings, and many others who were styled "The Great," "The Earth-Shaker," "The World Conqueror," and the like. They slaughtered millions and brought benefit to only a few. Most of these conquerors were highly intelligent, like Chinggis and Timur the Great. Ibn Khaldun, after several interviews with Timur, commented: "Some attribute to him knowledge, others attribute to him heresy . . . still others attribute to him the employment of magic and sorcery, but in all this there is nothing; it is simply that he is highly intelligent and perspicacious, addicted to debate and argumentation about what he knows and also about what he does not know."[11] Yet Timur also said, "The whole expanse of the inhabited part of the world is not large enough to have two kings."[12] Most great conquerors were intelligent megalomaniacs, leaving triumphal stelae, arches, and sculptures whose grandiose inscriptions and depictions boast more of the territories and peoples conquered than of the well-being of the realm. We can probably add rulers of less well-documented precolonial

American and African empires, such as Aztec rulers, the Songhai Empire's Sonni Ali or Chaka Zulu—and the failed world conqueror, Hitler.

Yet conquest produced what are interchangeably called "empires" and "civilizations"—Egyptian, Akkadian, Assyrian, Roman, Hellenic, Persian, Turkic, Muslim Arab, Mughal, Mongol, Chinese, Spanish, British, Aztec, Inca, Maya, American, and so on. These imperial civilizations *all* eventually replaced worlds of small peoples, tribes, and city-states, mainly through aggressive war. But they also developed mission statements that listed bringing order, freedom, civilization, and often the true faith to the conquered, and these became motives or pretexts for further wars. We should be cynical about most of these claims, and civilizations of multiple city-states also existed for long periods before their eventual conquest by empires—as was true of ancient Sumer, classical Greece, and Mesoamerica.

Conquerors depended on loyal followers and obedient clients, on compliant, militarized subjects, and on legitimacy of rule. Qin emperor Shi Huang also drew on legalist reforms, Chinggis cited earlier Mongol expansion, Napoleon inherited the *levée en masse*, Hitler had the Wehrmacht and the SS. They knew they had to extract material rewards for their followers and clients, in addition to tribute and taxes for themselves, but they also knew that victories would cement follower and client loyalty and their own fame and wealth. Men would follow a leader who had been successful, but conquerors were in a sense trapped by their own success, compelled to continue conquests by a mixture of Durkheim's "malady of infinite aspiration," the need to keep on rewarding followers, and fear that the militarism they had cultivated might produce threatening rivals should their conquests end. In these pages Mongol and Aztec rulers were conspicuously trapped by their ambitions. This was the tyranny exerted by their personal histories.

The great conqueror is now rare—though Putin would like to be one. Rarity is obsolete, for three reasons. First, the rise of nationalism legitimizes states inhabiting a sanctified world order of states; second is the replacing of interstate wars by civil wars; and third is the rise of electoral democracies with competitive elections and short-term rulers. Rulers in the twenty-first century have aspired to notions of "greatness" more elevated than base profit, but not amounting to conquest—with the major exception of Putin. Americans' sense of national greatness combines pride in idealized American values and the power of the U.S. military. Support for both is the undying refrain of politicians, baked into their ideology.

Benevolent American mission statements are backed by enormous military budgets, justified in terms less of national defense or material gain than of "defending American democratic values"—this by the Pentagon, the biggest authoritarian organization in the world! "Defense" is also meant to indicate self-defense, even though it is carried through aggression to the whole world. Not even the Romans had such pretensions—though they did share the American pretext for war that intervening abroad was merely defending one's allies.

So although, overall, wars have not declined through human history, some types of war have declined, especially those creating great civilizations. There is now one great global civilization, containing rival imperial cores exploiting very dispersed peripheries. But future wars between those imperial cores might end all human civilization, and 2022 has seemed to stoke such fears.

Ideological-Emotional Power

Ideologies and emotions fill in the gaps of human rationality when scientific knowledge and certainty fall short. They enable action in the absence of full knowledge, important here since war is usually a risky shot in the dark. Emotions play a major role in descents toward war amid uncertain environments conducive more to anxiety and feverish emotions than to calm calculation. Disputes may escalate through minor provocations, hostile words, saber rattling, a clash of patrols, the sinking of a ship, maltreatment of citizens abroad, and rumors of atrocity. Hatred, anxiety, fear, and desire for honor, status, and domination combine into complex emotional states. Publicizing the other's escalations and atrocities intensifies hatred, making further escalation likelier. Some rivals are seen as "evil" or "terrorists." America is the Great Satan, Iran was a part of the Axis of Evil. Negotiating with evil is difficult, and for the United States it is currently illegal. Hatred is countered not by love for the enemy but by pragmatic appeals for a compromise solution. Emotions are invoked more for war, pragmatism for peace. Emotions intensify during war, making it harder to disengage.

Some political scientists also stress that emotional overconfidence or unreasonable fear (or both) lead into modern war. Lebow, analyzing twenty-six twentieth-century wars, says failure of decision making was mainly due not to imperfect information or commitment problems (as Realists say), or to material interests (as Marxists and economists say), but to sentiments of honor, status, or revenge.[13] Weakening rulers seek to defend or recover political status, especially domestically, while dominant rulers rarely rest satisfied, wanting ever more status. All want to maintain a sense of honor. Aggression derives from rash overconfidence or an exaggerated fear of an external threat, both boosted by indignant self-righteousness overriding contradictory information that might counsel peace. When both sides exhibit these emotions, damaging mutual brinkmanship follows. Most spectacular was the downward spiral of decisions leading to World War I, where brinkmanship, reluctance to back down, maintaining rulers' status and that of their states, and demonstrating fidelity to allies combined to make war the path of honor rather than reason. For Austria-Hungary and Russia, honor was seen as necessary for the dynasties' very survival. A monarchy without honor is illegitimate, said Habsburg and Romanov courtiers in 1914.

Van Evera examined modern cases of provocation by a ruler that caused others to actually start the fighting. He says great powers have been overrun by unprovoked aggressors twice, but six times by aggressors provoked by the victim's "fantasy-driven defensive bellicosity." The major threat to states, he says, is "their own tendency to exaggerate the dangers they face, and to respond with counterproductive bellicosity." He emphasizes fear.[14] White stresses overconfidence, saying that twentieth-century rulers starting wars underestimated the resistance of the target or the chances of others intervening to help the target because of a "lack of realistic empathy with either the victims or their potential allies."[15] We saw mixtures of fear, overconfidence, and lack of empathy in earlier warfare too. These modern studies did not include colonial wars where empathy was even less in evidence.

The bonding effect that societies exert on their members was identified in Arab armies and societies of his time by Ibn Khaldun as *asabiyya*, normative solidarity generating a collective will to pursue further goals. He argued that this was the fundamental bond of human society and the basic motive force of history, and it was at its purest in the nomadic Arab societies of his time. This concept permeates his world history. He focused on bonding between followers and rulers, strong at the beginning of a dynasty, but then weakening through successive rulers, as they began to merge with conquered populations, so losing their original tribal collective strength. Durkheim's theory of solidarity was more static. He stressed the normative solidarity of a whole society conferring trust and confidence in the strength and virtues of one's own group. In war *asabiyya* led to solidarity, commitment, and bravery by soldiers, especially in religious and communist forces and among long-distance freebooters such as Vikings or conquistadores.

But solidarity had an external downside, for it involved a lack of empathy with and understanding of the enemy—society as a cage, imprisoning the people within its stereotypes of the other. In wars the troops confidently marched singing into battle, expecting to be home soon, unable to imagine enemy troops at that moment doing likewise, with the same brio. Because rulers deny justice to the enemy's cause, they underestimate its sense of righteousness and the morale of its soldiers. Putin is the latest example of this. Such rulers view enemy resources opaquely, guided by external signifiers of strength and intentions, like rumors of political disunity or discontented generals, lower soldier morale, a supposedly inferior race or religion, or cultural decline or cowardice, or the accession of a child, a woman, or a supposed weakling (a comedian perhaps) to power—mixing understandable mistakes with self-delusion.

Overconfidence also results from blurring fact and value. Rational-choice theory strives to be scientific, keeping fact and value apart. "What is" governs the world, not "what should be." We social scientists are all taught this. Yet human beings do not operate like this, including social scientists on our days off. We all blur fact and value. In war this most often appears as the belief that our cause is just, and so we *should* achieve victory. The English word "should" has a double meaning—our cause is just, so victory is morally desirable, but also our victory is probable. Both Union and Confederate soldiers were convinced in 1860 that they should win quickly because their cause was just. In World War I, British troops should be back home by Christmas, German troops before the autumn leaves fell. Roman senators believed all their wars were just, blessed by the gods, and so they would always win, adding righteousness to their aggression. Chinese Confucian and legalist theorists saw this as a philosophical problem. They mostly concluded that a just and virtuous ruler would defeat an unjust and despotic one because the people would offer him more support. Right makes might. Whether this is true is debatable, but if rulers believe their cause is just, they tend to think they should win (in both senses). If only one side feels especially righteous, its morale may be higher and its battle performance better, as ancient Chinese theorists and Ibn Khaldun argued. But if both sides have that feeling, the result is a more murderous war, like the Thirty Years' War or World War II. For the protagonists, wars are moral as well as material clashes. Such emotional distortions tend to be universal in human groups, although not all lead to war.

Rarer are ideologies in the sense of generalized meaning systems combining grandiose claims to knowledge and values, a clear distinction between good and evil, and sometimes the goal of imposing these on the conquered, such as a religion or fascism or democracy. Yet here overconfidence and distortion especially grow. Putin demonized Ukrainians. American administrations demonized the ayatollahs, Saddam, and Gaddafi, and some members wanted to forcibly export democracy there. But they were very overconfident. They knew military power would bring victory in the field, but they were deluded about political aftermaths, for they believed in the global justice of their cause, and in good versus bad guys. They "should" be welcomed by Iraqis, they "should" achieve order and democracy. Yet killing the dictator and destroying his regime made things worse than if he had managed to keep order. A degree of repression is better for most people than the disorder resulting from a failed intervention.

Religions in historical wars played varied roles. Aztecs and Incas had clothed war in divine rituals, some of them quite savage. Medieval Christians often preached peace, but they went on crusades and massacred heretics, while many peasant revolts became millenarian. Islam had initially expanded as a warrior religion, but thereafter it became more tolerant of religious minorities than was Christianity, though disrupted by the cyclical wars identified by Ibn Khaldun, in which purist Islamic warriors swept into the decadent cities, only to gradually succumb to city pleasures, lose their *asabiyya*, and suffer defeat, usually in the fourth generation of a dynasty, at the hands of the next wave of purists. Most Japanese wars were secular, yet the feudal period saw some armies of Buddhist monks, and Buddhism was manipulated to support early twentieth-century Japanese militarism as well as today's militarism in Myanmar. Confucians were ambivalent about war, whereas Buddhists and Daoists were more pacific, yet their popular rebellions were sometimes fired by religious millenarianism.

Overall, however, most ideological warfare against an "evil" enemy has been modern, contradicting Weber's assertion of the increasing rationalization of modern society. I identified three waves of ideological warfare that began in Europe: sixteenth- and seventeenth-century wars of religion; French revolutionary wars leading to global nineteenth- and twentieth-century wars of national liberation; and twentieth-century global wars between communist, fascist, and liberal capitalist regimes.

Some suggest a current fourth Islamic wave, but though jihadists are strongly ideological, most recent wars between Muslims have not been, and they have also involved Western imperialism, as we saw in chapter 14. Racial ideologies were also key to modern European and Japanese colonial wars, dooming their empires to a short life, since they prevented the assimilation of natives into the imperial identity, unlike peoples conquered by the ancient Romans and Chinese.

Symmetric and Asymmetric Wars

Three typical power balances affect the chances of success in war. The first is where one party is so superior in power resources that its victory and consequent gains seem certain. It may be rational for sharks to attack and swallow minnows or weakening big fishes. U.S. secretary of state John Hay rejoiced in a letter to Theodore Roosevelt in July 1898 of victory over the Spanish Empire and its wooden ships: "It has been a splendid little war, begun with the highest motives, carried on with magnificent intelligence and spirit, favored by that Fortune which loves the brave." The second and third types are more puzzling. Why do minnows go to war against sharks, rather than submit? And why do evenly matched powers launch wars against each other, given probable mutual devastation?

I consider first the shark's reasoning. Gross military inequality has been common in wars of imperial conquest, usually the result of economic and political inequality. In ancient China and medieval western Europe and Japan, as in pre-Columbian America, rulers mobilizing more efficient states in more fertile lands could achieve low-cost military victories against less well-developed peoples on the periphery, which gave them an incentive to make aggressive war. Conquered lands were given to military veterans or settlers, and natives might be enslaved or enserfed. In Europe the core powers developed more effective states and more science-based capitalist economies, thereby conferring enough military superiority to conquer most of the world. Gross power inequalities conferred by uneven economic development help explain why some regions and periods of history saw more wars of imperial conquest than others.

That war is rational for sharks faced with minnows is morally deplorable and is in principle criminal under UN norms, though prosecutions have not occurred since Nuremberg. Yet the sharks need not conform to Realist theory by carefully calculating the odds. Their obvious superiority makes victory likely. Nor did Realist "anarchy" figure where one party was much stronger than the other, in many wars seeking regime change as well as in wars of imperial conquest, from Rome to China to Europe—and probably to other expanding civilizations, too. Stronger rulers have rarely felt insecure, except against domestic opponents.

History, however, has not always favored the sharks. "Barbarians," with their lesser economic and political development, had cavalry superior in flattish terrains to the bigger infantry-centered forces of agrarian states. Here, uneven modes of economic and military power made war more likely. Marxists stress the role of uneven economic development in history. I extend unevenness to military development. This also set off a dialectical development of warfare. Swift in-and-out raiding by war bands brought easy pickings, but a sequence of raids brought forth larger punitive retaliation from the agrarian state. In response, a few barbarian rulers developed their loose tribal confederacy into a more cohesive state and added infantry and siege warfare, which enabled them to fight back and even conquer. Both sides borrowed each other's military techniques and fought combined arms warfare, conquered territories, and even achieved a partial merging of the two peoples, a dialectical process. For the few triumphant rulers and their rewarded followers, this was highly rational, but it was not for the masses. Did the scale of Emperor Qianlong's warfare—mobilizing 600,000 soldiers and laborers while committing genocide against the Zunghars—benefit the peoples of China? I doubt it, even though some revisionist historians have bizarrely hailed his reign an Age of Enlightenment because of his artistic dabbling.

Today, we see a great white shark thrashing helplessly amid the shallows. The United States has the world's most powerful economy and military, far superior to those of its recent enemies. Yet battlefield victories have not led to desired results, for three reasons. First, the United States cannot (and does not want to) directly rule foreign territories, nor can it find reliable local clients through whom it can rule indirectly, except perhaps in Latin America, where conservative elites share its goals. The nationalist and religious ideologies of modernity prevent the recruitment of many local clients, as achieved by earlier empires. Where clients are recruited, this may exacerbate local ethnic or religious divisions—as in Afghanistan, Iraq, and Libya. Military interventions have brought disorder, and order is the primary political goal of most peoples, on which any democracy would have to be grounded. Second, weapons of the weak (the guerilla cell, the Kalashnikov, the suicide bomber, and so on) can sustain asymmetric warfare against a technologically superior enemy. Third, most Americans are only armchair warriors, unwilling to serve or to see wars drag on if they cause many American casualties. The financial cost is no obstacle, but the human cost is. This reflects the fact that American society (despite its proliferation of guns) is not at its core militaristic. But these three weaknesses ensure that American wars are not simply a series of understandable mistakes. They predictably fail, and so are irrational in terms of ends.

The second type of case comes when, for minnows, suing for peace and submitting might seem more rational than fighting. Rulers who submit can usually keep their domains if they swear allegiance to the more powerful or shift toward compliance with its policies. Some did take this route to survival, and conquerors often gave them the alternative of submission or possible death. The Inca specialized in this. Saddam Hussein could have survived this way, as have other dictators who cozy up to the United States. Yet often minnows choose to fight. They may try to balance the odds by counting on allies. Yet as Realists note, allies' words may not translate into deeds, or they may be bribed into switching sides (and the great conquerors were usually good at this diplomatic strategy). Sometimes the sharks even feast together on the minnows lying between them. Poland was partitioned three times by the surrounding great powers. Balancing rarely works in the long term unless strong normative trust is shared by the allies.

The other two reasons involve emotions and constraints. First, minnows are often overoptimistic because of the tyranny of history. Having survived a sequence of wars against lesser foes, they are unprepared for a superior one, and they are "caged" within the constraints of their own society, which limits accurate perception of the enemy and enables ideologies and emotions to distort vision. When the war is one of self-defense, they also believe their cause is just, meaning that they "should" both morally and probably win. This has been evident among Ukrainians. Native people confronting the first waves of European imperialists were often unaware that behind these small forces would come wave after wave of soldiers and settlers. The natives may have already committed a few atrocities against white people, which enraged the imperialists. Yet they were doomed anyway. In modern times only the Japanese and then the Chinese found the space and time to build up effective resistance to foreign imperialists.

Second, minnow rulers feel compelled to fight to maintain honor and status. Feudal rulers often went down fighting with honor. They felt they had no choice. Saddam self-destructed for status and honor. He did not allow himself to be seen complying with U.S. demands on chemical weapons (when he really was) because defiance was his badge of honor. That was his contribution to his doom. Tiny states have survived on all continents, but through submission, not battle (unless in a region of tiny states, like Central America, where several attempts at regional hegemony failed). A weaker ruler choosing resistance in the sights of a strong one was likely to die, and his kingdom, too.

The proliferation of vanishing kingdoms casts a shadow over defensive Realism's belief that survival is states' major goal, for overwhelmingly they have failed to survive. This was as true in pre-Columbian America as anywhere, though it was not true of postcolonial Latin America, where balancing against would-be hegemons was successful in six wars (and failed in none), aided by local terrain and colonial border legacies. After the 1830s all its states survived. In contrast, only one of over seventy polities in post-Zhou China survived. Sixteenth-century Japan saw over two hundred polities reduced to just one. The more than three hundred states of Europe were whittled down to thirty by the twentieth century, a process lasting many centuries in the West but coming in a nineteenth-century rush in central Europe. An unknown but large number of states and tribes disappeared from Italy and around the Mediterranean as Rome came to dominate.

Human "civilizations" have expanded by eliminating most of the world's polities. They did this in three main ways: defeat in war; submitting to the threat of force; and entering a union through marriage or inheritance contracts. In three admittedly smallish studies, of sixteenth-century Japan, medieval and modern Europe, and the world since 1816, most vanishing states died in battle, say John Bender, Norman Davies, and Tanisha Fazal.[16] This was less so of pre-Columbian America, where threats usually sufficed for the Inca, and where the Aztecs conjoined war and intermarriage in their strategies. But vanishing no longer occurs. Iraq survived when Saddam was killed, for the survival of states in the post-1945 world is almost guaranteed by international institutions and nationalist sentiments. Rulers are defeated and killed, but the countries survive. Conquest followed by direct imperial rule may be finished, with the possible exception of Ukraine.

The third type of odds is symmetric warfare between near equals, like Greek city-states, the Chinese Warring States, Han Chinese dynasties struggling against ex-barbarian empires, wars among the major Japanese daimyo, and wars between the major powers of modern Europe. A strategic premodern reason tempted rulers into attacking a near equal, for it gave the advantage of occupying enemy soil so that the attacker's troops could live off the land, wasting enemy resources while not wasting their own. But a defender who avoided defeat yet failed to throw back the invader would retreat, laying waste to his own domains in the path of the invader, to deprive him of the ability to live off the land. The more the retreat, the longer became the supply lines of the attacker. The initial advantage was exhausted and the armies became bogged down in stalemate, as we repeatedly saw. The extreme was the ability of Russian rulers to use their landmass to lure their enemy on to defeat.

Great powers fighting each other seem irrational because of the scale of destruction and death. Yet two ways to lessen the pain existed. The first was to develop rules of wars that kept the death rate in battle low for the dominant classes. This was extreme in Aztec "flower wars," but common in China during the Spring and Autumn period, and in Europe in the Middle Ages, and then again in the century following the Peace of Westphalia in 1648. War was not absent in these periods, but it was mutually regulated, which reveals a rational calculation of ends. War might not be so costly—for rulers and the upper classes. But that did not last.

The second way to lower pain was through wars of deflection. In ancient China and in Europe, wars between the major core powers could be partially deflected on to less powerful peoples on the periphery or on to the lesser allies of the other. Here the major powers were not occupying the entire space of geopolitics. Empires were built on expansion into the peripheries, much as Rome expanded around the Mediterranean, or Zhou rulers of ancient Chinese states expanded among the "people of the field," or Britain and France fought each other repeatedly across the world in the eighteenth century, when their peace treaties typically conferred territorial gains on both of them at the expense of colonized natives. This developed into a division of the spoils in the "Scramble for Africa" and in late imperial China, where the major foreign powers contributed military units to a joint force repressing Chinese resistance—a WEPO perhaps (West Pacific Organization), long before NATO. Wars of deflection cost less and brought territory, treasure, and imperial status. Major powers in Asia and Europe could expand cheaply across their peripheries, and Europeans then did so across the globe. The Cold War deflected superpower conflict onto lesser clients as the United States and the Soviets fought each other only indirectly, in proxy wars using client states and movements, a rational strategy for the superpowers, though not usually for their clients.

Realist theory has been based on data on wars since 1816, mainly in Europe, which had a particular geopolitics: its states occupied the whole space first of Europe and then of the world. There were soon very few small kingdoms to vanish, just major states and their colonies and client states. And because rulers were caged inside their domains, ignorant of their rivals' intentions and capacities, this might appear to them as a Realist security dilemma amid geopolitical anarchy. There have been other cases of rival rulers filling up the whole space of a geopolitical system, but there have been periods and places where this was not so, where expansion and deflection were possible, and so war was not simply grinding frontal confrontations between major powers. Yet Roman and European expansion, and Chinese and Japanese unification, culminated in life-and-death struggle between sharks. Occupying the whole space of the regional geopolitical configuration, and unable to regulate or deflect war, they fought predictably costly frontal battles against each other. This is the key puzzle of the third type of case. Why did they continue fighting each other?

Again the preservation of status and honor was important, but warring was amplified by ideological-emotional sentiments and by contexts invoking anxiety, fear, and hatred of "evil" rivals, as in those European-initiated waves of ideological warfare. Here the aggressor wished to transform the society of those it attacked, while the latter wished to protect their way of life. The most extreme example of this was Soviet resistance to Nazi Germany, for death or slavery awaited Jews, communists, and even all Slavs if the Nazis won in the east. For these groups, self-defense involved a truly desperate survival rationality.

But more frequently the aggression of sharks against equals resulted from path dependence—rulers faced with rivals were tempted to follow the paths that had brought them past success. Victories begat confidence, which made war a more likely outcome of a dispute. Cumulative swallowing meant that Rome, the last few Chinese Warring States, the last few Japanese daimyo, and the surviving major rulers in early modern Europe had grown accustomed to victory. Most finally got their comeuppance, but the sequence of victories had baked in the culture and institutions of militarism. Earlier success also strengthened martial virtues, the praising of heroes over traders; rulers perceived war, not trade, as the way to wealth, career success, social status, honor, and glory. In this way military power was elevated over other sources of power. The Roman Republic was the extreme case of baking in, but although Roman

militarism was unusually long-lived, war was also baked in to the Warring States of ancient China, the ex-barbarian dynasties ruling imperial
China, the Aztec and Inca dynasties, the early rulers of Arab dynasties,
sixteenth-century daimyo lords in Japan, medieval European princes,
Prussia-Germany and Japan in modern times, and today Putin's Russia.

Baking in also helps define friend and foe, as it does in current
American foreign policy, which defines Iran as the enemy, the Saudis as
friends, and Israel as a truly intimate friend, all for reasons—handed
down from the past and today possessing less relevance—that amplify
Israeli-Palestinian conflict and an incipient civil war between Shi'a and
Sunni Muslims. This is geopolitical immobility, not anarchy, history's
tyranny; it saves rulers beholden to entrenched pressure groups the trouble of figuring out where today's interests lie. Other examples were the
Song dynasty's inability to figure out changing power relations among
ex-barbarian polities, Yuan dynasty wars continuing in hostile ecologies,
and Napoleonic and Hitlerian overreaching.

Conversely, repeated war defeats or costly draws lower ambition,
eventually undermining militarism—a delayed-reaction Realism, as in
imperial Rome after repeated inconclusive wars with the Parthians and
northern barbarians. Since mutual exhaustion was common in Latin
American wars, rulers were not repeat offenders. They came to prefer
saber rattling followed by mediation. Japan's terrible civil wars in the sixteenth century produced widespread yearning for peace, which aided
Tokugawa hegemony. More common was a shorter-term effect. Four
times in Western Europe its worst wars—the Thirty Years' War, Napoleonic Wars, World War I, and World War II—produced a postwar period
of greater diplomatic activity. In the first three this was, alas, only temporary. Will the fourth period last longer? China under some Han and Song
dynasty rulers reacted to defeat with conciliatory diplomacy, as did American politicians for a decade after defeat in Vietnam. It is unclear whether
the recent spree of unsuccessful wars will result in long-term caution by
American rulers since they have discovered risk transfer militarism, the
contemporary form of wars of deflection, deflecting the risk of death
away from one's own troops onto enemy soldiers, civilians in war zones,
and hired contractors and mercenaries, all dying far from the public gaze.

We can perceive an outline of the development of warfare through
the ages. Each region in which states and class divisions emerged saw
intermittent warfare by those states against the clan, tribal, and stateless
groups on their peripheries, then absorbing them. When possessing

military advantages, peripheral groups could hit back, but this also involved their forming their own states. As each region was filled with states, their warfare turned more against each other, although incentives for conquering further peripheral peoples continued. The militaristic institutions and culture that had grown up on profitable little wars were then turned on bigger wars against each other. This warfare was at best zero-sum: for some to gain, others must lose, but since the losers disappeared, so did their history. What is recorded for our consumption is the success of imperial civilizations, whether these consisted of a single state or several competitors. But in present-day societies the whole world is filled up with states whose legitimacy is supported by international institutions. War between the major states can no longer be rational—although there is no guarantee that rulers will be rational. Contemporary battlefields have been largely transferred to the spaces inside weak states. So wars are historical sequences in which the experience of past generations lies heavily on the brains of the living, sometimes (as Marx said) as nightmare, but more often as exciting fantasy.

Conclusion

I began with the question why rulers choose war to achieve ends rather than relying on softer sources of power—economic exchange, cooperative ideologies, or geopolitical diplomacy. Rulers do exercise some freedom of choice. But *choice* is not quite the right word, since decisions also embody social and historical constraints of which the actors are not wholly aware, constituting part of their taken-for-granted reality. Sociology sees humans as creating social structures, which then become institutionalized, constraining subsequent action. Decisions are influenced by constraints deriving from overconfidence, social caging, varied emotions, intolerant ideologies, domestic politics, militarism baked in to institutions and cultures, and the tyranny of history. There are thus different levels of war causes—motives, emotions, ideologies, as well as ecological, geopolitical, and historical contexts, and erratic processes of escalation. Their varied interactions through time and space may defeat any simple theory of causes, as Raymond Aron noted. In response, some Realists have broadened rational choice to include all these factors, but their different metrics make it difficult to assign them relative weights, and if all these are regarded as rational, the theory becomes circular and we cannot identify irrationality. I did, however, simplify the motives contributing to causes into the main three: greed, status-honor-glory, and the enjoyment of domination.

On rationality, rulers' decisions over whether to make war or peace were sometimes careful, calculating pros and cons, but miscalculation occurred too often to support a rational-choice model, though there was also a delayed-reaction rationality, whereby rulers realize they have bitten off more than they can chew. But in an age of nuclear weapons and climate change, delayed-reaction Realism would be too belated for human survival. Combined economic and military power—seizing material resources through war—is the heart of Realist and Marxist theory. This is sometimes rational for the winners, although it is overwhelmingly zero-sum, where for some to benefit, others must suffer. But the perennial intervention of emotions and ideological and political motives weakens the rationality of both means and ends.

The offensive wars that go according to plan are mostly those in which sharks attack minnows, or in which wars among the sharks are deflected onto the minnows. Their military superiority means they do not need much calculation of odds, for they are likely to reap the benefits of victory. And since the winners write history, and the losers vanish, victory in war is seen as commoner, more profitable, more rational, and more glorious than it really has been. But war does not often pay, for all sides lose where war involves material costs greater than its spoils can justify, where there is no clear winner, or where war does not resolve the dispute in question. These probably constitute the majority of wars. Raiding might pay off if it does not become too repetitive, in which case retribution comes. Regime change or support might be done cheaply, but benefiting only one party, as in Latin America, or expensively, with war and without benefit, as in recent American ventures. Some wars over slivers of territory have brought benefit for the winners where valuable economic or strategic resources were obtained, but these wars are also intensified by emotional revisionism. Imperial wars of conquest benefited victorious rulers and attendant merchants, bankers, settlers, clerics, and officials of empire—but not usually the colonizer's people as a whole, and certainly not the exploited, enslaved, or exterminated natives of the colonies. Wars in self-defense are generally considered as both rational and legitimate, and some are both. But in many, submission would be more rational. The benefits of war are rarely shared widely.

War is the one instance where losing one's temper may cause the death of thousands. War pays us back more swiftly for mistakes than any other human activity. Humans are not calculating machines—more's the pity, since peace is more rational than war. If the social world did conform to rational theory, if rulers did carefully calculate the costs and benefits of war, trying hard to set emotions and ideologies aside and ignoring domestic political pressures, they would see that most wars are too risky and inferior to economic exchange, the sharing of norms and values, and diplomacy as ways of securing desired goals. Realism is fine as a normative theory, showing rulers how they should act for maximum benefit, but it is not a description of reality, for they do not act in this way. So we actually need more Realism, for this would bring more benefit through peace!

War is the least rational of human projects, but humans are only erratically rational creatures, as we know from our everyday lives, and from my examples of business start-ups and gambling. Rulers are asked in matters of war and peace to make decisions with momentous consequences, though they are armed only with the sketchy information, the ideologies, and the emotions of their imprisonment within the blinkers of their societies amid anxiety-producing, unfolding environmental and geopolitical constraints and the tyranny of history. The task of surmounting this is often beyond rulers, as it might be beyond us, too. Human beings are not genetically predisposed to make war, but our human nature does matter, if indirectly. Its tripartite character, part rational, part emotional, part ideological, when set inside the institutional and cultural constraints of societies, makes war an intermittent outcome. Human nature does matter, and that is why when wars are fought, they are mostly fought for no good reason.

Han Fei remarked in the third century BCE: "No benefit is more constant than simplicity; no happiness more constant than peace." It is better and simpler to choose peace, which is more rational, less lethal, simpler, and less risky, tomorrow being more or less like today.

Notes

Chapter One. Military Power and War

1. Mann, 2003.
2. Nietzsche, 1923: 43.
3. Ratchnevsky, 1992: 153.
4. Aron, 1973: 65–69.
5. Weber, 1978: 24–26, 399–400.
6. Sun Tzu, 1993: 3.2.
7. Clausewitz, 1976: 75.
8. Ibid.: 101.
9. Goertz et al., 2016: 27.

Chapter Two. Is War Universal?

1. Ibn Khaldun, 1958: 346.
2. Lahr et al., 2016.
3. Meyer, 2018.
4. López-Montalvo, 2018.
5. Dolfini et al., 2018.
6. Ferguson, 2003; Kelly, 2000; Nakao et al., 2016.
7. Malešević, 2017: 73–83.
8. Eckhardt, 1992: 24.
9. Keeley, 1996.
10. Ferguson, 1997, 2013a, and 2013b.
11. Gat, 2006, 2017.
12. Ferguson, 1995.
13. Gat, 2017: 27.
14. Kimber, 1990: 163.
15. Warner, 1958: 158.

16. Walker et al., 2011: table 2; Fry, 2007, 2013.
17. Ember and Ember, 1997.
18. Santos-Granero, 2010.
19. Fry and Söderberg, 2013.
20. Dyer, 1985: 8–9.
21. Mann, 1986: chap. 2.
22. Malešević, 2010: 90–92.
23. Coker, 2014: 202.
24. Otterbein, 2004.
25. Scott, 2017: 7; emphasis in original.
26. Graeber and Wengrow, 2021.
27. Malešević, 2022: chap. 1.
28. De Waal, 2006: 148; cf. MacMillan, 2020: 13–14; Malešević, 2022: 19–21.
29. Coker, 2021.
30. Gat, 2017: 37; 2006.
31. Pinker, 2011.
32. Collins, 2008.
33. Ibid.: 27.
34. Ibid.: 28–29.
35. Malešević, 2017.
36. Parkin, 1987.
37. Ibn Khaldun, 1958.
38. Gleditsch, 2004.
39. Wesseling, 1989: 8–11; 2005.
40. Luard, 1986; Levy, 1983.
41. Luard, 1986: 24, 35, 45.
42. Lemke, 2002: 167–71, 181; Centeno, 2002: 38–43.
43. Malešević, 2010: 95.
44. Webster, 2000.
45. Laffineur, 1999.
46. Graeber and Wengrow, 2021: 434–39.
47. Hsu, 1965: 56, 64.
48. Coker, 2014, 2021.

Chapter Three. Theories of the Causes of War

1. Clausewitz, 1976: 77.
2. Gilbert, 1947: 266.
3. More, 1952: 201.
4. Levy, 1988: 666–70; Blainey, 1971.
5. Mann, 2005.
6. Levy, 1988: 662.
7. Robinson, 2001.
8. Crawford, 2007.

9. Bueno de Mesquita and Smith, 2012; Reiter and Stam, 2002.
10. Downes, 2009.
11. Desch, 2002.
12. Ibid.: 44.
13. O'Brien and Prados de la Escosura, 1998.
14. Mack, 1975; Arreguín-Toft, 2005.
15. See Sanderson, 1999: 34–49; Turner and Maryanski, 2008: 170–74. For archaeological objection, see Weisdorf, 2005.
16. Blanton et al., 1993; Hayden, 2001: 251–54.
17. Halsall, 2007; Heather, 2010.
18. Pedersen, 2014.
19. Fearon and Laitin, 2003.
20. Ibid.
21. Jervis, 1978.
22. Wendt, 1999.
23. Waltz, 1979: 92, 118.
24. Mearsheimer, 2001: 31.
25. Bueno de Mesquita, 1981.
26. Howard, 1983: 14–15, 22; emphasis added.
27. Fearon 1995: 380.
28. Cf. Jackson and Morelli, 2011.
29. MacMillan, 2020: 24.
30. Mearsheimer, 2009: 246.
31. Lebow, 1981.
32. Ibid.: 147.
33. Waltz, 1979: 138; Wendt, 1999: 279.
34. Levy, 2011.
35. Van Evera, 1999: 256.
36. Bueno de Mesquita and Lalman, 1988.
37. Levy, 2011: 25–26.
38. Kant, 1891: 47.
39. Van Evera, 1999.
40. Sherman, 1879.
41. Clausewitz, 1976: 86, 101.
42. Ibn Khaldun, 1958: 354.
43. Kant, 1891.
44. Bull, 2002.
45. Katzenstein, 1996: 4–6.
46. See Malešević's critique, 2010: 64–70.
47. Lebow, 2010.
48. Van Evera, 1999: 16–34.
49. Blainey, 1973: 112–15.
50. Ibid.: 47–54, 159, 122.
51. Wright, 1957: 267.

52. Collins, 2008.
53. Owen, 2010.
54. Black, 1998: 22.
55. Cooney, 1997.
56. Lebow, 2010: 74.

Chapter Four. The Roman Republic

1. Harris, 1979: 10.
2. Sallust, 1992: 4.67.16.
3. Tacitus, 2010: chap. 30.
4. Harrer, 1918.
5. Livy, 1.32.5.
6. Ager, 2009; Harris, 1979: 166–75; Rosenstein, 2007: 338; Erskine, 2010: 38–39.
7. Hoyos, 2019a: 160–63.
8. Harrer, 1918.
9. Quoted by Eckstein, 2006: 308.
10. Thucydides, 1972: chapter 17.5.
11. Eckstein, 2006.
12. Terrenato, 2019.
13. Ibid.: 153.
14. Ibid.: xv.
15. Ibid.: 192.
16. Ibid.: 185.
17. Ibid.: 248.
18. Scheidel, 2009: 59–60.
19. Terrenato, 2019: 254
20. Raaflaub, 1991: 570.
21. Harris, 1979: 178–82; Beard, 2015: 163.
22. Eckstein, 2006: 47, 53, 215–16.
23. Alonso, 2007.
24. Harris, 1979, 2016.
25. Hoyos, 2019b; Gruen, 1986.
26. Gruen, 1986: 730.
27. Ibid.: 397–98.
28. Ibid.: 730.
29. Podany, 2010.
30. Ager, 2009.
31. Ibid.: 24.
32. Rosenstein, 2012: 217–18.
33. Oakley, 1993.
34. Polybius, 1889: 36.4.
35. Barton, 2007: 250–52.

36. Mattern, 1999: 194.
37. Rich, 2008.
38. See, for example, Harris, 1979; Hoyos, 2019a.
39. Scheidel, 2009: 74.
40. Tan, 2017.
41. Mattern, 1999: 65–79.
42. Rich, 2004: 58–59; Morley, 2010: 27.
43. Gruen, 2004.
44. MacMullen, 2000.
45. Kay, 2014.
46. Beard and Crawford, 1985: 76–77.
47. Ward-Perkins, 2005.
48. Rosenstein, 2012: chap. 6.
49. Harris, 1979: 34–35.
50. Suetonius, 1913: 77.
51. Morley, 2010: 25–29, 33; Rich, 2004; Rosenstein, 2007.
52. Tacitus, 1996: book 15.53.
53. Mattern, 1999.
54. Gruen, 1986: 288–315.
55. Ibid.: 418.
56. Scheidel, 2019: 80.
57. Sallust, 1899: chap. 4.
58. Hoyos, 2019a: 38.
59. Harrer, 1918: 35.
60. Gruen, 2004; Mattern 1999: chap. 4.
61. Taylor, 2015, 2017.
62. Rich, 2004.
63. Mattern, 1999: chap. 4.
64. Scheidel, 2019: 67.
65. Clark, 2014: chaps. 2–5.
66. Taylor, 2015: 18–19.
67. Rosenstein, 2007: 226–37; Beard, 2015: 163–65; Harris, 2016: chap. 2; Scheidel, 2019: 64–69.
68. Eckstein, 2006: 254–57.
69. Terrenato, 2019: 112–18; Beard, 2015: 154–56; Eckstein, 2006: 126–27.
70. Morley, 2010: 26; Beard and Crawford, 1985: 74.
71. Erskine, 2010: 12–15; Rosenstein, 2007; Mattern, 1999: 115.
72. MacMullen, 2000.
73. Pilkington, 2019; Miles, 2010; Hoyos, 2015.
74. Harris, 2006.
75. Hoyos, 2019b: chap. 4; Terrenato, 2019: 86–92.
76. Pilkington, 2019.
77. Whittaker, 1978: 71; Miles, 2010: 76.
78. Miles, 2010: 43, 76, 95, 367.

79. Harris, 2006: 150–90.
80. Hoyos, 2019b: 187–91.
81. Whittaker, 1978.
82. Palmer, 1997.
83. Polybius, 1889: 1:10, 11.
84. Pilkington, 2019: 170.
85. Polybius, 1889: 1:13.10–13.
86. Ibid.: 1:63; emphasis in original.
87. Hoyos, 2015: 76–77.
88. Whittaker, 1978: 89–90; Hoyos, 2019b: 179–85.
89. Rosenstein, 2012: 126; Harris, 1979: 201–5.
90. Rosenstein, 2012: 127–75.
91. Livy, 1853: 22.58.
92. Ibid.: 22.51.
93. Taylor, 2015: 38; Hoyos, 2015: 132–90.
94. Rosenstein, 2007: 238, 248.
95. Erskine, 2010: 44.
96. Hoyos, 2015: 270–76.
97. Rosenstein, 2012: 233.
98. Morley, 2010: 14.
99. Hoyos, 2019b: 66–67, 77, 81.
100. Plutarch, 1960: 15.5.
101. Beard and Crawford, 1985: 74, 85.
102. Hoyos, 2019b: chaps. 5, 6.
103. De Souza, 2008; Brunt, 2004.
104. Lee, 2008.
105. Kulikowski, 2019.
106. Scheidel, 2019: 69.

Chapter Five. Ancient China

1. Hsu, 1965: 56, 64; Hui, 2005: 150–55; Li, 2013: 182, 186–87.
2. Zhao, 2015.
3. Lewis, 1990: 33–35; Hsu, 1999: 566.
4. Lewis, 1990: 39; Zhao, 2015: 126.
5. Hsu, 1999: 557.
6. Walker, 1954: 56–58.
7. Hsu, 1999: 569.
8. Hui, 2005: 54–64.
9. Li, 2013: 163–64; di Cosmo, 2002a: 120–23.
10. According to Hui, 2005: 152, 156.
11. Elvin, 2004: 96–98.
12. Gumplowicz, 1899.

13. Di Cosmo, 2002a: chap. 3; Falkenhausen, 1999: 453, 584–89; Li, 2013: 178–80.
14. Sun Tzu, 1993: 7.20.
15. Hsu, 1965.
16. Lewis, 1999: 603; Hsu, 1965: 8–11.
17. Andrade, 2016: chap. 11.
18. Graff, 2002: 23; Sun Bin, 2003: 31–37.
19. Lewis, 1990: chap. 2; Rosenstein, 2009: 25–27; Li, 2013.
20. Hsu, 1965: 62–65; Hui, 2005: 54–64.
21. Hsu, 1965: 58–62, 68, 77, 89; Hsu, 1999: 554; Kiser and Cai, 2003.
22. Li, 2013: chap. 10.
23. Yates, 2008: 46–49.
24. Pines, 2012.
25. Storry, 1982: 60.
26. Gittings, 2012; Sun Bin, 2003: 95; De Bary and Bloom, 1999: 179.
27. Pines, 2018.
28. Sun Bin, 2003: 110, 112.
29. Quoted in Paul, 2004: 73.
30. Sun Tzu, 1993: 9.25.
31. Turchin et al., 2021.
32. Di Cosmo, 2002a: 155–59.
33. Turchin et al., 2021.
34. Hsu, 1999: 553–62; Lewis, 1999: 593–97; Falkenhausen, 1999: 525–26.
35. Hsu, 1999: 568.
36. Lewis, 1999: 619–20; cf. Lewis, 1990: chaps. 1 and 2, pp. 172–73.
37. Kiser and Cai, 2003; Zhao, 2015; Li, 2013: 223.
38. Sun Tzu, 1993: 113.
39. Hui, 2005: 78.
40. Zhao, 2015.
41. Lewis, 2007: 17.
42. Ibid.: 37.
43. Hui, 2005: 68, 73–79.
44. Hsu, 1965: 91, 107–16; Lewis, 1990: 48–49, 54; 2007: 30–35; Zhao, 2015; Li, 2013: 234–40.
45. Lewis, 2007: 47–52.

Chapter Six. Imperial China

1. Andrade, 2016: 312–15.
2. Dabringhaus, 2011; Li, 2013: chap. 12, esp. 284; de Crespigny, 2016: 321–22.
3. Zhao, 2015: 274–79.
4. Ibid.: 282, 15.
5. De Crespigny, 2016: 508.

6. Wang, 2013a.
7. Paul, 2003.
8. Fairbank, 1974.
9. Wang, 2011.
10. Ibid.: 32.
11. Wang, 2013a.
12. De Crespigny, 2016: 121–26, 164; cf. Loewe, 1974.
13. Wang, 2013a: 239–44.
14. Johnston, 1995.
15. Lorge, 2014.
16. Ibid.: 2.
17. Skaff, 2009: 171.
18. Kang, 2010: 82–106.
19. Zhang, 2015: 12–15.
20. Kang, 2010: 89–93, 105.
21. Graff, 2002.
22. Swope, 2009; Lorge, 2005: 131–39.
23. Lee, 2017: 84, 141.
24. Kang et al., 2018.
25. Wang, 2011: 152–56.
26. Phillips, 2011: 151–56.
27. Zhang, 2015: 160.
28. Fairbank, 1974; Wang, 2011: chap. 6.
29. Kang, 2010: chap. 6.
30. Yates, 2008: 35–40.
31. Kang, 2010; Zhang, 2015.
32. Lee, 2017.
33. Ikenberry, 2011: 61.
34. Cox, 1981: 139, 38.
35. Scheidel, 2019: 281–82.
36. Ibn Khaldun, 1958: 347.
37. Kradin, 2019.
38. Di Cosmo, 2002b.
39. Khazanov, 2015: 362; Paul, 2003.
40. Perdue, 2005: 35.
41. Biran, 2004, 2017.
42. Scheidel, 2019: 289.
43. Khazanov, 2015: 360.
44. Rosenstein, 2009: 42–44; Li, 2013: 269–78.
45. Di Cosmo, 2002b.
46. Johnston, 1995: 247; 1996: 219–21; Kang, 2010: chap. 7; Wang, 2011: 136–37.
47. Tao, 1983: 81.
48. Perdue, 2005: 31–32.
49. Yu, 1967: 6–19, 45–46; cf. de Crespigny, 2016: 162–63.

50. Tillman, 2005: 147; Wang, 2011.
51. Zhang, 2015: 150–51; Rossabi, 1983.
52. Wang, 2011.
53. Wang, 2013b.
54. Hansen, 2019; Zhao, 2015.
55. Worthy, 1983: 38.
56. Wang, 1983; Franke, 1983; Tao, 1983.
57. Wang, 2011.
58. Tao, 1983.
59. Lorge, 2015: 125–30.
60. Ibid.: 282.
61. Lorge, 2008.
62. Tillman, 2005; Rossabi, 1983; Wang, 1983: 54–62; Hansen, 2019.
63. Tillman, 2005.
64. De Weerdt, 2016.
65. Smith, 2015; Lorge, 2015.
66. Wang, 2011: 60.
67. Andrade, 2016: chap. 1.
68. Hansen, 2019.
69. Peterson, 1983: 224–31; Tao, 1983: 71.
70. Lorge, 2015; Smith, 2015.
71. Lewis, 2000; Graff, 2002: 247.
72. Lorge, 2015.
73. Ratchnevsky, 1992: 40–41, 89–90, 152, 159–60; cf. Biran, 2004.
74. Biran, 2004.
75. Hassig, 1988; Isaac, 1983.
76. Lamb, 1927: chap. 7; Ratchnevsky, 1992: 188–96.
77. Kim, 2009.
78. Rossabi, 1988: 101.
79. Lorge, 2005: 150–54.
80. Dardess, 2012.
81. Wang, 2011: chap. 5.
82. According to Andrade, 2016: 113.
83. Zhang, 2015: 119–52.
84. According to Dardess, 2012.
85. According to Swope, 2014.
86. Perdue, 2002: 376.
87. Elliott, 2009: 86.
88. Elliott, 2001; Dabringhaus, 2011; Waley-Cohen, 2009.
89. Perdue, 2002: 393.
90. Lorge, 2005: 165.
91. Perdue, 2002: 390.
92. Ibid.: 283.
93. Perdue, 2005: 284–87.

94. Theobald, 2013: 9, 5.
95. Elliott, 2009: 88–92, 100.
96. Dabringhaus, 2011.
97. Fairbank, 1968; Arrighi, 2007: 314–20; Andornino, 2006; Wang, 2013.
98. Lorge, 2005: 172; Chia, 1993.
99. Giersch, 2006: 47.
100. Ibid.: chap. 4; Dai, 2004: 182–83.
101. Giersch, 2006: 12–14.
102. Wang, 2018.
103. Andrade, 2016: 8, 238.
104. Sun Bin, 2003: 110, 112.

Chapter Seven. Medieval and Modern Japan

1. Friday, 2004: 6.
2. Farris, 2006: 164, 185–87.
3. Conlan, 2003: 219, 7; cf. Turnbull, 2008.
4. Friday, 2004: chap. 5.
5. Morillo, 2001.
6. Friday, 2004: 155–59.
7. Farris, 2006: 194–98.
8. Berry, 1994.
9. Ibid.: 23.
10. Ibid.: 48; 2005: 835–36.
11. Farris, 2006: 209.
12. Lamers, 2000: chap. 1.
13. Bender, 2008.
14. Lamers, 2000.
15. Farris, 2006.
16. Berry, 1982: 29–34.
17. Lamers, 2000: 76, 98, 103–4.
18. Berry, 1982: 161; cf. Stalker, 2018: chaps. 5 and 6; Turnbull, 2002.
19. Berry, 1982: 126–30; quote, 81.
20. Lamers, 2000: 163, 170.
21. Berry, 1986: 243–47; Roberts, 2012: 7; Ikegami, 1995: 152–63.
22. Berry, 1982: 81, 150–55.
23. Berry, 1986: 242–43.
24. Ferejohn and Rosenbluth, 2010.
25. Farris, 2006.
26. Ibid.: 211.
27. Berry, 1982: 107–10; Turnbull, 2002: 73.
28. Berry, 1982: 113–20.
29. Moore, 1988.
30. Ikegami, 1995.

31. Totman, 1988: 48, 63.
32. Tarling, 2001: 25.
33. Metzler, 2006: chap. 2.
34. Duus, 1995; Matsusaka, 2001; Brooks, 2000.
35. Duus, 1995: 175–84.
36. Lone, 2000: 100–105.
37. Dickinson, 1999: 256; Evans and Peattie, 1997: 124.
38. Shimazu, 2001, 2009.
39. Duus, 1995; Lone, 2000: chaps. 8–10.
40. Duus, 1995: 203, 399–423; Eiji, 2002.
41. Duus, 1995: 431, 284–88.
42. Kim and Park, 2008; Eckert, 1996; Chou, 1996; Cha, 2000; Ho, 1984; Maddison, 2003: table 4.
43. Gluck, 1985: 90, 216–17.
44. Dickinson, 1999: 151, 242–56.
45. Hata, 1988: 282–86.
46. Peattie, 1975: 29, 57–63.
47. Metzler, 2006: 128.
48. Peattie, 1975: 100.
49. Iriye, 1997: 50–62.
50. Peattie, 1975: 96–98; Barnhart, 1987; Jordan, 1987.
51. Humphreys, 1995.
52. Wilson, 1995: 253–55; Young, 1998.
53. Iriye, 1997: 13–26.
54. Ibid.: 26–28.
55. Benson and Matsumura, 2001: 21–38; Nish, 2002.
56. Taira, 1988: 578–89.
57. Woodiwiss, 1992: 58–66; Gordon, 1985: 416–25, 251; 1991: 203.
58. Garon, 1987: 198–218; Taira, 1988: 637–46; Odaka, 1999: 150–57; Gordon, 1985: 250–51; 1991: 287–92.
59. Berger, 1977: 85, 225, 333–34, 345–46; Snyder, 1991: 134.
60. Gordon, 1991: 302–15.
61. Nakamura, 1988: 464–68.
62. Metzler, 2006: 199–256.
63. Berger, 1977: 105–17, 346; Gordon, 1985: chaps. 9–10; Nakamura, 1988.
64. Lockwood, 1954: 117; Iriye, 1974; Duus, 1995: xv–xviii; Sugihara, 2004.
65. Brooks, 2000: chap. 5.
66. Peattie, 1975: 114–33.
67. Bix, 2001: 228–41.
68. Matsusaka, 2001: 354.
69. Barrett and Shyu, 2001.
70. Mitter, 2000.
71. Maddison, 2003: 25.
72. Young, 1998: 307; cf. Nish, 2002: 177–82.

73. Wilson, 2002.
74. Brooks, 2000: 200–207; Nish, 2002: 180.
75. Tarling, 2001: 42.
76. Peattie, 1975: 186–90; Hane, 1992: chap. 12; Bix, 2001: 308–13.
77. Bix, 2001: 317–23.
78. Barnhart, 1987: 89.
79. Ibid.: 90, 104–14.
80. Berger, 1977: 67–74.
81. Bix, 2001: 254.
82. Kershaw, 2007: 91.
83. Kennedy, 1999: 501–2.
84. Tsunoda, 1994; Toland, 1970: 144–45.
85. Lynn, 2003: 238–40.
86. Miller, 2007; Barnhart, 1987.
87. Miller, 2007: 242.
88. Kershaw, 2007: 91–128.
89. Kennedy, 1999: 513–14.
90. Quoted ibid.: 515.
91. Iriye, 1987: 149–50; 1991.
92. Evans and Peattie, 1997: 447, 471–82.
93. Tarling, 2001: 76–78; Kershaw, 2007: 365.
94. Kershaw, 2007: 128, 478.
95. See, for example, Wood, 2007.
96. LeMay, 1965: 387.
97. Pike, 2015.
98. Lynn, 2003: 248–49, 262–80.

Chapter Eight. A Thousand Years of Europe

1. According to Heather, 2010.
2. Ward-Perkins, 2005.
3. Scheidel, 2019: 159, 162–64; Bisson, 2009.
4. Black, 1998: 47.
5. Keen, 1984.
6. Kaeuper, 1999: 38; Keen, 1999: 4–5.
7. Bartlett, 1994.
8. Turchin, 2003.
9. Luard, 1986: 24–34.
10. Howard, 1983: 14.
11. Davies, 2011.
12. Rogers, 2000; Lynn, 2003: chap. 3.
13. Rogers, 1993.
14. Howard, 1983: 14–15.
15. Luard, 1986: 193–95.

16. Lynn, 2003: 80.
17. Honig, 2001: 119.
18. Honig, 2012.
19. Honig, 2001: 117.
20. Andrade, 2015.
21. Pascua, 2008: 194–96.
22. Mann, 1986: 463–69.
23. Owen, 2010.
24. Luard, 1986: 195–205.
25. Ibid.: 204.
26. Scheidel, 2019.
27. Ibid.
28. Wendt, 1999.
29. Holsti, 1991: 64, 84; Luard, 1986: 44–52.
30. Quoted in Lynn, 2003: 132–36.
31. Howard, 1983: 13.
32. Quoted in MacMillan, 2020: 25.
33. Lynn, 2003: 140–41.
34. Ibid.: 155–56.
35. Holsti, 1991: 108–9, 112; Luard, 1986: 205–12.
36. Dalrymple, 2019: 329.
37. Yazdani, 2017.
38. Grinin and Korotayev, 2015.
39. Owen, 2010: chap. 4.
40. Parker, 1971; Ellis, 2003: 9.
41. Fazal, 2007.
42. Holsti, 1991: 141; Luard, 1986: 52–56.
43. Holsti, 1991: 142–45.
44. Owen, 2010: 278.
45. Yazdani, 2017.
46. See Mann, 1993, 2012, for fuller explanations.
47. Aron, 1973: 24–25.
48. Mann, 1993: 764–66.
49. Clark, 2012; Otte, 2014.
50. Otte, 2014: 506.
51. Judson, 2016.
52. Otte, 2014: 508.
53. Malešević, 2010; MacMillan, 2020.
54. Owen, 2010: chap. 5.
55. Kershaw, 2007: 254–56.
56. Ibid.: 290.
57. Kershaw, 1998: chap. 13.
58. Kershaw, 2007: 479.
59. Simms and Laderman, 2021.

60. Kershaw, 2007: 382–430.
61. MacMillan, 2020; Marwick, 1975.
62. Mann, 2004.
63. See Mann, 2012: chap. 9; Mann, 2013: chaps. 2–4.
64. Wimmer, 2013.
65. Luard, 1986: 205.

Chapter Nine. Seven Hundred Years of South and Central America

1. Townsend, 2019; Berdan, 2014, 2021; Cervantes, 2020: chaps. 6–9; all use these sources.
2. Hassig, 2007: 314–15.
3. Ibid.: 312.
4. Berdan, 2014: 169–70.
5. Isaac, 1983.
6. Townsend, 2019: chap. 2.
7. Berdan, 2014: 157–59.
8. Townsend, 2019: 79, 249–55.
9. Cervantes, 2020: chap. 9.
10. Hassig, 1988: 128–32, 172; Townsend, 2019: 53.
11. Daniel, 1992; Hassig, 1988: 75–94.
12. Hassig, 1988: 236–50; Berdan, 2021: 181–82.
13. Townsend, 2019: 72.
14. Graeber and Wengrow, 2021: 370–73.
15. Townsend, 2019: chap. 5.
16. Cervantes, 2020: 173.
17. Rostworowski, 1999; D'Altroy, 2014; McEwan, 2006; Cervantes, 2020: chaps. 13–15.
18. McEwan, 2006: 127.
19. Rostworowski, 1999.
20. Julien, 2007: 342–44.
21. McEwan, 2006: 127.
22. D'Altroy, 2014: 340–41.
23. Hyslop, 1984; McEwan, 2006: 118–28.
24. Covey, 2020: 61–63.
25. D'Altroy, 2014: 324.
26. Bray, 1992: 230.
27. D'Altroy, 2014: 349.
28. Rowe, 2006.
29. Rostworowski, 1999: 46.
30. Cervantes, 2020: chap. 14.
31. Andreski, 1966: 211.

32. Holden, 2004: 4.
33. Scheina, 2003: part 10; Loveman, 1999: 43–59, 105–14.
34. Lemke, 2002; Gochman and Maoz, 1984: 607; Franchi et al., 2017: 12.
35. Mares, 2001: 37; Mares and Palmer, 2012: 2.
36. Franchi et al., 2017: 10–11.
37. Jones, 2014.
38. Lemke, 2002: 167–71, 181; Centeno, 2002: 38–43; Arocena and Bowman, 2014: 52–53.
39. Gochman and Maoz, 1984: 605.
40. Palmer et al., 2015: 230.
41. Gochman and Maoz, 1984: 609; Palmer et al., 2015: 235; Ghosn et al., 2004: 151.
42. Mares and Kacowicz, 2016: table 9.1; Hensel, 1994.
43. Dominguez and Mares, 2003; Battaglino, 2012: 131.
44. Dominguez and Mares, 2003: 13.
45. Centeno, 2002.
46. Tilly, 1975: 42; cf. Mann, 1986, 1993.
47. Centeno, 2002: 66, 87, 122.
48. Ibid.: 194.
49. Mazzuca, 2021.
50. Burr, 1967.
51. Holsti, 1996: 156–57.
52. Mares, 2001: 17.
53. Ibid.: 113–30.
54. Ibid.: chaps. 3–4; cf. Dominguez and Mares, 2003.
55. Gibler, 2012.
56. Grafe and Irigoin, 2006: 240.
57. Mazucca, 2021.
58. As listed in Grafe and Irigoin, 2006: appendix 2; cf. Dominguez and Mares, 2003.
59. Carter and Goemans, 2014.
60. Goertz et al., 2016: chap. 7.
61. Scheina, 2003: 427.
62. Centeno, 2002: 49.
63. Whigham, 2002, section 2; Leuchars, 2002; Henderson, 2016.
64. Braumoeller, 2019: 106–7; Whigham, 2017: 580.
65. Fazal, 2007: 41.
66. Whigham, 2017; Leuchars, 2002.
67. Bethell, 1996: 8.
68. Ibid.: 4.
69. Whigham, 2017.
70. Collier, 2003: 51–52.
71. Ibid.
72. Burr, 1967; Sater, 2007; St. John, 1994.

73. Sater, 2007: 21–25, 347–56; Henderson, 2016.
74. Burr, 1967.
75. Henderson, 2016.
76. Braumoeller, 2019: 107.
77. Zook, 1960; Niebuhr, 2018.
78. Chesterton, 2013.
79. Shesko, 2015.
80. Ibid.
81. Mares and Palmer, 2012; Zook, 1964.
82. Zook, 1964.
83. Mares and Palmer, 2012.
84. Ibid.: 67.
85. Ibid.; Mares, 1996.
86. Mares and Palmer, 2012: 130.
87. Durham, 1979; Anderson, 1981.
88. Henderson, 2016.
89. Corbacho, 2003; Mares, 2001: 155–58.
90. Mares, 2001: 157–58.
91. Centeno, 2002: 129; Holsti, 1996: 166–67.
92. Henderson, 2016.
93. Migdal, 2001: 137–50.
94. Mares and Palmer, 2012: 132.
95. Mann, 2013.
96. Arocena and Bowman, 2014: 52–63.
97. Haftel, 2007.

Chapter Ten. The Decline of War?

1. Excellent summaries of social thought on wars can be found in Joas and Knoeble, 2013; and Malešević, 2010: 17–50.
2. Joas, 2003: 128–33.
3. Ward, 1903.
4. Go, 2013.
5. Sumner, 1898.
6. Clausewitz, 1976: 260.
7. Gumplowicz, 1899: 116–24.
8. Treitschke, 1916: 395–96.
9. Weber, 1988: 60–61. I thank Stefan Bargheer for help in translating this.
10. Luft, 2007.
11. Simmel, 1903: 799.
12. Caillois, 1939, 2012.
13. See, for example, Joas, 2003; Malešević, 2010; Joas and Knoeble, 2013.
14. Mueller, 2009; Gat, 2006, 2017; Pinker, 2011; Goldstein, 2011.
15. Mueller, 2004: 17–18, 161.

16. Elias, 2012.
17. Durand, 1960; Fitzgerald, 1961; Scheidel, 2019: 43–45.
18. Hanson, 2005.
19. Flory, 2006.
20. Brunt, 1971.
21. Weatherford, 2004: 118; Morgan, 2007; Frankopan, 2015: 162.
22. Di Cosmo, 2002a: 6.
23. Biran, 2018.
24. Anonymous, 2011.
25. Khazanov, 2015.
26. Ratchnevsky, 1992: 129, 151; Giessauf, 2011; Biran, 2018.
27. Joveyni quoted in Spuler, 1972: 32–39.
28. Ratchnevsky, 1992: 129–33.
29. Lorge, 2005: 85–88.
30. Schmidt, 2011; May, 2007: 118–20; Sverdrup, 2017: 347.
31. Sverdrup, 2017: 347–48.
32. Frankopan, 2015: 161.
33. Morgan, 2007: 82, 137–38; May, 2011.
34. Anonymous, 2011.
35. Pinker, 2011: 195.
36. Braumoeller, 2019.
37. Eckhardt, 1992: 131.
38. Malešević, 2010: 119–20.
39. Cederman et al., 2011.
40. Blainey, 1988: 4.
41. Gat, 2017: 131–36.
42. Braumoeller, 2019: 94.
43. Sarkees et al., 2003: 65; Sarkees and Wayman, 2010.
44. Walter, 2017.
45. Wesseling, 2005.
46. Etemad, 2007: 92.
47. Tocqueville quoted ibid.: 86.
48. Mann, 2005: 100–107.
49. Wesseling, 1989.
50. Ibid.
51. Etemad, 2007: 89.
52. Ibid.: 93.
53. Kimber, 1990: 160.
54. Evans and Ørsted-Jensen, 2014.
55. Wesseling, 2005.
56. Bairoch, 1997: 638.
57. Etemad, 2007: 94.
58. Aron, 1997: 227.

59. Mueller, 1988.
60. Gat, 2017.
61. Goldstein, 2011: 15.
62. Ibid.: 309.
63. Roser, 2016.
64. Migdal, 2001.
65. Fazal, 2007.
66. Roser, 2016; Strand and Hegre, 2021.
67. Braumoeller, 2019: 86–92, 114; Cirillo and Taleb, 2016.
68. Marshall, 2017.
69. Clauset, 2018.
70. Beard, 2018.
71. Dupuy et al., 2017; Strand et al., 2019.
72. Hensel, 2002.
73. Themnér and Wallensteen, 2014; Dupuy et al., 2017; Pettersson and Eck, 2018; Strand et al., 2019; Braumoeller, 2019: 85.
74. Harrison and Wolf, 2012, 2014.
75. Goertz et al., 2016; cf. Roser, 2016.
76. Braumoeller, 2019: chap. 8.
77. Marshall, 2017.
78. See, for example, Melander et al., 2009.
79. Crawford, 2015.
80. Goldstein, 2011: 260–64.
81. Lacina and Gleditsch, 2005.
82. UNHCR, 2020, 2021; Marshall, 2017.
83. Caplan and Hoeffler, 2017.
84. Eisner, 2003, 2014.
85. Du Roy and Simbille, 2018.
86. Somashekhar and Rich, 2016.
87. Sharara et al., 2021.
88. Thome, 2007.
89. All figures are from Lopes da Silva et al., 2022.
90. Collins, 1974.
91. Kaldor, 1999; Münkler, 2005.
92. Wimmer, 2013; Malešević, 2010: 311–14.
93. Arreguín-Toft, 2005.
94. Ibid.; cf. MacMillan, 2020.
95. Quoted in Malešević, 2010: 83.
96. Quoted in Bourke, 1999: 209.
97. Wezeman et al., 2022.
98. Strand et al., 2019: figures 3 and 4.
99. As did Cirillo and Taleb, 2016.
100. Gat, 2006: 662.

Chapter Eleven. Fear and Loathing on the Battlefield I

1. Holmes, 1985: 210.
2. Stanhope, 1888: 18.
3. This is all covered in Raaflaub, 2007.
4. Goldsworthy, 1996: 30, 244–47.
5. Melchior, 2011.
6. Keegan, 1976: 78–116.
7. Ardant du Picq, 1947: 88–90, 154.
8. Keegan, 1976: 97–107, 171–74.
9. Collins, 2008: 83–133.
10. Josephus, 1987: bk. 6, chap. 8, sections 44–46.
11. Tolstoy, 2009: bk. 10, chap. 36.
12. Holmes, 1985: 84.
13. Linderman, 1987; Hess, 1997; McPherson, 1997; Manning, 2007; Adams, 2014; Steplyk, 2018.
14. Linderman, 1987: 7–17, 61.
15. Steplyk, 2018: 27, 75; McPherson, 1997: 68–69, 100–101.
16. Manning, 2007: 21, 31.
17. Marshall, 1947.
18. Grossman, 1995.
19. Laidley, 1865: 69; emphasis in original.
20. Malešević, 2010: 220, 221, 229; cf. Jacoby, 2008: 90.
21. Rottman, 2013.
22. Adams, 2014: 114–15; cf. Steplyk, 2018.
23. Griffith, 1989: 86.
24. Ibid.: 84–90.
25. Keegan, 1976.
26. Adams, 2014: 63.
27. Griffith, 1989: 111–13.
28. Hess, 1997: 57–59.
29. Ardant du Picq, 1947: 263–73.
30. Ibid.: 115.
31. Ibid.: 120.
32. Ibid.: 111–12.
33. Griffith, 1989: chap. 2.
34. McPherson, 1997: 72, 77.
35. Hess, 1997.
36. McPherson, 1997: 72–74.
37. McPherson, 1997: 6–7, 79; Adams, 2014: 111–12, 115.
38. Hess, 1997: 150.
39. Linderman, 1987: 261–62.
40. Hess, 1997.
41. Adams, 2014: 111.

42. Griffith, 1989: 50.
43. Hess, 1997: 74–93.
44. Ibid.: 75.
45. Adams, 2014: 70.
46. McPherson, 1997: 39–42.
47. Sherman to Major General Logan, December 21, 1863, ehistory.osu.edu.
48. Brown, 1970: 86–93; Stannard, 1992: 171–74.
49. Adams, 2014: 166.
50. McPherson, 1997: 163–66.
51. Weitz, 2008: 284–85.
52. McPherson, 1997: 46, 47.
53. Ibid.: 49–51.
54. Hess, 1997: 114–17.
55. McPherson, 1997: 87.
56. McPherson, n.d.; McPherson, 1997: 87.
57. Holmes, 1985: 84.

Chapter Twelve. Fear and Loathing on the Battlefield II

1. Roynette, 2018: 260.
2. Ibid.: 261.
3. Strachan, 2006.
4. Sheldon, 2005: 292.
5. Lebow, 2010: 137.
6. Sheldon, 2005; Middlebrook, 1972.
7. Ziemann, 2017: 74.
8. Horne, 2005: 909; my translation.
9. Holmes, 1985: 204–5, 182, 267–69; cf. Bourke, 2005: 199; Rousseau, 1999: 155.
10. Bourke, 2005: chap. 7; Rousseau, 1999: 155–60.
11. Rousseau, 1999: 223, 228.
12. Malešević, 2022: 184.
13. Jones, 2006: 239–41.
14. Audoin-Rouzeau and Becker, 2002: 93–103.
15. Cf. Horne, 2005.
16. Smith et al., 2003: 101–12.
17. Rousseau, 1999.
18. Ibid.: 309; my translation.
19. Maurin, 1982: 599–637.
20. Cochet, 2005; Loez, 2010.
21. Loez, 2010: 43.
22. Bond, 2002.
23. Ziemann, 2007; Ashworth, 1980.
24. Rousseau, 1999: 111–18.

25. Ashworth, 1980.
26. Ibid.: 173–75.
27. Ziemann, 2007.
28. Rousseau, 1999: 229–30.
29. Sheldon, 2005: 391.
30. Audoin-Rouzeau and Becker, 2002: 21–25.
31. Ziemann, 2017: 26–27.
32. Ashworth, 1980: 215.
33. Audoin-Rouzeau and Becker, 2002: 39–42.
34. Ashworth, 1980: 215–16.
35. Watson, 2008.
36. Smith, 1994.
37. Saint-Fuscien, 2011.
38. Pedroncini, 1967; Smith, 1994; Horne, 2005; Loez, 2010.
39. Keegan, 1976: 335; 1999: 331–50, 401.
40. Jones, 2008.
41. Audoin-Rouzeau and Becker, 2002: 40.
42. Ziemann, 2017: 32–33, 103–19; Maurin, 1982: 522.
43. Wildman, 1980: 203–45.
44. Keegan, 1976: 274–78, 314–17.
45. Watson, 2008: 66.
46. Ibid.: 69.
47. Ibid.: 70.
48. Wilcox, 2014.
49. Sanborn, 2003.
50. Mann, 2012: 176–85.
51. Ziemann, 2007: 142–53.
52. Cf. Boff, 2014.
53. Dollard with Horton, 1943.
54. Kershaw, 2012: xvii.
55. Shils and Janowitz, 1948.
56. Bartov, 1991; Fritz, 1995; Cintino, 2017.
57. Bartov, 1985; Lower, 2005; Bartov, 1991: 132.
58. Cintino, 2017: 3.
59. Ibid.: 158–62.
60. Bartov, 1991: 26.
61. Fritz, 1995.
62. Ibid.: 10.
63. Ibid.: 188–97.
64. Ibid.: 146–49.
65. Cintino, 2017.
66. Hellbeck, 2015.
67. Beevor, 1998.
68. Merridale, 2006.

69. Hellbeck, 2015: 58.
70. Reese, 2011: 160–73.
71. Merridale, 2006: 199.
72. Reese, 2011: 13.
73. Quoted in Merridale, 2006: 214.
74. Hellbeck, 2015: 53, 61.
75. Ibid.: 51.
76. Ibid.: 19.
77. Merridale, 2006: 63–68.
78. Hellbeck, 2015: 149.
79. Ibid.: 43.
80. Ibid.: 188.
81. Ibid.: 22.
82. Ibid.: 181, 22.
83. Ibid.: 67–68.
84. Ibid.: 67.
85. Ibid.: 50.
86. William Slim, speech to the officers of the Indian army, quoted by Lewin, 1976: 71.
87. See, for example, Collins, 2008: 43–54; Dyer, 1985: 118–19; Holmes, 1985: 58; Keegan, 1976: 74; Malešević, 2010: 220–21; 2022: 179; Jacoby, 2008: 90–91; Ferguson, 2006: 521.
88. Marshall, 1944, 1968, 1969.
89. Marshall, 1947: 54, 79.
90. Spiller, 1988; Glenn, 2000; Chambers, 2003; Engen, 2008, 2011.
91. Malešević, 2010, 2022.
92. Stouffer et al., 1949: table 3, 201; Collins, 2008: 46–49.
93. Kaufman, 1947.
94. Bourke, 2005: 289.
95. Stouffer et al., 1949: 283
96. Glenn, 2000: 30.
97. Blake, 1970.
98. Quoted ibid.: 340–41.
99. Bourke, 1999.
100. Ibid.: 2.
101. Ibid.: 19.
102. Ferguson, 1999: 357–58; cf. MacMillan, 2020: 81.
103. King, 2013: 48–49; emphasis in original.
104. Bourke, 1999: 155.
105. Ibid.: 154.
106. Ibid.
107. Ibid.: 229.
108. Blake, 1970: 342–43.

109. Stouffer et al., 1949: 159; Bourke, 1999: 145–49; Malešević, 2010: 224–25; MacMillan, 2020: 78–79.
110. Collins, 2008: 77, 67–70.
111. Bourke, 1999: 219, 208.
112. King, 2013: 45–48.
113. Marshall, 1968: 56.
114. King, 2013: 170–80.
115. Steckel, 1994; van Creveld, 1982.
116. Reiter and Stam, 2002.
117. Engen, 2008, 2009, 2011.
118. Cameron, 1994: 51, 201.
119. Shalit, 1988: 142.
120. Stouffer, et al., 1949: 98–100, 135–40.
121. Junger, 2011: 229.
122. Bartov, 1991: chap. 2.
123. Moskos, 1970: 73.
124. Shils, 1950: 22–24.
125. Mansoor, 1999; Rush, 2001.
126. Stouffer et al., 1949: 150.
127. Moskos, 1970.
128. Keegan, 1976: 335; Holmes, 1985: 214–16, 326.
129. Dyer, 1985: 144.
130. Hamner, 2011: 11.
131. Sherwood, 1996: 71.
132. Gurney, 1958: 258; Sherwood, 1996: 77–78; Wells, 1995: 49; Zhang, 2002.
133. Collins, 2008: 387–99.
134. Wells, 1995: 31.
135. Sherwood, 1996: 79.
136. Wells, 1995: 48.
137. Werrell, 2005: 125.
138. Toliver and Constable, 1997: 348.
139. Sherwood, 1996: 77–79; Werrell, 2005: 137–38, 144–45, 166.
140. Sparks and Neiss, 1956.
141. Wells, 1995: 105, 129.
142. Blake, 1970: 339.
143. Wells, 1995: 99; cf. Blake, 1970: 339.
144. Sherwood, 1996: 71, 91–94.
145. Bourke, 2005: 209–10.
146. Werrell, 2005: 196, 278.
147. Sherwood, 1996: 98–99.
148. Wells, 1995: 45–46, 115.
149. Stouffer et al., 1949: chap. 7.
150. Chancey and Forstchen, 2000: 80, 131–36.
151. Sherwood, 1996: 6, 38, 67.

Chapter Thirteen. Fear and Loathing on the Battlefield III

1. Blechman and Kaplan, 1978.
2. Kaplan, 1981.
3. Quoted in Cumings, 2010: 14.
4. Li, 2014: 39.
5. Johnston, 1996.
6. Edwards, 2006: 143–46.
7. Tomedi, 1993: 22, 110.
8. King, 2013: 181–82.
9. Tomedi, 1993: 67; Watson, 2002.
10. Watson, 2002: 176.
11. Marshall, 1951: 4, 61–62.
12. Glenn, 2000: 41–46.
13. Little, 1964.
14. Li, 2014.
15. Mahoney, 2001; Li et al., 2001; George, 1967.
16. Li, 2007: 91.
17. Li et al., 2001: 63, 67–69, 115–16.
18. George, 1967: 27–35.
19. Ibid.: 88.
20. Quoted ibid.: 25.
21. Mahoney, 2001.
22. Edwards, 2018: 59–61; Fehrenbach, 1963: 103, 137, 170.
23. Mahoney, 2001: 109.
24. Tomedi, 1993: 129, 136.
25. Mahoney, 2001: chaps. 5 and 6.
26. Ibid.: 94.
27. Edwards, 2018: 59–61.
28. Li, 2014.
29. Mahoney, 2001: 83.
30. Li et al., 2001.
31. Li, 2014: 61.
32. George, 1967: 133.
33. Li, 2014: 111–23, 132–33, 180.
34. Ibid.: 219–21.
35. Li et al., 2001: 149–55, 175.
36. Fehrenbach, 1963: 109, 264.
37. Li, 2014: 239.
38. Li et al., 2001: 43.
39. Birtle, 2006: 36.
40. Cockerham and Cohen, 1981.
41. Moskos, 1970: 136, 141.
42. Moskos, 1975.

43. Marshall and Hackworth, 1967.
44. Glenn, 2000.
45. Ibid.: 36.
46. Ibid.: 46–48, 160; cf. Collins, 2008: 52–59.
47. Marmar et al., 2015.
48. *All Things Considered*, National Public Radio, December 16, 2017.
49. Hendin, 1991.
50. Dennis et al., 2016; cf. Marx et al., 2010.
51. Maguen et al., 2009.
52. Holmes, 1985: 86.
53. Lepre, 2011.
54. Cf. Moskos, 1970: 78–80.
55. See Hunt, 2008: appendix, for a critique.
56. Donnell et al., 1965.
57. Halberstam: 1972: 366; Elliott, 2010: 70–74.
58. Elliott, 2003: chap. 14.
59. Hunt, 2008: 38–46.
60. Elliott, 2003: chap. 11.
61. Ibid.: 355, 374, 454.
62. Ibid.: 378–80.
63. Henderson, 1979.
64. Ibid.: 40.
65. Ibid.: 89.
66. Ibid.: 73.
67. Ibid.: 94.
68. Gouré et al., 1966.
69. Elliott, 2003: chap. 13; Gouré et al., 1966.
70. Elliott, 2010: chap. 3; Robin, 2001; 190–93.
71. According to Elliott, 2010: 182–84.
72. Hunt, 2008: 117–35.
73. Elliott, 2003.
74. Ibid.: 1133.
75. Taylor, 1999.
76. Li, 2007: 205, 220–22.
77. Elliott, 2003: 937–39.
78. Quoted in Welch, 2011: 121.
79. Hiam, 2006: chap. 5; Elliott, 2010: 193–95; Elliott, 2003: chap. 13.
80. Li, 2007: 250–59; Li, 2014: 248.
81. O'Brien, 1990: 65.
82. Collins, 2008: 57–59.
83. Report of the General Accounting Office, quoted by Buncombe, 2005.
84. Malešević, 2022: 154.

Chapter Fourteen. Recent Wars in Muslim Countries

1. Grinin, 2019.
2. Ibid.: 30.
3. World Islamic Front Fatwa, February 23, 1998:1.
4. Huntington, 1996.
5. Owen, 2010.
6. Pape, 2006.
7. Sharp, 2022.
8. Derluguian, 2021.
9. Ibid.
10. Agha and Malley, 2019.
11. Yazbek, 2015: 234–37, 246–47.
12. Ibn Khaldun, 1958: 297.
13. Donner, 2007: 299–300.
14. "Samer," 2017.
15. Weiss and Hassan, 2015.
16. Wood, 2016; McCants, 2015.
17. Khatib, 2015.
18. McCants, 2015: chap. 5.
19. Ibn Khaldun, 1958: 394.
20. The effects are horrifically described by Yazbek, 2015.
21. Khatib, 2015.
22. Callimachi, 2018; Speckhard and Ellenberg, 2020.
23. Weiss and Hassan, 2015: 222–24.
24. Ginkel and Entenmann, 2016; Dodwell et al., 2016; Wilson, 2017; and Speckhard and Ellenberg, 2020.
25. Atran et al., 2018.
26. Sagramoso and Yarlykapov, 2020.
27. Khosrokhavar, 2017; Speckhard and Ellenberg, 2020: table 5.
28. Wilson, 2017.
29. Wilson, 2015.
30. Dodwell et al., 2016.
31. Fishman and Felter, 2007.
32. Hegghammer, 2021.
33. Mitts, 2019.
34. Khosrokhavar, 2017: 21.
35. Knights and Almeida, 2020.
36. Hegghammer, 2021.
37. Khosrokhavar, 2017: 38.
38. Hansen, 2013; International Crisis Group, 2018.
39. Quinlivan, 1999; Kandil, 2016.
40. Sassoon, 2012: 129–61; Blaydes, 2018: 266–304.
41. Cheney, 2003.

42. Fukuyama, 2011.
43. Draper, 2020.
44. Mann, 2003.
45. Pew Research Center, 2011, 2016.
46. Junger, 2011.
47. Skelly, 2006; Sheehan-Miles, 2012.
48. Kudo, 2011.
49. Brereton Report, 2020.
50. O'Grady and Gunter, 2022.
51. Hoge et al., 2004.
52. Litz et al., 2009.
53. Maguen and Litz, 2012.
54. Finkel, 2013.
55. Ibid.
56. Bandura, 1999.
57. Phillips, 2019; Cooper et al., 2019.
58. Hattenstone and Allison, 2014.
59. Shaw, 2002.
60. Khan and Gopal, 2017.
61. Moore, 2019.
62. Pew Research Center, 2011: chap. 5.
63. Chappelle et al., 2010, 2014; cf. Armour and Ross, 2017.
64. Cole, 2017.
65. Mead, 2014.
66. Lewis and Holewinski, 2013.
67. Mashal, 2020.
68. Massing, 2021.
69. Mann, 2003.
70. Alshaibi, 2022.
71. Herring and Rangwala, 2006: 147–59.
72. Crawford, 2021.
73. Gibbons-Neff, 2021.
74. Mann, 1988: 183–87.
75. Sharp, 2020.
76. Nye, 1990.
77. Donner, 2007; Niditch, 2007.

Chapter Fifteen. Possible Futures

1. Zhao, 2006.
2. Ramzy and Buckley, 2019.
3. Friedrich et al., 2016.
4. Aron, 1973: 15.
5. Goldstein, 2011: 328.
6. Eisenhower, 1953.

Conclusion

1. Eckstein, 2006.
2. Small and Singer, 1970.
3. Reiter and Stam, 2002.
4. Lebow, 2010.
5. White, 1990.
6. Luard, 1986: 268–69.
7. Ibn Khaldun, 1958: 263, 355–65.
8. Thies and Baum, 2020.
9. Fearon, 1994.
10. Ibn Khaldun, 1958: 227–29.
11. Ibid.: 12.
12. Barthold, 1956: 60.
13. Lebow, 2010.
14. Van Evera, 1999: 192.
15. White, 1990.
16. Bender, 2008; Davies, 2011; Fazal, 2004.

Bibliography

Adams, Michael. 2014. *Living Hell: The Dark Side of the Civil War*. Baltimore: Johns Hopkins University Press.

Ager, Sheila. 2009. "Roman Perspectives on Greek Diplomacy." In Claude Eilers, ed., *Diplomats and Diplomacy in the Roman World*, 15–43. Leiden: Brill.

Agha, Hussein, and Robert Malley. 2019. "The Middle East's Great Divide Is Not Sectarianism." *New Yorker*, March 11.

Alonso, Victor. 2007. "Peace and International Law in Ancient Greece." In Kurt Raaflaub, ed., *War and Peace in the Ancient World*. Oxford: Blackwell.

Alshaibi, Wisam. 2022. "Transborder Opposition and Foreign Policy Elites: The Making of Regime Change in Iraq." Unpublished paper, UCLA Department of Sociology.

Anderson, Thomas. 1981. *The War of the Dispossessed: Honduras and El Salvador, 1969*. Lincoln: University of Nebraska Press.

Andornino, Giovanni. 2006. "The Nature and Linkages of China's Tributary System under the Ming and Qing Dynasties." *Working Papers of the Global Economic History Network*, London School of Economics, no. 21/06.

Andrade, Tonio. 2015. "Late Medieval Divergences: Comparative Perspectives on Early Gunpowder Warfare in Europe and China." *Journal of Medieval Military History* 13:247–76.

———. 2016. *The Gunpowder Age: China, Military Innovation, and the Rise of the West in World History*. Princeton: Princeton University Press.

Andreski, Stanislav. 1966. *Parasitism and Subversion: The Case of Latin America*. London: Weidenfeld & Nicolson.

———. 1968. *Military Organization and Society*. 2nd edition. London: Routledge & Keegan Paul.

Ardant du Picq, Charles-Jean-Jacques-Joseph. 1947 [1880]. *Battle Studies: Ancient and Modern*. Harrisburg, Pa.: Military Service Publishing.

Armour, Cherie, and Jana Ross. 2017. "The Health and Well-Being of Military Drone Operators and Intelligence Analysts: A Systematic Review." *Military Psychology*, December 13: 83–98.

Arocena, Felipe, and Kirk Bowman. 2014. *Lessons from Latin America: Innovations in Politics, Culture, and Development.* Toronto: University of Toronto Press.

Aron, Raymond. 1973. *Peace and War: A Theory of International Relations.* Abridged edition. New York: Doubleday.

———. 1997. *Thinking Politically: A Liberal in the Age of Ideology.* New York: Transaction.

Arreguín-Toft, Ivan. 2005. *How the Weak Win Wars: A Theory of Asymmetric Conflict.* Cambridge: Cambridge University Press.

Arrighi, Giovanni. 2007. *Adam Smith in Beijing: Lineages of the Twenty-first Century.* New York: Verso.

Ashworth, Tony. 1980. *Trench Warfare, 1914–1918: The Live and Let Live System.* London: Pan Books.

Atran, Scott, et al. 2018. "The Islamic State's Lingering Legacy among Young Men from the Mosul Area." *CTC Sentinel* 11:15–22.

Audoin-Rouzeau, Stéphane. 2005. "Vers une anthropologie historique de la violence de combat au XIXe siècle: Relire Ardant du Picq?" *Revue d'Histoire du XIXe Siècle* 30:85–97.

Audoin-Rouzeau, Stéphane, and Annette Becker. 2002. *14–18: Understanding the Great War.* New York: Hill and Wang.

Bairoch, Paul. 1997. *Victoires et déboires: Histoire économique et sociale du monde du XVIe siècle à nos jours*, vol. 2. Paris: Gallimard.

Bandura, Albert. 1999. "Moral Disengagement in the Perpetration of Inhumanities." *Personality and Social Psychology Review* 3:193–209.

Barnhart, Michael. 1987. *Japan Prepares for Total War: The Search for Economic Security, 1919–1941.* Ithaca: Cornell University Press.

Barrett, David, and Larry Shyu, eds. 2001. *Chinese Collaboration with Japan, 1932–1945.* Stanford: Stanford University Press.

Barthold, V. V. 1956. *Four Studies on the History of Central Asia.* Leiden: Brill.

Bartlett, Robert. 1994. *The Making of Europe: Conquest, Colonization and Cultural Change, 950–1350.* Princeton: Princeton University Press.

Barton, Carlin. 2007. "The Price of Peace in Ancient Rome." In Kurt A. Raaflaub, ed., *War and Peace in the Ancient World.* Oxford: Blackwell.

Bartov, Omer. 1985. *The Eastern Front, 1941–1945: German Troops and the Barbarisation of Warfare.* London: Macmillan.

———. 1991. *Hitler's Army: Soldiers, Nazis, and War in the Third Reich.* Oxford: Oxford University Press.

Bateman, Robert. 2002. *No Gun Ri: A Military History of the Korean War Incident.* Mechanicsburg, Pa.: Stackpole.

Battaglino, Jorge Mario. 2012. "The Coexistence of Peace and Conflict in South America: Toward a New Conceptualization of Types of Peace." *Revista Brasileira de Política Internacional* 55:131–51.

Beard, Mary. 2015. *SPQR: A History of Ancient Rome.* London: Profile Books.

Beard, Mary, and Michael Crawford. 1985. *Rome in the Late Republic: Problems and Interpretations.* London: Duckworth.

Beard, Steven. 2018. "Is There Really Evidence for a Decline of War?" *One Earth Future Research*, May 8. https://oefresearch.org/think-peace/evidence-decline-war.

Becker, Jean-Jacques. 1977. *1914: Comment les français sont entrés dans la guerre*. Paris: Presses de la Fondation Nationale des Sciences Politiques.

———. 1985. *The Great War and the French People*. Translated by Arnold Pomerans. Leamington Spa, U.K.: Berg.

Beckham, J. C., et al. 1998. "Atrocities Exposure in Vietnam Combat Veterans with Chronic Posttraumatic Stress Disorder: Relationship to Combat Exposure, Symptom Severity, Guilt, and Interpersonal Violence." *Journal of Traumatic Stress* 11:777–85.

Beevor, Anthony. 1998. *Stalingrad: The Fateful Siege, 1942–1943*. New York: Viking.

Bender, John. 2008. "The Last Man Standing: Causes of Daimyo Survival in Sixteenth Century Japan." MA dissertation, University of Hawai'i.

Benson, John, and Takao Matsumura. 2001. *From Isolation to Occupation: Japan, 1868–1945*. Harlow, U.K.: Longman.

Berdan, Frances. 2014. *Aztec Archaeology and Ethnohistory*. New York: Cambridge University Press.

———. 2021. *The Aztecs: Lost Civilizations*. London: Reaktion.

Berger, Gordon. 1977. *Parties Out of Power in Japan, 1931–1941*. Princeton: Princeton University Press.

Berry, Mary. 1982. *Hideyoshi*. Cambridge: Harvard University Press.

———. 1986. "Public Peace and Private Attachment: The Goals and Conduct of Power in Early Modern Japan." *Journal of Japanese Studies* 12:237–71.

———. 1994. *The Culture of Civil War in Kyoto*. Berkeley: University of California Press.

———. 2005. "Presidential Address: Samurai Trouble: Thoughts on War and Loyalty." *Journal of Asian Studies* 64:831–47.

Bethell, Leslie. 1996. *The Paraguayan War (1864–1870)*. University of London Institute of Latin American Studies, research paper no. 46.

Biran, Michal. 2004. "The Mongol Transformation: From the Steppe to Eurasian Empire." *Medieval Encounters* 10:338–61.

———. 2017. "Periods of Non-Han Rule." In Michael Szonyi, ed., *A Companion to Chinese History*, 129–42. Oxford: Wiley Blackwell.

———. 2018. "Violence and Non-Violence in the Mongol Conquest of Baghdad." In Robert Gleave and István Kristó-Nagy, eds., *Violence in Islamic Thought from the Mongols to European Imperialism*, 15–31. Edinburgh: Edinburgh University Press.

[Birtle, A. J.]. 2006. *The Korean War: Years of Stalemate*. Washington, D.C.: U.S. Army Center for Military History.

Bisson, Thomas. 2009. *The Crisis of the Twelfth Century: Power, Leadership, and the Origins of European Government*. Princeton: Princeton University Press.

Bix, Herbert. 2001. *Hirohito and the Making of Modern Japan*. New York: Harper-Collins.

Black, Jeremy. 1998. *Why Wars Happen*. London: Reaktion.

Blainey, Geoffrey. 1971. "The Scapegoat Theory of International War." *Australian Historical Studies* 15, no. 57: 72–87.

———. 1988. *The Causes of War*. 3rd edition. New York: Free Press.

Blake, Joseph. 1970. "The Organization as Instrument of Violence: The Military Case." *Sociological Quarterly* 11:291–432.

Blanton, Richard, et al. 1993. *Ancient Mesoamerica: A Comparison of Change in Three Regions*. Cambridge: Cambridge University Press.

Blaydes, Lisa. 2018. *State of Repression: Iraq under Saddam Hussein*. Princeton: Princeton University Press.

Blechman, Barry, and Stephen S. Kaplan. 1978. *Force without War: U.S. Armed Forces as a Political Instrument*. Washington, D.C.: Brookings Institution.

Boff, Jonathan. 2014. "The Morale Maze: The German Army in Late 1918." *Journal of Strategic Studies* 37:855–78.

Bond, Brian. 2002. *The Unquiet Western Front: Britain's Role in Literature and History*. New York: Cambridge University Press.

Bourke, Joanna. 1999. *An Intimate History of Killing: Face-to-Face Killing in Twentieth-Century Warfare*. New York: Basic Books.

———. 2005. *Fear: A Cultural History*. London: Virago.

Braumoeller, Bear. 2019. *Only the Dead: The Persistence of War in the Modern Age*. New York: Oxford University Press.

Bray, Tamara. 1992. "Archaeological Survey in Northern Highland Ecuador: Inca Imperialism and the País Caranqui." *World Archaeology* 24:218–33.

Brereton Report. 2020. Inspector-General of the Australian Defence Force. Afghanistan Inquiry Report. Canberra.

Brooks, Barbara. 2000. *Japan's Imperial Diplomacy: Consuls, Treaty Ports, and War in China, 1895–1938*. Honolulu: University of Hawai'i Press.

Brown, Dee. 1970. *Bury My Heart at Wounded Knee*. New York: Holt, Rinehart & Winston.

Brunt, Peter. 1971. *Italian Manpower, 225 B.C.–A.D. 14*. Oxford: Clarendon Press.

———. 2004. "Laus Imperii." In Craig Champion, ed., *Roman Imperialism: Readings and Sources*. Oxford: Blackwell.

Bueno de Mesquita, Bruce. 1981. *The War Trap*. New Haven: Yale University Press.

Bueno de Mesquita, Bruce, and David Lalman. 1988. "Empirical Support for Systemic and Dyadic Explanations of International Conflict." *World Politics* 41:1–20.

Bueno de Mesquita, Bruce, and Alastair Smith. 2012. "Domestic Explanations of International Relations." *Annual Review of Political Science* 15:161–81.

Bull, Hedley. 2002. *The Anarchical Society: A Study of Order in World Politics*. 3rd edition. New York: Columbia University Press.

Buncombe, Andrew. 2005. "US Forced to Import Bullets from Israel as Troops Use 250,000 for Every Rebel Killed." *Independent*, September 25.

Burr, Robert. 1967. *By Reason or Force: Chile and the Balancing of Power in South America, 1830–1905*. Berkeley: University of California Press.

Caillois, Roger. 1939. *L'homme et le sacré*. Paris: Gallimard.

———. 2012 [1950]. *Bellone ou la pente de la guerre*. Paris: Flammarion.

Callimachi, Rukmini. 2018. "The ISIS Files." *New York Times*, April 4.

Cameron, Craig. 1994. *American Samurai: Myth, Imagination, and the Conduct of Battle in the First Marine Division, 1941–1951*. Cambridge: Cambridge University Press.

Caplan, Richard, and Anke Hoeffler. 2017. "Why Peace Endures: An Analysis of Post-Conflict Stabilization." *European Journal of International Security* 2:133–52.

Carter, David, and H. E. Goemans. 2014. "The Temporal Dynamics of New International Borders." *Conflict Management and Peace Science* 31:285–302.

Cederman, Lars-Erik, Camber Warren, and Didier Sornette. 2011. "Testing Clausewitz: Nationalism, Mass Mobilization, and the Severity of War." *International Organization* 65:605–38.

Centeno, Miguel. 2002. *Blood and Debt: War and the Nation-State in Latin America*. College Park: Pennsylvania State University Press.

Cervantes, Fernando. 2020. *Conquistadores: A New History of Spanish Discovery and Conquest*. London: Penguin.

Cha, Myung Soon. 2000. "The Colonial Origins of Korea's Market Economy." In A. J. H. Latham and Heita Kawakatsu, eds., *Asia-Pacific Dynamism, 1550–2000*. London: Routledge.

Chambers, John Whiteclay. 2003. "S. L. A. Marshall's Men against Fire: New Evidence Regarding Fire Ratios." *Parameters* 33, article no. 6., U.S. Military War College.

Chancey, Jennie Ethell, and William Forstchen. 2000. *Hot Shots: An Oral History of the Air Force Combat Pilots of the Korean War*. New York: Morrow.

Chappelle, Wayne, et al. 2010. "Prevalence of High Emotional Distress and Symptoms of Post-Traumatic Stress Disorder in U.S. Air Force Active Duty Remotely Piloted Aircraft Operators." https:// apps.dtic.mil/sti/citations/ ADA577055.

Chappelle, Wayne, et al. 2014. "Symptoms of Psychological Distress and Post-Traumatic Stress Disorder in United States Air Force 'Drone' Operators." *Military Medicine* 179:63–70.

Cheney, Dick. 2003. Interview by Tim Russert. *Meet the Press*, NBC News, March 16. https://www.nbcnews.com/id/wbna3080244.

Chesterton, Bridget. 2013. *The Grandchildren of Solano López: Frontier and Nation in Paraguay, 1904–1936*. Albuquerque: University of New Mexico Press.

Chia, Ning. 1993. "The Lifanyuan and the Inner Asian Rituals in the Early Qing (1644–1795)." *Late Imperial China* 14:60–92.

Chou, Wan-yao. 1996. "The Kominka Movement in Taiwan and Korea." In Peter Duus et al., eds., *The Japanese Wartime Empire, 1931–1945*. Princeton: Princeton University Press.

Christensen, Jonas. 2004. "Warfare in the European Neolithic." *Acta Archaeologica* 75:129–56.

Cintino, Robert. 2017. *The Wehrmacht's Last Stand: The German Campaigns of 1944–1945*. Lawrence: University Press of Kansas.

Cirillo, Pasquale, and Nassim Nicholas Taleb. 2016. "The Decline of Violent Conflicts: What Do the Data Really Say?" *Nobel Foundation Symposium 161: The Causes of Peace*. https://www.fooledbyrandomness.com/violencenobelsymposium.pdf.

Clark, Christopher. 2012. *The Sleepwalkers: How Europe Went to War in 1914*. London: Allen Lane.

Clark, Jessica. 2014. *Triumph in Defeat: Military Loss in the Roman Republic*. Oxford: Oxford University Press.

Clarke, Humphrey. 2011. "How Bad Were the Mongols?" *Quodlibeta* blog, December 13. https://bedejournal.blogspot.com/search?q=how+bad+were+the+mongols%3F.

Clauset, Aaron. 2018. "Trends and Fluctuations in the Severity of Interstate Wars." *Science Advances* 4, no. 2. https://www.science.org/doi/10.1126/sciadv.aao3580.

Clausewitz, Carl von. 1976 [1832]. *On War*. Edited by Michael Howard and Peter Paret. Princeton: Princeton University Press.

Cochet, François. 2005. *Survivre au front, 1914–1918: Les poilus entre contrainte et consentement*. Saint-Cloud: 14–18 Éditions.

Cockerham, William, and Lawrence Cohen. 1981. "Volunteering for Foreign Combat Missions: An Attitudinal Study of U.S. Army Paratroopers." *Pacific Sociological Review* 24:329–54.

Coker, Christopher. 2014. *Can War Be Eliminated?* Cambridge, U.K.: Polity Press.

———. 2021. *Why War?* Oxford: Oxford University Press.

Cole, Chris. 2017. "Interview of Former RAF Reaper Pilot 'Justin Thompson' (a pseudonym)." Drone Wars UK. www.dronewars.net.

Collier, Simon. 2003. *Chile: The Making of a Republic, 1830–1865: Politics and Ideas*. Cambridge: Cambridge University Press.

Collins, Randall. 1974. "Three Faces of Cruelty: Towards a Comparative Sociology of Violence." *Theory and Society* 1:415–40.

———. 2008. *Violence: A Micro-Sociological Theory*. Princeton: Princeton University Press.

Conlan, Thomas. 2003. *State of War: The Violent Order of Fourteenth-Century Japan*. Ann Arbor: University of Michigan Press.

Conway-Lanz, Sahr. 2005. "Beyond No Gun Ri: Refugees and the United States Military in the Korean War." *Diplomatic History* 29:49–81.

Cooney, Mark. 1997. "The Decline of Elite Homicide." *Criminology* 35:381–407.

Cooper, Hélène, Maggie Haberman, and Thomas Gibbons-Neff. 2019. "Trump Says He Intervened in War Crimes Cases to Protect 'Warriors.'" *New York Times*, November 26.

Corbacho, Alejandro. 2003. "Predicting the Probability of War during Brink-manship Crises: The Beagle and the Malvinas Conflicts." Universidad del CEMA Documento de Trabajo no. 244.

Covey, Alan. 2020. *Inca Apocalypse: The Spanish Conquest and the Transformation of the Andean World*. Oxford: Oxford University Press.

Cox, Robert. 1981. "Social Forces, States and World Orders: Beyond International Relations Theory." *Millennium: Journal of International Studies* 10:126–55.

Crane, Stephen. 1895. *The Red Badge of Courage*. New York: Appleton.

Crawford, Neta. 2007. "The Long Peace among Iroquois Nations." In Kurt Raaflaub, ed., *War and Peace in the Ancient World*, 348–68. Oxford: Blackwell.

———. 2015. "War-Related Death, Injury, and Displacement in Afghanistan and Pakistan, 2001–2014." Costs of War Project. Watson Institute, Brown University.

———. 2021. "The U.S. Budgetary Costs of Post-9/11 Wars." Costs of War Project. Watson Institute, Brown University.

Cumings, Bruce. 2010. *The Korean War: A History*. New York: Modern Library.

Dabringhaus, Sabine. 2011. "The Monarch and Inner-Outer Court Dualism in Late Imperial China." In Jeroen Duindam et al., eds., *Royal Courts in Dynastic States and Empires: A Global Perspective*, 265–87. Leiden: Brill.

Dai, Yingcong. 2004. "A Disguised Defeat: The Myanmar Campaign of the Qing Dynasty." *Modern Asian Studies* 38:145–89.

Daley, Paul. 2014. "Why the Number of Indigenous Deaths in the Frontier Wars Matters." *Guardian*, July 15.

Dalrymple, William. 2019. *The Anarchy: The East India Company, Corporate Violence, and the Pillage of an Empire*. London: Bloomsbury.

D'Altroy, Terence. 2014. *The Incas*. 2nd edition. Malden, Mass.: Wiley-Blackwell.

Daniel, Douglas. 1992. "Tactical Factors in the Spanish Conquest of the Aztecs." *Anthropological Quarterly* 65:187–94.

Dardess, John W. 2012. *Ming China, 1368–1644: A Concise History of a Resilient Empire*. Lanham, Md.: Rowman & Littlefield.

Davies, Norman. 2011. *Vanished Kingdoms: The History of Half-Forgotten Europe*. London: Allen Lane.

De Bary, Theodore, and Irene Bloom. 1999. *Sources of Chinese Tradition*, vol. 1. 2nd edition. New York: Columbia University Press.

De Crespigny, Rafe. 2016. *Fire over Luoyang: A History of the Later Han Dynasty, 23–220 AD*. Leiden: Brill.

Deng, Kent. 2015. "China's Population Expansion and Its Causes during the Qing Period, 1644–1911." London School of Economics, Department of Economic History, Working Paper no. 219.

Deng, Kent, and Lucy Zheng. 2015. "Economic Restructuring and Demographic Growth: Demystifying Growth and Development in Northern Song China, 960–1127." *Economic History Review* 68:1107–31.

Dennis, Paul, et al. 2016. "Moral Transgression during the Vietnam War: A Path Analysis of the Psychological Impact of Veterans' Involvement in Wartime

Atrocities." U.S. Department of Veteran Affairs. https://www.ncbi.nlm.nih.gov/pmc/articles/PMC5299042/.

Derluguian, Georgi. 2021. "A Small World War." *New Left Review* 128 (March–April): 25–46.

Desch, Michael. 2002. "Democracy and Victory: Why Regime Type Hardly Matters." *International Security* 27:5–47.

De Souza, Philip. 2008. *The Ancient World at War: A Global History*. London: Thames and Hudson.

De Weerdt, Hilde. 2016. *Information, Territory, and Networks: The Crisis and Maintenance of Empire in Song China*. Cambridge: Harvard University Asia Center.

Dickinson, Frederic. 1999. *War and National Reinvention: Japan in the Great War, 1914–1919*. Cambridge: Harvard University Press.

Di Cosmo, Nicola. 2002a. *Ancient China and Its Enemies: The Rise of Nomadic Power in East Asian History*. Cambridge: Cambridge University Press.

———. 2002b. "Introduction: Inner Asian Ways of Warfare in Historical Perspective." In Di Cosmo, ed., *Warfare in Inner Asian History (500–1800)*. Leiden: Brill.

———, ed. 2009. *Military Culture in Imperial China*. Cambridge: Harvard University Press.

Dodwell, Brian, et al. 2016. *The Caliphate's Global Workforce: An Inside Look at the Islamic State's Foreign Fighter Paper Trail*. West Point, N.Y.: Combating Terrorism Center.

Dolfini, Andrea, et al., eds. 2018. *Prehistoric Warfare and Violence: Quantitative Methods in the Humanities and Social Sciences*. New York: Springer.

Dollard, John, with Donald Horton. 1943. *Fear in Battle*. New Haven: Institute of Human Relations, Yale University.

Dominguez, Jorge, and David Mares. 2003. *Boundary Disputes in Latin America*. Washington, D.C.: United States Institute of Peace.

Donnell, John, et al. 1965. *Viet Cong Motivation and Morale in 1964*. Report prepared for the Office of the Assistant Secretary of Defense. Santa Monica: Rand Corp.

Donner, Fred. 2007. "Fight for God—but Do So with Kindness." In Kurt Raaflaub, ed., *War and Peace in the Ancient World*. Oxford: Blackwell.

Downes, Alexander. 2009. "How Smart and Tough Are Democracies? Reassessing Theories of Democratic Victory in War." *International Security* 33:9–51.

Draper, Robert. 2020. *To Start a War: How the Bush Administration Took America into Iraq*. New York: Penguin.

Dupuy, Kendra, et al. 2017. *Trends in Armed Conflict, 1946–2016*. Oslo: Oslo Peace Research Institute.

Durand, John. 1960. "The Population Statistics of China, A.D. 2–1953." *Population Studies* 13:209–56.

Durham, William. 1979. *Scarcity and Survival in Central America: Ecological Origins of the Soccer War*. Stanford: Stanford University Press.

Du Roy, Ivan, and Ludo Simbille. 2018. "Décès au contact des forces de l'ordre: Une nouvelle mise à jour de notre base de données." *Basta*, December 4. https://basta.media/Deces-au-contact-des-forces-de-l-ordre-une-nouvelle-mise-a-jour-de-notre-base.

Duus, Peter. 1995. *The Abacus and the Sword: The Japanese Penetration of Korea, 1895–1910*. Berkeley: University of California Press.

Duus, Peter, et al., eds. 1996. *The Japanese Wartime Empire, 1931–1945*. Princeton: Princeton University Press.

Dyer, Gwynne. 1985. *War*. New York: Crown.

Eckert, Carter. 1996. "Total War, Industrialization and Social Change in Late Colonial Korea." In Peter Duus et al., eds., *The Japanese Wartime Empire, 1931–1945*. Princeton: Princeton University Press.

Eckhardt, William. 1989. "Civilian Deaths in Wartime." *Bulletin of Peace Proposals* 20:89–98.

———. 1992. *Civilizations, Empires, and Wars: A Quantitative History of War*. Jefferson, N.C.: McFarland.

Eckstein, Arthur. 2006. *Mediterranean Anarchy, Interstate War, and the Rise of Rome*. Berkeley: University of California Press.

Edwards, Paul. 2006. *The Korean War*. Westport, Conn.: Greenwood Press.

———. 2018. *The Mistaken History of the Korean War*. Jefferson, N.C.: McFarland.

Einsiedel, Sebastian von. 2017. "Civil War Trends and the Changing Nature of Armed Conflict." *United Nations University Centre for Policy Research Occasional Paper* no. 10.

Eisenhower, Dwight D. 1953. Address to the American Society of Newspaper Editors, Statler Hotel, Washington, D.C., April 16.

Eisner, Manuel. 2003. "Long-Term Historical Trends in Violent Crime." *Crime and Justice* 30:83–142.

———. 2014. "From Swords to Words: Does Macro-Level Change in Self-Control Predict Long-Term Variation in Levels of Homicide?" *Crime and Justice* 43. https://www.journals.uchicago.edu/doi/abs/10.1086/677662?journalCode=cj.

Elias, Norbert. 2012. *On the Process of Civilisation: Sociogenetic and Psychogenetic Investigations*. Translated by Edmund Jephcott. Dublin: University College Dublin Press.

Elliott, David. 2003. *The Vietnamese War: Revolution and Social Change in the Mekong Delta, 1930–1975*, 2 vols. Armonk, N.Y.: M. E. Sharpe.

Elliott, Mai. 2010. *RAND in Southeast Asia: A History of the Vietnam War Era*. Santa Monica: Rand Corp.

Elliott, Mark. 2001. *The Manchu Way: The Eight Banners and Ethnic Identity in Late Imperial China*. Stanford: Stanford University Press.

———. 2009. *Emperor Qianlong: Son of Heaven, Man of the World*. New York: Pearson.

Ellis, Geoffrey. 2003. *The Napoleonic Empire*. 2nd edition. New York: Palgrave Macmillan.

Elvin, Mark. 2004. *The Retreat of the Elephants: An Environmental History of China*. New Haven: Yale University Press.

Ember, Carol R., and Melvin Ember. 1997. "Violence in the Ethnographic Record: Results of Cross-Cultural Research on War and Aggression." In Debra L. Martin and David W. Frayer, eds., *Troubled Times: Violence and Warfare in the Past*. New York: Routledge.

Engen, Robert. 2008. "Killing for Their Country: A New Look at 'Killology.'" *Canadian Military History* 9:20–28.

———. 2009. *Canadians under Fire: Infantry Effectiveness in the Second World War*. Montreal: McGill-Queen's University Press.

———. 2011. "S. L. A Marshall and the Ratio of Fire: History, Interpretation, and the Canadian Experience." *Canadian Military History* 20:39–48.

Erskine, Andrew. 2010. *Roman Imperialism*. Edinburgh: Edinburgh University Press.

Etemad, Bouda. 2007. *Possessing the World: Taking the Measurement of Colonisation from the Eighteenth to the Twentieth Century*. New York: Berghahn Books.

Evans, David, and Mark Peattie. 1997. *Kaigun: Strategy, Tactics, and Technology in the Imperial Japanese Navy, 1887–1941*. Annapolis: Naval Institute Press.

Evans, Raymond, and Robert Ørsted-Jensen. 2014. "'I Cannot Say the Numbers That Were Killed': Assessing Violent Mortality on the Queensland Frontier." https://ssrn.com/abstract=2467836.

Fairbank, John, ed. 1968. *The Chinese World Order: Traditional China's Foreign Relations*. Cambridge: Cambridge University Press.

———. 1974. "Introduction: Varieties of the Chinese Military Experience." In Frank Kiernan and John Fairbank, eds., *Chinese Ways of Warfare*. Cambridge: Harvard University Press.

Falkenhausen, Lothar von. 1999. "The Waning of the Bronze Age: Material Culture and Social Developments, 770–481 B.C." In Michael Loewe and Edward Shaughnessy, eds., *The Cambridge History of Ancient China: From the Origins of Civilization to 221 B.C.* Cambridge: Cambridge University Press.

Farris, William. 2006. *Japan's Medieval Population: Famine, Fertility, and Warfare in a Transformative Age*. Honolulu: University of Hawai'i Press.

Fazal, Tanisha. 2004. "State Death in the International System." *International Organization* 58:311–44.

———. 2007. *State Death: The Politics and Geography of Conquest, Occupation, and Annexation*. Princeton: Princeton University Press.

Fearon, James. 1994. "Domestic Political Audiences and the Escalation of International Disputes." *American Political Science Review* 88, no. 3: 577–92.

———. 1995. "Rationalist Explanations for War." *International Organization* 49:379–414.

Fearon, James, and David Laitin. 2003. "Ethnicity, Insurgency and Civil War." *American Political Science Review* 97, no. 1: 75–90.

Fehrenbach T. R. 1963. *This Kind of War: The Classic Korean War History*. New York: Macmillan.

Fennell, Jonathan. 2011. *Combat and Morale in the North African Campaign*. Cambridge: Cambridge University Press.

Ferejohn, John, and Frances Rosenbuth, eds. 2010. *War and State Building in Medieval Japan*. Stanford: Stanford University Press.

Ferguson, Brian. 1995. *Yanomami Warfare: A Political History*. Santa Fe, N.M.: School of American Research Press.

———. 1997. "Review of Lawrence Keeley, *War before Civilization: The Myth of the Peaceful Savage*." *American Anthropologist* 99:424–25.

———. 2003. "Introduction: Violent Conflict and Control of the State." In Ferguson, ed., *The State, Identity, and Violence: Political Disintegration in the Post–Cold War World*. London: Routledge.

———. 2013a. "Pinker's List—Exaggerating Prehistoric War Mortality." In Douglas Fry, ed., *War, Peace, and Human Nature: The Convergence of Evolutionary and Cultural Views*, 112–31. New York: Oxford University Press.

———. 2013b. "The Prehistory of War and Peace in Europe and the Near East." In Douglas Fry, ed., *War, Peace, and Human Nature: The Convergence of Evolutionary and Cultural Views*, 191–240. New York: Oxford University Press.

Ferguson, Niall. 1999. *The Pity of War: Explaining World War I*. New York: Basic Books.

———. 2006. *The War of the World: Twentieth-Century Conflict and the Descent of the West*. New York: Penguin.

Finkel, David. 2013. "The Return: The Traumatized Veterans of Iraq and Afghanistan." *New Yorker*, September 9.

Fishman, Brian, and Joseph Felter. 2007. *Al-Qa'ida's Foreign Fighters in Iraq*. West Point, N.Y.: Combating Terrorism Center.

Fitzgerald, Charles. 1961. *China: A Short Cultural History*. 3rd edition. New York: Praeger.

Flory, Stewart. 2006. "Review of Hanson: *A War Like No Other*." *Bryn Mawr Classical Review*. https://bmcr.brynmawr.edu/2006/2006.03.40/.

Franchi, Tassio, et al. 2017. "Taxonomy of Interstate Conflicts: Is South America a Peaceful Region?" *Brazilian Political Science Review* 11:1–23.

Franke, Herbert. 1983. "Sung Embassies: Some General Observations." In Morris Rossabi, ed., *China among Equals: The Middle Kingdom and Its Neighbors, 10th–14th Centuries*. Berkeley: University of California Press.

Frankopan, Peter. 2015. *The Silk Roads: A New History of the World*. London: Bloomsbury.

Friday, Karl. 2004. *Samurai, Warfare and the State in Early Medieval Japan*. New York: Routledge.

Friedrich, Tobias, et al. 2016. "Nonlinear Climate Sensitivity and Its Implications for Future Greenhouse Warming." *Science Advances* 2, no. 11.

Fritz, Stephen. 1995. *Frontsoldaten: The German Soldier in World War II*. Lexington: University Press of Kentucky.

Fry, Douglas. 2007. *Beyond War: The Human Potential for Peace*. New York: Oxford University Press.

———, ed. 2013. *War, Peace, and Human Nature: The Convergence of Evolutionary and Cultural Views*. Oxford: Oxford University Press.

Fry, Douglas, and Patrik Söderberg. 2013. "Lethal Aggression in Mobile Forager Bands and Implications for the Origins of War." *Science* 341:270–73.

Fukuyama, Francis. 2011. *The Origins of Political Order: From Prehuman Times to the French Revolution*. New York: Farrar, Straus & Giroux.

Gal, Reuven. 1986. *A Portrait of the Israeli Soldier*. Westport, Conn.: Greenwood.

Garon, Sheldon. 1987. *The State and Labor in Modern Japan*. Berkeley: University of California Press.

Gat, Azar. 2006. *War in Human Civilization*. New York: Oxford University Press.

———. 2017. *The Causes of War and the Spread of Peace*. Oxford: Oxford University Press.

Gee, David. 2007. *Informed Choice? Armed Forces Recruitment Practice in the United Kingdom*. foreceswatch.net/wp-content/uploads/informedchoicefull.pdf.

George, Alexander. 1967. *The Chinese Communist Army in Action: The Korean War and Its Aftermath*. New York: Columbia University Press.

Ghosn, Faten, et al. 2004. "The MID3 Data Set, 1993–2001: Procedures, Coding Rules, and Description." *Conflict Management and Peace Science* 21:133–54.

Gibbons-Neff, Thomas. 2021. "Documents Reveal U.S. Officials Misled Public on War in Afghanistan." *New York Times*, August 29.

Gibler, Douglas. 2012. *The Territorial Peace: Borders, State Development, and International Conflict*. Cambridge: Cambridge University Press.

Giersch, C. Patterson. 2006. *Asian Borderlands: The Transformation of Qing China's Yunnan Frontier*. Cambridge: Harvard University Press.

Giessauf, Johannes. 2011. "A Programme of Terror and Cruelty: Aspects of Mongol Strategy in the Light of Western Sources." In Frank Krämer, Katharina Schmidt, and Julika Singer, eds., *Historicizing the "Beyond": The Mongolian Invasion as a New Dimension of Violence?* Heidelberg: Universitätsverlag Winter.

Gilbert, Gustav. 1947. *Nuremberg Diary*. New York: Farrar, Straus.

Gillespie, Colin. 2017. "Estimating the Number of Casualties in the American Indian War: A Bayesian Analysis Using the Power Distribution Law." *Annals of Applied Statistics* 4:2357–74.

Ginkel, Bibi van, and Eva Entenmann, eds. 2016. *The Foreign Fighters Phenomenon in the European Union: Profiles, Threats & Policies*. The Hague: International Centre for Counter-Terrorism.

Gittings, John. 2012. "The Conflict between War and Peace in Early Chinese Thought." *Asia-Pacific Journal* 10, no. 12. https://apjjf.org/2012/10/12/John-Gittings/3725/article.html.

Gleditsch, Kristian Skrede. 2004. "A Revised List of Wars between and within Independent States, 1816–2001." *International Interactions* 30, no. 4: 231–62.

Gleditsch, K. S., and S. Pickering. 2014. "Wars Are Becoming Less Frequent: A Response to Harrison and Wolf." *Economic History Review* 67:214–30.

Glenn, Russell. 2000. *Reading Athena's Dance Card: Men against Fire in Vietnam*. Annapolis: Naval Institute Press.

Gluck, Carol. 1985. *Japan's Modern Myths: Ideology in the Late Meiji Period*. Princeton: Princeton University Press.

Go, Julian. 2013. "Sociology's Imperial Unconscious: Early American Sociology in a Global Context." In George Steinmetz, ed., *Sociology and Empire*, 83–105. Durham: Duke University Press.

Gochman, Charles S., and Zeev Maoz. 1984. "Militarized Interstate Disputes, 1816–1976: Procedures, Patterns, and Insights." *Journal of Conflict Resolution* 28:585–615.

Goertz, Gary, et al. 2016. *The Puzzle of Peace: The Evolution of Peace in the International System*. Oxford: Oxford University Press.

Goldstein, Joshua. 2011. *Winning the War on War: The Decline of Armed Conflict Worldwide*. New York: Dutton.

Goldsworthy, Adrian. 1996. *The Roman Army at War, 100 BC–AD 200*. Oxford: Clarendon Press.

Gordon, Andrew. 1985. *The Evolution of Labor Relations in Japan: Heavy Industry, 1853–1955*. Cambridge: Harvard University Press.

———. 1991. *Labor and Imperial Democracy in Prewar Japan*. Berkeley: University of California Press.

Gouré, Leon, Anthony J. Russo, and Douglas Scott. 1966. *Some Findings of the Viet Cong Motivation and Morale Study: June–December 1965*. Report prepared for the Office of the Assistant Secretary of Defense. Santa Monica: Rand Corp.

Graeber, David, and David Wengrow. 2021. *The Dawn of Everything: A New History of Humanity*. New York: Farrar, Straus and Giroux.

Grafe, Regina, and Maria Alejandra Irigoin. 2006. "The Spanish Empire and Its Legacy: Fiscal Redistribution and Political Conflict in Colonial and Post-Colonial Spanish America." *Journal of Global History* 1:214–67.

Graff, David. 2002. *Medieval Chinese Warfare, 300–900*. London: Routledge.

Greitens, Sheena, et al. 2020. "Understanding China's 'Preventive Repression' in Xinjiang." Brookings Institution, March 4. https://www.brookings.edu/blog/order-from-chaos/2020/03/04/understanding-chinas-preventive-repression-in-xinjiang/.

Griffith, Paddy. 1989. *Battle Tactics of the Civil War*. New Haven: Yale University Press.

Grinin, Leonid. 2019. "Islamism and Globalization." *Journal of Globalization Studies* 10:21–36.

Grinin, Leonid, and Andrey Korotayev. 2015. *Great Divergence and Great Convergence: A Global Perspective*. Cham: Springer.

Grossman, Dave. 1995. *On Killing: The Psychological Cost of Learning to Kill in War and Society*. Boston: Little, Brown.

Gruen, Erich. 1986. *The Hellenistic World and the Coming of Rome*. 2 vols. Berkeley: University of California Press.

———. 2004. "Material Rewards and the Drive for Empire." In Craig Champion, ed., *Roman Imperialism: Readings and Sources*. Oxford: Blackwell.

Gumplowicz, Ludwig. 1899. *The Outlines of Sociology*. Philadelphia: American Academy of Political and Social Sciences.

Gurney, Gene. 1958. *Five Down and Glory: A History of the American Air Ace*. New York: Arno.

Haftel, Yoram. 2007. "Designing for Peace: Regional Integration Arrangements, Institutional Variation, and Militarized Interstate Disputes." *International Organization* 61:217–37.

Hagopian, Amy, Abraham Flaxman, Tim Takaro, et al. 2013. "Mortality in Iraq Associated with the 2003–2011 War and Occupation: Findings from a National Cluster Sample Survey by the University Collaborative Iraq Mortality Study." *PLOS Medicine*. https://journals.plos.org/plosmedicine/article?id=10.1371/journal.pmed.1001533.

Halberstam, David. 1972. *The Best and the Brightest*. New York: Random House.

Halsall, Guy. 2007. *Barbarian Migrations and the Roman West, 376–568*. Cambridge: Cambridge University Press.

Hamner, Christopher. 2011. *Enduring Battle: American Soldiers in Three Wars, 1776–1945*. Lawrence: University Press of Kansas.

Hane, Mikiso. 1992. *Modern Japan: A Historical Survey*. Boulder, Colo.: Westview.

Hansen, Stig Jarle. 2013. *Al-Shabaab in Somalia: The History and Ideology of a Militant Islamist Group, 2005–2012*. Oxford: Oxford University Press.

Hansen, Valerie. 2019. "The Kitan-Liao and Jurchen-Jin." In Victor Cunrui Xiong and Kenneth J. Hammond, eds., *The Routledge Handbook to Imperial Chinese History*, 212–28. New York: Routledge.

Hanson, Victor. 2005. *A War Like No Other: How the Athenians and Spartans Fought the Peloponnesian War*. New York: Random House.

Harrer, G. A. 1918. "Cicero on Peace and War." *Classical Journal* 14:26–38.

Harris, William. 1979. *War and Imperialism in Republican Rome, 327–70 B.C.* Oxford: Clarendon Press.

———. 2016. *Roman Power: A Thousand Years of Empire*. Cambridge: Cambridge University Press.

Harrison, Mark. 1988. "Resource Mobilization for World War II: The U.S.A., U.K., U.S.S.R., and Germany, 1938–1945." *Economic History Review* 41:171–92.

Harrison, Mark, and Nikolaus Wolf. 2012. "The Frequency of Wars." *Economic History Review* 65:1055–76.

———. 2014. "The Frequency of Wars: Reply to Gleditsch and Pickering." *Economic History Review* 67:231–39.

Hassig, Ross. 1988. *Aztec Warfare: Imperial Expansion and Political Control*. Norman: University of Oklahoma Press.

———. 2007. "Peace, Reconciliation, and Alliance in Aztec Mexico." In Kurt Raaflaub, ed., *War and Peace in the Ancient World*, 312–38. Oxford: Blackwell.

Hata, Ikuhiko. 1988. "Continental Expansion, 1905–1941." In Peter Duus, ed., *The Cambridge History of Japan*, vol. 6, *The Twentieth Century*. Cambridge: Cambridge University Press.

Hattenstone, Simon, and Eric Allison. 2014. "Post-Traumatic Stress Disorder." *Guardian*, October 24.

Hayden, Brian. 2001. "Richman, Poorman, Beggarman, Chief: The Dynamics of Social Inequality." In G. Feinman and T. Price, eds., *Archaeology at the Millennium: A Sourcebook*, 231–72. New York: Springer.

Heather, Peter. 2010. *Empires and Barbarians: The Fall of Rome and the Birth of Europe*. Oxford: Oxford University Press.

Hegghammer, Thomas. 2021. "Resistance Is Futile: The War on Terror Super-charged State Power." *Foreign Affairs*, September–October. https://omnilogos.com/resistance-is-futile-war-on-terror-supercharged-state-power/.

Hellbeck, Jochen. 2015. *Stalingrad: The City That Defeated the Third Reich*. New York: Public Affairs.

Henderson, Peter. 2016. "Border Wars in South America during the 19th Century." *Oxford Research Encyclopedia of Latin American History*. https://oxfordre.com/latinamericanhistory.

Henderson, William Darryl. 1979. *Why the Vietcong Fought: A Study of Motivation and Control in a Modern Army in Combat*. Westport, Conn.: Greenwood.

Hendin, Herbert. 1991. "Suicide and Guilt as Manifestations of PTSD in Vietnam Combat Veterans." *American Journal of Psychiatry* 148:586–91.

Hensel, Paul. 1994. "One Thing Leads to Another: Recurrent Militarized Disputes in Latin America, 1816–1986." *Journal of Peace Research* 31:281–97.

———. 2002. "The More Things Change . . .: Recognizing and Responding to Trends in Armed Conflict." *Conflict Management and Peace Science* 19:27–53.

Herring, Eric, and Glen Rangwala. 2006. *Iraq in Fragments: The Occupation and Its Legacy*. Ithaca: Cornell University Press.

Hess, Earl. 1997. *The Union Soldier in Battle: Enduring the Ordeal of Combat*. Lawrence: University Press of Kansas.

Hiam, Michael. 2006. *Who the Hell Are We Fighting? The Story of Sam Adams and the Vietnam Intelligence Wars*. South Royalton, Vt.: Steerforth.

Ho, Samuel Pao-San. 1984. "Colonialism and Development: Korea, Taiwan and Kwantung." In Ramon Myers and Mark Peattie, eds., *The Japanese Colonial Empire, 1895–1945*. Princeton: Princeton University Press.

Hoge, C. W., et al. 2004. "Combat Duty in Iraq and Afghanistan, Mental Health Problems, and Barriers to Care." *New England Journal of Medicine* 351:13–22.

Holden, Robert. 2004. *Armies without Nations: Public Violence and State Formation in Central America, 1821–1960*. Oxford: Oxford University Press.

Holmes, Richard. 1985. *Acts of War: The Behavior of Men in Battle*. New York: Free Press.

Holsti, Kalevi. 1991. *Peace and War: Armed Conflicts and International Order, 1648–1989*. Cambridge: Cambridge University Press.

———. 1996. *The State, War, and the State of War*. New York: Cambridge University Press.

Honig, Jan Willem. 2001. "Warfare in the Middle Ages." In Anja Hartmann and Beatrice Heuser, eds., *War, Peace and the World Orders in European History*. London: Routledge.

———. 2012. "Reappraising Late Medieval Strategy: The Example of the 1415 Agincourt Campaign." *War in History* 19:123–51.

Hopkins, Keith. 1977. "Economic Growth and Towns in Classical Antiquity." In Philip Abrams and E. A. Wrigley, eds., *Towns in Societies: Studies in Economic History and Historical Sociology*. Cambridge: Cambridge University Press.

———. 1983. "Murderous Games." In Hopkins, *Death and Renewal*, chap. 1. Cambridge: Cambridge University Press.

Horne, John. 2005. "Entre experience et mémoire: Les soldats français de la grande guerre." *Annales, Histoire, Sciences Sociales*, 60:903–19.

Howard, Michael. 1983. *The Causes of War and Other Essays*. London: T. Smith.

Hoyos, Dexter. 2015. *Mastering the West: Rome and Carthage at War*. New York: Oxford University Press.

———. 2019a. *Carthage's Other Wars: Carthaginian Warfare outside the "Punic Wars" against Rome*. Barnsley, U.K.: Pen and Sword.

———. 2019b. *Rome Victorious: The Irresistible Rise of the Roman Empire*. London: Tauris.

Hsu, Cho-yun. 1965. *Ancient China in Transition: An Analysis in Social Mobility, 722–222 B.C.* Stanford: Stanford University Press.

———. 1999. "The Spring and Autumn Period." In Michael Loewe and Edward L. Shaughnessy, eds., *Cambridge History of Ancient China*. Cambridge: Cambridge University Press.

Hui, Victoria Tin-Bor. 2005. *War and State Formation in Ancient China and Early Modern Europe*. New York: Cambridge University Press.

Humphreys, Leonard. 1995. *The Way of the Heavenly Sword: The Japanese Army in the 1920s*. Stanford: Stanford University Press.

Hunt, David. 2008. *Vietnam's Southern Revolution: From Peasant Insurrection to Total War*. Amherst: University of Massachusetts Press.

Huntington, Samuel. 1996. *The Clash of Civilizations and the Remaking of World Order*. New York: Simon & Schuster.

Hyslop, John. 1984. *The Inka Road System*. Orlando: Academic Press.

Ibn Khaldun. 1958 [1377]. *Muqaddimah: An Introduction to History*. Translated by Franz Rosenthal. Princeton: Princeton University Press.

Ikegami, Eiko. 1995. *The Taming of the Samurai: Honorific Individualism and the Making of Modern Japan*. Cambridge: Harvard University Press.

Ikenberry, John. 2011. *Liberal Leviathan: The Origins, Crisis, and Transformation of the American World Order*. Princeton: Princeton University Press.

International Crisis Group. 2018. "Al-Shabaab Five Years after Westgate: Still a Menace in East Africa." *Report 265*, Africa, September 21.

Iriye, Akira. 1974. "The Failure of Economic Expansionism, 1918–1931." In Bernard Silberman and Harry Harootunian, eds., *Japan in Crisis: Essays on Taishō Democracy*. Princeton: Princeton University Press.

———. 1987. *The Origins of the Second World War in Asia and the Pacific*. New York: Longman.

———. 1991. "Japan's Defense Strategy." *Annals of the American Academy of Political and Social Science* 513:38–47.

———. 1997. *Japan and the Wider World: From the Mid-Nineteenth Century to the Present*. New York: Longman.

Isaac, Barry. 1983. "Aztec Warfare: Goals and Battlefield Comportment." *Ethnology* 22:121–31.

Jackson, Matthew, and Massimo Morelli. 2011. "The Reasons for Wars: An Updated Survey." In Christopher Coyne and Rachel Mathers, eds., *The Handbook on the Political Economy of War*. Cheltenham, U.K.: Edward Elgar.

Jacoby, Tim. 2008. *Understanding Conflict and Violence*. London: Routledge.

Jervis, R. 1978. "Cooperation under the Security Dilemma." *World Politics* 30:186–213.

Joas, Hans. 2003. *War and Modernity*. Translated by Rodney Livingstone. Cambridge, U.K.: Polity.

Joas, Hans, and Wolfgang Knoeble. 2013. *War in Social Thought*. Princeton: Princeton University Press.

Johnston, Alastair. 1995. *Cultural Realism: Strategic Culture and Grand Strategy in Chinese History*. Princeton: Princeton University Press.

———. 1996. "Cultural Realism and Strategy in Maoist China." In Peter Katzenstein, ed., *The Culture of National Security: Norms and Identity in World Politics*, 216–68. New York: Columbia University Press.

Jones, Daniel, et al. 1996. "Militarized Interstate Disputes, 1816–1992: Rationale, Coding Rules and Empirical Patterns." *Conflict Management and Peace Science* 15:163–213.

Jones, Edgar. 2006. "The Psychology of Killing: The Combat Experience of British Soldiers during the First World War." *Journal of Contemporary History* 41:229–46.

Jones, Halbert. 2014. *The War Has Brought Peace to Mexico: World War II and the Consolidation of the Post-Revolutionary State*. Albuquerque: University of New Mexico Press.

Jordan, Donald. 1987. "The Place of Chinese Disunity in Japanese Army Strategy during 1931." *China Quarterly* 109:42–63.

Josephus, Flavius. 1987 [ca. 75 CE]. *Wars of the Jews*. Translated by William Whiston. Peabody, Mass.: Hendrickson.

Judson, Pieter. 2016. *The Habsburg Empire: A New History*. Cambridge: Harvard University Press.

Julien, Catherine. 2007. "War and Peace in the Inca Heartland." In Kurt Rafflaub, ed., *War and Peace in the Ancient World*, 329–47. Oxford: Blackwell.

Junger, Sebastian. 2011. *War*. London: Fourth Estate.

Kaeuper, Richard. 1999. *Chivalry and Violence in Medieval Europe*. Oxford: Oxford University Press.

Kaldor, Mary. 1999. *New and Old Wars: Organized Violence in a Global Era*. Stanford: Stanford University Press.

Kallet-Marx, Robert. 1995. *Hegemony to Empire: The Development of the Roman Imperium in the East from 148 to 62 B.C.* Berkeley: University of California Press.

Kandil, Hazem. 2016. *The Power Triangle: Military, Security, and Politics in Regime Change*. Oxford: Oxford University Press.

Kang, David. 2010. *East Asia before the West: Five Centuries of Trade and Tribute*. New York: Columbia University Press.

Kang, David, et al. 2018. "War, Rebellion, and Intervention under Hierarchy: Vietnam-China Relations, 1365 to 1841." *Journal of Conflict Resolution* 63, no. 4: 896–92.

Kant, Immanuel. 1891 [1784]. *Principles of Politics*, including *Perpetual Peace: A Philosophical Sketch*. Translated by W. Hastie. Online Library of Liberty. https://oll.libertyfund.org/title/hastie-kant-s-principles-of-politics-including-his-essay-on-perpetual-peace.

Kaplan, Stephen. 1981. *Diplomacy of Power: Soviet Armed Forces as a Political Instrument*. Washington, D.C.: Brookings Institution.

Katzenstein, Peter, ed. 1996. *The Culture of National Security: Norms and Identity in World Politics*. New York: Columbia University Press.

Katzman, Kenneth. 2011. *Bahrain: Reform, Security, and U.S. Policy*. Washington, D.C.: Congressional Research Service, March.

———. 2020. *Bahrain: Unrest, Security, and U.S. Policy*. Washington, D.C.: Congressional Research Service, September.

Kaufman, Ralph. 1947. " 'Ill Health' as an Expression of Anxiety in a Combat Unit." *Psychosomatic Medicine* 9:104–9.

Kay, Philip. 2014. *Rome's Economic Revolution*. Oxford: Oxford University Press.

Keegan, John. 1976. *The Face of Battle*. London: Jonathan Cape.

———. 1999. *The First World War*. New York: Alfred A. Knopf.

Keeley, Lawrence. 1996. *War before Civilization: The Myth of the Peaceful Savage*. Oxford: Oxford University Press.

Keen, Maurice. 1984. *Chivalry*. New Haven: Yale University Press.

———. 1999. *Medieval Warfare: A History*. New York: Oxford University Press.

Kelly, Raymond. 2000. *Warless Societies and the Origins of War*. Ann Arbor: University of Michigan Press.

Kennedy, David. 1999. *Freedom from Fear: The American People in Depression and War, 1929–1945*. New York: Oxford University Press.

Kershaw, Ian. 1998. *Hitler, 1889–1936: Hubris*. New York: Norton.

———. 2007. *Fateful Choices: Ten Decisions That Changed the World, 1940–1941*. London: Penguin.

————. 2012. *The End: The Defiance and Destruction of Hitler's Germany, 1944–1945*. New York: Penguin.

Khan, Azmat, and Anand Gopal. 2017. "The Uncounted." *New York Times*, November 16.

Khatib, Lina. 2015. *The Islamic State's Strategy: Lasting and Expanding*. Washington, D.C.: Carnegie Endowment for International Peace.

Khazanov, Anatoly. 2015. "Pastoral Nomadic Migrations and Conquests." In Benjamin Kedar and Merry Wiesner-Hanks, eds., *The Cambridge World History*, vol. 5, *Expanding Webs of Exchange and Conflict, 500 CE–1500 CE*. Cambridge: Cambridge University Press.

Khosrokhavar, Farhad. 2017. *Radicalization: Why Some People Choose the Path of Violence*. New York: New Press.

Kim, Duol, and Ki-Joo Park. 2008. "Colonialism and Industrialisation: Factory Labour Productivity of Colonial Korea, 1913–37." *Australian Economic History Review* 48:26–46.

Kim, Hodong. 2009. "The Unity of the Mongol Empire and Continental Exchanges over Eurasia." *Journal of Central Eurasian Studies* 1:15–42.

Kimber, R. G. 1990. "Hunter-Gatherer Demography: The Recent Past in Central Australia." In Betty Meehan and Neville White, eds., *Hunter-Gatherer Demography: Past and Present*. Sydney: University of Sydney Press.

King, Anthony. 2013. *The Combat Soldier: Infantry Tactics and Cohesion in the Twentieth and Twenty-first Centuries*. Oxford: Oxford University Press.

Kiser, Edgar, and Yong Cai. 2003. "War and Bureaucratization in Qin China: Exploring an Anomalous Case." *American Sociological Review* 68:511–39.

Kissel, Hans. 1956. "Panic in Battle." *Military Review*, July: 96–107.

Knights, Michael, and Alex Almeida. 2020. "Remaining and Expanding: The Recovery of Islamic State Operations in Iraq in 2019–2020." *CTC Sentinel* 13:1–16.

Kolbert, Elizabeth. 2011. "Peace in Our Time: Steven Pinker's History of Violence." *New Yorker*, October 3.

Kradin, Nikolay. 2019. "Social Complexity, Inner Asia, and Pastoral Nomadism." *Social Evolution and History* 18:3–34.

Kudo, Timothy. 2011. "On War and Redemption." *New York Times*, November 8.

Kulikowski, Michael. 2019. *The Tragedy of Empire: From Constantine to the Destruction of Roman Italy*. Cambridge: Belknap Press of Harvard University Press.

Lacina, Bethany, and Nils Gleditsch. 2005. "Monitoring Trends in Global Combat: A New Dataset of Battle Deaths." *European Journal of Population* 21:145–66.

Laffineur, Robert, ed. 1999. *Polemos: Le contexte guerrier en égée à l'âge du bronze: Actes de la 7e Rencontre égéenne internationale, Université de Liège, 1998*. Université de Liège.

Lahr, Mirazon, et al. 2016. "Inter-Group Violence among Early Holocene Hunter-Gatherers of West Turkana, Kenya." *Nature* 529:394–98.

Laidley, T. T. S. 1865. "Breech-Loading Musket." *United States Service Magazine* 3:67–70.

Lamb, Harold. 1927. *Genghis Khan: The Emperor of All Men*. Garden City, N.Y.: Garden City Publishing.

Lamers, Jeroen. 2000. *Japonius Tyrannus: The Japanese Warlord Oda Nobunaga Reconsidered*. Leiden: Hotei.

Lebow, Richard Ned. 1981. *Between Peace and War: The Nature of International Crisis*. Baltimore: Johns Hopkins University Press.

———. 2010. *Why Nations Fight*. Cambridge: Cambridge University Press.

Lee, Doug. 2007. "Warfare and the State." In Philip Sabin et al., eds., *The Cambridge History of Greek and Roman Warfare*, vol. 2, *Rome from the Late Republic to the Late Empire*. Cambridge: Cambridge University Press.

———. 2008. "Treaty-Making in Late Antiquity." In Philip de Souza and John France, eds., *War and Peace in Ancient and Medieval History*. Cambridge: Cambridge University Press.

Lee, Ji-Young. 2017. *China's Hegemony: Four Hundred Years of East Asian Domination*. New York: Columbia University Press.

Lemarchand, Guillermo. 2007. *Defense and R&D Policies: Fifty Years of History*. Presentation for INES Council Meeting, Berlin, June 1–4.

LeMay, Curtis. 1965. *Mission with LeMay: My Story*. Garden City, N.Y.: Doubleday.

Lemke, Douglas. 2002. *Regions of War and Peace*. Cambridge: Cambridge University Press.

Lepre, George. 2011. *Fragging: Why U.S. Soldiers Assaulted Their Officers in Vietnam*. Lubbock: Texas Tech University Press.

Leuchars, Chris. 2002. *To the Bitter End: Paraguay and the War of the Triple Alliance*. Westport, Conn.: Greenwood.

Levy, Jack. 1983. *War in the Modern Great Power System, 1495–1975*. Lexington: University Press of Kentucky.

———. 1988. "Domestic Politics and War." *Journal of Interdisciplinary History* 18:653–73.

———. 2011. "Theories and Causes of War." In Christopher Coyne and Rachel Mathers, eds., *The Handbook on the Political Economy of War*. Cheltenham, U.K.: Edward Elgar.

Lewin, Ronald. 1976. *Slim: The Standardbearer*. Hertfordshire, U.K.: Wordsworth.

Lewis, Larry, and Sarah Holewinski. 2013. "Changing of the Guard: Civilian Protection for an Evolving Military." *Prism* 4, no. 2: 57–66.

Lewis, Mark. 1990. *Sanctioned Violence in Early China*. Albany: State University of New York Press.

———. 1999. "Political History of the Warring States." In Michael Loewe and Edward Shaughnessy, eds., *The Cambridge History of Ancient China*. Cambridge: Cambridge University Press.

———. 2000. "The Han Abolition of Universal Military Service." In Hans van der Ven, ed., *Warfare in Chinese History*, 33–76. Leiden: Brill.

———. 2007. *The Early Chinese Empires: Qin and Han*. Cambridge: Harvard University Press.

Li, Feng. 2013. *Early China: A Social and Cultural History*. Cambridge: Cambridge University Press.

Li, Xiaobing. 2007. *A History of the Modern Chinese Army*. Lexington: University Press of Kentucky.

———. 2014. *China's Battle for Korea: The 1951 Spring Offensive*. Bloomington: Indiana University Press.

Li, Xiaobing, et al., eds. and trans. 2001. *Mao's Generals Remember Korea*. Lawrence: University Press of Kansas.

Linderman, Gerald. 1987. *Embattled Courage: The Experience of Combat in the American Civil War*. New York: Free Press.

Little, Roger. 1964. "Buddy Relations and Combat Performance." In Morris Janowitz, ed., *The New Military: Changing Patterns of Organization*, 195–224. New York: Norton.

Litz, Brett, et al. 2009. "Moral Injury and Moral Repair in War Veterans: A Preliminary Model and Intervention Strategy." *Clinical Psychology Review* 29:695–706.

Livy. 1853. *History of Rome*. Translated by D. Spillan. Project Gutenberg. https://www.gutenberg.org/files/19725/19725-h/19725-h.htm.

Lockwood, William. 1954. *Economic Development of Japan*. Princeton: Princeton University Press.

Loewe, Michael. 1974. *Crisis and Conflict in Han China, 104 BC to AD 9*. London: Allen & Unwin.

Loez, André. 2010. *14–18: Les refus de la guerre: Une histoire des mutins*. Paris: Gallimard.

Lone, Stewart. 2000. *Army, Empire and Politics in Meiji Japan: The Three Careers of General Katsura Taro*. New York: St. Martin's.

Lopes da Silva, Diego, Nan Tian, Lucie Béraud-Sudrea, et al. 2022. "Trends in World Military Expenditure, 2021." SIPRI Fact Sheet. Stockholm: SIPRI, April.

López-Montalvo, Esther. 2018. "War and Peace in Iberian Prehistory: The Chronology and Interpretation of the Depictions of Violence in Levantine Rock Art." In Andrea Dolfini et al., eds., *Prehistoric Warfare and Violence: Quantitative Methods in the Humanities and Social Sciences*. New York: Springer.

Lorge, Peter. 2005. *War, Politics and Society in Early Modern China, 900–1795*. London: Routledge.

———. 2008. "The Great Ditch of China and the Song-Liao Border." In Don Wyatt, ed., *Battlefronts Real and Imagined: War, Border, and Identity in the Chinese Middle Period*, 59–74. New York: Palgrave Macmillan.

———. 2014. "Discovering War in Chinese History." *Extrême-Orient Extrême-Occident* 38:21–46.

———. 2015. *The Reunification of China: Peace through War under the Song Dynasty*. Cambridge: Cambridge University Press.

Lower, Wendy. 2005. *Nazi Empire-Building and the Holocaust in Ukraine*. Chapel Hill: University of North Carolina Press.

Luard, Evan. 1986. *War in International Society: A Study in International Sociology*. London: Tauris.

Luft, Sebastian. 2007. "Germany's Metaphysical War: Reflections on War by Two Representatives of German Philosophy: Max Scheler and Paul Natorp." http://works.bepress.com/sebastian_luft/27.

Lynn, John. 2003. *Battle: A History of Combat and Culture*. Boulder, Colo.: Westview.

Mack, Andrew. 1975. "Why Big Nations Lose Small Wars: The Politics of Asymmetric Conflict." *World Politics* 27:175–200.

MacMillan, Margaret. 2020. *War: How Conflict Shaped Us*. New York: Random House.

MacMullen, Ramsay. 2000. *Romanization in the Time of Augustus*. New Haven: Yale University Press.

Maddison, Angus. 2003. *The World Economy: Historical Statistics*. Paris: OECD Development Centre.

Maguen, Shira, and Brett T. Litz. 2012. "Moral Injury in Veterans of War." *PTSD Research Quarterly* 23:1–6.

Maguen, Shira, Thomas J. Metzler, Brett Litz, and Karen Seal. 2009. "The Impact of Killing in War on Mental Health Symptoms and Related Functioning." *Journal of Traumatic Stress* 22:435–43.

Mahoney, Kevin. 2001. *Formidable Enemies: The North Korean and Chinese Soldier in the Korean War*. Novato, Calif.: Presidio Press.

Malešević, Siniša. 2010. *The Sociology of War and Violence*. Cambridge: Cambridge University Press.

———. 2017. *The Rise of Organized Brutality: A Historical Sociology of Violence*. Cambridge: Cambridge University Press.

———. 2022. *Why Humans Fight: The Social Dynamics of Close-Range Violence*. Cambridge: Cambridge University Press.

Mallet-Marx, Robert M. 1995. *Hegemony to Empire: The Development of the Roman Imperium in the East from 148 to 62 B.C.* Berkeley: University of California Press.

Mann, Michael. 1984. "The Autonomous Power of the State: Its Origins, Mechanisms and Results." *Archives Européennes de Sociologie* 25:185–213.

———. 1986. *The Sources of Social Power*, vol. 1, *A History of Power from the Beginning to A.D. 1760*. Cambridge: Cambridge University Press.

———. 1988. *States, War and Capitalism*. Oxford: Blackwell.

———. 1993. *The Sources of Social Power*, vol. 2, *The Rise of Classes and Nation-States, 1760–1914*. Cambridge: Cambridge University Press.

———. 2003. *Incoherent Empire*. London: Verso.

———. 2004. *Fascists*. Cambridge: Cambridge University Press.

———. 2005. *The Dark Side of Democracy: Explaining Ethnic Cleansing*. Cambridge: Cambridge University Press.

———. 2012. *The Sources of Social Power*, vol. 3, *Global Empires and Revolution, 1890–1945*. Cambridge: Cambridge University Press.

———. 2013. *The Sources of Social Power*, vol. 4, *Globalizations, 1945–2011*. Cambridge: Cambridge University Press.

———. 2016. "Have Human Societies Evolved? Evidence from History and Pre-History." *Theory and Society* 45:203–37.

Manning, Chandra. 2007. *What This Cruel War Was Over: Soldiers, Slavery, and the Civil War*. New York: Alfred A. Knopf.

Mansoor, Peter. 1999. *The G.I. Offensive in Europe*. Lawrence: University Press of Kansas.

Mares, David. 1996. "Deterrence Bargaining in the Ecuador-Peru Enduring Rivalry: Designing Strategies around Military Weakness." *Security Studies* 6:91–123.

———. 2001. *Violent Peace: Militarized Interstate Bargaining in Latin America*. New York: Columbia University Press.

———. 2012. *Latin America and the Illusion of Peace*. New York: Columbia University Press.

Mares, David, and Arie Kacowicz. 2016. *Routledge Handbook of Latin American Security*. New York: Routledge.

Mares, David, and David Scott Palmer. 2012. *Power, Institutions, and Leadership in War and Peace: Lessons from Peru and Ecuador, 1995–1998*. Austin: University of Texas Press.

Marmar, Charles, et al. 2015. "Course of Posttraumatic Stress Disorder 40 Years after the Vietnam War: Findings from the National Vietnam Veterans Longitudinal Study." *Journal of the American Medical Association Psychiatry* 72, no. 9: 875–81.

Marshall, Monty. 2017. "Major Episodes of Political Violence, 1946–2016." Vienna, Va.: Center for Systemic Peace.

Marshall, S. L. A. 1944. *Island Victory: The Battle of Kwajalein Atoll*. New York: Penguin.

———. 1947. *Men against Fire: The Problem of Battle Command*. New York: Morrow.

———. 1951. *Commentary on Infantry Operations and Weapons Usage in Korea, Winter of 1950–51*. Johns Hopkins University: Operations Research Office, Department of the Army. (Declassified 1998.)

———. 1968. *Bird*. New York: Warner.

———. 1969. *Ambush: The Battle of Dau Tieng* and *Bird: The Christmastide Battle*. New York: Nelson Doubleday.

Marshall, S. L. A., and David Hackworth. 1967. *Vietnam Primer: Lessons Learned*. Washington, D.C.: Headquarters, Department of the Army. https://archive.org/details/Vietnam_Primer_Lessons_Learned.

Marwick, Arthur. 1975. *War and Social Change in the Twentieth Century: A Comparative Study of Britain, France, Germany, Russia and the United States*. New York: St. Martin's.

Marx, Brian, et al. 2010. "Combat-Related Guilt Mediates the Relations between Exposure to Combat-Related Abusive Violence and Psychiatric Diagnoses." *Depression and Anxiety* 27:287–93.

Mashal, Mujin. 2020. "How the Taliban Outlasted a Superpower: Tenacity and Carnage." *New York Times*, May 26.

Massing, Michael. 2021. "The Story the Media Missed in Afghanistan." *New York Review of Books*, October 20.

Matsusaka, Yoshihisa. 2001. *The Making of Japanese Manchuria, 1904–1932*. Cambridge: Harvard University Press.

Mattern, Susan P. 1999. *Rome and the Enemy: Imperial Strategy in the Principate*. Berkeley: University of California Press.

Maurin, Jules. 1982. *Armée—Guerre—Société: Soldats Languedociens, 1899–1919*. Paris: Sorbonne.

May, Timothy. 2007. *The Mongol Art of War*. Barnsley, U.K.: Pen and Sword.

———. 2011. *The Mongol Conquests in World History*. London: Reaktion.

Mazzuca, Sebastián. 2021. *Latecomer State Formation: Political Geography and Capacity Failure in Latin America*. New Haven: Yale University Press.

McCants, William. 2015. *The ISIS Apocalypse: The History, Strategy, and Doomsday Vision of the Islamic State*. New York: St. Martin's.

McEwan, Gordon. 2006. *The Incas: New Perspectives*. Santa Barbara: ABC-CLIO.

McPherson, James. 1997. *For Cause and Comrades: Why Men Fought in the Civil War*. New York: Oxford University Press.

Mead, Corey. 2014. "A Rare Look inside the Air Force's Drone Training Classroom." *Atlantic*, June 14.

Mearsheimer, John. 2001. *The Tragedy of Great Power Politics*. New York: Norton.

———. 2009. "Reckless States and Realism." *International Relations* 23:241–56.

Melander, Erik, et al. 2009. "Are 'New Wars' More Atrocious? Battle Severity, Civilians Killed and Forced Migration before and after the End of the Cold War." *European Journal of International Relations* 15:505–36.

Melchior, Aislinn. 2011. "Caesar in Vietnam: Did Roman Soldiers Suffer from Post-Traumatic Stress Disorder?" *Greece & Rome* 58, no. 2: 209–23.

Merridale, Catherine. 2006. *Ivan's War: The Red Army, 1941–45*. London: Faber & Faber.

Metzler, Mark. 2006. *Lever of Empire: The International Gold Standard and the Crisis of Liberalism in Prewar Japan*. Berkeley: University of California Press.

Meyer, Christian. 2018. "Patterns of Collective Violence in the Early Neolithic of Central Europe." In Andrea Dolfini et al., eds., *Prehistoric Warfare and Violence: Quantitative Methods in the Humanities and Social Sciences*. New York: Springer.

Middlebrook, Martin. 1972. *The First Day on the Somme, 1 July 1916*. New York: Norton.

Migdal, Joel. 2001. *State in Society: Studying How States and Societies Transform and Constitute One Another*. Cambridge: Cambridge University Press.

Miles, Richard. 2010. *Carthage Must Be Destroyed: The Rise and Fall of a Civilization*. New York: Viking.

Miller, Edward. 2007. *Bankrupting the Enemy: The U.S. Financial Siege of Japan before Pearl Harbor*. Annapolis: Naval Institute Press.

Mitter, Rana. 2000. *The Manchurian Myth: Nationalism, Resistance, and Collaboration in Modern China*. Berkeley: University of California Press.

Mitts, Tamar. 2019. "From Isolation to Radicalization: Anti-Muslim Hostility and Support for ISIS in the West." *American Political Science Review* 113:173–94.

Moore, Adam. 2019. *Empire's Labor: The Global Army That Supports U.S. Wars*. Ithaca: Cornell University Press.

Moore, Barrington, Jr. 1988. "Japanese Peasant Protests and Revolts in Comparative Historical Perspective." *International Review of Social History* 33:312–28.

Morgan, David. 2007. *The Mongols*. 2nd edition. Malden, Mass.: Blackwell.

Morgenthau, Hans. 1946. *Scientific Man versus Power Politics*. Chicago: University of Chicago Press.

———. 1948. *Politics among Nations: The Struggle for Power and Peace*. New York: Alfred A. Knopf.

Morillo, Stephen. 2001. "Cultures of Death: Warrior Suicide in Medieval Europe and Japan." *Medieval History Journal* 4:241–57.

Morley, Neville. 2010. *The Roman Empire: Roots of Imperialism*. London: Pluto.

Morris, Ian. 2005. "Military and Political Participation in Archaic-Classical Greece." Princeton/Stanford Working Papers in Classics no. 120511.

Moskos, Charles. 1970. *The American Enlisted Man*. New York: Russell Sage.

———. 1975. "The American Combat Soldier in Vietnam." *Journal of Social Issues* 31: 25–37.

Mueller, John. 1989. *Retreat from Doomsday: The Obsolescence of Major War*. New York: Basic Books.

———. 2004. *The Remnants of War*. Ithaca: Cornell University Press.

———. 2009. "War Has Almost Ceased to Exist: An Assessment." *Political Science Quarterly* 124:297–327.

Münkler, Herfried. 2005. *The New Wars*. Cambridge, U.K.: Polity.

Nakamura, Takafusa. 1988. "Depression, Recovery, and War, 1920–1945." In Peter Duus, ed., *The Cambridge History of Japan*, vol. 6, *The Twentieth Century*. Cambridge: Cambridge University Press.

Nakao, Hisashi, et al. 2016. "Violence in the Prehistoric Period of Japan: The Spatio-Temporal Pattern of Skeletal Evidence for Violence in the Jomon Period." Royal Society, March 1. https://royalsocietypublishing.org/doi/10.1098/rsbl.2016.0028.

Niditch, Susan. 2007. "War and Reconciliation in the Traditions of Ancient Israel." In Kurt Raaflaub, ed., *War and Peace in the Ancient World*. Oxford: Blackwell.

Niebuhr, Robert. 2018. "The Road to the Chaco War: Bolivia's Modernisation in the 1920s." *War and Society* 37:91–106.

Nietzsche, Friedrich. 1923 [1895]. *The Anti-Christ*. Translated by H. L. Mencken. New York: Alfred A. Knopf.

Nish, Ian. 2002. *Japanese Foreign Policy in the Interwar Period*. Westport, Conn.: Praeger.

North, J. A. 1981. "The Development of Roman Imperialism." *Journal of Roman Studies* 71:1–9.

Nye, Joseph. 1990. *Bound to Lead: The Changing Nature of American Power*. New York: Basic Books.

Oakley, Stephen. 1993. "The Roman Conquest of Italy." In John Rich and Graham Shipley, eds., *War and Society in the Roman World*. London: Routledge.

O'Brien, Patrick, and Leandro Prados de la Escosura. 1998. "The Costs and Benefits for Europeans from Their Empires Overseas." *Revista de Historia Economica* 1:29–92.

O'Brien, Tim. 1990. *The Things They Carried*. Boston: Houghton Mifflin.

Odaka, Konosuke. 1999. " 'Japanese-Style' Labour Relations." In Tetsuji Okazaki and Masahiro Okuno-Fujiwara, eds., *The Japanese Economic System and Its Historical Origins*. Oxford: Oxford University Press.

O'Grady, Hannah, and Joel Gunter. 2022. "SAS Unit Repeatedly Killed Afghan Detainees, BBC Finds." BBC World News, July 12. https://www.bbc.com/news/uk-62083196.

Oguma, Eiji. 2002. *The Genealogy of "Japanese" Self-Images*. Translated by David Askew. Melbourne: Trans Pacific.

Oppenheimer, Franz. 1975 [1908]. *The State*. New York: Free Life Editions.

Otte, Thomas G. 2014. *July Crisis: The World's Descent into War, Summer 1914*. Cambridge: Cambridge University Press.

Otterbein, Keith. 2004. *How War Began*. College Station: Texas A&M University Press.

Owen, John, IV. 2010. *The Clash of Ideas in World Politics: Transnational Networks, States, and Regime Change, 1510–2010*. Princeton: Princeton University Press.

Owen, Wilfred. 1921. *Poems, with an Introduction by Siegfried Sassoon*. London: Chatto and Windus.

Palmer, Glenn, et al. 2015. "The MID4 Dataset, 2002–2010: Procedures, Coding Rules and Description." *Conflict Management and Peace Science* 32:222–42.

Palmer, Robert. 1997. *Rome and Carthage at Peace*. Stuttgart: Franz Steiner.

Pape, Robert. 2006. *Dying to Win: The Strategic Logic of Suicide Terrorism*. New York: Random House.

Parker, Harold. 1971. "The Formation of Napoleon's Personality: An Exploratory Essay." *French Historical Studies* 7:6–26.

Parkin, Diana. 1987. "Contested Sources of Identity: Nation, Class and Gender in Second World War Britain." PhD dissertation, London School of Economics.

Parsons, Talcott. 1971. *The System of Modern Societies*. Englewood Cliffs, N.J.: Prentice-Hall.

Pascua, Esther. 2008. "Peace among Equals: War and Treaties in Twelfth-Century Europe." In Philip de Souza and John France, eds., *War and Peace in Ancient and Medieval Europe*, 193–210. Cambridge: Cambridge University Press.

Patterson, John. 1993. "Military Organization and Social Change in the Later Roman Republic." In John Rich and Graham Shipley, eds., *War and Society in the Roman World*. London: Routledge.

Paul, Gregor. 2004. "War and Peace in Classical Chinese Thought: With Particular Regard to Chinese Religions." In Perry Schmidt-Leukel, ed., *War and Peace in World Religions*, 72–75. London: SCM Press.

Paul, Jürgen. 2003. "The State and the Military: A Nomadic Perspective." In Irene Schneider, ed., *Militär und Staatlichkeit: Beiträge des Kolloquiums am 29. und 30.04.2002*. Halle: Orientwissenschaftliche, 12:25–68.

Peattie, Mark. 1975. *Ishiwara Kanji and Japan's Confrontation with the West*. Princeton: Princeton University Press.

Pederson, Neil. 2014. "Pluvials, Droughts, the Mongol Empire, and Modern Mongolia." *Proceedings of the National Academy of Sciences* 111, no. 12: 4375–79.

Pedroncini, Guy. 1967. *Les mutineries de 1917*. Paris: Presses Universitaires de France.

Perdue, Peter. 2002. "Fate and Fortune in Central Eurasian Warfare: Three Qing Emperors and Their Mongol Rivals." In Nicola di Cosmo, ed., *Warfare in Inner Asian History (500–1800)*. Leiden: Brill.

———. 2005. *China Marches West: The Qing Conquest of Central Eurasia*. Cambridge: Harvard University Press.

Perlo-Freeman, Sam, et al. 2015. "World Military Expenditures." Stockholm International Peace Research Institute Fact Sheet, April.

Peterson, Charles. 1983. "Old Illusions and New Realities: Sung Foreign Policy, 1217–1234." In Morris Rossabi, ed., *China among Equals: The Middle Kingdom and Its Neighbors, 10th–14th Centuries*. Berkeley: University of California Press.

Pettersson, Therese, and Kristine Eck. 2018. "Organized Violence, 1989–2017." *Journal of Peace Research* 55:535–47.

Pew Research Center. 2011. *The Military-Civilian Gap: War and Sacrifice in the Post-9/11 Era*. Washington, D.C.: Pew Research Center.

———. 2016. *Public Uncertain, Divided over America's Place in the World: Growing Support for Increased Defense Spending*. Washington, D.C.: Pew Research Center.

Phillips, Andrew. 2011. *War, Religion and Empire: The Transformation of International Orders*. Cambridge: Cambridge University Press.

Phillips, Dave. 2019. "Trump Clears Three Service Members in War Crimes Cases." *New York Times*, November 16.

Pike, Francis. 2015. *Hirohito's War: The Pacific War, 1941–1945*. London: Bloomsbury.

Pilkington, Nathan. 2019. *The Carthaginian Empire, 550–202 BCE*. Lanham, Md.: Lexington Books.

Pines, Yuri. 2012. *The Everlasting Empire: The Political Culture of Ancient China and Its Imperial Legacy*. Princeton: Princeton University Press.

———. 2018. "Legalism in Chinese Philosophy." Stanford Encyclopedia of Philosophy. https://plato.stanford.edu/entries/chinese-legalism/.

Pinker, Steven. 2011. *The Better Angels of Our Nature: Why Violence Has Declined*. New York: Viking.

Plutarch. 1960 [75 CE]. *Plutarch's Lives*. Translated by John Dryden. New York: Modern Library.

Podany, Amanda. 2010. *Brotherhood of Kings: How International Relations Shaped the Ancient Near East*. Oxford: Oxford University Press.

Pollack, Kenneth. 2002. *Arabs at War: Military Effectiveness, 1948–1991*. Lincoln: University of Nebraska Press.

Polybius. 1889 [1568]. *Histories*. Translated by Evelyn S. Shuckburgh. London: Macmillan.

Quesada, Alejandro de, and Philip Jowet. 2011. *The Chaco War, 1932–35: South America's Greatest Modern Conflict*. Oxford: Osprey.

Quinlivan, James. 1999. "Coup-Proofing: Its Practice and Consequences in the Middle East." *International Security* 24:131–65.

Raaflaub, Kurt. 1991. "City-State, Territory, and Empire in Classical Antiquity." In Anthony Molho, Kurt Raaflaub, and Julia Emlen, eds., *City States in Classical Antiquity and Medieval Italy*, 565–88. Ann Arbor: University of Michigan Press.

———, ed. 2007. *War and Peace in the Ancient World*. Oxford: Blackwell.

Ramzy, Austin, and Chris Buckley. 2019. " 'Absolutely No Mercy': Leaked Files Expose How China Organized Mass Detentions of Muslims." *New York Times*, November 16.

Rance, Philip. 2007. "Battle." In Philip Sabin et al., eds., *The Cambridge History of Greek and Roman Warfare*, vol. 2, *Rome from the Late Republic to the Late Empire*. Cambridge: Cambridge University Press.

Ratchnevsky, Paul. 1992. *Genghis Khan: His Life and Legacy*. Oxford: Blackwell.

Rawski, Evelyn. 1996. "Presidential Address: Re-envisioning the Qing: The Significance of the Qing Period in Chinese History." *Journal of Asian Studies* 55:829–50.

Reese, Roger. 2011. *Why Stalin's Soldiers Fought: The Red Army's Effectiveness in World War II*. Lawrence: University Press of Kansas.

Reiter, Dan, and Allan Stam. 2002. *Democracies at War*. Princeton: Princeton University Press.

Rich, John. 2004. "Fear, Greed, and Glory: The Causes of Roman War Making in the Middle Republic." In Craig Champion, ed., *Roman Imperialism: Readings and Sources*. Oxford: Blackwell.

———. 2008. "Treaties, Allies and the Roman Conquest of Italy." In Philip de Souza and John France, eds., *War and Peace in Ancient and Medieval History*. Cambridge: Cambridge University Press.

Richardson, John. 1996. *The Romans in Spain*. Oxford: Blackwell.

Roberts, Adam. 2010. "Lives and Statistics: Are 90% of War Victims Civilians?" *Survival: Global Politics and Strategy* 52:115–36.

Roberts, Luke. 2012. *Performing the Great Peace: Political Space and Open Secrets in Tokugawa Japan*. Honolulu: University of Hawai'i Press.

Robin, Ron. 2001. *The Making of the Cold War Enemy: Culture and Politics in the Military-Industrial Complex*. Princeton: Princeton University Press.

Robinson, Eric. 2001. "Reading and Misreading the Ancient Evidence for Democratic Peace." *Journal of Peace Research* 38:593–608.

Rogacz, Dawid. 2017. " 'Spring and Autumn Annals' as Narrative Explanation." In K. Brzechczyn, ed., *Towards a Revival of Analytical Philosophy of History: Around Paul A. Roth's Vision of Historical Sciences*, 254–72. Leiden: Brill-Rodopi.

Rogers, Clifford. 1993. "The Military Revolutions of the Hundred Years' War." *Journal of Military History* 57:241–78.

———. 2000. *War Cruel and Sharp: English Strategy under Edward III, 1327–1360*. London: Boydell.

Römer, Felix. 2013. "Milieus in the Military: Soldierly Ethos, Nationalism and Conformism among Workers in the Wehrmacht." *Journal of Contemporary History* 48:125–49.

Rosenstein, Nathan. 2007. "War and Peace: Fear and Reconciliation at Rome." In Kurt A. Raaflaub, ed., *War and Peace in the Ancient World*. Oxford: Blackwell.

———. 2009. "War, State Formation, and the Evolution of Military Institutions in Ancient China and Rome." In Walter Scheidel, ed., *Rome and China: Comparative Perspectives on Ancient World Empires*, 24–51. Oxford: Oxford University Press.

———. 2012. *Rome and the Mediterranean, 290 to 146 BC: The Imperial Republic*. Edinburgh: Edinburgh University Press.

Roser, Max. 2016. *Our World in Data: War and Peace after 1945*. https://ourworldindata.org/war-and-peace.

Rossabi, Morris. 1983. "Introduction." In Rossabi, ed., *China among Equals: The Middle Kingdom and Its Neighbors, 10th–14th Centuries*. Berkeley: University of California Press.

———. 1988. *Khubilai Khan: His Life and Times*. Berkeley: University of California Press.

Rostworowski de Diez Canseco, María. 1999. *History of the Inca Realm*. New York: Cambridge University Press.

Roth, Jonathan. 1999. *The Logistics of the Roman Army at War (264 B.C.—A.D. 235)*. New York: Columbia University Press.

Rottman, Gordon. 2013. *The Big Book of Gun Trivia*. Oxford: Osprey.

Rousseau, Frédéric. 1999. *La guerre censurée: Une histoire des combattants européens de 14–18*. Paris: Éditions du Seuil.

———. 2008. "Consentement: Requiem pour un 'mythe savant.' " *Matériaux pour Notre Temps*, no. 91: *Les Français dans la Grande Guerre*, March: 20–22.

Rowe, John. 2006. "The Inca Civil War and the Establishment of Spanish Power in Peru." *Ñawpa Pacha: Journal of Andean Archaeology* 28:1–9.

Roynette, Odile. 2018. "La fabrique des soldats." In Bruno Cabanes, ed., *Une histoire de la guerre, XIXe–XXIe siècles*, 259–69. Paris: Éditions du Seuil.

Rush, Robert. 2001. *Hell in Hürtgen Forest*. Lawrence: University Press of Kansas.

Sagramoso, Domitilla, and Akhmet Yarlykapov. 2020. "What Drove Young Dagestani Muslims to Join ISIS? A Study Based on Social Movement Theory and Collective Framing." *Perspectives on Terrorism* 14:42–56.

Saint-Fuscien, Emmanuel. 2011. *À vos ordres? La relation d'autorité dans l'armée française de la Grande Guerre*. Paris: Éditions de l'École des Hautes Études en Sciences Sociales.

Sallust. 1899 [ca. 40 BCE]. *The Jugurthine War*. Translated by John S. Watson. New York: Harper & Brothers.

———. 1992. *Histories*. Translated by Patrick McGushin. Oxford: Oxford University Press.

"Samer" (pseudonym). 2017. *The Raqqa Diaries: Escape from "Islamic State."* Edited by Mike Thompson. Translated by Nader Ibrahim. London: Hutchinson.

Sanborn, Joshua. 2003. *Drafting the Russian Nation: Military Conscription, Total War, and Mass Politics, 1905–1925*. DeKalb: Northern Illinois University Press.

Sanderson, Stephen. 1999. *Social Transformations: A General Theory of Historical Development*. Oxford: Blackwell.

Santos-Granero, Fernando. 2010. *Vital Enemies: Slavery, Predation, and the Amerindian Political Economy of Life*. Austin: University of Texas Press.

Sarkees, Meredith Reid, and Frank Whelon Wayman. 2010. *Resort to War: A Data Guide to Inter-State, Extra-State, Intra-State, and Non-State Wars, 1816–2007*. Washington, D.C.: CQ Press.

Sarkees, Meredith Reid, Frank Wayman, and J. David Singer. 2003. "Inter-State, Intra-State, and Extra-State Wars: A Comprehensive Look at Their Distribution over Time, 1816–1997." *International Studies Quarterly* 47:49–70.

Sassoon, Joseph. 2012. *Saddam Hussein's Ba'th Party: Inside an Authoritarian Regime*. Cambridge: Cambridge University Press.

Sater, William. 2007. *Andean Tragedy: Fighting the War of the Pacific, 1879–1884*. Lincoln: University of Nebraska Press.

Savranskaya, Svetlana, and Tom Blanton. 2017. "Who Promised What to Whom on NATO Expansion?" *National Security Archive*, briefing book no. 613, December 12. https://nsarchive.gwu.edu/briefing-book/russia-programs/2017-12-12/nato-expansion-what-gorbachev-heard-western-leaders-early.

Scheidel, Walter, ed. 2009. *Rome and China: Comparative Perspectives on Ancient World Empires*. Oxford: Oxford University Press.

———. 2019. *Escape from Rome: The Failure of Empire and the Road to Prosperity*. Princeton: Princeton University Press.

Scheina, Robert. 2003. *Latin America's Wars*, vol. 1, *The Age of the Caudillo, 1791–1899*. Washington, D.C.: Brassey's.

Schmidt, Katharina. 2011. "With Hearts of Iron and Swords for Whips—the Mongols as Specialists of Violence." In Frank Krämer, Katharina Schmidt, and Julika Singer, eds., *Historicizing the "Beyond": The Mongolian Invasion as a New Dimension of Violence?* Heidelberg: Universitätsverlag Winter.

Scott, James. 2017. *Against the Grain: A Deep History of the Earliest States*. New Haven: Yale University Press.

Shalit, Ben. 1988. *The Psychology of Conflict and Combat*. New York: Praeger.

Sharara, Fablina, Eve E. Wool, Gregory Bertolacci, et al. 2021. "Fatal Police Violence by Race and State in the USA, 1980–2019: A Network Meta-Regression." *Lancet* 398, October 2. https://www.thelancet.com/journals/lancet/article/PIIS0140-6736(21)01609-3/fulltext.

Sharp, Jeremy. 2020. *Yemen: Civil War and Regional Intervention*. Washington, D.C.: Congressional Research Service, revised April 23.

———. 2022. *U.S. Aid to Israel*. RL 33222. Washington, D.C.: Congressional Research Service, February 18.

Shaw, Martin. 2002. "Risk-Transfer Militarism, Small Massacres and the Historic Legitimacy of War." *International Relations* 16:343–59.

Sheehan, James. 2008. *Where Have All the Soldiers Gone? The Transformation of Modern Europe*. Boston: Houghton Mifflin.

Sheehan-Miles, Charles. 2012. "Finding Forgiveness for Murder." Blog posted May 8. https://sheehanmiles.com/blog/2012/05/08/finding-forgiveness-for-murder/.

Sheldon, Jack. 2005. *The German Army on the Somme, 1914–1916*. Barnsley, U.K.: Pen and Sword.

Sherman, William Tecumseh. 1879. Speech delivered at the Michigan Military Academy, Orchard Lake, June 19.

Sherwood, John Darrell. 1996. *Officers in Flight Suits: The Story of American Air Force Fighter Pilots in the Korean War*. New York: New York University Press.

Shesko, Elizabeth. 2015. "Mobilizing Manpower for War: Toward a New History of Bolivia's Chaco Conflict, 1932–1935." *Hispanic American Historical Review* 95:299–334.

Shils, Edward. 1950. "Primary Groups in the American Army." In Robert Merton and Paul Lazarsfeld, eds., *Continuities in Social Research: Studies in the Scope and Methods of the American Soldier*. New York: Free Press.

Shils, Edward, and Morris Janowitz. 1948. "Cohesion and Disintegration in the Wehrmacht in World War II." *Public Opinion Quarterly* 12:280–315.

Shimazu, Naoko. 2001. "The Myth of the 'Patriotic Soldier': Japanese Attitudes towards Death in the Russo-Japanese War." *War & Society* 19, no. 2: 69–86.

———. 2009. *Japanese Society at War: Death, Memory and the Russo-Japanese War*. New York: Cambridge University Press.

Simmel, Georg. 1903. "The Sociology of Conflict: III." *American Journal of Sociology* 9:798–811.

Simms, Brendan, and Charlie Laderman. 2021. *Hitler's American Gamble: Pearl Harbor and Germany's March to Global War*. New York: Basic Books.

Skaff, Jonathan. 2009. "Tang Military Culture and Its Inner Asian Influences." In Nicola di Cosmo, ed., *Military Culture in Imperial China*. Cambridge: Harvard University Press.

Skelly, James. 2006. "Iraq, Vietnam, and the Dilemmas of United States Soldiers." *Open Democracy*, May 25.

Small, Melvin, and David Singer. 1970. "Patterns in International Warfare, 1816–1965." *Annals of the American Academy of Political and Social Science* 391:145–55.

Smith, Leonard. 1994. *Between Mutiny and Obedience*. Princeton: Princeton University Press.

Smith, Leonard, et al. 2003. *France and the Great War, 1914–1918*. Cambridge: Cambridge University Press.

Smith, Paul Jakov. 2015. "A Crisis in the Literati State: The Sino-Tangut War and the Qingli-Era Reforms of Fan Zhongyan, 1040–1045." *Journal of Song-Yuan Studies* 45:59–137.

Snyder, Jack. 1991. *Myths of Empire*. Ithaca: Cornell University Press.

Somashekhar, Sandhya, and Steven Rich. 2016. "Final Tally: Police Shot and Killed 986 People in 2015." *Washington Post*, January 6.

Soufran Center. 2015. *Foreign Fighters: An Updated Assessment of the Flow of Foreign Fighters into Syria and Iraq*. New York: Soufran Center.

Sparks, Blair, and Oliver Neiss. 1956. "Psychiatric Screening of Combat Pilots." *U.S. Armed Forces Medical Journal* 7:811–19.

Speckhard, Anne, and Molly Ellenberg. 2020. "ISIS in Their Own Words: Recruitment History, Motivations for Joining, Travel, Experiences in ISIS, and Disillusionment over Time—Analysis of 220 In-Depth Interviews of ISIS Returnees, Defectors and Prisoners." *Journal of Strategic Security* 13:82–127.

Spiller, Roger. 1988. "S. L. A. Marshall and the Ratio of Fire." *RUSI Journal* (formerly *Royal United Services Institution Journal*) 133:63–71.

Spuler, Bertold. 1972. *History of the Mongols Based on Eastern and Western Accounts of the Thirteenth and Fourteenth Centuries*. Translated by Helga and Stuart Drummond. Berkeley: University of California Press.

Stalker, Nancy. 2018. *Japan: History and Culture from Classical to Cool*. Oakland: University of California Press.

Stanhope, Philip. 1888. *Notes of Conversations with the Duke of Wellington, 1831–1851*. London: Longmans Green.

Stannard, David. 1992. *American Holocaust: The Conquest of the New World*. New York: Oxford University Press.

Steckel, Francis. 1994. "Moral Problems in Combat: American Soldiers in Europe in World War II." *Army History* 31:1–8.

Steplyk, Jonathan. 2018. *Fighting Means Killing: Civil War Soldiers and the Nature of Combat*. Lawrence: University Press of Kansas.

St. John, Ronald. 1994. "The Bolivia-Chile-Peru Dispute in the Atacama Desert." International Boundaries Research Unit, University of Durham, *Boundary and Territory Briefing* 1, no. 6.

Stockholm International Peace Research Institute. 2019. *Fact Sheet: Trends in International Arms Transfers, 2018*. Stockholm: SIPRI.

Storry, Richard. 1982. *A History of Modern Japan*. Harmondsworth, U.K.: Penguin.

Stouffer, Samuel, et al. 1949. *The American Soldier*, vol. 2, *Combat and Its Aftermath*. Princeton: Princeton University Press.

Strachan, Hew. 2006. "Training, Morale, and Modern War." *Journal of Contemporary History* 41:211–27.

Strand, Håvard, and Håvard Hegre. 2021. "Trends in Armed Conflict, 1946–2020." *Conflict Trends* 3. Oslo Peace Research Institute.

Strand, Håvard, Siri Aas Rustad, Henrik Urdal, and Håvard Nygård. 2019. "Trends in Armed Conflict, 1946–2018." *Conflict Trends* 3. Oslo Peace Research Institute.

Suetonius. 1913 [121 CE]. *The Lives of the Twelve Caesars*. Translated by J. C. Rolfe. Loeb Classical Library. Cambridge: Harvard University Press.

Sugihara, Kaoru. 2004. "Japanese Imperialism in Global Resource History." *LSE Working Papers of the Global Economic History Network*, no. 07/04.

Sumner, William Graham. 2013 [1899]. *The Conquest of the United States by Spain*. Indianapolis: Liberty Fund.

Sun Bin. 2003 [ca. 4th century BCE]. *The Art of Warfare*. Edited by D. C. Lau and Roger Ames. Albany: State University of New York Press.

Sun Tzu. 1993 [ca. 5th century BCE]. *The Art of Warfare*. Edited by Roger Ames. New York: Random House.

Sverdrup, Carl. 2017. *The Mongol Conquests: The Military Operations of Genghis Khan and Sübe'etei*. Solihull, U.K.: Helion.

Swope, Kenneth. 2009. *A Dragon's Head and a Serpent's Tail: Ming China and the First Great East Asian War, 1592–1598*. Norman: University of Oklahoma Press.

————. 2014. *The Military Collapse of China's Ming Dynasty, 1618–44.* London: Routledge.

Tacitus. 2010 [ca. 98 CE]. *Agricola* and *Germania.* Hardmondsworth, U.K.: Penguin.

————. 1996. *The Annals of Imperial Rome.* Harmondsworth, U.K.: Penguin.

Tackett, Nicolas. 2017. *The Origins of the Chinese Nation—Song China and the Forging of an East Asian World Order.* Cambridge: Cambridge University Press.

Taira, Koji. 1988. "Economic Development, Labor Markets, and Industrial Relations in Japan, 1905–1955." In Peter Duus, ed., *The Cambridge History of Japan,* vol. 6, *The Twentieth Century.* Cambridge: Cambridge University Press.

Tan, James. 2017. *Power and Public Finance at Rome, 264–49 BCE.* New York: Oxford University Press.

Tao, Jing-Shen. 1983. "Northerners or Barbarians: Northern Sung Images of the Khitan." In Morris Rossabi, ed., *China among Equals: The Middle Kingdom and Its Neighbors, 10th–14th Centuries.* Berkeley: University of California Press.

Tarling, Nicholas. 2001. *A Sudden Rampage: The Japanese Occupation of Southeast Asia, 1941–1945.* Honolulu: University of Hawai'i Press.

Taylor, Maxwell. 1971. "Briefing by Ambassador Taylor on the Current Situation in South Vietnam, 27 November 1964." In *Pentagon Papers,* Gravel Edition, 3:666–73. Boston: Beacon Press. https://www.mtholyoke.edu/acad/intrel/pentagon3/doc242.htm.

Taylor, Michael. 2015. "Finance, Manpower, and the Rise of Rome." PhD dissertation, University of California, Berkeley.

————. 2017. "State Finance in the Middle Roman Republic: A Reevaluation." *American Journal of Philology* 138:143–80.

Taylor, Sandra. 1999. *Vietnamese Women at War: Fighting for Ho Chi Minh and the Revolution.* Lawrence: University Press of Kansas.

Terrenato, Nicola. 2019. *The Early Roman Expansion into Italy: Elite Negotiation and Family Agendas.* Cambridge: Cambridge University Press.

Themnér, Lotta, and Peter Wallensteen. 2014. "Patterns of Organized Violence, 2003–12." Stockholm International Peace Research Institute Yearbook. Oxford: Oxford University Press.

Theobald, Ulrich. 2013. *War Finance and Logistics in Late Imperial China: A Study of the Second Jinchuan Campaign (1771–1776).* Leiden: Brill.

Thies, Clifford, and Christopher Baum. 2020. "The Effect of War on Economic Growth." *Cato Journal,* Winter: 199–212.

Thome, Helmut. 2007. "Explaining the Long-Term Trend in Violent Crime: A Heuristic Scheme and Some Methodological Considerations." *International Journal of Conflict and Violence* 1, no. 2: 185–202.

Thucydides. 1972. *History of the Peloponnesian War.* Translated by Rex Warner. Harmondsworth, U.K.: Penguin.

Tillman, Hoyt. 2005. "The Treaty of Shanyuan from the Perspectives of Western Scholars." *Sungkyun Journal of East Asian Studies* 5: 135–55.

Tilly, Charles. 1975. "Reflections on the History of European Statemaking." In Tilly, ed., *The Formation of National States in Western Europe*. Princeton: Princeton University Press.

Toland, John. 1970. *The Rising Sun: The Decline and Fall of the Japanese Empire, 1936–1945.* New York: Random House.

Toliver, Raymond, and Trevor Constable. 1997. *Fighter Aces of the U.S.A.* Atglen, Pa.: Schiffer.

Tolstoy, Leo. 2009 [1867]. *War and Peace*. London: Penguin.

Totman, Conrad. 1988. *Politics in the Tokugawa Bakufu, 1600–1843*. Berkeley: University of California Press.

Townsend, Camilla. 2019. *Fifth Sun: A New History of the Aztecs*. Oxford: Oxford University Press.

Treitschke, Heinrich von. 1916. *Politics*, vol. 2. New York: Macmillan.

Tsunoda, Jun. 1994. *The Final Confrontation: Japan's Negotiations with the United States, 1941.* Vol. 5 in James Morley, ed., *Japan's Road to the Pacific War*. New York: Columbia University Press.

Turchin, Peter. 2003. *Historical Dynamics: Why States Rise and Fall*. Princeton: Princeton University Press.

Turchin, Peter, et al. 2021. "Rise of the War Machines: Charting the Evolution of Military Technologies from the Neolithic to the Industrial Revolution." *Plos One*, October 20. https://journals.plos.org/plosone/article?id=10.1371/journal.pone.0258161.

Turnbull, Stephen. 2002. *War in Japan, 1467–1615*. Oxford: Osprey.

———. 2008. *Samurai Armies, 1467–1649*. Oxford: Osprey.

Turner, Jonathan, and Alexandra Maryanski. 2008. *On the Origins of Societies by Natural Selection*. Boulder, Colo.: Paradigm.

United Nations. 2019. "United in Science: High-Level Synthesis Report of Latest Climate Science Information." Science Advisory Group of the UN Climate Action Summit.

United Nations High Commissioner for Refugees. 2020. *Global Report*. Geneva: UNHCR.

———. 2021. *Global Report*. Geneva: UNHCR.

United Nations Intergovernmental Panel on Climate Change. 2021. *Sixth Assessment. Climate Change: The Physical Science Basis.*

Van Creveld, Martin. 1982. *Fighting Power: German and US Army Performance, 1939–1945.* Westport, Conn.: Greenwood.

Van Evera, Stephen. 1999. *Causes of War: Power and the Roots of Conflict*. Ithaca: Cornell University Press.

Waal, Frans de. 2006. *Our Inner Ape: The Best and Worst of Human Nature*. Cambridge, U.K.: Granta.

Waley-Cohen, Joanna. 2009. "Militarization of Culture in Eighteenth-Century China." In Nicola di Cosmo, ed., *Military Culture in Imperial China*. Cambridge: Harvard University Press.

Walker, Richard. 1954. *The Multi-State System of Ancient China*. Hamden, Conn.: Shoe String Press.

Walker, Robert, et al. 2011. "Evolutionary History of Hunter-Gatherer Marriage Practices." *Plos One*, April 27. https://journals.plos.org/plosone/article?id=10.1371/journal.pone.0019066.

Walter, Dierk. 2017. *Colonial Violence: European Empires and the Use of Force*. Oxford: Oxford University Press.

Waltz, Kenneth. 1979. *Theory of International Politics*. Reading, Mass.: Addison-Wesley.

Wang, Gungwu. 1983. "The Rhetoric of a Lesser Empire: Early Sung Relations with Its Neighbors." In Morris Rossabi, ed., *China among Equals: The Middle Kingdom and Its Neighbors, 10th–14th Centuries*. Berkeley: University of California Press.

Wang, Jinping. 2018. *In the Wake of the Mongols*. Cambridge: Harvard University Press.

Wang, Yuan-Kang. 2011. *Harmony and War: Confucian Culture and Chinese Power Politics*. New York: Columbia University Press.

Wang, Zhenping. 2013a. *Tang China in Multi-Polar Asia: A History of Diplomacy and War*. Honolulu: University of Hawai'i Press.

———. 2013b. "Explaining the Tribute System: Power, Confucianism, and War in Medieval East Asia." *Journal of East Asian Studies* 13:207–32.

Ward, Lester. 1903. *Pure Sociology: A Treatise on the Origin and Spontaneous Development of Society*. New York: Macmillan.

Ward-Perkins, Bryan. 2005. *The Fall of Rome and the End of Civilization*. Oxford: Oxford University Press.

Warner, Lloyd. 1958. *A Black Civilization: A Social Study of an Australian Tribe*. Revised edition. New York: Harper & Brothers.

Watson, Alexander. 2008. *Enduring the Great War: Combat, Morale and Collapse in the German and British Armies, 1914–1918*. Cambridge: Cambridge University Press.

Watson, Brent. 2002. *Far Eastern Tour: The Canadian Infantry in Korea, 1950–1953*. Montreal: McGill-Queen's University Press.

Weatherford, Jack. 2004. *Genghis Khan and the Making of the Modern World*. New York: Crown.

Weber, Max. 1978 [1922]. *Economy and Society*. Translated by Ephraim Fischoff. 2 vols. Berkeley: University of California Press.

———. 1988 [1923]. *Gesammelte Politische Schriften*. Tübingen: Mohr Siebeck.

Webster, David. 2000. "The Not So Peaceful Civilization: A Review of Maya War." *Journal of World Prehistory* 14:65–119.

Weisdorf, Jacob. 2005. "From Foraging to Farming: Explaining the Neolithic Revolution." *Journal of Economic Surveys* 19:561–86.

Weiss, Michael, and Hassan Hassan. 2015. *ISIS: Inside the Army of Terror*. New York: Regan Arts.

Weitz, Mark. 2008. *More Damning Than Slaughter: Desertion in the Confederate Army*. Lincoln: University of Nebraska Press.

Welch, David. 2011. *Painful Choices: A Theory of Foreign Policy Change*. Princeton: Princeton University Press.

Wells, Mark. 1995. *Courage and Air Warfare: The Allied Aircrew Experience in the Second World War*. London: Frank Cass.

Wendt, Alexander. 1999. *Social Theory of International Politics*. Chicago: University of Chicago Press.

Werrell, Kenneth. 2005. *Sabres over MiG Alley: The F-86 and the Battle for Air Superiority in Korea*. Annapolis: Naval Institute Press.

Wesseling, Henk. 1989. "Colonial Wars: An Introduction." In Japp de Moor and Henk Wesseling, eds., *Essays on Colonial Wars in Asia and Africa, 1870–1914*. Leiden: Brill.

———. 2005. "Imperialism and the Roots of the Great War." *Daedalus* 134:100–107.

Wezeman, Pieter, Alexandra Kuimova, and Siemon Wezeman. 2002. "Trends in International Arms Transfers, 2001." Stockholm, SIPRI Fact Sheet, March.

Whigham, Thomas. 2002. *The Paraguayan War*, vol. 1, *Causes and Early Conflict*. Lincoln: University of Nebraska Press.

———. 2017. *The Road to Armageddon: Paraguay versus the Triple Alliance, 1866–70*. Calgary: University of Calgary Press.

White, Ralph. 1990. "Why Aggressors Lose." *Political Psychology* 11: 227–42.

Whittaker, C. R. 1978. "Carthaginian Imperialism in the 5th and 4th Centuries." In P. D. A. Garnsey and C. R. Whittaker, eds., *Imperialism in the Ancient World*. Cambridge: Cambridge University Press.

Whittaker, Dick. 1993. "Landlords and Warlords in the Later Roman Empire." In John Rich and Graham Shipley, eds., *War and Society in the Roman World*. London: Routledge.

Wiedemann, Thomas. 1995. *Emperors and Gladiators*. London: Routledge.

Wilcox, Vanda. 2014. "Morale and Battlefield Performance at Caporetto, 1917." *Journal of Strategic Studies* 37:829–54.

Wildman, Allan K. *The End of the Russian Imperial Army: The Old Army and the Soldiers' Revolt (March–April, 1917)*. Princeton: Princeton University Press.

Wilson, Lydia. 2015. "Lydia Wilson: What I Discovered from Interviewing Imprisoned Islamic State Fighters." Interview by Amy Goodman. *Democracy Now!* November 17.

———. 2017. "Understanding the Appeal of ISIS." *New England Journal of Public Policy* 29:1–11.

Wilson, Sandra. 1995. "The 'New Paradise': Japanese Emigration to Manchuria in the 1930s and 1940s." *International History Review* 17:249–86.

———. 2002. *The Manchurian Crisis and Japanese Society, 1931–33*. London: Routledge.

Wimmer, Andreas. 2013. *Waves of War*. Cambridge: Cambridge University Press.

Wood, Graeme. 2016. *The Way of the Strangers: Encounters with the Islamic State*. London: Allen Lane.

Wood, James. 2007. *Japanese Military Strategy in the Pacific War: Was Defeat Inevitable?* Lanham, Md.: Rowman & Littlefield.

Woodiwiss, Anthony. 1992. *Law, Labour, and Society in Japan: From Repression to Reluctant Recognition*. London: Routledge.

Worthy, Edmund, Jr. 1983. "Diplomacy for Survival: Domestic and Foreign Relations of Wu Yüeh, 907–978." In Morris Rossabi, ed., *China among Equals: The Middle Kingdom and Its Neighbors, 10th–14th Centuries*. Berkeley: University of California Press.

Wright, Quincy. 1957. "Design for a Research Project on International Conflicts." *Western Political Quarterly* 10:263–75.

Wyatt, Don. 2009. "Unsung Men of War: Acculturated Embodiments of the Martial Ethos in the Song Dynasty." In Nicola di Cosmo, ed., *Military Culture in Imperial China*. Cambridge: Harvard University Press.

Yates, Robin. 2008. "Making War and Making Peace in Early China." In Philip de Souza and John France, eds., *War and Peace in Ancient and Medieval History*. Cambridge: Cambridge University Press.

Yazbek, Samar. 2015. *The Crossing: My Journey to the Shattered Heart of Syria*. London: Routledge.

Yazdani, Kavah. 2017. *India, Modernity and the Great Divergence: Mysore and Gujarat (17th to 19th C.)*. Leiden: Brill.

Yoffee, Norman. 2005. *Myths of the Archaic State: Evolution of the Earliest Cities, States, and Civilizations*. Cambridge: Cambridge University Press.

Young, Louise. 1998. *Japan's Total Empire: Manchuria and the Culture of Wartime Imperialism*. Berkeley: University of California Press.

Yu, Ying-shih. 1967. *Trade and Expansion in Han China: A Study in the Structure of Sino-Barbarian Economic Relations*. Berkeley: University of California Press.

Zhang, Feng. 2015. *Chinese Hegemony: Grand Strategy and International Institutions in East Asian History*. Stanford: Stanford University Press.

Zhang, Xiaoming. 2002. *Red Wings over the Yalu: China, the Soviet Union, and the Air War in Korea*. College Station: Texas A&M University Press.

Zhao, Dingxin. 2015. *The Confucian-Legalist State: A New Theory of Chinese History*. Oxford: Oxford University Press.

Zhao, Gang. 2006. "Reinventing China: Imperial Qing Ideology and the Rise of Modern Chinese National Identity in the Early Twentieth Century." *Modern China* 32:3–30.

Ziemann, Benjamin. 2007. *War Experiences in Rural Germany, 1914–1923*. Translated by Alex Skinner. New York: Berg.

———. 2017. *Violence and the German Soldier in the Great War: Killing, Dying, Surviving*. Translated by Andrew Evans. London: Bloomsbury.

Zook, David. 1960. *The Conduct of the Chaco War*. New York: Bookman.

———. 1964. *Zarumilla-Marañón: The Ecuador-Peru Dispute*. New York: Bookman.

Index